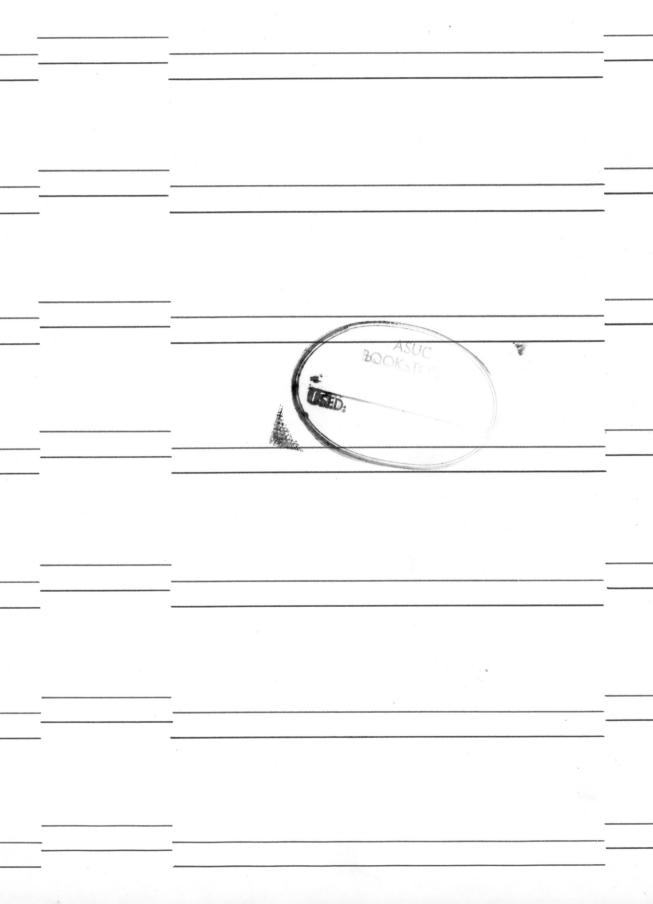

Municipal Management Series

The Practice of Local Government Planning

The International City Management Association is the professional and educational organization for chief appointed management executives in local government. The purposes of ICMA are to enhance the quality of local government and to nurture and assist professional local government administrators in the U.S. and other countries. In furtherance of its mission, ICMA develops and disseminates new approaches to management through training programs, information services, and publications.

Managers, carrying a wide range of titles, serve cities, towns, counties, and councils of governments in all parts of the United States and Canada. These managers serve at the direction of elected councils and governing boards. ICMA serves these managers and local governments through many programs that aim at improving the manager's professional competence and strengthening the quality of all local governments.

The International City Management Association was founded in 1914, adopted its City Management Code of Ethics in 1924, and established its Institute for Training in Municipal Administration in 1934. The Institute, in turn, provided the basis for the Municipal Management Series, generally termed the "ICMA Green Books." ICMA's interests and activities include public management education; standards of ethics for members; *The Municipal Year Book* and other data services; local government research; and newsletters, *Public Management* magazine, and other publications. ICMA's efforts for the improvement of local government management—as represented by this book—are offered for all local governments and educational institutions.

Contributors

Jonathan Barnett

Frank Beal

Alexander J. Darragh

Richard Ducker

Stephen Belais Friedman

Laurence Conway Gerckens

Judith Getzels

Elizabeth L. Hollander

Elizabeth Howe

Eric Damian Kelly

Constance Lieder

Carl V. Patton

Leslie S. Pollock

Jeffry D. Reckinger

Sandra Rosenbloom

Paul H. Sedway

Frank S. So

Israel Stollman

William Toner

Municipal Management Series

The Practice of Local Government Planning

Second Edition

Published for the
ICMA Training
Institute

By the
International
City
Management
Association

Editors

Frank S. So
American Planning
Association

Judith Getzels
American Planning
Association

Municipal Management Series

Library of Congress Cataloging-in-Publication Data

The practice of local government planning.
  (Municipal management series)
  Bibliography: p.
  Includes index.
  1. City planning—United States. I. So, Frank S.
II. Getzels, Judith.   III. Series.
HT167.P7 1988   352.9'6'0973   87-35273
ISBN 0-87326-077-5

Printed in the United States of America.

949392919089
5432

Foreword

Since the International City Managers' Association first published *Local Planning Administration* in 1941, the successive volumes on local planning have probably been the most widely read and influential books in the Municipal Management Series. Two qualities—continuity and change—have made possible the strength and quality of each edition of the local planning volume.

Local Planning Administration, the first of the ICMA planning volumes, was prepared by planning consultant Ladislas Segoe and six associates. Since then, the book has undergone four revisions: in 1948, 1959, 1968, and 1979. By 1979, when the book first appeared under its current title, the planning field had expanded to a degree that required the creation of two volumes: one on urban planning and one on state and regional planning. In 1986, the American Planning Association (APA) published *The Practice of State and Regional Planning* as part of the Municipal Management Series.

Several characteristics have remained constant in the ICMA volumes on local planning. First, planning is viewed from a management perspective: it is assumed that readers of the book are or will be involved in daily policy analysis and decision making, and both the descriptive text and examples are designed to address management issues from a practical as well as a theoretical perspective. Second, contributors to the volume are chosen for their ability to integrate research, personal experience, and knowledge of general practice;

the result is chapters that give a vivid, authoritative picture of planning at the local level. Third, the editors of each successive volume have been committed to documenting and exploring changes in the planning profession.

Like its predecessors, this volume reflects those changes. The introductory chapter to the book, with its discussion of planning environments, begins the examination of new developments in the planning field. Each chapter considers, in its turn, the influences that shape current planning practice. For example, in recent years, the shifting role of the federal government has been one of the greatest sources of change. As federal funds for a number of programs have decreased or been withdrawn, local and state governments have had to rethink their services and discover ways to make up the difference. The nature of the planning profession—which is characterized by a long-term perspective—has made planners central to this process.

As both administrators and policy-making bodies have come to rely on the breadth of knowledge conferred by planning expertise, planners in numerous municipalities have assumed increasingly important roles in local government—and often find themselves mediating among a number of competing interests and needs. Although this position can be a difficult one for planners who view themselves as neutral technicians, other planners have chosen to become advocates for groups whose needs might otherwise be overlooked. Whichever path a planner chooses, there is no question that planning has become an increasingly politicized field.

Readers familiar with the 1979 edition will note that these and other changes receive careful attention in this volume. They will also note that, like its predecessors, this book is designed as a basic reference for planners, professional local government administrators, and students of planning and public administration.

The books in the Municipal Management Series are prepared for ICMA's Training Institute, which offers in-service training specifically designed for local government administrators. ICMA has sponsored the institute since 1934.

Creating the second edition of *The Practice of Local Government Planning* was a cooperative effort that could not have been accomplished without the expertise and commitment of a number of organizations and individuals. First among these are the editors: Frank S. So, Deputy Executive Director, APA; and Judith Getzels, Director of Research, APA. We also extend thanks to the APA itself, which provided valuable support for the project.

We are grateful to the chapter authors, not only for their excellent contributions but also for their commitment and cooperation during the revision process.

Chapter 6, on transportation planning, was reviewed by a number of individuals whose invaluable assistance we wish to acknowledge: Dr. David Hartgen, Transportation and Statistics and Analysis Section, New York State Department of Transportation; Kevin Heanue, Director of Highway Planning, Federal Highway Administration; Lee Mertz, also of the Federal Highway Administration; Joseph P. Giselman, Study Coordinator, Austin Transportation Study, Austin, Texas; and Larry Dallam, Principal Planner, Howard Needles Tammen & Bergendoff, Minneapolis, Minnesota.

A number of ICMA staff members contributed to the project: Barbara H. Moore, Director, Book Division, who worked with the editors to plan the initial scope and conception of the book; Sandra Chizinsky Leas, who oversaw the project; Alice R. Markham, who copy edited the manuscript; Dawn M. Leland and Rebecca A. Geanaros, who managed illustrations and production; and Mary W. Blair, publications secretary.

William H. Hansell, Jr.
Executive Director

International City
Management Association

Washington, D.C.

Contents

Part one:
The context and history of comprehensive planning

1 Introduction

Planning environments

The nature of local government planning can vary considerably in focus, substance, and style, depending on the type of community or area being planned. Planning for midtown Manhattan will be quite different from planning for the downtown of a rural Iowa community. This first section of the introduction provides an overview of a number of different environments in which planning is practiced: older central cities, Sun Belt cities, inner-ring, residential, and high-growth suburbs, small rural towns, and resort towns.

Older central cities

Older central cities, such as Cleveland, Gary, and Newark, are what come to mind when the media refer to "the city." Most of these cities developed during the nineteenth century; their economies were based on smokestack industries; they were the early financial and retail centers; and they housed wave after wave of immigrants during the nineteenth and early twentieth centuries.

A number of related factors accelerated dislocations in economies of these cities. The federally supported development of the interstate highway system, for example, made it easy for middle-class families to move out of the cities into the suburbs and continue to commute to city jobs—at least for a while. Federal housing mortgage insurance programs lent support to this migration to the suburbs. Urban factory owners seeking to expand and modernize their crowded old multi-story plants joined the exodus to the suburbs; land for efficient one-story factories was readily available at reasonable prices outside the city boundaries. Furthermore, quick and flexible truck access to these factories became possible as a result of their new locations on the new highways. Outmoded city plants were often simply abandoned; many of them still stand empty. The result for the cities was loss of middle-class populations as well as loss of industrial jobs.

During the 1950s, these older cities made efforts to improve and renew their declining central business districts—the source of a large portion of the tax revenue needed to run city government. Early efforts focused on the creation of pedestrian malls (perhaps to copy the suburban shopping centers), but it soon became clear that retailing was generally moving to the suburbs and that central business districts had to build their futures on banking, finance, government, and other service functions.

Other early efforts to rejuvenate the older cities focused on the construction of urban expressways, which public officials thought would bring in shoppers from the suburbs. In fact, the expressways simply made it easier to move to the suburbs.

During the 1970s and 1980s, changes in the nation's economy took their toll on older cities. In particular, many of the cities in the East and Midwest that had depended on smokestack industries such as steel and automobiles found their economies tumbling as these industries moved overseas. The decline in manufacturing employment created a decline in disposable income, which hurt retail business; decline in retail, in turn, created serious urban tax base problems. The economic decline and consequent shortage of jobs in some older central cities caused large numbers of young people to move away from these areas. This factor, combined with the more general migration of population to the suburbs, contributed to population decline in some older central cities.

Because of a complex interaction of social and economic factors, many older cities have serious housing problems. From the late 1940s through the early 1960s, the nation's public investment in urban housing was at its peak. In many instances, however, "urban renewal" consisted of totally clearing vast inner-city areas and building acres of high-rise public housing, an approach that turned out to be socially disastrous. Although parts of the urban housing market are vigorous—high-income apartment construction and the rejuvenation of declining residential areas by "urban pioneers"—the magnitude of housing needs continues to create significant challenges for older cities. For example, in the mid-1980s, sectoral unemployment, a decrease in the amount of inexpensive inner-city housing, and the deinstitutionalization of dependent populations worsened the problem of homelessness nationwide but put particular pressures on older central cities. Even the renewal of older neighborhoods, generally referred to as gentrification, is a cause of concern. Although planners and public officials alike are pleased to see declining areas renewed on a private basis, the purchase of housing by upper-income groups tends to displace lower-income residents.

The drop in federal housing support has placed an additional burden on cities, and planners have had to seek new ways to finance housing construction and rehabilitation. Many states have created housing authorities, and public-private partnerships are being forged to obtain new money from older urban financial institutions. In some high-growth downtown areas, cities charge fees to builders to create a pool of money that can be drawn on for housing loans.

Although older cities often appear to be a locus for national social and economic problems, they nevertheless remain the destination of immigrants seeking to build a new life. Immigrants tend to start from the bottom of the social and economic ladder and work their way up. To do this, they need inexpensive housing and suitable jobs—neither of which is easy to find in many older cities.

As bleak a picture as this is, older cities are and will be centers of commerce and services as well as good places to live. Planning in these cities may face formidable obstacles but is also an area of vigorous action and accomplishments.

Central business districts have come to emphasize services, rather than continue their past dependence on retailing. Retailing has come to be divided into those activities that are most economically delivered in suburban shopping centers and those that are most effectively delivered in a central area—such as department stores committed to a central anchor location. Central business districts have also been rejuvenated through the construction of new hotels, convention centers, and sports stadiums, all of which encourage tourism. Increasing tourism has been one of the primary goals of harbor, waterfront, and riverfront renewal programs. Older cities have also invested in centers for cultural activities and the arts. Federal and state funds have enabled many cities to retain or expand arts programs, including orchestras, dance, theatre, and fine arts.

Older cities have also come to recognize the importance of preserving historically significant downtown buildings and residential areas. The rich architectural legacy of older cities is increasingly seen as a valuable resource in the rejuvenation of urban areas. Along with historic preservation has come a greater interest in urban design. Cities are paying close attention to the creation of pedestrian plazas and other street-level amenities as well as to the design of new private buildings.

Economic development planning is crucial to the health of older central cities. Programs include business and job retention, job training, and the creation of financial mechanisms—such as tax abatement—to promote development. Cities

The once and future suburb

"Suburbia is a squishy term," says Census Bureau geographer Richard Forstall, explaining that the bureau talks about metropolitan statistical areas and urban areas, but not suburbs per se. Some "central cities," he notes, include many areas that look like suburbs, and some areas that are considered suburban look suspiciously urban. . . .

Nor can suburbs be pigeonholed by function as bedroom communities, for today they're as likely to be office centers and even cultural and recreational centers. . . .

Demographic stereotypes won't do, either. Because of the vagaries of terminology, the Census Bureau's Forstall can't tell us exactly how many people live in the "suburbs." But he can say that 105 million people live outside the central city boundaries, as opposed to 74 million inside. . . .

What all this adds up to is a citylike entity but without the traditional core. Freed from dependence on rail lines that limited the location of the earliest suburbs, the new ones are spreading into the countryside. "Ring cities," Rutgers University's George Sternlieb aptly calls them. The newest developments attract the jobs, while the older suburbs are left with such city-type problems as homelessness, substandard housing, and decaying commercial strips. . . .

In *Pride of Place*, his recent book and television series, architect Robert Stern waxes lyrical about the early planned suburbs like Olmsted's Roland Park outside Baltimore. And, as well-to-do enclaves, many of these communities are thriving. But other older, inner-ring suburbs, not so well-favored to begin with, are showing signs of residential and commercial decay.

Quoted recently in an article about the old blue-collar suburbs, University of Miami geographer Peter Muller noted that they face stiff competition from the new downtowns—"the outer city," in his phrase. "Entire communities are considered used up," he said, "and they're being discarded like so many beer cans."

Source: Excerpted from Ruth Eckdish Knack, "The Once and Future Suburb," *Planning* (July 1986), 6–12.

---

even plan their capital facilities to improve the community as a business environment.

In spite of past difficulties, some older cities, such as Boston, San Francisco, and parts of Chicago and New York, are experiencing a turnaround reflected in significant new growth in downtown development. In fact, in such cities the development pressures are great enough to generate concern about traffic, parking, and the replacement of historically significant low-density buildings by high-rise, high-density buildings. In some cities, increased land values have driven up housing costs to the extent that the middle class has difficulty finding affordable housing.

Sun Belt cities

Sun Belt cities may be as old as cities in the North and East, but they are developing rapidly. Pleasant climates, coupled with a general shift of economic activity to the South and West, have created high rates of growth in cities such as Atlanta, Houston, Dallas, Phoenix, and Los Angeles. Suburbs near these cities are also high-growth areas. Some Sun Belt cities are business and financial centers for a regional economic hinterland. Central areas in such cities experience a variety of planning problems, such as boom-and-bust cycles in office development; insufficient public transit; and excessive automobile traffic (which is accompanied by air pollution). In some Sun Belt cities, such as Phoenix and

Atlanta, efforts are being made to reverse sprawling development patterns by more intense, multinucleated development.

In rapidly growing cities, the climate for planning and development controls can undergo abrupt swings. On the theory that growth is "good," a city may go through a boom with little planning. It may then become clear that growth without quality has caused traffic congestion and air pollution and is generally destroying the "good life" that residents originally sought. The response may be more vigorous planning and regulatory mechanisms, which can set off yet another cycle in which major real estate interests experience losses and blame planning and land use controls—regardless of whether regulation is at fault.

Many growing Sun Belt cities in the Southwest have developed in desertlike conditions and are now faced with a major natural resource problem: water. Urban and agricultural interests are often in conflict over the allocation of water. Some urban officials look to other regions for sufficient water supply, and future interregional political conflict on this issue is likely.

Inner-ring suburbs

In many ways the problems of older, inner-ring suburbs mirror those of central cities: because most of the land has been built out, these areas are not the focus of the kind of development interest that is being directed toward "outer-ring" suburbs. As the suburbs have matured, school enrollments have declined, and local governments are faced with the special needs of an aging population. Competition with outlying regional shopping centers has damaged the commercial centers of many older suburbs: the traditional small central business districts are experiencing on a smaller scale the same decline in retail activities that the central cities have experienced. A variety of renewal and rehabilitation efforts have succeeded, however, in preserving the functions of the older suburban downtowns.

The new suburban "downtown"
Thirty miles northeast of midtown Manhattan, Stamford, Connecticut (pop. 102,000), has become one of the leading corporate headquarters cities in the world. In Houston, the Galleria–Post Oak area would be the ninth-largest downtown in America—if it were a downtown, instead of a quasi suburb ten miles away. . . .

All across the country, a new kind of "downtown" is emerging. Like the traditional urban downtown, it is a center for employment, commerce, and culture. But it is usually located far from the center of the old city, in an area that until recently was thought of as a bucolic suburb. Some of these centers are emerging almost overnight in older, traditionally low-rise suburban shopping areas. Others are being planned from scratch on raw land, much as the new towns of the 1960s were. . . .

In simplest terms, suburban downtowns are employment centers, representing a shift of jobs away from central cities. Office employers—the lifeblood of the postwar downtown—have been heading for the suburbs in increasing numbers. . . .

"All the stuff that doesn't *have* to be downtown is moving to the suburbs," says David Dowall, professor of urban and regional planning at the University of California, Berkeley.

Because of this massive employment shift, a whole new kind of city is being created in the suburbs. But as real estate consultant Christopher Leinberger, managing partner of California-based Roberts Charles Lesser, Inc., puts it: "Nobody has an image of what that city should be." Developers want to build at urban densities. Planners demand suburban-style height and

Like that of older central cities, the housing stock of some older suburbs is aging. Given the decline in federal support for housing, these suburbs will have to look to the private market and to local government to help conserve the housing stock.

Residential suburbs

Residential suburbs include those that developed in the late 1940s and early 1950s as well as more recently. Suburban housing is predominantly single-family, with a small proportion of multifamily townhouse developments and low-rise apartment buildings. Residential suburbs generally include some commercial development, such as community and regional shopping centers, and business development along major arterial streets. Some suburbs may also sustain a limited amount of light industry along arterial streets or expressways.

The most common planning issues in such communities concern the orderly development of residential areas. Normally, zoning and land subdivision regulations can cope with new residential development. Increasingly, suburbs have begun to impose special fees or to require developers to participate in the financing of off-site improvements. Some suburban communities are still wary of the construction of multifamily dwellings, but this attitude is less common than it was in the past.

Public services and facilities are normally provided by the local governments that provide police and fire protection (sometimes volunteer fire departments), libraries, and public schools. During the 1950s and 1960s, school construction often lagged behind need. However, as family size has decreased, or as families have postponed having children, shortages of schoolrooms are relatively rare, and some older suburbs are experiencing declines in school enrollment and are seeking new uses for school buildings.

As more business and industry move to suburban locations, suburban residents

---

parking requirements. And residents often rebel at the resulting traffic congestion.

The result, says Leinberger, is something that is "neither fish nor fowl." The new downtowns aren't really suburban. They employ up to 100,000 people, often in tall office buildings. And even when they're located close to commuter rail stations, they're frequently characterized by massive traffic jams.

But new downtowns aren't really urban, either. Most are designed for the automobile, with little concern for pedestrians or transit riders and with few of the urban characteristics that can make a downtown job enjoyable. And some of the businesses are reporting difficulty finding employees for lower-paying jobs. Having moved to the suburbs partly to draw upon the attractive suburban work force, they're inaccessible to the urban working

class—a group that, ironically, could become more important as the number of suburban women looking to reenter the work force dwindles. "It's increasingly difficult to find housewives in the suburbs sitting at home not working," says Dowall. . . .

Why have whole new cities sprung up over the last ten years without much attention from planners or designers? . . . "We've been ignoring a major part of our urban landscape," says J. Thomas Black, staff vice-president of the Urban Land Institute, which is just beginning to research the subject. "There is a tremendous bias among urban designers, who don't like to admit that the suburban centers exist. There's a real shortage of concepts as to what the alternatives are."

Source: Excerpted from William Fulton, "Office in the Dell," *Planning* (July 1986), 13–17.

no longer look to the city's central business district as the primary place of employment. More and more suburban residents commute to jobs in other suburbs.

High-growth suburban centers

In the mid-1980s, a new type of suburb began to emerge that will pose significant challenges to planners. Some planners call them "centers," but there is as yet no common term for high-growth suburbs such as DuPage County, Illinois, and Route 1 near Princeton, New Jersey. The development of the "new" type of suburb began when the traditional suburb—consisting largely of single-family housing with a little multifamily housing and some business development—came to be seen by major businesses as a highly desirable location for office, research, or industrial facilities. The second phase of development occurred when enough businesses had relocated to the suburbs to transform them into job generators. High-rise office buildings and sprawling business parks now cluster along major suburban arterial streets and expressways. Regional offices for major insurance companies, research laboratories, and similar businesses and services are turning what were once residential suburbs into high-density, mixed-use developments. In some suburban centers, major business buildings and regional shopping centers are in close proximity. The total land and floor area devoted to commercial and business use may surpass the size of the central business district in many smaller cities.

These new suburban centers generate significant amounts of automobile traffic; few such communities have mass transit other than feeder bus service to commuter railroad lines. Thus, almost everyone drives to work, but most suburban expressways were built in an era when the journey to work was from suburb to central city. Now that work trips are from suburb to suburb, the cost of providing adequate roads presents a serious problem to local planners. First, suburban roads are generally considered local and therefore may not qualify for federal highway grants. Second, the density of development is so great and the land development pattern so set that no vacant land may be available for additional arterial streets. The result is suburban gridlock. Increasingly, local governments are requiring developers of shopping centers and office buildings to pay additional fees to finance roads beyond the boundaries of their own developments. Frustrated by the inability of local government to fund road improvements, some developers have chosen to finance road improvements on their own.

High rates of business growth in suburban centers have generated conflict between the development community and the local government on the one hand and citizen groups on the other. Developers and the local government see business and industrial growth, and the resulting tax revenues, as a desirable way to finance community services, especially in residential areas—which commonly do not pay their own way. Citizen groups, however, see high-density business development as destructive to the suburban way of life.

Suburban centers represent a new type of metropolitan development that is not like the old central city and not like the residential suburb of the last several decades. Because of the proliferation of neighboring suburban governments that share facilities—such as roads—and resources—such as water—intergovernmental planning mechanisms will be needed to deal with problems created by growth. The necessary cooperation may be difficult to achieve in areas where suburbs compete with each other to attract businesses.

Rural small towns

The rural small town is a distinct type of environment for planning. These often-isolated communities serve as the centers for the county or township in an

Summer fun? According to the city manager of Ocean City, Maryland, a vacation spot for people from the Washington, D.C.–Baltimore area, the changes that summer brings are logistical "nightmares." Population increases from 10,000 to 200,000 during peak summer months. Water use rises from 1 million gallons per day to 13. And trash pickup expands from a winter average of 30 tons per day to 600 tons per day. Meeting the increased demand means hiring 1,200 seasonal employees to supplement the 500 regular full-time staff. Despite the fact that summer homeowners generate a good portion of the city's operating funds through payment of their property taxes, many residents (including summer residents) want the seasonal flood of visitors to dry up. And the Ocean City Council has, in fact, put a cap on development density in an effort to keep the situation under control.

Wildwood, New Jersey, near Atlantic City and home of the largest beach on the Jersey shore, cites an influx of nearly 245,000 visitors (compared with a fixed population of 5,000) "on any

given summer day." And, unlike Ocean City, Wildwood does not have the benefit of deriving much property tax from the visitors. Most of the burden falls on the permanent residents. In addition, the community is one of the few that doesn't charge a beach access fee. This may have to change. Hiring 525 seasonal employees to help out the regular staff of 245 cost $882,000 in 1987 as opposed to the $680,000 it cost in 1986.

Southhampton, the largest town on Long Island's East End, doubled its charge for a nonresident seasonal beach pass to $100 in 1987 both to discourage more visitors and to pay for services. The community hires forty provisional police officers and another thirty who issue tickets but don't carry guns. Parking and traffic are the biggest problems in the area, and no remedy is in sight.

Source: *Public Investment*, a special quarterly edition of the Planning Advisory Service (PAS) memo (Chicago: American Planning Association, June 1987), 4.

---

agricultural, resource-based, or other nonmetropolitan economy. They may have as few as 1,000 people; many are in the 2,500-to-5,000 population range. Many such communities have lost population to metropolitan areas; many have declined because of drops in the surrounding agricultural economy.

Small towns in poor or declining regions present special problems. Often, they do not have sufficient public funds to provide good public services. The cost of replacing a system of private wells and septic tanks with a modern water or sewerage system may be more than a small community can afford, and maintenance and replacement costs for public facilities can be quite high. Providing modern medical services is also a special problem for small communities.

In small rural towns, increased economic activity can be as much of a problem as poverty or decline. For example, a small community chosen as the site of a small industrial plant or in the vicinity of such a plant may have difficulty coping with the resulting growth. Local governments in rural areas often lack sufficient technical staff to analyze the private sector's development proposals. Moreover, they are not prepared to do the necessary public planning and must seek immediate help from private consultants or state technical assistance agencies. One of the most serious problems is providing public improvements such as sewer and water facilities, which must be constructed *before* the local government begins to receive tax revenues from the new economic activities. Public debt must be carefully planned, and efforts must be made to negotiate with the private sector to install some facilities before they are needed. As new economic activity generates new housing needs, additional pressure is created for adequate public facilities. New populations require a host of public services, including schools, police protection, and fire protection.

A distinct category of rural small town is one whose economy is based on a resource such as oil or coal. Problems in such communities are often related to their economic dependence on a particular resource. If the resource becomes depleted, the local economy suffers. Miscalculation of the value of a resource can create problems, too. For example, in the mid-1970s a number of Great Plains towns expected to grow substantially because of oil shale deposits, but as world oil prices dropped during the 1980s, extracting oil from shale ceased to be economically feasible. Some small communities in Texas and Oklahoma have suffered because of the decline in oil prices and the decline of the U.S. oil industry.

Resort towns

The resort community is another planning environment that poses special challenges to planners. Resort communities in rural areas share many of the problems of other growing rural areas: growth in a rural environment often occurs without sufficient governmental oversight. Even when adequate technical planning services are available, rapid growth in a resort area can cause public services to lag behind the pace of development.

The fact that resort areas often take root in environmentally fragile areas poses special planning problems. A resort established in a beautiful natural area may find that growth takes its toll on the recreational value—open space, clean air, and a sense of wilderness.

A number of problems associated with resort areas are less related to growth than to the seasonal character of the communities. For example, the seasonal influx of tourists may create traffic jams for only part of the year, but the streets must be adequate to the stress of those months. Other systems, such as sewer and water facilities, are subject to the same temporary strains. In communities where there are a number of second homes, building code standards must be established on the basis of peak occupancy. In a number of communities, second homes are becoming year-round residences, but the local governments cannot provide adequate services for a year-round population.

Planning and plans

Planning and plans are common to life, business, and government. To most of us, planning conveys the idea of preparing for the future or getting from here to there. This seems simple enough. However, within the context of local government, and to the various practitioners who work in it, *planning* and *plans* can have a variety of meanings depending on the situation. The discussion that follows describes what *planners* mean by "the planning process" and what various levels of "plans" are.

Planning as a process

At the most general level of planning and management, the planning process is divided into five major steps:

1. Basic goals. For local planning, determining basic goals may mean asking questions such as the following: Do we want to grow? Do we want to arrest decline? Do we want to be a center for high-tech industry? What balance do we want between investment in highways and in mass transit?
2. Study and analysis. Among other things, planners study land use, population trends, the economic base of the community, and physiographic features.

3. Plan or policy preparation. A plan or policy is prepared for the community as a whole or for a segment of it. It is a basic statement of how the community will develop, in what direction, and perhaps at what pace.

4. Implementation and effectuation. To carry out plans, planners use tools such as zoning ordinances, land subdivision regulations, capital improvements programs, and general guidelines for private development and public investment.

5. Monitoring and feedback. The last step determines, for example, how well the plans and policies are being carried out, whether the goals were realistic, and whether the study and analysis foresaw new occurrences. Feedback may become the basis for a redesign of the plans and even of the planning system.

These five steps describe the planning process in the abstract. In reality, most local planning consists of three steps: (1) examining inventories and trends in land use, population, employment, and traffic; (2) forecasting the "demand" (in some ways this is a "free market" approach); and (3) planning facilities and services of sufficient capacity to accommodate future demand. This traditional

---

Portraits of planners: The feminist

"Basically," says Charlotte Birdsall, "I'm a midlife planner." Trained as a social worker, Birdsall was an activist in her Cincinnati neighborhood when her three children were growing up. In 1976, at age 40, she joined the city planning department, after earning a master's degree in community planning from the University of Cincinnati.

"I never expected to go into a traditional land use agency," she says. "But I've never regretted my decision. I feel there's a definite place in an agency like this for someone with a social policy orientation."

As senior planner in the advanced planning division, Birdsall heads a small housing section, which, in addition to planning and monitoring programs, works on such special projects as shared housing for the elderly. She defines her job as "using traditional land use skills and background as the basis for recommending social policy."

Planners, she notes, have "a certain credibility that social workers lack—a credibility that comes from dealing with the hard stuff, the land."

Birdsall, who is divorced, lives in a racially integrated neighborhood. She grew up in Detroit. She's a liberal Democrat who, however, voted for Richard Nixon in 1960—the result of the influence of her politically conservative father. Since then, she says, "my eyes got opened."

The women's movement has been the "guiding value" of her life, she says, and she's on the board of a university's women's studies program. She's also active in her Unitarian church. She subscribes to *Ms.*, the *New Yorker*, and the *Atlantic*, and recommends Italo Calvino's novel *If on a Winter's Night a Traveler*. She says she doesn't watch television but does like movies—"anything with Meryl Streep."

Although Birdsall says she values her AICP membership, she is concerned about a state licensing program: "How would we write a licensing law that would include me?" she asks. But regarding residency requirements, another issue that planners have had to face in some jurisdictions, she has no doubts. "I'm all for them."

Source: Excerted from Ruth Eckdish Knack, "Here's Looking at You," *Planning* (March 1986), 9–15.

method of planning is an inexact process, depending as it does on forecasting. No matter how sophisticated the forecasting methods, trends are difficult to forecast—especially when a freewheeling entrepreneur makes a locational decision that will have major consequences for a city. Nevertheless, planners must become adept at analyzing a number of dependent interrelated systems.

Furthermore, public planners must be able to take responsibility for understanding what the community wants and for shaping the future of the community's land uses to reflect those desires. Although strong believers in the free market may not be comfortable with this notion, it is at the core of planning. Even some Sun Belt cities that initially welcomed a boomtown atmosphere are reassessing the role of public planning because of declining air quality, crowded streets and highways, and an inability to keep up with public service demand.

Multi-step planning

Planning agencies are now refining their procedures in order to help facilitate both forecasting and implementation of community goals. The first step consists of taking inventories and analyzing trends. In the second step, however, the forecasts are made on a different basis. Instead of assuming that the forecast is a given, the planning agency considers it to be a "what if" statement; the community can then evaluate the pluses and minuses of each forecast.

The third step is the identification of goals and objectives. Many communities have undertaken communitywide or business-led goal studies, which are useful ways of getting residents to think about the community. The identification of goals should be based on widespread participation; goals are not to be set by top officials. The role of the planning agency is to raise issues where there are choices. For example, what are the housing choices in the community? Are all income groups adequately served by the private market? Everyone wants a clean river in town, but how do we define "clean," and what are we willing to pay to clean up the river? How do we weigh standards for air pollution, noise, and water quality against economic development opportunities? Do we want to establish population density ceilings in particular areas?

The fourth step is to formulate, test, and compare alternative policies and plans. Unfortunately, only the most sophisticated transportation planning agencies have the methodological capacity to be precise in testing alternatives in terms of quantitative analysis, and even methods of transportation analysis have

---

The context of planning   These issues are traffic lights and warning signals that need to be observed.

Legal   Is it lawful? Can it be done?

Political   Is it acceptable?

Social   Who wins? Who loses?

Economic   What are the costs? What are the benefits?

Fiscal   Where is the money?

Intergovernmental   What agencies are directly responsible?

Aesthetic   What are community preferences and values?

Environmental   What is the impact?

Management   Who's in charge?

Source: Sam M. Cristofano and William S. Foster, eds., *Management of Local Public Works* (Washington, DC: International City Management Association, 1986), 75.

---

shortcomings, as discussed in chapter 6, "Transportation Planning." Recently, interesting and useful efforts have been made to test plan or policy alternatives with a combination of quantitative and nonquantitative methods. However, these methods are most useful for answering very narrow policy questions. Given the complexity of interactions within urban areas with respect to land use, transportation, land economics, and so on, evaluating alternative general plans remains a difficult task.

The fifth step is to compare and evaluate alternative plans on the basis of such criteria as financial capacity, the extent to which community goals are met, public acceptability, the legal and social constraints on implementation, and the stress placed on limited resources or facilities.

The sixth step is to select the most acceptable plan and review the forecasts and assumptions. The purpose of this review is to consider two questions: How congruent are the plan and the data obtained in step one? How much compromise was necessary to create the preferred plan? For example, population forecasts may indicate the need for a variety of public facilities, but further analysis may show that public revenues will not permit the funding of those facilities. Thus, some desirable projects may be delayed, scaled down, or eliminated.

The seventh step is to prepare detailed plans for elements (e.g., housing, transportation) of the comprehensive plan and for community facilities and programs.

The eighth step is to implement plans and policies through both public and private means. Implementation usually involves regulation, some incentives, and some cooperation.

The final step is not a step at all but a continuous evaluation of the process as a whole. The purpose of the evaluation is to discover blind alleys, redo plans that seem impossible to implement, and change regulations that are creating problems.

Throughout the planning process, the planning agency conducts its own in-house work, hires consultants, consults with other local government departments, establishes task forces and advisory committees, confers with other governmental levels, and has numerous meetings with officials, technicians, and the public. The approach is complex and can be frustrating, yet it seems to be the only way we know how to conduct the local democratic planning process. Thus, planning is not just a series of "rational" steps but is also constantly interwoven into a continuous process of agency management.

Plans

The preceding discussion emphasizes the process of planning, but planning must create products. As shown in Figure 1–1, these products vary with the type and level of plan being prepared.

At the broadest and most general level is the comprehensive plan, at one time called the master plan and also known as the general plan. More recently, products of this kind have been called strategic plans. The comprehensive plan is a document (in multiple volumes for very large jurisdictions) that is the result of lengthy and intensive study and analysis. The geographic scope is the entire community and its regional environment. The time scale is long range or indefinite. Such a plan is comprehensive in that it tries to link long-range objectives to a number of interdependent elements, including population growth, economic development, land use, transportation, and community facilities.

The comprehensive plan discusses the principal issues and problems of growth or decline facing the community. It will also indicate the main trends that seem inevitable and that need the attention of public or public-private programs. Plans usually contain a mixture of suggestions, proposals for which the means of implementation have not yet been identified, and actual commitments of local governments. For at least a decade plans have tended not to be presented in map form because of the difficulty of identifying precise sites or dimensions; instead, most plans are a series of policy statements.

Depending on the size of the community, a comprehensive plan may also contain chapters on public utility and facility systems if general policies have been established for these systems. However, the degree of detail is nowhere near that in system plans, shown in the second level of Figure 1–1. System plans are more detailed than the comprehensive or general plans yet do not necessarily approach engineering specifications. A system plan summarizes the plans, policies, and programs for a specific network of communitywide facilities—the entire sewer system, the entire fire protection system, or the park and recreation system. System plans deal with specific facilities in specific places.

At the third level are area plans, which include details about certain geographic parts of the community. The most common type is a plan for the central business district. Other area plans are for industrial districts, civic and cultural centers, individual neighborhoods, the community or district encompassing several neighborhoods, and waterfronts. Details in area plans may go down to the block level. The area plan identifies the issues and problems facing a geographic area, develops plans for the future, and provides guidance to local decisionmakers reviewing private development proposals.

The style of planning can vary with the area. For example, a plan for a central business district may emphasize urban design components and the involvement of the private sector, whereas neighborhood-level planning involves citizen groups and neighborhood organizations.

The fourth type of plan is a detailed engineering plan for components of subsystems, such as trunk sewer lines, major water mains, and street extensions. These plans are based on systemwide plans and typically are prepared under the direction of the public works department.

Portraits of planners: Opposite numbers   Instead of answering our survey question about "how you spend your leisure hours," Lawrence Carter scribbled in the margin, "You don't know anything about rural life, do you?"

Carter, it turns out, is a part-time farmer (two acres of produce, several hogs, 1,000 chickens), besides being planning director of very rural Bedford County, near Altoona, Pennsylvania.

Most planners, he says, occupy an "alien world" with far different values from Carter's. It's the world he saw as a teacher in a Cleveland suburb in the early 1970s—"middle-class American, Organization Man, not for me." He left in midyear, and after a short stint running the county's children's home ("a quick burnout"), returned to the Altoona area, where he had grown up. For several years, he worked for a newly formed health systems agency, acquir-

ing on-the-job training in systems analysis and health planning, skills that he says separate him from typical planners, who, in Carter's view, are hung up on land use.

In 1981, Carter, who is now 40, became county planning director. He describes himself as "a bit of a maverick" because he isn't a "trained planner—whatever that is." But he insists that his undergraduate social sciences degree qualifies him to deal with a job that he sees as primarily educational. "Our job is to help local governments determine what policy direction *they* want to take." In practice, that means that Carter spends a lot of time "soapbox stumping—teaching people about themselves."

Carter "won't go near" the AICP exam because "it will be full of things I haven't had to deal with," and he thinks planning will remain an

Figure 1–1 Types and
levels of plans.

1. **Comprehensive plans**
   Plans containing basic policies for
      land use—residential, commercial,
      industrial, public—and general
      policies for public systems

2. **System plans**
   Land use
   Sewers
   Water
   Storm drainage
   Transportation: streets and mass transit
   Solid waste
   Parks and recreation
   Libraries
   Government administration
   Police
   Fire
   Health
   Public works buildings and facilities
   Cultural
   Institutional

3. **Area plans**
   Central business district
   Industrial districts
   Civic and cultural centers
   Community districts
   Waterfronts
   Neighborhoods

4. **Plans for subsystem components**
   Engineering plans for construction of
      trunk sewer line, major water main, or
      a street extension

5. **Site plans**
   Library
   Fire station
   Neighborhood park

At the fifth level are site plans for facilities such as libraries, fire stations, and neighborhood parks. Such facilities require land purchase, architectural and engineering drawings, scheduling in the capital improvements program, possible public hearings for site selection, meetings with neighborhood or community groups, and coordination with neighborhood development plans. System plans are considered separately from site plans, because linear systems provide the basic network for planned development. If the systems are not in, development

"immature profession" until it emphasizes systems and policy.

We weren't necessarily looking for an exact opposite to Larry Carter when we called our next planner. But we found it anyway in Mark Strauss. Not only is Strauss a city dweller and traditionally trained in land use planning—but he believes anyone involved with physical planning should be trained as an architect, as he himself is.

Strauss has an architecture degree from Cornell, but he concluded after enrolling in Jonathan Barnett's graduate planning program at the City University of New York that he liked the broader picture planning can provide. As head of planning for a New York architecture firm, he views planning as a "support for architecture," and he spends much of his time going after projects. His forte is showing clients

and local officials how a proposed development will fit into the character of a city. Registered as an architect, Strauss has not taken the AICP exam. "As an architect," he says, "I feel I have a license to do planning."

On the survey, Strauss said he was a political independent. He voted for Mondale but said "in some ways I could be a Republican if it meant getting rid of the waste in government." What holds him back is his concern over social issues.

Strauss grew up in suburban Nassau County, Long Island, "a place with no sense of place." In a way, he says, "that's what made me decide to become a planner."

Source: Excerpted from Ruth Eckdish Knack, "Here's Looking at You," *Planning* (March 1986), 9–15.

may not occur. After they are constructed, the availability of utilities may accelerate development. In other words, these linear systems shape urban development.

The context of planning

Public planning is never as simple and direct as a textbook makes it sound. A planner must learn to be a jack-of-all-trades. Today's planner works in a complex intergovernmental web of plans, policies, and regulations. Planners must have the patience and the understanding to work in the changing world of politics. Planners must comply with a large body of land use law and must be ready to contribute to the making of that law. To make reasonable forecasts, planners need a working knowledge of practical economics. Planners must understand how a community's fiscal situation will limit or support the implementation of a plan. Planners must understand how to protect the natural environment and how to encourage development that most people will find aesthetically attractive. Finally, planners must learn to participate in the management of planning programs.

Scope of this book

The purpose of this book is to provide an introduction to and an overview of the way planning works in local government. When Ladislas Segoe and his

---

What do planners do? In 1986, *Planning* magazine sent out some 20,000 questionnaires, surveying almost the entire membership of the American Planning Association. The 6,669 responses *Planning* received are the basis for the statistics that follow.

Asked to choose the three areas in which they did most of their planning, our respondents did what we thought they might do. Almost 44 percent checked off the old workhorse, zoning and subdivision regulation; in fact, nearly 4 percent (231 people) checked *only* that area. The other two top choices were policy planning and coordination (40 percent) and—the field of the 1980s—economic development (35 percent).

We suspect that a decade ago, environmental planning, fourth on our list with 24 percent, would have come in higher, and so would housing, eighth on our list with 14 percent, and historic preservation, eleventh with 8 percent. And two decades ago, transportation, sixth today with 15 percent, would surely have ranked near the top.

And where are the newcomers—those with less than a year of experience?

Besides the popular fields noted above, they're doing more demographics (5 percent vs. 2 percent for those with more than 25 years experience); information processing (7 percent vs. 3 percent); and mapping (3 percent vs. 1 percent). Fewer seem to be going into environmental planning: 5 percent vs. 8 percent of the group with over 25 years of experience.

People's views of what they *should* be doing often differ greatly from what they, in fact, do. And planners, apparently, are no exception. For only 4 percent picked zoning and subdivision approvals—the number one area of work—as their "ideal role."

What did reach the top of this list was interagency coordination (20 percent) and providing data (13 percent). We note with interest that political liaison (fourth on the list) picks up adherents from the old-timers (25-plus years of experience) and that many more of the newcomers chose social advocacy than did their older counterparts.

Source: Excerpted from Ruth Eckdish Knack, "Here's Looking at You," *Planning* (March 1986), 9–15.

associates produced the first edition of this series in 1941, *Local Planning Administration*, the book summarized the current state of knowledge in the field of local planning. This was possible because planning was then relatively young (for example, the American Institute of Planners had fewer than 200 members). During the last half-century, the field has expanded considerably (The American Planning Association now has about 20,000 members), becoming more complex and specialized. It is possible to be a comprehensive planner, but it is also possible to specialize in such areas as transportation, health, or the environment. Thus, this book cannot summarize all the knowledge in the field, nor can it cover all existing subfields.

The goal of this book is not to explain how to do planning but to show how planning is done. The editors assume that the serious student will acquire technical expertise in other courses. The book introduces the planning student or new planner to some of the fundamental issues of the field by illustrating how planners approach the problems and challenges of their field. It is important for a planning student to understand the economic, political, and social factors that affect local planning *before* he or she begins to study the finer technical aspects; this approach will, it is hoped, prevent the mistaken conclusion that planning could accomplish more were it not for economic, political, and social constraints.

Although the book does provide a comprehensive introduction to local government planning, it cannot, because of space limitations, cover other important aspects of planning in practice. Thus, teachers and students will need to supplement this book, depending on the objectives of the course, with readings on topics such as educational program facilities; planning for the arts and cultural activities; engineering and planning for sewer, water, and storm drainage facilities; citizen participation; planning of business and industrial areas; health planning; refuse collection and disposal; and planning for facilities such as libraries, fire stations, community centers, and recreation. Finally, the reader interested in activities at the state and regional levels should refer to the companion to this volume, *The Practice of State and Regional Planning*.

This book gets underway in chapter 2, a historical overview of local planning that places planning in its political and social context. Particular attention is given to the development of planning as a function of local government and to the evolution of basic planning and regulatory tools.

Chapter 3, which also starts from a historical perspective, traces the development of the general or comprehensive plan. The chapter covers the functions and components of the plan as well as the professional debate concerning its scope and nature.

Chapter 4 describes planning for the districts of a community; geographic subareas may include central business districts, interrelated neighborhoods, or a corridor of business activities. The chapter describes the kinds of data that are collected to prepare district-level plans and explains the steps in plan preparation.

Chapter 5 focuses on the ways in which local government has integrated environmental factors into the planning processes. Of course, many environmental issues are of concern at the national and state levels, but this chapter focuses on the methods used by local government planning agencies to provide greater compatibility between local development and environmental systems.

Transportation has always been an extremely important part of local planning. Chapter 6 describes how transportation planners approach the task of planning major arterial street systems and transit systems. Particular emphasis is placed on the evolution of transportation planning as a technical process and on the more efficient use of existing systems.

For many decades design was granted less importance than other planning considerations. Chapter 7 describes the developing role of urban design in local planning, focusing particularly on development controls and public investment, the two primary means of local government influence on urban design.

Chapter 8 offers a detailed look at land subdivision regulation, a land use control technique that is particularly important in developing communities. Subdivision regulation guides private development when vacant land is converted to residential, commercial, or industrial use. In addition, subdivision regulation ensures that public facilities such as streets and sewer and water lines are constructed to specific technical standards.

Chapter 9, "Zoning," covers a topic that is important to both mature and developing cities. The chapter discusses the legal basis of zoning, its implementation, and its relation to other regulatory mechanisms.

Planning for economic development, the focus of Chapter 10, is an increasingly important aspect of local planning, especially in mature communities. The chapter explains the national and international context of local economic development, describes the types of data that are required for careful planning, and discusses a variety of strategies to retain or attract business or industry.

Using three examples—demographic change, unemployment, and location of facilities for mentally handicapped people—Chapter 11 illustrates the inter-

---

Portraits of planners: The "typical" planner   Steve Tuckerman comes from East Providence, Rhode Island, where his father was an engineer. And Tuckerman himself intended to study civil engineering when he enrolled at Worcester Polytechnic Institute. A freshman course in city planning sidetracked him permanently. He went straight from WPI to the graduate regional planning program at the University of Massachusetts.

Tuckerman's first job in 1979, where he stayed until 1985, was with East Hampton, Connecticut, a growing community of 9,000 twenty miles from Hartford. He was the first in-house planner in the town's history, and his job included revamping the zoning and subdivision regulations. He's proud of having gotten a new mixed-use zoning district passed to encourage people to invest in unused factory sites.

In East Hampton, Tuckerman was, as he puts it, "a one-man show." Because he wanted to get experience in management, he decided in 1985 to take a job in nearby Coventry, a rural town near the University of Connecticut. Things didn't work out, though, and he moved again, this time to Southington (pop. 40,000), another of the contiguous semi-industrial towns in the Hartford metropolitan area.

As Tuckerman views his job, inter-agency coordination—"getting different agencies to talk to each other"—and zoning and subdivision approvals are equally important roles. The latter he refers to as "the meat and potatoes of planning."

Tuckerman is 31 years old and married to a pediatrician. They live in neighboring New Britain in the downstairs portion of a two-family house they own. Southington, he notes, does not have a residency requirement for city employees, but if it did, he would be opposed. In fact, he thinks planners can be more impartial if they don't live in the town they work in. He's a nonpracticing Episcopalian who checked liberal Democrat for our political question and added the word "ultra." With a laugh, he says that means he "subverts from within."

He's an AICP member but doesn't believe in registration or licensing beyond that. "Ours is too diverse a field," he says.

Tuckerman's comment is reminiscent of the definition once offered by the late Harvey Perloff, dean of UCLA's planning and architecture school. A planner, said Perloff, is a "generalist with a specialty."

Source: Excerpted from Ruth Eckdish Knack, "Here's Looking at You," *Planning* (March 1986), 9–15.

action between economic and physical development and social processes. The chapter also covers the origins and use of social-impact assessment and the use of social elements in comprehensive plans.

A community is first and foremost a place for people to live. In the United States, the private market constructs most housing, meeting the needs of people with moderate or high incomes; people with lower incomes, however, have always faced difficulty finding affordable, adequate, safe, and low-cost housing. Although the federal government once provided significant financial resources to help local governments fund housing, it has largely withdrawn housing support. Chapter 12, "Planning for Housing," examines changing governmental roles. It also considers the dynamics of housing supply and demand, housing standards, and the elements of a housing plan.

Planning is a management activity, and planning must be managed. Chapter 13 focuses on the evolution and organization of local planning agencies within the overall governmental structure; the management of the agency's planning program—with an emphasis on strategic planning; and the interaction of planning with the host of other government agencies—local, state, and national—that affect planning.

To successfully design and implement plans, planners must understand the local government budgetary process. Chapter 14 provides an overview of the operating budget and capital improvements programming. It also discusses a number of the ways in which local governments finance capital improvements.

Local government planning is professional, rational, and objective to the extent to which it can gather, analyze, and apply information. Chapter 15 describes techniques for obtaining data, sources for data, and basic methods of data analysis.

Chapter 16, on the values of the planner, brings the book to a close by discussing issues that are of central concern to all professionals in local government planning. Planners must balance the desire for beauty with the desire for efficiency. Planners must find ways to guide growth while conserving resources. Planners who operate in local government must deal with issues of equity, pluralism, individuality, and democratic participation. Planning is a valued-laden field.

The bibliography at the back of the book, which is divided chapter by chapter, lists a number of standard works for the new planner or student. It is intended not as a comprehensive scholarly list but as a guide to the next places to go following this book.

 # Historical development of American city planning

This chapter traces American city planning from early colonial times through the nineteenth century and then focuses on subsequent developments grouped into five periods: 1900 to 1920, 1920 to 1940, 1940 to 1960, 1960 to 1980, and since 1980. Decennial census figures are presented as guideposts, and highlights are given in sociology, economics, and technology to support historical generalizations about planning.

Before 1900

The history of American planning in the years before 1900 can be divided into three phases: the colonial era, the period of expansion and westward migration, and the years following the Civil War. In the rest of this section, each of these periods—and its contribution to the development of modern urban America—will be considered in detail.

The colonial tradition

Preplanned community development was the norm for European colonial settlements in the New World beginning in the late 1500s, when the Law of the Indies fixed the form of Spanish municipalities in the Americas.

New Haven, Connecticut, established in the 1630s, was laid out as a grid of nine square blocks. The grid pattern was also used in Philadelphia (1682), Detroit (1700), New Orleans (1718), and Savannah (1733). In Williamsburg (1699) a geometric variation was used in which a main avenue was paralleled by two secondary streets and a mall intersected the main axis, all of which created visual and symbolic linkages between the College of William and Mary, the colonial capitol, and the governor's palace.

These early settlements consisted of residences, streets, open public spaces, and a few specialized structures such as churches, government buildings, and warehouses. Even the largest of the American colonial cities was quite low in density, consisting of one- and two-story structures interspersed with large areas of gardens and arbors. At the time of the American Revolution, New York City, the largest American city, had only 33,000 people, while the village-cities of the frontier were mere hamlets.

American colonial town planning was predicated on a European concept of the powers of municipal government, which was derived in turn from the development of the free town and the charter city during the Middle Ages. Such medieval communities were municipal corporations of considerable authority commonly capable of owning and disposing of all vacant land in the city. They were generally authorized to play a major role in guiding the physical development of the community as well as in setting social and economic policies. Such was commonly the case with American colonial towns.

As a result of the American Revolution and the subsequent adoption of the Constitution, however, American cities became creatures of their respective states. Almost all local authority belonged to state governments, with counties

Figure 2–1 Robert Montgomery's 1717 scheme for a Georgia settlement to be known as the "Margravate of Azilia." The town was to be ringed by a greenbelt and 640-acre estates.

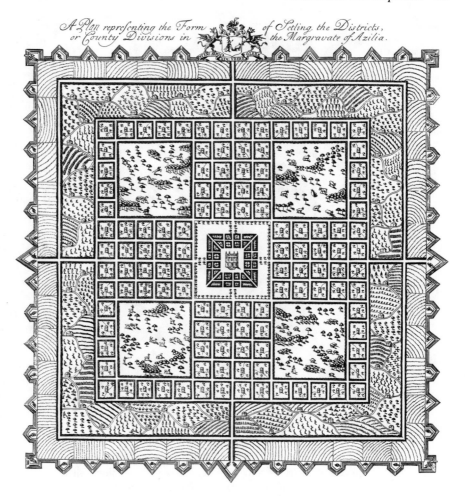

acting as agents of the states and with cities and towns (usually designated as municipal corporations) functioning under city charters or legislative enactments that gave them only certain designated powers. These powers were few, were strictly controlled by the states, and were concerned primarily with the maintenance of order and the provision of basic services. Cities had no clear authority to control, let alone direct, the development of private property, and the states failed to exercise their authority in this area.

The early republic

The Ordinance of 1785, which established a system of rectangular survey coordinates for virtually all of the country west of the Appalachians, opened the American West to rapid settlement and resulted in rampant land speculation for private gain.

The late eighteenth century also witnessed the evolution of an agrarian ethic which held that a life rooted in agriculture is the most valuable way of life; this outlook was inherently antiurban and supported a nonrestrictive and minimal role for government. Agrarian philosophy—eagerly adopted by American intellectuals and rapidly internalized by political theorists—combined with the decline of municipal government and enormous increases in land speculation to sound the death knell of the American colonial town planning tradition.

The first order of business for the new country, upon attainment of independence, was the establishment of a capital for the new federal government.

Figure 2–2   Peter Gordon's view of Savannah in 1734 shows James Oglethorpe's tidy division into four wards, each with forty house lots and four public building sites arranged around an open space.

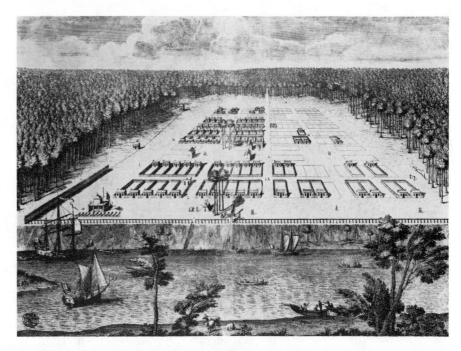

In 1790 Congress designated Philadelphia as the temporary seat of the government until 1800, when a new capital city on the Potomac was to be ready for occupancy. With President Washington, the three commissioners appointed to arrive at a plan for the capital commissioned Pierre Charles L'Enfant to design the new city.

L'Enfant's plan was centered on the Capitol and the "President's Palace" (now the White House), both situated on rises of ground commanding views of the river and connected by a large diagonal boulevard, Pennsylvania Avenue. From this center, L'Enfant developed a vast radial plan incorporating these and other major public structures and providing large public open spaces and plazas as well as two vast green intersecting malls—one behind the Capitol and the other behind the President's Palace—on the east bank of the Potomac River. A small-grid street plan was superimposed over this grand composition of radial streets, public structures, plazas, and vast malls.

When one of the commissioners requested changes in his plan, L'Enfant became difficult, and he was ultimately dismissed. The task of laying out the capital city was entrusted to Andrew Ellicott, who replicated L'Enfant's scheme and provided the necessary adjustments. Almost immediately the city became the focus of speculative attention; it was abundantly evident that the municipal authorities needed to demand compliance with the plan's requirements were seriously lacking. The presence of a plan—but the absence of the means to enforce it—was a clear indication of the urban future that lay before the country in the century ahead, as land speculation, free of municipal control, became the dominant force in shaping the American city.

Elsewhere in the country, at the beginning of the nineteenth century, large-scale city plans developed along the lines of traditional American colonial towns fared badly, commonly being ignored in favor of land-speculation-based plans. For example, the governor and judges' plan for Detroit, authorized by Congress in 1806 after a fire leveled the settlement on 11 June 1805, was a vast radial plan of boulevards, parade grounds, and "circuses" intended to cover the burned-out area of the original city and an additional area of more than 1,600 acres of the adjoining wilderness of the Michigan Territory. When disagreements developed between the creator of the plan, Judge Woodward, and the governor and the other judges, the plan was repealed and replaced by a grid system more amenable to minimal government expenditure and maximum potential for land speculation.

Similarly, the plan by Joseph Mangin (surveyor and architect for the city of New York) for the expansion of New York City—a plan based on public squares, public structures, and wide boulevards—was rejected in favor of a plan that was more in keeping with the new urban realities of minimal governmental responsibility, rampant land speculation, and minimal interference with private property. The approved plan, filed in 1811, was an unbroken grid-street plan extending to the north for over 100 blocks, irrespective of the rough terrain of the island, relieved by just one parade ground, a single public market, and five small parks sited on terrain undesirable for private development. This plan provided for a minimum number of public amenities and activities and a maximum number of identical speculative building lots.

Also in 1811, the Cumberland Road (the National Road), the first major road in the United States constructed with federal funds, was begun at Cumberland, Maryland; it reached Columbus, Ohio, in 1833 and terminated at Vandalia, Illinois, in 1840. Constructed at a cost of approximately $7 million, the National Road became a conduit for immigration from the East Coast to the seemingly limitless farmlands of the interior.

The Erie Canal, begun in 1817 and operational in 1825, complemented the National Road as the way to the American West. For a brief period, settlements vied with each other to be on the main line and feeder lines of canal systems, but the canal was soon to be supplanted by the railroad as a major means of transportation. The railroad corporations, which ultimately became the New York Central, the Pennsylvania, and the Baltimore and Ohio, were formed between 1823 and 1831. Railroad track in the United States increased from 20 miles in 1830 to over 2,500 miles in 1840.

Expansion: Its rapidity and its results

A small grid-plan town was laid out on the site of present-day Chicago in 1830, at which time the first tenement houses were being built in New York City. These tenements would be occupied in the 1840s by the first of the massive waves of European immigrants who swelled the size of American cities. In 1840 only three American cities had populations of more than 100,000. By 1850 there were nine such cities, and over 4.5 million Americans lived in cities and towns.

The three major ports of entry for immigrants were New York City, which had been provided with a grid plan in 1811; Philadelphia, which was founded as a grid city in the 1680s; and the new grid city of Chicago. This form of street planning was generally unfamiliar to the Northern European peasants and to the residents of the European medieval organic towns who began to flock to our shores in midcentury. To many of these immigrants, the plan of these ports of entry become symbolic of their lives in the New World, and they carried this grid plan with them as they moved inland to build the thousands of grid-plan communities west of the Appalachians. This development was reinforced by the rectangular land survey system established by the Ordinance of 1785.

In addition to these frontier agricultural settlements, another form of city was evolving in America in the mid-nineteenth century—the great industrial city. These cities were based on railroad transportation, as the public road system was scarcely developed. Such cities contained center-city factories surrounding power sources; their extent was circumscribed by the efficient transmission of steam power by means of flywheels and belts. Large brick industrial mills, usually three to six stories high, arose near the core of the city. Because the system employed a vast amount of cheap labor, it required a population within easy walking distance of the mill; in consequence large concentrations of tenement flats grew up around factory sites.

Fifty major "firsts" in modern American city planning

1811   First federal interstate highway authorized–U.S. Route 40 from Baltimore through the Northwest Territory, part of a nationally sponsored regional economic development program.

1867   New York State passes the first major tenement house law restricting physical conditions.

1867   San Francisco enacts the first land use zoning restricting the location of obnoxious uses.

1892   A survey of large-city slums is the first federal government recognition of the problems of slums and cities.

1899   A Massachusetts state court is the first to support restriction of building height.

1903   In Cleveland, Daniel H. Burnham, John M. Carrere, and Arnold W. Brunner create the first local "civic center" plan in the country.

1906   In San Francisco, "City Beautiful" principles are applied for the first time to a major American city on the mainland, in a plan by Daniel H. Burnham and Edward Bennett.

1907   Connecticut legislature creates the first official, local, and permanent town planning board, for Hartford.

1907   The Russell Sage Foundation begins the first comprehensive city survey, in Pittsburgh.

1909   In Chicago, Daniel H. Burnham and Edward H. Bennett develop the first metropolitan regional plan.

1909   Wisconsin passes the first state enabling act for planning.

1909   First national planning conference is held in Washington, D.C.

1909   Los Angeles institutes the first major use of land use zoning to direct future development.

1910   Forest Hills Gardens, on Long Island, is the first American test of the neighborhood unit idea.

1913   First major American textbook on planning: *Carrying Out the City Plan*, by Flavel Shurtleff.

1913   George B. Ford and Ernest P. Goodrich create The Technical Advisory Corporation in New York City, the first private planning consulting firm.

1913   New Jersey becomes the first state to institute mandatory referral of subdivision plats, the beginning of modern subdivision control.

1914   Newark, New Jersey, hires the first full-time municipally employed planner, Harland Bartholomew.

1915   California becomes the first state to institute extraterritorial mandatory referral of subdivision plats.

1916   Congress passes the Federal-Aid Road Act, the first federal-aid highway act.

1916   New York City adopts the first comprehensive zoning code.

1916   The Miami Conservancy District (Ohio) adopts the first regional functional authority plan.

1917   The American City Planning Institute elects Frederick Law Olmsted, Jr., first president of an American professional planning association.

1919   The Ohio State Conference on City Planning (now The Ohio Planning Conference) creates the first statewide citizens' organization in support of planning.

1919   First American parkway: The Bronx River Parkway, New York.

1921   First bi-state functional authority is created: The Port of New York Authority in New York and New Jersey.

1922 Los Angeles creates the first county planning board.

1922 First suburban, auto-oriented shopping center is constructed: Country Club Plaza at Kansas City, Missouri.

1925 Cincinnati planning commission is first to officially adopt a comprehensive plan for a major American city.

1926 In *Village of Euclid* (Ohio) v. *Ambler Realty Company*, the Supreme Court supports comprehensive zoning for the first time.

1926 New York is the first state to provide a public subsidy for housing.

1933 First U.S. National Planning Board is created (abolished, as the National Resources Planning Board, in 1943).

1933 Ohio passes the first state public housing act.

1934 First federally supported public housing for the general population is constructed, via PWA (Cedar-Central in Cleveland, the first to be begun; Clark-Howell-Techwood in Atlanta, the first to be occupied).

1934 Alfred Bettman of Cincinnati becomes the first president of the American Society of Planning Officials (parent organization of the American Planning Association).

1935 The "greenbelt" towns are begun, the first federally built new towns to be constructed in peacetime.

1937 The Housing Act of 1937 makes the first major federal legislative commitment to public housing.

1945 Pennsylvania passes the first state urban redevelopment act.

1948 Cincinnati is the first American city to adopt a metropolitan comprehensive plan following World War II.

1949 The Housing Act of 1949 creates the first federal urban redevelopment program (clearance).

1949 First regional shopping center is built: Town and Country Shopping Center (the "Miracle Mile"), east of Columbus, Ohio.

1954 The Housing Act of 1954 creates the first federal conservation and rehabilitation program and establishes the first federal 50-50 funding for preparation of general plans.

1961 The Housing Act of 1961, section 221(d)3, creates the first federal housing subsidy program.

1965 Robert C. Weaver is appointed first Secretary of the U.S. Department of Housing and Urban Development (HUD).

1972 First rapid transit built for fast center-to-center service: the Bay Area Rapid Transit (BART) system, San Francisco.

1972 First federal revenue-sharing program is created.

1972 First national land use legislation is introduced (aborted).

1974 First federal block grant system is introduced, replacing the categorical grant system.

1978 Hawaii introduces the first statewide zoning system.

1979 Israel Stollman becomes the first Executive Director of the American Planning Association (a merger of AIP and ASPO).

Source: Adapted from Steven I. Gordon, ed., *The Review Book: American Institute of Certified Planners Written Examination* (Columbus, OH: The Ohio State University, City and Regional Planning Department, 1985). Reproduced by permission.

In the mid-nineteenth century, workers, in New York City and other large U.S. industrial cities frequently lived in "railroad flats," long, narrow apartments in which going from one room to another required passage through consecutive spaces, as in a railroad passenger train. These walk-up structures, generally five to seven stories high, were constructed solidly in rows across entire block faces with four apartments on each floor surrounding a central common staircase, with just one room in each apartment provided with a window or two for light and air. The small rear yard contained a multi-seat outhouse and often a well, resulting in deplorable sanitary conditions.

During the first half of the nineteenth century, virtually no governmental actions were initiated to control or redirect private development in order to ameliorate worsening housing and living conditions. As a result of this laissez-faire policy, the weakness of municipal authority in the new state-centered political system, and the antiurban bias of agrarian philosophy, some of the worst housing and living conditions of the modern era were created in America during the next half century.

The rapid growth of New York City in the early 1850s brought to public attention the lack of public open space in the plan of 1811. This deficiency was rectified in 1853 when the New York State legislature authorized purchase of a site for a great "central park." Frederick Law Olmsted, Sr., was appointed superintendent of construction in 1857; in the following year, in association with Calvert Vaux, he won the competition for the design of the park. His "greens-ward" plan for Central Park consisted of a vast English garden of "natural" terrain and lakes, curved paths, and irregular plantings. The first English garden to be realized in America on so large a scale, Central Park, became the model for all American city parks.

The postwar era to the turn of the century

Under the impetus of war production, American cities of the North grew enormously during the Civil War, intensifying already serious housing problems. Housing reformers denounced the do-nothing attitudes of government and demanded public control of housing conditions. In 1867 the first New York Tenement House Law was enacted, legitimizing the railroad flat with a few improvements and prohibiting by law the construction of anything worse. In the same year, a San Francisco ordinance prohibited development of slaughter-houses, hog storage facilities, and hide curing plants in certain districts of the city. This 1867 ordinance, which was preventive rather than after the fact and restricted land uses by physical areas of the city, set the stage for the further evolution of land use zoning in the United States.

The period between 1860 and 1870 also saw the beginning of suburbanization in the United States, with the creation of small settlements beyond the cities for the residences of owner-managers capable of affording them. Riverside, Illinois, west of Chicago on the Des Plaines River, was planned by Frederick Law Olmsted, Sr., and Calvert Vaux in 1869. Here, as in Central Park, Olmsted and Vaux applied the principles of the English garden and produced a system of gently curving tree-lined streets and single-family detached houses with deep setbacks of lawn and shade trees. This suburban, quasi-rural, and exclusively residential pattern of perimeter development became the status symbol of the owner-manager class in the United States. The Riverside pattern has been copied in the suburban development of virtually every major city in the country and still dominates concepts of land subdivision for single-family detached units.

In 1877, in *Munn* v. *Illinois*, the Supreme Court of the United States made the following ruling:

When, therefore, one devotes his property to a use in which the public has an interest,

Figure 2–3 One of Jacob Riis's many photographs of tenement life.

he, in effect, grants to the public an interest in that use, and must submit to be controlled by the public for the common good, to the extent of the interest he has thus created.

This decision paved the way for future governmental intervention in private development. The development controls enacted in the New York Tenement House Law of 1867 were expanded in 1879 to require that new tenements provide a narrow air shaft between adjacent structures with windows opening onto this air shaft from the interior rooms. This law, known as the "Old Law," also required two toilets on each floor accessible from the common stair hall and a window opening of at least one square yard in each room.

The U.S. census of the following year, 1880, showed that New York had become the first American city of over 1 million population. The massive immigration of the next decade, in which some 5 million people entered the United States, increased urban congestion and led to the rapid construction of tenement houses. In Chicago new business buildings rose to sixteen or more stories in response to the soaring land values of the 1880s, introducing the now-commonplace vertical character of downtown business areas. The first practical electric trolley—soon to become the dominant means of urban transportation in America—moved over the streets of Richmond, Virginia, in 1888.

At the beginning of the 1890s, business and industrial uses were intermixed throughout the core of the American city. On the congested streets of the city—frequently of mud and often strewn with garbage—the contrast between the personal wealth of the few and the abject poverty of the many was startling. Political corruption of the worst sort generated little enthusiasm for increased governmental responsibilities in a system where *public* meant *of poor quality*.

The deplorable conditions of tenement house life in New York City were exposed by Jacob Riis in *How the Other Half Lives* (1890)[1] and *The Children of the Poor* (1892).[2] These disclosures outraged the public, with the result that in 1892 the U.S. Congress appropriated $20,000 for an investigation of slums in

Figure 2–4   View of the World Columbian Exposition of 1893.

cities of over 200,000 population. This study was the first federal recognition of the problems of slums and urban housing in America.

In 1890, to commemorate the 400th anniversary of the discovery of America, Congress designated Chicago as the site of a great world's fair. This fair, the World's Columbian Exposition, opened on the first of May, 1893. It was designed by a team headed by the Chicago architect Daniel H. Burnham and including Charles Follen McKim of the architectural firm of McKim, Mead and White; Frederick Law Olmsted, Sr.; and Augustus St. Gaudens, the sculptor. This team produced the first example in the United States of a great group of public buildings and public spaces that were conceived in relation to each other and that were specifically designed to delight and impress the citizen-visitor and to fulfill that citizen's every need. The fair became a model for urban America: well over 2 million Americans flocked to see this "White City," and many left committed to realizing some elements of that citizen-centered good order in their home communities. Burnham came to be known as the father of city planning in the United States for his contributions to American city planning during the first decade of the twentieth century, contributions based on his experiences at Chicago in 1893.

The recession being experienced by the rest of the nation in 1893 had been temporarily forestalled in Chicago by the positive effects of the Columbian Exposition. When the exposition closed, Chicago and its environs became enveloped in the same economic pressures that threatened the rest of the country. In Pullman, Illinois, a "model" industrial city built in 1881 a short distance from Chicago, a violent confrontation occurred as a result of layoffs and unemployment, and federal troops were called in. The Pullman Strike of 1894 intensified social discord in Chicago and effectively halted the creation of model industrial communities like Pullman for decades.

In the spring of 1897, with the social discord and economic conditions that had created the Pullman Strike still fresh in mind, Burnham urged that public works planning be undertaken in Chicago on a massive scale, both to create employment and to encourage a socially unifying civic pride. Much to Burnham's disappointment, the city's commercial and political leadership failed to act on his suggestions, and the notion of effecting socioeconomic reform through large-scale construction of public facilities was to lie dormant for several years. Burnham's proposals were based on the ideas developed between 1850 and 1870 by Baron Haussmann for Paris, where two decades of social peace and the greatest period of capital formation in French history resulted from a policy of eliminating unemployment through massive public works projects. Because Paris, "The City Beautiful," had inspired Burnham's efforts, such proposals come to be referred to as examples of an American "City Beautiful" movement.

In 1898, Ebenezer Howard, a stenographer to the British Parliament, published *To-Morrow: A Peaceful Path to Real Reform* (reissued four years later as *Garden Cities of To-Morrow*).[3] Howard proposed to solve problems of the industrial slums of the Western world by creating small, self-sufficient "garden cities" of finite population surrounded by greenbelts of publicly held land permanently committed to agriculture—thus precluding urban expansion and eliminating speculative land costs. These garden cities were to be built around green open spaces and public buildings. Schools were to be located at the center of subunits separated by major streets, and limited industrial establishments were to be located at the perimeter. Urban growth was to be accommodated through additional static satellite units established around a similarly limited and structured central city providing common services. The concept of the neighborhood unit, the basic building block of the American city following World War II, and the greenbelt towns constructed by the U.S. government during the Depression, evolved from Howard's concepts.

The American city became increasingly congested and complex at the turn of the century. An elevated railroad wound around the downtown section of Chicago to form the Loop, and the first American electric underground railroad subway system was constructed in Boston in 1897. Tall buildings, rising everywhere in response to rising land values, blocked sunlight and inhibited the free flow of air to the streets below. In 1898 a Massachusetts statute was passed limiting the height of buildings around Boston's Copley Square to 90 feet. In 1899, in a landmark decision (*Attorney General* v. *Williams*), the Massachusetts Supreme Court upheld the statute, establishing the public's right to protect and preserve light and air by regulating maximum building height.

The year 1899 saw the close of a century of extraordinary national and urban population growth, during which time the population of the United States grew from 5 million to 76 million. In 1900, 40 percent of that population lived in cities, thirty-eight of which had more than 100,000 inhabitants.

From 1900 to 1920

In spite of efforts during the nineteenth century to regulate tenement housing in New York City, conditions in that city's tenements at the turn of the century were appalling. Lawrence Veiller, the first full-time housing reformer in America and founder of the National Housing Association, led a massive effort to improve these conditions that resulted in a voluminous report on housing conditions in New York City and the passage in 1901 of a "New Law" that Veiller wrote. Unlike earlier tenement laws, the New Law was vigorously enforced. It *required* permits for construction, alteration, and conversion; inspection upon completion; and penalties for noncompliance. Most significantly, it provided for a permanent tenement house department to administer and enforce the law. Among other conditions, the New Law required wide light and air courts between structures and a toilet and running water in each apartment. The New Law became the model for tenement laws throughout the United States.

A new era of plans

In 1900, an annual meeting of the American Institute of Architects was held in Washington, D.C., to commemorate the centennial of the capital city. This meeting called attention to L'Enfant's plan, to the "White City" of the Columbian Exposition, and to the disorderly condition of both Washington and the American city in general that had resulted from unrestrained free enterprise, land speculation, and public neglect. Senator James McMillan of Michigan, impressed by this meeting, appointed a subcommittee of his Senate Committee on the District of Columbia and charged it with the restoration of L'Enfant's plan. The McMillan Committee, headed by Daniel Burnham, was the same basic team that had designed the World's Columbian Exposition, with substitution of F. L. Olmsted, Jr., for F. L. Olmsted, Sr., who was in ill health at the time. This was the first group in America to be identified as experts on city planning and to be given the status of professional city planning consultants. The McMillan Committee Plan, reported in 1902, focused on restoration of the Mall, the siting of new public buildings, the creation of a regional park system, and the location of monuments. President Theodore Roosevelt's enthusiastic endorsement of the plan established a federal sanction for city planning.

The planning movement that grew out of the McMillan Plan was a reform movement. Burnham considered himself a leader of the American Republican Progressive movement, which was attempting, through public works project siting and design by public policy, to reduce graft in the placement and construction of public buildings, and to improve the quality of the public environment for all to enjoy. The movement also intended to effect a transfer of wealth from the rich to all citizens through investment in public buildings, plazas, and parks that would be available to all, be owned by all, and become objects of a socially unifying civic pride.

In 1902, Tom Johnson, reform mayor of Cleveland, convinced Burnham to head a team charged with preparing a plan for a group of public buildings in downtown Cleveland. Johnson intended this project to eliminate a notorious slum area, to provide necessary public facilities, and to encourage in Cleveland citizens an intense civic pride that would create a feeling of allegiance to the city and its government. The result of this work, the Cleveland Group Plan of 1903, stimulated similar "civic center" plans throughout the United States.

In 1904 a civic association in San Francisco, headed by former mayor James D. Phelan, invited Burnham to prepare a plan for the city. Burnham and his new planning assistant, Edward H. Bennett, produced a plan that was not limited to a grouping of structures in the civic center: it was a plan of radial and concentric highways, a highway outer belt, extensive shoreline parks, and a mass transit subway. Smoke-producing industry was located on the basis of wind-drift patterns, and residential districts were bounded by major streets to reduce through traffic. These aspects of the plan became city planning dogma in America for the next three generations. This plan, published in 1906, was the first application of Burnham's principles to an entire large American city on the mainland.

The first official, local, and permanent town planning board in the United States, the Hartford Commission on a City Plan, was created by the Connecticut legislature in 1907. Similar boards were created in Milwaukee in 1908 and in Chicago, Detroit, and Baltimore in 1909. These early boards were created to sponsor the development of a city plan, to oversee its execution, and to encourage financial support of public construction projects. Because they lacked departmental status, these boards had little direct contact with operating agencies of city government, and the chairmen of the boards lacked equal status with department heads in dealing with the municipal executive officer.

Ebenezer Howard's garden city concept was realized for the first time at Letchworth, England, begun in 1903. Designed as a city for some 35,000 people,

Figure 2–5 A diagram from Ebenezer Howard's *To-Morrow* (1898) depicting a central city and six garden cities connected by canals, railways, and roads.

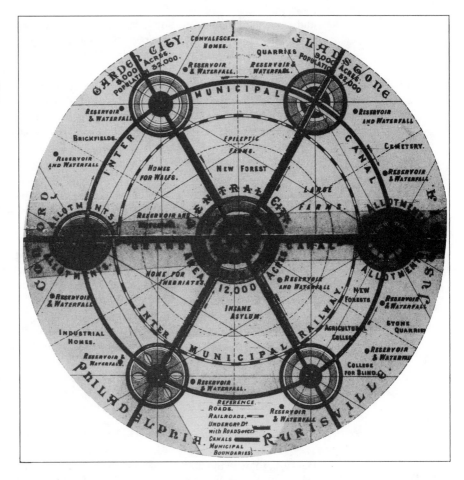

surrounded by an extensive greenbelt, Letchworth was planned in full detail by Barry Parker and Raymond Unwin. Shortly thereafter, Unwin was challenged by a wealthy social worker to create an area of London with healthy housing available to residents with a wide range of incomes and provided with a full range of civic activities. Unwin's efforts resulted in the first comprehensive neighborhood design, Hampstead Garden Suburb, built at the northern terminus of the London subway system in 1907. Unwin modified Howard's idea of satellite towns to create small satellite residential districts that would never grow, being bounded by major streets, with segregated industry (in Howard's scheme at the perimeter, in Unwin's in London) and with the entire area centered around major green open spaces and public facilities.

In 1907 the United States experienced its highest level of immigration: 1,285,000 people in one year. Immigrants flooded into the New Law tenements of New York City and into every other major city of America, including the steel city of Pittsburgh, where housing and public health conditions were deplorable. In 1907 the first systematic statistical city survey in America was begun in Pittsburgh. Housing, health, and social conditions were carefully surveyed, compiled, and plotted with respect to geographic location. The subsequent correlations and analyses established the foundation for a kind of data-based city planning that was not to emerge fully in the United States until a generation later.

Burnham spent virtually all of 1907 and 1908 working on a plan of Chicago commissioned by the Commercial Club, a prestigious businessmen's association. This plan, released on 4 July 1909, was the first metropolitan-regional plan in the United States. Burnham's daring proposals covered a vast area, projecting a great outer belt of regional parks and reservations, an intricate web of radial and concentric highways, and a lakefront park system more than twenty miles in length. The plan also grouped and relocated railroad lines and terminals, created many center-city parks and broad, radial, tree-lined boulevards, straightened the Chicago River, and projected a vast new civic center and a two-level boulevard (now Wacker Drive) parallel to the Chicago River.

The fact that the plans for Chicago (1909), San Francisco (1906), Cleveland (1903), and Washington, D.C. (1902), dealt almost exclusively with public buildings, parks, and streets, proposing no changes to or control over private property, was neither accidental nor solely a function of the nature of Burnham's planning theories. Control of private development by public law lacked clear support from state and federal supreme courts. Publicly owned lands and facilities, on the other hand, were clearly susceptible to public control. Planners based their practical designs on the knowledge that they could be implemented. But in 1909, in *Welch* v. *Swasey*, the Supreme Court established the first nationwide authority enabling communities to regulate the development of private property by limiting building heights and by varying these heights according to zone.

In 1909 Wisconsin passed the first state enabling act granting municipalities within its borders a clear right to engage in city planning. In the same year the first formal course in city planning was offered at Harvard, followed shortly thereafter by a course at the University of Illinois.

A land use zoning ordinance passed in Los Angeles in 1909 created a multitude of use zones applicable to large areas of undeveloped land. Virtually all previous land use zoning had been established to protect existing patterns of development. This ordinance signaled the beginning of an era in which zoning could be used to shape future development. The year 1909 also saw the first national conference on city planning, held in Washington, D.C.

Expansion in the second decade

By 1910 there were almost 92 million Americans, 46 percent of whom were urban, and over fifty cities of more than 100,000 inhabitants. There were also 500,000 automobiles registered in the United States. This plaything of the rich was about to flood the streets of cities built for horsecars, trolleys, and foot traffic. These same cities were about to undergo vast pre–World-War-I growth generated by extended railroad access and expanded trolley routes.

In reaction to this growth, the Russell Sage Foundation, impressed by Unwin's neighborhood design at Hampstead Garden Suburb, sponsored the first demonstration of Unwin's concept in the United States. This project, Forest Hills Gardens, located at a site along the Long Island Railroad near New York City, was designed by Frederick Law Olmsted, Jr., and Grosvenor Atterbury, with the advisory services of Unwin. Initiated in 1910 and completed in 1913, it served as a model for American suburban land development.

When Daniel Burnham died in 1912, leadership in American city planning passed to Frederick Law Olmsted, Jr. Unlike Burnham, Olmsted believed that the city plan should include all uses of land, private as well as public, and that plans should be continuously updated to ensure that they remained relevant to current urban issues and to the citizens' evolving aspirations. Olmsted's vision of municipal planning and control of private development gained momentum in 1912, when the Supreme Court declared in *Eubank* v. *City of Richmond* that municipal control of the horizontal location of buildings on private property, via setback legislation, was constitutional.

Eighteen cities in America had planning boards in 1913. Shortly thereafter this number increased markedly, as state after state passed enabling acts permitting municipalities to engage in planning. In 1913 New Jersey required all land subdivision plats to be reviewed by the local planning board. This was the beginning of land subdivision control as a function of city planning in the United

States. In 1913, Massachusetts made planning mandatory for its local governments.

Land use zoning, which was of critical importance to planning for and municipal control of private land development, came to the U.S. Supreme Court in 1915 in *Hadacheck* v. *Sebastian*. Until that year, few American communities had enacted land use control ordinances because the Court might have held that restriction of higher future profit uses was an unconstitutional taking of property without just compensation. In *Hadacheck*, the Court agreed with the California Supreme Court that "regulation was not precluded by the fact 'that . . . the value of investment made . . . prior to any legislative action will be greatly diminished.' " If the Court did not consider reduction in value of real prior investments valid grounds for declaring the ordinance unconstitutional, it was highly improbable that a reduction of potential future value would be held to invalidate an ordinance. Many municipal leaders, interpreting this case to mean that the Supreme Court had granted implicit approval of land use zoning, began to prepare land use control programs.

A New York commission had been created in 1913 to devise a scheme for the effective control of future urban development of the city. Under the leadership of Edward M. Basset, this commission arrived at the concept of a comprehensive zoning code—a single ordinance that would integrate land use controls, controls on building height, and control of building setbacks and yards. With the issuance of the *Hadacheck* decision in 1915, the Supreme Court had given explicit or implied constitutional approval to all three of these elements (height control by zone in *Welch* v. *Swasey*; building setback control in *Eubank* v. *City of Richmond*; land use control in *Hadacheck* v. *Sebastian*). The New York Zoning Code, the first comprehensive zoning code in the United States, was adopted in 1916. The code was unrelated to a general plan for the fulfillment of community aspirations (in fact, it was a substitute for such a plan), was generally protective of current land interests, and was not based on a forecast of future land use demand. New York's "comprehensive" zoning ordinance was rapidly adopted by many other large American cities, signaling a major shift in the means of governmental control of urban development. Formerly, local governments used public works projects to direct urban growth and to ensure that development corresponded to a definition of the public interest. "Comprehensive" zoning ordinances shifted the emphasis from public to private construction and instituted highly conservative legal and administrative forms of control.

Another significant event in 1916 was the signing of the Federal-Aid Road Act. At a time when the nation's intercity road system was barely passable, this act assisted state highway construction, providing two-lane concrete roads in a countrywide interstate system. There were 4.7 million automobiles on the streets of America in 1917, an increase of 4.2 million since 1910.

Approximately two thousand people attended the ninth national planning conference, held at Kansas City, Missouri, in 1917. At this meeting a small group of members decided to create a professional society and established the American City Planning Institute (ACPI), now known as the American Institute of Certified Planners. The fifty-two charter members of the ACPI included architects, landscape architects, engineers, attorneys, and developers. Frederick Law Olmsted, Jr., served as the institute's first president.

The United States became an urban nation as it entered the 1920s. The census of 1920 reported that 51 percent of the 106.4 million persons residing in the United States at that time lived in urban areas.

From 1920 to 1940

The twenty years between 1920 and 1940 were decades of contrast. In the twenties, prosperity and rapid increases in automobile ownership made possible

Figure 2–6   Even in 1917, New York's Fifth Avenue was congested with auto traffic.

the first massive migration of middle-income residents from the central city to the suburbs. In this period of extensive suburbanization, city planning emphasized development control at the perimeter of the city and the construction and widening of streets to accommodate the automobile. Land use zoning of undeveloped areas, land subdivision controls, and other regulatory devices became the focus of planning efforts, and now engineers, lawyers, and administrators rose to positions of planning leadership, in addition to the architects, landscape architects, and business leaders of the previous decade. Advocates of "The City Efficient" and "The City Administrative" began to supplant the earlier advocates of The City Beautiful. The same years also saw the creation of the first comprehensive plan and of several landmark housing projects.

By the 1930s, the economic hardships of the Depression years shifted emphasis in planning to the creation of massive public works projects. Appalling housing conditions and a slump in housing construction brought large-scale federal intervention through a number of programs, including the Federal Housing Administration (FHA), created in 1934; FHA requirements gradually became the basis for housing standards that still dominate the housing industry today.

An era of unprecedented growth

Local governments reacted to rapid residential and commercial expansion in the 1920s by instituting controls on development. The basic legal framework for the control of private development in the United States was created in the 1920s. This framework emphasized control and protection, by ordinance, of the physical character of the new middle-income residential areas constructed at the perimeter

Figure 2–7 Kansas City's Country Club Plaza in the 1920s.

of the city, maintenance of the status quo in the central city, and fulfillment of the interests of business and industry—which took the form of extensive over-zoning for commercial and industrial uses.

By 1920 many American cities required planning board approval of land subdivision plats based on the application of standards for width of right-of-way, maximum block length, and conformance with the predetermined location of major streets. These standards and mapped locations were established in ordinances creating an official *major street plan*, also commonly termed an *official map*. These requirements often included necessary dedication of streets to the public by gift from the developer prior to the platting of abutting property. The courts upheld this requirement, holding that there is no "taking of property" in such a required "gift" of street right-of-way, as the giving is just a precondition to platting, which the developer must initiate by request; the "gift" is therefore free of municipal coercion. This logic would be expanded in the 1930s to require the mandatory dedication of parklands through land subdivision control.

With rise in automobile ownership, suburban expansion of American cities in the 1920s outstripped municipal annexation, resulting in development of vast areas beyond municipal boundaries. In addition to fostering extraterritorial controls, this led to the creation of county planning authorities capable of dealing with the areas surrounding the central city. In 1922 Los Angeles County created the first county planning board in the United States.

Explosive suburban expansion led the Russell Sage Foundation to undertake a monumental study of the future of the New York metropolitan area, the *Regional Survey of New York and Its Environs*.[4] Begun in 1922, this study was not completed until 1929.

A charter member of the ACPI, J.C. Nichols, responded to the new expansion of the American city by creating the world's first automobile-oriented shopping center, Country Club Plaza, at the outskirts of Kansas City, Missouri, in 1922.

The compact retail sales and business areas of the pre-1920 era, clustered at the core of the city and centered around railroad terminals and trolley stops, began to move outward with the spread of the automobile, making every major street a potential commercial district. Thus, the prosperity of the 1920s, combined with the automobile and complemented by commercial zoning of virtually every major street, resulted in extensive lineal strip commercial development. Vastly increased automobile traffic and its resulting street congestion, together with gross commercial overconstruction, decreased access to these strip commercial areas, which was ultimately reflected in extensive areas of vacant or poorly maintained business facilities along major streets—a condition that can still be seen in hundreds of cities.

Although most land use zoning in the early 1920s was based on broad use categories such as *residence, business,* and *industry,* many communities were making finer distinctions. Some were creating zones in which the single-family detached residence was the only type of residence permitted. State courts supported such regulations, generally basing their support, as in the Massachusetts case of *Brett* v. *Building Commissioner of Brookline* (1924), on protection of public health through reduced danger of fire and increased light and air and on an inability to find that such control bears no conceivable relationship to the protection of the public health, safety, morals and/or welfare. In *Miller* v. *Board of Public Works of the City of Los Angeles* (1925), the state court based its decision in support of single-family-only districts on a presumed relationship between inducement of ownership and community stability, interest in public affairs, and good citizenship. The issue of such finely delineated land use zoning categories had not been tested in the U.S. Supreme Court; nor had another issue—that of zoning totally undeveloped land for uses other than those that the free market would dictate. In 1925 the California Supreme Court supported the zoning of undeveloped land areas in *Zahn* v. *Board of Public Works of the City of Los Angeles*, stating, "Zoning . . . looks not only backward . . . but forward to aid in the development of new districts according to a comprehensive plan having as its basis the welfare of the city as a whole."

The first such "comprehensive plan having as its basis the welfare of the city as a whole" to be officially adopted by a major American city was adopted in Cincinnati in 1925. Alfred Bettman, a Cincinnati attorney, was heavily involved in the work of the United City Planning Committee of Cincinnati, a citizen group dedicated to integrating urban planning with the ongoing processes of the Cincinnati city government. The pro-planning policies of this citizen committee were adopted as elements of the platform of a reform group, the Charter Committee, that came to power in 1924 and immediately implemented Bettman's program. A key element in this program was official adoption of a statement of the long-term goals and policies of the city with regard to its urban form and structure, including both public and private development; this statement was to be followed by the city council in the creation of control devices, such as zoning and subdivision control ordinances, and in the expenditures, of public funds.

The comprehensive plan as pioneered by Bettman and the city of Cincinnati in 1925 became a cornerstone of American city planning. In this concept, legal control of community development is used as a tool for, and is subservient to, the realization of a set of comprehensive, long-range community goals; this is in distinct contrast to comprehensive zoning as presented in the New York City Zoning Code of 1916, in which controls were established without reference to long-range community development policies and projected land use needs.

Prior to 1926 the land use control component of comprehensive zoning rested on a weak constitutional foundation. The New York City Zoning Code of 1916 had never been tested in the U.S. Supreme Court, and its land use element had been adopted solely on the basis of an implication of constitutionality in *Hadacheck* v. *Sebastian*. In 1926 the U.S. Supreme Court heard *Village of Euclid* v. *Ambler Realty Co.*, in which the constitutionality of comprehensive zoning and all of its parts was contested. The Court had decided, informally, to respond in favor of Ambler, striking down the comprehensive zoning package, when Alfred Bettman, fulfilling a charge from the Ohio State Conference on City Planning, was permitted to file an *amicus curiae* brief in support of Euclid and comprehensive zoning. Following Bettman's presentation, the Court, by a 6 to 3 vote, found in favor of Euclid.

This case established the constitutionality of comprehensive zoning and all of its parts. The *Euclid* decision became the basic constitutional building block of American city planning. For Bettman, however, this was a hollow victory. City after city, armed with the constitutional pronouncements of *Euclid*, proceeded to adopt comprehensive zoning ordinances that were unaccompanied by the comprehensive long-range planning he believed essential to the public welfare.

In 1926 the New York Commission on Housing and Regional Planning, created in 1923 and chaired by Clarence S. Stein, published the first state planning report. As a result of this study, in 1926 the state of New York passed an act establishing a state housing board empowered to provide tax exemptions for twenty years to limited-dividend housing corporations willing to provide housing for lower-middle-income people and to abide by a maximum rent schedule. This first public program for housing subsidy in the United States resulted in the construction of 6,000 housing units in fourteen projects.

Clarence Stein, together with Henry C. Wright, realized a model project in 1926 in the construction of Sunnyside Gardens at a site on Long Island near New York City. Sunnyside provided town houses and garden apartments of varying setback on full-block lots, eliminating the narrow side yards and small rear yards of speculative lot-by-lot subdivisions and pooling the land into large common center-of-the-block parks and playgrounds. These units, models for many future "garden apartment" projects, were two rooms deep and were sited parallel to the street.

The peak year for housing production in the United States during the 1920s was 1927. During that year 810,000 dwelling units were built. During this boom, the City Housing Corporation, sponsors of Sunnyside, undertook another model project by Stein and Wright, Radburn, at Fairlawn, New Jersey, which was constructed in 1928. Radburn consisted of large superblocks containing center-of-the-block parks bounded by two-story single-family houses. Pedestrian paths led from the houses through the center-of-the-block parks to the local school and to a nearby shopping center, thus separating pedestrian and vehicular traffic. This project, an evolution of the neighborhood idea explored at Hampstead in London and at Forest Hills Gardens on Long Island, became the prototype for most of the "advanced" American land development planning for the next fifty years.

In 1928 the U.S. Department of Commerce, under Secretary Herbert Hoover, published a new Standard City Planning Enabling Act and recommended its adoption by state legislatures. Although this act was useful in that it promoted city planning, it also confused the comprehensive plan with the zoning plan, leading communities to prepare zoning proposals without reference to long-range, comprehensive public policy issues. By recommending separate adoption of pieces of the plan, the act denied the importance of the comprehensive plan as an integrated statement of public policies. By suggesting that the planning commission, a semi-independent agency, receive and adopt the comprehensive plan and oversee the planning staff (rather than leave these tasks to the municipal legislative body), the act weakened the emerging role of planning as an integral element of government. Many states acted on this suggested enabling act; its

Figure 2–8   An aerial view of Radburn, New Jersey.

Figure 2–8   An aerial view of Radburn, New Jersey.

provisions are still the common basis for municipal planning in many states today.

The *Regional Survey of New York and Its Environs*, prepared by the Russell Sage Foundation and published in 1929, analyzed regional economic, demographic, and governmental problems by combining a vast mass of information on current conditions with projections of the future. This reliance on data, critical to Bettman's concept of a comprehensive plan, became the norm in the years to come as other cities modeled their plan-making processes after this monumental undertaking. In one section of this monumental regional plan for New York City, Clarence A. Perry, a resident of Forest Hills Gardens, codified Unwin's neighborhood ideas and propounded the "neighborhood unit" as the basic building block of the city. The neighborhood unit would have an elementary school at its center and would be bounded by arterial streets at the perimeter. The distance from school to perimeter would be based on a comfortable walking distance for a school-age child; there would be no through traffic or industrial or commercial uses inside the unit. Perry's concept of the neighborhood unit reinforced a local school-centered pattern, with segregation of uses, that was to become the cornerstone of American suburban development after World War II.

The depression years

Franklin Delano Roosevelt, pledging a New Deal to the American people, was elected President in 1932. With 13 million people out of work, New Deal programs focused mainly on unemployment. The New Deal supported planning for the future by means of detailed studies and projections, as well as careful budgeting of resources, bringing economists, statisticians, and sociologists into the planning profession. In many ways the New Deal programs resembled application on a national scale of Burnham's program to restore civic pride and confidence through great public projects designed to provide employment, help ensure social peace, and redistribute wealth to those in need.

The president's uncle, Frederic Adrian Delano, who had been a major supporter of Burnham's 1909 plan for Chicago and had been the chairman of the *Regional Survey of New York and Its Environs,* now came to Washington to chair America's first national planning board.

The National Planning Board, founded in 1933, encouraged state and municipal governments to plan for development over long periods of time and encouraged formulation of twenty-year comprehensive plans founded upon statistical pro-

Figure 2–9
Construction of the
Cherokee Dam in
Tennessee, a project of
the Tennessee Valley
Authority.

jections of future conditions. The board also stimulated the creation of state planning boards.

The year 1933 also saw the creation of the Tennessee Valley Authority, an independent, multifunctional government agency created for the regional planning and development of the Tennessee River valley. Its extensive programs ranged from flood protection and water management to recreational development and power generation.

In 1933 housing development in the United States was at its lowest point in a century. The new administration, focusing on employment in the construction trades and on the condition of slum housing, undertook to construct new dwellings and to rebuild deteriorated central city areas. To do this, the Public Works Administration (PWA) and the Federal Housing Administration (FHA), were created in 1934.

Initially, and for a short time, PWA was authorized to lend up to 85 percent of the cost of housing projects to public and private limited-dividend corporations. Only seven housing projects were produced under this program, which was replaced in 1934 by a new and radically restructured PWA Housing Division with authority to make grants and low-interest loans to limited-dividend housing authorities, usually local housing authorities. The most radical parts of the program were the federal government's power of eminent domain to acquire housing sites and its power to engage directly in the construction of these projects. This program produced fifty projects before it was terminated in 1937.

The FHA was established to expand construction jobs for the unskilled by attracting private funds to residential construction. It did so by providing government insurance of private home loans, removing the financial risk in such investments. To assure nondefault on these loans, the FHA established minimum standards for housing financed under this program. Designed to meet the housing desires, in purchase and resale, of the upper-middle-income group—those least likely to default—these FHA standards were the first federal minimum housing "standards" adopted in the United States. Because they were rapidly reflected in local zoning codes, in building codes, and in private loan manuals as the minimum standards for *all* housing construction in the country, housing that the middle- and lower-income groups could afford quickly became a priori "substandard" and undesirable and thus was "zoned out" of most American cities, severely restricting the amount of housing available to middle- and lower-income groups. The FHA's focus on labor-intensive construction of owner-occupied, single-family detached units stimulated an enormous suburban expansion as a by-product, especially in the decades of the 1950s and 1960s.

The American Society of Planning Officials (ASPO) was created in 1934 to bring planning commissioners, city managers, and other officials more actively into the planning movement, to serve as a clearinghouse for information, and to increase communication among planners. (In 1978 ASPO consolidated with the American Institute of Planners to become the American Planning Association [APA].) Alfred Bettman of Cincinnati served as ASPO's first president.

In 1935 the Resettlement Administration, within the U.S. Department of Agriculture, undertook to design and construct four communities collectively referred to as the "greenbelt towns." Greenbelt, Maryland; Greenhills, Ohio; Greendale, Wisconsin; and Greenbrook, New Jersey. The new towns were to assist in local employment and to create model communities to guide future development. The greenbelt towns, modified neighborhood units in the countryside surrounded by extensive greenbelts of public land and serving as dormitory suburbs for nearby metropolises, were built and operated by the federal government. Greenbrook was never built, because in 1936 the U.S. Court of Appeals for the District of Columbia, in *Township of Franklin* v. *Tugwell*, ruled that the Emergency Relief Appropriation Act on which the program was based was invalid and that the federal government had no constitutional authority to use its power of eminent domain in states for housing purposes.

The entire PWA Housing Division system was abandoned in 1937, as by that time it was clear that the finding in *Tugwell* applied equally to the PWA programs. Local housing authorities also resented federal dominance, and the radical "pump priming" for jobs that was needed in 1934 seemed not so necessary with the emerging economic recovery of 1937. The PWA Housing Division was replaced in the Housing Act of 1937 by the U.S. Housing Authority (USHA). This 1937 act became the foundation for most future federal public housing programs. Under USHA, local housing authorities used their state-granted power of eminent domain to acquire housing sites. About 168,000 dwelling units were constructed by local housing authorities under this program between 1937 and the outbreak of World War II. Given that New York City alone had over 800,000 Old Law tenements (1897–1901) and railroad flats (pre–1879), it is clear that

Figure 2–10 Aerial and street-level views of Greenbelt, Maryland.

these New Deal programs were capable of revealing the depth of the housing problem but could do little to solve it.

A decade after proposing the concept of the neighborhood unit in the *Regional Survey of New York and Its Environs,* Clarence Perry elaborated on it in his book, *Housing for the Machine Age.*[5] Perry held that the neighborhood structure, if it is to create true community, must bring together people of identical background and interest. He also held that the problems of juvenile delinquency could be coped with only by the provision of single-family detached residences with individual backyard playgrounds. He therefore recommended that the basic building block of the city, earlier suggested by Perry and others as a fairly high-density apartment-based unit, be an area of owner-occupied, single-family detached homes. This modified version of the neighborhood unit was to become the basic structuring unit for post–World War II development.

On 1 January 1939 the American City Planning Institute (ACPI) was renamed the American Institute of Planners (AIP). At this time the United States was recovering from the Depression, and there was much agitation for the elimination of government involvement in housing and other aspects of American life. As the prospect of a European war appeared with increasing clarity, interest in housing and urban development issues subsided.

From 1940 to 1960

Planning for anything but the war effort was largely neglected for the first half of the 1940s, which left the country unprepared for the rapid growth that was to occur in the second half of the decade. Most of that postwar growth took place in suburban areas, and by the onset of the fifties, population decline and physical deterioration had arisen as problems in central cities. Particularly with the advent of the Housing Act of 1954, which provided the first federal funds earmarked for community planning, planning activities expanded, as efforts were made both to preserve urban centers and to manage the development of communities at the perimeter.

The war and after

The United States census of 1940, the first decennial census to include data on housing quality, reported that one out of every eight urban dwellings had no indoor bathing or toilet facilities and that one out of every seven had no running water or plumbing of any kind. Rapid uncontrolled construction of urban housing units, the pride of the nineteenth century, had become the housing crisis of the twentieth century.

Threat of war resulted in the creation in June 1940 of the Office of the Housing Coordinator, established to coordinate all federal housing programs and to determine housing needs relative to critical defense industries. The USHA low-rent public housing program was abolished, and 100-percent loans were made available to local housing authorities for the construction of defense housing. In this brief period between the depths of the Depression and the onslaught of World War II, the International City Managers' Association published *Local Planning Administration*, by Ladislas Segoe,[6] a distinguished planning consultant who had played a major role in preparing the Cincinnati plan of 1925. This book codified planning methods, processes, and standards that had developed since the early 1920s and became both the primary text for students in planning programs at American universities and the basic municipal reference work that guided community development during the postwar era.

From 1942 to 1945 war planning replaced rather than complemented city planning. The national commitment to planning for the war effort and for the war effort alone was at its most harmful in 1943, when the National Planning

Figure 2–11 A neighborhood in Levittown, New York, a large postwar suburban development.

Figure 2–12 The Point Park, Pittsburgh, in the mid-1970s.

Board was abolished and its functions were distributed among committees of Congress. This absence of concern for the urban future left the country and its cities totally unprepared for the urban problems that would arise at the end of the war.

In February 1942 all federal housing agencies were consolidated in the National Housing Agency (NHA). In contrast to the World War I era, when federal government corporations were empowered to build defense industry housing, the approach taken during World War II was to build on the successful 1934 FHA model, stimulating construction of war housing by private enterprise. To ensure the success of this program, the Housing Act of 1937 was amended to provide FHA mortgage insurance of 90-percent loans (10 percent down) of twenty-five-year duration. Over 1,850,000 dwelling units for war workers were constructed through this wartime mortgage insurance program. At the end of World War II the nation faced a shortage of over 7 million urban housing units. To meet these needs, especially for returning service personnel, the liberal and highly effective 90-percent–twenty-five-year mortgage insurance terms of the war housing program were extended to FHA and Veterans Administration (VA) housing programs. This action was a major factor in the housing boom of the late 1940s and early 1950s.

Because there had been little advance planning for peacetime, the rapid metropolitan growth of the postwar period generally took place without benefit of comprehensive plan guidelines other than remnants of long-range plans executed in the 1930s and earlier. A vast expansion of the suburban fringes of American cities occurred after 1945; this expansion was heavily influenced by federal and state highway construction programs, national prosperity (which fostered extensive automobile and home ownership), and the FHA and VA housing programs. Mass transit companies, which operated fleets of gasoline-powered, rubber-tired motorbuses that had replaced the electric trolleys in the 1920s and 1930s, began to find it difficult to serve this spread-out, low-density population pattern.

The larger cities created well-staffed planning agencies to cope with this postwar suburban explosion. These staffs devoted most of their time to immediate concerns, such as day-to-day zoning and subdivision control, and to urban redevelopment programs.

Interest in central city redevelopment arose when the census of 1940 indicated that central cities were beginning to lose population to surrounding suburban areas. In response, urban land and business interests urged creation of public redevelopment authorities capable of using state-granted powers of eminent domain to acquire and demolish deteriorated districts. Supporters of this plan wanted the federal government then to subsidize private corporations to encourage reconstruction—for nonhousing purposes—on these cleared sites. The advent of the war forestalled further development of this idea, but intense interest arose again in 1945. In that year, Pennsylvania passed the first state urban redevelopment act that granted a subsidy for the reconstruction of deteriorated central city areas for uses other than housing; the primary result was the Golden Triangle project in Pittsburgh.

In 1947 all federal housing programs, including the FHA mortgage insurance program, were relocated to a new Housing and Home Finance Agency (HHFA), and the first of the massive postwar FHA suburban housing projects to be supported by mortgage insurance emerged at Levittown, New York, followed by Park Forest, Illinois, in the following year.

Unwin's concept of the neighborhood unit, as expanded upon by Perry in the *Regional Survey of New York and Its Environs* in 1929 and as modified by him in 1939 to exclude all but single-family detached units, became the basis of postwar FHA and VA mortgage insurance requirements. A new minimum national standard arose, in effect, from the priority given by Perry in 1939 to the single-family detached residence. As specified in the FHA mortgage insurance requirements of the 1930s, these residences were to be located in uniform owner-occupied districts, on curved streets with green front-yard setbacks and two trees per lot. This accrued pattern was codified in the American Public Health Association's publication *Planning the Neighborhood* in 1948.[7]

Residential suburban decentralization of the American city in the late 1940s was accompanied by the beginning of the dispersal of manufacturing plants from their long-established locations in the core of the city to locations along major railroads and highways at the perimeter. This dispersal was made possible by major improvements in highway systems, subsidized development of over-the-road freight trucking fleets, and widespread automobile ownership among factory workers. These conditions were pointed up in 1949 with the establishment of the first regional shopping center in the United States. In that year Don M. Casto opened the Town and Country Shopping Center (known at the time as "The Miracle Mile") at the outskirts of Columbus, Ohio, beyond the new suburban developments.

The Housing Act of 1949 created a federal program for central-city redevelopment based on the model of the Pennsylvania Act of 1945. Under the program, physically deteriorated areas became eligible for federal support for clearance and redevelopment for any reuse. With the aid of federal subsidies, huge areas of central cities were cleared by local redevelopment authorities and reconstructed by and for private enterprise. The 1949 act made city planning an important activity in the United States, as it required that any federally aided urban redevelopment program conform to a plan for the entire community, creating an instant demand for professionally trained city planners.

Planning concerns at midcentury

The Census of 1950 reported a population of 151 million Americans, owning 48 million automobiles, with 84.5 million people living in metropolitan areas. Suburban fringe areas had increased in population by 35 percent since 1940, whereas central cities had increased by only 13 percent. This Census also reported that 2.5 million of the 40 million American urban homes were dilapidated. The 1949 Housing Act, as actually appropriated, provided for just 26,000 new low-income public housing units a year. At that rate, the 2.5 million dilapidated units occupied by the urban poor would be replaced shortly before A.D. 2050.

Many communities, feeling the pressure for residential development, sought to preserve the rural character of their communities, to maintain high land values, and to preserve their social character (excluding all but the reasonably affluent) by enacting minimum lot area requirements of one-half to one acre or more and minimum residential floor areas that would preclude less than substantial construction. Armed with state court support, and using the neighborhood unit composed of owner-occupied, single-family detached homes as a basic building block, community after community enacted similar regulations, usually with standards far beyond minimal protective needs. Over time, central cities became surrounded by suburban ordinances whose cumulative effect was to deny entry to lower-middle- and lower-income groups—often racial minorities—who were residents of the central city.

The Housing Act of 1954 extended the clearance programs of the 1949 act to the rehabilitation of areas in the process of deteriorating and to the conservation of nondeteriorating areas in danger of deteriorating. The act's emphasis on conservation strongly encouraged adoption and enforcement of housing codes. The act also required a "workable program" for the elimination of future deterioration, from which the concept of the community renewal plan emerged. Among the elements of this program were neighborhood analyses, housing for displaced persons, and citizen participation in the redevelopment process. These emphases led local urban redevelopment staffs to direct their attention away from commercial redevelopment of the city core and toward efforts to improve the opportunities of poor residents of the inner city, paving the way for the "social advocacy" planning of the 1960s.

The Housing Act of 1954, in which urban redevelopment was retitled "Urban Renewal," specifically required that urban redevelopment projects be part of a comprehensive city plan, complete with surveys and projections. To ease the financial burden of preparing such plans, Title I, section 701, provided for fifty-fifty federal-local funding of such plans for communities of under 25,000 people. Since such communities could not afford permanent staffs for this work, it fell to private planning consultants. The "701" program not only created vast employment opportunities for planners but also created a major private urban development consulting industry in America. These "701" projects were coordinated through state planning offices, providing an incentive to rekindled state planning efforts. Increased professional opportunities were immediately reflected in academic systems: between 1950 and 1960 the number of graduate planning programs in America more than doubled.

The latter half of the 1950s saw a major shift of retail centers to the urban perimeter in the form of shopping centers located at or near the intersection of radial and concentric perimeter highways. Undoubtedly the most influential of these developments was Northland Shopping Center in Detroit, designed by Victor Gruen and Associates, which opened in March 1954 and served as a model for new shopping centers throughout the country.

In response to the loss of commercial vitality in the historic city core, downtown business groups and city governments initiated efforts to revitalize central areas. These plans commonly provided an inner belt freeway around the commercial core with radial freeways leading to the suburban areas, large perimeter parking garages, and a central area of street malls reserved solely for pedestrian use. During the next decade, many cities adopted the inner belt freeway and radial freeway components of this design as a result of the Interstate Highway Act of 1956, which provided for a $60-billion defense highway construction program consisting of over 40,000 miles of limited-access highways linking every major city in the nation.

Concurrent with the large-scale relocation of production industry to the perimeter of the city during this period, the "industrial park" emerged. Highly desirable industrial sites along major rail lines and highways were identified by developers and were provided with generous sites and utilities to meet industrial needs. The better designed industrial developments were often surrounded by bands of landscaped and earth-bermed open space, creating highly functional and environmentally attractive industrial accommodations in the suburbs or near the open countryside.

From 1957 until the end of the decade, the major planning activities undertaken in the United States included urban renewal clearance projects, center-city rehabilitation projects, preparation of new long-range (twenty-year) comprehensive plans based on the now-classic methods, and day-to-day zoning and subdivision control work. In addition, the planning staffs of some cities, notably New York and Washington, D.C., proposed building height and bulk controls that would be more flexible than simple limits on height and setback. Included among these experimental concepts was control by floor area ratio; this ratio indicates the maximum permitted relationship between building floor area and net site area and allows virtually any shape and height of building as long as this ratio is not exceeded.

The Housing Act of 1959 made matching funds available for the preparation of comprehensive plans at the metropolitan, regional, state, and interstate levels. By 1960 half of the costs of comprehensive planning in America were being subsidized by the federal government as an inducement to all levels of government to participate in this activity.

By 1960, 70 percent of the nation's 180 million Americans were living in urbanized areas, and megalopolis, the regional city, was a reality, spreading from Boston to northern Virginia.

From 1960 to 1980

The primary influence on planning in the decades between 1960 and 1980 came from changing federal priorities, primarily in the areas of economic and community development. The next two sections consider these developments in detail, tracing a shift from the broad social programs of the 1960s to the "New Federalism" of the 1970s.

The programs of the 1960s

In the late 1950s, more flexible land use controls—such as the floor area ratio and performance standards—created greater diversity in development patterns. In 1961 this trend was continued when the New York City Zoning Code of 1916 was replaced by a new code that specified site area requirements per room (a room-density device); incorporated special incentives such as bonuses for provision of plazas, arcades, and pedestrian walkways; created a flexible building setback system; and provided for development control by open space ratio.

The Housing Act of 1961, in section 221(d)3, provided for an interest subsidy to private nonprofit corporations, limited-dividend corporations, cooperatives, and some public agencies to construct rental housing for low- and moderate-income families. This interest subsidy program became the basic federal housing program of the 1960s.

Membership in the American Institute of Planners (AIP), founded in 1917 as the American City Planning Institute with 52 charter members, had grown to over 3,000 by 1962. In that year, New Jersey became the first state to license the practice of planning, followed in 1966 by Michigan, which licensed use of the title *planner* but not the practice of planning. AIP members were generally unenthusiastic about these actions because they had the effect of defining the planning profession at a time when planners believed that dynamic role changes were required to respond to the planning needs of a rapidly changing society.

In 1963 the Community Renewal Plan (CRP) efforts of many cities were redirected toward assisting lower-income groups to improve their economic standing and their opportunities. Citizen participants in these programs began to press for planning activities extending far beyond the classic city planning confines of land use, building bulk, and utilities and transportation facilities. The mid-1960s also saw initiation of a new scale in private merchant-builder housing efforts, as numerous privately constructed new towns were begun, including Reston, Virginia, and Columbia, Maryland. These new towns were generally satellite dormitory suburbs for the upper middle class.

The creation in 1965 of the U.S. Department of Housing and Urban Development (HUD) provided urban interests with a cabinet-level position, such as rural interests enjoyed through the Department of Agriculture, for the first time in American history. The first secretary of HUD was Robert Weaver. The Housing and Urban Development Act of 1965, the most comprehensive extension of federal urban development and housing programs since 1949, provided rent supplement payments for those below the local poverty line, loans at 3-percent interest for low- and moderate-income families, and subsidies for an additional 240,000 low-rent public housing units. This was followed by enactment of the Model Cities program through the Demonstration Cities and Metropolitan Development Act of 1966.

The Model Cities program, initiated by President Johnson, was unique in the history of American city planning; in earlier federal programs designed for local implementation, problems were identified and defined and responses or solutions devised at the federal level. In the Model Cities program, residents of subdistricts designated as Model City districts created their own quasi-political organization, decided on their problems and priorities, and proposed their own means of arriving at solutions. These organizations and their proposed programs were then funded by the federal government. Although this federal incentive to initiate local district planning—in which urban users defined solutions to their own problems—encountered serious difficulties, the Model Cities program solidly established policy formulation by citizens as an essential part of almost every future urban development program.

The Civil Rights Act of 1968 ended the legality of racial discrimination in the sale or rental of 80 percent of American housing. Later in that same year, in *Jones* v. *Alfred H. Mayer Co.*, the Supreme Court ruled that section 1982 of the Civil Rights Act of 1866 prohibited racial discrimination in all housing in America.

In recognition of the need for more and better housing for low- and moderate-income families, the Housing and Urban Development Act of 1968 included programs for the construction of 6 million subsidized housing units during the next ten years. Section 235 extended home ownership to low- and moderate-income families with FHA-mortgage-insured loans by means of a monthly payment from HUD to the mortgage holder, reducing the owner's monthly costs. Section 236 provided federal interest supplements for mortgages on multifamily rental and cooperative housing, thus reducing the cost of these units.

In response to the way in which many communities had used zoning ordinances to lock out low-income groups, in 1969 Massachusetts passed the Law for Low- and Moderate-Income Housing. This law authorized the state to review and to override local zoning laws when they had the effect of making it uneconomical to build housing for low-income families.

In 1961 Congress passed a law permitting states to legalize ownership of a housing unit without title to the land on which the site is located. This stimulated condominium developments throughout the United States in the late 1960s.

In the early 1950s, single-family detached housing units, the basic building block of the neighborhood unit, accounted for more than 90 percent of the nation's new housing starts, a proportion that decreased to 60 percent in the late 1960s and to less than 50 percent in the early 1970s. One of the major reasons for the drop was the rising cost of the new single-family detached house, which by the late 1970s was beyond the reach of about 70 percent of American families; the higher costs were created by a combination of rising minimum standards, land costs, financing costs, property taxes, and building material costs.

Planned unit development (PUD) zoning provisions had begun to appear in response to the new scale of residential development following World War II. Earlier zoning standards assumed lot-by-lot development rather than area development, but in the late 1960s, interest in large-scale condominium development and cluster patterns led to the establishment of special PUD zones, in which normal development controls were waived upon special approval of a project. Once experience proved such flexible project planning zones desirable, variable density provisions were created, allowing experimentation in site design. Provisions for varied residential types and mixed land use followed, continuing the evolution toward flexible performance control of urban development.

In 1969, implementing the Intergovernmental Cooperation Act of 1968, the U.S. Office of Management and Budget issued Circular A-95, which required areawide regional planning agency review of all proposals for local participation in federal development programs. This stimulated the creation of a network of regional clearinghouses charged with receiving and disseminating project information as well as coordinating applications for federal assistance. Circular A-95 helped establish an administrative base for regional planning and coordination in the 1970s.

New directions in the 1970s

As the decade began, the Nixon administration announced that, in fulfillment of its New Federalism programs, many federal urban development programs would be terminated and replaced by a system of community development based on decentralized programs and federal revenue sharing. President Nixon signed the State and Local Fiscal Assistance Act in October 1972, creating a multi-billion-dollar general revenue sharing program.

Two years later, in 1974, Congress passed the original Community Development Block Grant (CDBG) legislation, which furthered the revenue-sharing aspect of the New Federalism. Local governments had discretion in the use of these block funds, and local councils—generally more conservative than Congress on these issues—tended to direct these funds away from broad socioeconomic programs and toward "safe" capital projects, such as parks, firehouses, swimming pools, and tennis courts. These federal funds were often sufficient to make such projects possible without an increase in local taxes. The Democrat-controlled Congress believed that funds appropriated to benefit minorities and lower-income groups were being abused, and in the CDBG legislation Congress required that these funds be used for their originally allocated purposes. The Nixon and Ford administrations illegally ignored this congressional directive and encouraged the use of block grant funds in lieu of general local revenue, thus gutting the congressionally approved programs.

Serious conflicts developed between the Democrat-dominated Congress and the Republican administration under Ford. Congress continued to try to further the goals of the New Frontier and the Great Society as articulated by the Kennedy and Johnson administrations and as provided for in congressional actions; but the Ford administration, following the policies of the Nixon administration, continued to abolish, to delay implementation, and to deflect the funds provided for the social programs enacted by Congress.

When Carter took office in 1976, he was obliged by law and by campaign promises to honor congressional directives. HUD announced that by August 1977, all planning agencies desiring "701" planning funds would have to have a housing element that met the requirements of the 1974 act: to increase housing opportunities, disperse lower-income housing, and ease racial and economic segregation. But as HUD began to redirect its programs, it encountered serious resistance from local officials, both Democrats and Republicans. By 1977 local governments had become accustomed to a steady stream of federal funds with no strings attached. To return these funds to their congressionally authorized purposes, local governments believed that they would have to institute unpopular increases in local taxes. Local officials throughout America pressured Congress and the Carter administration to ease the requirements of the 1974 act.

HUD Secretary Patricia R. Harris argued for a new Housing and Community Development Act (CDA) that would redirect the community development programs to the benefit of low- and moderate-income families, as originally charged by Congress. But the Housing and Community Development Act of 1977 provided that only 75 percent of CDA funds would be used for their original purposes, and this amount was negotiated downward annually. The act also extended "701" comprehensive planning funds on an annual appropriation basis, which meant that they, too, would be phased out. Finally, a stagnant economy led Congress to amend Title 7 of the 1970 Housing and Urban Development Act to require a "national urban policy" statement from the president (starting in 1978), rather than an "urban *growth* policy" statement.

Between 29 January and 2 February 1978, five hundred participants in The White House Conference on Balanced National Growth and Economic Development gathered to advise President Carter. The conference recommended a strong federal role in long-range planning for the impact of federal policies and investments; the establishment of national economic and employment goals; a national energy policy; federal encouragement of state planning; metropolitan tax-base sharing; and the creation at the federal level of a unit to advise the president on national growth and development and to coordinate federal activities related to national growth objectives. But President Carter's 1978 State of the Union message indicated that his administration's policies would be focused differently:

Government cannot solve our problems. It can't set our goals. It can't define our vision. Government cannot eliminate poverty or provide a bountiful economy or reduce inflation, or save our cities or cure illiteracy or provide energy. . . . We simply cannot be the managers of everything and everybody.

In his *Urban Policy Message* of 27 March 1978, President Carter announced "a new partnership to conserve America's communities" in which the private sector and state and local governments would take on a greater leadership and financial role to help reduce the burden of the $80-billion federal deficit.

By mid-1978 it was clear that the United States did not have, and would not have, anything that could be termed a national urban policy. The programs of the 1960s—Model Cities, Urban Renewal, Manpower Training—were in disuse and disfavor. Revenue sharing, the principal urban policy of the earlier 1970s, continued to provide general support for local communities but precluded use of these funds for national social programs, while passage of Proposition 13 in California in the summer of 1978, mandating a rollback in property taxes, encouraged similar efforts throughout the United States to limit funds available to state and local governments for social programs.

In 1978 the Carter administration implemented the Urban Development Action Grant (UDAG) program, created by Congress in 1977 to assist distressed cities and urban counties through "leveraging": providing limited federal funds to induce private investment in areas of economic and neighborhood stagnation. UDAG program criteria were set to ensure that funds would be directed to older declining cities, economically stagnant neighborhoods, areas of extensive poverty and unemployment, and areas of slow population and employment growth. Although only 28.4 percent of UDAG funds went to central-city neighborhoods in the first year of the program, HUD did require all recipient communities to show through housing and equal employment opportunities that they had an ongoing commitment to low- and moderate-income persons and to minorities.

By the autumn of 1979, the UDAG program had become the centerpiece and virtually the only surviving element of President Carter's urban initiatives. Congress increased UDAG funding almost 70 percent in 1979, in spite of a General Accounting Office finding that many million-dollar UDAGs were not serving their intended purpose. Congress again significantly decreased "701" Comprehensive Planning Programs funds, the House Appropriations Committee arguing that since $11 billion in CDBG funds had flowed to metropolitan areas since 1975, local communities themselves should be allocating some portion of these federally provided funds to support planning services; thus, "701" funds were no longer needed. Congress again significantly cut "701" funds in the 1980 budget, and as American communities entered the eighties, they were, for the first time since 1954, without specific federal funds earmarked in support of planning.

Despite the withdrawal of federal policies in support of planning, important new directions were taken by planners during the decade of the 1970s. The protection of the natural environment and the extension of housing to underserved populations became objectives of planning efforts in the early 1970s. The energy crisis and the economic recession provided further challenges for planners in mid-decade.

Housing in the suburbs

Throughout the decade, housing for low- and moderate-income families continued to be a difficult problem. Although the U.S. census of 1970 reported that more Americans were living in the suburban fringes of metropolitan areas than in central cities, lower-income families, particularly racial minorities, generally did not share in this suburban dispersal of American housing. This fact can be attributed in large part to exclusionary zoning practices. Mary Brooks brought this subject into the open in *Exclusionary Zoning*, published by The American Society of Planning Officials in 1970.[8] In the same year, in an attempt to correct exclusionary practices, Dale Bertsch, executive director of the Miami Valley Regional Planning Commission, prepared a Regional Housing Dispersal Plan for the Dayton, Ohio, region that came to be known as the Dayton Plan. This plan allocated new, low- and middle-income housing units throughout a five-county regional metropolitan area on a "regional fair share" basis. The concept of "fair share" had considerable influence on subsequent zoning regulations.

In the late 1960s, responding to the same housing needs, the Southern Burlington County chapter of the NAACP brought suit against the township of Mount Laurel, New Jersey, challenging the developing suburban township's zoning ordinance for its failure to provide a variety of housing opportunities, particularly for families of low and moderate income. In 1975 the New Jersey Supreme Court found in favor of the NAACP, ruling that local land use regulations "cannot foreclose the opportunity . . . for low- and moderate-income housing and . . . must affirmatively afford that opportunity, at least to the extent of the municipality's fair share of the present and prospective need thereof." The court gave Mount Laurel ninety days to revise its zoning ordinance to correct these deficiencies, thereby becoming the first state supreme court to impose an affirmative, "inclusionary" land use obligation on local governments throughout the state.

During the following years, however, the court's decision in *Mount Laurel* resulted in few changes in municipal zoning policies and little opportunity for the construction of low- and moderate-income housing. Early in 1977, the New Jersey Supreme Court clarified and expanded upon the *Mount Laurel* decision. In *Oakwood at Madison* v. *Township of Madison et al.*, the court held not only that the township had an obligation to provide its regional fair share of low- and moderate-income housing but also that such developing communities must overzone for "least cost" housing to encourage low land costs. During the 1980s the Supreme Court of New Jersey found it necessary to tackle the same issues once again in a case known as "*Mt. Laurel II.*"

The U.S. Supreme Court, in contrast, did not undertake actions in support of the HUD-based programs of the early 1970s. In *Village of Arlington Heights et al.* v. *Metropolitan Housing Development Corporation et al.* (1978), the Court held that if there is no record of proof of an intent to discriminate in the adoption of an exclusionary ordinance, the act of discrimination does not exist. Although proof of intent is difficult to establish, this principle became the foundation for the Court's future approach to civil rights issues.

Although HUD did undertake to disperse federally assisted housing projects in the suburbs in the late 1960s, its efforts were often effectively blocked by the requirement that a local referendum be held prior to initiation of a project. White—and generally relatively affluent—residents of suburban areas tended to vote to exclude such projects; the only districts in which minorities and the poor could count on heavy support were those areas they currently occupied.

In the *Valtierra* cases (1971), the U.S. Supreme Court upheld these referendum requirements, stating: "Provisions for referendums demonstrate devotion to democracy, not to bias, discrimination or prejudice."

Numerous referenda against public housing, low-income housing, and multifamily housing followed the Supreme Court decision in the *Valtierra* cases. In northeastern Ohio, land use change came virtually to a halt as one community after another introduced referenda on proposed developments. Eastlake, Ohio, amended its zoning ordinance to require a citywide referendum and at least 55-percent voter approval of *any* change in existing land use legislation. On 21 June 1976, the U.S. Supreme Court upheld Eastlake's referendum requirement (*Forest City Enterprises* v. *Eastlake*), a decision that prompted many suburban communities to adopt similar referendum requirements.

California, which had experienced soaring housing costs in the 1970s, took a direct approach to the need for low- and moderate-income housing. The state took the lead in creating inclusionary housing programs, which provide by law for a broad range of housing, by income. Palo Alto and Davis, California, adopted ordinances requiring tract home builders to sell 10 percent of their new units *below cost* to moderate-income families who could not otherwise afford them. By the end of 1979, Boulder, Colorado, and Montgomery County, Maryland, also had adopted inclusionary housing requirements. In that same year, the California Coastal Commission held that the state's inclusionary laws applied to luxury beachfront hotel rooms; the commission required hotel builders to rent a fixed number of rooms in each new development at half price to permit middle-income families access to the shoreline.

On taking office in 1974, President Ford signed the Housing and Community Development Act, which abolished categorical, purpose-specific grants and replaced them with a block-grant system that merged previously separate grant programs into lump sums, to be allocated on the basis of a formula. This program, mandated by Congress as part of a Housing Assistance Plan (HAP), required submission of a three-year development plan identifying "both short- and long-term community development objectives which have been developed in accordance with area-wide development planning." The act also required that the HAP

assess the housing assistance needs of lower-income persons . . . residing in or expected to reside in the community [to] promote a greater choice of housing opportunities and [to] avoid undue concentrations of assisted persons in areas containing a high proportion of low-income persons.

The act further indicated its primary objective as

the development of viable urban communities by providing decent housing and a suitable environment and expanding economic opportunities, principally for persons of low and moderate income. . . . The federal assistance is for the support of . . . reduction of the isolation of income groups within communities and geographical areas and the promotion of an increase in the diversity and vitality of neighborhoods through the spatial deconcentration of housing opportunities for persons of lower income.

This marked the first time that congressional action was directed toward economic as well as racial segregation.

Although the Community Development Block Grant programs required that the Housing Assistance Plan provide for the regional distribution of low- and moderate-income housing and primarily benefit low-income persons and racial minorities, the Ford administration in the mid-1970s did not implement these requirements. Community Development Block Grants were made to suburban communities free of these obligations; many of the communities then used these funds for entirely different purposes. Nor did HUD, under President Ford, implement its congressional mandate to disperse low-income housing projects, continuing instead to concentrate them in deteriorated areas of central cities.

This pattern became so blatant that district court orders were sought to require HUD to fulfill its congressionally mandated duty as required by the 1974 law. In *Carla A. Hills* (Secretary of HUD) v. *Dorothy Gautreaux et al.* (1976), the U.S. Supreme Court found HUD guilty of violating the Constitution and federal statutes through "sanctioning and assisting [the Chicago Housing Authority's] discriminatory program."

Summing up the federal housing policies of most of the decade in a 619-page report released on 8 January 1978, the American Bar Association's Advisory Commission on Housing and Urban Growth charged that the housing policies of federal, state, and local governments during previous administrations had overtly and covertly discriminated on the basis of race or income and had created and maintained purposefully exclusionary systems.

Growth management and the environment

In his 1970 State of the Union message, President Nixon stressed the need to preserve the natural environment. This emphasis was consistent with increasing public concern for clean air, clean water, and the protection of natural resources. During his time in office, Nixon established both the Environmental Protection Agency (EPA) and the President's Council on Environmental Quality. The task of the council was to set policy to implement the provisions of the Environmental Policy Act of 1970. The major provision of this act required all government agencies and licensees to file an environmental impact statement, documenting the probable effects of the undertaking, each time new construction was contemplated.

During the 1970s, those who advocated opening suburban areas to the less affluent often collided with environmentalists, who propounded no-growth or slow-growth policies for the metropolitan fringes. Proposals for "growth management" for rapidly developing suburban areas were grounded not only in concern for the environment but also in the need to control municipal expenditures for capital improvements. In *Golden* v. *Planning Board of the Town of Ramapo* (1972), for example, the New York Court of Appeals upheld a zoning ordinance that made issuance of a development permit contingent on the presence of public utilities, drainage facilities, parks, road access, and firehouses. Although the community did intend to provide the required facilities in the future, new development could proceed promptly only if its location would not demand new facilities in advance of Ramapo's schedule. The community developed an elaborate point system to determine under what circumstances a developer could be granted a permit. Ramapo reported in 1974 that this program had reduced housing starts by one half. In the 1980s, however, the program, which was so influential in its time, was abandoned because the community's development situation had radically changed.

In the wake of *Ramapo*, many communities at the perimeter of metropolitan areas undertook no-growth or slow-growth programs. In 1971 Petaluma, California, in the San Francisco area, adopted an Official Statement of Development Policy that specified a geographically balanced strategy of new residential construction based on a quota of 500 building permits per year. In the previous year 2,000 had been granted. In 1975 the Ninth U.S. Circuit Court of Appeals (*Construction Industry Association of Sonoma County* v. *City of Petaluma*) upheld this process, stating that "the concept of the public welfare is sufficiently broad to uphold Petaluma's desire to preserve its small-town character, its open spaces and low density of population and to grow at an orderly and deliberate pace." Upon appeal, the U.S. Supreme Court refused to review the case, upholding the circuit court opinion. In 1976, building on the growth control and performance zoning actions pioneered in *Ramapo* and in *Petaluma*, the California Supreme Court, in *Associated Home Builders of the Greater East Bay* v. *City of Livermore*,

Figure 2–13   Quincy
Market and Faneuil Hall,
Boston.

upheld the denial of the issuance of *all* building permits for residential construction until certain specific performance criteria were met for the city as a whole.

In November 1976, as Jimmy Carter won election to the presidency of the United States, the voters of California approved the *California Coastal Zone Act*, by far the most far-reaching environmental legislation to be ratified by any of the thirty coastal states, creating a Coastal Zone Commission with broad powers to control the development of coastal areas. Concern for environmental issues was in the forefront of the American consciousness in 1976.

Historic preservation

As the end of the decade approached, historic preservation and rehabilitation, important causes that would be taken up by planners in communities across the country, were brought to public attention both by law and by example. In 1978 the completion of Boston's historic Faneuil Hall marketplace adaptation, featuring restaurants and shops, created a successful new center for urban life in Boston. During the same year, in New York, the controversy surrounding the preservation of the Grand Central terminal was settled by the U.S. Supreme Court. In *Penn Central Transportation Co. et al.* v. *City of New York et al.*, the Court held that the company was not entitled to compensation when the terminal was designated a historic landmark; backed by the Court's decision, New York City prohibited construction of a fifty-three story office building over the terminal. Although all fifty states and more than five hundred municipalities had passed landmark preservation laws by 1978, until *Penn Central* many state and local governments had hesitated to designate prime commercial properties as landmarks for fear of future financial liability. The Supreme Court decision permitted states and localities to move ahead safely with landmark designations.

Professional planning

By 1977, sixty years after its founding at Kansas City in 1917, the American Institute of Planners had grown to over twelve thousand members in forty chapters, and there were over fifty degree-granting planning programs in American colleges and universities. In mid-1978, the members of the American Institute of Planners and the members of the American Society of Planning Officials voted to consolidate into a single organization—the American Planning Association (APA). At this time, the new association has a membership of about twenty thousand planning commissioners, professionals, students, and interested citizens.

Since 1980

The 1980 Census reported 226.5 million Americans, 76 percent living in metropolitan areas. Yet, 48 of the 100 largest American cities lost population between 1970 and 1980. St. Louis, which had been the fourth largest city in the United States at the beginning of the century, lost 27 percent of its population during that decade, the greatest decline of any American city. During the same decade, Chicago lost 600,000 people, primarily white families moving to suburban areas, and for the first time blacks and Hispanics composed more than half of the city's population.

In response to strong criticism by central-city community groups, HUD committed 90 percent of UDAG funds to neighborhood projects in the first two quarters of 1980. Just one month before the presidential election, President Carter signed into law the Housing and Community Development Act of 1980, which expanded federal aid to low- and moderate-income housing programs by 30 percent. Under the Carter administration, CETA jobs increased 400 percent, 95 percent of which went to the disadvantaged population; furthermore, subsidized housing starts increased from 15,000 a year under the Ford administration to 265,000 a year under Carter.

Ronald Reagan was elected president in November 1980. During the campaign, Reagan had faulted Carter's social programs, arguing that releasing free enterprise from regulation would solve the economic and social problems of America without government intervention. The first half of the 1980s under Reagan was characterized by a federal emphasis on deregulation and on local rather than national determination of priorities. National programs in support of customary public planning initiatives were in abeyance. Local planners found it increasingly necessary to develop and rely on state and local assistance for their programs and to form alliances with private-sector groups. Economic development programs had high priority for planners, and sophisticated fiscal devices began to be introduced into planning, such as computer-based local impact fees charged to private developers for the provision of infrastructure.

In March 1981, Representatives Jack Kemp and Robert Garcia introduced a bill (H.R. 7094) promoting "enterprise zones," a concept imported from England that provided various incentives to investors in industrial developments within certain depressed areas of central cities. Suspension of minimum wage requirements for enterprise zone residents was among the elements proposed. Although federal legislation authorizing designated enterprise zones died twice in congressional conference committees, the idea was taken up by a number of states. From 1982 to 1986, twenty-five states adopted enterprise zone legislation.

The Supreme Court's 1981 decision in the case of *San Diego Gas and Electric Company* v. *City of San Diego* suggested that an expansion of government liability might be in store: specifically, that government might be held liable for money damages for an unconstitutional temporary taking caused by excessive land use regulation.

Also in 1981, in *Wilson and Voss* v. *County of McHenry*, the Second District Court of Illinois upheld a zoning regulation that required a minimum one-quarter-square-mile lot in an agricultural zone, noting that the preservation of farmland is a valid public purpose and that the regulation was "reasonable," being based on a duly adopted comprehensive plan. The need to determine the "reasonableness" of public policy and regulation, particularly in light of the possibility of public liability for the impact of policy decisions, led in the early 1980s to a renewed interest in developing long-range, comprehensive plans. Where such plans existed, the wish to minimize municipal and personal liability encouraged adherence to them.

In 1981 the Section 8 housing subsidy program was terminated. That same year, American housing starts fell to a thirty-six-year low. The CETA jobs program was eliminated, as were many other categorical aid programs. Fiscal stress experienced by many American cities, including New York City's near-bankruptcy and Cleveland's default on bank loans, worsened in 1982. The national unemployment rate edged over 10 percent, and many firms in the steel, auto, and farm implement industries either closed or significantly cut back production. In 1982 President Reagan cut urban-directed programs by 10.6 percent, followed by another 8.1 percent in 1983. Federal cuts in urban aid forced cities to deal directly with a number of social problems. An increase in the number of homeless persons—resulting from a complex interaction of economic factors and public health decisions—posed a significant and difficult problem in many cities. Federal budget cuts in social services had negative effects primarily in the North and the Midwest, while increased military spending benefited primarily the Pacific Coast, Texas, and New England.

Community planning and development programs generally stagnated in the early 1980s, and many planning staffs were cut. In the Sun Belt, however, large-scale development continued to encourage widespread physical planning. In many ways, developments at the federal level in the early 1980s had the greatest effect on regional planning agencies. Their coordinating roles conflicted directly with the federal emphasis on decentralization, and their one major power, approval or disapproval of federal categorical grants, died with the onset of block grants and revenue sharing.

Between 1980 and 1982, 33 of the 100 largest American cities continued to lose population. In 1983, 178 million Americans lived in metropolitan areas, an increase of 6 million people in three years, while the population of most central cities stabilized or continued to decline. As the national unemployment rate reached approximately 9.6 percent and federally funded jobs and social support programs were curtailed, the number of Americans living in poverty increased. In midsummer 1983 the Census Board reported that in 1982 alone, 2.6 million people had been added to the number below the poverty line, that 15 percent of the population was below the poverty line, and that one of every two black children was living in poverty. Between 1981 and 1983, the Reagan administration had eliminated sixty-two urban grant programs, and 10 percent of the remaining programs had been combined into block grants whose purpose would be determined locally. Under the Carter administration, UDAG and CDBG programs generally had been targeted to disadvantaged residents of central cities. Under the Reagan administration, however, neighborhood programs in most cities were terminated or lost their federal funding; UDAG and CDBG funds were applied to hotels and office buildings in city centers.

The Environmental Protection Agency (EPA), centerpiece of President Nixon's environmental program, languished during the early 1980s. In 1983 mismanagement of the EPA came to light amid charges of unethical conduct, including attempts to afford private industry special treatment in the toxic waste program. The assistant administrator of the EPA was fired and the head of the EPA resigned.

The appreciation for and economic use of historic resources continued to grow during the beginning of the 1980s. In New York City, phase one of a rejuvenated South Street Seaport opened in 1983, a re-creation of the old East River waterfront near Fulton Street projected to cost $351 million and to involve more than twenty-five buildings and a pier. St. Louis, in response to dramatic decline in the population of the central city, became a leader in the use of investment tax

Figure 2–14   Pier 17 and Schermerhorn Row, both parts
of New York City's South Street Seaport.

credits to rehabilitate older buildings. In 1984 alone, $51 million was spent in
St. Louis to renovate properties listed on the National Register of Historic Places,
and another $35 million was spent on redeveloping historic districts in the city.
The Rouse Company spent $135 million to rehabilitate St. Louis's Union Ter-
minal, transforming it into a festival marketplace and hotel.

   In 1984 San Francisco demonstrated its commitment to historic preservation
with a far-reaching new downtown plan and zoning ordinance. The ordinance
proposed the transfer of development rights as an incentive to historic preservation, steering new development away from the historic downtown area to a

thirty-square-block "special development district" on South Market Street, far from the historic core of the city. The plan also included developer charges to support low- and moderate-income housing, a means of supporting housing that several other cities are attempting to incorporate into their plans and ordinances.

In his 1984 National Urban Policy Report, President Reagan reiterated his view that maintaining noninflationary growth, increasing state and local responsibilities, and encouraging public-private cooperation were the keys to dealing with urban problems. During the early and mid-1980s, planners focused on long-range physical planning for capital construction to ensure the least possible expenditure of now-scarce tax funds in the provision and operation of infrastructure. Projects originating in the private sector replaced broad social programs, and public-private partnerships, negotiation and arbitration, and consensus making became daily concerns of the planning community.

President Reagan was re-elected in November 1984. By 1985 there were 237.1 million Americans. Since 1980, 90 percent of the population growth had been in the West and the South. Metropolitan areas continued to grow at a faster rate than the rest of the country, central-city populations continued to decline, and 35.3 million Americans lived in poverty.

Conclusion

Planning for American urban settlements is as old as the settlements themselves. The physical form of cities was of great concern to the founding fathers, who carefully set down those community forms they believed most conducive to realizing functional and humanly self-fulfilling settlements. Although the industrialism and massive immigration of the nineteenth century seriously compounded America's urban problems when the country was politically least capable of coping with them, the nineteenth century saw significant accomplishments in the development of large city parks, the first attempts to control the worst housing conditions, the beginning of planned suburbs, the development of mass transit and commuter railroads, and, at the end of the century, the first federal government programs and legal authorities designated to deal with urban development problems.

The years from 1900 to 1920 saw the advent of the automobile as a major factor in American cities, the birth of the planning profession in the creation of the American City Planning Institute (subsequently the American Institute of Planners and now the American Institute of Certified Planners), the development and expansion of land use zoning and comprehensive zoning, the formation of the first official citizen planning commissions, and the creation of civic centers and long-range city plans. The most notable city plan by far was Daniel Burnham's bold proposal for Chicago (1909), which called for a metropolitan approach to planning.

The years of prosperity and depression, 1920 to 1940, saw the rapid spread of comprehensive zoning (sanctioned unequivocally by the Supreme Court) and land subdivision controls. The extraordinary growth in automobile production, along with the growth of streets and highways, created new land development problems for the still-new planning field. During the 1920s several model housing developments were undertaken, including Sunnyside, New York, and Radburn, New Jersey, which influenced much of the land development in this country for years to come. Federal laws passed in 1934 and 1937 created the basis for public housing in America and, through the Federal Housing Administration, for mortgage insurance programs that established the standards for the millions of single-family detached houses that were to be built in suburban America after World War II.

After the war the nation saw a vast expansion of suburban housing, the establishment of planning as an ongoing activity of local governments, the development of more technically refined zoning and subdivision controls, a significant growth in the number of planning schools, large-scale urban renewal activities, extensive citizen participation, and the development of the interstate highway system.

In the 1980s, with decreased financial resources and the elimination of federal support for city and regional planning, the practice of planning is once again in competition for local support dollars and is being sold locally on its value in creating a functionally and economically efficient community system for the delivery of needed goods and services at the lowest community costs for capital construction and operations. Urban and regional planners are at work across the entire range of local governments, especially in management and finance, as they deal with critical social, functional, and economic development issues. The constantly changing world of the planners, in a professional and functional sense, is set forth in the rest of this book to help meet the changing needs of urban development for America in the 1990s.

1   Jacob A. Riis, *How the Other Half Lives.* Reprint (Williamstown, MA: Corner House, 1972. Original published 1890).

2   ———, *The Children of the Poor.* Reprint (New York: Johnson Reprint Corp., 1971. Original published 1892).

3   Ebenezer Howard, *Garden Cities of To-Morrow.* Reprint, F. J. Osborn, ed. (Cambridge: MIT Press, 1965. Original published 1898).

4   Regional Plan Association, *Regional Survey of New York and Its Environs.* 10 vols. (New York, 1928–1931).

5   Clarence Perry, *Housing for the Machine Age* (New York: Russell Sage Foundation, 1939).

6   Ladislas Segoe, *Local Planning Administration* (Chicago: International City Managers' Association, 1941).

7   American Public Health Association, *Planning the Neighborhood* (Chicago: Public Administration Service, 1948).

8   Mary Brooks, *Exclusionary Zoning,* Planning Advisory Service Report no. 254 (Chicago: American Society of Planning Officials, 1970).

3 General development plans

The general development plan has been the cornerstone of American planning theory and practice since the early 1900s. During this century there has been a continuing redefinition of what a plan is and what it does. The concept of the plan has evolved to keep pace with changing needs and new theories of public decision making. As a result, a plan of the 1990s will bear little resemblance to the typical general plan prepared at the turn of the century.

General plans have masqueraded under a variety of names—city plan, development plan, urban plan, master plan, growth management plan, comprehensive plan, policy plan, and many more. These name changes reflect, in part, the evolving idea of what the plan is supposed to do. In some cases, the name change is a public relations effort on the part of one local administration to disassociate itself from the planning efforts of a previous administration. Largely for convenience, this chapter will use the term *general plan*.

Despite changes in name and concept, some consistent elements characterize the general plan. First, it is a *physical plan*. Although a reflection of social and economic values, the plan is fundamentally a guide to the physical development of the community. It translates values into a scheme that describes how, why, when, and where to build, rebuild, or preserve the community. This emphasis on the physical has been the source of much controversy and debate. Some planners have argued that the physical emphasis ignores people, but this argument has by and large been put to rest. A consensus has developed in the field that the general development plan is not a social service delivery plan, or a health plan, or a plan for economic promotion, although it may reflect or incorporate elements of all of these.

A second characteristic of the general plan is that it is *long range*, covering a time period greater than one year, usually five years or more. In years past the general plan was largely a snapshot or frozen image of what the community would look like twenty, thirty, or forty years later; but there was, unfortunately, little guidance as to how to get from the present to the utopian future. It is now recognized that an effective plan expresses current policies that will shape the future, rather than showing a rigid image of the future itself. Nevertheless, a good plan should be slightly utopian. It should challenge and inspire us with a vision of what might be. It should also tell us how to get there.

A third characteristic of a general development plan is that it is *comprehensive*. It covers the entire city geographically—not merely one or more sections. It also encompasses all the functions that make a community work, such as transportation, housing, land use, utility systems, and recreation. Moreover, the plan considers the interrelationships of functions.

Fourth, the general plan is a *statement of policy*, covering such community desires as quantity, character, location, and rate of growth (be it no growth, slow growth, rapid growth, or decline) and indicating how these desires are to be achieved.

In some states the general plan has essentially no legal status. It is a piece of advice that can be ignored with little or no penalty. In other states its standing has been enhanced by new laws or judicial rulings that give it substantial authority to compel action. Although the plan is not a zoning ordinance, a subdivision regulation, an official map, a budget, or a capital improvements program, it should be a guide to the preparation and the execution of these components of the planning process.

Finally, a plan is a guide to decision making by the planning commission and the governing board and the mayor or manager.

This chapter reviews evolving concepts of the general plan from its U.S. origins in the City Beautiful movement to the concerns of the present day; analyzes major purposes of the plan with respect to policy, decision making, and legal requirements; and reviews the issues in preparing a plan, including considerations of policy, procedure, intergovernmental relations, technical processes, review processes, and major kinds of coverage. There is a brief evaluative conclusion.

Evolving concepts of the general plan

The modern general plan has developed over time and has been shaped by numerous legal, political, and social forces. Understanding these root forces is a prerequisite to understanding what the plan is and what it can and cannot accomplish. The essential point of this review is that the general plan reflects the social and cultural values of the times. The plan can be understood only by understanding the community that prepares it and the current social environment. (The history of local planning in general in the United States is reviewed in detail in Chapter 2.)

The conscious design of cities and towns is a practice as ancient as civilization. Our most familiar and admired roots in city design are the Greek and Roman cities, which were planned with well-developed ideas of city function and built with great engineering skill. The earliest American plans reflected some of these ancient roots in that they were primarily concerned with the layout of new communities. These plans ranged from the simple gridiron of the land surveyor to the visions of L'Enfant and William Penn for the cities of Washington and Philadelphia.[1]

In the latter part of the nineteenth century the major cities of the United States experienced remarkable population growth, and planners shifted their attention from design of new communities to methods of improving conditions in existing cities. Immigrants streamed into cities such as Boston, New York, Chicago, and Philadelphia, along with the young from the farms looking for work. Older cities doubled or tripled in population,[2] and this growth brought the attendant difficulties of land speculation, residential overcrowding, inadequate sanitary systems, traffic congestion, and rapid, unplanned construction and land subdivision. In the early part of this century there were two major responses to these conditions—the City Beautiful movement and the social reform movement—that have greatly influenced local planning to the present day.

The City Beautiful movement and social reform

The City Beautiful movement epitomized by the Chicago world's fair of 1893 (officially the World's Columbian Exposition) promoted an "ideal" city of broad streets and monumental public buildings. The fair generated demand throughout the country for replanning the ugly mix of factory and tenement and the congested, smelly streets of the "real city." The talents of architects, landscape architects, and engineers were sought for citywide improvement plans that focused on aesthetics.

The most important plan to emerge from this movement was Daniel Burnham's 1909 plan for Chicago (Figure 3–2). It is characteristic of the City Beautiful movement in depicting an aesthetic vision of the city, but it also contains chapters on rapid transit, suburban growth, a comprehensive park system, transportation and terminals, streets and subdivision control, and problems in the central city.

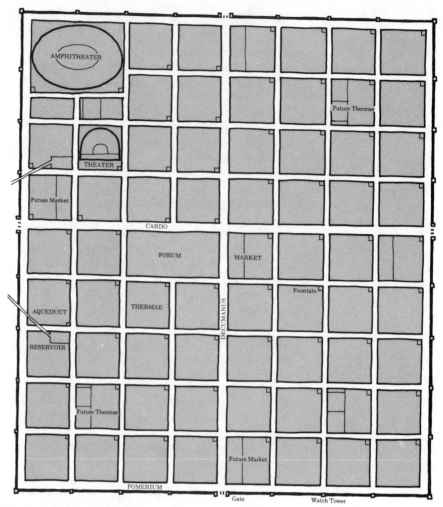

Figure 3–1   The idealized layout of the imaginary city of
Verbonia (circa 25 B. C.; above) contrasts with the land
use patterns in the Barrington area, northwest of
Chicago. The Verbonia master plan, designed to
accommodate about 50,000 people, shows the sites for
the entertainment complex, the forum, the public market,
the public baths, and the major water line serving the
city.

The chapter on the central city treats not only civic buildings but the problem
of congestion and the menace to the health of the community posed by the
slums.

The condition of the slums created a second major response to the burgeoning
city. A social reform movement concerned with overcrowding in windowless
tenements, infant mortality, and frequent epidemics grew up during this same
period. In his book *How the Other Half Lives,* Jacob Riis, a police reporter in
New York, was the most dramatic spokesman for social reform.[3]

The reformers saw the interrelated problems of congestion and crime, unemployment and transit, density and recreation space. They aimed at a coordinated
and comprehensive approach based on surveys of existing conditions. Solutions
to social and physical needs were sought in physical change: street widening,
rehabilitation, and zoning (which was then practiced in German cities).

By 1917 city planning was enough of a profession to stimulate the formation
of a professional organization, the American City Planning Institute. By this

Land use

Existing private open space

Existing public open space

Proposed public open space

Business

Not in Barrington Area Council of Governments plan

Residential

1 or more units/acre

1 unit/ 1–2 acres

1 unit/ 2.5 acres

1 unit/ 5 acres

Office/ light industry

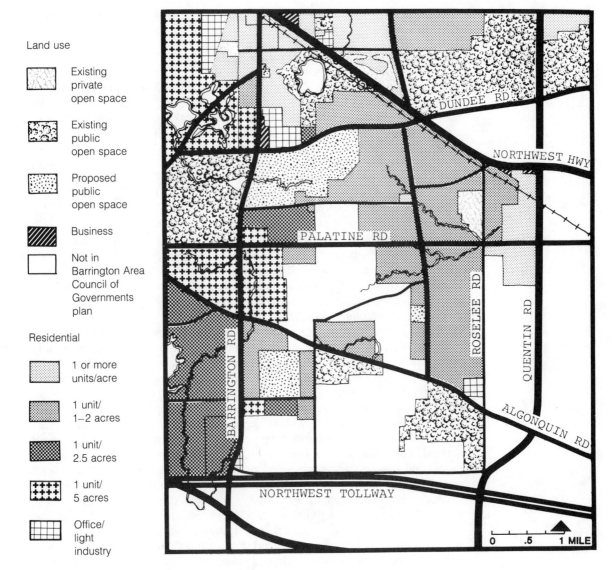

Figure 3–1 *continued.*

time the City Beautiful was giving way to the "city practical" or city functional, with an emphasis on scientific data analysis and efficient management. Regional planning and a popular interest in zoning also characterized planning in the age of the automobile and the skyscraper (the 1920s). The extent to which comprehensive planning concepts had developed had been articulated by the distinguished city planner Frederick Law Olmsted, Jr., in 1911:

We must disabuse the public mind of the idea that a city plan means a fixed record upon paper of a desire by some group of individuals prescribing, out of their wisdom and authority, where and how the more important changes and improvements in the physical layout of the city are to be made—a plan to be completed and put on file and followed more or less faithfully and mechanically, much as a contractor follows the architect's drawings for a house. We must cultivate in our own minds and in the mind of the people the conception of a city plan as a device or piece of administrative machinery for preparing, and keeping constantly up to date, a unified forecast and definition of all the important changes, additions and extensions of the physical equipment and arrangement of the city which a sound judgement holds likely to become desirable and practicable in the course of time, so as to avoid so far as possible both ignorantly wasteful action and ignorantly wasteful inaction in the control of the city's physical growth.[4]

The standard zoning and planning enabling acts

The model zoning and city planning enabling acts, which were published by the U.S. Department of Commerce in the 1920s,[5] have had an extraordinary influence in defining the general plan. These model acts were eventually adopted by almost all the states, and for more than fifty years they have served as the principal *legal* description of the general plan.

Although these model acts did much to promote local zoning and planning efforts throughout the country, they are most notable for three weaknesses: failing to define the relationship between planning and zoning; establishing incomplete coverage of the plan; and sanctioning piecemeal adoption of plan components.

The Standard State Zoning Enabling Act came first in 1922 and provided that zoning regulations be in "accordance with a comprehensive plan." However, the nature of a comprehensive plan was not yet clear. The Standard City Planning Enabling Act, which followed in 1928, indicated that a zoning plan should be included in the master plan and that the zoning commission should become part of the planning commission. However, there is no indication of the essential difference between zoning as regulation of existing land uses and comprehensive planning as a long-range view of what those uses should be. Perhaps even more important, there was no indication of how the two activities should be related. The drafters were of the view that zoning should be based on a comprehensive understanding of current land uses and future needs. However, the timing of the two model laws and a lack of clarity did little to stop a trend in many cities to adopt a zoning ordinance without any comprehensive planning at all.

Another weakness of the planning act was that the content of plans was not defined. Only five areas of concern were cited: streets, other public grounds, public buildings, public utilities, and zoning. A footnote indicates that at least some of the drafters had a more comprehensive view of the plan elements.[6] However, in many communities planning was limited to the five areas cited in the act. Moreover, although the act indicates the interrelatedness of the planning activities, it also allows for adoption and publication of portions of the plan, which inadvertently encouraged uncoordinated functional planning.[7] A number of municipalities prepared and adopted master functional plans—such as a master transportation plan.

The 1930s and early 1940s were characterized by major national and state involvement in planning activities related to New Deal public works programs and the war effort. In his book on TVA David Lilienthal says:

Here is the life principle of democratic planning—an awakening in the whole people of a sense of this common moral purpose. Not one goal, but a direction. Not one

Figure 3–2 Daniel Burnham's 1909 Chicago plan, probably the most influential general plan ever drafted in the United States, provided for traffic circulation, railway stations, parks, boulevards, public recreation areas, a yacht harbor, and a civic center. Developed by Daniel H. Burnham and Edward H. Bennett, it has been a constant reference point in both the history and the current practice of planning. Many of the features shown in the diagram have been built, including the major parks, yacht harbor, and other facilities along the lake front; major streets (now freeways); and the straightening of the South Branch of the Chicago River. The photo (bottom) shows the Chicago skyline as it appeared in the mid-1980s.

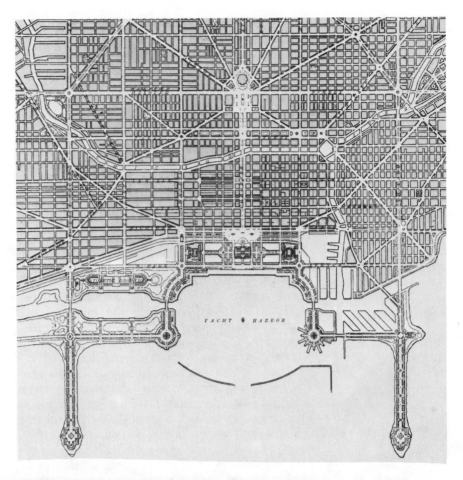

plan, once and for all, but the conscious selection by the people of a succession of plans.[8]

Toward the end of World War II, there was a resurgence of interest in local planning efforts in many municipalities as they anticipated postwar adjustments. The focus of these efforts was on questions of employment and industrial development.[9]

Postwar: The housing acts and "701" plans

After World War II American cities again were teeming with overcrowded slums. The industrialized cities had attracted migration from southern and rural areas. Housing was in short supply, and there was great interest in eliminating blight, rebuilding central cities, and expanding the housing supply.

All of these aims were addressed in the Housing Act of 1949. The focus of the act was on redevelopment projects. The act contained language requiring redevelopment to conform to "general plans for the development of the locality as a whole." When the limits of the redevelopment approach became apparent, federal legislation gave additional emphasis to citywide planning efforts, land use regulations, and maintenance of the housing stock. The Housing Act of 1954 required "workable programs" from local governments applying for urban renewal assistance. One of the requirements of the workable program was a long-range general plan (zoning, subdivision regulations, code enforcement, and citizen participation were also required). By 1959 money for comprehensive planning was available to cities, counties, and state and interstate agencies. As a result of federal financial support, there was "more urban planning in the U.S. in the latter half of the 1950's than at any previous time in history."[10]

The support of the federal government spawned a library of "701" plans, named after the section of the federal housing act that authorized the funding. Many of these plans were of immense value to the cities and villages that sponsored them; others, however, were prepared only because they were required as a condition of eligibility for urban renewal funds. Planners suffered much criticism for the rather mechanical and unimaginative way in which the plans were prepared. Although much maligned, the "701" plans and the planning process played a major role in institutionalizing the planning function in local government. They also provided a general plan format that has served as a basis for plan development to this date.

While the typical "701" plan was being turned out by the hundreds in the 1950s and 1960s, the traditional approaches to developing the plan were being reexamined. It was a time of ferment within the profession as it became more and more apparent that the static, goal-oriented master plan approach was not having the desired results. Planners were aware that the shape of urban centers was being determined by forces outside the control of the local government planning function and that efforts to reshape the city had social and economic consequences that had not been well anticipated. Moreover, planners were increasingly aware that the long-range, general policy guidance of the classic plan was having little influence on the short-term, incremental decision making that was characteristic of most local governments.

Bridging this gap between long-range goal setting and short-term implementation was the focus of much of the reexamination of planning during this period. In 1956 Martin Meyerson issued a call for a "middle-range bridge" between decision making and long-range planning.[11] Others stressed the need for a planning "process" with emphasis on efficient gathering and integrating of data on which to base alternative courses of action.[12] There was increasing interest in examining the social and economic consequences of physical planning.[13]

In a number of large cities, these new perspectives resulted in the creation of development departments that combined planning and development functions. Other planning departments turned to vast data collection efforts made more feasible by new computer technology. Some departments gave up the traditional planning document that described the city of the future graphically and verbally and focused instead on general goal statements accompanied by budgeting and programming procedures.[14] This was the period in which the "policy plan" was developed.[15]

The 1960s was also a time of considerable debate concerning social versus physical planning. Social activists argued that the physical planners ignored people. The physical planners responded by arguing that their plans took social values into account. In the end the debate was neither won nor lost as each side grudgingly accepted some of the points made by its adversary. A great interest in social planning was one result of the attention given to human problems during President Johnson's War on Poverty and the Model Cities program. In 1967, the broader concept of planning was institutionalized by the American Institute of Planners in its definition of the professional planner. No longer did the professional planner have to be concerned primarily with physical development and land use.

Advocacy and issue-oriented planning

By the late 1960s and the early 1970s the whole concept of the plan and planning was rather battered and beleaguered. Critics were sniping at "cookie cutter" plans that were not responsive to local needs, at elitist plans prepared and adopted by "establishment" planning commissions, and at plans that ignored the needs of minorities and low-income families. Critics argued that no one could or should try to articulate the goals for something as complex as a city.

Dissatisfaction with planning as it was being practiced led to the development of advocacy planning. As used in the late 1960s, advocacy planning referred to the right of a neighborhood or other group to advocate plans directed to its own interests. In this view, these interests should form the basis for government action, and participation in plan making should therefore be as important as the plan itself—especially in central-city neighborhoods with large poor and minority populations.

Meanwhile, in suburban and resort areas, general plans began to take more account of community issues and the needs of special-interest groups. Plans were no longer based on assumptions of continued growth, and the planner was not expected to be a neutral or apolitical technician.

Preeminent among community concerns in the late 1960s and 1970s was the environment. In response to this concern, strategies for environmental and resource conservation were introduced into the comprehensive planning process. Plans indicated how future development could be more energy efficient and protect the natural environment. Many communities recognized that existing trends and patterns of development conflicted with notions of environmental conservation and prepared plans that identified the type of future development that could best reduce such conflicts.

During the 1970s, local advocacy and environmental protection were coupled with increasing concern about the rising costs of development, including urban infrastructure. A highly significant planning trend—growth management—was the result. In the 1960s, every town wanted new industry and more people; by the 1970s, this goal was being questioned. Communities across the nation had begun to recognize that growth inevitably had its costs and that growth at any cost was not a reasonable objective. New growth might bring new tax revenues, but it also brought demands for services such as roads, schools, libraries, fire protection, and sewers. The cost of these services at times exceeded the revenues gained through taxes. Even when the new growth was not a fiscal problem for

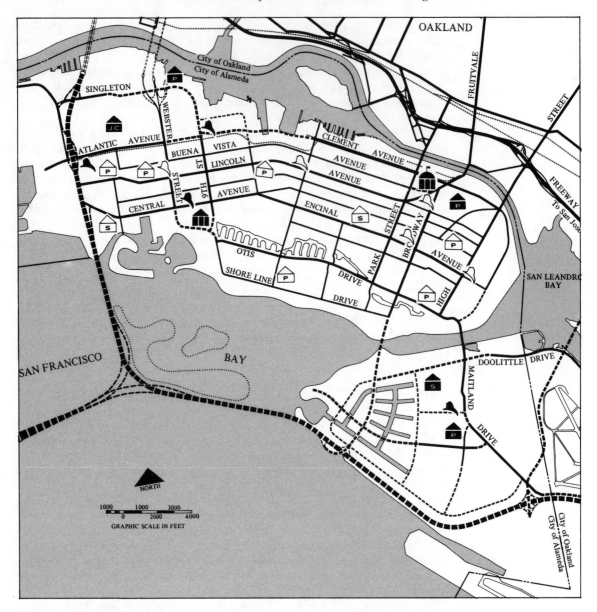

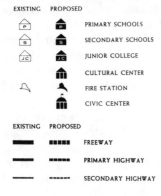

EXISTING	PROPOSED	
P	P	PRIMARY SCHOOLS
S	S	SECONDARY SCHOOLS
JC	JC	JUNIOR COLLEGE
		CULTURAL CENTER
		FIRE STATION
		CIVIC CENTER

EXISTING	PROPOSED	
━━━	■■■■■	FREEWAY
───	─────	PRIMARY HIGHWAY
──	------	SECONDARY HIGHWAY

Figure 3–3   Public buildings and transportation elements of the general plan for Alameda, California, prepared in 1968. This is the horizon (broad overview) for just two elements of the general plan proposed for development by 1990. Other plan elements include land use, urban aesthetics, circulation, public buildings, recreation, and utilities.

local governments, it caused other kinds of problems. New developments might destroy a favorite wooded area, disrupt the ecology of a marsh, overcrowd a school, cause pollution, create traffic congestion, or simply disrupt a way of life that townspeople wanted to preserve. This resulted in the realization that planning has as much to do with maintaining a desired quality of life as with giving order to growth. Thus, local planning came to incorporate the idea of "growth management," which recognized that growth came at a price and that such growth should be managed so as to achieve community goals in a cost-effective manner.

The effort to preserve a "way of life" has been the Achilles' heel of growth management, since some localities used their apparent concern for the environment and the municipal treasury as an excuse to keep out the "wrong kind" of people. The "wrong kind" could mean anyone with a family income below theirs and could also mean a member of a minority group.

Early growth management efforts were labeled *nongrowth*, as some local governments wanted to put an absolute stop to all new growth. Later efforts were more sophisticated and sought to control the amount, timing, and location of new growth on an annual basis by establishing some form of quota or by tying each increment of new growth to the installation of sewers or the provision of other expensive municipal services.

When viewed from one perspective, little is new about growth management other than a label. One of the purposes of planning has always been to influence, manage, and direct the growth of communities. What is distinctive is that past planning assumed that growth was good and bigger was better. Today communities want growth on their own terms. The difference is that growth management is viewed not as a new *activity* but as a new *goal* of local government.

Elements of growth management

Local growth management is . . . a conscious government program intended to influence the rate, amount, type, location, and/or quality of future development within a local jurisdiction. Growth management programs may include a statement of growth policy, a development plan, and various traditional and innovative implementation tools—regulations, administrative devices, taxation schemes, public investment programs, and land acquisition techniques. . . . It should be noted that this definition, which in fact focuses on actively guiding growth, differs from the popular notion of stopping growth completely.

As defined, the growth management process attempts to influence the "primary" characteristics of growth: rate, amount, type, location, and quality. These are the essential input features of urban growth—the major avenues through which the overall form and nature of development can be affected.

It is also possible to distinguish a secondary set of growth features that could be called "impact" characteristics. These features, such as environmental impact, fiscal impact, or impact on regional parity, are outputs that result from the development process itself. Analyzing the impacts of development is one way to judge the effectiveness and equity of growth management. A local government may attempt to limit negative growth impacts by managing primary growth characteristics—by minimizing the fiscal impact of new growth, for example, by directing it to locations already served by water and sewer systems and limiting its rate to a level that can be accommodated by planned public facilities.

Source: Excerpted from David R. Godschalk, David J. Brower, Larry D. McBennett, and Barbara A. Vestal, *Constitutional Issues of Growth Management* (Chicago: American Society of Planning Officials, 1977), 8–9.

There is, however, another perspective, a perspective that suggests that growth management is really the coming of age of planning. Growth management finally brings together the plan and the tools of implementation. Growth management programs have designed and implemented new ways to control growth—new ways to use the traditional powers of zoning and capital investment. The interest in growth management has enhanced the status of the general plan, because it is the plan that forms the foundation for political acceptance. The public, the developer, and political leaders will accept the restrictions of a growth management program if they can be certain that the program has been soundly conceived (that is, based on a plan). As will be indicated later in this chapter, the courts, too, are insisting that community efforts to manage growth must be based on a plan.

Another major event of the 1970s was the adoption in 1975 of the American Law Institute's *A Model Land Development Code*.[16] The code may have a major effect on all our land development practices in the next several decades, much as the model codes of the 1920s have had. The section on local (municipal) planning reflects the challenges to the traditional comprehensive planning process made in the 1950s and 1960s. It stresses the use of long-term goal setting and data collection and analysis as bases for public action. Social and economic impacts are recognized, and study of them is required (although physical development is the central concern). Planning is clearly viewed as a continuing process intended to serve those who must take public action.

The code provides for a "local land development plan" that contains long-term policies and goals regarding the use and development of land. However, these goals "are primarily important as a framework for the short-term programming"[17] required in other sections. The code's major concern is with the "preparation and evaluation of specific programs of public action."[18] A short-term program of one to five years is required; it identifies planning reports, their sequence, and the agency responsible.

The organizational location of planning in local government is not specified in the model code, but the client for the plan is the legislative body of the municipality, and adoption of the plan by that body is necessary to give the plan legal standing. Adoption is required in order to ensure that the attention of legislators is focused on "problems of physical development and location of activities that use land and on concrete programs aimed at their solution."[19]

Updating requirements in the code are designed to ensure that a continuing planning process is maintained and that the plan continues to reflect relevant trends and viewpoints. Periodic local land development reports must be adopted within a year from the end of the short-term program period to maintain the legal status of the plan.

The drafters of the code are clearly interested in a close and comprehensible relationship between planning efforts and short-term land use regulation, including zoning. Unlike the Standard Planning Enabling Act of 1928, which sanctioned both but did not link them well, this code is designed to provide the broader perspective necessary for noncapricious land regulation, as well as a shorter-term program that gives a clear indication of the intentions of public agencies in carrying out the goals.

During the mid-1980s local governments began to experiment with preparing "strategic plans," a concept borrowed from the private sector. Corporations prepare strategic plans to change their products, services, and marketing strategies.

At the most basic level, the strategic planner analyzes the factors *internal* to the company (e.g., marketing, manufacturing processes) and *external* to the company (e.g., the general economy, technology, competition, government regulation). In conducting internal and external assessments, the strategic planner seeks to identify the company's strengths, weaknesses, opportunities, and threats.

Based on the analysis, corporate planners and executives choose missions, objectives, and strategies that build on strengths, correct weaknesses, take advantage of opportunities, and deal, as best as can be done, with threats.

Because the application of the strategic planning concept to the public sector is still in an experimental stage, judgments about the efficacy and applicability of the technique must be withheld. Some communities have merely used the corporate labels to produce traditional plans. Some have accomplished widespread citizen and business community participation in establishing goals for limited purposes, such as economic development.

Comprehensive planning as a process

The establishment of growth management as a major function of local planning departments recognizes that planning is a continuing process and that the development and implementation of physical improvements must be linked to the local budget, cooperation with other units of government, and the needs and capabilities of the private sector. This has led general development plans to take on a more flexible, policy orientation. Aspects of fixed land use planning are now used to illustrate the application of policies rather than as a firm statement of the community's future image. Furthermore, the use of policy-oriented plans rather than fixed land use plans demonstrates a recognition that general plans are implemented through a series of incremental decisions rather than through major construction programs that rely on the plan as a static blueprint for the future.

The comprehensive plan as a static guide to the community's future is giving way to a comprehensive planning *process* that includes and coordinates various plans, programs, and procedures. Within this continuing process, certain aspects of general development plans are produced and revised over a specific time period. Communitywide plans are becoming more generalized, with highly spe-

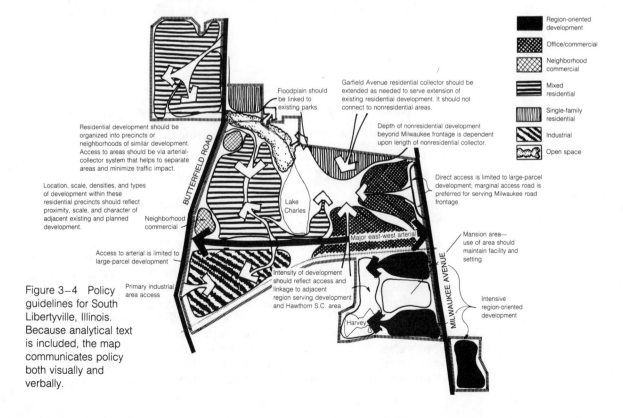

Figure 3–4 Policy guidelines for South Libertyville, Illinois. Because analytical text is included, the map communicates policy both visually and verbally.

cific physical planning being directed to districts where specific growth or redevelopment issues need to be resolved. (See Chapter 4 for an extended discussion of district plans.)

This approach is not necessarily new. For example, Chicago incorporated a district planning approach in its comprehensive plan of 1968. However, of note is the fact that this approach is now being used by smaller communities, especially those that face significant growth. This reflects the fact that flexible zoning techniques such as planned unit developments and the market-driven nature of private development have reduced the utility of master plans, which specify land use on a parcel-by-parcel basis. As a result, growth management comprehensive plans tend to rely more on development guidelines than on fixed maps. Growing communities have begun formulating a general development plan that provides a broad, communitywide land use framework and is refined through district plans with detailed guidelines for land use decision making.

As comprehensive planning continues to evolve, it is most likely that it will come to refer to a process that produces various products needed to guide local development decisions. Included would be documents stating the goals and objectives of the community; policy plans that provide rules or courses of action to achieve the objectives; broad land use plans that outline an image of the community and coordinate the development of communitywide system plans for utilities, transportation, parks, schools, and the like; and district plans that provide detailed recommendations for specific geographic areas. In addition, the comprehensive planning process would provide a place to lodge the newly emerging concept of strategic planning discussed in the preceding section.

Evidence of the institutionalization of the comprehensive planning process is quite broad. For example, many communities have "advanced planning" divisions within their planning agencies to undertake the long-range, comprehensive planning process. Many comprehensive plans contain provisions for scheduled review and updating. Others require that any rezoning request that differs from the comprehensive plan recommendation first be evaluated and approved as an amendment to the comprehensive plan. These examples indicate that general development planning is increasingly being looked upon by decision makers as a key tool in effective local government.

Functions of a general plan

Court strikes down city zoning decision—no general plan.

Civic organization decries city decline—calls for coordinated approach.

Planning commission announces new plan as required by state law.

Developers call city plan outmoded—stops new investment.

State coastal zone planning to be turned back to cities and counties.

Utility announces site for nuclear power plant—village board calls for impact assessment.

These are some of the headlines that might appear in the local press, indicating the need for a general plan. We can see from the list that local governments are likely to undertake plans in response to a combination of local circumstances or to the requirements of state and federal laws or regulations.

As indicated in these fictitious headlines, conditions within a municipality itself are an important generating force for a comprehensive planning effort. Burgeoning growth or rapid decline may ignite the concern of both private citizens and public servants. For example, a major new facility such as an automobile plant may require a comprehensive plan for the future of a city or town. An industry pullout may prompt an economic development plan.

A local resource such as an attractive coastal location, a lake, or a historic site may generate development pressures that require a plan. It may become apparent that new growth is destroying the resource that attracted development in the first place. Pressures may arise to restrict new growth in order to preserve the resource. A general plan becomes a useful tool for sorting out what the community wants, whether limits should be imposed, and what interests are being served by such action.

The courts increasingly have looked for a rationale behind a local zoning ordinance that can be used to weigh the relative merits of zoning changes or to justify the costs that compliance with a zoning ordinance may require. The general plan articulates long-range development goals for the community against which shorter-term zoning administration can be measured.

The functions performed by a general plan are many and complex, but they can be grouped under three principal categories:

1. The plan is an expression of what a community wants. It is a statement of goals, a listing of objectives, and a vision of what might be.
2. The plan, once prepared, serves as a guide to decision making. It provides the means for guiding and influencing the many public and private decisions that create the future of the community.
3. The plan in some cases may represent the fulfillment of a legal requirement. It may be a necessary obligation. Such a mandated plan can, of course, still fulfill the first two functions, but the fact that it is required adds a distinctive dimension to the planning process.

How, one might ask, can a single document fulfill such broad and complex functions? The answer is that the plan document by itself does not do the job. The value is derived from the *process* of preparing the plan and the *use* of the plan after its preparation.

When planners point out that planning is a process, they mean that it is naive to assume that a single document can answer all questions or solve all problems. Conditions change, resources are shifted, and goals are altered, making it necessary to revise, adapt, and update the plan. The point of a plan is to focus attention on the process—to create a basis for debate, discussion, and conflict resolution. Planning must be a continuous and continuing activity designed to produce the best possible decisions about the future of the community. The *plan* represents a periodic bringing together of the activities of planning. The essence of a plan is that it is a statement of policy, an expression of community intentions and aspirations. When recognized as a statement of policy, the plan can have tremendous influence; but that influence is realized only within the context of a total planning program.

The plan as a statement of policy

Central to all notions of the general plan is that the plan is an expression of what the community wants. It is a statement of goals, a listing of desires, an expression of ambitions. A good plan should be all these things. However, although there is widespread agreement as to the importance of goal setting, actual practice often falls short of ideal expectations. This is not surprising when one considers the immense difficulty of setting goals for something as large and diverse as a city. How can conflicts between the goals of competing interest groups be resolved? Is it possible to define goals that are specific enough to be useful? Can long-term planning goals be made compatible with short-term political goals?

The problems of goal setting are many and complex, but since 1960 there has been continuing and substantial improvement in the ability of local governments to prepare plans that embody meaningful statements of policy. Part of this improvement is the result of the changing context of local planning. Traditional planning methods are being replaced in response to new demands.

To a considerable degree the traditional methods of planning were borrowed from work done in architects' offices, single-function government agencies, or private corporations. These methods were well suited to the single site and the unitary setting, but they have not been as well suited to the complex and mercurial city. Traditional planning method was predicated on such factors as basic agreement on goals, ability to predict the future with precision, and centralized control over the resources needed to achieve the goals. Early local planning, of course, was privately supported and was under the control of respected community leaders who shared a common vision of the future of their community. In this consensus, environmental goals were implied rather than stated, since the leadership agreed and everyone else either did not care or did not have the power to be heard.

Today planning occurs in a different political and social environment. Decision-making processes are more open and more democratic. A more sophisticated citizenry wants to know what the local government "plans" to do and wants to be part of the plan-making process.

Traditional planning was essentially a technical exercise. Modern planning practice is both normative and technical, concerned with both ends and means. Normative planning develops the broad, general basis for action, whereas technical planning is concerned with specific, established purposes and the procedures employed in achieving those purposes. One is concerned with values, the other with methods. An effective plan should deal equally with the normative and the technical, since a planning department has a dual role in the affairs of government. A planner should function in a middle zone between the politician (a normative planner) and the bureaucrat (a technical planner). The planner has special competence and training in both areas, and his or her plans should reflect both.

The policies or goals that are contained in a plan may already exist in various forms or places within a community and may simply be brought together and organized. Or they may be the result of a long and sophisticated goal-setting process. In either case they must be sufficiently unified to express clear direction and purpose, so that citizens have little doubt as to what the community believes in and stands for.

Some will resist using a plan as a statement of policy. Elected officials may be reluctant to commit themselves too far into the future, preferring instead to keep their options open. Special-interest groups may also see some danger in using the plan as an expression of policy: If the adopted policies are antithetical to their perceived interests, they would prefer to have no plan at all. It should be kept in mind, however, that a good plan does not foreclose future decisions by prescribing the future in detail. The policies of the plan say, in effect, "When we encounter this situation we will probably act this way for these reasons." This approach has the advantage of stating a position in advance of heated controversy. To deviate from a policy in the plan will require an argument and a rationale as convincing as the one in the plan. Departing from the precepts of a plan should always be possible—although not necessarily easy.

The advantages of viewing the plan as an instrument of policy include the following:

1. The essential and uncluttered statements of policy facilitate public participation in and understanding of the planning process.
2. A plan that is a statement of policy encourages or even demands involvement on the part of public officials.
3. The plan as policy provides stability and consistency, in that it is less likely to be made obsolete by changing conditions.

4.   Finally, the plan guides the legislative bodies responsible for adopting land use controls, the commissions or boards that administer them, and the courts that must judge their fairness and reasonableness.

The plan as a guide to decision making

If the first function of a plan is to express community goals and objectives, then the second is to serve as a guide to decision making. A plan needs to make a difference. Those who make decisions about the community need to take account of what the plan says.

There are many ways in which a plan can make a difference. The most common way in which the plan is used as a guide to decision making is in the zoning process. Certainly, the enactment and amendment of a zoning ordinance should be guided by the contents of the plan. In addition, the week-to-week administration of the zoning process is best done through reference to the policies and principles set forth in a comprehensive plan. As will be indicated later in this chapter, this relationship between the plan and the zoning ordinance is being defined by law rather than by convention. Some state legislatures are requiring that the zoning ordinance be consistent with the city or county plan, and some courts are hesitant to uphold a land use control measure that is not supported by a plan.

Subdivision regulations (Chapter 8) and zoning ordinances (Chapter 9) should also be designed and administered in accordance with the recommendations of a plan. In the same way, the official map is another tool of community development that is designed to reflect the goals set forth in the plan.

The capital improvements program and budget (Chapter 14) have traditionally been thought of as implementation devices that were guided by the contents of a plan. Planning departments are frequently responsible for putting together the

---

The worth of the comprehensive plan   Ever since I was awarded a degree in city planning from a school that stressed, I thought, the worthiness of comprehensive, long-range physical planning for urban areas, I have heard that whole notion criticized. Repeatedly, I have heard the quality, content, usefulness, and effectiveness of the comprehensive plan challenged, as often as not by those who teach city planning. The critics say that the comprehensive plan is too vague, too subjective, too biased, too specific. It is elitist and divorced from the people, . . . full of end-state visions that are unrelated to the real issues of a dynamic world. . . .

There are certainly elements of truth in these assertions. But, in general, they coincide neither with my sense of reality nor with the centrality of the idea. Comprehensive plans have always been policy documents, even if they have not been read that way. They have become less and less end-state, static pictures of the future. They regularly deal with pressing current issues: housing, transportation, jobs, public services, open space, urban design. . . . Any planning efforts are remarkable in a society that could never be accused of having a bias toward city planning in the first place, a society that has tended to look at land and urban environments as little more than high-priced consumable commodities. And isn't it grand that plans are visionary! Why shouldn't a community have a view, a vision of what it wants to be, and then try to achieve it?

Source: Excerpted from Allan B. Jacobs, *Making City Planning Work* (Chicago: American Society of Planning Officials, 1978), 307.

capital improvements program and setting priorities among the competing demands for a share of the capital budget.

A rather dramatic illustration of the plan as a guide to decision making as reflected in budgeting exists in Atlanta, Georgia.[20] In 1974 a new city charter integrated the planning and budgeting process in a new department of budget and planning. The city's plan, known as the Comprehensive Development Plan (CDP), is the cornerstone of an elaborate and continuing process that relates the city's goals to its budgets. According to the 1974 charter amendment, the operating and capital budgets *must* be based on the CDP. Public hearings are required for both the CDP and the budgets, and the city council must formally adopt each of these each year.

The CDP includes "plans" for one, five, and fifteen years in a program format. Summary information on current or proposed projects and programs to achieve those plans, as well as cost figures, are also included in the document. The Base Plan, rewritten every five years, is the major planning statement. The 1984–1988 plan has major sections on economic development, housing, public service systems, citizen participation, public-private partnerships, and financing.

Few, if any, cities are as advanced in this process as is Atlanta, but Atlanta's experience is indicative of a trend toward making the plan a significant document that will be used to guide the many decisions controlling local development. It is clear that by integrating planning and budgeting and by requiring that no budget be adopted without reference to an adopted general plan, a general plan takes on major significance in Atlanta. In short, it does indeed function as a guide to decision making.

A general plan can and should be used to guide or influence a variety of decisions. Allan Jacobs illustrates the importance of the plan as he reviews his experiences as the former planning director of the city of San Francisco:

As time passed and with a growing and more solidly based set of plans to rely upon, individual short-range proposals . . . could be viewed in the light of long-range considerations. . . . We could review the location of a subsidized housing development in the context of the housing plan element. We could measure a neighborhood re-zoning proposal against the housing and urban design elements. When a piece of public land was to be sold or leased, we could check it against a policy of the plan, as we could the vacation or widening of a street. We could relate a small renewal project in Chinatown to both the city-wide and neighborhood plans that we had prepared and we could advocate such a project. City planning was especially pleasing when the projects and programs were clearly the outcome of our plans. We were exhilarated when all our research, meetings, presentations, reconsiderations, confrontations and responses to demands led to concrete actions, or even when all we knew was that the ideas had a fighting chance of becoming reality.[21]

Jacobs goes on to say that the functions of coordination, zoning admin-istration, subdivision regulation, design review, and the design of renewal and redevelopment projects are extremely important activities but that all require some framework within which to function and make recommendations.

That framework is the general or master plan. Without it, city planners have a much harder time explaining why their ideas and their proposals are preferable to anyone else's. There were times when I might have argued otherwise, most notably in the early San Francisco months when I was impatient to get on with the action, to respond to the burning issues. . . . Taking the time to decide what we want our communities to be and then acting to achieve those goals seemed more and more worthwhile in San Francisco as time passed. It was a route that proved more practical as well.[22]

Most often a plan is used to guide the decisions of the planning department itself, the planning commission, the council, and the mayor or manager. How-ever, there are others who use the plan as a guide. Other departments of local

How to use development plans The good planning agency does not keep its plans on dusty shelves but uses plans in day-to-day decision making. This example shows how planning agencies use plans.

Let us say that a private developer wants to build a 150-acre development that is predominantly residential (135 acres) and partly commercial (15 acres). Let us assume that a mixture of housing types—single-family homes, rental apartments, and condominium apartments—is proposed. How does the planning agency use plans in reviewing such a development?

The agency first checks the land use plan to determine whether the general area is designated residential, then examines the proposed densities to see how well they fit with the plan's proposals and projections. The planning staff also checks to determine any physiographic characteristics—soil conditions, stream profiles, and important stands of trees—to see the environmental constraints that will influence site planning. The staff also determines the land use plan policies concerning the amount and location of commercial space in the center of the community.

On the basis of the land uses and anticipated population to be served, the staff in turn checks other plans for sanitary sewers, storm runoff, major and minor streets, and public facilities to determine how well the proposed development "fits into" the community's plans. For example, the parks and recreation plan may call for a neighborhood park site within the general area. Or the school plan may have identified the area as being served by an existing school; therefore, no additional school facilities are anticipated. The staff also examines the capital improvements program to determine how public facilities that are or are not programmed in the future will serve the new development.

There will be times when the development raises major policy issues not covered by the general plans. Perhaps the plan is out-of-date, or perhaps it was not detailed enough to make a judgment. In these cases planning staffs will carry out supplemental studies that amplify or update a plan element.

Finally, the planning staff prepares a staff report that will be presented to various decision makers in government, such as the planning commission, the mayor, the local manager, and the local council.

government, for example, might have need for the guidance offered by a plan. A fire department might use it in designing its service areas. And state government and metropolitan planning commissions may have occasion to use the plan. What is perhaps most important is that a well-designed plan should influence the decisions of the private sector. Builders, land developers, and businesses can learn of the local government's intentions as indicated by the plan and be guided accordingly.

Obviously, a plan that is used to guide decision making must be well prepared. It must be specific, must outline clear programs and priorities, and must avoid the trap of vague generalities.

General development plans also are a source of basic information about existing and expected conditions in the community. Although clearly secondary to the directives of the plan, the plan's function as a source of local information is an important one. The end users of the plan—elected and appointed officials, private developers, and the planners themselves—change over time. The plan, as a compendium of local information, is a ready educational tool that ensures

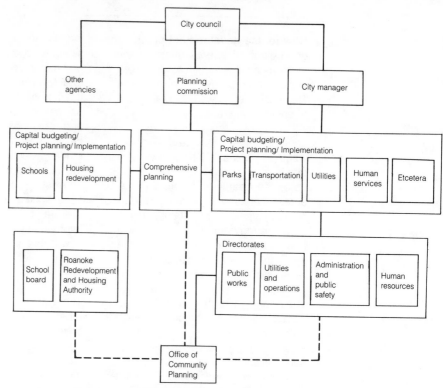

Figure 3–5   Proposed administration of comprehensive plan for Roanoke, Virginia. Administering a comprehensive plan requires coordination among legislative bodies, boards and commissions, operating departments, administrators, and quasi-independent agencies.

that all participants in the local development process will have similar background information and definitions of key terms, both of which are needed to establish the perspective for decision making.

The plan as a legal document

Increasingly, local governments are preparing plans because they have to, not necessarily because they want to. This fairly recent phenomenon has resulted from state mandates that local governments create a plan, or court requirements that some form of planning document be presented as the basis for land use controls.

This trend toward the required plan gained considerable momentum during the decade of the 1970s and promises to have a profound and lasting effect on our views of planning and plans. The trend reflects, more than anything else, a coming of age of planning and a recognition that a plan can and should really mean something. The plan is no longer a formality to be prepared and forgotten. It is rapidly becoming a requirement—and one that must contain certain elements; it is becoming a requirement that has for all practical purposes the force of law, or a requirement that must be fulfilled if the municipality is to receive federal or state funds or other benefits.

This trend appears to result primarily from a shifting attitude on the part of the courts as they review land use regulations. The Standard State Zoning Enabling Act of the 1920s stated that zoning "shall be in accordance with a comprehensive plan." For decades this language has been the subject of intensive debate, but for decades the courts rendered their opinions on zoning matters without requiring that a local government have a plan, or requiring the zoning to be consistent with a plan if there should be one.

This judicial attitude was not surprising considering the rather static nature of early zoning practice. In those days it was assumed that a local government would prepare a zoning map that outlined areas of residential, commercial, or industrial use and that any amendments to or variances from the zoning map would be few and far between. Property owners needed only to look at the map and the zoning text to determine what they could or could not do with their property. In short, the zoning map and text became the plan, and the courts needed to look no further to determine what the community wanted.

Two major changes in land use control practices have eroded the willingness of the courts to accept a zoning ordinance without reference to a general plan. The first change was the increasing use of flexible land use controls. As local governments became unwilling to specify in advance where everything would be or what it would look like, they adopted a "wait and see" attitude toward development, using such devices as floating zones, planned unit developments, large-lot zoning, special-use permits, and wholesale amendments or variances. Property owners no longer knew in advance exactly what they could or could not do with their property, and they came to expect to go before the local authorities and negotiate an agreement.

This trend toward negotiated agreements resulted in part from an appreciation of our inability to predict the future. It seemed that no matter how carefully a local government would prepare its zoning ordinance, something unanticipated would make it inappropriate or out of date. The other reason for negotiated agreements was that communities wanted to be able to attract the "right" kind of use and prohibit the "wrong" kind. The flexible controls allowed them to say yes to electronics factories and stately homes on two-acre lots and no to smelting plants and apartment houses for low-income residents. Although this may have suited a community's need to control its own destiny, the courts began to doubt the fundamental fairness of the system. The zoning ordinance had ceased to be predictable and prescriptive and had become merely a set of procedures one had to go through to find out what might be done with one's property. In the courts' view, it was a system that could be subject to abuse.

The second change in land use control practice has been the increasing adoption of growth management programs. Traditionally, planning and land use control systems have been concerned with the location and character of growth. In the 1970s planners added a third dimension: timing. It was no longer assumed that all growth was good. Growth had its negative consequences, and some communities went so far as to adopt a no-growth policy. Most, however, were satisfied to control the rate of growth (for example, x number of housing units per year).

Again, the courts have begun to say that if a municipality wants to control the rate of growth, it will have to show some evidence of a coordinated approach in order to avoid charges of arbitrary and capricious enforcement. In short, the courts would like to see a plan.

When vast acres of land were zoned for all manner of use far in advance of need, it did not matter much whether there was a plan. Now that land use control has become a finely tuned, flexible tool for controlling the most minute detail of development, including timing, a plan has become increasingly important.

The landmark case in which the judiciary recognized a plan as a valid defense of a local growth program is *Golden* v. *Planning Board of the Town of Ramapo* (1972).[23] Ramapo Township amended its zoning ordinance to implement a permit system for all new residential development. A permit would be granted only if the development were adequately served by public facilities; adequacy was determined by a point system based on the proximity of the development to available services such as sewage treatment or water supply. In upholding the timing control system, the court relied heavily on the fact that the challenged ordinance was implementing a well-designed general plan for the community. In the absence of the plan, it is unlikely that the court would have ruled in favor of the township.

Two Oregon cases further illustrate judicial interest in a general plan. In *Fasano* v. *Board of County Commissioners* (1973), the Oregon Supreme Court rejected the notion that amendments to the zoning ordinance are legislative and instead determined that they were quasi-judicial, thus completely shifting the presumption of validity usually applied to legislative acts. The court's opinion placed heavy weight on the comprehensive plan as a justification for zoning amendments and noted that "the more drastic the change, the greater will be the burden of showing that it is in conformance with the comprehensive plan as implemented by the ordinance."[24]

In *Baker* v. *City of Milwaukie* (1975), the Oregon Supreme Court unequivocally gave the general plan a central role in local zoning:

We conclude that a comprehensive plan is the controlling land use planning instrument for a city. Upon passage of a comprehensive plan, a city assumes a responsibility to effectuate that plan and conform prior conflicting zoning ordinances to it. We further hold that the zoning decisions of a city must be in accord with that plan.[25]

The issues being raised in the courts concerning the status of the general plan are also being debated in state capitols. A number of states have begun to *require* local governments to prepare plans or to *require* zoning and other land use control measures to be consistent with local plans, or both. State legislatures are being pushed and pulled into this posture. They are being pushed by the courts and pulled by their own desire to gain greater control over the development process.

California was one of the first states to enact legislation requiring local governments to adopt a plan. California also requires local zoning to be consistent with the adopted plan. The Florida Local Government Comprehensive Planning Act of 1975 mandates planning by counties, municipalities, and special districts. It further requires that all land development regulations enacted or amended be consistent with these comprehensive plans. Kentucky, Nebraska, Colorado, and Oregon also have some form of mandatory planning or "consistency" requirements.

Not everyone agrees with this movement to require local governments to plan. Some argue that the only meaningful plan is one that is generated from local needs and desires, not one imposed by some higher level of government. The debate on this issue will doubtless continue, but it is probable that the decade of the 1980s will see the plan emerge as an "impermanent constitution," a term coined a quarter of a century ago by Charles M. Haar. Haar argued as follows in 1955:

If the plan is regarded not as the vestpocket tool of the planning commission, but as a broad statement to be adopted by the most representative municipal body—the local legislature—then the plan becomes a law through such adoption. A unique type of law, it should be noted, in that it purports to bind future legislatures when they enact implementary materials.[26]

The implications of the mandated plan and the rulings that the control of land use be consistent with the plan are far-reaching. The plan ceases to be an exercise in platitudes. It must do more than be for motherhood and against sin. It must be carefully and accurately crafted, for it will have the force of law. This is not to suggest that the traditional functions of a plan, those of education, information, persuasion, and coordination, are lost. On the contrary, these functions will always be central purposes of the plan. However, as the status of the plan changes to that of an impermanent constitution, it will become more important, it will be taken more seriously, and it will have a greater effect on people's lives.

Components of a general plan

Although there is no set format for a general plan, the following components are usually represented:

1. Demographic conditions, which outlines existing and expected population and employment composition of the community.
2. Land use, which describes current and projected land use within the community and adjacent unincorporated areas.
3. Transportation, which outlines proposals for adding to or improving the street and highway systems and mass transit system and may contain proposals for other aspects of the transportation system including bicycles, pedestrians, airports, and harbors.
4. Community facilities, which treats the capital plant of the community and includes schools, parks, libraries, and other public buildings such as the city hall, museums, and the like.

Many plans contain additional components. The issues that are considered of most importance to a particular community's future and the policy orientation of the community at the time of the plan's development will certainly influence the contents of the plan. For example, many plans have components that treat housing, historic preservation, urban design, energy, employment, and the delivery of human services. Many plans have a section outlining the steps needed to implement the recommendations of the plan itself.

The content of a plan often reflects the development status of the community. Communities can be viewed as developing or mature. In developing communities, which have substantial amounts of open land that is or will be subject to development pressures, the primary role of the plan might be to determine how best to organize development on that land and provide the necessary service systems. Mature communities, on the other hand, may have little or no remaining undeveloped land. Hence, plans for such communities are concerned with recycling developed lands, repairing or maintaining existing systems, and replacing outmoded facilities. Most often, plans of mature communities concentrate on specific portions of the community needing attention and guidance, such as individual neighborhoods or the downtown.

Although the organization may vary, each component of a general plan usually consists of three portions: (1) a description of existing conditions, (2) a statement of goals and objectives, and (3) a description of future needs and proposals for meeting those needs.

The description of existing conditions establishes a context for the plan's recommendations; it provides a comprehensive record of conditions during the preparation of the plan, defines key terms, and educates community residents about the current status and needs of the community. Because a sound information base is required to determine the extent of needs and identify ways to meet them, the preparation of this material often consumes a substantial percentage of the time devoted to the development of a general plan.

Goals and objectives represent the plan's statement of community desires. These statements give direction to the plan. They represent the community's aspirations and outline the ends that should be reached if the plan's proposals are properly implemented. Goals are value-based statements that are not necessarily measurable. Objectives are more specific, measurable statements of desired ends. For example, a goal might be "a community containing a balanced variety of housing types." Objectives appropriate to attaining this goal might include "Increase the amount of multifamily units," "Increase the amount of housing accessible to the elderly," and so on.

Identifying how best to meet the needs of the community is at the heart of the plan. These needs are derived from projections that are exogenous to the plan, such as population growth, economic growth, and energy costs, as well as from the goals and objectives of the plan. Approaches to meeting these needs— the recommendations of the plan—are usually described in the form of policies, programs, and projects. Policies are rules or courses of action that indicate *how* the goals and objectives of the plan should be realized. Programs are a series of related, mission-oriented activities aimed at carrying out a particular policy or group of policies. Programs often consist of a series of projects, which are specific actions or "brick-and-mortar" recommendations.

How these policies, programs, and projects are described in a plan depends on the nature of the recommendations, and the orientation of the plan. Certain policies can be expressed in graphic form—such as the proposed land use pattern or the thoroughfare system for a town. Other policies are usually written.

Preparing a general plan

A number of elements are involved in the preparation of a general plan, including the initiation, direction, and performance of the work and the relationship between the planning process and affected citizens and surrounding communities. The eleven sections that follow consider each aspect of plan preparation in detail.

Who initiates?

The development of a general plan is most often initiated by the local public authority—the council, mayor, planning commission, manager, or planner (not necessarily in that order). The reason for undertaking the plan in theory, and perhaps in best practice, is local concern over the future orderly growth and development of the community. Concern may stem from lagging growth, burgeoning growth, or stagnation.

State requirements for and funding of general plans are currently an important motivating force for undertaking a plan. Federal requirements for general plans have varied over the years, but some coordinative plan has been a requirement for federal local development monies, and federal monies have been available in greater and lesser amounts to pay for plans.

The trend in state enabling legislation to require local plans has already been noted. While there is increasing national concern about rational use of land and protection of farmland and natural resources (such as coastal zones), there is continuing political pressure to maintain the "local" nature of land use decisions. The result is state planning efforts that delegate comprehensive planning responsibility to local municipalities. One of many examples is the coastal-zone planning program in Oregon, where coastal cities are required to prepare general plans that include provisions for use of the coastal area.

It is important to note that there is also a long American tradition of initiation of comprehensive planning efforts by concerned citizens as well as by public servants; the Burnham plan is the best-known historical example. In 1984 the San Francisco Chamber of Commerce funded the preparation of a strategic plan—the first corporate-style plan for a large city.

The initiation of a comprehensive planning effort in response to public concern over the future of the municipality is, in many ways, the ideal circumstance for the undertaking. One of the aims of the planning effort is to generate widespread discussion about the future development of the municipality. As many planners have discovered, it is often difficult to gain the attention of any but a few of the public. This is particularly true of plans generated by a planning department or commission simply in response to federal or state requirements.

Who directs the work?
And who else should be involved?

Although a comprehensive planning effort may be financed and directed wholly outside the public sector, this is the exception and not the rule. The majority of municipalities over 25,000 in population now have planning departments or commissions with paid staff, one of whose tasks is to prepare comprehensive development plans for the municipality.

It is evident that the locus of responsibility for planning will vary from one community to another and that a planning staff must often serve a combination of local elected officials, appointed advisers, and hired managers. As Alan Black so aptly put it: "The planning function does not fall neatly into either the 'line' or 'staff' activities in government. The proper placement of planning in the municipal organization chart has long been a matter of dispute."[27]

The dispute over the placement of planning is commonly traced to the fears of corrupt municipal government held by the reformers of the 1920s. These reformers were somewhat romantic proponents of the notion that rational people serving on an independent planning commission outside of political influence could improve the municipality. It is now a commonplace, however, to emphasize the need to bring the planning function closer to those who make public investment decisions (the legislators, the mayor, and the city manager).

This approach to the planning function is reflected in the creation of planning or planning and development departments where the staff is responsible to the chief executive but also is advised by a planning commission. There are also a significant number of cities with joint city-county commissions.

The city manager's role in the planning function is especially prominent in smaller cities, where he or she is most likely to have major responsibility. In many larger cities, deputy managers may be responsible for planning.

If the plan is going to be used following its preparation—to guide zoning decisions, to provide the basis for planning community development activities, to set priorities for street improvements—it is essential that those who are expected to use it be involved in its preparation. Local elected and appointed officials who will be ruling on zoning changes should have been through the process of examining population trends, housing patterns, and commercial development and should have had to sort out goals for future development. And officials who will be developing and adopting the capital improvements program should be familiar with the community's long-range goals.

If the planning function is located in a municipal department, the staff will have to seek input from private investors (lending institutions, real estate developers, businesspeople, industrialists, and others with a vital interest). Also, it behooves the staff to seek the involvement of municipal department heads, local elected officials, or the mayor's office as necessary to gain support for required public investment.

The public must be involved in plan preparation. The public comes in several forms. It can include individual citizens with a particular interest in plan making, and it can include the organized public. The latter includes a broad range of groups—labor unions and minority organizations, promoters of environmental quality or historical sites, and neighborhood groups, to name a few. Both the individual citizen and organized publics should have an opportunity to participate in plan development. Advisory committees, radio and television presentations and call-in shows, surveys, and public meetings are some of the many techniques for gaining public participation in a plan. Now that participation has become widely recognized as an integral part of the planning process, many highly developed techniques are available to the planner. It is also essential that the schedule of plan preparation reflect the amount of time it takes to gain the interest and involvement of the larger community.

Citizen participation

Since the tumultuous era of the 1960s, citizen participation has become an important part of the plan development process. However, the nature and extent of such participation can vary considerably. At a minimum is the citizen's involvement through the public hearing process, which comes prior to plan adoption. In some communities, however, residents are deeply involved in the development of plans through participation in citizen committees that make recommendations to the planning commission. In many communities the planning process is initiated through communitywide surveys to identify planning issues. Surveys are often followed by structured activities that include nominal group or other public participation techniques; these activities help determine issues to be treated in the comprehensive plan and identify possible approaches to their resolution.

Whether local government is working in partnership with a community group or in a more adversarial role, the involvement of neighborhood residents in self-assessment of neighborhood conditions and needs can help broaden understanding at the community level of the factors involved in neighborhood decay. Such awareness can bring about, for example, a heightened interest in maintaining the flow of home financing monies into neighborhoods—an interest that can be reflected, in turn, by "anti-redlining" laws. Neighborhood self-assessment also provides insights for the planner into "how things work" in a particular neighborhood, insights that can be important to the design of new housing sites, street layout, and location of commercial facilities.

Relationship to county, metropolitan, and regional planning

What about the other end of the spectrum? How should the comprehensive planning effort of a municipality be related to the larger context of which it is a part—the county, the metropolitan area, the region?

The development of most communities is immediately affected by their surrounding environs. Depending on prevailing annexation laws and practices and the history of development, communities may be struggling with a declining tax base as development occurs outside their limits. Local governments may be members of councils of governments or may have intermunicipal arrangements for the provision of services ranging from water supply to schools.

The context in which the local planning effort is undertaken is increasingly complex. Counties, metropolitan areas, states, and interstate regions all may have comprehensive planning efforts that to a greater or lesser extent must be considered by the local municipality.

State involvement in land use planning varies greatly from state to state. Some municipalities will find themselves undertaking comprehensive planning efforts because of state programs delegated to them. The greatest impact of state planning on individual localities over the next decade may be in revised state planning acts and in the identification of geographic areas of particular concern to the state because of their unique ecological, historical, or economic significance. Should such sites be identified in or near municipalities undertaking a planning effort, they would be important considerations in the planning effort.

Regional or metropolitan planning programs encompassing a community will certainly have important implications for local transportation, growth projections, overall land use allocations, competing business centers, housing distribution, and natural resources management. Other issues of importance to the locality that may be addressed at a regional level include water supply, solid waste disposal, and flood control.

Many local governments work closely with regional agencies in plan development. Smaller cities may even rely on a regional planning staff to prepare the plans. There are also instances of city-county joint plans, prepared by joint staff and adopted by both city council and county commission.

Differences of perspective at the local and regional levels mean that there is often some friction between the two planning efforts. Large, older central cities very often feel underrepresented on regional commissions, whose membership is not always (or even usually) based on population. Suburban communities experiencing growth pressures may or may not find regional estimates of growth acceptable or even reasonable. Discussion of the need for and location of low- and moderate-income housing is very often controversial.

One of the greatest challenges for the planners of the next decade will be to sort out the jurisdictional level at which to plan various services and land uses. Our greater understanding of ecological systems, our communication technology, and our national energy needs are a few of the factors that have heightened our awareness of interdependence. At the same time, we have a continuing commitment to local community control over decision making and to involvement of people in the decisions that will affect their lives.

A general plan should identify the local government's role in the region of which it is a part and should describe how that role may be changing because of growth or decline. A realistic assessment of the alternative futures open to a community must take into account regional trends. However, it is the local planners who should know best how the particular strengths and weaknesses of the community will influence its future development.

Who does the technical work in plan preparation?

When a locality has a planning staff, it is the responsibility of that staff to prepare plans. However, given the diverse technical skills necessary to identify environmental, transportation, utilities, and other needs of the community, most planning staffs will require additional assistance. In some cases this assistance can be provided by other municipal departments such as public works or engineering. Consultants are also frequently used in the preparation of particular components of the plan. In small cities, consultants may undertake all of the technical work under the direction of the planning staff, planning commission, or city manager.

When consultants are used, it is important that the local staff and policymakers stay closely involved in the evolution of the plan—examining data, formulating policy, and reviewing alternative schemes. If the consultants prepare all the material on their own and present a finished product to the community, it is much less likely to be useful. In addition, it is often valuable to involve consultants in some aspects of plan implementation. This guards against planning work that is irrelevant to the needs of a particular community and the mechanisms available to it for implementation.

How much money is needed?

Planning is certainly not an expensive task of local government compared with providing services such as police and fire protection. Plans rarely cost more than 0.5 percent of the cost of the municipal capital investments that the plan is designed to guide. However, because the payoffs from planning are not seen as immediate and tangible, the planning budget is often considered expendable. This is particularly true in times when funds are short. It can, of course, be argued that when money is short, it is most important for local officials to know the anticipated impact of public investment. However, it is exactly at this point that planning is often seen as a luxury.

In the last decade federal monies were available to municipalities specifically for comprehensive planning. It is difficult to predict whether such funds will be available in the next decade. This means that each locality will have to make its own case for planning. The task will be easiest in localities experiencing major growth or decline. It is also likely to succeed where the planning effort is designed to assist local officials in making investment decisions. A clear link between the planning effort and the management of the municipality must be established.

How much time is needed?

The length of time needed to prepare a development plan varies with the factors shown in Figure 3–6. Because there are at least as many incentives for prolonging the planning process as for shortening it, deadlines must be set at the outset that specify the availability of specific products. On the one hand, such deadlines must be realistic in terms of the time it takes to collect and process information; on the other hand, they must take into account that prolonged planning efforts may be obsolete by the time their findings are printed.

When a short time frame is required, an interim policy plan is one useful technique for providing a general plan in a timely manner. The interim policy plan allows for a statement of goals and objectives that is subject to further refinement upon completion of more complex and time-consuming studies. Although such a general statement may lack specificity, it is a useful way for planning commissions and legislative bodies to make broad judgments on issues such as growth rates, balancing growth with environmental factors, promoting economic development, preserving historic districts, and so on.

In determining the timing of a plan, it is important to remember that planning is an ongoing process. No comprehensive plan can be the "last word" on the future development of the community. Factors beyond the influence of local administrators and beyond their predictive capacities are likely to cause change and to require new plans. Inherent in comprehensiveness is a tendency toward

	More time	Less time
1. Is it an initial effort?	X	
2. Are there highly technical elements to be prepared, such as analysis of hazard areas?	X	
3. Will widespread public involvement be sought?	X	
4. Is there a critical investment decision contingent upon plan completion?		X
5. Are there legislative requirements?		X
6. Are there rewards for early completion?		X
7. Are staff available and on board?		X
8. Are commissioners', council members', or mayors' terms coincident with the planning period?		X
9. Is there an imminent changeover in the local administration?	X	
10. Is there information available on the municipality in regional or state planning agencies?		X
11. Does the plan have to be consistent with a regional or state plan?	X	
12. Are things changing very rapidly in the municipality that make the planning of high interest?		X
13. Are there deep divisions in the municipality about what the future of the community should be?	X	
14. Is there more than one local agency with significant planning responsibilities?	X	

Figure 3–6   Factors affecting the time required for a development plan.

exhaustiveness. Exhaustive data that are known only to the planning director and planning staff and are never used to formulate policies or describe trends are neither helpful nor worthy of the expenditure.

Who adopts the plan?

How important is formal adoption of the general development plan by the council, or formal endorsement by the mayor? If, indeed, the intent of the plan is to make a public statement of the community's policies on future physical development, formal adoption or endorsement is *the* act of political support.

Adoption is no guarantee of implementation or even of full support. However, it is an important step in the process of articulating, publicizing, and endorsing municipal goals for physical development. Adoption does ensure that those adopting the plan will be informed of the plan's goals and policies. (It is to be hoped, of course, that at least some of them have been actively involved in their preparation.) The plan also can provide strong leverage for zoning ordinance revision (if necessary) and enforcement.

It is essential that a plan give the elected officials an understanding of the conditions that require public action—hence the need for a public policy. The drafters of the plan should not assume that the officials know why the community needs a plan at all. The plan should describe the current situation in the community: growth trends, functions, and population mix, as well as the adequacy of its infrastructure to serve those who live there and those expected to come there. A brief history often enhances understanding of the current situation.

What that is inherent in the current situation requires public action? If matters continue as they are with no attempt to influence them, what consequences will follow that are considered undesirable? Shortfalls in the local housing stock, abandoned neighborhoods, scattered development of agricultural land, overuse of a local natural resource that threatens its future—these are some of the conditions that should be presented to officials to show the necessity for a plan.

Establishing an overall strategy

A general plan contains a series of policies concerning land use, provision of housing, location of new transportation facilities, and the like. These individual policies should reflect an overall strategy for local development that is articulated at the outset. In growing communities, this strategy may center on approaches to affect the rate and location of growth and new development or on schemes for slowing or directing growth. In older areas with stable or declining populations, the focus of the strategy should concern the public resource and investment priorities that will help and upgrade the community.

The policies in a general plan are often supported by a series of goals for the community's development, including the amenities the local government should provide and to whom it should provide them.

Because of the comprehensive nature of the plan and the consensus approach to policy formulation often inherent in plan development, goals statements often have an inclusive quality that makes it difficult to determine priorities for action. Improvement of "quality of life" and provision of "decent, safe, and sanitary housing for all" are typical planning goals that are not specific enough.

A good plan is one that pushes beyond a laundry list of generalized goals to a series of more concrete policy recommendations. Priorities should be clear. Goals must be translated into specific and measurable objectives.

The larger the community, the more difficult it is to determine priorities. Many activities are going forward at the same time in both the public and private sectors. One approach to such complexity is to build an overall development strategy out of a series of neighborhood plans. Whatever the approach and direction of the plan's overall strategy, the strategy should be stated at the outset, and it should be possible to relate the recommendations of individual plan components to it.

What should the plan look like?

Plans come in more varied sizes and shapes than most public documents, perhaps because of the design training of many of those responsible for them. Many plans are printed in a series of volumes so that no one document is unwieldy. Many are summarized in short pamphlets for wide public distribution. Some agencies use a loose-leaf notebook in which individual plan components may be added (or subtracted) as they are completed or updated. This is a visual reflection of the ongoing nature of plan making.

Should maps be used?

Maps have always been a primary communication tool for planners. They can be very helpful in making graphic and site specific the policies contained in the plan. Some cities, such as Philadelphia, report that their maps are the tools most heavily used by those trying to relate specific proposals to the plan. However, they also report difficulties in keeping the maps updated.

Action	By whom	Proposed schedule (year) 1	2	3	4	5
1. Revised land development regulations						
Complete draft regulations	OCP	•				
Planning Commission/Council review and approval	PC/CC	···•				
Revise zoning map/review and approval	OCP/PC/CC	····•				
Detailed design guidelines where applicable	OCP/PC	······•				
Implementation of new regulations	PC		··········	··········	··········	········►
Continuing review of regulations	OCP/PC				··········	········►
2. Administering the plan						
Revise plan administrative structure	PC/City	····•				
Initiate continuing planning activities	PC/OCP		··········	··········	··········	········►
Establish comprehensive data system	OCP/PC		··········	··········	····•	
Revise zoning administrative structure	PC/BZA/ARB	····•				
Establish improved review/reporting procedures	OCP		········•			
Implement continuing planning/zoning reviews	OCP		··········	··········	··········	········►
3. Partnership approach						
Enlist participation of private advisory groups	PC/OCP/RNP	····•				
Create new public-private vehicles: Housing Corp., etc.	City/PC/RNP		··········	·········•		
Continue coordination of partnership activities	PC/OCP/RNP		··········	··········	··········	········►
4. Planning and development actions						
Prepare neighborhood data inventory	OCP/RNP	······•				
Prepare detailed component plans	City/OCP/RNP	·······	·····•			
Select priority neighborhoods for initial efforts	PC/OCP/RNP	···•				
Initiate neighborhood action planning	PC/OCP/RNP	•····	·····•	··········	·····•····	····►
Technical assistance for defined action projects	City/OCP/RNP	······	··········	··········	··········	····►

CC: City Council • City: City Administration • PC: Planning Commission • BZA: Board of Zoning Appeals • ARB: Architectural Review Board • OCP: Office of Community Planning • RNP: Roanoke Neighborhood Partnership

Figure 3–7   Five-year action schedule for Roanoke, Virginia. Planning implementation requires identifying what must be done, by whom, and when.

There is also a point of view that people come to rely too heavily on the maps and ignore important policy statements. Some plans specifically state that if there is a conflict between the map and the policy statements, the written word rules.

Adopting and applying the plan

Although planning law varies from state to state, in general the planning commission is charged with developing a general plan and submitting it to the local council for public hearing and adoption. Without such adoption, the merit and utility of the plan are markedly reduced. Once adopted, the plan should be viewed as the basic set of policy guidelines governing local development decisions. As such, it is a key source document for zoning decisions, capital improvements planning, budgeting, and establishing policy responses to particular issues.

The link between general development plans and zoning is quite apparent. That is, the plan identifies a pattern of desired land use development, and zoning ordinances specify the range and conditions of use that can occur on parcels of land. In this view the zoning ordinance is clearly a tool to implement the land use recommendations of the general plan, and certain states have made the development and linkage of a plan to local zoning a mandatory requirement. This was first required in California during the mid-1970s; Florida now requires all municipalities to develop a comprehensive plan and to link their zoning ordinances to that plan.

Capital improvements planning refers to the planning of major local facilities such as sewer, water, transportation systems, and public buildings. These systems need to be planned to reflect the policies of the general development plan. In fact, it is usually the case that the broad outlines of these systems are depicted in the general plan. The adoption of the general plan should initiate a process wherein the municipal capital improvements program is refined to reflect the recommendations of the development plan and, hence, affect the budgeting of local monies for public improvement. As might be expected, budgeting money to build the recommended improvements within the time identified by the plan and capital improvements program is one of the keys to plan implementation.

In addition to using the plan to direct zoning decisions, establish capital improvements programs, and allocate municipal funds, local governments should also use the plan as a basis for general policy review. The plan development process usually uncovers a host of issues which, if treated, receive a specific policy response. Once adopted, however, many of these policies are never used and often are forgotten until a crisis arises. Through the council or planning commission, the local government should conduct a policy review on a timely basis, perhaps every two years, to evaluate the policies contained within the plan, note those that should be changed and those that should be removed, and develop new policies if necessary. Policy review ensures that the decision makers keep the plan current and are aware of the directives contained within it.

Conclusion: Looking ahead

One of the major themes of this chapter is that a general plan reflects the times. A good plan must be responsive to the social and cultural mix that characterizes each particular place and era. How else can we explain the wide range and character of the various plans that have been produced during the last half century? Yet within that variation, the essence of the idea of a plan has remained intact, and we must conclude that it will continue to survive.

Declarations of what the general plan of the 1990s will be like are risky. Declarations of what it should be like are foolish. Nevertheless, there is merit in attempting to project some of the current trends to see what might be in store.

First, and most important, general plans will continue to be produced, regardless of what they are called, because the compelling logic behind them will not subside. That logic is simply that it is wise to look ahead, to anticipate rather than to react, to coordinate rather than to compete, and to make decisions that are based on shared community objectives.

Second, the production of the general plan will be better integrated into local government and will no longer be the exclusive province of the planning department or commission. Many of the major principles of planning are becoming commonplace in local government management. No longer is the planner seemingly the only spokesman for the long-range, comprehensive point of view. Managers, budget officers, and department heads increasingly espouse and practice a form of planning that the planning profession has long advocated. This trend toward greater acceptance of planning principles is a welcome sign and a challenge to the planning profession. If the profession does not continue to grow and advance, it will be swallowed up by its own success. It will have no special skills or principles to offer to the local government management agenda. The challenge will be to continue to lead in the development of tools and techniques of planning and management.

Third, it is likely that future general plans will focus increasingly on resource management—be it water, energy, land, or air. The nation is becoming increasingly sensitive to the limits of these finite resources and the constraints that these limits impose on future development. The concept of carrying capacity will cease to be merely an academic issue and will become a central feature of a growing number of general plans.

Finally, we will continue to see more efforts to define the legal dimensions of the general plan. The trend toward mandated plans will no doubt continue. There will be increasing experimentation with laws that require development regulations to be "consistent" with published plans. The result will be the production of general plans that carry the authority of the law as well as the authority of their own logic.

1   John W. Reps, *The Making of Urban America: A History of City Planning in the United States* (Princeton, NJ: Princeton University Press, (1965).

2   Mel Scott, *American City Planning since 1890* (Berkeley: University of California Press, 1969) 2.

3   Jacob Riis, *How the Other Half Lives* (New York: Dover, 1971).

4   From a speech presented by Frederick Law Olmsted, Jr., at the Third National Conference on City Planning, Philadelphia, 15–17 May 1911, quoted in Scott, *American City Planning*, p. 141.

5   U.S. Department of Commerce, Advisory Committee on Zoning. *A Standard State Zoning Enabling Act* (Washington, DC: U.S. Government Printing Office, 1922); and U.S. Department of Commerce, Advisory Committee on City Planning and Zoning, *A Standard City Planning Enabling Act* (Washington, DC: U.S. Government Printing Office, 1928).

6   Bassett's view of a plan as limited to several elements probably dominated over the broader views of Olmsted and Bettman.

7   Alan Black, "The Comprehensive Plan," in William I. Goodman and Eric C. Freund, eds. *Principles and Practice of Urban Planning* (Washington, DC: International City Management Association, 1968), 353–55.

8   David Lilienthal, *TVA: Democracy on the March* (New York: Harper & Brothers, 1954), quoted in:

Charles M. Haar, *Land Use Planning: A Casebook on the Use, Misuse and Reuse of Urban Land* (Boston: Little, Brown & Co, 1971), 712.

9   Scott, *American City Planning*, 397.

10   Ibid.

11   Martin Meyerson, "Building the Middle-Range Bridge for Comprehensive Planning," *Journal of the American Institute of Planners* 22 (Spring 1956): 58–64.

12   Melville C. Branch, *Continuous City Planning*, Planning Advisory Service Report no. 290 (Chicago: American Society of Planning Officials, April 1973). There were also challenges to the planner's claim to comprehensive understanding of the functions of the city (Altschuler: Braybrooke and Lindblom) and the planner's predictive capacities. Others asked whose goals were being articulated and challenged the activity as promoting the interests of those in power—often in conflict with the interests of those affected (Davidoff: Gans). The effects of general plans on particular neighborhoods and on city life-styles were also pointed out by Herbert Gans and Jane Jacobs. See Alan Altshuler, "The Goals of Comprehensive Planning," *Journal of the American Institute of Planners* 31 (August 1965): 186–95; David Braybrooke and Charles Lindblom, *A Strategy of Decision* (New York: The Free Press of Glencoe, 1963); Paul Davidoff,

"Advocacy and Pluralism in Planning," *Journal of the American Institute of Planners* 31 (November 1965): 331–38; Herbert Gans, *The Urban Villagers: Group and Class Life of Italian Americans* (New York: The Free Press, 1965); and Jane Jacobs, *The Death and Life, of Great American Cities* (New York: Random House, 1961).

13 See Melvin M. Webber, "The Role of Intelligence Systems in Urban Systems Planning," *Journal of the American Institute of Planners* 31 (November 1965): 289–96, and William L. C. Wheaton and Margaret Wheaton, "Identifying the Public Interest: Values and Goals," in *Urban Planning in Transition,* ed. Ernest Erber (New York: Grossman, 1970).

14 Scott, *American City Planning,* 560.

15 Franklyn H. Beal, "Defining Development Objectives," in Goodman and Freund, eds. *Principles and Practice of Urban Planning*, 335–40.

16 American Law Institute, *A Model Land Development Code,* complete text, adopted by the American Law Institute May 21, 1975, with Reporter's Commentary (Philadelphia: American Law Institute, 1976).

17 Ibid., Article III, 136.

18 Ibid.

19 Ibid., 155.

20 American Society of Planning Officials, *Local Capital Improvements and Development Management: Case Study Draft Report—Atlanta,* prepared by the American Society of Planning Officials under contract to the U.S. Department of Housing and Urban Development and the National Science Foundation (Chicago: American Society of Planning Officials, 1978), 4.

21 Allan B. Jacobs, *Making City Planning Work* (Chicago: American Planning Association, 1978), 304–5.

22 Ibid., 306.

23 *Golden* v. *Planning Board of the Town of Ramapo,* 30 N.Y. 2d 359, 285 N. E. 2d 291, 409 U.S. 1003 (1972).

24 *Fasano* v. *Board of County Commissioners of Washington County,* 264 Ore. 574, 582, 507 P.2d 23, 27 (1973).

25 *Baker* v. *City of Milwaukie,* 533 P.2d 722 (1975).

26 Charles M. Haar, "The Master Plan: An Impermanent Constitution," *Law and Contemporary Problems* 20 (Summer 1955): 375.

27 Black, "The Comprehensive Plan," 357.

Part two: District, environmental, and transportation planning

4 District planning

An overview of district planning

Planning for a district—that is, a *portion* of a municipality—cannot be perceived simply as comprehensive community planning at a lesser scale, or in a segmented manner. District planning involves major distinctions in approach, perspective, scope, and other characteristics dictated by the ultimate purpose of the plan. The district plan can encompass many of the same elements as a comprehensive plan, but it deals with an area that has detailed and specific needs within the overarching policies of a comprehensive plan. Three unique requirements characterize planning for a district or a part of a community: the need to relate closely to the residents, or users, of the district; the need to define carefully the boundaries of the district; and the need to relate the district to its larger setting in terms of circulation, open space, natural resources, visual form, land uses, and public services and facilities. The scale of a district plan typically warrants a strong urban design focus and often calls for specific housing or traffic circulation programs. Given the more limited scale of the district plan, it is especially important to involve landowners as well as special-interest groups and associations in the planning process. The more manageable scale also provides opportunities for detailed opinion surveys of residents and other participants in the planning process. On the other hand, the district planning process does involve many steps that correspond to those in the conventional comprehensive planning process: a complete survey of existing land uses and public facilities; projections of future needs and expectations; clear documentation of the district's economic and social role in the larger community; and an inquiry into the objectives of the district's residents, businesses, employees, and organizations.

These steps lead, in various ways, to an array of major options for development of the district, which are sketched out at first and amplified during the later stages of the planning process. The options are subject to scrutiny and review, a selection is made, and preliminary and final plans are prepared. The implementation needs are examined early in the program so that the implementation component can be more easily prepared. These steps may be carried out by different participants. For instance, technical start-up work is usually done by staff or consultants. Options are presented to planning committees, planning commissions, and, most desirably, elected governing bodies (although the latter may resist early decisions). Preliminary and final plans and implementation components typically are adopted by planning commissions and governing bodies.

Many opportunities and refinements are available when planning is pursued at a smaller geographic scale. District planning departs from areawide or jurisdictionwide planning primarily in its level of detail. The inventory, the first element in a planning process, is typically scrupulously detailed at the district level. For instance, the land use survey can and should be done parcel by parcel and presented in a correspondingly detailed format. Surveys of business establishments examine numbers of employees, amounts of space occupied, and even condition of structures. Land use, population, and employment projections may be based on a disaggregation from larger projections for an entire area (just as the jurisdiction's own projections may be extrapolated from regional projections). However, economic projections for a district can involve far more than normal population and employment statistics; they can be based on a focused market analysis, which is ordinarily not feasible for an entire jurisdiction. Similarly, goals and objectives can be based on full-scale or large sample surveys and interviews rather than determined in a gross or cursory manner. Once the preferred plan is proposed, actual copies can be made available to all interested parties.

The implementation program for a district must correspond to the detail of the plan, and indeed there is great incentive for ensuring that it does. Zoning can be parcel specific. In the realm of regulation, the "specific plan" (authorized in some states, such as California), can be used to advantage, since it is a plan-zoning hybrid with direct regulatory effect, superseding more general zoning. Hence, it can almost mirror the district plan and provide a direct policy-regulatory link. Capital improvements programs need not be presented in oversimplified chart or matrix formats; a plan at the district level can provide specific documentation, including precise locations, costs and sources of funding, and priorities and timing.

The implementation of a district plan can extend to managing new growth. For instance, a specific amount of commercial development can be permitted each year on the basis of potential buying power, or allowable residential development can be based on the availability of services and public facilities.

Problems in district planning

What are the obstacles and shortcomings of district planning? One of the first difficult considerations is the selection of the general locus for such planning.

Figure 4–1   Overview of the district planning process.

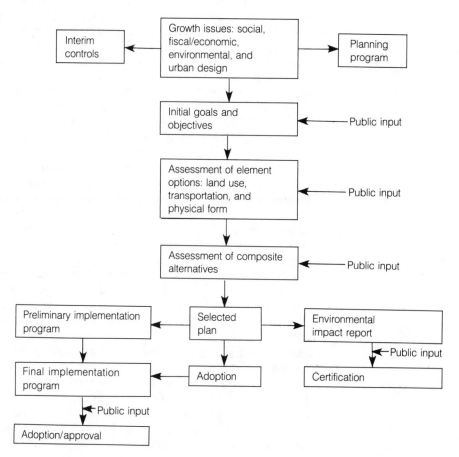

This is often controversial, since it implies a preference for one district over another. However, if done as part of a larger program of multidistrict planning, it is more politically defensible. Giving representation to a larger area can mitigate political fallout from directing official and staff attention to a single district of the community.

Ultimately, district boundaries must be specifically delineated. Common names and neighborhood recognition often dictate this geographic choice. Major natural features such as rivers also should not be overlooked as potential boundaries. A typical problem occurs, however, when a major street is used as a boundary, because this does not allow appropriate planning for the corridor created by the street on *both* sides.

Residents unfamiliar with the planning field can easily confuse a district planning program with comprehensive planning. Where this potential exists—for instance, where a downtown is closely identified with its larger community—it must be made clear that this is merely one portion of the community; otherwise, boundaries may appear arbitrary or biased, and concurrent or later general planning efforts may seem redundant. Published maps are the best vehicle for portraying this distinction.

The "imageability" of the district is another typical problem. It is necessary to choose a central physical focus in the district that can provide an easily understood image or symbol. Choosing an image for a central business district, for example, is easy, because most people know the "downtown." However, in multinucleated commercial districts, a single physical focus may be more elusive, and it may be necessary to redefine the district or even to divide it further into more understandable subareas. This may be useful in any case to document highly localized characteristics.

The need for consistency between the district plan and the comprehensive plan is a particular challenge in district planning. Consistency is most easily achieved when district planning follows soon after adoption of the comprehensive plan. When a comprehensive plan is itself out-of-date, the challenge is greater. Although it is fruitless to try to ensure consistency with an obsolete plan, portions of the plan may still be usable. For example, district goals and objectives could be related to policies corresponding to a citywide open-space system based on immutable natural features.

Although consistency with the larger plan often is ignored, consistency with "live," if dated, regulatory instruments cannot be. One of the purposes of the district plan is to update development review policies for the particular district. Hence, a jurisdiction may be required to modify a portion of an old zoning ordinance to correspond with a newly adopted district plan while leaving the remainder untouched. This provides a particular challenge for the planner but can be achieved creatively by use of a "specific plan," a new zone, an overlay zone, or some other tailored regulatory approach, pending overall modification of the entire ordinance.

District plan types and elements

Five kinds of district plans are most prevalent: (1) the downtown or central business district plan; (2) the residential neighborhood or commercial area plan; (3) the facilities complex plan (such as for a civic or government center, a transportation center, or an education center); (4) the area plan for a new suburban development; and (5) the natural resource plan (such as for wetlands or hillsides). In addition, there are other emerging plan types, such as those involving a corridor for a major arterial or a transit line; joint development plans relating to a transit station; or plans relating to the environs or impact area of a major facility (e.g., a university, stadium, or convention center).

Like comprehensive plans, district plans are clearer and more accessible when they are divided into elements, such as open space, circulation, related public facilities, and visual form. This division is useful in district planning no matter what type of area is involved, because it provides an analytical framework and allows interrelationships to be studied.

Yet there are major drawbacks to such an approach. Dividing the district plan into discrete physical elements may cause reciprocal relationships among elements to be ignored. Moreover, such elements can be viewed as driving or constraining the plan, rather than more appropriately serving or supporting it. Finally, although the segmented plan may lend itself to "bite-sized" consumption, it also can foster biases among public-interest groups or professional entities, which are inimical to a comprehensive approach.

Properly done, and without inordinate emphasis (e.g., special committees), physical system elements can contribute significantly to a thorough district plan and also can be a sound way of clarifying issues and trade-offs.

Planning prerequisites

There are certain prerequisites to the establishment of a district planning program. A general plan for the community should be formulated and adopted prior to development of a district plan. This overall guide indicates the role of the district in the community and acts as a point of departure for the district study. The general plan also will have placed the community in its proper relationship to other communities in the region.

Community support is essential. Major property owners and tenants in the district must be convinced of the need for the plan to ensure its acceptance and success. Financial contributions to the planning program by these groups can strengthen their involvement and support and also may be necessary to undertake an adequate program.

A plan advisory committee or committees can provide advice and information and serve as a sounding board for political feasibility and community acceptance. However, it should be made clear to committee members that the plan is for the benefit of the entire district—and its larger community—and not merely to serve the interests of local businesses or interest groups. Moreover, committee members must comprehend that they are serving only as conduits and interpreters for public officials and do not have ultimate authority.

The role of such a committee should be distinguished clearly from that of the planning commission. The former serves to reflect the particular area involved and to convey a fuller knowledge of that area—still in the context of the larger city. However, the planning commission maintains the larger perspective—and the legal authority—to approve and recommend the plan to the governing body.

Adequate administrative organization, understanding, cooperation, and support of the planning program by all departments of local government are as important as citizen participation. A technical advisory committee consisting of representatives of the manager or administrator, of the public works department, and of other departments and agencies should be considered. One of the most difficult aspects of district plan formulation is the reconciliation of institutionalized biases of different agencies and professional groups with responsibility for a single function that may too often be viewed in isolation from other functions. For instance, a housing agency may wish to ensure that additional housing opportunities are provided, an economic development agency may find housing intruding on a proposed commercial function, and a parks agency may find either of these uses inimical to environmental quality. It is the responsibility of the planning program to convey the trade-offs and overall costs and benefits involved.

Planning start-up

The first step in the development of a district plan is the preparation of a detailed program of study setting forth study phases, completion dates, and staff allocations. The program will reveal the need for any staff increases or consulting services and permit budget commitments to be established.

Tentative boundaries of the district should be established, subject to later adjustment. Factors to be considered are geographical features, man-made facilities, census tracts, and traditional demarcations. The total study district should be sufficiently large to include all contiguous areas that are significantly interdependent.

Goals and policies should be formulated concurrently with the initial data-collection phase of the study to provide direction to the research and survey program. However, goals and policies should remain flexible and subject to reconsideration as research progresses.

Goals and policies provide the most significant and binding statements of the community's commitment to its districts. Those formulated during the early phase of district plan development should focus on anticipated issues and be specific enough to permit interim decision making. Although publication of a report on goals and policies at an early stage in the district planning program may be a valuable means of focusing community attention on the planning program and demonstrating the community's commitment to the program, care should be taken that the program not get bogged down in the detailed verbiage of goal and policy statements.

Data inventory and analysis

The data collection and analysis phases are the foundation of an intellectually honest program. Although the eventual decisions may be made in a highly political context, the facts speak for themselves and continue to be useful as reference points.

To facilitate understanding of the constraints and opportunities that must be addressed, a series of inventories and analyses is conducted at the start of the program. This work provides the description of existing conditions often required for environmental reporting and a data baseline for the assessment and comparison of alternatives. Among the aspects to be addressed are:

Current land use

Land supply available for new construction or reconstruction

Traffic conditions and status of transportation facilities

Historic and architectural resources

Amount and type of employment, employees' places of residence, and means of transportation used for work-related trips

Potential growth in office, retail, and residential uses

Existing and anticipated private and public construction projects

Capacity of public utilities

Potential sources of financing for public- and private-sector development and improvements.

The next eight sections consider each of the major elements included in the data gathering and analysis stage of district plan development. In each case, the topics covered encompass the type of data to be gathered; possible means of

Figure 4–2
A composite land use,
physical form, and
circulation diagram for
downtown Novato,
California.

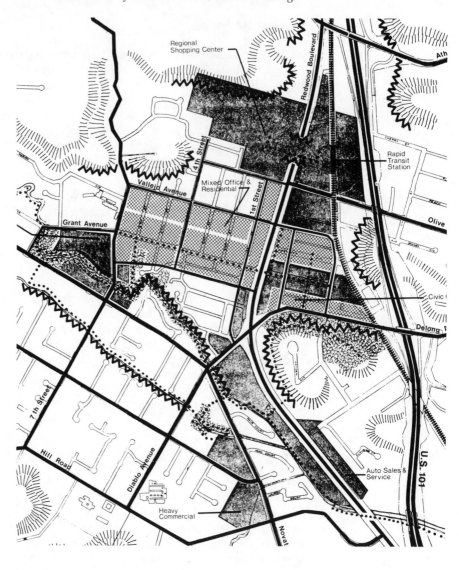

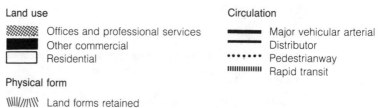

Land use

▨ Offices and professional services
■ Other commercial
□ Residential

Physical form

〰 Land forms retained
ᐯᐯ Visual edge
▓ Natural areas preserved

Circulation

━ Major vehicular arterial
─ Distributor
•••••• Pedestrianway
▥ Rapid transit

obtaining data or sources from which to obtain it; potential difficulties in the
gathering and analysis of the data; and the end product of the analysis.

Land use

Key determinants of the final plan relate to land use—its supply and demand.
This analysis involves three basic steps: inventorying what is there, analyzing
land developability (i.e., supply), and assessing future requirements for various
uses (i.e., demand).

Land use inventories constitute the most important part of any district planning survey. Each use and establishment in the district should be inventoried according to a standard classification system. Information should be gathered about employment and floor space for each activity as well as for each facility (building or parcel). For purposes of analysis, the district may be divided into smaller areas established for statistical manageability or because of special characteristics (e.g., a civic center or produce market).

The survey of land uses provides (1) a quantified description of current land uses that serves as a basis for transportation, parking, environmental, and economic analyses, and (2) an up-to-date description of the functional organization of the district and its subareas. Any land use data previously assembled should be updated to include major land use changes. A supplementary survey should be conducted to document street-level uses and the status of housing units. Land use maps documenting street-level and upper-level uses by parcel can be prepared along with tables summarizing the floor area of commercial, office, warehousing or manufacturing, and other building space; the number of housing units and parking spaces for each block in the district; and a generalized land use map depicting land use and functional organization.

A land-supply (or developability) analysis then provides the foundation for major segments of the planning process. This analysis documents land available for new construction as a result of vacancies or economic underutilization and determines the development capacity of this land supply based on current zoning. It identifies where future growth can be accommodated, provides the basis for identifying alternative land use patterns and intensities, and provides a foundation for determining traffic implications of land use alternatives.

Land developability is best determined by means of a two-step process. In the initial step, assessor's data is used to determine and map the ratios between land value and the value of improvements on the land and to identify where assemblage of smaller parcels has occurred. By identifying those parcels with significant economic underutilization, this analysis reveals the potential for reinvestment and intensified development. A follow-up analysis is done to determine more accurately the points at which reinvestment and intensified development are likely to occur. Since the location, types of uses permitted, and amount of floor area permitted will influence the results, sample parcels should be selected from the various subareas. The product is a map of the district showing levels of economic underutilization and potential for major land assemblage. A table can be used to summarize the development potential of underutilized land.

Both employment and floor-space projections should be made for each separate activity classification. These projections should, in turn, be translated into land requirements. (Methodologies, including all assumptions, should be carefully spelled out to permit subsequent review and modification, if necessary.) Significant advances in research techniques (aided by increasing availability of electronic data-processing equipment) ought to result in far greater reliability of such projections. The use of modeling, however, should be avoided at this scale. The subsequent section on economic and market analysis presents more specific information on this essential step.

Circulation

Traffic and circulation studies should be undertaken concurrently with land use studies. Development of a circulation system to serve the district should be a team effort, if possible, involving the community planner, traffic engineer, public works director, and transit and highway officials. The purpose of traffic and circulation studies is to evaluate the relationships between current and future land use patterns, transportation facilities, and travel habits. Data for the evaluation should be gathered through origin and destination studies and through surveys of traffic volumes, travel times, street capacities, and parking information. Traffic and circulation studies have three parts: an analysis of travel patterns and modes, an analysis of transportation capacity, and an assessment of parking supply and demand.

Few, if any, district study budgets permit the development of information necessary for a sophisticated analysis of existing and projected travel modes and patterns. Agency staff must ordinarily rely heavily on fundamentally simple or previous studies. Travel patterns and travel modes are analyzed by (1) determining current and forecasting future places of residence for persons employed in the district, and (2) documenting current and predicting future means of transportation used by area employees. This analysis provides a basis for testing traffic impacts of district land use options. Random samples of district employees can be used to determine (1) place of residence; (2) means of travel for work trips; (3) number of persons per automobile, if this is the means used; (4) location of parking used; and (5) times of arrival for morning and evening work trips. The survey should be done at various places of employment that typify current patterns or are representative of future trends. The survey should be supplemented by information gathered from prior surveys. The products of the analysis of traffic patterns and modes are technical memoranda indicating in graphic and tabular form desired travel corridors and modes of transportation for current and future district employees.

Transportation capacity is analyzed by determining the capacity of existing transportation facilities and services to accommodate future district growth and by identifying improvements or programs that can increase the capacity of district-serving transportation facilities and services. Current traffic volumes on district streets and freeways and on the arterials serving the district are documented. Critical intersections and other constraining segments are identified and volume–capacity ratios calculated for the existing conditions, with the use of data from previous district studies. Projected traffic volumes and patterns, based on forecasted employment and activity, are assigned to the street system, with deficiencies noted. The potential to increase capacity through minor improvements—such as signal changes and removal of curbside parking—is determined. Survey results are used to forecast future places of residence of district employees. A report should be prepared indicating in map and tabular form critical traffic conditions and potential means for expanding roadway capacity. The report should distinguish between external capacity constraints, such as freeways, and localized constraints affecting only limited portions of the district.

Parking supply and demand are assessed by documenting the current parking space supply, usage, and demand and by determining future parking demand by number and location. Information on parking spaces from prior studies, from parking operators (public and private), and from land use data is compiled. This information is supplemented by documentation of on-street supply and usage from community records and the employee survey. Additionally, estimates of parking demand are made on the basis of existing land uses and forecasted growth. The demand estimate for existing land uses applies conventional parking ratios to the land uses documented and shows the relationship between this estimated demand and the actual supply. The forecasted demand is presented in a range based on varying levels of commercial growth and alternative assumptions on future auto and transit use by district employees and shoppers. The product of this analysis is a report that documents existing conditions and identifies future parking needs in terms of supply, location, and financing.

Visual form surveys

Surveys and studies focusing on design should be undertaken in the district. Visual quality looms large in the planning process because of the district's relatively small scale. Elements to be considered include natural features, man-made features, and combinations of both that result in vistas, panoramic views, and other visual combinations. Visual assets and liabilities are surveyed to (1) document conditions that either contribute to or detract from the appearance and environmental quality of the district; (2) provide an initial identification of visual assets that can be used more effectively; and (3) determine means by which adverse visual conditions can be eliminated or reduced.

A field survey documents significant visual assets and liabilities. Aspects to be addressed include (1) major views of important open spaces and of visually or functionally important buildings; (2) street spaces with scale, architecture, and street-level use that are especially attractive to pedestrians; (3) visually important open spaces and the components that contribute to or detract from the appearance and use of these spaces; and (4) poorly maintained private and public areas, inappropriate remodelings of older structures, and visually unattractive street-front conditions, including chaotic sign use, barren facade design, and obsolete storefronts and displays. Survey work can be supplemented by opinions obtained through public workshops. A map record and a photo record of surveyed conditions should be prepared, with a preliminary listing of approaches to better use of assets and of techniques for eliminating visual liabilities.

A survey of urban design should be undertaken to identify places and structures that enrich the appearance of the district through either historic associations or visual interest and to determine the importance of design elements. Findings can be compiled for the district and coordinated with a district inventory. Design elements should be classified into three categories: (1) elements with major historic or architectural significance; (2) elements with historic or architectural significance resulting primarily from street facade appearance or major contributions to the overall urban context; and (3) elements with less design value that contribute to the visual appearance of the district because of height, materials used, or distinctive architectural features. Products include a map of urban design resources according to class of resources, preliminary guidelines for preservation or reuse, and identification of the potential for creation of historic districts.

Economic and market analysis

The forecast of economic growth establishes a sound basis for estimating short- and long-term market demand for space and thus provides a basis for determining future land use and transportation requirements. The district's ability to capture a share of local and regional growth in employment and space depends on how well the community is able to compete with other cities or counties on locational attributes and the price of space. The regional market consists of several submarkets related to business functions, such as corporate headquarters, government, information processing, and business services. These functions have different locational and space requirements and can vary with respect to potential future employment growth. Such factors must be considered in evaluating the likelihood that the district will be a preferred location for establishing new businesses, accommodating expanding businesses, or transferring certain functions of existing businesses now located elsewhere.

The analysis of employment and space potentials for the district can draw on other assessments of future growth, such as regional inventories of activity, regional employment projections, and market studies. This information should be supplemented by information from representatives of the real estate and investment communities and interviews with selected employers.

The amount of future retail employment and space in the district will be affected by many factors. First, retail activity is influenced by the workers' spending patterns. Changes in employment are likely to influence worker-related retail sales; such changes include an influx of new workers created by the addition of office space and changes in the characteristics of the existing district work force. Second, retail demand in the district is affected by spending patterns of district residents. Additional housing, for example, is likely to increase demand for certain retail goods and increase overall retail sales. Third, a portion of retail activity results from attracting customers to stores offering high-quality goods, specialty items, and a wide array of general merchandise.

The district may function as a subcommunity or neighborhood shopping district for many residents. An important determinant of future retail activity is the likelihood of enlarging the district's share of spending by attracting other residents to its stores and expanding these localized markets.

Retail activity forecasts and studies consider these factors and evaluate how they are likely to affect future spending in the district. The forecasts are based on several sources of information, including sales tax data, housing and population forecasts, and spending patterns. The study also considers the ability of district retail stores to compete with other shopping districts and shopping centers.

The office and retail forecasts should be presented as order-of-magnitude estimates for the district as a whole. The intent is not to produce detailed, sector-by-sector forecasts but to identify the approximate level of additional employment and floor space that can reasonably be anticipated. The forecasts should be presented as a range, including the levels of likely growth that should be considered in the land use, transportation, urban design, and implementation studies. Short- and long-term forecasts should be provided, with a general indication of the likely timing of growth. The incentives to and constraints on district growth should be summarized and their anticipated effects on forecasts identified.

In addition to the forecasts, the analysis conducted in this task summarizes the important economic and market factors that are likely to affect the location of future office and retail activity within the district. It discusses differences in growth potential among districts as well as their interrelationships. This summary evaluation provides background information for the economic feasibility analyses conducted in subsequent tasks.

Housing and residential analysis

A housing market analysis provides a sound basis for subsequent housing policy and program decisions; it determines the type of housing that can and should be promoted in the district, identifies existing housing stock that should be protected, and indicates appropriate locations for new housing.

The district should be considered a submarket of the community (and the region), and estimates should be made of the demand for housing units by tenure, price, rent, and type of household. The analysis should use information already developed for the region and the community and should be supplemented by original research where necessary. Housing-related questions can be incorporated into an employee survey of place of residence and mode of travel. Population analysis may be undertaken to project demand and absorption rates for residential facilities. A housing report describes the housing potential, identifying opportunities for retention and expansion of housing and noting issues and possible housing programs.

Ongoing and proposed building projects must be documented to provide a current estimate of existing and future land uses, building space, and development commitments. Interviews should be held with representatives of the real estate and development communities to identify projects that might be in an early stage of consideration. The survey would include smaller-scale commercial and residential rehabilitation projects. Products include (1) a map identifying approved or proposed projects by parcel; (2) a tabular summary by building or project showing uses, square footage, number of parking spaces, and expected occupancy date; and (3) a brief physical description of the proposals, including design (height, bulk, and street-level treatment) and uses or structures displaced.

Public facilities and services

Public facilities and services are surveyed to determine whether existing public facilities will limit future growth or require significant expansion to accommodate growth. The following public facilities, utilities, and services should be inventoried to determine potential capacity problems and, if applicable, to identify surplus capacity that could attract new development: water service, sewers (both collection and treatment capacity), storm drainage, power, schools, police, fire protection, and street and park maintenance. The survey should determine the extent to which limitations are localized, document plans and programs for upgrading public facilities and services, and identify functional and financing opportunities for upgrading. A report should document the status of existing facilities and services and identify opportunities for improvement or expansion.

Regulatory adequacy

Current regulations are analyzed to determine their effectiveness and guide development in a manner beneficial to the community. The application of regulations to past projects should be reviewed, with special attention given to effects of current parking policies and regulations, effects of district floor area ratio (FAR) regulations, and effectiveness of existing design guidelines and design review procedures. The analysis should include a review of selected projects to document the final effects of community regulations and procedures. This investigation should be supplemented by a review of the public hearing minutes and interviews with staff responsible for development review, with the applicants, and with the planning commission. The resulting report should document: (1) issues and problems created by regulations and procedures; (2) provisions or procedures that have been effective; and (3) changes that should be considered in regulatory provisions and procedures, or the specific application of these regulations in the district.

Financial resources

Existing and potential resources for financing district capital improvements and services are surveyed to provide a firm basis for assessing the financial feasibility and fiscal implications of development options to be identified in subsequent tasks. This information serves also as a basis for determining the feasible level of transportation improvements and thus the allowable trip-generation budget and overall development capacity of the district.

Many of the desired improvements and programs for a district can be achieved only through the combined efforts of the community and the private sector (including developers, property owners, and businesses). The private sector may be able to provide for some public facilities and services. Other improvements, however, may require public financing or joint public-private participation. Public financing could include the funding of physical improvements and public facilities as well as public subsidies and assistance to induce development. An analysis of financial resources identifies the techniques available to finance public expenditures in the district, such as tax increment financing, assessment and maintenance districts, revenue bonds, lease-purchase financing, joint development and value-capture techniques, and sale-leaseback arrangements. Incentive programs to be evaluated include loan guarantees, loan assistance, historic-rehabilitation bonds, grants, land assembly and write-down, and mortgage revenue bonds.

Revenue sources must be identified and matched with the financing mechanisms that show the most promise for feasibility and implementation. Public and private acceptance of financing mechanisms depends, in many cases, on which revenue sources are used, how the revenue burden is distributed, and the level of risk to the community or private sector associated with long-term revenue potentials. Moreover, the ability to finance the cost of certain improvements and programs is contingent on the revenues that can be generated. The revenue potentials of the district will influence the number and type of financing approaches needed to realize community objectives.

The planners must estimate the amount of money needed to finance public improvements under different funding mechanisms, including the total project and annual revenue requirements. Revenues to be considered include the property tax (for tax increment financing), sales tax, development fees, assessment fees, and revenue sources for retiring revenue bonds. Revenue requirements should be evaluated in light of the district's potential to generate future revenues from development. This evaluation provides information on whether revenue potentials are likely to cover revenue requirements, the effects of timing on the availability of revenues, the appropriateness of various means of financing long-term debt, and the need for multiple techniques to achieve the desired improvements and programs.

The financing mechanisms and revenue sources that have potential for use in the district should be summarized in a report highlighting their advantages and disadvantages and identifying the most appropriate uses for them. For each alternative, the relationship between public facility costs and district revenue potentials should be evaluated. The analysis should describe how the different financing arrangements and revenue sources are likely to affect different interests in the district, such as private developers and property owners, businesses, and residents. Issues to be considered include the effects of financial risk, the distribution of the revenue burden, the implications of the cost of doing business, and the likelihood of encouraging or discouraging development interest in the district.

Documentation of existing conditions should be succinct and should focus on factors that will influence the plan and that can be used also as data sources for any environmental impact statements. Graphics are a good way to communicate the data in an existing-conditions report.

Determining plan scope and content

On the basis of the inventory and analysis findings, the scope and format of the plan are defined. This definition

Identifies major issues that must be addressed

Identifies opportunities for improvement of the district

Reviews prior plans and identifies any objectives and land use, transportation, urban design, and implementation recommendations that are still applicable and those that must be revised

As necessary, redefines, expands upon, or clarifies community objectives for the district

Identifies the plan subareas that should compose the study district and determines the level, type, and priority of attention to be given to each subarea

Further refines the work program to reflect selected priorities and emphases.

Identifying major issues to be addressed in the plan focuses attention and resources to achieve the maximum benefits from the study. Public meetings are used to solicit residents' opinions. Conclusions should be distilled regarding major issues, concerns, and opportunities. A report should be prepared identifying these issues, concerns, and opportunities, with a discussion indicating the relative importance of each and implications for the scope and content of the plan.

The planner clarifies community objectives for the district to focus the study effort and provide a basis for judging the policies and programs under consideration. Study findings can be used to draft an interim statement of objectives, which is then reviewed and modified to reflect comments received. (It is anticipated that the statement of objectives will be refined further, once the analysis of options has clarified the implications and practicality of these objectives.)

District subareas and priority project sites are defined to establish a basis for further and subsequent planning and programming work and to identify locations that merit particular attention because of either problems or opportunities. The findings of this task should be reviewed and recommendations prepared that cover the following areas: plan subarea boundaries, priority project sites, and level, type, and priority of attention for each site. These recommendations should be reviewed with the various agencies or groups that have a significant interest in, or responsibilities for, the identified sites. A report should be prepared that depicts designated plan subareas and priority sites and indicates the planning and programming work to be done for each.

The identification of issues, objectives, and planning areas and subareas, and the general inventory and understanding of the area should help to define the scope and proposed content of the plan. Care should be taken that the focus is on the important current and anticipated problems and that resources are not squandered simply for the sake of comprehensiveness or equitable treatment of all elements or issues.

The planner then refines the district plan work program to more closely reconcile the program to those items that should be most productive. The initial program should be reviewed and refined on the basis of information and insights gathered and comments received.

Preparation and assessment of options

All of the studies are used to identify potential improvement programs and methods for accomplishing them. These exploratory analyses help to define options by addressing (1) the central, districtwide organization of land use, transportation, structures, and spaces (including urban design considerations); (2) the specific uses and development patterns of the subareas of the district plan; (3) special design and program conditions for smaller-scale problem or opportunity sites or parts of the various components of districtwide systems such as pedestrianways, transit facilities, or parking; and (4) implementation techniques and programs dealing with such aspects as financing, regulatory methods, and capital improvements programming.

Options should be developed in two steps. The first step addresses plan subareas, smaller-scale projects, or segments of districtwide systems to determine the range of possibilities on this "finer-grain" scale. The second step addresses districtwide concerns and prospects—in particular, land use, transportation, and urban design, taking into consideration the smaller-scale options found feasible and worthy of further investigation in the first step. The second step emphasizes the aggregate and cumulative effects of districtwide choices.

During each of these steps, an ongoing assessment of possible options considers the following: (1) economic and market feasibility; (2) functional performance; (3) fiscal consequences; (4) environmental effects; (5) visual impacts; (6) socioeconomic effects (e.g., dislocation of residents or businesses, income enhancement, and expanded or decreased housing opportunities); and (7) implementation feasibility (e.g., availability of financing, sufficiency of regulatory means, and acceptance by political groups and the community). Responses to the options should be solicited from the community and officials.

Land use and development options for the plan subareas must be prepared in sufficient depth to permit the feasibility and benefits of the options to be assessed and to make possible the review and early resolution of critical issues. Sketch plans and programs for each of the plan districts should address (1) varying land use mixes and intensities; (2) alternative local circulation and parking arrangements; (3) urban design choices; and (4) implementation and programming prospects.

The level of attention given to each subarea should correspond to its potential for significant change and to the need for early resolution of critical development issues. Each sketch plan should be evaluated for feasibility as well as for compatibility with the objectives of the plan and with development elsewhere in the district. This evaluation should focus primarily on economic feasibility, socio-economic effects, projected traffic conditions, and implementation feasibility.

Preparation and assessment of district options would evaluate development and improvement actions for portions of the district in sufficient detail to determine their feasibility and in turn the feasibility of districtwide options. Sketch plans for selected subareas establish both physical requirements (such as amount of land, permissible floor space, parking needs, and vehicular access) and constraints (such as dislocation of residents or businesses or land assemblage problems). The assessment at this scale focuses on economic feasibility. The economic residual analysis tests two things: the economic feasibility of proposed changes and the capacity of various types of projects to generate revenues. The financial criteria determine whether projects can support themselves and whether they can also support mitigation of their impacts. Examples of typical changes (e.g., varying permitted uses, allowable floor areas, and required parking) should be selected and the residual analysis performed to test the economic feasibility and the ability of the types of projects to finance impact fees or dedications for public facilities and services, amenities, or housing assistance.

Preparation and assessment of districtwide land use, transportation, and urban design options should identify the implications of alternative policies for the district. Districtwide policies should be considered in an integrated manner and combinations formed that permit major policy choices for the district to be tested. The districtwide options should incorporate, as appropriate, the program requirements of the various subareas and special elements and sites found to be desirable and feasible. Major policy issues to be addressed in the preparation and selection among districtwide options might include

Relative priority of transit versus automobile access

Modifications to current parking policy, including consideration of alternative parking arrangements—for example, decentralized parking provided by each property owner, centralized and peripheral systems of parking structures and lots, and variations in parking requirements to promote either transit or automobile use

The level of district growth that can be permitted on the basis of the ability to finance required transportation improvements or to institute effective transportation systems management (TSM) programs

The degree of protection to be given to historic or architectural resources

The level of emphasis to be placed on retailing, housing, and office uses

The pattern and structure of growth in the district, for example, concentration of major office and retail activity to increase efficiency and cost-effectiveness of transit

Figure 4–3 District planning options and subarea options should be specific enough to allow for a detailed determination of their implications. This diagram, which shows the existing setting and two different scenarios for growth, conveys some of the physical form implications of designated options in the San Francisco Downtown Plan Phase I.

Existing

Option 1

Option 2

The extent to which height and other design limitations should be imposed on future buildings to protect views, improve the street-level pedestrian environment, protect the setting of historic buildings, preserve distinctive districts, or promote other urban design objectives.

Developing districtwide options is a three-stage process. The first stage involves the preparation of separate options for land use, transportation, and urban design. The land use options identify alternative ways of distributing projected growth, giving different emphases to retail, office, and residential uses. The transportation options give varying emphases to automobile and transit access. For each transportation option, improvements required and judged capable of being financed and constructed would be identified and allowable trip generation data developed for each choice. The urban design options should address major policy variations in heights, historic architectural preservation, and alteration of the use and intensity of special districts. The second stage tests and determines the consistency among various combinations of land use, transportation, and urban design policies. For example, what land use limitations are imposed by a transportation option relying primarily on automobile access? Will a dispersed pattern of office use undermine the feasibility of improved transit service? In the third stage, several districtwide options found to be internally consistent and potentially desirable are selected and assessed. A meeting should be held to solicit residents' responses.

Following these reviews, an overall assessment of the options should be prepared that addresses the following: the ability of the proposed transportation system to accommodate the traffic generated by the associated land uses; the effects on air quality associated with each option; and the ability to finance improvements and services generated by projected growth under each option. This assessment can consider both short-term financing requirements and longer-term needs generated by the cumulative districtwide effect of incremental growth.

A report should be written identifying the districtwide options under consideration, summarizing the effects associated with each, and perhaps indicating which option is recommended. If time permits, the selected option may be refined and amplified in a further report for public distribution, wherein the identified effects of the selected option are considered and reflected in a more complete, yet still synoptic, proposal.

The resources available for implementing the plan options must be identified and the applicability and effectiveness of the techniques assessed. Initially identified financing, regulatory, and other institutional means for implementing the plan should be expanded upon and their potential application to the various options investigated further. A summary report should be prepared (1) to rate the techniques on effectiveness—that is, the probability of continuing availability of financial resources, the degree of support from affected parties, and the soundness of the legal foundation for regulatory techniques—and (2) to describe the application of the techniques to specific conditions, issues, or projects.

The following are among the implementation methods that could be explored:

Procedures establishing a permissible trip-generation budget for properties in the district

Means of financing major public capital expenditures necessitated by district growth

Ways of protecting historic and architectural resources

Means of supporting and encouraging new private investment that promotes district objectives

Means of increasing use of and dependency on public transit.

Figure 4–4 One set of options for the Kittredge Street Area, a subarea of a plan prepared for the University of California at Berkeley.

Option 1: Low-rise mixed use

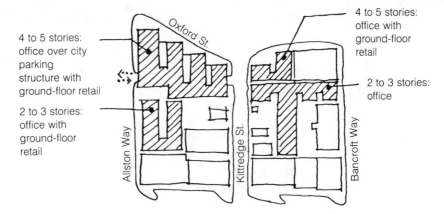

4 to 5 stories: office over city parking structure with ground-floor retail

2 to 3 stories: office with ground-floor retail

4 to 5 stories: office with ground-floor retail

2 to 3 stories: office

Oxford St.

Allston Way

Kittredge St.

Bancroft Way

Option 2: Office/residential mixed use

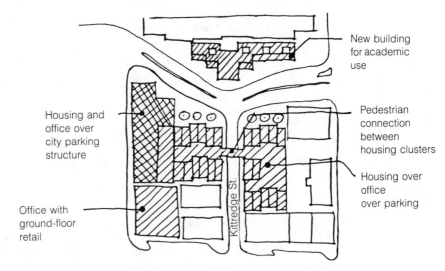

Housing and office over city parking structure

Office with ground-floor retail

New building for academic use

Pedestrian connection between housing clusters

Housing over office over parking

Kittredge St.

Option 3: Hotel/conference/office

Remodeled 2223 Fulton for academic or administrative use

Hotel with ground-floor retail along Allston Way

Office over city parking structure

Office with ground-floor retail

Addition to existing structure

Office over parking

Kittredge St.

Figure 4–5 A summary initial assessment of the impact of various options on the Kittredge Street Area.

	Option 1	Option 2	Option 3	
	Low-rise mixed use	Office/ residential mixed use	Hotel conference/ office	University extension building site
Economic factors				
Financial feasibility	+	**+**	**+**	−
Employment opportunities	+	**+**	**+**	0
Cost-revenue impact on city	+	**+**	**+**	0
Joint-venture opportunities	**+**	**+**	**+**	na
Circulation factors				
Potential transit utilization	+	**+**	**+**	+
Vehicular traffic impacts	−	−	−	0
Land use factors				
Downtown vitality	+	**+**	**+**	+
Housing opportunities	0	**+**	0	na
Land assembly potential	0	**+**	+	na
Social and community factors				
Historic preservation	0	−	−	0/m
View protection	0	0/m	0/m	0
Open space protection	na	na	na	−

KEY
+	Very positive	−	Very negative
+	Positive	?	Uncertain
0	Neutral	na	Not applicable
−	Negative	m	With mitigations

Composing the plan

Integrating the various elements into a single, comprehensive district plan document is perhaps the most difficult and certainly the most intensive phase of the planning program. It involves responding to selected options while ensuring that sound planning principles are applied. The process is partly consensual, partly intuitive, and partly based on an understanding of market forces, and on what is politically possible in any given community.

Space for the expansion of activities should be allocated in light of current trends, circulation proposals, and impacts on visual form and character. The circulation scheme should be designed as a total system, with trafficways, transit, pedestrianways, and parking facilities properly integrated and related to land use proposals. The visual aspect of the plan should not be treated as a side issue but should influence both land use and circulation decisions.

Preliminary plan proposals, or alternate proposals, should be reviewed by technical and lay advisory bodies so that technical adjustments can be made and consensus reached on a final plan.

The draft district plan and its elements

Prior findings should be used to select the land use, transportation, and urban design provisions that will make up the individual elements of the plan. Policies should be set for plan subareas, and more definitive development/conservation specifications should be drafted for each subarea. The level of specificity will correspond to the degree of control desired.

Planning objectives need to be refined at this point. Some objectives may be deleted because they are not attainable or because they would conflict with other more highly valued objectives. It may be necessary to elaborate on specific objectives to ensure clarity. A recommended set of new objectives should be incorporated into the final plan document.

Districtwide land use, transportation, and urban design elements are the three central components of the plan. They should be internally consistent and consistent with districtwide objectives. Internal consistency is especially important. The trip-generation allowances of the transportation component should be congruent with the type and intensity of permitted land uses, and provisions for land use should be consistent with urban design provisions. Text and districtwide plan diagrams should be prepared for inclusion in the final document.

Proposals should be refined and developed further for the plan subareas. Final adjustments should be made in the district plan provisions to reflect districtwide concerns as well. For example, proposed transportation improvements may require specific land use and urban design modifications. The localized land use, transportation, and urban design provisions of the plan could be further delineated, with the level of detail varied according to the level of public intervention proposed, the degree of coordination required because of land ownership patterns or preservation objectives, and the likelihood that improvement actions will occur quickly. Text and graphics for the district plan elements should be prepared.

Figure 4–6   District plan diagram for town center, Anchorage, Alaska.

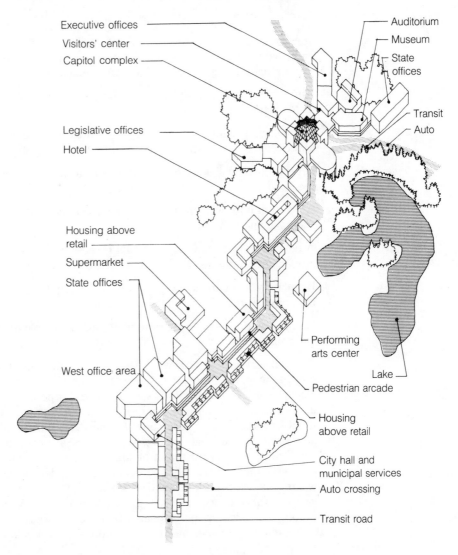

The plan should be sufficiently long range to allow for significant change and make interim phasing possible, and sufficiently detailed to provide adequate policy guidance. It should be flexible enough to accommodate technological change and architectural innovation and be presented so that the lay person can understand the major proposals. Careful editorial attention is required to meet these diverse and potentially conflicting needs.

The final plan should contain the following: a summary of the goals and policies of the plan; a description of the plan's overall organization in physical and locational terms; land use, circulation, and visual elements; and an implementation section, spelling out in as much detail as possible the methods for carrying out the plan, including costs and priorities.

Adoption of the final plan should occur after public hearings held by the community governing body. The plan should be published and made available to the public at little or no cost and should be amended periodically in light of changing conditions and policies.

Implementation

Policy implementation is one of the most neglected facets of district planning, despite its obvious importance. Including a complete implementation program directly in the plan is advantageous because it specifies in a single document the effectuation proposal, the legal basis for the proposal, and the organization that should effect the planning program. The implementation process will be more responsive to real needs if it is borne in mind while the plan is being developed.

A great portion of the overall effort should be devoted to preparing the implementation program. Implementing actions should be refined concurrently with preparation of the draft plan. An implementation program should include

An overall strategy for maximizing the effectiveness of public- and private-sector actions

A financing program establishing procedures for funding public-sector improvements and attracting and assisting private projects when necessary

A procedure for linking permitted growth to the transportation capacity of the district

An overall improvement program identifying needed capital improvements and assigning them priority

A development review and approval process, including environmental assessment requirements

Regulatory procedures and provisions necessary to secure compliance with plan objectives and program specifications

Guidelines for promoting a community's equal employment and minority enterprise goals.

Regulatory system recommendations are critical and should be as specific as possible to guide future development. A maximum trip-generation procedure may constitute a major effort, setting a level for permissible development measured in floor space. Additional land use requirements specifying permitted uses should be required. Other conventional development concerns that must be addressed include height, siting, building design, coverage, required parking (if permitted), use and treatment of street-level commercial space, and signs. This portion of the plan should both recommend regulatory mechanisms and indicate where these mechanisms should be applied. Recommended regulatory provisions (not in final ordinance format), maps and diagrams indicating districts of application, and a description of related procedures should be included.

A capital improvements program should identify and establish priorities for public capital improvements. On the basis of the provisions of the overall development strategy, both a short-term (3 to 5 years) and a long-term (5 to 15 years) capital improvements program should be prepared. The long-term program should address, in particular, transportation improvements that may require protection of a right-of-way, collection of fees, or assessment to provide for the future financing of the improvements. The programs should assign priorities to the improvements and identify prerequisite actions, thus delineating the necessary sequence of improvements.

A program of suggested development projects should recommend specific projects for implementation. On the basis of the options analysis and decisions on an overall development strategy, short-term projects should be identified that are capable of having significant early positive impact on the district. The projects selected may be private developments that would benefit from community assistance and support, community redevelopment activities, or districtwide or localized

Figure 4–7 After the plan receives approval, more specific guidelines for development should be included to guide landowners, developers, and designers.

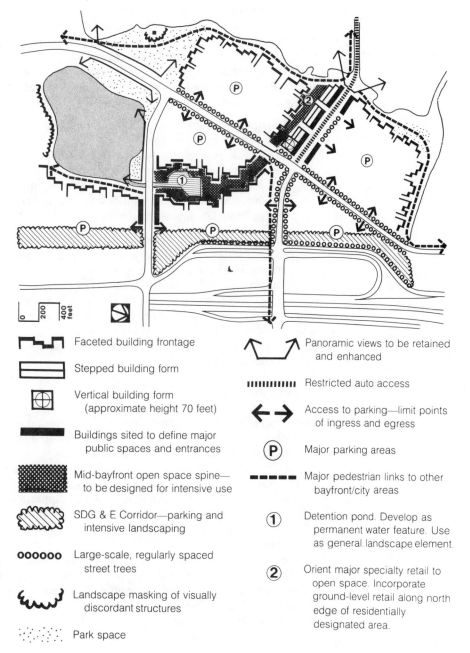

Symbol	Description
Faceted building frontage	
Stepped building form	
Vertical building form (approximate height 70 feet)	
Buildings sited to define major public spaces and entrances	
Mid-bayfront open space spine— to be designed for intensive use	
SDG & E Corridor—parking and intensive landscaping	
oooooo Large-scale, regularly spaced street trees	
Landscape masking of visually discordant structures	
Park space	

Panoramic views to be retained and enhanced

‖‖‖‖‖ Restricted auto access

←→ Access to parking—limit points of ingress and egress

(P) Major parking areas

▬ ▬ ▬ ▬ Major pedestrian links to other bayfront/city areas

(1) Detention pond. Develop as permanent water feature. Use as general landscape element.

(2) Orient major specialty retail to open space. Incorporate ground-level retail along north edge of residentially designated area.

enhancement programs, such as improved maintenance of public district or street landscaping and building facade improvements.

Most plans do not give sufficient emphasis to implementation. The problem lies in devising methods to carry out plans in ways that are equitable and protect property rights but at the same time are effective in achieving plan objectives. Many new techniques use more equitable implementation systems, such as incentives for development in accordance with plans, transferring of development rights, and guaranteed governmental oversight and cooperation.

Preparing the final document

The planning team should assemble the final plan into a single document summarizing key provisions. Graphics are a good way to ensure clarity and succinctness. The plan report should be accompanied by a technical report describing in more detail the analyses underlying the plan and including program recommendations and expanded descriptions of programs, projects, or recommended regulations. The report also should provide necessary data for subsequent environmental impact reports.

A comprehensive but easily understandable description of the recommended program is essential. Work products should be compiled into a single, usable document. Editing and reformatting as needed ensure a well-organized and understandable document. The plan should consist of the following sections:

1. Description of purpose and organization, and how to use plan materials
2. Statement of objectives
3. Districtwide plan elements consisting of separate but integrated sections dealing with land use, transportation, and urban design
4. Plan provisions for district subareas, including more specific provisions for land use, transportation, urban design, and implementation
5. An implementation program.

Technical documentation should provide an in-depth description of the basis for plan recommendations and assemble relevant data for use in subsequent assessments. Data and analysis prepared in preceding phases should be compiled into a single report. The materials should be organized into the following major sections: (1) description of existing setting; (2) assessment of options; and (3) description of the basis for selecting the final program recommendations. Although a draft environmental impact report is not required in most states, the materials should be compiled to permit their use for this purpose. A methodology description should be included in an appendix.

Making the final presentations

Following publication of the document, an extended period should be devoted to further presentation and promotion of the plan, including final meetings with committees, schools, and media representatives.

Materials for media release should ensure widespread community awareness of the plan and encourage public attendance at final presentations. A packet should be prepared with both a written and a graphic description of the program. The materials should be suitable for use by newspapers, television, or radio, and a press conference should be held to present the program to media representatives.

Concluding presentations should explain the entire program and provide any necessary clarification. Concluding meetings should be held with the public and officials after publication and transmittal of the report. Following these meetings, additional public meetings may be held with officials to ensure that the momentum of the plan is maintained.

5 Environmental land use planning

Conceptually, environmental land use planning is simple: Environmental land use planners apply their understanding of natural and health sciences to land use decisions. In practice, environmental land use planning extends from the federal and state to the local government level; geographically, it extends from urban to suburban and rural areas; legally, it extends from a simple floodplain ordinance to the complex National Environmental Policy Act.

The work of the environmental land planner is not easily classified. Such planners are found at all levels of government. Some are engaged mainly in environmental impact assessments or in the development of environmental land use plans. Others focus on the preparation and administration of environmental land use regulations. Specific projects or tasks might include preparing an environmentally oriented land use plan for a city or county, preparing a "critical area" plan for a resource of statewide import, administering a local floodplain ordinance, assessing the environmental impact of a change in federal surface mining policy, tracking down the sites of abandoned hazardous waste areas, or conducting a site plan review of a large planned development.

As should be evident, environmental land planners function in many different settings. They are found in cities, counties, regional agencies, states, and the federal bureaucracy. They might also be employed by consulting firms, development companies, public utilities, or quasi-public organizations, especially those with environmental interests. As part of a large bureaucracy, an environmental land planner might perform very specialized tasks, such as evaluating the environmental impact of tourism on Yellowstone Park or other national parks. Alternatively, a small town or rural county might employ only one planner, who would juggle environmental work with many other responsibilities.

In all cases the work of environmental land planners is done in a difficult setting where political, social, and economic interests must be taken into account. Like any aspect of planning, environmental land planning is both an art and a science. But unlike some other planning specialties, environmental land planning is well accepted by most people and is well integrated into American society.

In the past twenty-five years, environmental planning has become an American institution. The U.S. Environmental Protection Agency (EPA), established in 1971, is now one of the most powerful and best-known agencies of the federal government. Throughout the mid-1980s, Congress continued to support environmental legislation, passing important amendments to the Safe Drinking Water Act and the Comprehensive Emergency Response, Compensation, and Liability Act, also known as Superfund. In 1987 the 100th Congress passed amendments to the Clean Water Act. Although the amendments were vetoed by President Reagan, Congress overrode the veto.

Survey after survey has shown that Americans give unquestioning support to environmental goals.[1] Whereas environmental impact statements were once a source of controversy, they are now a matter of fact, a customary procedure accompanying most major developments. Whether groundwater ought to be protected is no longer a question, and floodplains are now typically reserved for their natural function. Environmental land planning is simply another dimension of planning theory and practice, and every planner needs an understanding of it.

Surveys of local planning practice demonstrate the extent of environmental planning at the local level. After a 1975–1976 survey of county governments, the National Association of Counties reported that of 1,747 respondents (there are 3,044 counties in the U.S.), 49 percent had zoning authority over unincorporated areas, and 30 percent were engaged in coastal zoning or in the control of air, water, or noise pollution.[2] A 1986 survey of growth management practices in various cities and counties identified 282 jurisdictions that use their fiscal or police power to control the rate, timing, location, or amount of population or economic growth with the goal (among others) of protecting local environmental quality.[3]

In 1979 the National Agricultural Lands Study reported that 270 jurisdictions across the nation were using zoning to protect agricultural lands and agricultural operations.[4] Considering that agricultural lands account for roughly two-thirds of all privately held lands in the United States, it is clear that agricultural zoning also provides some protection for most of the environmental resources associated with those lands. A more recent survey of agricultural zoning determined that 342 jurisdictions, in just three states—Wisconsin, Minnesota, and Iowa—were zoning to protect agricultural land.[5] Agricultural zoning is extensive in several other states, such as California and Oregon, which means that the number of communities using zoning to protect agricultural land has increased by several hundred and that most of the increase has occurred within the past ten years.

Granted, these surveys have not covered the entire population of more than forty thousand general-purpose local governments, nor even a defensible sample of them. But, at a minimum, these data indicate that there is substantial local activity in environmental land use planning and that it covers a broad spectrum of environmental issues.[6]

Although support for environmental protection is high, much remains to be done. In El Paso, Texas, a developer eager to put up a shopping center leveled a forty-six-foot hill after "donating" its cactus and yucca plants to the University of Texas at El Paso. The *El Paso Times* noted that "for the most part, the mountain . . . is gone—its granite blasted to pieces and hauled away . . . to fill swampland."[7] The EPA estimated that of the 35 million tons of hazardous waste

Figure 5–1 Transport of hazardous waste from an abandoned site to a legal disposal site. The truck must be decontaminated before leaving the site.

disposed of in 1979, 90 percent was improperly handled.[8] A real estate ad in the *Courier Press*, a rural Wisconsin newspaper, reads, "Are you a good swimmer? . . . There isn't a swimming pool here, but the house is in the floodplain; nevertheless, it isn't priced that high and this floodplain stuff doesn't scare a good Kickapoogian anyway!"[9]

Houses continue to slide down hills or subside into old open dumps. Hazardous-waste disposal sites are discovered in small towns, big cities, and rural areas. Wells are polluted, and the Ogallala Aquifer (one of the largest water-bearing stratas in the United States, extending from South Dakota to Texas) shows extensive local water-level declines in Texas, New Mexico, and Kansas, as a result of overpumping for agricultural irrigation. High water levels in Lake Michigan send waves pounding into lakefront homes, and beach erosion continues. Clearly, the need for environmental land use planning is as great as ever.

Origins of environmental planning

Earth Day 1970 was unique in American experience. A vivid demonstration of commitment to environmental protection, it featured lectures, demonstrations, marches, and cleanups all over the nation. Schoolchildren cleaned garbage out of ponds. Automobiles, symbols of pollution, were buried. Media coverage was extensive, and it is perhaps for that reason that many people assume environmental land use planning to date from Earth Day 1970. Earth Day was, in fact, followed shortly by an abundance of environmental legislation at the federal, state, and local levels. But what Earth Day represented was only the latest resurgence of a spirit that runs deep in American history and thought.

In 1864 George Perkins Marsh (1801–1882), diplomat, world traveler, geographer, and keen observer, wrote a book that summarized a growing body of scientific evidence of the impact of human action on the earth. Looking at the vast changes wrought in Europe and elsewhere by deforestation, erosion, sedimentation, flooding, and climate modification, Marsh turned his attention to North America, a continent that, by comparison with Europe, had been little affected by lumbering, agriculture, mining, and urbanization. Marsh's *Man and Nature: or, Physical Geography as Modified by Human Action,* set forth a convincing argument for environmental land use planning that would both conserve natural resources and restore degraded resources to better condition.[10] This book, the first American text of environmental land use planning, influenced a whole generation of writers and researchers on this continent and elsewhere and remains a classic in the field.

Shortly after Marsh published *Man and Nature*, Major John Wesley Powell, Director of the U.S. Geographical and Geological Survey of the Rocky Mountain Region, transmitted his *Report on the Lands of the Arid Region of the United States* (1878) to the U.S. Congress.[11] Powell's report translated Marsh's ideas into proposed policy. Powell was the first in the history of our country to suggest a public land policy anchored in the capabilities of the land rather than in the allocation of fixed acreages (e.g., 80 or 160 acres) regardless of whether the land is suited for cultivation, grazing, or timber. Powell classified the land by its suitability for timber, grazing, and irrigation and then suggested that land use reflect the capabilities. The report was, in a sense, the forerunner of many environmental land use plans.

The conservation and city planning movements also contributed to the development of environmental land use planning. Most notable of the planner and landscape architects were Frederick Law Olmsted, Sr., H.W.S. Cleveland, and Ebenezer Howard, whose designs for parks, cities, and new towns reflected increasing emphasis on natural principles of land use. Olmsted's new town of Riverside, Illinois, designed in 1868 with Calvert Vaux, exemplifies interest in natural drainage, contour development along natural topographic lines, and extensive use of open space. Cleveland viewed cities as part of a continuum that extended to rural areas, thus incorporating rural open space into cities and cities into rural open space. In Cleveland's view, the country was part of the city, and good planning would keep it that way. He was also a staunch critic of grid patterns of development and favored development that followed natural contours. Ebenezer Howard's *Garden Cities of To-Morrow* (1898) gave high priority to the protection of agricultural land, partly for its productive value, partly because Howard's ideal garden city was to be surrounded by a greenbelt that would limit the size of the city as well as protect it from the sprawl of nearby cities.[12]

Although the roots of environmental land use planning are often traced to the city planning movement, it can be argued that its real origins are rural, for it was in rural areas that environmental land use received sustained attention. The Country Life Movement, which was something of a rural version of the American Civic Association, grew out of Theodore Roosevelt's Commission on Country Life. Although dedicated to a broad set of rural interests, the movement gave considerable attention to soil erosion and depletion, landscape preservation, and conservation of forests.[13]

A number of writers addressed planning issues more directly. In *Rural Planning and Development* (1917), Thomas Adams suggested for the Canadian Commission of Conservation a broad program of rural planning that included landscape preservation, the elimination of poorly planned rural subdivisions, the preservation of agricultural land, and the classification of rural lands according to their suitability for various uses.[14] In two early texts on rural planning, *Rural Improvement* (1914) and *Country Planning* (1924), Frank A. Waugh, a landscape architect, considered a variety of environmental land issues—the importance of natural contours, landscape preservation, soil erosion and depletion, and forestry management.[15]

The conservation movement, led by Gifford Pinchot (chief forester of the United States), President Theodore Roosevelt, and others, created an awareness of the value of public lands and of the need to establish forest preserves and national parks. But the great impetus for local environmental land use planning occurred during the Depression and Franklin D. Roosevelt's administration. Roosevelt's administration sponsored a variety of planning initiatives whose legacy is apparent today. Among these were the Soil Conservation Service of the U.S. Department of Agriculture (USDA). From its beginning, the Soil Conservation Service concerned itself with major environmental problems of rural areas—erosion, flooding, sedimentation, and aridification. And to address such problems, over 3,000 local soil and water conservation districts were formed under state enabling legislation, roughly one per county, for each county in the nation. Today these independent local districts remain principal advocates of environmental land use planning in rural areas and work with counties, cities, townships, and other local governments.

The Roosevelt administration, through the USDA and its Bureau of Agricultural Economics, established planning committees in 2,400 counties to deal with a host of environmental problems including soil erosion, deforestation, flooding, forest fires, runoff, and water quality. These committees, while independent of local general-purpose government, advised local decisionmakers and the USDA. In addition, they often advocated local plans and land use regulations. Such local efforts were complemented by the work of Roosevelt's National Resources Planning Board. Although this board focused mainly on national resource issues, it also sponsored state planning boards and regional planning agencies across the nation that focused on environmental issues. Although the work of the National Resources Planning Board and the Bureau of Agricultural Economics was eventually stopped by the U.S. Congress, their legacy is still apparent across the nation.

World War II brought a halt to many of the programs of the Roosevelt administration, but the period also saw the publication of Edward H. Graham's extraordinary book, *Natural Principles of Land Use* (1944).[16] Graham's text integrated ecological principles with those of land use and prescribed land management practices for various rural land classes. Graham brought together the work of soil scientists, hydrologists, geologists, biologists, and botanists in an ecological view of land use planning. The distinguishing feature of Graham's overlooked classic is that it established a clear relationship between environmental land planning and the public interest, while at the same time establishing a methodological framework that would dominate environmental land planning in the decades that followed. Notwithstanding his pivotal contribution to environmental land planning, Graham is seldom cited or given credit for his work.

In 1969 Congress passed the National Environmental Policy Act (NEPA), which established a new national policy on environmental protection, set up the Council on Environmental Quality, and required the preparation of environmental impact statements for major federal projects. Two years later, Ian McHarg, following the century-old tradition of George Perkins Marsh, published *Design with Nature*, which quickly became a model for environmental land planning and influenced a whole generation of local, regional, and state plans.[17]

But *Design with Nature* and the NEPA merely foreshadowed things to come; in a welter of legislation, the federal government, along with states and localities, further institutionalized environmental policy. Federal legislation during the 1970s included the Clean Water Act, the Safe Drinking Water Act, the Solid Waste Management Act, the Resource Conservation and Recovery Act, the Toxic Substances Control Act, the Surface Mining Control and Reclamation Act, the Clean Air Act, the Coastal Zone Management Act, the Wild and Scenic Rivers Act, and the Flood Disaster Protection Act.

Similar legislation surfaced at the state level, but states, unlike Congress, added land use reforms. States including Oregon, California, Florida, Hawaii, Vermont, Colorado, and New Jersey adopted major new land use planning and regulatory programs that gave heightened protection to environmental resources. Dozens of states adopted specialized programs to protect specific lands—wetlands, woodlands, floodplains, watercourses, aquifers, agricultural lands, scenic areas, and critical environmental areas.

Localities followed suit, but they expanded their areas of concern to specifically local problems—erosion, runoff, wildlife habitats, watersheds, woodlands, steep slopes, historic and archeologic areas, dunes, migratory routes, sinkholes, scenic areas, seismic zones, and so on. Local activity and concern are evidenced in the thousands of plans and regulations designed to prevent public harm and protect public welfare by preserving the natural environment.

Thus, by end of the 1970s, environmental land use planning was solidly entrenched in American life, and planners found themselves handling increased responsibility and facing high expectations on the part of the American public.

The ecology of environmental planning

Ecology can be defined as the study of the relationship between an organism and its environment. The relationship between an environmental land planner and his or her environment constitutes the ecology of an environmental land planner. The context of environmental land planning is made up of a broad and complex set of institutions, laws, and practices. Environmental land planning is a multidisciplinary activity in which the planner's primary task is to gather the wealth of available information and expertise and apply it to the problem at hand. To do so, however, planners must not only have a solid grasp of natural and health sciences but must also have a keen understanding of the legal and political factors that influence their work.

Environmental land planners operate in a complex political environment. Because environmental land planning and regulation inevitably impinge on private property, landowners have an obvious interest. Developers have a similar interest, but they are more likely to become involved on a case-by-case basis; landowners, in contrast, are likely to be vocal at key points in the planning process such as in the development of plans and land use regulations. A host of special-interest groups beyond landowners and developers are likely to seek involvement in the planning process, including historic preservationists, chambers of commerce, open space advocates, clean air and water proponents, hunting and fishing associations, environmental health groups, and numerous neighborhood and good-government interests.

Practitioners are well advised to show sensitivity to the often conflicting interests of such groups, to open up the planning process to them, and to ensure a fair hearing for all parties. Few things are more provoking to a special-interest group than having been locked out of the planning process and simply given a

---

Getting help: Good sources   To obtain information, local planners need only identify general sources, dial a telephone number, and ask for help. Public information officers at state and federal agencies are especially helpful in identifying appropriate staff members or offices. Despite the demands on the staff of state and federal agencies, planners will be pleasantly surprised by the attention and assistance given them by outside experts. The help may range from setting up an initial inventory of natural and health-science data to providing expert opinion on the impacts of development.

The U.S. Environmental Protection Agency, for example, provides expertise to planners on a host of environmental issues—from low-level radiation to trace metals in groundwater. The U.S. Department of the Interior's Fish and Wildlife Service, National Park Service, and Geological Survey house similar information. The U.S. Department of Agriculture's Forest Service and Economic Research Service are especially knowledgeable about agriculture, forestry, and rural development. Planners should also be aware of the special expertise of the U.S. Department of the Army, Corps of Engineers, the National Weather Service, the National Oceanic and Atmospheric Administration, the National Aeronautics and Space Administration, and the Occupational Safety and Health Administration.

Of special import for local planning is the expert assistance available from the Soil Conservation Service, an arm of the U.S. Department of Agriculture. Soil conservationists are affiliated locally with 3,000 Soil and Water Conservation Districts. Other data, especially air photographs, may be available through the Agricultural Conservation and Stabilization Service, also an arm of the U.S. Department of Agriculture and also found in 3,000 local conservation offices.

Assistance similar to that available at the federal level is often available through state agencies and departments, such as departments of conservation, environment, agriculture, and fish and wildlife; geological and water surveys; and offices of environmental quality.

Locally, planners are well advised to regard special-interest groups as important resources. Local governments themselves often house useful environmental information in a number of departments, including health, public safety, transportation, and library. Quasi-public organizations such as arboretums, zoos, historical societies, and botanic gardens are also helpful resources.

fait accompli. Moreover, it is likely that members of these groups have considerable expertise and experience that ought to be brought to bear on environmental issues. For example, in one case involving the siting of a sanitary landfill, a hastily formed citizens' group that opposed a particular site had expert knowledge of agricultural drainage tiles (used to drain excess water from fields) and local wells. This information did not appear on any of the official inventories and was, in fact, unknown to any but these few people. The location of private wells and agricultural drainage tiles is an important consideration in landfill siting, and the failure of planners to seek out this information from special-interest groups could have resulted in flooded farm fields and polluted wells.

Like the political environment, the governmental context of environmental land planning is complex. Large cities or populous counties may have a number of staff members with environmental expertise, whereas small towns and rural areas may have one generalist planner. Regional agencies may assist urban municipalities or urban counties on specialized aspects of environmental land planning, but in rural areas regional agencies often serve as staff to towns and counties. Environmental expertise may also be found in the staffs of special districts, townships, and even some villages. Thus the governmental setting is broad and inclusive.

Yet whether the local staff is large or small, common environmental problems often require extensive intergovernmental cooperation. For example, the proposed dredging of a single small wetland might easily involve the U.S. Army Corps of Engineers, the U.S. Department of Interior's Fish and Wildlife Service; state departments of conservation, agriculture, or environmental protection; and local drainage districts, soil and water conservation districts, water-supply districts, and counties or municipalities. Juggling the interests of numerous agencies as well as the interests of the host jurisdiction is no easy matter and demands great skill in coordination and communication.

Still, if the complex governmental setting can be troublesome, it can also be the source of a tremendous array of environmental expertise. This expertise is available to environmental land planners almost for the asking (see sidebars).

Getting help: A case in point

Twenty-five or thirty years ago, long before Grundy County, Illinois, adopted zoning, Material Services Corporation (a subsidiary of General Dynamics) began extracting sand and gravel along the banks of the Illinois River near Morris, Illinois. Citizens of Grundy have charged that during those years, Material Services has changed the surface hydrology of two creeks—resulting in extensive flooding, erosion, and destruction of roads and bridges. Citizens filed complaints with the state for years, but nothing was done; by state law, Material Services' sand and gravel operation was exempt from county land use controls.

Joseph Duffy, director of planning for Grundy County, contacted the U.S. Army Corps of Engineers and asked them if Material Services had a permit to conduct their operation along the Illinois River. It did not, and the Corps scheduled hearings on the matter. Duffy, along with other county officials, involved a number of state and federal agencies in the permit process to focus their expertise on what the county perceived as the major problems.

Although the permit has yet to be issued, Material Services Corporation has made a raft of improvements along both creeks and paid for the replacement of a bridge. The corporation is now addressing problems that had been the subjects of citizen complaints for more than a decade. Federal and state agencies can often be extremely helpful in addressing local problems. But local jurisdictions must begin by asking for help.

Environmental land planners can and should avail themselves of the geologists, hydrologists, soil scientists, botanists, biologists, meteorologists, chemists, and others employed by local, regional, state, and federal governments.

Data gathering in environmental land planning nevertheless has its hazards—one of which stems from the tremendous reservoir of experience and expertise that planners can call on: the amount of information available often outruns a planner's ability to assimilate it. Hence, a key strength of any planner is the ability to locate information, synthesize it, and bring it to bear on the immediate problem.

The practice of environmental planning

Although any planner should be sensitive to environmental values and incorporate those values into his or her work, environmental land planning is developing into a specialty in itself. What do environmental land planners do? What is the stuff of environmental land planning? What should a planner concerned with the environment know?

As was mentioned earlier, the environmental planner brings aspects of the natural and health sciences to the planning process. This means that the planner must be able to develop plans and land use regulations that will serve two broad goals: First, to protect people and property from natural and man-made hazards; second, to protect and maintain important natural and man-made values.

A hazard is a natural or man-made feature or process that threatens the health, safety, or welfare of people or their property. An EPA publication titled *Chemical Emergency Preparedness Program: Interim Guidance*, reviews health hazards associated with a variety of acutely toxic chemicals that are commonly stored for use in industrial and chemical processing plants around the country.[18] These chemicals represent a substantial man-made hazard, and the EPA report provides guidance for plans and land use regulations to protect people and property from these chemicals. Using information on the location, volume, and type of acutely toxic chemicals, along with EPA data, planners would be able to (1) define a hazard zone; (2) minimize population density within it; and (3) minimize incompatible land uses within or adjoining the hazard zone.

A value is a natural or man-made feature or process that enhances the health, safety, or welfare of people or their property. For example, land that is fertile, tillable, moist, and well drained is highly suited, other things being equal, to agricultural use. Properly conducted, agriculture may be practiced on such land without degrading it while, at the same time, maximizing its productive value. Such land exhibits important environmental values and, as such, ought to be protected from land uses that do not maintain or protect these environmental values.

In fact the case of prime agricultural land provides a good example of how a community, by not protecting an important environmental value, may actually convert such a value into an environmental hazard. For example, let us say that a municipality permits a thirty-unit, low-density subdivision to be built on prime agricultural land amid large blocks of prime agricultural land. Clearly, the land on which the subdivision is built is likely to be taken out of agricultural use, and thus an important environmental value will be destroyed.

Yet the subdivision also sets the stage for long-term, protracted land use conflicts between residents of the subdivision and nearby farmers. Farmers find themselves victimized by increases in theft and vandalism of crops, equipment, and buildings. They may also experience damage to farm animals, cut fences, subdivision gardens creeping out into farm fields, midnight dumping of trash in fields, children converting cultivated earth into play areas, and sundry other troubles that lower productive values of the land.

For the new suburbanites, who love the idea of agriculture but loathe its practice, another set of problems emerges. Agriculture proves to have a number of characteristics in common with heavy industry at times—twenty-four-hour operations, heavy equipment, noise, dust, odors, and applications of pesticides, fertilizers, and insecticides. Some of these agricultural practices are hazardous to the health of the subdivision residents.

Still another facet of this conflict concerns public services, public finance, and regulation of agricultural practice. The new suburbanites, although living in a distinctly rural setting, often begin to demand suburban rather than rural levels of public service—increased fire and police protection, sanitary or storm sewers, snow removal, street cleaning, and the rest. Such service increases are then translated into increased property taxes, which, of course, weigh most heavily on farmers. Furthermore, suburbanites may succeed in getting ordinances passed limiting the times or nature of agricultural operations.

Thus, a common result of allowing large subdivisions on prime agricultural land amid large blocks of prime agricultural land is the certain loss of the agricultural values of the subdivided land. In addition, the values on adjoining agricultural lands diminish, and the prospect of health hazards increases for the residents of the new subdivision.

The general goals of protection from hazards and preservation of values suggest something of the education of an environmental land use planner. Such an education must include a basic introduction to the health sciences plus a grasp of key concepts in geology, hydrology, meteorology, botany, biology, and soils. More important, the planner must understand the interactions among various elements of physical geography so that he or she can trace the impact of a change—for example, the effect of a new shopping center on wildlife, flood-plains, or soil erosion. Furthermore, environmental land planners must be able to take these overall concepts and relate them to the larger (extra-local) environment and the interactions among the elements of that larger environment. Knowledge of the natural and health sciences, coupled with a standard planning education, is requisite for effective practice.

The most significant work of environmental land use planners falls into three categories—preparation of land use plans, assessment of proposed developments, and preparation of land use regulations. In the preparation of land use plans, the most common methodology that planners use is land suitability analysis (LSA). To assess proposed developments, planners turn to environmental impact assessment (EIA).

It is important to understand the distinction between LSA and EIA. In local planning work, planners generally use suitability analysis to evaluate the fitness

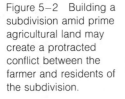

Figure 5–2 Building a subdivision amid prime agricultural land may create a protracted conflict between the farmer and residents of the subdivision.

of land for various uses. For example, a planner might use LSA to identify various alternative sites for a proposed landfill. To do so, the planner would likely examine large segments of the entire land base of a community before identifying potential sites. But once such alternative sites were selected, the planner would then use a far more detailed environmental impact assessment to determine more precisely the environmental consequences of a landfill on a specific site. Thus, a principal difference is that LSA is undertaken at a general level, often in a communitywide study, whereas EIA focuses on one or more particular land uses at specific locations. A further distinction between LSA and EIA is that EIA explicitly considers alternatives to the proposed land use as well as actions that might be taken to mitigate negative consequences of the project. Finally, both LSA and EIA incorporate a variety of methodologies; each phrase refers to a class of methodologies and not necessarily to any single one.

Although land suitability analysis and environmental impact assessment are two different techniques, there is nothing to prevent a planner from using suitability analysis as a technique of environmental impact assessment. Generally, however, land suitability analysis is not a common methodology in environmental impact assessment, and the processes will be treated separately in this chapter.

Land suitability analysis

Land suitability analysis is associated with a variety of methodologies and applications.[19] The methodologies are generally used to produce maps depicting the appropriateness of land areas to various land uses. Since suitability is dictated at least partially by environmental criteria, the maps depict an allocation of land use that is at least partially anchored in environmental criteria. Suitability may also be dictated by economic, social, or even political criteria.

County soil surveys (available free from the county Soil and Water Conservation District office) provide a clear example of LSA. County soil surveys are simply an inventory, description, and evaluation of the soils within a county. Historically, soil conservationists have used such surveys to draft conservation plans for farms, and farmers have used them to help plan for crops. The county soil survey classifies all soils in a county into soil series; there may be several dozen soil series in any one county. The classification is based on characteristics of the soil, including texture (percentage of sand, silt, clay), permeability, slope, parent material, wetness, and so on.

In Kendall County, Illinois, for example, soil scientists have classified the county's 320 square miles into 44 distinct soil series. The soils in each of these 44 series are then rated against potential land uses, including recreational development, dwellings, septic tanks, and sewage lagoons. The characteristics of the soils—wetness and permeability, for example—suggest a range of appropriate and inappropriate land uses.

If the rating system used for the Kendall County soil survey were extended to cover a range of suburban or urban land uses, the result would be a suitability map for land use anchored in data on soil characteristics. If in addition to the evaluative data on soils one were to include data on hydrology, geology, flora, fauna, climate, slope, and so on, the resulting suitability map would allocate land uses on the basis of wide-ranging environmental data.

Land suitability analysis includes four main steps:

1. Selecting and defining a classification system for all resources within a land area
2. Classifying the land area according to the system
3. Selecting and defining a classification system for land use
4. Comparing each of the classified land uses to each of the classified land areas.

A simple example illustrates the process. Let us say that we will use LSA to evaluate the suitability of a parcel of land for two land uses. The two classes selected are wet soils and dry soils (step 1). Wet soils are those having standing water within one foot of the surface for more than 180 days per year. Dry soils are all others. This definition of a classification system distinguishes between the two classes (wet and dry soils) on the basis of their relative values and hazards to people or property. For example, wet soils would be hazardous to residences but would offer values for recreation. Conversely, dry soils would offer values for residences but might be inferior for recreation.

On the basis of the county soil survey, the parcel of land is classified into two categories, which are shown on a map (step 2). The two land use categories are residential and recreational (step 3). The classification system evaluates the two land use classes (residential and recreational) according to values and hazards, so that the optimum location for each use can be determined.

A residence, for example, requires dry, well-drained soils (a value) and would be damaged by flooding or foundation problems on wet soils (a hazard). Recreation, in contrast, might profitably occur on wet soils in the form of boating, fishing, and scenic viewing (a value) but not on dry soils. In this instance although the value of recreation on wet soils exceeds the value of recreation on dry soils, dry soils do not represent a hazard to recreation but merely a lesser value.

The land areas are classified as wet and dry soils and the land uses are classified as residential and recreational. Wet soils are suited to recreational use but not to residential. Dry soils are more favorable to residential use. The correspondences between the two classes are easily mapped (step 4). Thus, LSA may be used to allocate future land use at least partially on the basis of environmental criteria.

The simplified example presented here illustrates the principles of LSA. In practice, however, LSA is much more complex. The combination of numerous classifications of land areas, including, for example, hydrologic, geologic, historic, botanic, physiographic, and soil resources, coupled with a dozen or so classes of land use, results in a far more difficult process. Moreover, the definition of hydrologic resources may itself include ten or more separate aspects—such as wetlands, recharge areas, floodplains, and water quality—and for each of these, the planner will make a value and hazard assessment. Then add the remaining classes (with all their aspects) and the accompanying value and hazard evaluations and the data problem is clear.

Not only are the costs of acquiring the data high, but so are the costs of manipulating the data. Furthermore, the combination of resources and land uses creates a complex rating process that may be mathematically suspect.[20] The use of numerous overlay maps to illustrate suitability can become troublesome when there are simply too many maps to read at once and the combinations of lines and colors cloud interpretation.

Despite its disadvantages, LSA is a standard technique of environmental land use planning. Recent advances in computer programs, including personal computer programs, hold promise in dealing with the problem of data manipulation. Ian McHarg, the landscape architect most closely associated with this technique, provides several examples of LSA in *Design with Nature*, and another excellent example was the plan done for Medford, New Jersey.[21]

Environmental impact assessment

Environmental impact assessment is generally used to evaluate a proposed land use in a specific location. Compared to LSA, EIA is typically more detailed and more focused. Furthermore, EIA often includes an evaluation of various alternatives to the proposal, some assessment of irreversible impacts, and recommendations for measures to minimize negative impacts. Conceivably, EIA might demonstrate

Values and hazards inherent in soils used for residential development

Values On soils neither too wet nor too impervious, sewage from buildings with septic tanks is properly purified. Since septic tank runoff travels neither too fast nor too slowly through the soil, odor and germs are removed. The chances of polluting groundwater or wells is very low.

On proper soil, buildings are provided with good, stable support. The changes from shifting, slumping, or settling are minimized.

On moderate or minor slopes, soil will tend to erode less. The costs of foundation construction, septic system or sewer installation, and roadbuilding are lower.

Hazards Too-permeable soils (such as sand) permit sewage to run through it too quickly to be purified—polluting groundwater and wells.

Soils not permeable enough (such as clay) will cause sewage to seep to the surface—creating wet, smelly, and unsanitary conditions.

Bedrock too close to the surface will cause sewage to be deflected back to the surface—also creating unsanitary conditions.

Improper soils—even on moderate or minor slopes—may be unable to bear the weight of construction equipment, buildings, or traffic. Settling, shifting, and slipping can result in damage and constant maintenance problems.

On steep slopes, soils present severe problems for buildings, roads, and septic systems. Septic runoff may be difficult or impossible to control: the tendency for soil to erode if disturbed is high—as is the danger of slumping (collapse) under weight. The costs of engineering foundations and installing septic or sewer and other utility systems skyrocket.

Source: Bruce Hendler, *Caring for the Land: Environmental Principles for Site Design and Review*. Planning Advisory Service Report no. 328 (Chicago: American Society of Planning Officials, 1977), 52–53.

that the environmental effects of a proposed project are so severe that the project ought to be drastically revamped or abandoned entirely.

Environmental impact assessment covers a wide range of applications. A comprehensive plan, for example, may be the subject of such an analysis, as may a proposed airport or sewage plant. Planned unit developments or other large-scale proposals are also common candidates for EIAs, as are major land use policies proposed by the federal government. Grazing policies of the USDA's Bureau of Land Management, for example, would be subject to EIA, as would proposed federal policies dealing with land use in national parks or policies governing control of agricultural soil erosion. Many states have passed legislation requiring EIAs on major capital improvements and new land use policies undertaken by the state. Environmental impact assessment occurs in a number of contexts and can take various forms. It can be conducted as a formal, independent study (often to meet legal requirements) or as part of a larger study process—often a site plan review. If an EIA is conducted as a formal, independent study, the goals of the study are outlined in the legislation requiring it; occasionally, the legislation will also specify the general study approach. If the EIA is conducted as one part of a larger study, the goals of the study and the general study approach are determined more by the principal investigator (for example, a planning director) than by the legislation authorizing the study.

The National Environmental Policy Act is an example of such legislation. It requires that an EIA

1. Describe current conditions
2. Identify alternative means of accomplishing the objective
3. Enumerate the likely impacts of each alternative
4. Identify the preferred alternative and the method used to select it
5. Describe the impact of the selected alternative in detail
6. List possible actions to minimize negative impacts of the selected alternative.[22]

When an EIA is conducted as part of a larger study, the requirements of the study are generally less well defined, which means that the planner has considerable discretion in choice of methodology and some discretion with respect to the goals of the study.

Among the most commonly used EIA methodologies, five are particularly important: ad hoc approaches, checklists, matrices, networks, and overlays.[23] These methods are not mutually exclusive and are often used in combination.

Ad hoc approaches, which are simply quick responses to EIA requirements, feature planners' best estimates of primary environmental impacts and rarely deal with secondary impacts. For example, a primary impact of a new subdivision might be erosion, and a secondary impact might be the sedimentation of a wetland downstream from the subdivision. Ad hoc approaches, by definition, lack the structure that is required for detailed assessment and thus are rarely used, except when a project requires an extremely quick assessment and thus precludes more time-intensive methods.

Checklists, a refinement of ad hoc approaches, are created by various experts who may also provide instructions on how to perform analyses of the items on the checklist. Most checklists are simply a prepackaged set of questions to help planners assess the project. It is the structure provided by the questions that makes the checklist different from ad hoc approaches, in which all estimates stem from the brains of the investigators rather than from responses to a set of prepared questions. Checklists are particularly useful in the evaluation of smaller developments or minor land use changes.

Matrices offer an understandable and comparatively easy method of EIA. In a matrix, proposed actions are identified along the horizontal axis, and impact areas are identified along the vertical axis. The relative severity of the impact is noted within each box of the matrix.[24]

Networks, which offer an in-depth look at environmental impacts, trace a single action through a series of iterations to demonstrate the cumulative consequences of a proposed action. For example, in the case of the subdivision that would cause erosion, the network method would trace the erosion through the watershed to determine its effect on all hydrologic resources, which might reveal a series of secondary and tertiary impacts. In this case, erosion might lead to sedimentation of a wetland, which in turn, might damage the wildlife habitat in the wetland. Damage to the wildlife habitat might affect hunting, the tourist industry, or water quality. Thus, a network provides a more realistic view of both short- and long-term impacts of a project on the environment as a whole.

Cartographic techniques use LSA to estimate the likely impact of a proposed action. As mentioned earlier, this approach relies on the preparation of interpretive maps illustrating resource areas or processes, each of which is rated and mapped with respect to land use suitability. The technique provides a relatively quick evaluation of the primary impact of a proposed project but offers little information on secondary or tertiary impacts. Still, the use of LSA in EIA illustrates one of the side benefits of using LSA to generate land use plans. Once

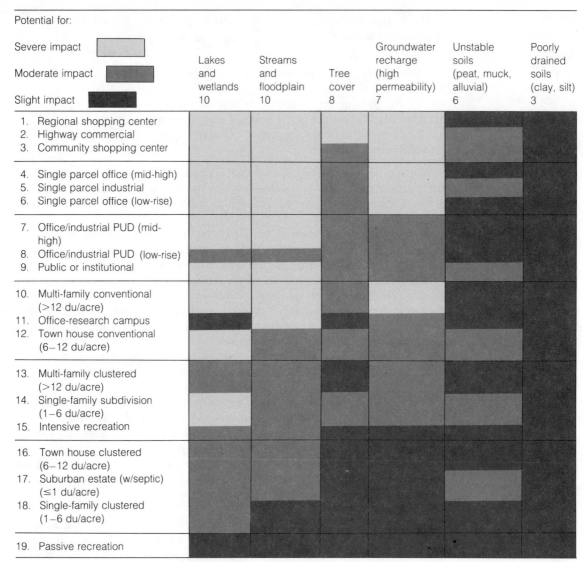

Figure 5–3   A matrix showing environmental impact potentials.

the maps delineating land suitability are developed, they can be used repeatedly to evaluate any number of proposals.

Environmental land use regulation

For most planners, the heart and soul of environmental land use planning is in the regulations that implement those plans. Land use regulations usually appear in zoning ordinances or subdivision regulations, although some jurisdictions adopt separate ordinances governing environmental matters. Land use regulations are generally based on the same evaluation of values and hazards that guide the land use plans. That is, regulations are designed to protect or maintain resource areas or processes that have value and to protect people or property from hazards associated with resource areas or processes.

Typical resource areas are wetlands, woodlands, and watercourses; common examples of resource processes are runoff, erosion, sedimentation, and flooding. Regulations affecting resource processes usually apply throughout a jurisdiction, whereas resource area regulations apply only in defined zones.

The first step in ordinance design is to identify the functions to be protected;

Figure 5–4 A map
showing distribution of
environmental impact
potentials.

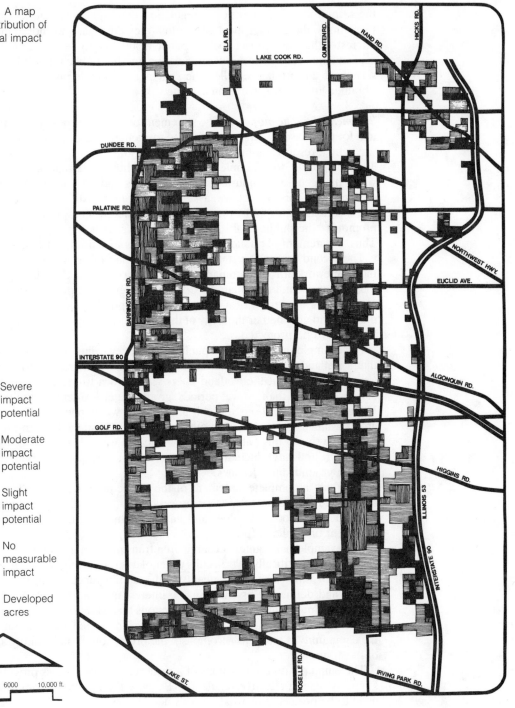

the second step is to develop a regulation that will do so. In developing such regulations, the planner must ensure that they are clearly anchored in the public interest—that they reflect specific public health, safety, and welfare issues. The explicit connection between the regulation and the public interest is made in the section of the ordinance called the statement of public purpose, the statement of public intent, or some similar name.

Statement of public purpose   The statement of public purpose or intent is important for two reasons: First, it explains to the general public in an easily understood way why a resource area or process is important and why it must be protected. To some people, for example, a wetland is nothing more than an area of standing water that generates thousands of mosquitoes and occasionally smells bad. To someone with this perspective, a wetland protection ordinance makes little sense, and a statement of public purpose that says merely that protecting the wetland promotes "the public health, safety, and welfare" is not especially convincing. Thus, a statement of public purpose must focus specifically on values or hazards.

The second reason the statement of public purpose is important is that it sets the framework for the ordinance itself and becomes a checklist against which the ordinance can be evaluated. A detailed statement of public purpose precisely identifies the functions of a resource area or process. A simple review should make it evident whether the body of the ordinance addresses each of the resource functions to be protected.

For example, a statement of public purpose regarding wetlands would explain that a wetland performs many functions and is typically related to groundwater. One function is that the wetland filters water down to recharge groundwater in dry periods, and then, in wet periods, groundwater is discharged to the wetland. Under natural conditions the ebb and flow of water between the wetland and groundwater is retained, and both resources are sustained. With rapid urbanization, however, this balance is upset, and the water level in both the wetland and the groundwater fluctuates wildly. As a result, the quality of both the wetland and the groundwater declines.

To create a complete statement of the public interest, the planner must first understand the resource area or process; only then will he or she be able to spell out the associated values and hazards, which are then translated into the statement of public purpose.

For example, an aquifer recharge area transmits surface water to the groundwater; more specifically, it transmits water of a certain quality at a certain quantity per unit of time. The water quality and quantity functions of the aquifer are critical and define the essential public interest in protecting it. A statement of purpose or intent that reflects these functions makes clear to the public—including landowners, developers, county commissioners, judges, and others—what the community is trying to accomplish: the protection of the quantity and quality of its groundwater.

The emphasis on the functions of a resource area or process provides another key to designing effective regulation. Because the functions define what values need to be protected or what hazards need to be guarded against, they provide insight into critical regulatory criteria. In the example of the recharge area, the central features of the regulation ought to protect and maintain water quality and water quantity. As long as these functions are protected, the regulation will maintain the essential values of the recharge area.[25]

Although it may seem evident that planners must first define the functions that need to be protected (values) or protected against (hazards) and then incorporate those into a statement of public purpose and finally into regulatory standards, it is really not all that simple. Resource areas and resource processes are complex and highly site specific, and it is often difficult to define functions. And once defined, these complex, site-specific functions need to be translated

Statement of purpose

The Township Board of _____ Township finds that growth, the spread of development, and increasing demands upon natural resources have had the effect of encroaching upon, despoiling, or eliminating many of its groundwater recharge areas and processes associated therewith, which, if preserved and maintained in a properly managed condition, constitute important, physically aesthetic, recreation and economic assets to existing and future residents of the community.

Specifically, the Township finds:

1. That a major portion of public and private water supplies is derived from wells which extend into underground bodies of water known as aquifers.
2. That as water is used, the aquifer is replenished, or recharged, primarily by rainfall within areas which, due to soil type, geologic formation, and geographic proximity to surface waters, have the greatest ability to transmit water to the aquifer(s).
3. That unrestricted development of these areas will decrease the recharge capability of such areas by reducing natural area available for

absorbing rainfall and by increasing the volume and speed of surface runoff. Further, natural vegetation within the recharge area, as well as interaction between surface water and aquifers, provides for filtration of water, reducing the amount of natural and man-made pollutants reaching the aquifers.

Therefore, the purposes of this Article (Ordinance) are:

1. To manage groundwater recharge areas to maintain the present or natural rate of recharge, when possible, to enhance the rate of recharge to ensure dependable future water supply.
2. To provide for the nondegradation of groundwater quality in usable aquifers and protect the Township's fresh water supply from the damages of drought, overdraft, pollution, or mismanagement.
3. To provide for the paramount public concern for these natural resources in the interest of health, safety, and general [well-being of the] residents of this township.

Source: *Model Groundwater Recharge Area Preservation Ordinance*, draft. (Lansing, MI: Tri-County Regional Planning Commission, 1983), Appendix C-3.

---

with care into a clear statement of public purpose. Finally, knowledge of the functions of a natural resource or process does not lead to an automatic translation into regulatory criteria but requires a patient, careful, precise rendering that explains complex phenomena in clear, effective, legally defensible regulatory language. The previously given example of the aquifer recharge area is deliberately simplified to highlight the methodology involved. When one considers that resource areas and resource processes are extremely complex and poorly understood (examples might be a cranberry bog, a winter deer-feeding range, a mangrove swamp, a prairie remnant, microclimates, or redwood forest ecology), the difficulty and importance of developing effective regulation become more evident.

Performance and conventional zoning   The regulatory approach follows two basic models—performance zoning or conventional zoning. An ordinance based on performance criteria requires applicants to demonstrate that the current functions of the resource area or process will be maintained or improved. The ultimate standard in performance zoning is a precise measurement of the way in which the community wishes the function "to perform" after any proposed land use is in place. For example, in the case of the aquifer recharge, the ordinance might require applicants to demonstrate that the recharge area, following development, will continue to transmit water at y quality and at x quantity per unit of time. Such a standard, of course, requires precise understanding of the functions of the aquifer as well as a measurement method that, upon trial, will produce consistent results.

Performance standards for environmental regulation are extremely useful provided that the functions of the natural resource or process can be precisely measured. As environmental research continues, these measures are easier to obtain;[26] often, however, the functions are not easily measured—nor is the optimum measurement known)—and planners must rely on conventional zoning to protect resource areas and processes.

Conventional zoning ordinances contain lists of permitted uses, prohibitions of certain practices (dredging of wetlands, for example), density restrictions, setback requirements, height limits, and so forth. Unlike performance standards, this regulatory scheme does not approach the functions of the resource area or process directly but instead relies on indirect controls to achieve the result. However, both performance and conventional zoning ordinances are designed to protect the functions of the resource area or process.

Relationship of resource areas and processes   Although resource areas and processes have been discussed as if they were discrete phenomena, they are part of the same system, and failure to protect resource processes will likely lead to degradation of resource areas. For example, a community may enact strict regulations to protect wetlands and the functions that wetlands perform—as sediment traps, flood-holding areas, wildlife habitats, groundwater or surface water recharge areas, and so forth. Yet the wetland is inextricably linked to the larger watershed, and failure to control runoff, erosion, and sedimentation in the watershed typically will lead to the degradation of the wetland. Therefore, a major principle of environmental land use regulation is that resources and processes must be treated as a system in which the degradation of one will likely lead to the degradation of others.

Emerging issues

The strength and vitality of any profession is evidenced by the emergence of new research areas. The field of environmental land planning and regulation is likely to be expanding its focus for years to come. For new planners, new issues suggest directions for research that ought to generate significant advances in environmental protection—not to mention jobs.

Hazardous waste, for example, dominates the headlines, and it includes wastes generated by business and industry as well as by households. Health hazards stemming from hazardous waste—contaminated water, air, soil, flora, and fauna—are well documented. Since households served by landfills generate huge amounts of hazardous waste, all landfills are hazardous-waste disposal sites, differing only in degree of hazard. As distinctions between what is and what is not a hazardous-waste disposal site become increasingly unclear, one implication for planners is that all new landfills might have to be sited as if they were hazardous-waste disposal sites, and all existing landfills—operating or recently closed—would be treated as any hazardous waste site would be treated. Likewise, it would be necessary to identify and analyze older abandoned dumps and older landfills as well as sites of abandoned gasoline tanks, oil tanks, or other abandoned structures housing toxic chemicals. Many of these may have been abandoned forty or fifty years ago and many may be buried deep underground with no telltale sign left at the surface. Consider, for example, how many thousands of gasoline stations, each with an underground tank, containing some toxic residue, have been aban-

Figure 5–5 This figure illustrates the range and frequency of potential contamination sites in Michigan. Also to be considered are the thousands of abandoned sites that pollute or threaten to pollute groundwater and that remain unidentified.

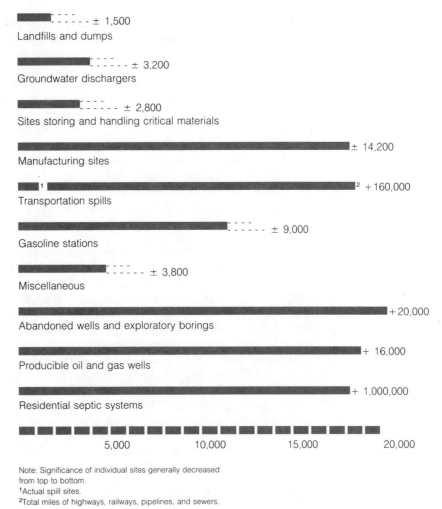

Landfills and dumps ± 1,500

Groundwater dischargers ± 3,200

Sites storing and handling critical materials ± 2,800

Manufacturing sites ± 14,200

Transportation spills [1] [2] + 160,000

Gasoline stations ± 9,000

Miscellaneous ± 3,800

Abandoned wells and exploratory borings + 20,000

Producible oil and gas wells + 16,000

Residential septic systems + 1,000,000

5,000   10,000   15,000   20,000

Note: Significance of individual sites generally decreased from top to bottom.
[1]Actual spill sites.
[2]Total miles of highways, railways, pipelines, and sewers.

doned since, for example, 1930! Transporting hazardous waste, siting new facilities, and identifying or reclaiming old sites are all promising research endeavors.

Linear zones of pollution, perhaps better described as linear zones of hazardous waste, present another major set of planning problems. These zones are those in a linear corridor along major traffic routes and beyond right-of-way areas where deposits from automobile and truck traffic accumulate, polluting soil, water, and vegetation.

Because many sensitive land uses are concentrated in these corridors, linear zones of pollution endanger the health of the most sensitive segments of the population—elementary-school children, hospital patients, park visitors, and residents of retirement homes. Studies of contaminants along traffic arterials in Illinois showed dangerous levels of lead in many urban, suburban, and rural areas, and studies in Urbana, Illinois, showed high concentrations of a variety of other toxins.[27] Given the nation's extensive automobile transportation network, it is reasonable to assume that linear zones of hazardous waste extend throughout virtually all urban and many suburban and rural areas. Very little planning or regulatory work has focused on this problem.

The protection of farms and farmland is another issue receiving increasing attention from planners. In hundreds of communities, farms and farm operations are subject to more stringent protection from incompatible uses than ever before.

Formerly, such lands were viewed as urban reserves or unrestricted districts in which most uses were permitted regardless of their impact on agriculture. Communities are now protecting their agricultural resources not only to protect farms and farm operations but also to promote more compact development, to reduce public-service costs, to safeguard environmental resources, and to maintain the agricultural economic base. Since agriculture is a basic industry (and, in many communities, a critical if not dominant industry), the protection of agriculture is really a protection of the economic core of a community. This public purpose is broader than merely protecting the operations of any one farmer or any one patch of farmland. Considerable efforts are now being made at state and local levels across the nation to ensure that agricultural lands are maintained in agricultural use. Similar work needs to be done, however, on the environmental problems generated by industrialized agriculture, which include extensive erosion and sedimentation; pollution of surface and groundwater by fertilizers, pesticides, and other chemicals; and disposal of animal wastes.

Groundwater protection requires the prevention of groundwater pollution and groundwater depletion.[28] Groundwater pollution is inextricably tied to the pollution of surface land areas, particularly aquifer recharge areas. Protecting the quality and quantity of groundwater requires that planners understand how to deal with a host of potential sources of pollution. Groundwater depletion stems from groundwater withdrawals and the proliferation of impervious surfaces in recharge areas. The depletion of groundwater means that the amount of water available in an aquifer has declined. Often, such a decline is due to one or more of three factors: (1) Reduced precipitation; (2) overpumping of groundwater for agriculture, mining, other industries or commercial or residential uses; or (3) placement of impervious surfaces such as parking lots, streets, and buildings over an aquifer recharge area, which is simply the area that most efficiently transmits water from the earth's surface to the aquifer. Once a recharge area is largely covered with impervious surfaces, water can no longer be transferred to the aquifer in sufficient amounts to sustain the water-table level, and so the level falls.

Because of the character of groundwater movement and the geographic size of many recharge areas or aquifers, programs for groundwater protection may need to extend throughout a region or across several states, which would require increasing activity at state and regional levels. There is also room, however, for considerable local activity, especially in water conservation programs. Like many emerging areas of research, groundwater protection efforts are hampered by lack of understanding: the knowledge of groundwater hydrology is generally inadequate, as is the understanding of how to protect groundwater. The field presents considerable opportunity for research.

Still another emerging specialty in environmental land use planning is resource area reclamation. Following the extensive destruction of such critical resources as wetlands and watercourses, many jurisdictions are trying to determine how to reclaim them. Efforts are also being made to reclaim segments of the great canal systems that once traversed much of the Northeast and Midwest. As more and more states and communities discover the values of these resource areas, reclamation planning is likely to emerge as a promising research topic.

The production, use, and storage of hazardous material is another area of increasing importance to land use planning. In 1985 the EPA, in conjunction with the chemical industry, published interim guidelines for communities; the guidelines cover buffers, setbacks, and other measures designed to protect people and property from hazardous materials. Although these guidelines represent a first effort, they are important for planners and suggest that major changes will have to be made in both plans and regulations. This, too, is an area that would benefit greatly from additional research.

Radon, a colorless, odorless, radioactive gas emitted by underlying geological

Figure 5–6   Solidified chemicals at an abandoned hazardous waste drum site.

material, is a known carcinogen associated particularly with lung cancer. Radon can concentrate in energy-efficient homes, exposing residents to unhealthy levels of radiation. Although the research is fairly recent, the problem appears to be substantial and may affect millions of homes, schools, work places, hospitals, and other sensitive land uses. Remedial measures that building owners or occupants can take to lower radon levels are not required by law. Furthermore, almost no work has been done in land use planning to prevent the problem in newly developing areas. Radon is an issue on which states and localities are likely to take action, and they will need the expertise of environmental land use planners.

This brief presentation of emerging environmental issues suggests the increasingly complex scope of the land use planning field. Moreover, the issues identified include only relatively new policy areas and thus do not include a myriad of others, such as coastal zone planning, planning in arid or arctic zones, and planning in mountainous areas or in prairie country.

Conclusion

Environmental land planning has a long and distinguished history in the United States. Public awareness of environmental issues and support for environmental improvements remain strong and are evidence of public commitment to the work of environmental land planners. The work itself has become increasingly complex, both in terms of knowledge of resource areas and resource processes and in terms of the governmental institutions that have been established to deal with them. In their practice, environmental land planners must continue to develop their planning and regulatory techniques to keep pace with the intricate institutional setting and the rapidly expanding knowledge of the environment. For this important work, more capable, dedicated, and qualified planners are needed who understand the natural environment.

1   George Gallup, Jr., "October 31: Public Opinion Referendum," in *The Gallup Poll: Public Opinion 1982* (Wilmington, DE: Scholarly Resources, Inc., 1983); George H. Gallup, "December 16: Environmental Protection," in *The Gallup Poll: Public Opinion 1984* (Wilmington, DE: Scholarly Resources, Inc., 1985); and "The Harris Survey, September 1981," in Elizabeth Hann Hastings and Philip K. Hastings, eds. *Index to International Public Opinion, 1981–1982* (Westport, CT: Greenwood Press, 1983).

2   National Association of Counties and International City Management Association, *The 1977 County Year Book* (Washington, DC, 1977). Aggregate figures based on Section D, table 1/2, 103–151.

3   Robert Gray, President, Resource Consultants (Washington, DC, December 10, 1986), personal communication.

4   William Toner, "Land Use Controls: Agricultural Zoning," in Robert E. Coughlin et al., eds., *National Agricultural Lands Study. The Protection of Farmland: A Reference Guidebook for State and Local Governments* (Washington, DC: U.S. Government Printing Office, 1981), 104.

5   William Toner, "Ag Zoning Gets Serious," *Planning* 50, no. 12 (1984): 19–24.

6   Other evidence of the institutionalization of environmental land use planning is found in professional journals and associations. One of the professional divisions of the American Planning Association (APA) is the Environmental Planning Division, and the Association of American Geographers (AAG) has a similar division. Journals and other publications of the APA and the AAG give considerable attention to environmental land use planning. A number of other journals also include extensive material on environmental land use planning, including *Environmental Management, Landscape Journal, Journal of Soil and Water Conservation,* and *The Environmental Professional,* to name just a few key sources.

7   *El Paso Times* (May 5, 1986), 7–A.

8   U.S. Department of the Interior, Geological Survey, *Water Fact Sheet* (Reston, VA, November 1983).

9   *Courier Press* (June 6, 1977), 5.

10   George Perkins Marsh, *The Earth as Modified by Human Action* (New York: Arno Press, 1970). (Original published in 1874 as *Man and Nature.*)

11   John Wesley Powell, *Report on the Lands of the Arid Region of the United States.* Reprint, Wallace Stegner, ed. (Cambridge, MA: Harvard Common Press, 1983. Original published 1878).

12   Ebenezer Howard, *Garden Cities of To-Morrow.* Reprint, F. J. Osborn, ed. (Cambridge: MIT Press, 1965, Original published 1898).

13   L. H. Bailey, *The Country Life Movement in the United States* (New York: Macmillan 1915).

14   Thomas Adams, *Rural Planning and Development: A Study of Rural Conditions and Problems in Canada* (Ottawa: Commission of Conservation, 1917).

15   Frank A. Waugh, *Rural Improvement* (New York: Orange Judd Company, 1914); and Frank A. Waugh, *Country Planning: An Outline of Principles and Methods* (New York: Harcourt, Brace and Co., 1924).

16   Edward H. Graham, Jr., *Natural Principles of Land Use* (New York: Greenwood Press, 1944).

17   Ian L. McHarg, *Design with Nature* (Garden City, NY: Doubleday, 1971).

18   U.S. Environmental Protection Agency, *Chemical Emergency Preparedness Program: Interim Guidance,* draft (Washington, DC, 1985).

19   Three excellent articles consider methodologies and applications in LSA: Lewis D. Hopkins, "Methods for Generating Land Suitability Maps: A Comparative Evaluation," *Journal of the American Institute of Planners* 43, no. 4 (1977): 386–400; Frederick Steiner, "Resource Suitability: Methods of Analysis," *Environment Management* 7, no. 5 (1983): 401–420; and Frederick Steiner and Kenneth Brooks, "Ecological Planning: A Review," *Environmental Management* 5, no. 6 (1981): 495–505.

20   See Hopkins, "Generating Land Suitability Maps," 386–400.

21   See McHarg, *Design with Nature,* 31–41, 55–65, 103–115, and Narendra Juneja, *Medford: Performance Requirements for the Maintenance of Social Values Represented by the Natural Environment of Medford Township, New Jersey* (Philadelphia: University of Pennsylvania, Department of Landscape Architecture and Regional Planning, Center for Ecological Research in Planning and Design, 1974).

22   Lewis D. Hopkins et al., *Environmental Impact Statement: A Handbook for Writers and Reviewers,* IIEQ no. 73–8, Illinois Institute for Environmental Quality, report no. PB 226 276/AS (Springfield, VA: National Technical Information Service, 1973).

23   An excellent article by Shopley and Fuggle identifies, defines, and evaluates a series of EIA approaches. See J. B. Shopley and R. F. Fuggle, "A Comprehensive Review of Current Environmental Impact Assessment Methods and Techniques," *Journal of Environmental Management* 18, no. 1 (1984): 25–47.

24   The most common example of the matrix method is that used in L. B. Leopold et al., *A Procedure for Evaluating Environmental Impact,* Geological Survey Circular no. 645 (Washington, DC: U.S. Department of the Interior, Geological Survey, 1971).

25   Frank DiNovo and Martin Jaffe, *Local Groundwater Protection: Midwest Region* (Chicago: American Planning Association, 1984).

26   William M. Marsh, *Landscape Planning: Environmental Applications* (Menlo Park, CA: Addison-Wesley Publishing Co., 1983).

27.   Anne Whiston Spirn, *Granite Gardens* (New York: Basic Books, 1984).

28.   DiNovo and Jaffe, *Groundwater Protection.*

6

Transportation planning

Cities came into being for protection and to allow households and business enterprises to interact easily with one another. Transportation systems that facilitate access to employment, labor, goods, and services are crucial to the economic and social well-being of a community. No other public service so affects development patterns or is so affected by them.

Transportation planning considers questions that range from the global—How can transportation systems be used to create desirable urban forms?—to the particular—How many parking spaces does a suburban office complex need?

Like all planning questions, these examples can be answered in several ways. The transportation planning profession has developed objective standards and methods to address many transportation issues; the public and many planners believe that there are empirically verifiable answers to such questions. In fact, however, most of the presumably value-free methods contain both implicit values and unstated assumptions. Even if there is an empirically correct description of the current situation, there simply is no one right way to describe or predict the future. Planners must inevitably respond to events outside their control, and to do so they must make assumptions about what those events will be. Transportation projections are based on assumptions about future land use patterns, household and business behavior, and transport system costs and services; commonly used parking and highway standards value uncongested highways, unrestrained auto travel, and readily available parking.

These values may be those of the majority of society or not; the "objective" judgments may be reasonable and professional or not. But because the objective methods are based on some subjective or normative judgments, debates over transportation expenditures cannot be resolved simply by disseminating more information to all participants. In the past, planners were not often called upon to defend or even expose the assumptions underlying their methods; today, the public and decisionmakers are more sophisticated, and they may publicly challenge the inherent values of the transportation planning process.

Historically, transportation planners have accepted as given that land use patterns would develop largely through market decisions, generally continuing current trends; planners' methods supported and perhaps encouraged those decisions through the construction of infrastructure. Overall, transportation planners assumed that growth in demand for transportation was a given and that their job was to supply the appropriate transportation resources to serve the ever-growing demand. Today a variety of political and economic forces have significantly changed the environment in which transportation planners work.

First, continuing growth in demand is no longer assumed, nor are funds available to supply increasing demand. There is persistent criticism of planning's tendency to build transportation facilities to meet demand instead of directing growth in line with societal goals for urban form.

Second, because the nation's highway and transit infrastructure is in need of extensive rehabilitation and maintenance, transportation planners have had to develop methods to determine which facilities should be repaired and when. Third, transportation planners have become active participants in transportation financing through developing and implementing innovative ways to raise revenue for the construction or repair of transportation infrastructure.

Now that the addition of new facilities is not their primary concern, transportation planners must search for ways to use existing transportation systems more efficiently. Moreover, federal and state requirements have added new dimensions to the jobs of transportation planners, who are now expected to understand the social, environmental, and ethical implications of various transport options and the land use patterns that they support.

Finally, transportation planning has become an increasingly politicized field. Planners often find themselves caught between the technical side of their discipline and the world of devising compromises among the wishes, hopes, interests, and needs of many different groups. Transportation planning is perhaps the most technical of the planning disciplines because it relies extensively on statistical tools and projection methods. However, despite its technical orientation, transportation planning, like most types of planning, is in part a social science that evaluates how people interact and then projects their future needs.

Transportation planning today is a blending of technology and social science that occurs within a highly political environment and is shaped by the formal processes and agencies that regulate the planning process. This chapter will discuss the major facets of transportation planning: what is and is not known about land use and transportation, the organizations and institutions within which transportation planning occurs, the laws and regulations that govern those organizations and the planning process, the technical tools that planners use, and the political nature of planning decisions.

Transportation and land use

The relationship between transportation and land use underlies all the activities that we call transportation planning, but the land use–transportation relationship is complex and changing; trying to pin it down to simple rules or formulas is like trying to focus on a moving target. Any number of projects come under the heading of transportation planning: financing a regional rail system, making transit services accessible to disabled residents, predicting the impact of a new shopping mall on highway traffic. But in no instance can transportation planning be concerned with transportation services alone. Every transportation decision has implications for land use, and part of a planner's job is to determine, as nearly as possible, how altering one side of the equation will affect the other.

Two factors contribute to the complexity of the land use–transportation equation. First, the relationship between transportation and land use is reciprocal: land use patterns affect travel decisions, and travel decisions affect land use patterns—perhaps simultaneously, perhaps sequentially. Second, the activity patterns of businesses and families change, *independently of land use and transportation*, in response to changing values, norms, and preferences. The development of transportation planning as a discipline is the history of the struggle to understand land use on the one hand and household and business behavior on the other.

Reshaping the city

To what extent can—or should—planners use transportation facilities to shape a "livable city?" For the past fifty years, observers of urban life from Lewis Mumford to Jane Jacobs have argued that it is the responsibility of transportation planners to use their professional skills to improve the urban form. At issue is whether cities ought to develop in response to millions of individual, private market decisions or be shaped by an overall plan that interferes with the market in the name of "public interest." Zoning and building codes historically have prevented the implementation of some private decisions about land use; local governments already take an active role in determining development patterns by providing or withholding public services. How much further can or should intervention go?

The fact that transportation planners have expertise in a wide range of areas does not necessarily mean that they ought to be assigned primary responsibility for shaping urban development. Arguing that it is a planner's role to act in the public interest leaves a number of important questions unanswered: For example, how is the "public interest" to be defined? How can planners ensure that they do not simply impose their values on others?

Two interrelated aspects of urban development draw a majority of critics' concern: suburban development and the preeminence of the car. On the positive side, our current transportation system, with its heavy reliance on the private car, has given unparalleled mobility to the majority of American families, allowing them to live and work where they wish. Families have often chosen to live in the suburbs, enjoying a suburban style of life and lower housing costs. Furthermore, families have found it even cheaper to own a car; the costs of automobile ownership have decreased steadily in real terms. Critics observe, however, that millions of Americans too disabled or too poor to drive have actually suffered real losses in mobility as suburbanization has increased. Although the effective costs of owning one car have dropped, a 1983 study by the Organization for Economic Cooperation and Development found that American families spend more of their income on transportation than families in thirteen major industrial countries, perhaps reflecting second-car purchase. While auto-related deaths have been dropping, more than 44,000 people still die each year on our nation's highways. Moreover, the mobility enjoyed by so many auto drivers exacts a

---

A miscarriage of modern technics   As soon as the motor car became common, the pedestrian scale of the suburb disappeared, and with it, most of its individuality and charm. The suburb ceased to be a neighborhood unit: it became a diffused low-density mass, enveloped by the conurbation and then further enveloping it. . . . Under the present suburban regime, every urban function follows the example of the motor road; it devours space and consumes time with increasing friction and frustration, while under the plausible pretext of increasing the range of speed and communication, it actually obstructs it and denies the possibility of easy meetings and encounters by scattering the fragments of a city at random over a whole region.

At the bottom of this miscarriage of modern technics lies a fallacy that goes to the very heart of the whole underlying ideology: the notion that power and speed are desirable for their own sake, and that the latest type of fast-moving vehicle must replace every other form of transportation. . . . It is an absurdly impoverished technology that has only one answer to the problem of transportation; and it is a poor form of city planning that permits that answer to dominate its entire scheme of existence.

Under the present dispensation we have sold our urban birthright for a sorry mess of motor cars. As poor a bargain as Esau's pottage. Future generations will perhaps wonder at our willingness, indeed our eagerness, to sacrifice the education of our children, the care of the ill and the aged, the development of the arts, to say nothing of ready access to nature, for the lopsided system of mono-transportation, going through low-density areas at sixty miles an hour, but reduced in high density areas to a bare six.

Source: Lewis Mumford, *The City in History*, copyright © 1961 by Lewis Mumford. Reprinted by permission of Harcourt, Brace Jovanovich, Inc.

Private versus public transit   The reason for preferring private over public transit is not, as often alleged, the perversity of the consumer or his ignorance of economics. Part of the reason can be ascribed to public policy that has favored the car, but the basic reason why most urban trips are made by automobile is that the family car, despite its shortcomings, is superior to any other method of transportation. It offers comfort, privacy, limited walking, minimum waiting, and freedom from schedules or routing. It guarantees a seat; protects the traveler from heat, cold, and rain; provides space for baggage; carries extra passengers at no extra cost; and for most trips, except those in the center city, gets there faster and cheaper than any other way. The transit rider confronts an entirely different situation. He must walk, wait, stand, and be exposed to the elements. The ride is apt to be costly, slow, and uncomfortable because of antiquated equipment, poor ventilation, and service that is congested in rush hours, infrequent during any other time of day, inoperative at night, and nonexistent in suburbia.

Source: Wilfred Owen, *Transportation for Cities: The Role of Federal Policy* Washington, DC: The Brookings Institution, Copyright 1976.

price in environmental damage and the consumption of nonrenewable fossil fuels.

It can be argued that the market has given the public what it wants—multi-nucleated, decentralized communities heavily dependent on the private car. Critics respond, however, that certain government infrastructure decisions, including massive financing of the highway system, have interfered with the market process in ways that predetermined the outcome.

Although the use of transportation facilities as a deliberate tool of land use control has not been a part of the American approach to city planning, several European national-level governments have used regional rail and highway investments in an effort to relieve congestion in central cities and direct new growth to concentrated areas or corridors. In the United Kingdom, the growth of New Towns was facilitated by major highway and rail links. In France, massive extensions of the Paris regional Metro support satellite cities, which are intended to relieve housing demand in Paris.

The difference between the traditional American approach and these European approaches to land use and economic development is fundamental. Even if the American approach were to change in the coming years, transportation and other planners would require a great deal of empirical information about the land use–transportation equation before they would be able to implement more active approaches to land use control.

What do we know about managing city form?

Although a connection between the transportation system and the location of households and businesses is clear, planners cannot predict with any accuracy the direction or the strength of that connection, nor can they be sure which is effect and which is cause. For example, does the existence of a rail-transit system *create* the dispersed suburbanization so characteristic of modern cities around the world? Do people want to own and use cars, or have they been forced into doing so by lack of adequate alternatives?

A look at empirical evidence about the impact of highways and transit on development patterns shows mixed results, and it appears that the findings may for commercial and industrial land uses may be different from those for residential ones. While it is clear that transportation facilities often have a profound and measurable effect on immediately adjacent land, consequences at greater distances are less certain. Even where impacts seem clear, they are not always what critics might have expected or desired; there is substantial evidence, for example, that even public *transit* improvements have facilitated low-density residential development.

Critics blame the proliferation of suburbs on the automobile and on government support for highway construction; however, studies suggest that suburbs of many cities developed before they were readily accessible by highway or transit, as residents sought relief from the congestion and problems of the central city.

Beginning in the late nineteenth century, rapid-transit technology offered significant improvements in speed and coverage over previous systems, making it easier to move out from the central city. After World War I, decentralization in cities as different as Los Angeles and Shaker Heights was facilitated by trolleys and intraurban electric trains. There is strong evidence that the new modern rapid-transit systems in San Francisco, Toronto, and Washington, D.C., have contributed to increased residential suburbanization by effectively reducing the costs of traveling long distances to the central city.

Although they are easy to spot once they occur, the potential negative effects of highway and transit systems have been difficult to anticipate. In suburban Washington, D.C., traffic congestion near "park-and-ride" stations hasbecome a substantial problem. In Austin, Texas, a citywide system of synchronized transfer stations was seriously delayed because neighbors and merchants protested the bus and pedestrian congestion that would result. In San Francisco's East Bay, elderly residents whose neighborhoods were deliberately targeted for service by the BART rail system have been forced to move because of increases in land values near the transit line and commercial and residential gentrification.

The European experiences offer further indications of the complexity of the land use–transportation equation. The British have generally conceded that although

Figure 6–1 Rapid-transit technology facilitated city-to-suburb travel before the advent of the automobile. The photograph shows an inspection trip by the mayor and council of Laurel, Maryland, on the first Washington, D.C.–Laurel trolley, 21 September 1902.

the New Towns have met other social goals, they have failed to redistribute residential development in the desired ways, resulting instead in increased suburbanization and low-density residential development. Nor have the satellite cities surrounding Paris successfully channeled growth in that region.

The European programs also demonstrate the difficulty of understanding all the human factors underlying travel behavior. In Britain, for example, the first New Towns were built without parking facilities, because they were located along rail or transit lines. Because workers began to purchase automobiles as their standard of living rose, the government has since had to go back and build large parking structures.

Empirical evidence suggests that as *all* transport modes have allowed faster travel, households and businesses alike have indicated a preference for decentralized activity; they tend to relocate outside the central city, where land is cheaper and more plentiful and where households have access to suburban amenities. This sets off another phase of decentralized land use, because increasing development of suburban areas makes it less necessary for either households or businesses to locate in city centers to meet their needs.

Using transportation facilities and services to reshape urban form requires resolution of serious political and policy questions, as well as a better understanding of the forces that created existing urban structures and services. Although experience and research have provided a remarkable amount of information about the aggregate effects of transportation improvements on land use, significant questions remain. A number of normative and empirical debates will have to be resolved before a thorough revision of current approaches to transportation or land use planning can be undertaken.

Whenever transportation facilities do change land use patterns, whether or not in desired ways, transportation decisions are only part of a package of government tools; economic development, labor market, and housing policies and plans are involved also. The European efforts all involved substantial financial incentives to businesses and families locating in preferred areas, as well as stringent restrictions on growth and development in nonpreferred areas. Any resolution of normative or empirical debates must occur within a broader context than that of transportation planning alone. All of the disciplines and decisionmakers that affect a community's growth and development must be included.

A body of knowledge does exist, however, that allows transportation planners to suggest solutions daily to a myriad of small and large transportation problems and to formulate longer-range plans that are ready for public debate. Transportation planners rely on an ever-expanding knowledge of the land use–transportation relationship to predict needed transportation facilities given certain land use forecasts or to predict future land use development given transport system improvements. Although there are problems and gaps in the system, the profession has built up an impressive repertoire of techniques, methods, and guidelines.

If a community, or the society as a whole, wishes consciously to influence the urban form, transportation planners can make a constructive contribution to the debate. However, most transportation planners do not believe that they are responsible for the form of the city or for changing it; their contribution can be made only as part of a comprehensive public and political discussion of desirable urban forms and the price that decisionmakers and the public are willing to pay to achieve them.

The rest of the chapter discusses the structure of the traditional U.S. transportation planning process and the tools and methods applied to that process. The following section considers the ways in which early transportation planners dealt with the land use and transportation questions raised here; it will also examine the role of transportation planning in a comprehensive land use planning process.

The formal metropolitan transportation planning process

In any region or metropolitan community, a number of public agencies may be engaged in transportation planning. Most cities and counties have road and traffic departments; city and county planning agencies may also conduct transportation analyses. District or regional highway department offices, councils of governments, and transit operators also perform transportation studies and prepare plans.

Some agencies conduct transportation analyses as part of their primary mission; others engage in transportation planning only as a complement to their primary responsibilities. Some agencies build highway or transit systems; others only study their effects. Some agencies deal with both highway and transit issues while others deal with only a subset of highway problems, such as road maintenance. Some agencies interact with one another daily, others only infrequently. No matter how professional and analytical these agencies may be, they will always have differences in priorities and interests that may lead them to different conclusions and decisions about transportation issues.

However, all agencies in a metropolitan area that are involved in large-scale or regional transportation delivery engage in a fairly well-established set of planning procedures. Many, though not all, of these activities are defined by federal regulations, which require that a metropolitan area have a coordinated highway, transit, and land use planning process in order to receive federal funds for highway and transit improvements. Differences among agencies in regional plans, projections, or results generally must be resolved to satisfy these federal regulations.

The procedures followed by these agencies and the ways in which they coordinate their activities are the result of a metropolitan or regional planning process that has developed over the last forty years. This section of the chapter will consider the history and structure of that process; the next section will explore the procedures and techniques used by regional and metropolitan planners. Local transportation issues will be discussed in a later section.

Assumptions of the process

How has the formal metropolitan transportation planning process dealt with the land use and social questions raised in the opening section of this chapter? The formal transportation planning process that began in the early 1940s sidestepped many of the land use–transportation debates by accepting easy answers to both normative questions—What should a city look like? and empirical ones—What are the reciprocal effects of land use and transportation facilities?

First, it was assumed that transportation planning would take place as part of a comprehensive process in which community goals and objectives would be set. Then available techniques would—and could—be applied to develop the transportation alternative that would best meet community goals and objectives.

While planners recognized that some groups had interests different from those of the general public and that some groups might pay a heavier price or receive less benefit from a public project, they believed that there was a "public interest" that could be identified and served.

The so-called comprehensive, rational process assumed that clear-cut community goals could be implemented and that all planning techniques were scientific and value neutral. In other words, once community goals were set, transportation planning became a matter of applying technical expertise to the achievement of those goals. The assumption was that transportation planning problems had a "right" answer.

Second, transportation planners generally assumed that community goals and objectives were already known. For example, most early planners assumed that increased mobility and expansion of the highway—and in some cases, the transit system—were community norms. By extension, rapid suburbanization and increasing dependence on private cars were not viewed with concern.

This view of community norms fostered the development of two primary operational goals: transportation planners were to (1) reduce congestion and (2) increase travel speeds using the most cost-effective means. The result was the construction of new, uncongested, faster-flowing facilities, particularly those serving morning and evening peak periods created by home-to-work trips. Above all, the focus on reducing congestion generated solutions designed to accommodate vehicular traffic; emphasis was on developing ways to move more cars in the peak period, and little attention was given to nonvehicular traffic, nonwork trips, and noncentral destinations. Because new facilities were designed to meet (or nearly meet) peak-period demands, miles of expressway lanes were underused for most of the day.

Highway engineers and the intercity freeway   The relative influence of engineering and city planning considerations on decisions concerning the intercity freeway illustrated a fairly simple point: clarity of standards and strength of conviction were extremely important political variables. When standards were clear, and a profession felt confident that [the standards] were right or "the best available," conscientious men could look to them for guidance and take on from them the energy that flowed from unclouded conviction. . . .

It was a crucial element of the highway engineers in freeway disputes that they possessed and believed implicitly in a set of clear normative propositions, applicable to the most important of their problems and convincing to the vast majority of the people with whom they had to deal. . . .

1. Highway improvements were desirable.
2. The location of highway routes should be determined according to

engineering criteria, of which by far the most important were traffic service and cost.
3. The articulate public (in opposition to freeway construction) should never be confused with the entire public.
4. It was preferable, engineering considerations being equal, not to build a highway through a residential neighborhood or very far from existing areas of heavy investment. . . . Engineering considerations were, however, seldom equal.

Highway engineers emphasized that traffic and cost data were quantitative and impartial. They believed that they were able, therefore, to prove that they had selected (the right) highway routes without favoritism toward any group or interest.

Source: Alan A. Altshuler, *The City Planning Process: A Political Analysis* (Ithaca, NY: Cornell University Press, 1969), 76–78. Copyright © 1965 by Cornell University. Used by permission of the publisher.

Third, the formal process regarded future land use patterns as a given. Although planners did attempt to predict future spatial patterns, both the planning process and the techniques applied to it assumed that land use decisions would be made as they always had: by private market forces and not by government regulation of land use patterns to meet societal concerns.

Today, transportation planners are more likely to recognize that community goals and their operational implications are not always easy to determine—and that they may not be settled before the comprehensive planning process begins. Often, opposition to a planned transportation improvement surfaces only after the project has gone through the entire formal process. Although residents and interest groups may agree in principle with the general goals of that process, they often disagree violently over practical alternatives and plans.

Planners have also come to see that there may be no one best way to deal with a problem or to plan for the future. A number of legitimate views may remain in conflict throughout the entire planning process. This conflict may ultimately be settled, not by planners applying cost-benefit ratios but by elected officials responding to constituents' demands.

Planners working for agencies with differing missions and priorities often find themselves in conflict as advocates for plans or projects. Many issues formerly considered technical and professional "judgment calls" have become overtly political because of the implications of different assessments for transit and highway plans. Political decisionmakers unable to resolve difficult issues may put greater responsibility on planners—and on their technical tools—than in the past. Planners may be asked to produce additional plans, to delay the decision process, or to produce estimates and projections supporting political decisions that have already been made.

Although the assumption that planning is neutral and value free has been strongly challenged, it shaped a formal organizational and professional process that is still with us today. The process has many strengths as well as serious weaknesses. Perhaps the most severe problem is that the process is not designed to question the ultimate form of urban development. Historically, transportation planners have been compelled to make land use assumptions because other agencies and institutions failed to do so. In the 1960s, when transportation planners first began to evaluate the land use–transportation relationship, they were unable to obtain either the technical information or the political consensus on which to base infrastructure decisions. It is no easier today to achieve political consensus on future land use; local officials are often unwilling or unable to make difficult trade-offs among competing interest groups. Even if consensus were possible at the local level, it would be extremely difficult to achieve at the metropolitan level.

Federal mandates now require participating agencies and local governments to identify and evaluate land use projections on which transportation decisions are based; however, in most metropolitan areas, these projections are ultimately made by transportation planning agencies and not by land use planners.

History of metropolitan transportation planning

Although transportation planning takes place in a variety of agencies and at various levels of government, those agencies that wish to receive federal transportation assistance must cooperate with one another. There is a fairly standardized metropolitan planning process that coordinates the plans of most transit and highway agencies. This process has been structured by federal legislation and programs going as far back as the 1930s.

Highway planning at the state and local level was inaugurated by the Federal-Aid Highway Act of 1934, which permitted a state to use up to 1½ percent of construction funds for planning and economic evaluation. Activities first financed by these funds continue today: developing inventories and maps of the highway system, preparing traffic counts, and determining how to finance the construction and maintenance of highway facilities.

The Federal Highway Act of 1956, which launched the national Interstate Highway System, was the largest U.S. public works program ever undertaken. The 1956 act extended the planned system to 41,000 miles and, most notably, provided a means to pay for the construction of the system—the Highway Trust Fund.

The Interstate Highway System was the largest impetus not only for transportation planning but for comprehensive regional land use planning as well.

As cities and states began funding interstate highway links, they saw the need to develop plans that were based on regionwide, comprehensive analyses of proposed projects and their costs and benefits.

The Federal-Aid Highway Act of 1962 provided a major stimulus for a *formal* comprehensive process. Implemented in 1965, section 134 of the act legislated the first formal requirement that highway construction projects in urbanized areas of more than 50,000 population must be based on a continuing, comprehensive planning process carried out cooperatively (the "3-C" process) among states and local communities. The 1962 act further *required* states to spend 1½ percent of construction funds for planning; money not spent on planning was lost to the state. Generally the states spent some of that money themselves but also passed through a great deal to regional highway agencies and, increasingly, to regional councils of government to pay for the comprehensive planning process. These funds were significant because they led to extensive state research programs and contributed greatly to the development of local as well as state transportation planning expertise.

The 3-C process, born in 1962, had tremendous impact on the organizational arrangements developed at the local level to carry out highway and, ultimately, all transportation planning. First, the 3-C process set the planning scale at the regional or metropolitan level; second, the cooperation requirement brought about the creation of planning agencies or organizational arrangements designed to ensure communication and cooperation between all parties. Perhaps most significantly, the required organizational arrangements became the basis for cooperation among agencies planning for transit, urban rail transportation, air transportation, and waterways, as well as among those concerned with social, economic, and environmental effects of transportation improvements.

Although formal transit planning requirements did not appear until the 1966 amendments to the Urban Mass Transportation Act of 1964, many large urban areas, in advance of any formal requirements to do so, began coordinating their transit and other planning activities with the 3-C regional highway planning agencies. This process was facilitated by the 1973 Highway Act, which allowed states to set aside an additional ½ percent of construction funds specifically for the 3-C process; the funds generally went to regional planning organizations.

The 1973 Highway Act was in several ways a major impetus for regional planning. The act spoke for the first time of coordinating highway and transit planning in a Metropolitan Planning Organization (MPO), a term not in common currency at the time.

In 1975 the Federal Highway Administration (FHWA) and the Urban Mass Transportation Administration (UMTA) issued joint highway and planning regulations in support of the 1973 act. The joint regulations firmly placed in *one single agency*—the MPO—responsibility for preparing a comprehensive transportation plan for both highway and transit modes, with long-range (10- to 20-year) and shorter-range (5-year) elements.

Responsibilities in three areas were given to MPOs: coordinating the planning efforts of transportation and land use agencies in the region; conducting certain types of planning studies; and making decisions about highway and transit resource allocation when there were conflicts among agencies or when funds were not sufficient to cover all projects. To put these planning goals into operation, the MPOs were required to produce a number of consistent transportation plans and documents. Some of these responsibilities reflected the natural evolution of efforts already underway in regional councils of government and planning agencies. Other activities, particularly the resolution of conflicts about federal and local funding expenditures, were extremely controversial.

In 1983, in response to criticism of these regulations, the federal government issued new planning regulations that significantly relaxed the restrictions and requirements on states and MPOs. The important regulations and documents required between 1975 and 1983 are described in the following section; their ultimate impact on the planning process is also discussed.

Structure of the metropolitan transportation planning process

The metropolitan planning process that developed in response to federal regulations was not the same in every region; every element of the process was open to state and local interpretation and debate. However, despite the variations in local interpretation, two elements remained constant in the formal planning process: the organization performing regional planning functions and the planning functions performed.

Between the 1965 implementation of the 3-C planning requirement and the 1975 joint UMTA-FHWA regulations, most areas developed regional agencies to perform the required planning process. In 1972, 42 percent of these agencies were organized and staffed by the state highway department, 37 percent were regional councils of government, and 17 percent were city or county agencies. In those regions where a state highway or city or county agency performed the 3-C process, the regional council of government continued to perform other federally mandated planning and the A-95 regional clearinghouse function.

The 1975 joint regulations empowered the governor to designate the MPO for each metropolitan area in the state. However, the guidelines were written to encourage the designation of regional councils of governments (COGs) as MPOs. Since many COGs were not then performing the 3-C process, there was substantial opposition to this change, notably from state highway departments. By 1976, the Department of Transportation largely got its way; 82 percent of all MPOs were COGs. In 1983, when the restrictions were relaxed, the number of COGs designated as MPOs fell sharply—to 55 percent. However, the number of state highway department agencies designated MPOs fell even more sharply, to only 4 percent. The newly designated MPOs were city and county agencies and freestanding units organized solely to receive the MPO designation.

There are two distinct periods in the evolution of MPOs and of the regional planning agencies that preceded them: from 1965 to 1983 their responsibilities and the comprehensiveness of their role grew substantially. After 1983 their responsibilities were altered significantly; many of the planning activities previously required ceased to be mandatory, although they are permitted and even encouraged today.

From 1965 to 1983   In the first phase of their development, MPOs were required to prepare three major documents: a comprehensive long-range plan for transit and highway improvements; a three-to-five-year Transportation Improvement Program (TIP) that was to be based on a subset of the twenty-year long-range plan; and an annual element, a one-year program of activities. The TIP and the annual element were to be reviewed each year. MPOs were required also to prepare Transportation System Management (TSM) plans detailing how the region would make better use of existing transit and highway facilities.

In addition, MPO planning documents were required to take account of a number of environmental and social concerns. In response to energy shortages, MPOs had to develop energy conservation plans stressing transportation alternatives. To deal with environmental problems, they were obligated to carry out or coordinate environmental reviews of transportation projects. Plans involving private transit operators were also required to ensure the active involvement of the private sector. Finally, MPOs had to see that elderly and handicapped people were involved in the planning process and that regional plans were adequately responsive to their needs.

The many obligatory activities and documents were undertaken and prepared by different actors in each community. In most areas, each agency with responsibility for a particular mode of travel prepared its own plan: the transit operator the transit plan, the highway department the highway plan. The MPO then performed only the coordinating function, organizing meetings and ensuring that diverse agency plans were compatible and could be presented as part of the three documents required by the federal government.

Over the years, however, many MPOs began to prepare their own regional plans, and as federal regulations became more stringent, other agency plans were more and more closely coordinated with the process overseen by the MPO. Moreover, MPOs began to develop comprehensive data bases and regional planning models on which other agencies came to rely.

Since 1983   It is still too early to see the impact of the 1983 relaxation of federal requirements. The 1975 joint regulations and the TSM, environmental, and social requirements were strongly criticized for being too proscriptive and unresponsive to local needs. Furthermore, the federal government addressed issues piecemeal, as they arose, without regard for the overall planning process. Many of the TSM or environmental studies or plans were simply added on at the end of the lengthy regional planning process and could have little impact on how highway and transit agencies made their decisions.

New problems do arise, and it is not possible at the beginning of a process to identify all the issues that will concern the public and policymakers. For example, national concerns may take precedence over local rights; national policy may require localities to ensure that the environment is protected, that federally assisted highways are used efficiently, or that disabled citizens are adequately served by highway and transit systems built with public funds.

The 1975 joint planning requirements, though modified, are significant for the continuing direction they gave to regional transportation planning; their emphasis on multimodal planning (the planning of many modes in conjunction with one another) was particularly influential. The required TIP was the link between planning and programming; it brought together all highway and transit projects in a single document, and it included an annual element that could serve as the basis for federal funding decisions in any given year.

The federal government has continued its commitment to multimodal planning and to the 3-C planning process. Moreover, most states continue to support MPOs that carry out long-range multimodal planning efforts and that link comprehensive planning to operational decisions. Most of these MPOs retain the distinction between a multiyear program of activities and a biannually reviewed element, and most support the link between a comprehensive regional plan and individual agency activities.

Although the pre–1983 formal process had many critics, most observers agree that it brought a measure of coordination to the plans of various transportation agencies whose activities significantly affect one another. Moreover, by requiring overall consistency in transportation plans, the process also encouraged cooperating agencies to resolve conflicts in methods and assumptions.

Many observers have questioned how comprehensive the regional transportation planning process will be in the future. A 1984 report by the Advisory Commission on Intergovernmental Relations (ACIR) concluded that, as a result of relaxed federal regulations and lack of federal funding, most MPO planning will become "increasingly isolated, less comprehensive, and shorter range." Activities that are suggested but not required may not be performed at all, because the MPO has neither the political clout to ensure that individual agencies undertake such activities nor the funds to conduct supporting studies. There is strong pressure in some regions for decentralization—distribution of the MPO function among smaller coordinating and planning units. These trends in the organizational structure of regional planning complement trends in the technical aspects of the process. Increasingly, planners focus on smaller areas and use less comprehensive, less complex methods, sometimes using hand-held calculators rather than regional transportation models.

Transportation planning as a technical process

The core of the technical transportation planning process at the regional level consists of three interrelated activities: gauging the demand for transportation services and facilities; matching cost-effective supply options to that demand; and considering the impact of supply alternatives on the social, economic, and environmental characteristics of the community.

These activities are generally part of a highly structured and elaborate technical process that grew out of federal 3-C requirements and the need for an orderly and logical approach to planning future regional transportation facilities. Three features were typical of the comprehensive processes begun in the 1960s: (1) transportation planners often had to undertake land use planning because land use planning agencies had not done so; (2) there was a strong emphasis on the development of mathematical models and technical tools; and (3) planners devoted most of their efforts to estimating demand and gave less emphasis to supply-side and financial questions.

Methodology in context

The technical element of the regional transportation planning process does not exist in a vacuum; technical processes and methods are inextricably bound to political and institutional structures. The issues addressed by the technical process, the assumptions of that process, the ways in which data are handled—all of these are often determined by the interests of the institutions performing the studies and by the political realities of the metropolitan area.

The technical elements of the transportation planning process evolved alongside the institutional process described in the preceding section. Large-scale transportation planning techniques and regional land use models were developed primarily in response to the new comprehensive planning responsibilities placed on MPOs and their predecessors by the 1962 Highway Act (although earlier prototype efforts showed the way). These large-scale models were used to determine the regional impact of extensions of the federal highway system; increasingly over time, these models were used also to gauge the effects of rapid-rail extensions.

Historically, transportation planners were forced to make de facto policy decisions about future land use patterns and the role of highway and transit systems in shaping the urban environment. One of the major requirements for regional land use and transportation models was future land use projections or goals. Because these were rarely available when regional transportation modeling began, transportation planners themselves often became responsible for producing land use projections. Transportation planners rarely sought the role of de facto policymakers, although some did eventually become accustomed to making easy assumptions about land use development.

As MPO obligations became less comprehensive, planners began to develop and rely on simplified and streamlined analytical approaches. Today, planners more often focus on single growth corridors or subregional areas. They seldom run large-scale regional land use and transportation models to answer important policy questions, or they augment them with more sensitive tools.

Large-scale regional modeling efforts are, however, still important, particularly in high-growth areas; several large Sun Belt cities are considering the development of new regional models. Moreover, large-scale modeling efforts formed the basis of most urban transportation planning decisions in the past twenty years—which means that we are still living with the consequences and will continue to do so for some time.

Although the basic features of the traditional, large-scale planning process are easy enough to describe, the way the process is carried out varies from region to region. In some areas, one agency is responsible for all or most of what is described here; in other areas, a number of agencies undertake the various components, producing sometimes conflicting, sometimes complementary projections and plans.

Different projections and plans often arise from different assumptions. The entire technical process is driven by assumptions, ranging from estimates of future transportation costs to predictions of future household behavior patterns. Reasonable people can differ on these questions, and the interests of individual transportation agencies may cause them to accept one assumption over another. For example, transit agencies are likely to assume a shift to public transit in the future; highway agencies are likely to assume that auto use will continue at its current level or increase.

Policymakers, as well as the lay public, often have great faith in technology and can be dismayed to find that competent and professional technical efforts can produce different results. Because the technical process does not always give unambiguous answers, and because it has become extremely complex and time-consuming, it has lost some of its power with political decisionmakers. Nevertheless, when the process is used properly and is not expected to answer inherently political questions, it has tremendous planning power.

The technical process has a number of strengths: it gives meaning to large-scale land use and transportation patterns; it provides an understanding of social and commercial phenomena in a community; and it gives policymakers comparable measures by which to judge alternative transportation strategies. Overall, the technical process has given U.S. transportation planners an enviable record in predicting future transportation needs.

Nevertheless, it is important to recognize what cannot or should not be done with the results of the technical process. Modeling efforts cannot resolve basic policy debates about desirable land use or family living patterns. Statistical tools can only augment, never replace, professional judgment and experience. Planners can use models to evaluate the implications of various land use or cost assumptions, but they cannot tell which of several plausible assumptions will come true.

The sections that follow describe the growth and development of the comprehensive large-scale process as well as the streamlined methods that are now used to supplement the regional models and tools.

The comprehensive process

The conventional transportation planning process generally consists of technical methods designed to use and produce a uniform set of projections and analyses. Even though responsible agencies and actors vary, each region must have a regional transportation process that includes the following elements:

1. Future land use and economic projections
2. Estimations of travel demands
3. Ways to match demand to the capacity and service characteristics of supply alternatives
4. Estimations of costs and benefits of potential alternatives for the community as a whole and for various subgroups in the population
5. Procedures for mediating conflicts between interest groups and between the findings of different planning agencies in the community.

Land use forecasting   Of necessity, major regional transportation planning efforts in the 1950s and 1960s had to incorporate a number of steps to gather basic land use information and to estimate future land use and economic patterns. The ground-breaking Chicago Area Transportation Study (CATS) inaugurated the use of sophisticated, large-scale transportation network and land use modeling methodology. Although not all regional planning efforts of the 1960s were structured identically, many other regional planning agencies used CATS as a prototype and put a great deal of effort into forecasting land use and travel.

Highway and transportation planners did not initially expect to be involved in the first series of land use and economic projections; they assumed that some city or county planning agency "knew" what future land use and economic patterns would be. But early transportation planners found that cities did not know what their futures might look like; moreover, cities rarely had up-to-date population estimates or complete inventories of current land uses or traffic patterns.

Today, the role of the transportation planning office in projecting population growth, economic activity, and land use varies depending on the community. In some localities, transportation planners may assist planning departments in developing future projections, but the land planning agencies are the final authority. In other communities, although the land use planning process and transportation forecasting process are separate, transportation planners use inventories and traffic data from local land planning and traffic departments and do not develop their own. In still other communities, transportation planning agencies continue to develop their own economic and land use projections, and these forecasts may or may not be consistent with those of local land use planning agencies. Some of these conflicts are resolved or at least mediated by the MPO; others are not.

A land use forecast requires three interrelated steps: (1) determining future population growth; (2) determining future economic activity; and (3) determining future land use patterns, that is, determining where the forecasted population growth and economic activity will occur. The next stage of the forecast matches land use patterns to the generation and distribution of future travel by (1) estimating the number of trips generated by new residential and commercial activity; (2) determining the distribution of those trips; and (3) determining the mode that would be used to make those trips. The sections that follow examine only those elements of land use forecasting that are inherently related to transportation.

Estimating regional demand   To estimate demand, a regional planning agency begins by gathering data on current relationships between land use and economic activity on the one hand and travel choices on the other. Regional transportation planners then attempt to predict the number and kind of trips generated by and attracted to future land uses and the modes those trips might use. Augmenting this information with data on other communities, planners build mathematical models that portray those relationships.

Developing models   The estimation of demand relies on tools that can predict one side of the land use–transportation equation if the other side is known or postulated. However, before planners can use models to predict the future, they must be sure that the models can replicate existing travel patterns; this is called model calibration. Figure 6–2 illustrates the structure of this process in most metropolitan areas. Note that the models are usually derived from existing empirical data and that they are checked against existing data in the calibration process.

Of course, successful prediction depends on whether historically observed relationships will continue into the future or indeed on whether public policy

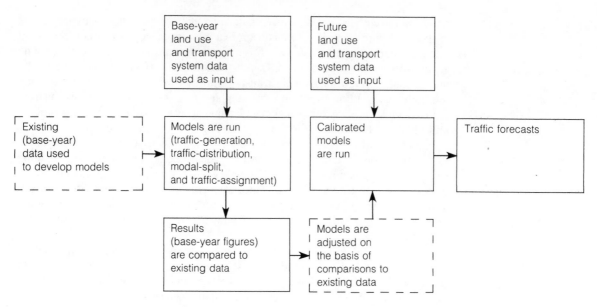

Figure 6–2   Traffic forecasting methodology.

will allow them to do so. Conventional models have been strongly criticized for the assumption that 1960 travel patterns will be equally valid for families and businesses in 1990 and beyond.

Because planners have been developing and using models for more than twenty years, most of the basic models already exist and need to be updated and modified rather than created from scratch. The technical process followed today usually relies on four separate models that are run independently. Each of these models has several major variations, in which both mathematical functions and underlying assumptions differ. The four basic models are

Trip-generation models, which estimate the number of trips generated by different types of land use

Trip-distribution models, which estimate where in the city the generated trips will go

Modal-split models, which estimate which trips will use transit and which will use private auto

Traffic-assignment models, which assign trips by each mode to actual or planned routes.

The fourth model, traffic assignment, is actually used for the supply side of the planning equation, which will be discussed in a later section.

These models were first developed by agencies conducting the major transportation studies of the 1960s and were updated and improved by subsequent regional planning studies, researchers at major universities, consultants, and the Federal Highway Administration (FHWA). The FHWA, now in conjunction with the Urban Mass Transportation Administration, has for a number of years developed and updated a series of standardized models that are part of the Urban Transportation Planning System (UTPS). UTPS packages are readily available to regional and municipal planning agencies, and the FHWA holds annual seminars and regional conferences on their use.

Using the models   The output of any one model is usually used as input for the next model, but the order in which the models are run is not totally standardized and varies, for example, from country to country. Figure 6–3 shows four sequences

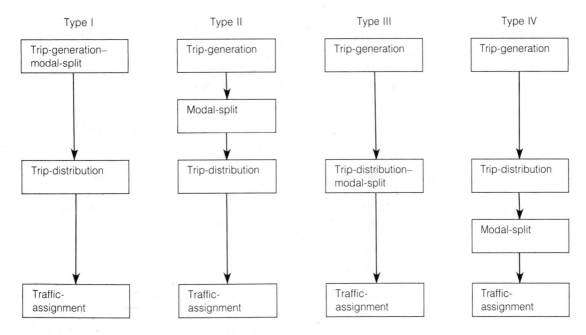

Figure 6-3 Four sequences in which transportation models can be used.

in which the models can be used. As the figure shows, all four sequences run the trip-generation model first and the traffic-assignment model last. The variation occurs in the positioning of the modal-split model. Clearly, the order in which the models are applied will affect the outcome of the process. Model sequences III and IV, for example, which place modal-split decisions after trip-generation and trip-distribution, assume that the availability of transit does not affect people's decisions about *whether* or *where* to travel. The implication is that for destinations not accessible by transit, people are financially and physically able to travel by car.

Type II sequences, which allot trips to the major modes and then distribute them throughout the region, were developed in the United States as part of early comprehensive planning efforts; among cities that have used this approach are Chicago, Pittsburgh, and Philadelphia. Type II sequences are generally considered more appropriate for communities with high transit use, where transit may significantly affect community growth. Type III and IV sequences, where modal-split decisions are made *after* trips have been distributed, were later developments; among cities that have used Type III or IV sequences are Washington, D.C.; Buffalo, New York; and Minneapolis-St. Paul, Minnesota.

Regional supply analysis The next step in the comprehensive transportation planning process is to match forecast demand to cost-effective supply options. As noted earlier, the traditional, supply-oriented approach is losing ground. Transportation planning today is not simply a matter of estimating future demand and determining the kind of additional facilities needed to meet that demand. Planners are now being asked to consider a wide range of alternative transportation options, to determine how the existing system could be redirected to meet future demands without extensive construction of new facilities, and even how to generate income to pay for the new facilities that should be built.

This section will examine the technical side of the traditional process: evaluating supply options in light of projected demands. Later sections will describe newer aspects of the transportation planning function, including transportation system management, supply management, and paratransit.

The purpose of the technical process is to match predicted demand to a number of possible supply options—including doing nothing—and to develop objective, comparative measures of the costs and benefits of each option. System costs can include engineering, right-of-way acquisition, construction, maintenance, operation, and enforcement; user costs can include loss of time and money and decreased convenience and satisfaction.

Transportation planners try to assess user costs and benefits by predicting the effect of various supply options on both travelers and their vehicles. To do so, transportation planners use models that are mathematical representations of the existing highway and transit network. (Note that for purposes of economic analysis, nonmonetary costs, such as congestion, are translated into monetary terms: decreased congestion equals decreased travel time, which in turn yields monetary savings.) Like the demand models described in the preceding section, network models are based on empirical examination of the existing system, then calibrated against the original data, or base year, to make sure that they are reliable. The network model includes information on the type, capacity, and service level of each route as well as the length of the route and average travel speed on it.

Once future demand has been identified, transportation planners generally perform three major analyses: first, they consider the implications of the do-nothing option by predicting the impact of future demand on the current network and describing what would happen to congestion and travel times for all riders, new and old. Second, they may propose new facilities built to the level of service considered appropriate, then modify the network model to represent the new facilities. The model would then be used to predict how the new and old travel demand would be distributed over the revised network. Third, planners may choose one or more potential but competing improvements for a given corridor or area—perhaps a rail system and a freeway extension—and predict comparative usage and impact.

Once transportation planners have an idea of how many riders or drivers will use a facility and what costs or benefits will accrue to users from increased or decreased congestion and travel times, they can compare the costs (both to the public and to users) of the proposed facility against the expected benefits. This evaluation allows planners and decisionmakers to understand the costs of various highway and transit options and to compare various routing and modal alternatives.

Transportation planners use a fairly well-defined set of street and highway characteristics to determine how existing and proposed transportation options should be represented in the network model. The characteristics of transit supply options are less well defined, in part because there are a number of ways to serve the same demand—light versus heavy rail, for example. Each assumption about the mode of supply can conceivably produce a different set of predictions about future transit or highway use.

Economic analysis of highway options   The authority on highway standards is the *Highway Capacity Manual (HCM)*, which is published by the Transportation Research Board and updated periodically. The *HCM* includes six *levels of service* that describe and define congestion and service characteristics on highways. The *HCM* bases its standards on a combination of empirical observation, judgment, and mathematical modeling.

Freeways and limited-access highways are described in terms that represent reasonable ranges in three critical dimensions: average travel speed, density, and flow rate. Figure 6–4 shows examples of the six levels of service, A through F, on an urban freeway. Planners can use these service-level measures in several ways. Levels of service can be used to describe current highway problems or as operational goals for new or expanded highways. They can be used to measure

Level of service A

Level of service D

Level of service B

Level of service E

Level of service C

Level of service F

Figure 6–4   Freeway levels of service.

effects on highways of increased travel demand or to determine the number of lanes needed to achieve a desired level of service for projected traffic flows. Planners use the capacity and speed standards to calculate savings and losses in time and convenience for new and old users, for alternative routes, and for the do-nothing alternative.

Most traffic-assignment models use these service standards to limit the number of autos allowed onto current or future highway facilities. For example, once a future facility reaches a specified capacity and service level, the model must allocate additional trips somewhere else. This enables planners to see if projected highways will meet all projected demand and to identify where additional congestion or pressure on the network will still occur.

Figure 6–5 Factors that influence transit capacity of urban streets.

Vehicle characteristics
Allowable number of vehicles per transit unit (i.e., single-unit bus, or several units-cars per train)
Vehicle dimensions
Seating configuration and capacity
Number, location, and width of doors
Number and height of steps
Maximum speed
Acceleration and deceleration rates
Type of door actuation control

Right-of-way characteristics
Cross-section design (i.e., number of lanes or tracks)
Degree of separation from other traffic
Intersection design (at grade or grade separated, type of traffic controls)
Horizontal and vertical alignment

Stop characteristics
Spacing (frequency) and duration
Design (on-line and off-line)
Platform height (high-level or low-level loading)
Number and length of loading positions
Method of fare collection (prepayments, pay when entering vehicle, pay when leaving vehicle)
Type of fare (single-coin, penny, exact)
Common or separate areas for passenger boarding and alighting
Passenger accessibility to stops

Operating characteristics
Intercity versus suburban operations at terminals
Layover and schedule adjustment practices
Time losses to obtain clock headways or provide driver relief
Regularity of arrivals at a given stop

Passenger traffic characteristics
Passenger concentrations and distribution at major stops
Peaking of ridership (i.e., peak-hour factor)

Street traffice characteristics
Volume and nature of other traffic (on shared right-of-way)
Cross traffic at intersections if at grade

Method of headway control
Automatic or by driver/trainman
Policy spacing between vehicles

Economic analysis of transit options   Describing current service or estimating the impact of new transit service is more difficult than conducting similar analyses for highways.

First, whereas standards for highway service are based on the three criteria of speed, density, and flow, transit standards must incorporate many more variables to be comprehensive. Figure 6–5 shows the seven major elements identified by the *HCM* as significantly affecting transit capacity. Table 6–1 shows peak-period *rail* standards of service, which are based on number of passengers and crowding (measured in square feet allotted to each passenger.) These level-of-service standards roughly correspond to the six levels of comparable highway service.

A second problem is that, with the exception of rail systems, most transit operates in mixed traffic; transit service standards must therefore take account of the movement of both people and vehicles. For those transit modes that operate on the highway system, standards reflecting both person-carrying and vehicle-carrying capacity are crucial.

At-grade transit services, generally buses and trolleys, create particular calculation problems. They are larger than autos, and their stopping and starting can significantly reduce the level of service on streets; if existing highway lanes

Table 6–1   Passenger-loading standards and levels of service for urban rail transit vehicles.

Peak-hour level of service	Approximate sq. ft./ passenger	Approximate no. of passengers/seat
A	15.4 or more	0.00 to 0.65
B	15.2 to 10.0	0.66 to 1.00
C	9.9 to 7.5	1.01 to 1.50
D	6.6 to 5.0	1.51 to 2.00
E-1	4.9 to 4.0	2.01 to 2.50
E-2 (Maximum scheduled load)	3.9 to 3.3	2.51 to 3.00
F (Crush load)	3.2 to 2.6[a]	3.01 to 3.80

Note: Fifty percent standees reflects a load factor of 1.5 passengers per seat.

[a]The maximum crush load can be realized in a single car but not in every car on the train.

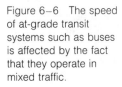

Figure 6–6   The speed of at-grade transit systems such as buses is affected by the fact that they operate in mixed traffic.

are removed to construct bus-only lanes, the level of service on the highway can fall correspondingly. In the calculation of total time and cost savings from alternative transportation options, losses to car drivers must be taken into account along with time and cost savings to transit riders. The *HCM* includes standards that allow planners to trade off vehicular capacity against passenger-carrying capacity. These standards, however, are not without controversy. There is disagreement, for example, over whether it is more important to facilitate transit by imposing costs on automobile drivers or to facilitate automobile traffic by imposing costs on transit.

A third problem with transit standards is the wide variation between the theoretical and observed capacity of a transit vehicle. Private cars have fairly low, but constant, occupancy, whereas occupancy of transit vehicles in the peak period varies widely by route and from one community to another. Just as significantly, it is difficult to predict the occupancy of future transit vehicles.

Should transit planners use theoretical or empirical occupancies when assessing transit options? This question has significant impact on current debates about urban rail transit systems. For example, there is now considerable public interest in light rail systems, which can have fairly high passenger-carrying capacity yet can cost significantly less than heavy rail systems. However, the overall cost-effectiveness of any rail system depends on the *actual* number of people that will be carried, a variable that is influenced by many design and policy considerations—from the number and location of stops to the extent of at-grade interaction with autos. Security, safety, convenience, and aesthetics all play a role in users' choices as well, but these features are not generally reflected in network models. Proponents of light rail systems believe that the network models should represent the potential rather than the observed rider time and cost features, because future systems will be safe, clean, reliable, and designed to meet current and projected land use patterns; in other words, future light rail systems will not suffer from the problems that have plagued the older systems and will therefore be the mode of choice for more travelers.

Resolution of this issue is difficult; whereas European cities have reported peak-hour maximum loads of up to 20,000 passengers, no U.S. light rail system has achieved volumes above 9,000 during the peak hour—and that was the older Pittsburgh system. (Although heavy rail volumes vary, the average U.S. peak-hour volume, excluding New York City, is about 12,000 passengers; New York's rail transit system carries over 40,000 passengers per hour during the peak on some lines.) On arterial streets, conventional buses with standing loads can carry more than 9,000 passengers per peak hour. The choice between heavy and light rail and other transit alternatives depends largely on whether theoretical or observed capacity is used and on actual cost differences.

Supply-side problems   Transportation planners face serious difficulties in matching supply to demand. First, they must estimate the costs of various supply options in the face of a number of unknowns. Choosing the most cost-effective alternative is difficult when so many cost and other variables may change—from inflation and interest rates to projected land use patterns. Second, providing supply may, of itself, change demand in ways that cannot be predicted. When travel patterns develop as predicted, planners often see this as an indication that their tools work; it may, however, be a self-fulfilling prophecy. For example, building a highway between two points might encourage people to go where they would not otherwise have gone, but it is difficult either to prove or to depend on this. Third, the effects of highways and transit systems are not always easy to measure in dollars or minutes. Even features traditionally quantified—like travel time savings—can be controversial; for example, a bank president, a teenager, a schoolteacher, and a retired person may each place a different

Figure 6–7   A car in Buffalo's light rail system.

Figure 6–8   Crystal City Station, part of Washington, D.C.'s heavy rail system.

value on time; and each may take a different view of time spent *waiting* for a bus versus time spent *riding* a bus.

Over the years the cost-benefit analysis of transportation alternatives has been expanded considerably to encompass a number of additional cost features—the environment, energy consumption, and neighborhood preservation, among others—but this has made the analysis even more complex. This complexity may make the results difficult for the public and political decisionmakers to work with or understand.

The complexity and ambiguity of demand models and the difficulty of analyzing supply options, combined with a growing public recognition that local government cannot continue to build new highway or transit systems, have encouraged the development of new approaches to meeting demand.

New approaches to regional planning

Many factors have created the need for new or modified approaches to regional transportation planning: the difficulty of achieving political consensus on region-wide developments; the growing complexity of regional supply and demand models and the expense of maintaining them; the need for immediate responses to pressing transportation problems; pressure from political decisionmakers; and growing maintenance and rehabilitation needs. Moreover, all of these pressures have been exacerbated by dwindling federal and state assistance for planning and for infrastructure construction and maintenance.

Planners have generally responded in three ways: First, as federal funds have become less available for needed transportation improvements—however need is defined—planners have sought ways to make the existing transport infrastructure more efficient and effective. Second, planners have sought new and innovative ways either to supply or to finance the transportation services and structures that still are required, including the active involvement of the private sector. Third, planners have developed new "quick-response" planning tools to augment, or even occasionally replace, the regional comprehensive modeling process. Each of these three approaches will be described in the sections that follow.

Increasing system efficiency

Planners are faced with two realities: first, money is no longer readily available to expand the existing highway and transit infrastructure; second, the existing system in many areas is inefficiently used. Because facilities are generally built to provide a high level of service during the peak period, they are often underused during the rest of the day. Even during the peak, inefficiencies in traffic flow and highway entry can reduce the effective capacity of the system.

There are a number of ways to redirect and redistribute travel demand to make better use of facilities or increase effective capacity: (1) *reduce* overall demand; (2) *redirect* demand to lower usage periods; (3) expand capacity through minor physical road and transit *improvements*; and (4) *increase occupancy* in the vehicles that use the system during peak periods.

The methods that fall into these categories range from road tolls on expressways during the peak period to encouraging transit and carpool use by offering reduced fares and creating special bus and carpool lanes on freeways. Before 1983 the federal government mandated that regional planning agencies prepare Transportation System Management (TSM) plans that considered which of the possible methods could and should be used. Figure 6–10 shows a number of potential TSM actions for cities of varying sizes. Although all regions must consider the implications of such options, they are not required to produce a TSM plan.

Many of these measures hold great promise, but there can be substantial

Figure 6-9 High-occupancy vehicles benefit from the use of highway express lanes.

Figure 6-10 Transportation System Management actions by goals category.

Mobility dominant goal	Conservation dominant goal
Larger cities	
"Add-a-lane" preferential facilities for high-occupancy vehicles (HOV)	"Add-a-lane" preferential facilities for high-occupancy vehicles (HOV)
Preferential parking for HOV	Preferential parking for HOV
Ride-sharing promotion	Ride-sharing promotion
Improvements in local bus fares, routes, and schedules	Improvements in local bus fares, routes, and schedules
Park-ride with express bus	Park-ride with express bus
Express bus operators	Express bus operators
Bicycle paths	Bicycle paths
Signal improvements	Ramp metering with HOV bypass
Pedestrian separations	Automobile restricted zones with HOV preference
One-way streets	Exclusive HOV ramps
Reversible streets	Through traffic restrictions with HOV preference
Turn restrictions	"Take-a-lane" HOV preferential facilities
Ramp metering	Parking duration limit with HOV preference
Channelization and widening	Facility and area tolls and taxes with HOV preference
Curb-parking restrictions	Parking duration pricing with HOV preference
Bus-stop relocation	
Loading zones	
Speed limits	
Truck enhancements controls	
Work rescheduling	
Motorists' aids, advisories	
Smaller, less congested cities	
Ride-sharing promotion	Ride-sharing promotion
Improvements in local bus fares, routes, and schedules	Improvements in local bus fares, routes, and schedules
Bicycle paths	Bicycle paths
Signal improvements	
Pedestrian separations	
One-way streets	
Turn restrictions	
Right turn on red	
Channelization and widening	
Curb-parking restrictions	
Bus-stop relocation	
Loading zones	
Speed limits	

difference between their theoretical possibilities and their observed impact. For example, of the TSM elements listed in Figure 6–10, increased carpooling would most reduce congestion on roadways; there is little controversy about this assertion. The average U.S. vehicle occupancy rate is a very low 1.4 and is even lower during the peak-period work commute trip. Increasing that figure to even two people per car would have a far more profound impact than *tripling* transit ridership, and it would do so without expensive capital acquisition. In practice, however, a range of programs designed to increase carpooling, from preferential highway use and parking schemes to regional computer matching programs, have had substantial effects only in very special circumstances; between 1970 and 1980 average U.S. vehicle occupancy rates actually went down.

Road pricing measures, which have substantially reduced congestion in experiments in Singapore and Hong Kong, could also significantly affect highway use in U.S. cities by reducing overall travel demand and by encouraging travel during off-peak times. Yet such tolls are politically controversial, because they raise equity questions: critics argue that they will leave the highways open only to those wealthy enough to pay the tolls.

Some of the measures shown in Fig. 6–10 have been effective in reducing congestion in a small area or in making better use of an existing street facility. Clearly, some of these measures are useful tools for local planners dealing with site-specific congestion. Although pedestrian malls and auto-restricted areas have been used effectively in many European cities as well as in the United States, such methods rarely have regional impact and may, in fact, simply redistribute congestion to adjoining neighborhoods.

Jurisdictional and institutional problems can arise in the planning and carrying out of such measures regionwide. The MPO, which is required to consider alternatives to rail or highway extensions, is rarely in a position to put any of them into effect. For example, parking strategies and preferential carpool treatment are generally the responsibility of municipal governments; strategies that involve reduced transit fares or higher levels of transit service require active cooperation from transit agencies. Although institutional arrangements are changing to facilitate such cooperation, implementing TSM measures is often a difficult organizational problem.

TSM measures, like major highway and transit extensions, do not benefit all participants equally; this has been one of the stumbling blocks to increased institutional cooperation. Although many measures would undoubtedly reduce peak-period congestion, thereby reducing the need for additional facilities, some affected parties might not receive direct benefits. Downtown merchants, for example, have traditionally opposed TSM measures, such as street preference for buses or parking strategies that significantly limit downtown parking, because they fear that business will be reduced. Many believe that strategies to decrease congestion will do more harm to sales than the congestion itself does.

Implementing TSM measures, which often have low capital costs, poses a real challenge to planners; in many ways it is easier to gain support for and to implement major highway or transit projects. Measures to increase use of existing facilities often have to be packaged together to achieve success; road pricing or parking space limitations, for example, would be disruptive and inequitable if not matched by increased transit service and preferential treatment for carpools. The task of planners is to fashion complicated solutions, gain acceptance for all components, organize institutional actors, and generate public support.

The impact of any TSM package on congestion and the use of existing facilities is city- and even site-specific. Although theoretical guidelines can be used to gauge potential impact, it is the planner's job to develop a locally effective package. For example, a planner can count on active transit agency cooperation for a restrictive downtown parking plan only if the transit system already has the capability to provide needed service during the peak period; many transit systems currently face the same peak-period congestion that highways do.

The political impact of the planner's package is no less city- and site-specific. Although it may be theoretically more efficient to convert an underused lane of highway traffic to a carpool or bus lane, political reality may dictate that a planner can do so only on *new* freeways. Not surprisingly, political support of complex TSM packages may be difficult to achieve. Although a package of TSM measures might bring important public benefits, it is not likely to create individual winners; this enables those who oppose the measures (or some part of them) to create more effective opposition. Large-scale capital projects, in contrast, often have substantial winners, such as the building trade unions, who actively lobby for them—even if the users who receive time and congestion savings do not.

Nontraditional supply approaches

The traditional approach to regional transportation planning focused only on the public component of any transportation system—the component directly supplied by the public sector. Today planners are working also with "hybrid" options, transport systems that combine public and private components. These newer supply options, described as paratransit, generally combine private auto characteristics with transit characteristics; they include carpooling, vanpooling, and subscription bus services (group service bought in advance) as well as taxis and demand-responsive transit services. In many cases, paratransit services are cheaper than comparable services provided by the public sector alone, although this varies.

Paratransit services can encompass a wide range of transportation modes. Although the public often interprets the term to refer to some kind of small vehicle, paratransit is defined by its service characteristics, not by the vehicles it employs.

Paratransit services are appealing for a number of reasons. First, they are automatically TSM measures when they increase the use of either existing modes or facilities, as group taxis and subscription buses do. Second, such services are often more tailored to the needs of today's families than are fixed-route, conventional transit services. Many paratransit modes carry more passengers than do private cars and still offer enough flexibility and convenience to be attractive to nontransit users. Third, paratransit services are often useful to people prevented by financial circumstances or disability from using general public systems. For example, people with low incomes currently use conventional private taxis for more of their trips than do those with higher incomes, possibly because it is cheaper to use a full-fare taxi occasionally than to own and operate a car. People with disabilities have used private wheelchair carriers and taxis for many years. In the past ten years, the public sector also has used paratransit providers to serve designated groups of elderly and handicapped people.

Paratransit services are not inherently public or private; a public transit agency may provide demand-responsive services for elderly people or contract with private bus companies for suburban subscription services. However, many paratransit providers *are* private operators, and local governments that wish to increase privatization of service have been particularly interested in paratransit for that reason.

Increasing the role of the private sector

Planners have responded to increasing financial constraints by involving the private sector in the delivery of services formerly provided by the public sector. Growing interest in paratransit services comes at the same time that planners are considering private provision of *all* types of transportation services traditionally operated by the public sector.

Privatization is also tied to recent federal emphasis on reducing government restrictions on private transit modes. At the local level, some communities have reduced the regulation of private taxi and other paratransit operators; this has been advocated as a way to increase the number of such vehicles on the road, thereby reducing the need for additional, public-sector transit and highway expenditures.

Increasing the role of the private sector in service delivery generally takes one of two forms: (1) free-market service provision or (2) public contracting for private-service delivery—where desirable services cannot be provided at a profit by the private sector. The term *privatization* does not always refer to the first of these alternatives; clearly, some traditionally public services cannot be provided at socially desirable levels by the private sector at a profit. There are instances, however, in which private operators can and do make profits by operating along certain routes or providing certain services, sometimes charging in excess of public transit fares. In such cases, planners are questioning whether government ought to expend scarce resources to duplicate existing services. For example, a number of private operators provide express bus service into Manhattan from suburban New Jersey and Connecticut. In the paratransit realm, several old jitney services legally ply their trade on selected routes in Atlantic City and San Francisco; there is evidence that illegal taxi and jitney operations offer similar services in other U.S. cities.

Most public officials are unwilling to allow the private sector to provide service only where they can make a profit; although only certain routes are potentially profitable, many socially desirable routes may not be. Moreover, the give-and-take of a purely competitive transportation system might produce unreliable service and incomplete coverage. Another objection to free-market service provision is that poor or handicapped people will not be able to afford privately provided services. One way to get around this problem is to make subsidies to such riders a matter of public policy. The subsidy would go directly to the riders, allowing them to chose their own transportation alternative. The government need not provide the operator with public funds, a strategy that, in effect, gives everyone, needy or not, a public subsidy.

Often, private operators can supply needed transit or paratransit services more cheaply than other alternatives but not at a profit. In such cases, public agencies and governments may contract for transit or paratransit services; directly or indirectly, a public-sector subsidy makes up the difference between revenues and costs, including profit.

The most common traditional or line-haul *transit* services contracted for are express bus services and suburban or downtown circulation systems.

Contract *paratransit* services usually fall into four major categories:

1. Demand-responsive or flexibly routed services in low-density areas; Phoenix and Ann Arbor have such arrangements.
2. Feeder services to traditional line-haul transit systems; San Diego and Memphis have experimented with these services.
3. Demand-responsive services for special target groups such as elderly or handicapped people; such systems are common throughout the U.S.
4. User-side subsidy programs that provide the rider with vouchers that may be redeemed by any participating taxi or paratransit provider; Milwaukee has one of the oldest and most successful programs.

Subsidies to providers can take several forms: The provider can charge the public agency for costs only in excess of fares received; or the public sector may hire the operator as a contractor, paying all costs and retaining the fares. The contractor may be allowed to continue service to its regular "private" customers, or the public agency may require service (vehicles and drivers) completely dedicated to public provision.

Like every other transportation issue, privatization is not without controversy. Although advocates argue that the private sector is inherently more efficient—and thus less costly—than the public sector in delivering identical services, most economists believe that it is only competition that keeps the private operator efficient. If one private provider is always awarded a contract, or other operators do not come forward to bid on contract services, it is doubtful that private service provision will remain either more efficient or cheaper. Because transit services have not generally been provided privately and competitively, only larger metropolitan areas may have enough private operators to compete—and to remain in business if a public contract is not awarded.

Critics have also questioned whether the public and private sectors provide the same level of service. Supporters of privatization argue that the private sector may provide even better service, as it tries to develop different markets, perhaps among people never before willing to forgo use of their cars. Opponents argue that the major savings achieved by private operators are in labor costs, and that these savings come at the expense of hiring nonprofessional, unreliable, and even dangerous drivers. Moreover, they argue that private vehicles are often poorly maintained and underinsured.

Experience suggests that contracts with private providers must specify performance and driver standards and must include backup options to keep the providers' costs reasonable and to guard against a failure to perform. Moreover, there must be a public-sector employee whose job it is to monitor the contract, and that person's time must be considered a cost of obtaining contract service.

Interestingly, the possibility of private competition may keep costs down in the *public* sector; unions keep costs down for fear that the service will be contracted out. Similarly, the ability of the public sector to take over should it become necessary can keep costs down in the private sector; in Houston, the private express bus company providing contract service to the Houston MTA lowered its costs by 20 percent when the MTA purchased enough buses to provide the express bus services themselves if they had to.

New financial strategies

The management of demand, TSM, paratransit, and privatization all have one thing in common: they are means of making the best use of existing resources. The environment of transportation planners today is one of limited resources—financial and otherwise. Planners are finding that their task often includes finding the financial support necessary to put projected plans into operation or to maintain those that already exist. In response to financial constraints, planners have begun to obtain substantial financial commitments from the private sector for the construction and operation of highway and transit improvements; they have learned also to evaluate alternative bond financing methods.

A recent trend is to allow or even require private developers and entities to pay some or all of the cost of constructing (or rehabilitating) transportation facilities. Private individuals have always been charged for local transportation improvements that directly benefit their property, such as curbs and gutters, but cofinancing by the private sector is a new and promising approach.

The private sector has recognized that public infrastructure improvements can in some cases increase the value of land and developments far in excess of tax revenues that would be returned to the local governments making those investments. Moreover, given the public sector's lack of funds, many developers realize that their projects may never get off the ground if they do not cover some or all of the infrastructure costs.

Cofinancing of transportation investments is not always voluntary. Several states, most notably California and Florida, have enacted legislation that permits localities to charge developers not only for on-site transportation improvements but for infrastructure additions needed in the entire regional transportation system. The courts have generally upheld such measures if developers are asked to pay only for *additional* improvements whose necessity is directly created by their development; they cannot be asked to share the cost of an existing structure if capacity is already available.

Because of such court rulings, many planners are developing models that attempt to predict the regional as well as the local transportation impact of residential or commercial development. For example, will level of service on a highway corridor fall from A to C once a development is established? In a related effort, planners are developing financial models to evaluate when and where impacts will be felt and how to match fees to those impacts.

The appropriateness of either voluntary or mandatory cofinancing is site specific. Low-growth areas that wish to encourage commercial or industrial development can harm themselves by adding to the costs of those enterprises. Communities worried about affordable housing may question the eventual impact of fees and charges for infrastructure on the cost of houses in the affected areas.

In considering cofinancing as an option, planners must be alert so that it does not radically change the priority of highways and transit facilities to be constructed. If a transportation project sought by developers is not scheduled for public construction in a given time period, it is usually because the regional planning process has generated a Transportation Improvement Program that gives higher priority to other projects. If projects are taken from the bottom of the list because cofinancing is available, meritorious proposals, originally rated higher but without such funding, will be displaced.

Streamlined analytical procedures

Traditional regional transportation planning methods were designed to evaluate regional transportation systems and to indicate aggregate travel movements. The lengthy process described earlier in this chapter took from one to three years to provide answers to local decisionmakers, and the complexity of the models often made the results too complicated, as well as too late, to be of help in deciding pressing local policy issues.

At the end of the 1970s, the National Cooperative Highway Research Program, as well as many metropolitan planning agencies, began developing travel estimation procedures that could give analytical responses to important policy questions in a matter of a few months rather than several years. The impetus for the research came from evidence that MPOs were shifting emphasis away from long-range, regional capital facility planning to short-range, subregional highway and transit improvements.

Although regions vary in the extent to which they use any given set of procedures, a body of travel estimation methods is developing that gives rapid answers to fairly proscribed planning questions. These methods generally supplement the traditional four-step procedure (trip generation, trip distribution, modal split, and traffic assignment). All of the streamlined methods simplify the computerized procedure by reducing the need for local calibration where there is evidence that important parameters are transferable among regions. Additionally, some methods actually substitute hand calculations for extensive computer modeling. Attempts are also made to reduce data input requirements and to produce output in a format that is useful to the public and to decisionmakers.

In addition, mathematical models at various scales and levels of detail, from predicting noise to gauging the capacity of intersections, are being used where the regional models do not directly address a local policy issue or have not done so recently.

The techniques that have been developed are generally called *sketch planning*. Armed with these new tools, regional planners are increasingly limiting their focus to one or several major corridors in an area rather than continuing to run large-scale models to predict regionwide changes and trends. At the same time, planners often consider far more alternatives but in less detail than the traditional supply approaches called for. For example, a broad range of transit, transit and highway, and highway-only alternatives might be considered to meet projected demand in a given corridor.

Sketch planning is thought to be appropriate for cities with populations from 100,000 to 3 million that have one or more concentrated travel corridors. The methods are useful for both short- and long-range analyses. Planners can begin by screening a large number of options according to simplified criteria; several highly rated alternatives can be chosen for more detailed analysis or what has been called "meso planning."

Although sketch and meso planning are more limited approaches that might seem to be a regression in purely methodological terms, they do address both political and technical problems in the comprehensive process. By simplifying both the assumptions and the methods underlying the analyses, these approaches clarify, for concerned professionals and elected officials, the planning process itself and the outputs of that process. The need to predict the impact of hundreds, if not thousands, of private-market land use decisions throughout an entire region, as well as their social, economic, and environmental effects, is obviated. Efforts are focused instead on trying to understand what will happen only in a given corridor of land that is already thought to be the site of planned development.

The local transportation planning process

In many important ways local transportation planners and traffic engineers undertake many of the same processes as those planning at the regional or metropolitan level: they estimate future demand or current travel need and match that need to cost-effective supply options. Unfortunately, the projections and activities of local transportation planners are not always coordinated with the regional planning process. Individual development projects are often approved at the local level without regard for the cumulative or regional impact.

Meeting high demand on local arterials—commonly thought of as *congestion*—is a frequent planning problem for both highway and transit systems because the demand for both facilities tends to be concentrated in narrow periods of the day. The ultimate goal of local transportation planning is to fashion an uncongested network of highways and transit services that will link neighborhoods to other neighborhoods and commercial areas.

The activities in which local transportation departments engage vary widely. Figure 6–11 shows the organization of the Dade County, Florida, Department of Traffic and Transportation. Are all of the activities in which transportation agencies are engaged considered "transportation planning?" It is difficult to draw the line between a traffic engineer and a transportation planner; increasingly there is significant "crossover" of specialists in both professions. In the rest of this section, the more traditional planning functions will be discussed.

Estimating demand

Like their regional counterparts, local planners attempt to predict the number, kind, and distribution of trips associated with various land use patterns and building types. However, there are two important differences: first, local planners are often concerned with individual parcels of land and with specific land uses.

Second, local planners can use a compendium of empirical information as a guide to determine travel patterns created by specific uses of a parcel of land.

The Institute of Transportation Engineers (ITE) publishes and updates a manual that gives ranges in the number of trips generated by and attracted to ten major types of land uses and several hundred subcategories of those land uses. The ten major categories are port and terminal, industrial and agricultural, residential, lodging, recreational, institutional, medical, office, retail, and services.

The ITE bases its findings on empirical observations made in as many cities as possible; it urges cities to use standard recording and observation methods and to report their findings for use in the manual. Unfortunately, the ITE has many observations for some types of land use and very few for other types. Moreover, observations for some types of land use are all based on one part of the country or in one type of city.

Local planners can easily use the ITE *Trip Generation Manual*, with or without additional data from local studies, to determine the demand for travel that will be created by a new or altered land use on one site, along an arterial corridor, or in an entire neighborhood. These demands can then be matched to cost-effective supply options.

Supply

Urban road facilities are generally grouped into four categories according to level of service and function: expressway, arterial, collector, and local. (Such facilities are covered in the *Highway Capacity Manual*, which was described in the section on analyzing regional supply options.) Local planners can use these standards to define the type of road facilities that could be constructed or provided to meet projected demand, given policy decisions on the appropriate level of service.

Local planners are also interested in providing pedestrian facilities; Again, the ultimate choice of type of facility depends not only on potential demand but also on policies on appropriate levels of service. Local transit planners, working in cooperation with traffic planners, can use similar standards to determine whether projected demand is high enough to give priority treatment to transit.

What does the future hold?

Transportation planning is a growing, developing, exciting profession. Planners often face conflicts between accepted societal goals such as adequate transportation on the one hand and environmental or community protection on the other. Highways that would benefit the community as a whole may disrupt a neighborhood. Roads may be badly needed in growing residential areas sited on environmentally sensitive land.

The uncertainty of the land use–transportation equation challenges local planners doing short-term work as well as regional planners making long-range predictions. There will always be substantial public debate over whether new transport facilities serve growth that would have occurred anyway—or whether those facilities create the growth. The highway versus transit controversy will always be embedded in this debate, as will the argument over the desirable city form—centralized or decentralized.

The need to resolve these issues is the core of transportation planning. Transportation planners will continue to be asked to resolve conflicts about future land use, an issue that demands political resolution. Transportation planners will continue to be asked to respond to questions that can have significant impact on local decision making: What will cars or gasoline cost ten or twenty years in the future? How much will those prices matter to households that have experienced steadily increasing real incomes?

Individual planners have their own responses to these issues. Planners who have been trained in the more technical approach to transportation planning often feel strongly that political issues should not affect their work. Other transportation planners believe that the only way to ensure that political bodies accept transportation plans is to incorporate efforts to resolve political conflict into the planning process.

Ethical issues also arise in transportation planning. Increasingly, planners are

Figure 6–11
Organization of the Dade County, Florida, Department of Traffic and Transportation.

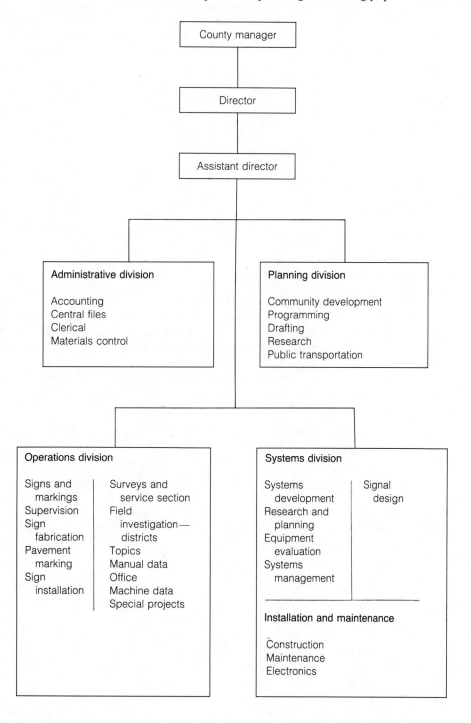

being asked to produce demand or cost estimates for transportation facilities that are strongly desired by political leaders. By manipulating the assumptions underlying the models (for example, by assuming a large increase in population or in the price of cars or gasoline) it is sometimes possible to obtain the desired results. What should transportation planners, whether in the public or the private sector, do about such pressures?

Ethical issues in forecasting

Technical experts are often employed by agencies which advocate particular solutions to certain problems: . . . highways vs. rapid transit in urban transportation, and so on. A forecaster might be in the employ of an engineering firm which received a small contract to estimate the need for a bridge. If the bridge is shown to be justified, additional consulting fees for design and engineering may produce hundreds of times the income derived from the preparation of the forecast itself.

It is indeed difficult to withstand pressures to produce self-serving forecasts which are cloaked in the guise of technical objectivity. . . . Advocates of particular positions gain strength for their arguments by virtue of the supposedly "unbiased" technical analysis which they can cite. And politicians who finally make resource allocations calmly accept forecasts which confirm their particular preconceptions with far less critical review than those who do not.

Source: Martin Wachs, "Ethical Dilemmas in Forecasting for Public Policy," in Martin Wachs, ed., *Ethics in Planning*, (Rutgers, NJ: The State University of New Jersey, 1985, 255–256).

There are additional pressures on the purely technical component of the transportation process. While a transportation project may benefit the community as a whole, it often benefits or costs some groups far more than others—groups that may wish to influence the planning process. In the political debate that follows, there is often considerable argument over the assumptions and data used in the planning process.

The most exciting and challenging part of transportation planning comes from the necessity for planners to be technical specialists and social scientists—while operating in a highly political environment.

Part three: Urban design and land use regulation

7 Urban design

Designing a city is much easier than persuading other people to take the design seriously or to carry it out consistently. Some of the most famous city designs were created in isolation, either as ideal cities or as visions of the way a city should look decades in the future: Filarete's Sforzinda, Ledoux's Chaux, Le Corbusier's Ville Contemporaine, the Archigram Group's Plug-In City. Such designs have often been influential, but usually in ways their authors did not intend. The nature of cities has proved too complex to be grasped in a single image, and the pace of social, technological, and economic change has been too rapid for any urban design concept to remain valid indefinitely.

Because city design is difficult, however, does not mean that it should not be done. The origins of the planning profession in the United States at the beginning of the twentieth century were closely tied to the City Beautiful movement. The design and construction of new civic centers, parks, and boulevards were part of beautification plans for entire cities. Gradually, however, the design aspects of planning came to be deemphasized. Planning became a branch of municipal engineering, and urban design decisions came to be seen as subjective judgments that were inappropriate for government to make. When interventionist design returned, it was in the context of slum clearance and urban renewal, and intervention was confined to those parts of the central city that had seriously deteriorated. The tower in the park, the design most characteristic of modernist architecture, was usually chosen for slum clearance and urban renewal projects. Seeing urban design primarily as a means of urban transformation was closely related to social philosophies built into the doctrine of modernist architecture.

Not until the mid-1960s were the entire city and metropolitan region again perceived as appropriate subjects for urban design, and this shift was accompanied by a fundamental change in emphasis. The search for principles that would shape all city design decisions, a search that had characterized both the City Beautiful movement and modernist architecture, was replaced by an awareness that a city is not designed by making pictures of how it should look at some indefinite point in the future. Although a coherent design concept is important, it can become a reality only through incremental steps that make design part of daily decision making. Cities are designed and redesigned continuously by the actions of real estate entrepreneurs and government agencies. To shape the city, urban designers must understand, and then learn to change, how these actions take place. It is of critical importance that urban designers participate in important decisions that shape the design of cities, as a failure to understand the design implications of their decisions does not absolve investors or public authorities of responsibility for the results. The path to a designed city can only be through these thousands of individual design decisions; and the ultimate goal may change many times, in keeping with the pace and pattern of urban change.

It is easy to think of places in any metropolitan area where design could have been much better if someone had dealt with the issues soon enough: the downtown street lined with new buildings, each with no relation to the next; the small, historic church jostled by the giant, mirror-glass office building; the neighborhood of houses broken by an apartment tower and its parking garage.

Where all development is new, the failure of the parts to add up to a coherent whole is particularly poignant. A highway interchange may have the equivalent of a small city center within its four quadrants: a hotel, office buildings, garden apartments, and a shopping mall; but each structure is separate, and a car is often needed to go from one to another. In an inner-city urban-renewal district there may be publicly aided housing on one corner, a school next door, a fire station down the street, and a block of store across the way, all built at much the same time with no functional or aesthetic coordination among them.

Such urban design failures are the by-product of otherwise perfectly rational decisions. Developers compete with each other for the advantage of individual properties; they purchase land secretly to conceal their intentions from competitors. For developers, coordinating the design of a city or district is a subsidiary issue at best. Government agencies are concerned primarily with carrying out their own responsibilities efficiently. They usually finance housing or build new streets with little thought about relationships to other private and public investments.

The role and education of urban designers

Somehow, the urban designer has to mediate and strive for harmony among competing private interests and the various imperatives of public programs. Urban designers may be either staff or consultants; they may work for government agencies, developers, or nonprofit groups. In any urban design situation, however, the powers of local government to regulate development and to provide development incentives are of fundamental importance.

Many urban designers can be found in planning agencies, because this is where zoning and street mapping powers are usually administered. Urban designers review subdivision plans and planned unit developments as well as other proposals that require some change in zoning or streets.

An urban renewal agency is another likely location for urban design staff. Cities today rarely subsidize the cost of acquiring land as they did when federal money was available. However, the power to assemble parcels of land is a powerful development incentive, because investors are unable to put together some urban projects without it. Land assemblage, as well as securing development in the public's economic interest, can help improve city design. If the government is the landowner, even for a brief time, it can put design conditions on the sale to private investors.

The writing of environmental impact statements requires an understanding of urban design, and the environmental impact procedure requires that developers and government agencies at least go through the motions of large-scale development coordination and design.

Urban designers help administer historic-district regulations, reviewing development proposals and making suggestions particularly when new buildings are being built in a historic area.

Some urban designers also work with local communities, either on assignment from their planning departments or through storefront community design centers in neighborhoods.

Real estate investors use urban design consultants to prepare large-scale development plans for residential communities, office parks, and downtown mixed-use developments, particularly when planning approvals involving design considerations are required. When development companies keep a long-term interest in a large project, they need to exercise urban design control over each portion of the project to maintain an appropriate level of design quality and to preserve the value of unbuilt parcels.

There are not as many urban designers as there should be in public works and transportation agencies, which have important urban design responsibilities but often operate in an atmosphere inimical to urban design. It would also be useful for more people trained in urban design to work for major investors in development, such as large life insurance companies. Real estate market trends and the quality of construction are carefully evaluated by permanent lenders; urban design considerations rarely receive the same attention.

However, people with urban design titles can be found in most planning and development agencies and in private consulting offices. A few people trained and experienced in urban design have begun to reach the higher, policy-making positions in local government and real estate investment companies. A modern practice of urban design has evolved that is beginning to produce some effective results, although a visit to any city or region makes it clear that there is no reason for complacency.

How should urban designers be educated? Design is a discipline that takes time to learn. It seems to use aspects of the mind not required in conventional academic subjects. Making a design differs fundamentally from analyzing what is right or wrong with the design after it is on paper. The designer has to be able both to postulate a design idea and then to decide whether it makes sense in a specific situation. Architecture, the most complex design discipline, is probably the best training. Landscape architects, however, learn techniques of managing the environment that are usually not taught to architects. Design can also be taught in a planning studio, although there is a danger that planners will never study either the internal arrangement of buildings or the modification of landscape and thus will not fully understand the range of design alternatives.

Once a person is proficient in design, the next step is to learn to make design decisions at the scale of the district, city, or region, either by participation in a studio or through a professional internship. Since most city design ideas are carried out by private developers and government agencies, it follows that an urban designer needs to understand real estate economics, public administration, and the legal framework that gives government the power to intervene or regulate matters related to city design. Case studies, also an important part of urban design education, acquaint students with the experience of one locality so that it can be applied in similar situations elsewhere.

Urban design theory: Four traditions of urban design

There is no single, coherent set of urban design theories that can provide a basis for all practical decisions—any more than there is a single theory of architecture or landscape design. Instead there are four well-established traditions: monumental city design, the garden city and garden suburb, the modernist city, and the megastructure, or the city as building. They have evolved in counterpoint to the evolution of urban areas themselves, from the walled cities of the preindustrial period to the spreading metropolis of today.

Monumental city design

The monumental, tree-lined boulevards, groups of columned civic buildings, and the art museum in the park to be found in many American cities are usually a legacy of the City Beautiful movement inspired by the World's Columbian Exposition held in Chicago in 1893. Perhaps the most famous planning document of the period is Daniel Burnham and Edward Bennett's 1909 Plan of Chicago, which imposed a boulevard system over local streets, laid out great waterfront parks and splendid civic buildings, and attempted to shape private development as well.

The Chicago Plan was strongly influenced by the extensive alterations carried out in Paris under the administration of Baron Georges Eugène Haussmann, the Prefect of the Seine during the reign of Napoleon III in the 1850s and 1860s.

Haussmann was able to impose a uniform architecture on Parisian boulevards because he could assume the limitation on building height that had been established since the beginning of history: the average building could be no taller than the number of stories that people would willingly walk up stairs. The invention of the elevator and the development of the steel frame made the skyscraper possible and took away one of the basic assumptions of monumental design.

No one knew more about the tall building than Daniel Burnham, whose firm had been among the pioneers of skyscraper architecture. The illustrations to the Chicago Plan show streets of tall buildings all at the same height, but the only controlling mechanism suggested in the Plan to make such uniformity possible is a vague injunction for "teamwork" among architects. The legal opinion in the Plan includes a discussion of condemnation as a means to achieve the design, but that would have made the city government the prime developer for the whole planned area, a radical idea even today. No one seems to have made a connection between the height limits in the design and regulatory powers of local government. Washington, D.C., had height limits at this time, as did the fire codes of other cities. Only four years later, work was to begin on New York City's zoning regulations, but no one sought to use zoning controls to achieve the uniformity demanded by monumental design.

As a result, the Burnham plan effectively shaped Chicago's public parks and buildings and the construction of some major streets, but it did not provide the comprehensive city design described in the illustrations.

Monumental city design has never been easy to implement. It evolved as a response to new concepts of space created by the rediscovery of perspective during the Renaissance. Ideas that first appeared in painting were readily translated into stage sets and then gardens, but the transition into city design required special circumstances. The long, straight streets that Pope Sixtus V caused to be built in Rome connected places of pilgrimmage across what were then vast, vacant stretches of the city. The great axial perspectives of Versailles asserted the symbolic domination of Louis XIV over the natural landscape, not over the crowded, twisting streets of Paris. In the reconstruction of London after the great fire of 1666, Christopher Wren sought to use long, straight vistas and avenues radiating from *ronds points*, but the complexities of the necessary property exchanges defeated him.

Incremental development of city squares brought Renaissance spatial concepts to cities by the eighteenth century, but Pierre Charles L'Enfant's plan for Washington, D.C., drawn during George Washington's administration, was one of the first large-scale monumental designs for cities to be carried out. However, it took a long time for the city to grow into the plan. Early visitors like Charles Dickens found an absurd contrast between the scale of the plan and the little, provincial city that had developed within it.

Monumental design principles made popular by the City Beautiful movement continued to be used through the 1930s for groups of governmental buildings and for college campuses. By the end of World War II, however, these principles had become discredited by their association with the architectural projects of Hitler and Mussolini and by the belief that modern architecture should sweep away the outmoded trappings of the past.

Modern architects continued to make use of monumental design principles, however, in default of other ideas about how to organize groups of buildings. For example, in 1964 the architects for the three principal components of New York's Lincoln Center for the Performing Arts agreed on a plaza with paving patterns modeled on Michelangelo's capitol in Rome and a central fountain placed on the axis of symmetry of the buildings. They also placed simplified colonnades on the plaza facades. Similarly the Pennsylvania Avenue Development

Plan for Washington, D.C., launched in 1967, is a design for a Haussmannesque boulevard.

More recently, as part of the change in architecture that is often referred to as "post modernism," there has been a great revival of interest in monumental city design ideas. In applying monumental concepts to cities, the major difficulty continues to be relating tall buildings and today's urban traffic to design concepts that were invented for the preindustrial city. One alternative is to inflate the scale of the whole architectural ensemble, a concept identified with the Barcelona architect Ricardo Bofill. Leon Krier is an articulate spokesman for a second viewpoint, which is that the tall building and the automobile were essentially mistakes and should be kept out of cities. A more moderate possibility is to set tall buildings in a context that could have been constructed in earlier centuries, an approach that responds more readily to monumental principles of organization and arrangement. The Fifth Avenue facades of New York's Rockefeller Center were designed on this principle: two pairs of six-story pavilions maintain a traditional-scale relationship with Fifth Avenue and frame the axes of the RCA and Associated Press building towers, which are set back behind them.

Garden suburbs and garden cities

Most suburban subdivisions embody the principles of the garden suburb, at least in a diluted form. The concept was already well defined by 1857, when Llewelyn Park, designed by Alexander Jackson Davis, was begun in what is now West Orange, New Jersey. Frederick Law Olmsted's 1868 design for Riverside, a railroad suburb of Chicago, is even more closely related to what came to be standard practice. In both suburbs, stretches of land were left clear for parks

Figure 7–1   Andrew Ellicott's drawing of Pierre Charles L'Enfant's plan for Washington, D.C., an example of monumental city design.

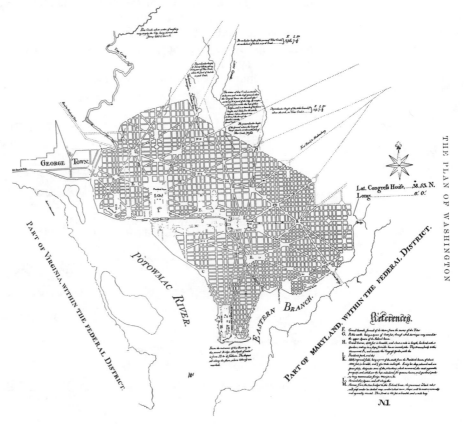

and greenways, and curving streets give access to somewhat irregularly shaped lots that are landscaped to provide a parklike setting for the houses.

The layout of the streets developed from the path system of English gardens, the embodiment of the picturesque sensibility. The picturesque in turn derived from two sources, Northern European landscape painting and the arrangement of Chinese gardens. In a picturesque garden the natural landscape was edited and recomposed to provide a series of changing views as the visitor moved along a carefully managed route.

The garden city, as opposed to the garden suburb, was the radical social proposal of Ebenezer Howard, who was not a designer or planner but a London courtroom stenographer. Howard invented the concept of self-contained, self-sufficient communities, surrounded by greenbelts and linked in clusters, that could serve as a substitute for the ever-spreading metropolis. A practical visionary, Howard was able to organize the construction of a prototype garden city, Letchworth, which started in 1903. The design for Letchworth, by Raymond Unwin and Barry Parker, drew on garden suburb prototypes, on model villages for farm workers, and on previous designs for model company towns. The result was a cottage vernacular that made Howard's radical social planning seem totally unthreatening.

In 1905, the designs developed for Letchworth were refined further for Hampstead Garden Suburb, where Unwin and Parker sought more architectural definition of open spaces and added the cul-de-sac to the vocabulary of winding streets. Hampstead was planned to have more upper-income residents than Letchworth; this circumstance provided opportunities for more elaborate buildings. The gifted architect Edwin Lutyens was responsible for the design of buildings in the central group, and other noted architects of the period contributed to an environment that was more distinguished than Letchworth. Hampstead, in its turn, had enormous influence on the design of other garden suburbs, such as Forest Hills Gardens in New York City. This development was one of the prototypes for the neighborhood unit, an idea defined by Clarence Perry, director of the Russell Sage Foundation, which sponsored Forest Hills Gardens.

A more systematic version of the cul-de-sac was employed at Radburn, a planned suburb in Fairlawn, New Jersey, designed in 1926 by Clarence Stein

Figure 7–2   British advertisements from the 1920s for Welwyn, a self-contained garden city.

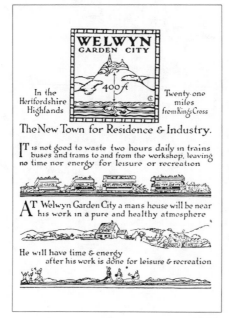

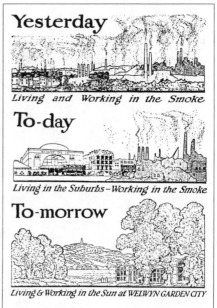

and Henry Wright. The Radburn separation of road traffic and pedestrian green-ways has become a standard element of planned unit developments.

There has been a recent revival of interest in the entire architectural vocabulary of the garden suburbs that were created in the earlier part of this century—in the house types and landscaping as well as in the road plans. The architect Robert A. M. Stern has been a notable advocate of this garden-suburb revival.

The garden city concept of planned, self-contained communities was widely adopted after World War II as a government policy to control the growth of large cities. Planned new towns were built in Sweden and Finland and were used as a major regional planning device in Great Britain and as a means of diverting the growth of Paris. Planned communities influenced by British exam-ples were constructed at Columbia, Maryland, and Reston, Virginia; the Irvine Ranch in southern California also has some resemblance to a British new town.

Figure 7–3   Plan for Radburn, New Jersey, a self-contained community on the model set forth by Ebenezer Howard.

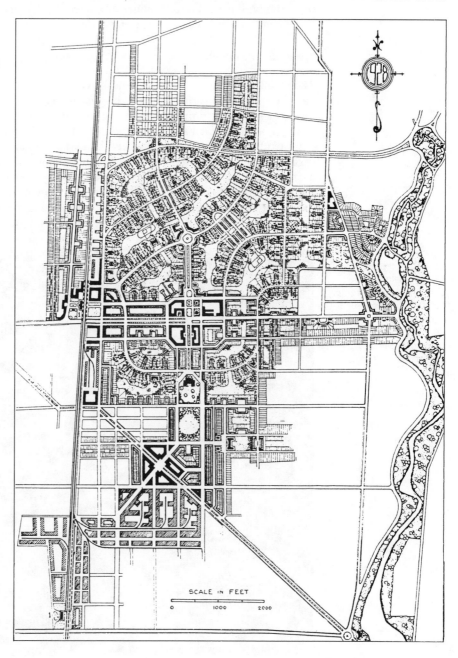

SCALE IN FEET

0   1000   2000

Under a now-defunct federal program, Title VII of the 1970 Urban Growth and New Communities Act, construction began on many other new towns, which were meant to be as self-sufficient as Howard's Garden Cities. However, most of these ventures failed because they could not survive the long wait for income sufficient to pay back the costs of land acquisition, roads, and infrastructure. A contributing factor was the absence of national planning policies like those that had supported the growth of planned new communities in Great Britain, France, and northern Europe. Although Congress had called for such policies as part of the 1970 act, the executive branch had never formulated them.

The Woodlands, a planned community on some 15,000 acres near the Houston airport, is one example of a recent, Howardesque development that is well on its way to completion, and other planned communities have been successful in resort areas. A commission to design at this scale is the ultimate urban design opportunity, but such opportunities are much more unusual than the chance to make constructive changes in existing cities.

Modernist city design

The idea that the modern city should be completely different from cities of the past has been a powerful influence on recent city design. The most compelling image of the modern metropolis is still the one created by Le Corbusier in his 1922 proposal for *La Ville Contemporaine*, a city of 3 million people.

Le Corbusier was not uninfluenced by earlier urban design ideas: The basic organization of his proposed city was monumental, with strong axial and diagonal avenues; and a greenbelt of the type advocated by Ebenezer Howard separated the managerial elite in the center of the city from workers and their factories located at the periphery. What was new about Le Corbusier's formulation was that it created a consistent urban image based on the tall building and the

Figure 7–4   The Loughborough Road housing estate in the London borough of Lambeth shows the strong influence of Le Corbusier's ideas on official design in England during the 1950s.

automobile. Le Corbusier was making drawings of limited-access highways long before any had actually been built; and he was illustrating his city designs with clusters of sixty-story office buildings when the tall building was still the exception in the United States and was hardly found in European cities at all. In later projects, Le Corbusier went on to define what came to be the elements of post–World War II urban renewal: highways sectioning existing cities into subdistricts; housing and office towers grouped in abstract formal relationships; buildings isolated from one another in a parklike setting from which all previous structures have been cleared; and stadiums, recreational facilities, or museums in parks along waterfronts.

Experimental subsidized housing projects in Europe, particularly in pre-Hitler Germany, were additional important sources of modernist urban design. The Weissenhof Housing Settlement in Stuttgart, planned under the direction of Ludwig Mies van der Rohe in 1927, was a demonstration of a unified architectural style of flat roofs, planar surfaces devoid of historical ornament, and boxlike building shapes. The Dammerstock district in Karlsruhe, planned by Walter Gropius in 1929, made use of a principle that emerged from several such projects to become almost a formula: Buildings should be sited for maximum exposure to sunlight and spaced so that they do not cast shadows on each other.

The ideals of modernist architecture and city design were promoted by the Congrès Internationaux d'Architecture Moderne (CIAM) and by historian-advocates like Sigfried Giedion, Nikolaus Pevsner, and J. M. Richards as a revolution against the architecture of the past. The CIAM's concepts of modernism were put forward so forcefully that they overwhelmed an alternative set of examples, equally modern, that were far more accepting of the existing city. Among these examples were Rockefeller Center, where tall buildings were fitted into the urban context, or the publicly subsidized Hillside Homes, designed by Clarence Stein in 1932 as a series of courtyards carefully related to surrounding streets.

The European modernist idea of separate buildings set in open space and oriented according to the compass became the standard for publicly subsidized housing, and the abstract, boxlike office or apartment tower set in plaza space is the underlying design idea behind most downtown development regulations in force today.

The recent reaction against the modernist vision of the city seeks to restore the street as a basic element of city design, to preserve older buildings and relate new structures to them, and to modify the boxlike shapes characteristic of modern architecture. Nonrevolutionary modern buildings by such architects as Raymond Hood or Clarence Stein are being looked at as models. Why is Rockefeller Center any less modern than the drawings of La Ville Contemporaine?

The megastructure, or the city as a building

The downtown atrium connected by pedestrian bridges to other downtown structures and the covered shopping mall are legacies of the megastructural approach to city design, which, during the 1960s and early 1970s, became almost a craze among urban designers, despite the impracticality of many of the design proposals.

The idea of cities as enormous structures has a long pedigree: royal palaces were often what amounted to self-contained cities, particularly when the loyalties of the populace were not certain. The great exhibition buildings of the nineteenth-century world's fairs were big enough to enclose many ordinary structures and were experienced as if they were enclosed city streets. These exhibition buildings, along with urban shopping arcades and department stores, were the ancestors of the modern shopping mall.

Around 1960 the idea of the city as a building became connected with the idea of cities of the future: cities of interchangeable capsules that could be plugged into immense urban frameworks, cities with new linear transportation systems, cities that could move under their own power or could be taken down and rebuilt in a new location. Interest in the megastructure was a reaction to the enormous urban growth that was going on at the same time. New and drastic measures seemed necessary to bring that growth under control, and for a time the megastructure seemed to many designers to be the right answer.

One problem with the megastructure was that it raised to a new level of difficulty the managerial and financial issues that had defeated so many new towns. To the land, grading, and infrastructure costs that must be borne during the initial stages of any large new development, the megastructure added the structural frameworks and vertical transportation systems that had to be in place before "plug-in" development could begin. Nor was it easy to progress incrementally; the whole idea of the megastructure was that development had to be done all at once on a very large scale.

Figure 7–5 A page from *Archigram 4*, the publication of the Archigram Group of English architects, whose work probably did the most to make the city as a building a popular idea within the architectural profession.

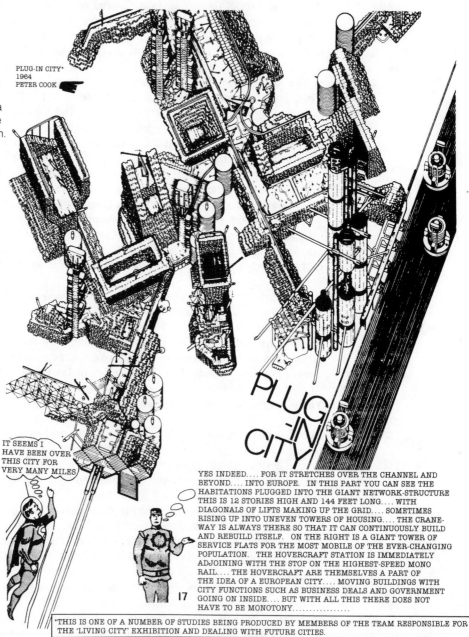

Habitat, housing designed by Moshe Safdie for Montreal's Expo '67, was a megastructure meant to be a prototype for mass-produced housing. Each apartment unit was a factory-constructed concrete module, but the potential economies of fabrication were negated by the expensive poured-in-place concrete supports. Research might eventually have solved this problem, but Habitat was completed just as the politics of urban development began to change decisively. The demand was for smaller, not larger, projects and for buildings that fit into existing cities, not structures that required that the existing city be removed.

Ideas developed for megastructures continue to influence individual buildings, but few of the original proponents of this kind of urban design are drawing megastructural city projects today. Paolo Soleri may be the only exception.

The changing context of urban design

The four city-design traditions have become a library of design ideas to be drawn upon as circumstances require rather than a series of mutually exclusive doctrines. This pluralism not only reflects similar developments in architecture, landscape architecture, and the other design professions but also reflects the changing nature of the city itself. Metropolitan areas now include both an old, densely developed central business district and suburban office parks; historic districts and new subdivisions; suburban downtowns and regional shopping centers; old factory loft areas and decentralized industrial parks. No single image of the city can encompass the variety and complexity of today's urban region.

In addition, in recent years urban design has become responsive to new and powerful influences. Community participation in planning, for example, has often reduced the size of individual proposals and made designs more receptive to social diversity. The city designer has had to come out of the office or studio and deal directly with the public, explaining the advantages of design ideas and winning political support for them.

Studies by environmental psychologists and sociologists of how the public uses open space have led to an increase in what might be called consumer awareness in urban design. An important work of this type has been William H. Whyte's *The Social Life of Small Urban Spaces*, which documents, often by time-lapse photography, actual behavior in different physical settings. Whyte's research has had a direct effect on design provisions in the zoning codes of New York City, Pittsburgh, and other localities.

Increased public support for historic preservation has also had a significant effect on city design. It has made designers more aware of the existing architectural context and has revived appreciation for monumental and garden suburb design as well as for works of nonrevolutionary modern architecture that are not part of a theory that calls for replacing all existing cities.

The environmental movement has made important changes in the way designers approach site planning. The procedure for determining the carrying capacity of land outlined by Ian McHarg in *Design with Nature* has now become standard practice. The environmental impact statement, in a clumsy way, forces social and economic analysis as well as studies of the physical environment. It mandates a comprehensive approach to the relationships among social, economic, and environmental requirements that parallels the mechanisms used by designers, who are used to juggling competing exigencies.

The urban design implications of planning decisions

The two aspects of planning that have the greatest effect on urban design are development controls and public investment. Development controls provide the framework for what the private investor constructs; public investment determines both what government builds directly and what is financed through incentives

Performance standards for urban design   The city of Pittsburgh uses a performance standard for urban design. All new development in downtown Pittsburgh is subject to project development plan review under the zoning ordinance. As the planning department becomes aware of individual development proposals, it publishes written criteria articulating design and planning issues before the architecture and development assumptions have become fixed. It is thus in the developer's interest to notify the planning department in the early stages of preparing for project development plan review.

The following are excerpts from urban design criteria issued for two buildings in downtown Pittsburgh. The illustrations show how the developers and architects undertook to solve the policy issues articulated by the city. At left is a view from Market Square of the completed PPG building; the other photograph shows the C. N. G. building in the left background and the Midtown Towers building at the right.

Excerpts from PPG Industries criteria
1.   Any office tower(s) should . . . block as little sunlight as possible from public open spaces such as Market Square. . . .

2.   The design relationships between new development . . . and nearby buildings should . . . minimize abrupt changes in scale.
3.   The elements of the . . . development that front on Market Square should complete the enclosure of the Square and be comparable in height, scale, and character to existing buildings fronting on the Square.

Excerpts from C. N. G. building criteria   The prevailing architecture of the Penn/Liberty district has walls of masonry. Both Heinz Hall and the Stanley Theater have brick facades of pleasing design. The Midtown Towers building has an interesting facade on its Liberty Avenue frontage. The design of new development on the Heinz Hall block should take into account the architectural character of its surroundings. . . . Long building frontages on Liberty Avenue should be modulated to pick up the sixty-foot dimension that is the width of the Midtown Towers building and of many other buildings in the Penn/Liberty district. . . . Tower design should also provide an appropriate height transition to Midtown Towers.

Source: Pittsburgh City Planning Department design guidelines.

for the private investor. An understanding of the urban design implications of planning decisions can add a strategic dimension to planning. It can create new opportunities for constructive change, opportunities missed all too often in the past.

Development controls and urban design

For zoning to be a useful means of influencing the design of cities, the regulations must restrict somewhat the amount of development. If the zoning envelope permits larger buildings than the market wishes to develop, zoning becomes essentially irrelevant. On the other hand, if the zoning seems impossibly strict, it may in fact be an invitation to suggest changes. Many localities deal with land use and building bulk through zoning maps that closely reflect existing conditions. Any suggested change is negotiated on a case-by-case basis, often by the creation of a planned development district. The advantage of a discretionary review, in which the planning authorities respond to a developer's proposal, is that special conditions of site and development programs receive individual consideration. The advantage of including explicit regulations in the zoning text is that the developer knows exactly what is required and the public knows exactly what to expect. However, both of these conventional alternatives have serious defects.

Defects of conventional zoning

The floor area and bulk controls in the zoning ordinance are very often direct prescriptions for development: if the developer wishes to create the most profitable investment and build to the permitted limits, there is often only one reasonable alternative. But if cities are getting the buildings called for in their zoning ordinances, why isn't development of better quality? It could be; the power to obtain better design is there. Sometimes zoning produces undesirable development because the design implications have just not been understood by the people who wrote the ordinance. In other cases, the design philosophy embodied in a zoning code may now be considered inappropriate. Many zoning codes were revised in the 1950s and 1960s to take account of design ideas associated with modernist architecture, particularly the concept of a tower surrounded by open space. Now that designers are more concerned with the relationship of buildings to neighboring structures and streets, such zoning codes may be preventing desirable solutions.

Aspects of zoning other than bulk controls also can strongly affect building and site design. Parking requirements, particularly on suburban sites, can become the most difficult element to solve in an entire design and thus the most important design determinant. However, parking requirements are rarely written with their design implications in mind.

The allocation of land use through zoning can also be an important urban design decision. A city's skyline is shaped not only by floor area controls but by the extent and location of building sites where tall buildings are permitted. Often, however, the full implications of zoning are not understood. A typical error is to zone more land for high-density office construction than the market can absorb for fifty or seventy-five years. The result is that property owners tear down existing, low-density buildings and hold the land as parking lots, hoping that the parcels will soon be major office sites. Another typical error has been to zone continuous commercial frontage along important streets in residential neighborhoods. The result is a spotty mixture of commercial and residential development and a bad juxtaposition between commercial parking lots and the yards of neighboring residences.

Environmentally sensitive areas and historic districts are becoming increasingly important to land use planning and thus city design. There may be conflicts between conservation objectives and the underlying zoning, the full implications of the conflict often not being understood until a particular proposal makes them clear. The replacement of historic districts and the natural landscape with disconnected, boxlike buildings surrounded by half-empty parking lots is often a direct response to the zoning ordinance. But the alternative method—changing restrictive zoning for each major development—has urban design perils of its own.

Defects of design review

Zoning changes are often made for a particular project. A developer requesting a zoning change will usually initiate a period of negotiation, during which the proposal will be adjusted to win approval for the zoning change. Although the design quality of the project may be a factor in the approval, planners are at a disadvantage in a conventional design-review situation. Because they usually do not see a design until it has been completed, changes that are necessary for public policy reasons can actually make the design worse than it was before. The nature of design is such that all elements must be part of a consistent system. Last-minute back-seat-driving makes such consistency hard to achieve, but changes may be necessary if the developer is pushing for advantages that the authorities do not wish to grant.

There is also a risk that, in the midst of a negotiation with a developer, planners will lose sight of basic principles that should have been maintained, whatever the attractions of the exception.

The critical elements in any discretionary design review situation are thus to

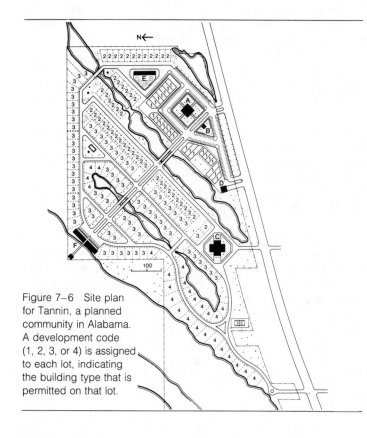

Figure 7–6 Site plan for Tannin, a planned community in Alabama. A development code (1, 2, 3, or 4) is assigned to each lot, indicating the building type that is permitted on that lot.

Guidelines for a large-scale suburban development Tannin is a planned community in southern Alabama designed by Andres Duany and Elizabeth Plater-Zyberk. A refinement of ideas the designers had originally developed for Seaside, Florida, the guidelines derive with elegant simplicity from elements to be found in any subdivision: streets, lots, setback and yard requirements, plus the fact that most developers offer buyers a choice among a range of models.

Many of the key design decisions for Tannin were made in the street plan, which is always true in a subdivision, but at Tannin the street configuration is more clearly part of an overall design concept. The site lies between a lake and a highway lined with commercial developments. Tannin's own strip shopping center is treated as a town square, with storefronts grouped around a green and a meeting hall.

have the criteria for review clearly articulated in advance and then to have a review procedure that permits a design to be looked at before every decision has been set.

Making urban design part of zoning

It is possible to enact design controls in zoning that are neither overly explicit nor overly discretionary. Such an approach combines a substratum of requirements set down in the zoning text with performance criteria for the design review of each building constructed.

The first level of design control deals with land use and density—issues that lend themselves to explicit regulation; the consistent planning policies and uniform administration that are constitutionally required cannot be maintained if land use and density are subject to negotiation every time a new development is contemplated. Although some of the traditional land use categories may now be out of date and require some redefinition, it still makes sense to segregate heavy industry, for example, and to separate residences and intensive commercial development in low-density regions. Limiting square footages of development, on the basis of the carrying capacity of the land, transportation, infrastructure, and expected market forces, remains a necessary part of development regulation.

The second level of design control shapes the physical bulk of a building. Setback lines, height limits, and percentages of required open space are some obvious examples of bulk restrictions. Building controls that are analogous to limits can convey a positive set of requirements: for example, buildings must be constructed *up to* a particular line, or a building must fill a certain percentage of the zoning envelope. It is possible to mandate such elements as pedestrian bridges between buildings, to require planted buffer zones, and to use formulas for the linear feet of seating required per square feet of public plaza space or

---

The main boulevard leads from the town center to a hotel and marina at the edge of the lake. The streets on either side of the boulevard are planned to create distinct precincts, each with either a public building or a body of water as its own focal point. Individual lots are coded 1, 2, 3, or 4, and each lot has its own house type, which can be built on that size lot and no other. (See the site plan shown in Figure 7-6.) Each type of lot comes with obligations for tree-planting and landscaping along the street.

As at Seaside, the regulatory system actually permits substantial architectural diversity. Requirements are set down in a code whose format has been copyrighted by the designers.

The enforcement mechanism at Tannin will be the condominium agreement, a document which is customarily far more detailed than any zoning approval. Approval was given under a Planned Unit Development Ordinance, which accepted the design plan and code as zoning for the whole planned community.

The superiority of Tannin's site plan over a typical subdivision is accomplished with some loss of market flexibility. If more buyers than predicted turn out to want Type-3 houses instead of Type-2s, or the other way around, whole segments of the plan would have to be recast, as streets and lots are tied together. On the other hand, Tannin is far more responsive to change than a planned unit development, where the building design is part of the site plan.

Source: Text by Jonathan Barnett, plan © Copyright 1985 Andres Duany and Elizabeth Plater-Zyberk, architects.

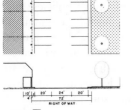

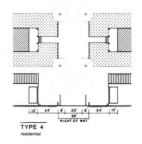

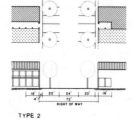
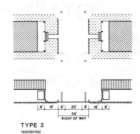

TYPE 1
retail & lodging

TYPE 2
residential

TYPE 3
residential

TYPE 4
residential

Types of housing permitted in Tannin, Alabama   The design ideas illustrated show what can be built in conformity to the code used at Tannin, although other design ideas are permissible. Different types of houses are not allowed to appear next to each other, however. Each house-type is set out in groups related to the design of the streets and to the overall land plan.

Type-1 lots occur only in the town center. The Type-1 building is likely to be constructed in increments of more than one lot, but conceptually is a two-story row house with an arcade and shop on the ground floor.

Type-2 lots require a two-and-a-half or three-story zero-lot-line house with a side garden and at least a partial side porch, a type characteristic of Charleston, South Carolina. The lots nearest the town center are coded for these Charleston houses.

Type-3 lots require conventional front, rear, and side yards. The permitted height is lower than for the Charleston houses, and at least a partial front porch is required. There is nothing in the code that actually requires a bungalow, but the one illustrated would fulfill the requirements of the lot. Type-3 houses also have to provide for off-street parking.

The high-rent district of Type-4 houses is located along the lake front, and there are more such houses across the street, backing onto a small pond. A two-story verandah is required across the front of these Type-4 houses, which, like the Type-3s, must have front, back, and side yards and provide off-street parking.

Source: Text by Jonathan Barnett, illustrations © Copyright 1985 Andres Duany and Elizabeth Plater-Zyberk, architects.

---

for the reduction of floor sizes above a certain height. All kinds of relatively subtle design issues can be objectified in this way.

A third level of control sets out performance requirements that become the basis for design review. These criteria can range from general suggestions about the shape of an office tower on the skyline to specific requirements for the size of truck docks or the location of curb cuts for garage entrances and exits. Issues within this spectrum might include architectural and functional relationships to surrounding structures, placement of public open space, or the use of ground floors for retailing to preserve the continuity of a shopping district. Some of these criteria can be embodied in a zoning text; major projects may require a mechanism that notifies planners to prepare review criteria for a specific site.

A fourth level of control can be obtained through the use of illustrative site plans and three-dimensional site models. There are self-evident dangers in producing such drawings or models, embodying what appear to be buildings, before there is either an architect or a client. As an adjunct to other forms of control, however, the illustrative plans and models can first, demonstrate that it is possible to design buildings that meet the requirements and second, show the kind of design that the planning authorities will look for in a review procedure.

Review of development proposals by a governmental body should normally take place in two stages. A preliminary approval permits the developer to proceed with the project; a second, more detailed review gives the public a chance to see elements of the scheme that, by the nature of the development business, would not have been worked out at the time the developer sought approval for the basic concept.

Land use strategies as a means of city design

Land use planning, once considered a relatively simple matter of matching real estate market projections and governmental services to available blocks or acreage, has rapidly become more sophisticated as local governments have become increasingly interventionist. At the same time, land use theory has become more arcane, as economics and urban geography increase their reliance on mathematical models.

The connection between land use and urban design is strongest when a locality seeks to promote development or strengthen a particular aspect of the local economy. The decision to promote retailing in downtown Milwaukee was reinforced by the design of the Grand Avenue project, where an indoor shopping environment was threaded through a combination of new and old buildings to connect the downtown department stores. The success of Grand Avenue, which seems to have restored downtown Milwaukee as the dominant retailing center in the region, in turn has implications for land use in the rest of the metropolitan area. Locating a festival marketplace in Baltimore's Inner Harbor was also a strategic land use decision. Because only so much retailing is possible in any market, using retailing to enliven the waterfront meant there was that much less demand available to support the traditional retail district. A choice of this kind is an urban design decision because it influences the functional organization of the whole city center.

The locations of landmark and National Register architecture and older buildings no longer required for their original use form an overlay to the traditional zoning map. Such older structures are still a valuable resource under current tax laws and, given the high cost of new building construction, will continue to represent an aspect of land use in the future. Not long ago the land under almost all older buildings was considered more important than the structures. Today the desire to find a new use for older buildings may encourage localities to change land use patterns by, for example, allowing residences or offices in former factories.

Environmental impact analysis as a mandate for area design

The paradox of the environmental impact procedure is that the analysis in itself neither responds to nor defines any set standard of what constitutes an acceptable environmental impact. The sole standard of acceptability is the adequacy of the statement in dealing in some way with all issues, and the only recourse for people who are opposed to a project for environmental reasons is to challenge the adequacy of a statement in the courts. A cynical administrator, after stating that the impact of a proposed development would be the end of life on earth as we know it, could then go ahead and approve the project. Not only that, but the statement might well be lawsuit-proof, as it would demonstrate that the most adverse potential impact had been considered.

A more sane procedure is followed by San Francisco, where the new downtown urban design plan embodies an environmental standard for the whole district. The environmental impact of any building that conforms to the plan has, by definition, already been evaluated. Such environmental zoning could ultimately be used to promote planning and urban design, because it requires political consensus about the future of substantial regions.

Public investment as a means of city design

Along with development regulations, projects that begin as items in a local government's capital budget are a major link between planning and urban design decisions. Not just public buildings, but streetlights, traffic signals, street and sidewalk paving, landscaping, and parks are important design elements. The design of a whole region can be shaped by investments in public transportation, highways, and water and sewer capacity. Development grants, tax subsidies, and other development incentives also have important urban design implications.

With its increasing activity in promoting development, the public sector frequently becomes a financial participant. This new public role carries with it an obligation to require a higher standard of design than might be expected from an unsubsidized entrepreneur, a standard that is often not achieved because of administrative problems.

Just as people learn not to hear continuous urban noise, they automatically ignore utility poles, overhead wires, and the ill-assorted collection of lights and signs to be found on most city streets. But constant exposure to a badly designed and confused environment does affect how people perceive their city; and local governments do have the ability to make significant improvements.

Most cities now have a downtown mall with special light fixtures, a framework system for traffic signals, and high-quality landscaping and sidewalk paving, all of which show what can be done with a little attention to design. These malls cost more than an ordinary street, but the cost difference is remarkably small considering the difference in effect.

If you walk around the corner, however, you will find the same old mixture of undesigned street elements, signs placed every which way, deteriorating sidewalks, and little or no amenity. City streets, lights, and traffic signals are renewed or replaced periodically, but the street environment usually ends up looking much as it did before. As relatively little more money would be needed to redesign these streets, the obstacles are usually administrative rather than financial. The authority for making changes is fragmented, and the people in charge may not be particularly sensitive to urban design issues, although they are making important urban design decisions by default. The crew from public works drills a hole in the sidewalk and puts in a new sign or bands a new sign to a light pole. A pole without a light is installed just to support a traffic signal. Workmen from a utility company dig up a terrazzo sidewalk and patch the hole with concrete. All of these decisions, each unimportant in itself, add up to a sense of total disorganization. A manual of design and placement for street signs, light fixtures, and traffic signals; a uniform standard of acceptable street and sidewalk finishes; and associations of property owners to plant and care for trees all could make a major difference at small additional cost.

Selecting sites for public buildings is rarely done with a full understanding of their implications for city design. Site selections for individual structures are based on implicit design assumptions about what the building should be. If a school, for example, can be a multi-story structure, its site requirements are different from those of a school that is all on one level. A sloping site might call for yet another type of building. Lack of awareness of design alternatives leads to site selection based on design stereotypes and to many a missed urban design opportunity.

In addition, because of the separation of agency responsibilities, housing, schools, police stations, and fire houses typically are built close to each other without any effort to coordinate their locations or their designs.

Although the nature of government administration probably makes rule-book architecture inevitable for the average public building, some rule books are far

Figure 7–7 The Brooklyn-Queens Expressway.

Figure 7–8 Paseo del Rio: The Downtown River Walk in San Antonio, Texas.

Figure 7–9   Acorn Street on Beacon Hill, Boston.

better than others, and officials should understand the implications of the regulations. To return to school buildings as an example, several big-city boards of education refused for years to accept the idea, common in many localities, that a primary school gymnasium could also be used as an auditorium. As a result, the number of pupils per school had to be larger to distribute the cost of the extra room, which meant that school sites had to be larger to accommodate the bigger building, and school districts had to be larger to supply the pupils. Thus, one simple design assumption made it far more difficult to find appropriate school sites and to plan housing and schools together.

Public investment and regional design

Extending streets and utilities to an area can decisively affect both the amount of future development and the way that development takes place. Ramapo, New York, and Petaluma, California, have become known for their decisions to use the allocation and construction of utilities to manage growth. Other governmental investments, such as downtown parking garages, can also help determine whether new development will take place.

Highway interchanges and rapid transit stations often become nodes for future development. Although this phenomenon is well known, it is not always taken into account when public policy is being made. There are, of course, timing problems; it is difficult for real estate development over the entrances to a transit station to proceed on the same schedule as the transit system itself. But if a public action substantially raises local real estate values, the public ought to receive development of higher quality in return.

In the days of federally administered urban renewal programs, individual buildings received extensive design reviews, and every local decision was restudied at regional and federal levels. The system proved far too cumbersome; by the time a proposal made it through all the layers of review, it might well

Figure 7–10 The Civic
Center, Denver,
Colorado.

Figure 7–11 The
Gallery at Market East,
Philadelphia.

Figure 7–12   The Grand Avenue, Milwaukee, Wisconsin.

Figure 7–13   Pike Place Market, Seattle, Washington.

be economically obsolete. As a consequence, more recent federal grant programs, such as Urban Development Action Grants, have been reviewed only for economic feasibility and appropriateness to the goals of the program. It has been up to local government to review the designs, if there is to be any design evaluation at all.

Developers, knowing that design is not a criterion for approval, are reluctant to spend money on designers before a grant application has been approved. The necessary drawings are often turned out in a few days by people who have never visited the city in question and who have no idea what is across the street, much less what the overall design character and planning policies of the area might be. Once a grant is approved, however, construction must usually begin as soon as possible so that financing arrangements will not unravel. The interval between "premature" and "too late" usually has proven to be breathtakingly short. As a result, many communities have lost control over the buildings being constructed with public subsidies. What is good for the developer is not necessarily good for a city or for the larger area.

The lesson of the recent federal grant programs has been that if you do not ask for urban design, you will not get it. At the same time, these programs have made developers much more aware of the kinds of development that are possible through a partnership of public and private interests. When the public is a partner in such developments, it has an obligation to set higher standards than those that might apply to an ordinary investment. When the public accepts this responsibility, there is potential for great improvement in urban design.

Cities can be designed

The designed city does exist—in fragments. Almost every city has some area that has been successfully designed, and just about every aspect of a city has been designed well somewhere. The challenge to urban designers is to achieve a consistently high standard of urban design, a task made more tantalizing by the evidence that achieving such a standard is possible.

The designed city is approached on highways carefully integrated into the natural landscape, like New York's Taconic State Parkway, passing service stations hidden behind landscaped berms, like the one at the Toronto airport. Billboards have been eliminated, as in the outskirts of Halifax, Nova Scotia. The road passes landscaped office parks like Las Colinas, near Dallas, and carefully sited heavy industry, placed where it will produce the minimal amount of pollution. As the highway enters the central city, it has the scenic interest of Storrow Drive in Boston or Lake Shore Drive in Chicago, and it is integrated with urban neighborhoods as successfully as the Brooklyn-Queens Expressway as it passes by Brooklyn Heights. Perhaps the mistakes of older freeway designs have been corrected by landscaped park decks, like those in Seattle, Washington, or Richmond, Virginia. The city's residential neighborhoods resemble Forest Hills Gardens in Queens and Chatham Village in Pittsburgh, and there are higher-density retail and residential centers similar to the Country Club Plaza in Kansas City.

Downtown, the waterfront is like the Riverwalk in San Antonio; it wanders past downtown neighborhoods like Boston's Beacon Hill and Back Bay or Philadelphia's Society Hill. There is a civic center like Denver's or San Francisco's, a downtown shopping street like Nicollet Mall in Minneapolis, or perhaps an indoor shopping center like The Gallery in Philadelphia or Grand Avenue in Milwaukee. Urban fountains, like those in Portland, Oregon, set off groups of office buildings like Rockefeller Center. Nearby, an old wholesale market has become the centerpiece of a lively new district like the Pike Market area in Seattle.

And so on—there are plenty of examples. The point is that such a city is possible; what is needed is the civic will and energy to bring it about.

8 Land subdivision regulation

To the general public, the term *subdivision* suggests a relatively large residential development of similar, single-family houses, often tract houses. By implication, *subdivision regulation* suggests the control government exercises over the development and construction of houses in a new neighborhood. From the planner's vantage point, the terms have a somewhat different meaning. In planning, subdivision is the process by which a tract of land is split into smaller parcels, lots, or building sites so that the parcels may eventually be sold, developed, or both. Land subdivision need not mean that the land subdivided will be developed soon; in some states, the sale of a large parcel of land from a farm may be subject to subdivision regulations even though the land will still be farmed after the sale. Nor does subdivision necessarily result in residential development; it can also produce industrial lots or space for lease in a shopping center. Although the subdivision of land may be accomplished by the sale of a portion of a parcel, subdivision may also occur prior to sale by the approval and recording of a plat, a map showing the newly defined lots or parcels. Although subdivision regulation is designed to control and record the process of subdividing, the product of this process is often the single-family residential development that fits the common conception.

Development of subdivision regulation

The importance of subdivision regulation is often underestimated, particularly in suburban and rural areas. As one authority has put it, "subdivision regulation has become so important that [it] is a more important public control than is zoning with respect to land being developed or redeveloped."[1] Yet the nature of subdivision regulation has changed dramatically over the years.

The function of the earliest platting and subdivision regulations was to govern the voluntary recording of plats and ensure that proper land records were made when land was described and sold. With the publication of the Standard City Planning Enabling Act by the Department of Commerce in 1928 and the adoption by many states of modern subdivision enabling legislation, these regulations evolved into development controls. First they began to include design standards for lots and blocks; later they incorporated design and construction standards for subdivision improvements. More progressive jurisdictions entered a third phase of regulation in the 1960s. As new residential development increased demands for public facilities, local governments responded by imposing compulsory dedication requirements on subdividers or by accepting money in lieu of dedicated land.

In the late sixties and early seventies, some communities began to question whether they were obligated to accommodate growth at its current pace and responded by establishing controls to limit or time growth. Such growth management programs focused on the impact of development on the community as a whole, or at least on a planning area much larger than a single subdivision. In the fourth phase of subdivision regulation, the regulations (or unified development ordinances) came to reflect the principles of growth management by

Figure 8-1 Public facilities and services that impinge
on and affect a residential subdivision. The range of
services that a household draws on in its daily living is
suggested here. Some are direct services to property,
such as streets and sewer and waterlines; other services
are available as needed, such as playgrounds, police
and fire protection, libraries, and schools.

requiring more serious examination of the external effects of a subdivision pro-posal. It was during this period that the "adequate public facilities" test first appeared in local ordinances, allowing approval of residential subdivisions only if a reviewing agency finds that existing public facilities (such as roads, utilities, schools, and drainage facilities are adequate to serve the growth generated by the subdivision.

The fifth and most recent phase of subdivision regulation, dating from the early eighties, is characterized by local governments' increasing use of impact fees and related financial exactions. Early growth management programs some-times created uncertainty about whose responsibility it was to provide areawide public facilities. Some local governments that wanted to accommodate growth but had difficulty financing the necessary areawide capital facilities turned to developers for "contributions," this time to finance their prorated shares of the costs of providing both on-site and off-site facilities. The allocation of costs for capital improvements and the determination of impact fees are complex matters that will demand increasing attention from planners.

This overview, however, does not do justice to the diversity of approaches used by local governments in regulating land subdivisions. Some towns and rural counties, for example, have not moved from the second phase of regulatory development to the third. A majority of local governments probably rely on regulatory approaches and requirements first used in the sixties or earlier. A number, however, have added innovations and embellishments in subdivision regulation derived from the growth management experiences of the seventies. The use of comprehensive impact fees, once confined largely to communities in Florida and California, is rapidly spreading.

Purposes of subdivision regulation

Over time, subdivision regulation has come to be regarded as a means of deter-mining who will finance capital improvements needed to serve new growth, but it serves a number of other purposes as well. By requiring the platting, or mapping, of newly created lots, streets, easements, and open areas, regulation requirements help to ensure the creation and preservation of adequate land records. Land titles can be determined much more easily if the "metes and bounds" (bearings and distances) descriptions of a property found in deeds are supplemented by, and refer to, a surveyed and recorded plat. Of course, plats are of particular value to tax assessors and are used to prepare land use and road and street maps. Jurisdictions that insist that developers provide "as built" drawings for streets, drainage facilities, and utilities find that these records save time and money when maintenance or other engineering work is undertaken.

Ensuring that subdivisions are properly designed is another key function of the subdivision review process. The manner in which land is subdivided, streets are laid out, and lots and houses are sold sets the pattern of community devel-opment for years to come. Once land is divided into building sites and streets, land ownership is only rarely consolidated, land is rarely resubdivided, and a particular site is only rarely redeveloped. Subdivision regulations often give a community its only opportunity to ensure that new neighborhoods are properly designed.

Subdivision review also allows a local government the opportunity to ensure that a new subdivision is properly equipped and that a public agency or private party will be responsible for maintaining the subdivision improvements that the developer provides. If the local government will have future responsibility for maintaining streets, sidewalks, drains and ditches, or parks, or for operating the utility system to which the subdivider will connect, it has an obvious interest in ensuring that these improvements and facilities are properly constructed and do not require an undue amount of maintenance. If the local government is not responsible for maintaining the facilities, it still has an interest in ensuring that it will not later be called on to make up for the developer's failure to provide adequate improvements when the land was subdivided. For example, if a developer is not required to provide adequate drainage facilities or if excessive street grades that cause soil erosion and washouts are allowed, experience has shown that the local government is often expected to solve the problem. Properly conceived regulations can protect the local government against future problems.

Subdivision regulations can also be viewed as consumer protection measures. At least in urban areas, lot purchasers rarely know what water line size or system pumping capacity will ensure adequate water pressure for their future homes. Nor are they likely to be able to evaluate the base and paving materials used to construct the streets that serve their houses. Establishing minimum standards for subdivision improvements and design is the traditional way to protect purchasers, who generally lack the specialized knowledge to evaluate improvements and design.

While the developer still controls the land, subdivision improvements are provided more easily and cheaply, and easements are more easily arranged. If improvements and easements are not provided until after the lots are sold, costs will be substantially greater than they would have been if the developer had provided the improvements and passed on the cost in the purchase price of the lot. Inflation nearly always increases the costs of materials and labor if improvements are delayed, and negotiating the purchase of easements after build-out is also likely to be expensive. Furthermore, costs that are passed on to the purchaser

---

Common deficiencies of subdivision ordinances

1. Ordinance lacks table of contents and is poorly organized.
2. Ordinance is not summarized or explained in information sheets, brochures, booklets, or manuals that are available to the public.
3. Ordinance and informational materials do not include flow chart of subdivision plat review procedure or indicate a timetable for completing the various steps in the procedure.
4. Ordinance fails to clarify the identity and indicate the authority of the official with responsibility for administering and enforcing the regulations.
5. Ordinance establishes requirements that are not properly related to the size and competence of the staff and boards who will be interpreting and enforcing the ordinance and inspecting subdivision improvements.
6. Ordinance lacks performance standards and provides developer with few choices or opportunities for trade-offs in meeting development standards.
7. Ordinance requires all subdivisions to meet inflexible set of standards, regardless of subdivision type, location, topography, or lot size.
8. Ordinance fails to establish abbreviated procedures for reviewing minor subdivisions.
9. Ordinance fails to provide workable standards governing the dedication and improvement of perimeter roads or facilities off site.
10. Ordinance requires application materials that are not actually used by the staff or reviewing agencies.
11. Ordinance makes no cross-references to zoning and fails to integrate plat approval process and review process required under zoning ordinance.
12. Ordinance fails to provide adequate development standards and inspection services for facilities and improvements not to be dedicated to the public.
13. Ordinance fails to describe exactly how properties and improvements offered for dedication to the public will be accepted and by whom.

can be financed over the term of a home mortgage loan. Despite concern about the affordability of housing, it is generally to the advantage of the property owner to finance improvements indirectly through a mortgage loan.

The purposes served by subdivision regulations are both legitimate and important. But local governments must also respect the concerns of those regulated and affected by development controls. First, a local government should be prepared to justify its substantive regulations and review procedures to developers or property owners. Local officials must be prepared to explain and defend not only the conceptual basis for government intervention in private land development but also the most obscure development standard. Second, the public has the right to expect staff and board members to be knowledgeable and competent. Members of the development review staff should deal directly with members of the public only after the staff has been properly trained and is conversant with local requirements. A local government should not attempt to administer regulations that demand competencies that its staff does not possess. Third, those affected by subdivision requirements have the right to have those requirements clarified at the earliest possible point in the development process. Standards and procedures should not require substantial interpretation by staff or plat review agencies in order to be made clear. Fourth, the development community is entitled to expect staff and board members to understand the importance of timeliness in the review process. It may not be unreasonable to expect a local government to increase its development review staff during periods of substantially increased development activity. Fifth, a subdivider may reasonably expect a local unit to designate a staff member to serve as liaison for purposes of completing the subdivision review process for a particular subdivision. That person can be expected to coordinate the review of the developer's plans by other agencies and departments, to shepherd the plats and plans through the approval process, to answer questions about the review process, to expedite the review process where possible, and to serve as official spokesperson for the local unit—to the extent that it is possible for a staff member to do so. Finally, a developer may expect that government will act in good faith. Developers should be promptly notified of possible changes in the regulations that may affect a particular subdivision, and the local unit should never attempt to exact concessions from a developer that do not reflect official policy or that are unlawful. Of course, any party subject to subdivision regulation deserves to be treated courteously and respectfully.

The regulatory setting

In every state of the union, units of local government are permitted to regulate the subdivision of land. How the regulations are administered—and by whom—varies from one jurisdiction to another. The next four sections consider the factors that shape the character and scope of subdivision regulations.

Units of government and their jurisdiction

Local governments derive their power to regulate subdivisions from state enabling legislation; virtually all states allow various classes of municipalities to exercise this power, and some states, such as Alaska, require certain units of government to do so.[2] In many states, the power to enact and enforce subdivision regulations—like zoning and certain other development controls—may be applied in a municipality's extraterritorial area.[3] Since a substantial amount of land subdivision occurs on the fringe of urban or suburban areas outside municipal boundaries, virtually all states also allow counties (or comparable units) to review subdivision plats. In a few states (e.g., Tennessee) regional agencies such as regional planning commissions may enjoy regulatory power over territory within municipal and county jurisdictions.[4]

Organizational arrangements within local government

The organizational arrangements for administering subdivision regulations vary substantially from jurisdiction to jurisdiction and from state to state. Most states have followed the suggestion of the Standard City Planning Enabling Act by delegating the power to regulate subdivisions to locally appointed planning commissions or boards. In some states (e.g., Connecticut) planning commissions are authorized both to adopt subdivision regulations and to review plats.[5] Elsewhere, such a commission may serve as the plat approval agency, but the local legislative body actually adopts regulations. In some states, (e.g., Arizona), the governing board both adopts ordinances and approves plats, which means that it serves in a legislative as well as an administrative capacity.[6] Not all jurisdictions rely on elected or appointed boards for plat approval. In many states, plat approval authority is delegated to staff technical review committees.

The range of possibilities is further expanded because most review procedures call for the preparation and approval of at least a preliminary plat in addition to a final, or record plat. The board that approves the first may not necessarily have responsibility for approving the second. Another variation is for the governing board to approve plats only after receiving recommendations from both the planning commission and staff.

Staff responsibility for administering subdivision regulations and coordinating the plat and plan review is often lodged in a municipal or county planning office or in a community development or environmental management super-agency. Most planning offices, however, do not include staff trained to inspect roads, drainage facilities, and utility layouts, so the task of ensuring compliance with regulations may fall to public works staff.

Local governments derive their authority to regulate subdivisions from state law. In states that permit substantial delegations of power to local government, home-rule cities and counties often have broad authority to impose dedication and fee requirements on developers. Most innovative growth management programs have been developed in jurisdictions that enjoy substantial home rule. Local governments that lack home-rule charters must rely on general state enabling legislation and are less likely to be able to use the same complement of regulatory techniques.

Subdivision regulations and other planning tools

Subdivision regulations are just one of a number of means communities use to carry out their planning programs. To be effective, subdivision regulations must be integrated with other local government plans, policies, and ordinances, such as the comprehensive or general plan and its capital improvement components, the zoning ordinance, the official map, utility extension policies, street improvement policies, environmental impact statement requirements, and various other development and environmental health regulations.

The most important of these may be the comprehensive or general plan and the capital improvements program. Ideally, the comprehensive plan should provide the policy and analytical basis for the design and improvement standards included in the subdivision regulations. In some states (such as Utah) a comprehensive street classification plan must be adopted before subdivision regulations can be enforced.[7] In a smaller number of states (such as California) only subdivision plats that are consistent with required comprehensive plan elements can be approved.[8] The link between subdivision regulations and the capital improvements program (CIP) is every bit as important. The capital improvements program is a schedule of public land acquisition and construction activity typically covering the succeeding five years; it indicates what improvements will be provided and where, when they will begin and be completed, what they will cost, and how they will be funded. When the CIP is recompiled each year, the first year of the program becomes the basis for the CIP portion of the current annual operating budget, and a new fifth year is added. In developing areas, subdivision regulations are an excellent means of linking a CIP to the development plans of developers and builders. Furthermore, the policy and analytical basis of the comprehensive plan and CIP strengthens the legal defensibility of the compulsory dedication, reservation, improvement, and fee requirements of the subdivision regulations.

Zoning regulates the use of land; subdivision ordinances regulate the division of tracts into building lots and the provision of infrastructure. Both zoning and subdivision ordinances may specify minimum lot size, shape, and access requirements; some of these standards from the zoning ordinance are typically incorporated by reference into the subdivision regulations. Although dedication and public improvement requirements have generally been imposed under subdivision authority, such exactions are now sometimes imposed along with various zoning permissions. Landscaping and environmental measures that once were evaluated only in zoning matters are now considered in the subdivision review process. The recordable plat required by virtually all subdivision ordinances is now occasionally required when zoning permission is sought for multifamily residential complexes, mixed use and planned unit developments, and commercial centers. As these examples indicate, the historically important distinctions between subdivision and zoning regulations are blurring. More and more local governments, especially charter cities, are seeking and using authority to adopt unitary land use ordinances that consolidate the authority, standards, and procedures of both in a single ordinance. Many innovative growth management programs have been based on unitary development ordinances. The increasing use of impact fees also encourages consolidated zoning and subdivision review, because these fees are often levied on commercial, industrial and multifamily residential developments as well as on residential subdivisions.

Scope of subdivision regulations

Not all divisions of land and property transactions are subject to public review and regulation, and determining which are and which are not is an administrative chore in itself. Many early statutes did not cover so-called metes and bounds subdivisions, so a subdivider became subject to regulation only by voluntarily choosing to prepare a plat for recordation or, in some cases, by selling lots with reference to a plat. Even today the "metes and bounds exemption" (exempting divisions of land for which no plat is offered for recordation and lots are described solely by survey bearings and distances) is alive and well in some jurisdictions. In most states the subdivision regulation enabling statutes define the term *subdivision,* and local governments must adhere to the scope of coverage this definition provides. Such definitions vary widely from state to state. An enabling statute from one state defines subdivision in part as "the division of a lot, tract or parcel of land into two or more lots, tracts, parcels, or other divisions of land for sale or development."[9] Other statutes define the term to include only those divisions resulting in a number of lots greater than two.[10] Such definitions provide a loophole for landowners who are willing to divide large tracts sequentially into a series of one- or two-lot subdivisions.

The language "division of land into . . . lots, tracts, parcels, or other divisions of land for sale or development" has generally been interpreted to exclude certain other property divisions. It may exclude condominium development, mobile home parks, and many shopping mall and commercial center developments. Unless the statutory definition is broadened, platting, dedication, and public improvement requirements that a local government may seek to impose on developments of this sort normally must be based on zoning or other regulations. Another question is whether subdivision regulations apply to divisions of land among heirs in an estate settlement. As a general rule, courts regard as outside the scope of subdivision regulation divisions of land made in a will or partitions of land among heirs who inherit tracts of land as tenants in common. The courts are generally unwilling to find that such division of land was made for "the purpose of sale or building development."

Certain large-lot subdivisions are typically exempt from regulation. Unfortunately, if regulations do not apply to 2-, 5-, or 10-acre lots, the pattern of an area may already be determined before land is divided into lots small enough to trigger government intervention. Legislation may also exempt small-scale subdivisions. In North Carolina, for example, land in single ownership whose entire area is no greater than two acres can be divided into not more than three lots, where no right-of-way dedication is involved and resulting lots meet municipal standards.[11] Other common exemptions include those applying to the recombination of lots, the division of strips of land to permit the expansion of right-of-way, and, occasionally, the division of land into parcels to be used for agricultural purposes. Such exemptions can create sizable loopholes in areas where small-scale contractors are active and rural property owners are inclined to subdivide their own land rather than to sell it to developers.

Elements of subdivision design

Properly handled, subdivision plat review can afford a community an outstanding opportunity to encourage the creation of attractive sites and visually appealing neighborhoods, to ensure that traffic circulation is efficient and convenient, to protect residential and other uses from traffic and incompatible land uses, to determine that individual lots are appropriately arranged and oriented, and to require that public improvements and facilities are coordinated with community plans and the character of surrounding areas. Unfortunately, many communities do not take sufficient advantage of the opportunity to influence the design of new subdivisions.

Although the compulsory dedication, fee, and public improvement requirements imposed on developers are greater than ever before, the quality of design in many new subdivisions has not appreciably improved. As communities have come to realize that good subdivision design is an art that does not necessarily lend itself to the imposition of numerical standards, regulations have begun to include more general design objectives or performance standards to guide design. Ironically, many local jurisdictions require that the preliminary plat include information that is useful in site design but make little use of it in the plat review process. Although one of the best means of encouraging good design is to see to it that subdivision designs are prepared by skilled designers, few jurisdictions require sketch plans and preliminary plats to be prepared by a registered landscape architect. To use the plat review process as an opportunity to encourage good design, communities should devise submission requirements that motivate developers to employ the services of a competent land planner.

Subdivision and the natural environment

Subdivision review should ensure that new development is properly integrated into the natural environment. The following elements need to be considered: hazard areas and critical environmental areas, stormwater management, soil erosion and sedimentation control, water quality, environmental impact statements, and landscaping and aesthetics.

Natural hazard and critical environmental areas   Whether and how to subdivide lands posing natural or man-made hazards is an issue for plat review boards and developers alike. Land subject to flooding, land that is too steep, land that is unstable because of geological or hydrological conditions, or land with unstable or dangerous subsurface conditions (abandoned mines, old landfills, or waste disposal sites) requires special attention. In some cases such areas may be subdivided, but only if the hazard is recognized and hazard areas are included in lots of sufficient size that the nonhazardous areas can accommodate building sites. Jurisdictions should also require that the final plat disclose the location and nature of hazard areas.

Another category requiring special attention might be called "critical areas" or "areas of environmental concern." These include special wetlands, ponds, waterways, and shorelands; habitats for endangered species; and areas of historical, architectural, or archeological importance. Most such areas are identified by and subject to state, regional, or federal legislation. Subdivision regulations should include language that will enable a local government to use subdivision design to help protect critical areas. Encouraging cluster or planned unit development design may be the best approach.

Land development definitions

Attached dwelling   A one-family dwelling attached to two or more other one-family dwellings by common vertical walls.

Basin   An area drained by the main stream and tributaries of a large river.

Berm   A raised and elongated mound of earth intended to direct the flow of water or to screen or buffer an area from its surroundings.

Cartway   The area of a street within which vehicles are permitted, including travel lanes and parking areas but not including shoulders, curbs, sidewalks, or swales.

Check dam   A small dam constructed in a gully or other small watercourse to decrease the stream flow velocity, minimize channel scour, and promote deposition of sediment.

Cul-de-sac   Turnaround at the end of a dead-end street.

Culvert   A drain, ditch, or conduit, not incorporated in a closed system, that carries drainage water under a driveway, roadway, railroad, pedestrian walk, or public way.

Cut and fill   To move earth by excavating part of an area and using the excavated material for adjacent embankments or fill areas.

Detention basin   A storage facility designed for the temporary storage of stream flow or surface runoff and for the release of the stored water at controlled rates.

Fill   To deposit sand, gravel, earth, or other materials in low-lying or underwater areas to build up or create usable land; the material so deposited.

Flag lot   A lot with a developable area connected to a public road by a narrow strip of land that includes a driveway; sometimes also refers to a landlocked lot that is connected to a public road only by a narrow right-of-way easement.

Gabion   A mattress, basket, or cage-like structure covered with wire, plastic mesh, or plastic netting, packed with stone and finer materials; may be used as a revetment, channel lining, weir, or groin.

Grade   (1) The slope of a road channel or of natural ground; (2) the finished surface of a canal bed, roadbed, top of embankment, or bottom of excavation; any surface prepared for the support of construction, such as paving or laying a conduit.

Grubbing   The process of removing roots, stumps, and low-growing vegetation.

Stormwater management The quantity, quality, and erosive effect of stormwater runoff should be reviewed whenever land is subdivided. Measures to control soil erosion, sedimentation, and downstream flooding and to protect water-supply watersheds should be incorporated into or coordinated with subdivision regulations whenever possible. The management of stormwater is often governed strongly by the drainage characteristics of the entire watershed. The traditional approach to handling stormwater, especially in urban areas, involves the installation of storm sewer and other pipe systems that rapidly remove stormwater from the site. More recent approaches are based on surface drainage and, where soils are permeable, the natural infiltration capacity of the land. These natural drainage systems use grassy swales to transport and dissipate the water; these drainage systems rely on existing topography and surface bodies of water to protect or create water impoundment areas.

Soil erosion and sedimentation control Soil erosion and sedimentation control programs protect the land from erosion and protect streams, reservoirs, and

Impervious surface Material that reduces or prevents the absorption of stormwater into the ground.

Impoundment An artificial collection or storage of water, such as a reservoir, pit, dugout, or sump.

Patio house A one-family, typically one-story dwelling located on and along at least one side-lot line, with a court or patio area enclosed by fences or walls.

Plat A map of land subject to a common development or sales plan that shows the location and boundaries of streets, individual lots or parcels, and other site information.

Retention basin A storage facility designed for the permanent storage of stormwater runoff.

Reverse frontage lot A through lot that is not accessible from one of the nonintersecting streets on which it fronts.

Revetment A facing of stone or other material, either temporary or permanent, placed along the edge of a stream to stabilize the bank and protect it from the erosive action of the stream.

Riprap Broken rock, cobbles, or boulders placed on earth surfaces, such as on the face of a dam or the bank of a stream, for protection against the action of water.

Sedimentation The settling out of the soil particles transported by water.

Swale An elongated earthen depression intended to direct the flow of water.

Through lot A lot that fronts on two streets that do not intersect at the corner of the lot.

Town house A one-family dwelling with two or three stories in a row of at least three units in which each unit has its own direct access to the outside, no unit is located over another, and each unit is separated from the next by a common fire wall.

Urban service boundary The boundary that defines the geographic limit of public facilities and services provided by an urban government, not necessarily coinciding with the unit's corporate boundary.

Watershed The geographic area drained by a particular river or major stream.

Weir A damlike structure built into the channel of a stream that forces the stream flow through a constricted outlet, thereby reducing the grade of the stream channel and dissipating the turbidity and velocity of the flowing water.

Zero lot line The configuration of a building on a lot such that one or more of the building's sides is located on and along the lot line.

other bodies of water from sedimentation. Control programs resulting from development usually limit the extent of the graded or disturbed areas and the length of time such areas are exposed without ground cover. An approved soil erosion and sedimentation control plan is often a prerequisite to a grading permit for the site. Construction of roads and installation of utilities as well as building construction can precipitate the need for erosion and sedimentation control.

A sedimentation control or grading plan should therefore be approved in conjunction with the preliminary plat, because the content of the plan will depend on the location of roads and utilities on the approved plat. The sedimentation control or grading plan should be based on an analysis of the soils, the hydrological features of the property, possible stormwater detention or retention areas, and the suitability of the land for proposed grading, grubbing, filling, and replanting.

Water quality   The quality of stormwater runoff should not be neglected. (See Figure 8–2.) Subdivision of land in water-supply watersheds may require special development standards. In some jurisdictions, to avoid surface or groundwater contamination of drinking water, newly subdivided lots in a water-supply watershed

Figure 8–2   Watershed management rating system, Guilford County, North Carolina. To be accepted, all plans must have 100 or more points and meet all other requirements. Subdivisions are rated prior to approval of preliminary plat.

Maximum point value	Factor	Point value	Points earned
20	**Zone**		
	B–3, O/I unsewered	5	
	B–3, O/I sewered	15	
	A–1	10	
	RA–40	10	
	R–PUD—mixed (single-family detached and cluster)	15	
	R–PUD—cluster exclusively	20	
25	**Impervious surface**		
	0–3%	25	
	3–7%	20	
	7–10%	15	
	10–15%	10	
25	**Proximity to floodway as defined by the Federal Insurance Administration**		
	>2000 feet	25	
	1000–2000 feet	20	
	500–1000 feet	15	
	100–500 feet	10	
	50–100 feet	5	
10	**Soil type as defined on page 29 of the Guilford County Soil Survey (U.S. Department of Agriculture Soil Conservation Service, Reference Table 7)**		
	Slight	10	
	Moderate	5	
25	**Drainage—protect and use natural drainageways**		
	Piped or improved drainage with riprap	5	
	Dispersed drainage or protected drainageways	10	
	Dispersed drainage and protected drainageways	20	
	Enhanced and protected natural drainageways	25	

must meet higher lot-size standards if individual sewage disposal systems such as septic tanks are to be used. Even where higher densities are justified because central utilities are available, development may need to be clustered on a portion of the site to reduce the area devoted to impervious surfaces such as roofs and pavement. These techniques can protect drinking water supplies by reducing the amount of pollutants that make their way into surface and groundwater supplies and the sediment load that makes its way into rivers, lakes, and reservoirs.

Environmental impact statements Occasionally a large-scale subdivision requires the preparation of an environmental impact statement or, alternatively, an environmental assessment to determine whether an impact statement is required. Such reporting may be required under the National Environmental Policy Act (NEPA) because a federal agency permit issued for some aspect of the development (e.g., a "Section 404 permit" for filling a wetland, administered by the Army Corps of Engineers and the Environmental Protection Agency) amounts to a major federal action that will significantly affect the quality of the environment. Or it may be required under the terms of a "little NEPA," a state environmental policy act that applies when a state or local government serves

Figure 8–2 *continued.*

Maximum point value	Factor	Point value	Points earned
25	Slope—low percentage of slope		
	0–6% average slope of subdivision of lot	25	
	6–10%	20	
	10–15%	5	
25	Land cover—high percentage of natural and stabilizing vegetation		
	Natural vegetation or stabilizing vegetation along drainage and on >25% of lot	25	
	Natural or stabilizing vegetation along drainage and on 15–25% of lot	20	
	Natural or stabilizing vegetation along drainage and on 10–15% of lot	15	
	Natural or stabilizing vegetation between units and water	10	
	Ornamental lawn on >5% of the lot	5	
	Vegetation on <5% of the lot	0	
25	Runoff control strategies		
	Maximum runoff retention	25	
	Moderate runoff retention	20	
	Runoff detention in excess of minimum requirements of Erosion Control Ordinance	15	
	Runoff detention equal to minimum requirements	5	
10	Sewage disposal		
	Public sewer system	10	
10	Road and driveway design		
	Impermeable road surface with vegetated ditches	10	
	Impermeable roads with piped drainage and/ or curb and gutter and energy dissipaters	5	
Total 200		Total _____	

as an approving or permitting agency. The impact statement or assessment is often available to a local government prior to subdivision plat review and can be a valuable source of environmental information for the agency approving the plats.

Landscaping and aesthetics   Many communities do not routinely require the landscaping of new subdivisions or the protection of existing vegetation, particularly if the location and orientation of buildings are unknown at the time of plat review. Some cities require the developer to plant street trees or to pay a fee to cover the cost for the local government to purchase and install the trees. More common are requirements for buffers or planting strips to shield new subdivision residents from the effects of adjacent land uses. One way to encourage the retention of trees and other vegetation is to avoid requiring that all vegetation in the right-of-way beyond the curb or road shoulder be cleared. Street sections allowing the flexible location of driveway cuts also minimize the clearing of land.

In addition to protecting existing greenery and requiring landscaping, communities also want to encourage site planners to think through the overall aesthetic aspect of subdivision design. Well-designed subdivision layouts take advantage of a tract's natural features; roads can be designed to provide visual interest for the driver, and lots can be designed to provide building sites with scenic vistas.

Street, block, and lot layout

The layout of streets, lots, and blocks is the essence of subdivision design. The next two sections consider the characteristics of good street design and lotting patterns.

Designing streets and access ways   Streets are critical to subdivision design. First, the streets themselves are space eaters, occupying a significant amount of subdivision land. Second, the arrangement of streets defines the shape and amount of land that is usable for development and influences the way in which lots are laid out. Third, street rights-of-way provide avenues for the transmission and distribution lines of many utilities, including gas, water, sewerage, electricity, telephone, and cable television.

A number of land use planning and traffic circulation principles should guide the design of subdivision streets.[12] Every local government should have a street-classification system that is consistent with an adopted thoroughfare plan. However, most thoroughfare plans focus on the arteries and highways that are designed to move traffic throughout the area. The classification of collector, subcollector, minor residential streets, and cul-de-sacs, those types of streets most often found in new subdivisions, is often neglected. A functional classification system for lower-order streets can be developed that recognizes that most subdivision streets are local, and their primary function is to provide vehicular and pedestrian access to abutting lots. Subdivision streets may be distinguished on the basis of their expected traffic volumes, the number of lots they serve, and the extent to which they will be used for on-street parking. Design and construction standards should be based on this street hierarchy, and subdividers should be expected to show how their proposed subdivision streets fit into it. A detailed street-classification system for lower-order streets can help to prevent the overdesign of streets and the disorder and neighborhood disruption that result when subdivision streets are undifferentiated.The following principles should be observed in the design of residential streets.

1. Street widths and patterns, intersection spacing, and the location of pedestrian ways should facilitate local access; streets should not be overdesigned.

2. Subdivision streets should discourage through traffic and excessive speeds. If streets are designed to limit traffic demand, a developer can avoid excessive paving and build less costly stormwater drainage systems.
3. The number of points where vehicular and pedestrian traffic can conflict should be limited, perhaps by the use of cul-de-sacs and looped streets. Separate pedestrian walkways should be built where feasible.
4. Land uses that generate substantial traffic should be located on or oriented to major streets peripheral to the subdivision. Even in moderate-density subdivisions, the designer should consider how the subdivision might be served by mass transit.
5. Street design should be compatible with the natural features of the site. Streets requiring less cut and fill are less costly to construct, less environmentally damaging, and more attractive. Street design should also be coordinated with stormwater management.

Figure 8–3 Elements in a street-classification system.

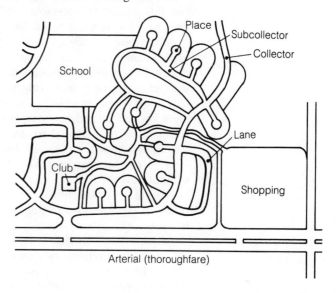

Figure 8–4 Project phasing and street stubs.

This type of stub is required only if connecting stub has been built or if street is planned as connector or arterial on adopted street plan

Phase 2

Phase 1

Street stub required as part of Phase 2

Phase 3

Street stub required as part of Phase 1

Stream crossing improvement provided as part of Phase 3

6.   Street design should promote energy conservation in the buildings served. The orientation of streets can allow builders to take advantage of wind breaks, cooling breezes, and the southern exposure that solar energy systems require. Furthermore, the less land that is devoted to paved streets, the smaller the heat buildup from roadway surfaces.

Several subdivision layout problems seem to come up repeatedly in the review process. One concerns the desirability of connecting new subdivision streets to existing or proposed streets in the surrounding area.[13] A local government may require a developer to extend a dedicated, improved street to the boundary of the development to connect with a street on adjacent property that is yet to be built. The developer is thus expected to provide a "stubout," a street with a temporary dead-end at the property line rather than a shorter street terminated with a permanent cul-de-sac. Such requirements may pit the local government not only against the developer but against home buyers as well. Potential purchasers of lots in the new subdivision may value the privacy provided by a series of subdivision cul-de-sacs more highly than the improved access to other parts of the community that the street may one day provide. Developers tend to dislike these stubout requirements, which force developers to build longer streets without appreciably increasing their lot count. Furthermore, a developer may legitimately wonder whether the stubbed-out street will ever be used as planned, given the difficulty the municipality or county may have in piecing together the segments of the planned roadway. Finally, in some cases the developer may legitimately view the required stubout as a windfall for the owners of relatively isolated neighboring land who may gain access through the new subdivision without paying for it.

Despite these objections, requiring stubbed-out streets or access ways is appropriate in the following circumstances. First, a street should be stubbed out in one stage of a subdivision plan if the street is to connect with a street built in a subsequent stage. Both portions of the street, of course, should be shown on the approved preliminary subdivision plat or development plan. Second, if a thoroughfare or street plan shows a future collector or arterial street bisecting the tract proposed for subdivision, and if the tract is large enough to generate enough traffic to support a higher-function roadway, the local government should be able to require the road to be built to that standard all the way to the property line of the subdivision. Finally, if a cluster of lots in an isolated portion of a subdivision is served by a single cul-de-sac or loop road, it is often wise to require an emergency-access easement along an unimproved road or path to the neighboring property. Such an easement, to be used only by emergency response or public service vehicles, can connect the end of the cul-de-sac or loop road with a similar access point on a road on adjacent property.

It is generally not a good idea to require a minor subdivision street to be extended to the property line if no exterior street connection is currently available. Both the function of the street to provide residential access and the legitimate privacy interests of potential lot purchasers should be protected.

It is desirable, however, to connect new subdivision streets with existing exterior streets that already extend to the subdivision boundary. Requiring the developer to extend existing collectors, arterials, and other thoroughfares into and through the subdivision can generally be justified if the traffic generated by the subdivision is sufficient to warrant a requirement that the developer build a higher-function roadway. A street extension is permissible even if the existing exterior street is a minor subdivision street, particularly if the street pattern beyond the subdivision boundaries has already been fixed. In most cases an expectation that the existing street will be extended has already been established.

Another problem in subdivision design involves the subdivision of land along major collector or arterial streets.[14] The function of providing access to adjacent residential lots is not performed well by streets that carry fairly heavy traffic volumes. Many subdivision ordinances provide authority to require the subdivider who owns frontage along such streets to orient the lots to interior streets, either at right angles or parallel to the collector or artery. Lots fronting on an interior street that back up to a major street should be deeper than normal or be screened from traffic by a wall or, less satisfactorily, by a landscaped buffer along the edge of the right-of-way (see Figure 8–6). A developer may also be required to establish a "non-access easement" along the major street right-of-way to prohibit abutting lot owners from gaining direct access to the street. A second option is to provide for the construction of a frontage or marginal access road running parallel to the collector or artery and located within its right-of-way, as shown in Figure 8–7. Because the frontage road serves lots only on one side, it may be built to standards lower than those that would apply to typical local-access streets. This approach may be more satisfactory in situations where the land to be subdivided is not deep enough to support two tiers of lots and an interior street.

Lots and blocks One of the most fundamental requirements of a subdivision ordinance is that new lots conform to the lot size and other lot-related standards of the zoning ordinance. Standards for lot size and width have been debated for some years. Studies of the impact of land use regulations on housing affordability have suggested a strong correlation between lot size and width and housing cost.[15] Unusually large or wide lots may cause disproportionate increases in the cost of providing those lots with utility improvements, such as paved streets and water and sewer lines, whose costs are a function of the linear distance the improvement is extended. In certain housing markets, large-lot zoning (and subdivision regulation) may effectively limit the construction of lower-income housing. On the other hand, larger lots may serve certain valuable purposes: for example, they may be required if central water and sewerage facilities are lacking. Substantially larger lot sizes (in excess of 25–40 acres) may also be appropriate in areas affected by an agricultural land-protection program. Smaller lots are also desirable in natural hazard zones, in water supply watersheds, and in fragile environmental areas.

Figure 8–5

"I GUESS THE SUBDIVISION REGULATIONS DIDN'T CALL FOR A WIDE ENOUGH CUL-DE-SAC."

Subdivision regulations should specify whether minimum lot-size requirements apply to all or only certain portions of a lot. Most regulations do not include areas within public street rights-of-way; some do not include areas within private streets, floodways, or certain utility easements.

Standard building lots have traditionally been rectangular, with a depth two to three times the lot width. Homeowners, particularly in urban areas, have simply become accustomed to more private open space in front or back than in side yards. However, most local governments find it necessary to permit variation in lot shape and frontage. For example, lot shape and frontage restrictions should be flexible enough to accommodate certain forms of higher-density, architecturally integrated developments, such as zero-lot-line housing, and to allow nonrectangular lots to be used at the ends of cul-de-sacs, as shown in Figure 8–8.

One debate about lot design concerns so-called flag, pipestem, panhandle, or spaghetti lots.[16] These lots are generally distinguished by the fact that the portion of the lot that fronts on the street or road is just wide enough to accommodate a driveway. By design or inadvertence, a local government may discourage such lots by measuring the required lot width at the required building setback line rather than at the actual building site. Various rationales are often given for restricting or prohibiting these lots. First, lots with complex sides often do not offer as much usable area for building sites and open space as their area suggests (although, if the lots are large enough, this may not make much difference.) Second, if the stem or handle of the lot abuts the street and the bulk of the lot

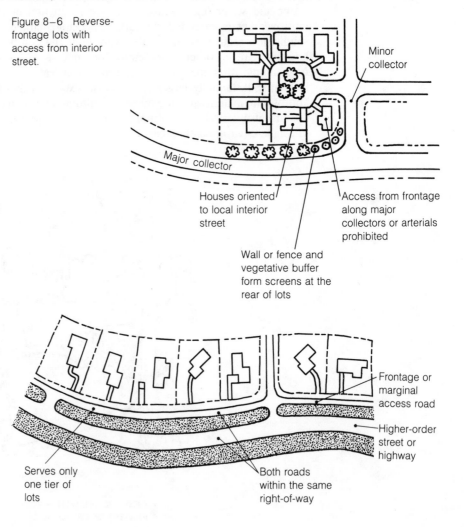

Figure 8–6   Reverse-frontage lots with access from interior street.

Minor collector

Major collector

Houses oriented to local interior street

Access from frontage along major collectors or arterials prohibited

Wall or fence and vegetative buffer form screens at the rear of lots

Frontage or marginal access road

Higher-order street or highway

Figure 8–7   Lots oriented to frontage or marginal access road.

Serves only one tier of lots

Both roads within the same right-of-way

is in the rear, lateral utility lines (such as for water and sewer) may require longer extensions, since the lines cannot be run perpendicularly from the street. On the other hand, the distance may be no greater than that between a house on a large rectangular lot and the road. Third, one effect of flag lots is to allow houses fronting the same road to be located at varying distances from the street, which means that in a subdivision with smaller lots, the front of one house may face the rear of the house next door. Furthermore, if the driveway entrances to flag lots ("stems") are bunched along the road, the arrangement can create potential traffic safety problems. However, proper planning and sensitive regulation can overcome many of these objections. For example, a spacing requirement will prevent driveways from being concentrated along a collector or arterial street. Lot-frontage requirements can ensure that a lot has sufficient frontage to accommodate driveways.

Nonrectangular lots have their advantages for the subdivision designer. For example, flag and pie-shaped lots can be useful in designing cul-de-sacs where frontage is at a premium and can help to reduce street length. In hilly or mountainous terrain, the lot designer may want to take advantage of a limited number of hillside or hilltop building sites, and rectangular lot requirements may be too limiting. "Spaghetti lots" (lots with long, thin strips with various twists and turns) are sometimes used in recreational or mountain-area subdivisions in which building sites are oriented around an attraction such as a lake or ski slope. The long, twisting shape provides each lot with exclusive access to a highway, which is likely to be located some distance from the building site.

Exactions and the financing of subdivision improvements

The questions of who will finance subdivision improvements and community facilities and how financing and maintenance will be handled are fundamental to subdivision regulation. Most jurisdictions now expect subdividers to provide certain public improvements at their own expense. These "exactions" may take the form of requirements for the dedication of land, the construction or installation of infrastructural improvements, or the payment of fees to finance these

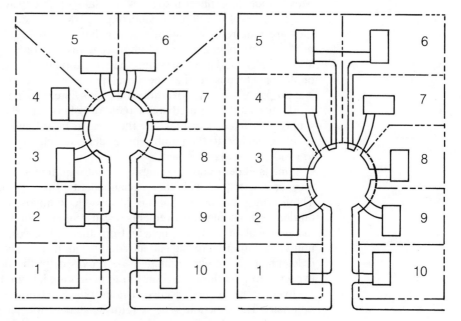

Figure 8–8 The drawing at left shows the design that may result when flag lots are prohibited; at right, an illustration of how flag lots can be used to reduce the length of a cul-de-sac.

improvements (e.g., fees in lieu of dedication, impact fees). However, some methods of arranging for the financing of subdivision improvements do not require the developer to assume all of the direct, front-end costs. The sections that follow describe the range of alternatives for providing and maintaining these improvements and community facilities.

Improvements and dedication of land

The most common form of exaction is a requirement that a subdivider provide infrastructural improvements to serve the land being developed. These improvements range from the more traditional (e.g., paved streets, utility lines, piped drainage systems, sidewalks) to the less traditional (e.g., sewage pump stations, bus shelters). Occasionally these improvements are required on lands or within easements that the developer does not own or control (e.g., the construction of a deceleration lane for a traffic artery adjacent to the site within the existing right-of-way). More commonly, these improvements will be made on site. If the improvements are to be available for public use or are to be connected to a public system, the locality will require the dedication of the land so improved and will accept the dedication only after the improvement has been completed and inspected. In some instances a community may expect a developer to provide an improvement that is clearly designed to serve a larger population than that expected in the subdivision. Many jurisdictions reimburse the developer for the portion of the costs of these "oversized" facilities that are not attributable to the new subdivision, providing the funds either when the facility is completed (common for roads and drainage facilities) or when future users tie into the system (common for water and sewer lines).

Strictly speaking, a dedication is a donation to the public of some interest in land for a particular range of uses. It may involve the fee simple title to the land, an easement, or some other property interest. A land dedication requirement may involve a ten-foot-wide easement astride a lot line to service a utility or the full title to a park site of several acres. The most controversial land dedications are those that permit off-street pedestrian access (e.g., easements between lots to connect a street with a lake or greenway) or those that involve sizable areas of developable land (e.g., park or school sites). If public facility sites are required, the subdivision regulations should be linked to an adopted public facility plan and capital improvements program. The regulations should also include standards governing the size, topography, utility, and accessibility of the site to ensure that the developer is not able to dedicate land that is inappropriate for the governmental unit's intended purpose. The amount of residential land dedicated for a park or school site should not be calculated simply as a fixed percentage of the area to be subdivided; rather the amount should be linked to the number of residents or schoolchildren that are expected to reside in the development.

Some land dedication and improvement requirements can be justified because they are consistent with the special-benefit principles of special assessments. Those principles suggest that it is permissible to impose on the development the burden of providing improvements because subdivision lot purchasers will enjoy the principal or exclusive benefit from them. The costs of minor streets and utility lines internal to the subdivision are often specially assessed; therefore, it is legitimate to require that they be provided by the developer, who can be expected to pass these costs on to the benefiting lot purchasers.

However, many subdivision exactions today are based on a somewhat different rationale. The exaction issue is reformulated to focus less on the question of whether lot purchasers will enjoy the principal or exclusive benefit provided by the facility and more on the question of whether a development bears a proportionate share of the costs of providing community facilities to serve new residents.

This new emphasis on prorating costs highlights the fact that traditional forms of exaction, such as land dedication and improvement requirements, are coarse tools for programming capital improvements in newly developing areas. Although the appearance of a number of new subdivisions in a given area may create the need for various improvements and public facilities, it may not be legitimate to assign the full cost of any one of them to an individual subdivider by means of a dedication or improvement requirement. Requiring the developer to provide a sewage-pump station, sections of arterial streets, or a major park or school site may not be an appropriate means of assigning capital costs, because one facility (or parcel of land) may serve an area larger than just one subdivision.

Requiring dedications and improvements from a number of developers can also pose problems. For example, the task of constructing or widening an arterial street cannot be divided easily among several developers, each of whom subdivides or develops at a different time. For that matter, a large areawide facility may be superior to several smaller ones. In the view of many municipal parks and recreation departments, open spaces or park areas of less than one acre are generally not as useful as larger tracts and are more difficult to maintain. For these reasons, fees in lieu of dedication and impact fee systems are beginning to displace more conventional dedication and improvement exactions, because they make it possible to apportion the costs of larger-scale improvements more systematically and equitably.

Fees in lieu of dedication

An alternative to compulsory dedication and improvement is to require or allow the subdivider to pay a fee that represents the value of the site or improvement that would have been dedicated or provided. Payment is usually made prior to and as a condition of final plat approval. In order to satisfy the constitutional tests outlined in a later section, these monies typically are placed in funds earmarked both by purpose (parks, school sites, etc.) and by the geographic area for which they were collected. "Fees-in-lieu" are typically used as an alternative to the dedication of park and school sites because these sites are most likely to serve areas beyond the boundaries of the subdivision and require prorating of the developer's contribution.

When compared to dedication, improvement, or other in-kind requirements, fees-in-lieu have several advantages. In-kind requirements may be infeasible if the subdivision is small; fees-in-lieu can be assessed against developments of all sizes. Developers may have an incentive to develop in piecemeal fashion to avoid the threshold application of certain dedication and improvement requirements; there is no such incentive where a sliding-scale schedule of fees is used. The local government receiving the funds can purchase the land or fund the improvement where it is most needed and when it is most convenient to do so. For example, administrators may find fees-in-lieu useful in financing drainage facilities, since large stormwater retention impoundments serving the entire drainage basin may be far more valuable than a number of drainage improvements sized in such a way that each serves only a single subdivision. Of course, in order to retain their "in-lieu" character, fees-in-lieu may be collected only for the types of sites or improvements for which a dedication or improvement requirement could have been imposed.

Some cities and counties are authorized to select the option (dedication or fees-in-lieu) that the subdivider must follow. Elsewhere the subdivider may have the right to choose, although the local government may be capable of influencing that choice by establishing fee and dedication schedules that make one option appear more attractive than the other.

Impact fees

Impact fees, also known as facility fees or project fees, are similar in concept and in function to fees in-lieu[17] but need not be directly tied to in-kind requirements and can more easily be applied to off-site as well as on-site facilities and improvements. Impact fees can be applied to apartment, condominium, commercial, and even office and industrial developments. Although such developments can create the need for new public facilities off-site, they often escape dedication and in-lieu requirements because subdivision regulations do not apply or because the land area to be dedicated is small. Another major difference between impact fees and typical subdivision exactions is that impact fees are generally collected when building permits are issued, usually just before the development creating the need for new services actually begins, rather than at the time of plat approval.

Impact fees are a systematic, comprehensive way of funding the new capital facilities required by new development. This approach contrasts sharply with the traditional method of funding capital improvements with revenues raised from the community at large. Although under appropriate circumstances impact fees could be used to fund new police stations, sanitary landfills, public health clinics, and community centers, most communities use impact fees to fund major street and highway projects, to expand water and sewerage systems, and, to a lesser degree, to obtain open space, park networks, and major stormwater control facilities.

The validity of a system of impact fees depends on the system's analytical basis. The steps that follow highlight the elements of a plan for the application of impact fees.

1. An estimate is made of the cost of acquiring land for and constructing each new public facility that is within the local government's jurisdiction, that must be provided during the planning period (e.g., twenty to twenty-five years), and that will be funded with impact fees. These estimates usually extend far beyond the time horizons used in a typical five- or seven-year capital improvements program.

2. The appropriate distribution of costs is determined on the basis of the costs of each facility that are attributable to, and that should be equitably borne by, both new and existing developments in each zone, service area, or planning district. Such a distribution of costs assumes that the community at large is obliged to provide public facilities such as roads and drainage improvements to serve existing residents at appropriate service standards. These costs are then allocated among the various development sectors—residential, commercial, and industrial.

3. A series of formulas or factors is used to allocate the appropriate portion of costs to each development project. For example, in the case of street improvements, the impact fee may be based on the number of trips generated by the land uses in the proposed development.

4. Once collected, these fees must be placed into trust funds or capital improvements funds, where they are earmarked both by type of facility and by the zone, service area, or planning district to be served.

5. When the funds reach appropriate levels, they are generally expended on the facilities for which they were collected so that residents of the new development actually benefit from the facilities; however, the fees may have to be refunded if they are not spent and facilities are not constructed within a reasonable time.

How an impact fee system meshes with the more traditional dedication and improvement requirements of subdivision regulations is an important emerging issue. A number of jurisdictions use impact fee systems simply to supplement more traditional in-kind subdivision contributions. The impact fees are used to help finance community facilities that normally serve an area substantially larger than a single subdivision, such as arterial and higher-function thoroughfares, community parks, and major trunk utility lines. Subdivision dedication and improvement requirements are applied independently and are confined primarily to on-site, local improvements that serve the immediate neighborhood of the subdivision. In most impact fee systems, fees in lieu of dedication are largely redundant and are not used.

In the future, however, many communities may experiment with unified impact fee systems that are designed to finance local neighborhood facilities located within the boundaries of a new subdivision as well as those serving a larger area. Such an arrangement presupposes that a subdividing developer may wish to provide the land for, and construct within the subdivision, some of those improvements called for in the capital improvements program. The value of such contributions should be credited against the amount of the impact fee assessed when the developer obtains building permits. In some cases, the impact fee system may allow developers credits for furnishing land or providing public facilities in areas some distance from the site for which development permission is sought and impact fees are owed. Impact fees are often used to finance new or expanded water and sewage facilities. One question that this practice raises is whether a developer may avoid the fees by establishing a private sewage-disposal or water-supply system. To meet the tests of constitutionality, it may be necessary to credit a developer for private facilities or improvements that serve the development in question, at least to the extent that the need for public ones is mitigated. It may also be necessary to credit a developer for the amount of future property taxes levied against the development that will be used to retire public facility bonds issued by the local government to serve the community as a whole. It may be useful to build some flexibility into impact fee requirements by including a procedure that allows a developer to submit evidence that the impact of a given development will differ from that predicted by the formula used in the fee schedule and to seek a corresponding revision in the fee.

Impact fees raise one other intriguing question: If a development contributes to the need for new capital facilities and if the developer might therefore be required to provide funds for their construction before construction ever begins, may not a developer be required to provide funds for the construction of those facilities that are already completed and in use? In other words, shouldn't a local government be able to recover through development fees the costs of needed capital improvements that it has already financed in anticipation of this very type of growth? Many municipal water and sewer utilities are experimenting with financial arrangements designed with this purpose in mind. The terminology for these arrangements is varied: capital cost-recovery systems, capacity-allo-cation plans, and capital improvement "buy-in" systems. Because they are based on revenue-producing public enterprises, the development fees may take the form of tap fees, connection charges, utility extension fees, acreage charges, or capital-recovery fees.

Often such charges are imposed to recover the costs of constructing a particular facility, such as a new wastewater treatment plant, rather than the costs of all systemwide improvements necessitated by new growth. To justify these charges and fees, a utility must be prepared to show that (1) it is not charging developers any of the costs of upgrading the existing system to adequately serve existing customers; (2) the developer is expected to "buy into" a portion of existing capacity that is no greater than necessary to serve the development; and (3) the portions of the facility costs financed through development fees, user charges imposed on future users, and reserve funds are equitably determined.

Exactions and the law

Most of the legal issues concerning developer exactions involve either a local government's authority to burden developers with a particular type of exaction or the constitutional question of whether an exaction is an appropriate application of government's regulatory power in a particular circumstance.

The issue of local government authority is still an important one for many cities and counties, particularly those that operate without home-rule charters. Many localities that depend on state enabling legislation for authority will find deficiencies in the legislation: for example, specific statutory authority to require dedication of parkland is available only in a minority of states. The lack of explicit authority is even more of a problem for communities that wish to charge either fees in lieu of dedication or development impact fees. In some states, broadly worded subdivision-control enabling legislation allows local units to "provide for" certain public facilities, such as parks, and courts have been willing to infer the implied power to use fees in lieu of dedication. In other states, however, the power to impose such fees must be explicit. Authorization problems can be most acute for communities that wish to impose impact fees. Cities and counties without home-rule charters must be able to find sufficient regulatory authority to charge such fees and must be able to show that an impact fee should not be characterized as a tax.

By their very nature, impact fees have been used to fund facilities such as schools, parks, and fire stations that traditionally have been financed from tax revenues. With this feature in mind, some courts have been inclined to characterize impact or similar capital improvement fees as taxes if the fees are based on a need for one type of capital improvement (e.g., parks) but apparently may be spent for another type (e.g., streets) or if the fees may be expended for capital improvements that will not necessarily provide sufficient benefit to the development for which they are imposed. If a court does label an impact fee a tax, it is likely to rule the fee invalid. Typically, a locality can levy a tax only by means of explicit state statutory or constitutional authority. In most states the power of local governments to levy special capital improvements taxes on developers is conspicuously absent.

Even if an impact fee is not characterized as a tax, specific enabling authority to impose impact fees as an exercise of the police power may be required in some states.

The constitutional aspects of exactions attract a great deal of attention. Unless exactions are flexibly applied, they may amount to an unconstitutional taking of private property for public use without just compensation, or a denial of the property owner's due process. For example, a requirement that a subdivider improve streets along subdivision boundaries or dedicate land for a park or school that serves an area substantially larger than the development might be vulnerable to such a claim. Similarly, the collection of fees in lieu of dedication or impact fees that are not earmarked by purpose and not expended in a timely way that sufficiently benefits the development in question may be legally vulnerable.

Courts around the country have formulated several tests for determining the constitutionality of a particular requirement imposed on a developer. Illinois, Ohio, and Rhode Island seem to adhere to the "specifically and uniquely attributable" test, under which a requirement is constitutional only if the burden cast upon the subdivider is specifically and uniquely attributable to the development. General public benefit from the dedication or improvement must be insignificant, and benefits must inure almost exclusively to the residents of the development. Adjacent and off-site street improvements generally will not meet this test; park and school site dedication requirements are likely to be acceptable only when applied to large, isolated, autonomous developments. A park site dedication requirement would probably not be legally defensible if the community had already provided suitable facilities nearby that could serve the development. under the specifically and uniquely attributable test, no dedication or improvement requirement is likely to pass muster unless the site or facility would be a candidate for special assessment.

In the past decade, state courts have chosen increasingly to use more flexible tests, generally some version of the "reasonably related" or "rational nexus" test. The first asks whether the requirement is reasonably related to the nature and impact of the development proposed; the second asks whether the exaction has a rational nexus to it. The more sophisticated versions of reasonably related and rational nexus tests first require that the need for the public facilities to be provided by the exaction be sufficiently attributable to the developer's activity to justify the imposition of the exaction. In other words, the cost burden to the developer cannot exceed the prorated portion of the total facility costs that can fairly be allocated to the development. The second requirement is that the facility provided by the developer or financed by the fees imposed on the developer sufficiently benefit the assessed subdivision. Courts using this test do not require the subdivision to enjoy the exclusive or even the principal benefit from the site, improvement, or fee. However, the timing of the benefits derived from a developer's contributions has emerged as a crucial factor in determining constitutionality. The developer cannot be expected to provide land or money for facilities that will benefit the development only at some distant time in the future. Although many courts have recognized the need for advance planning of community facilities, those that apply reasonably related and rational nexus tests have generally not tolerated exactions of land (for street extensions for example) if the community has no immediate plans to build and use the facility.

The emphasis on prorating costs and apportioning public facility burdens may imply that the job of devising a system of impact fees need not be complex. At least one court, however, the Utah Supreme Court in *Banberry Development Corporation* v. *South Jordan City*,[18] has suggested that the equitable share of capital improvement costs that may be assigned to newly developed properties may depend on a series of variables not specifically analyzed by other courts. These include the manner in which existing capital facilities were financed, particularly the extent to which they were provided by the municipality and financed by general taxation in other parts of the community; the extent to which newly developing properties have already contributed to existing facilities through the payment of general taxes, assessments, or user charges and may thus be entitled to a credit; the nature of any extraordinary costs that may arise in the servicing of newly developed properties; and the present value of amounts paid at different times. Courts that have applied the reasonably related and rational nexus tests to ad hoc exaction requirements by applying rough judgments of equity and fairness may be forced to develop more sophisticated legal tests for evaluating more sophisticated and systemic exactions.

California courts have used a constitutional test of their own that seems to be more liberal than tests used elsewhere. The dedication, improvement, or fee must be reasonably related to the nature and impact of the proposed development, but the link may be a bit more indirect. Courts applying this test apparently find no constitutional requirement that facilities derived from developer contributions serve or benefit exclusively or primarily development on which they are imposed: it is enough that existing facilities and facilities provided by dedications and fees from new development adequately serve existing and new residents alike and that a developer bear no more than an equitable share of the costs of providing facilities needed to serve new growth generally. Under this test, the mere fact that a developer happens to develop land close to an existing park does not enable the developer to avoid either a fee in lieu of dedication or an impact fee for parkland.

This California test, however, has been called into question by the U.S. Supreme Court case of *Nollan* v. *California Coastal Commission*.[19] In this decision, the Supreme Court ruled unconstitutional a California Coastal Commission requirement that a property owner dedicate for a public access easement a strip of land along the oceanfront portion of his lot as a condition to his obtaining approval for the demolition of an old house and the construction of a new, larger one. The Nollans' property was located in an area where dedications for public access had been made on nearly all of the beachfront parcels. The Court found that governments may not condition the approval of building plans upon agreements by property owners to surrender their property rights for public use without compensation—unless the condition is reasonably related to the burdens new construction would place on the public. It reversed the decision of a California Court of Appeal, which had upheld the dedication requirement under the California exaction test. Although the *Nollan* case should not jeopardize a well-conceived system of impact fees or similar capital-facility financing arrangements, it serves as a reminder that governments may not legally induce concessions from property owners simply because the development approval process can serve as a source of great leverage.

Exactions and developer opposition

The subdivision improvements and community facilities that a community exacts from a developer may have an important bearing on the profitability of a project. Exaction disputes do not necessarily result in litigation. Many subdivision review procedures and regulatory standards lend themselves to negotiated arrangements that defuse possible legal actions. Some developers in rapidly growing or selective communities may find it better to capitulate, provide what is required, and finish the project on time rather than fight town hall and miss the cresting market. A low-volume home builder working primarily in a single urban area may find it occasionally useful to concede in order to curry favor with the governmental unit that will be reviewing other of his projects in the years to come.

Certain circumstances, however, may incline a developer to contest exactions:

1. Not only will compliance with the requirement be costly, but the exaction is also unanticipated and is not reflected in the price the developer paid for the land. (Example: The developer is expected to redesign and replace an existing street intersection at one corner of the site.)
2. The same type of exaction has not been required of the developer's competitors.
3. The improvement or facility to be provided will benefit the general public more than it will benefit subdivision residents, and no arrangments have been made for prorated reimbursement. (Example: The developer is expected to construct a stormwater retention basin on the property to prevent downstream flooding.)
4. The improvement requirement may appear to primarily benefit subdivision residents, but the developer will have difficulty shifting its cost to lot purchasers because they do not value the improvement highly enough to pay the corresponding increment in the price of the lots. (Example: The developer must provide extra-wide streets or extra-thick street paving.)
5. The completion of a major public facility that will serve a large, phased development is required by the end of the first stage of development rather than by the end of the project. (Example: The developer must construct an extra traffic lane on an arterial street that runs along one boundary of the development.)

6. The local government insists that a public-facility site (e.g., a park or school site) be provided where some of the highest-priced building lots would otherwise be located or where public access to the site might substantially depreciate the value of adjacent lots.

The adequate public facilities test

Traditional land dedication, improvement and fee requirements seek to ensure directly that a subdivision bears the costs of local facilities that serve it. Although the provision of these facilities by the developer is generally required for plat approval, many growth management programs link new development and the provision of public facilities in rather different ways, such as timing, phasing, or quota controls. One popular approach has been to prohibit new development that is not served by adequate public facilities. For example, a subdivision may be approved only if the community finds that large-scale facilities such as major arteries and thoroughfares, schools, wastewater treatment plants, and areawide drainage facilities are adequate to serve the additional growth created by the subdivision.[20]

Advocates of growth managment believe that growth should be guided into areas best suited for it and that decisions about the sites for large-scale public facilities, the extension of utility systems, or the expansion of the road network should recognize and reinforce the suitability of various areas for development. Capital improvements should be programmed in an orderly way, both to make the most cost-effective use of tax dollars and to allow private property owners to rely on the local government to provide additional public-service capacity. Many growth management supporters argue that the adequacy of large-scale public facilities should be considered in the review of individual development projects because local governments are simply incapable of expanding capital facilities as fast as development can occur during periods of rapid growth. Allowing development to outstrip the provision of public facilities and services results in congestion, lower levels of service, and malfunctions that penalize old and new residents alike.

One approach to growth management is the technique of establishing service area boundaries for services such as water and sewer. The community determines the expansion of facilities and customer growth that it wishes to support within a particular planning period. It then commits itself to financing the major line extensions, treatment capacity expansion, and other infrastructural improvements necessary to serve development occurring within the service area boundary during the planning period. Typically the jurisdiction then refuses to bear the costs of providing services beyond the service area boundaries. It may even refuse to allow expansion of the utility system if the expansion is designed to accommodate areas beyond the service area boundaries or is ahead of schedule, even though a developer may propose to bear all of the costs.

The landmark adequate public facilities case is the New York Court of Appeals' decision in *Golden* v. *Planning Board of the Town of Ramapo* (1972).[21] Ramapo had adopted an eighteen-year capital improvements program and a comprehensive plan projecting future growth. All residential development except single-family detached dwellings required a special use permit granted by the governing board. A permit was granted if the developer's proposal rated a certain number of points based on the availability of five important services, even though not all of the services were controlled by the town. Adequacy was determined by the distance between the development and the public facility offering the service. To increase the point score and accelerate the development of the land, a developer could choose to provide some of the facilities. (Although the point system was in Ramapo's zoning ordinance, the system functioned much as it would in a subdivision ordinance.) New York's highest court upheld the constitutionality of the growth-management ordinance, rejecting "taking" and "exclusionary zoning" claims.

A number of rapidly growing communities have adopted some form of adequate public facilities test in a growth management or subdivision ordinance since the *Ramapo* decision, but this standard has its drawbacks. Traditional subdivision regulations generally make it clear that the developer is responsible for providing the required dedications, fees, and improvements to obtain plat approval. In an ordinance incorporating the adequate public facilities test, it may be less clear who bears the responsibility for enlarging public facilities, expanding their capacity, or improving service levels. Normally, certain capital improvements are the function of government because the benefits of these facilities are spread throughout the community. If a subdivision cannot be developed because community public facilities are inadequate but the community has no plan to upgrade or improve those facilities or offers no basis for its refusal to do so, it may be unconstitutional to apply an adequate public facilities test. If the community does offer a capital improvements plan to remedy the inadequacy, the local government nevertheless may be unable to adhere to its own schedule because of changes in federal and state funding programs, the need for voter approval of bond issues, policy changes brought on by governing board changes, or emergency needs for other facilities. In communities that permit a developer to arrange for the additional public facilities, the developer's only real option may be to finance a facility or improvement from which the new development will derive only fractional benefit and for which the developer can claim no reimbursement from others. The result is that the construction required to expand capacity or make service levels adequate is often delayed. In contrast to the effect of many dedication, improvement, fee-in-lieu, and impact fee requirements, the effect of an adequate public facilities test, whether intended or not, is more likely to limit growth than to accommodate it.

Other methods of financing subdivision improvements

Although the most important and popular methods of providing subdivision improvements place the full initial financial burden on the developer, several other financing methods are also used. At one time it was not uncommon for local governments to construct or pay for the construction of new facilities or to subsidize developers who provided them. Even today, some jurisdictions (especially very small towns) are so eager for growth that they subsidize the construction of local streets and utility lines within new developments. In some cases local governments provide labor or materials, in other cases partial reimbursement for the developers' costs.

Some local governments specially assess the costs of site improvements (particularly streets and utilities) against individual subdivision lots. In these communities, the developer submits a special-assessment petition, and the assessing authority (typically, but not necessarily, the general-purpose unit of local government) accepts the petition, uses the proceeds of special-assessment bonds or other debt instruments to finance the improvements, and imposes liens on the lots that benefit. Assessments may be collected relatively soon (within a year) after the assessment roll is approved or may be spread over a period as long as ten to fifteen years. In some cases the assessing authority may subsidize the project by assessing less than the full cost of the project against lot owners.

The creation or expansion of a special-improvement district is another important means of financing improvements. Particularly in unincorporated areas, developers of large subdivisions may find it advantageous to create or join a special district that includes the property being subdivided. Special districts commonly finance drainage facilities, water supply and sewage disposal systems, roads, parks, and various other improvements; they may or may not also be authorized to assume ongoing maintenance responsibilities. Such districts are generally empowered to issue improvement bonds and to impose special ad valorem property taxes against properties to service the debt.

When special-assessment authorities and special improvement districts finance the capital construction, the developer need not obtain front-end financing to build the facilities, and the lot purchasers can avoid the higher lot prices that might have otherwise resulted. The disadvantage of special-assessment authorities and special districts is that they tend to fragment the provision of government facilities and services and in some instances can undermine the control exercised by general-purpose units of government by offering competing services without the consent of the affected governmental units.

Compulsory reservation

Compulsory reservation of land may be useful where plans show that a site in a new subdivision would be the most desirable location for a major public facility but the local government cannot justify requiring the developer to dedicate the land free of charge. Compulsory reservation requires the developer to abstain from subdividing the reserved portion of the property and to keep it free from development for a specific period of time, during which the governmental unit or agency for whom the site was reserved may negotiate its purchase or begin eminent domain proceedings.[22] If the government fails to do so by the time the period expires, the reservation is lifted and the developer may subdivide and develop the reserved land.

Reserving sites and rights-of-way for public facilities under subdivision regulations is easiest if the community has adopted an official map, a document adopted by the governing board designating the exact location of existing and proposed streets, utilities, parks and playgrounds, and other public sites. Typically, once such a map is adopted, no building permit may be issued for a building or structure in the reserved areas.

For reservations to withstand the increasing skepticism of the courts, the nature and extent of the reservation requirements must be related to the ultimate development of the remaining land; the reservation period must be short (not more than several years); reasonable use of the reserved land must be allowed during the reservation period; and there must be some indication that the land will in fact be acquired and used by the appropriate unit of government. Although reservation has generally allowed units of government to obtain an option on reserved land without paying for it, some states (e.g., Pennsylvania) now require that owners of reserved land be paid a reasonable return for the use of the land forgone during the reservation period, regardless of whether the land is eventually acquired. Reservation is most useful for protecting public facility sites that do not demand a precisely surveyed location or alignment (such as sites for parks, schools, and fire stations) or for the widening of existing thoroughfares. It is more difficult to reserve right-of-way for a new highway thoroughfare.

Private ownership and maintenance of community facilities

Compulsory dedication and reservation requirements are based on the assumption that it is often desirable for a public agency to own, control, and maintain the open space, facilities, and improvements in new subdivisions. For example, a locality may wish to keep an access to a lake, stream, or the ocean open to the public. It may be useful for a municipality to be able to require the public dedication of a street that is a crucial link in the public street network. It may even be in a county's interest to create more business for a county water system with substantial capacity by requiring the public dedication and installation of water lines within a subdivision.

In many instances, however, it is neither possible nor practical for a government agency to accept and maintain the improvements and facilities that serve a new subdivision. Local governments should give careful thought to whether common facilities are made public or are allowed (or required) to remain private. However, if subdivision improvements and facilities do remain private, there is no reason for the applicable development standards to differ from those that apply to public facilities.

It may be necessary or desirable for a new development to rely on privately maintained common facilities. For example, reductions in federal funding for water purification and wastewater treatment facilities have made it increasingly difficult for local governments to offer unused treatment capacity to developers. Some communities may find that their growth depends on developments that have small, privately owned and managed decentralized wastewater treatment systems. Cost-conscious local governments may also discover that well-conceived private developments generate property tax revenues without the associated service burdens that their public counterparts are thought to impose. Of course, in some unincorporated areas, common facilities remain private because no unit or agency of government is either authorized to assume or capable of assuming responsibility for maintenance or operation.

Many communities review private maintenance arrangements as a part of final plat approval. Long-term maintenance and operation of common facilities by the developer is generally not a realistic option unless the development is large and is staged over many years. Even if long-term maintenance by the developer is not feasible, it is common for developers to be required to assume responsibility for streets, drainage facilities, and other improvements until the responsibility for operation and maintenance has been permanently accepted by some other private or public entity. A second and more common option is to require the developer to incorporate a property owners' or homeowners' association in which all lot owners are automatically members.[23] The association takes over the common areas and facilities and is empowered to maintain and operate them by assessing costs against the properties. Such community associations are common in planned unit developments and work best if their budgets are large enough to allow them to hire staff to manage the work. In some developments, operations and maintenance are handled by a trust, a private utility, or various other nonprofit entities. A third but less satisfactory arrangement used mainly for roads, requires the subdivider to include a facility-maintenance agreement in the restrictive covenants for the subdivision. Such an agreement explicitly assigns lot owners the responsibility for maintenance and provides a formula for allocating maintenace costs among them but establishes no formal organization for collecting the money and contracting for the work. One other approach, used in a few states, allows the local government to require the developer to post a maintenance bond or trust fund with a public agency to be used solely for future maintenance of a private facility, such as a private road. A final alternative is simply to allow lot purchasers to fend for themselves and maintain common facilities in any manner they can work out. A short rural road may never be maintained, or neighbors may chip in to buy a truckload of crushed stone to put on after the next spring thaw. The larger the number of properties served by the facility, the more unwieldy the arrangement becomes.

Administering subdivision regulations

The fundamental steps that most local governments follow in reviewing a subdivision plat have not changed substantially over the years. Particularly in the past decade, however, local government regulatory systems have come under increasing scrutiny; developers and citizens alike have attacked the development review process as too complicated, too slow, too unpredictable, and unfair. These concerns have required public officials and professional planners to focus attention on review procedures that were once taken for granted.[24]

A number of communities have attempted to reform the subdivision review process.[25] In some cases, regulations have been simplified to reduce the time needed to review a plat, thereby influencing one of the factors that increases the price of housing. Other reforms have been made to reduce the work load for elected and appointed public officials or to make the review process more open to the public and to make officials more accountable. Some communities have simplified procedures to gain a competitive edge in attracting new development. Of course, many planning departments have had to process subdivision plats more efficiently simply to survive budgetary limitations.

The other major change in subdivision review involves the exercise of discretion by plat approval agencies. Subdivision review has always involved negotiation among developers, staff, and reviewing agencies, but as long as the review focused on the impact of the proposal within the subdivision, the approval of a typical subdivision plat was a relatively straightforward and predictable matter. Innovative and flexible growth management techniques have broadened the focus of subdivision review to encompass wider, even communitywide impacts. Standards have become more general, and plat approval agencies now tend to wield more discretionary power. As the subdivision review process has come to include more bargaining and negotiation, the outcome of the process has become more uncertain.

Local governments review subdivision plats, using a variety of organizational arrangements, most of which rely on the decisions of a planning or governing board. Because subdivision regulations can be somewhat technical, however, a lay body may find it difficult to review complex subdivisions adequately. A board of elected officials or a planning commission may find that its role is redundant because it must either rely rather heavily on staff recommendations or be tempted to make technical judgments that it is not well qualified to make. Furthermore, many elected officials overestimate their authority to deny approval of subdivision plats. Subdivision regulations generally require plats to be approved if they meet the articulated standards of the ordinance. The fear of some elected officials that to delegate plat approval is to relinquish substantial discretionary power is often unfounded. If the law permits and a competent staff is available, there is much to be said for delegating plat review authority to the planning staff or to an interdepartmental technical review committee. In addition to technical expertise, staff can also generally offer swifter review than can a commission or council that meets only once a month. Developers tend to prefer staff approval for this reason.

The cyclical nature of the building industry and the seasonal nature of land development activity can create staffing problems in planning agencies. Planning directors, managers, and governing boards must anticipate increased work load during peak development review periods—or risk damaging staff morale and frustrating the development community. During peak periods, the planning directors may need to call in temporary or part-time help from within or outside the agency. Some large cities and counties have experimented with contracting out the review of subdivision plans and other development projects, but this can create problems of quality control and consistency.

Preapplication

Early consultation between developers and staff familiarizes developers with local development requirements and staff with proposed plans, reduces errors and omissions in applications, clarifies the proposal's impact on public facilities, and reveals possible conflicts with other projects, with past precedents, and with community feeling. Relatively little detail should be expected from the subdivider at this stage; one of the local government's objectives should be to help the subdivider to avoid the later redesign of the project. Of course, the planning staff or review committee may be unable to guarantee that a particular proposal will be approved, but these early negotiations can lead to changes in the developer's plans that might not easily be made later. Preapplication consultations will be more productive if the governing body provides the developer with a written outline of approval procedures (flow charts with approximate time frames are useful), a list of required application materials and information (checklists are helpful here), and a subdivision design manual that includes standards for subdivision improvements and illustrates solutions to subdivision design problems.

Preliminary plat review

The next important step in the review process is often the submission of a preliminary plat of the proposed subdivision, along with other documentation and plans. (In some communities this is the first step.) Figure 8–10 summarizes the preliminary plat review process. To call a subdivision map submitted at this stage "preliminary" is somewhat misleading, since the plat will, in large measure, fix the nature, design, and scope of the subdividing activity to follow. Furthermore, it serves as a general blueprint for whatever improvements or facilities the developer is to provide. Ordinarily, the subdivider will not be required to submit a site plan or building elevations to obtain subdivision plat approval, particularly if the subdivision is intended for single-family detached residences; but if construction of housing units is allowed before final site plan review, the site plan may be reviewed as if it were a preliminary plat. However, a final recordable plat is always required.

An effective review process depends on the adequacy of the information provided, and a unit need not proceed with a review until the application is complete. If the development project is complex, the local government's submission requirements are substantial, or special reports are required, an application may be deficient when first submitted or at some stage of the review. In many communities, the staff will halt the review process if the application is deficient. Because the costs of delay may be substantial for the subdivider, the local government should notify a subdivider as early as possible if application materials are incomplete. The application procedure should be designed to furnish the plat approving agency with information that will be used directly to approve or deny approval to the plat (and should therefore be geared to the authority the agency has in reviewing the plat), or it should be of use to some identifiable agency or private party.

The review of a typical subdivision plat (and the construction plans that will accompany it) may involve only a few departments, agencies, and units of government or a number of them. For example, an agency may be required to certify that the construction plans submitted meet that agency's standards for the improvement in question. In other cases, agencies such as the board of education are asked to review subdivision plans as a courtesy. A local government may be able to glean useful advice from an agency with no formal approval power. For example, in suburban and rural areas, a district soil conservationist may be able to furnish helpful advice about soils and drainage.

The review procedure works best when the departments and agencies (1) receive copies of the subdivision plats and accompanying documents well before their comments are expected; (2) make their recommendations and comments in writing; and (3) present those comments orally at a technical review committee

Figure 8–9 Combined preliminary subdivision plat and site plan for The Meadows in Chapel Hill, North Carolina.

meeting that includes representatives from all of the reviewing departments and agencies. Such a procedure encourages communication among the reviewing agencies as well as between each reviewing agency and the applicant. It also encourages prompt resolution of disagreements among departments or agencies, helps to familiarize the representatives with the concerns of other departments and agencies, and encourages agencies to meet the review schedule established by the plat approving unit. Many questions can be answered and disagreements resolved before the plat approval agency considers the plat. Ideally, the technical review committee provides a single recommendation that the planner or manager can carry to the planning or governing board.

Although some jurisdictions have delegated plat approval authority to staff, typically the preliminary plat is approved by the planning or governing board. State law and local regulations in a number of states require the plat approving board to hold a public hearing on the application before granting approval. In a few states (e.g., California and New Jersey) the board holding such a hearing functions in a quasi-judicial capacity, which requires it to hear evidence and make formal findings of fact; in many other jurisdictions the purpose of the public hearing is less clear. The risk of public hearings is that the planning or governing board will be tempted to base its decision on political factors extraneous to the regulations, thereby exceeding its power, and that the public will develop false expectations about the board's power to deny plat approval.

The customary practice is for a board to approve a plat, approve it with

Figure 8–10   Flow chart for preliminary plat review process.

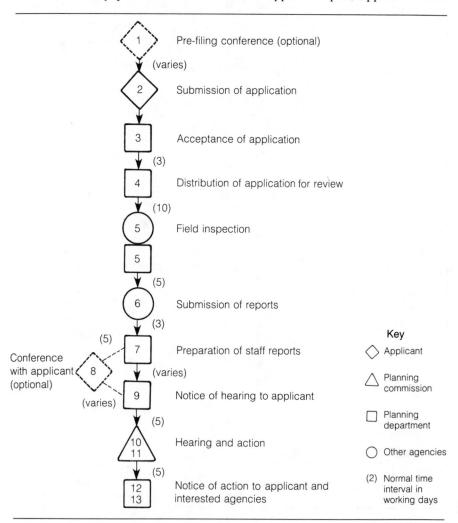

1   Pre-filing conference (optional)

(varies)

2   Submission of application

3   Acceptance of application

(3)

4   Distribution of application for review

(10)

5   Field inspection

5

(5)

6   Submission of reports

(3)

(5)

7   Preparation of staff reports

Conference with applicant (optional)   8

(varies)

9   Notice of hearing to applicant

(varies)

(5)

10
11   Hearing and action

(5)

12
13   Notice of action to applicant and interested agencies

Key

◇ Applicant

△ Planning commission

☐ Planning department

○ Other agencies

(2) Normal time interval in working days

conditions, or deny approval. Several alternatives are possible if changes are required to bring the preliminary plat into conformity with the regulations or if conditions are added that may require the redesign of the plat. The board can require the applicant to withdraw the plat, redesign the subdivision to incorporate the required changes, and then resubmit the revised plat. Alternatively, the board can approve the preliminary plat subject to the condition that the required changes be incorporated into the final plat. Requiring the redesign and resubmission of the preliminary plat will cost the applicant time and money, but permitting the applicant to "work out" the required changes in the final plat without resubmitting the preliminary version may produce a final plat that does not meet the board's expectations. The approach should probably depend on the extent of the required changes. The redesign of a cul-de-sac, for example, can probably be handled after the preliminary plat is conditionally approved, but complete relocation of a street may require that the stormwater management plan be revised and resubmitted prior to preliminary approval. One compromise may be for the board to delegate to staff the authority to approve redesigned preliminary plans prior to the submission of final plans.

Most regulations require final plans to be submitted and approved within a certain time (often a year or two) after the preliminary plat is approved. Approval of the preliminary plat generally implies approval of a final plat conforming substantially to the preliminary version, even if subdivision and zoning standards change during the intervening period. In a large, multiphased development, however, the final plats for some of the latter phases of the development may be submitted some years after the approval of the preliminary plat or master plan. An alternative is for the board to approve a flexible staging plan at the time the preliminary plat is submitted that allows final plats to be submitted over a much longer period. Approval of a staging plan also links the recording of final plats to the installation of the improvements necessary to serve the development phases. For this reason alone, approval of staging plans for larger subdivisions can be highly desirable.

Boards occasionally approve features of plats and plans that do not comply with the apparent terms of the subdivision regulations. Variances, exceptions, modifications, and waivers are some of the terms used to describe these kinds of permissions. Subdivision regulations and state statutes generally give only skimpy recognition to them, and there are no generally recognized standards for the granting of subdivision variances. To discourage abuse of these alternatives, some communities spell out which requirements may be modified and under what circumstances. For example, there is rarely a good reason to vary the minimum lot-size requirements of the regulations, but there may be some practical justification for allowing deviations from certain improvement standards. The best approach is to avoid variances by refining development standards and making them more flexible.

Many local governments classify subdivisions and establish different review processes for each class, which is an excellent way to streamline the regulatory process. In communities experiencing limited growth, an abbreviated review process can be used to handle a substantial majority of subdivisions. Some communities that categorize subdivisions divide them into "major" and "minor" classes. Major subdivisions may be subject to a three-stage review process (review of sketch plan, preliminary plat, and final plat). Minor subdivisions may be reviewed twice, at the sketch plan and final plat stages. A minor subdivision might be defined as a subdivision (1) involving not more than five lots, all fronting on an existing approved street or road; (2) requiring no new streets or roads (including those to provide access to interior property): and (3) requiring no extension of water or sewer lines or the establishment of new drainage easements to serve rear properties. To avoid submitting a development plan for the whole tract, a property owner might be tempted to submit a minor subdivision plan for only a portion of a large landholding. This abuse of the minor subdivision process can be prevented by permitting the minor subdivision review process to be used only where the subdivision includes all of the contiguous land owned by the sponsor.

Final plat review

The final plat is submitted in much the same way as the preliminary plat, with adequate copies for distribution to interested departments and to agencies that made recommendations or approved plans earlier in the process. Final plat review ensures that the recordable plat is in substantial accordance with plans approved earlier and that whatever subdivision improvements have been constructed conform to those plans.

Final plat review is also the occasion for reviewing the operation and maintenance of proposed private facilities and improvements. A local government needs to know that it will not be required at some point in the future to take over private roads or sewage disposal and treatment systems that have been improperly maintained. If the subdivision is part of a planned unit development, is clustered with common open space, or is simply a rural subdivision with private

Figure 8–11   Flow chart for final plat review process.

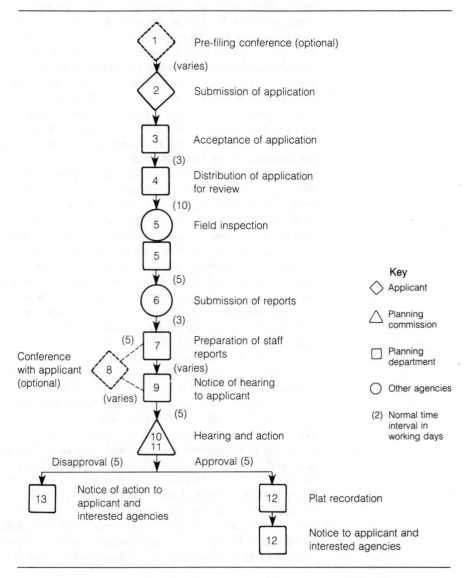

roads, the subdivider may be expected to document the existence of a mechanism or organization to handle maintenance responsibilities. Many jurisdictions review the restrictive covenants and maintenance agreements that apply to lot owners in a new development; as part of the final plat review, the agency may also review the articles of incorporation and bylaws for a proposed property owners' association.

The final plat is the subdivision map that is prepared for recording in the office of the registrar of deeds and is sometimes known as the *record plat*. In most states, such plats must be prepared by a registered surveyor or engineer. State statutes typically prescribe standards governing the quality of the survey and the platting conventions used, the format of the plat, and the certifications and other information displayed on the face of the plat. Most jurisdictions prefer that engineering information (e.g., the location and type of utilities and drainage facilities) not be included on the final plat; an engineering plat based on "as-built" drawings can be prepared when subdivision improvements are completed, but that plat is typically not designed to be recorded. All spaces, lots, and marks on the plat should either be self-explanatory or be explained by notes on the plat, by the approval resolution, or by the terms of the regulations or ordinance. An approved final plat commonly exhibits the following certifications: (1) a certificate of approval by the chair or head of the plat approval agency; (2) a certificate of accuracy and mapping by the surveyor; (3) a certificate of ownership and dedication; and (4) a certificate of registration by the registrar of deeds. In addition, various other statements and certificates may appear on the plat.

An important trend in some areas is for the local government to require various disclosure statements to be placed on or incorporated into the plat, although the use of such statements may be limited by the fact that most recordable plats are already crowded with information. Disclosure statements may show, for example, that the subdivision lots are located in a flood fringe area, are in an approach zone to an airport, are provisionally suitable for a septic tank system, are subject to coastal zone regulations, or are served by private roads to be maintained by individual lot purchasers.

Once the final plat for a subdivision (or a phase of the subdivision) is officially adopted by the plat approval agency, the plat may be recorded and lots sold. As a general rule, building permits for single-family detached houses in conventional subdivisions may not be issued until final plat approval and recording. Only then can plot plans based on recorded lots be presented and zoning requirements for each lot be applied.

Most regulations require the plat to be recorded within a month or two after it has been approved, to prevent the premature subdivision of land. This rule prevents subdividers from obtaining plat approval but resisting recording of the plat to avoid having their land assessed as building lots instead of as acreage. A few local governments assume responsibility for recording the approved plat to prevent it from being altered or tampered with before recording, but the risk of liability for mishandling of the plat makes this a questionable practice.

Checking both the submitted plats and the completed construction work can be costly. In addition, local governments are required to prepare special environmental or traffic impact reports for particular subdivisions; others are required to advertise the public hearings held on subdivision proposals. To recover some of these costs, many communities impose fees on the subdivider. Subdivision fees are generally based on the estimated rather than the actual costs of review, inspection, report preparation, and advertisement and generally are due before final plat approval. Although these fees must be related to actual costs, many local governments charge less than they could. A simple fee schedule may include a flat fee plus additional amounts for each lot or each linear foot of improvement installed. (These review, inspection, and related fees must be carefully distinguished from the impact fees and fees-in-lieu of dedication discussed earlier.

Guaranteed developer performance

Generally, a developer may not begin to construct subdivision improvements until the preliminary plat is approved. Although installation or construction of improvements may begin with approval of the preliminary plat, most jurisdictions do not require that improvements be completed before final plat approval. Typically, at least some of the improvements may be completed after final plat approval if the developer has guaranteed performance as a part of the final plat submission.

The most effective way to ensure that streets are properly constructed, drainage facilities properly provided, and water and sewer lines properly installed is to withhold final plat approval until these improvements are completed and inspected by the local government.[26] Only when the final plat is submitted and approved can the lots be sold and building permits be obtained. Although this procedure provides a local government with maximum leverage over the developer, most jurisdictions allow a subdivider to install or construct some or all of the required improvements after final plat approval, provided that the jurisdiction has a financial guarantee or some other form of leverage to ensure that the tasks will be performed.

A variation of this approach, sequential approval of required improvements, is used for staged developments. A developer may be allowed to assign a portion of the overall improvements to each development stage as part of the complete phasing plan. Final plat approval for each phase depends on completion of the required improvements for the preceding phase. (Financial security may be required before approval of the final phase.) Sequential approval of phased improvements eliminates the need for large financial guarantees and is adaptable to midsize subdivisions. Its primary drawback is that certain rather expensive large-scale improvements (a private wastewater treatment plant, for example) do not lend themselves to phasing. It may be unwise to allow phases of development to proceed before the treatment plant is ready, but requiring the completion of the entire sewage disposal system before the second phase of development is begun may be equally undesirable.

Some local governments have successfully used a hybrid approach. They require, for example, that certain improvements (such as the road base and drainage improvements) be installed before the final plat is approved and building permits are issued. Other improvements (including some or all of the paving work) may be subject to a financial performance guarantee and may be completed after lots are sold and building construction has begun.

More lenient jurisdictions try to exert leverage over the developer by withholding occupancy permits for the buildings erected until the necessary infrastructure improvements are provided. This approach works best for developers with integrated home-building operations and reduces development costs by requiring no financial guarantee. However, such a system requires more detailed record keeping than some smaller communities can manage and can penalize an innocent builder, contractor, or home buyer by making a house unavailable for occupancy on time.

Many local governments allow final subdivision plat approval only if the subdivider posts some form of security. The security, generally approved with the final plat, comes in a variety of forms: (1) the subdivider may obtain a performance bond from a surety company; (2) the subdivider may obtain an irrevocable letter of credit from a lender (often the lender who is providing construction financing); (3) the subdivider may place cash in an escrow account held in trust by the local government or by a financial institution; (4) the subdivider may escrow personal property (stocks, bonds, equipment) or mortgage or give a deed of trust on real property; or (5) the subdivider, the subdivider's lender, and the local government can enter into a three-party subdivision improvement agreement. If one of these options is used, the bond may not be released, the letter of credit withdrawn, the account closed, nor the contract completed until a representative of local government (often the engineer or public works director) has certified that the required improvements have been completed according to specifications.

Many jurisdictions have found the letter of credit to be the most satisfactory method of guaranteeing performance. Bonds are often costly—or worse, unavailable to smaller developers. Surety companies rarely allow a bond to be called without putting up some resistance. Cash deposits and escrow accounts require developers to make their assets available at the front end of the development process, when they need them most.

For communities that use financial performance guarantees, the most important question is when to declare a default. It may be unwise for a local government to do so unless lot purchases will suffer from the developer's failure to provide the improvements to which they are legitimately entitled. Even if the development is foreclosed or the developer goes bankrupt, the land can perhaps be sold to an investor or developer who is in a better position to complete the required improvements than is a governmental agency. In some instances it may be better for the local government to extend the completion deadline and allow renewal or extension of the developer's security. Declaring a default and taking over the completion of the improvements can be unexpectedly costly for a local government. The proceeds from security should, but often do not, reflect (1) the cost inflation of the labor and materials needed to complete the improvements; (2) the special administrative costs associated with declaring a default, bidding or programming the project, and completing it; and (3) the unforeseen costs of remedying the damage, deterioration, or faulty workmanship associated with the work that has already been done.

A second important matter is whether security should be released in stages. A local government may be under some pressure to release portions of the security as segments of the work are finished. Not only does this practice save the developer some expense in providing security, but contractors can use reduction of security as proof that portions of the work have been properly completed and that the developer owes them money. Reduction in the security typically requires more inspections and hence more expense for the local government. Many communities find that phased reductions in security are not warranted unless the development is staged by geographic area.

Although performance guarantees typically are used to secure the completion of improvements, they can also guard against defects in workmanship that appear after the improvements have been inspected, approved, and accepted. The developer can be required to provide a warranty against defects in improvements for a reasonable period (e.g., one year). The local government should retain a percentage of the security after improvements are completed for this purpose. Such security, rather than a maintenance bond, can serve as a form of construction guarantee.

Inspection and acceptance of improvements

Procedures for inspecting, approving, and accepting improvements should be made as explicit as possible. Constant tension exists between the local government, which needs to inspect improvements at several stages of completion, and the contractor and developer, who want to move on to other tasks. Inspection fees may be calculated as a percentage of the cost of the improvement, per linear foot of improvement, or by some other formula. Charging a fee for each site visit can prevent the inspector's time from being wasted. The list prepared by the engineer or inspector should be the basis for a report indicating whether the improvement is approved, partially approved, or rejected. It is a wise practice at this stage to require the developer to submit "as-built" plans or a certification that the working plans as approved represent what has actually been constructed or installed. The report and plans then serve as the basis for the release of the security and for acceptance of the improvements. Although many jurisdictions implicitly accept improvements by allowing maintenance and operation to begin, it is a better policy for the governing board to adopt a resolution explicitly accepting the subdivision improvements and the easements in which they are located.

Enforcement

The methods of guaranteeing performance just discussed are effective means of enforcing subdivision regulations if the developer submits subdivision plans for review and the development requires facilities or services. However, in small towns and rural areas, landowners often violate the subdivision ordinance by selling off lots without referring to an approved plat. Violation of an ordinance may be a misdemeanor crime, but few prosecuting attorneys are interested in these cases. Obtaining a court order to halt or remedy violations is often ineffective once lots have already been sold, and civil penalties are an unproven method of discouraging violation. In most states, registrars of deeds may not refuse to record a deed simply because it describes an illegally subdivided lot. One common administrative sanction is the withholding of building permits for lots in unapproved subdivisions. However, some courts have refused to authorize such withholding when the applicant has been an innocent lot purchaser, unless the lot standards of the zoning ordinance have also been violated.

Subdivision improvements

In the next seven sections, the setting of standards for required improvements is considered, as well as the types of improvements included in new subdivisions.

Setting improvement standards

Ensuring that arrangements have been made for physical improvements at the time land is subdivided is central to many of the purposes of subdivision regulation. The types of improvements typically required of developers are fairly standard and include paved streets (including curb and gutter where appropriate), surface and subsurface drainage facilities, sidewalks in some instances, water and sewer lines where service is available, and fire hydrants. More demanding municipalities may require street signs, streetlights, subdivision entrance signs, perimeter fences or walls, trash receptacles, or even bus shelters. Counties, especially less urban ones, generally require less. It is the quality and extent of these improvements that have become much more controversial.

Requirements that are appropriate for one type of subdivision may not be appropriate for another. Classes of subdivisions must be established and features of subdivisions distinguished. Standards for industrial subdivisions differ from those for a residential subdivision, those for a town-house subdivision from those for a subdivision with single-family detached houses. Improvement standards for residential subdivisions are generally scaled to lot size or development density (e.g., sidewalks may not be required for lots greater than 30,000 square feet). Requirements may also depend on the number of lots (e.g., private streets may serve only a limited number of lots), lot frontage (which may be linked to street width), the slope and topography of the land (which affects stormwater management measures), and other factors. Other jurisdictions may provide flexibility by allowing development standards to be varied in subdivisions that qualify for special treatment, such as planned unit developments, cluster subdivisions, or special demonstration projects. Regardless of how it is accomplished, some scaling of improvement requirements to the characteristics of subdivisions is essential if rigorous standards are to be applied.

Illustrating development standards in a design or improvements manual is often more useful than cataloguing them in a subdivision ordinance. The manual can serve as a reference for the zoning as well as for the subdivision ordinance and for improvements put out for bid as well as those installed or constructed by developers. Of course, if the subdivision regulations refer explicitly to portions of the manual, changes in the manual amount to changes in the ordinance and generally must be adopted by following proper ordinance-amendment procedures.

Many local governments express subdivision improvement standards as specification standards, but for certain improvements a variety of materials or designs may be equally adequate. One approach is simply to allow the developer to meet any of a series of specification standards deemed to be adequate. Another approach is to define the standard of performance the improvement is required to meet and then allow the developer to use any material or design that will accomplish the stated result. For example, a performance standard for erosion control might require that the velocity of stormwater runoff from a ten-year storm (a storm likely to occur only once every ten years and to have a certain duration) *after* the site is subdivided and developed not exceed the velocity of runoff from the site *before* it was subdivided and developed. A combination of soil erosion and sedimentation control devices and detention and retention basins might be used to meet this performance standard. It is important to note, however, that performance standards may make it more difficult to determine compliance, because they permit a wider variety of materials, designs, and techniques to be proposed. Unless the properties or performance of these materials, designs, or techniques have been determined by testing labs or research groups, a proposal's ability to meet a performance standard may turn out to be largely a matter of professional judgment. Many jurisdictions rely on a certified opinion rendered by a professional engineer, registered landscape architect, or surveyor; despite the potential for bias, they may also allow that opinion to be provided by someone under contract to the developer. A better approach may be to offer a variety of specification-based materials, designs, or techniques but to permit the developer the opportunity to demonstrate that others work as well as or better than those specifically allowed.

Water supply and sewage disposal

An important means of development control enjoyed by any local government with its own utility system is the power to determine where water and sewer line extensions will go and when capacity will be added to its water purification and wastewater treatment systems. Connecting to a central water or sewer system is an attractive possibility for many urban developers. Many local governments are permitted to offer utility service outside their limits when, where, and under virtually whatever conditions they choose. In some states, however, municipal utilities may be required to serve potential customers within their service area on a equitable basis.

The relative decline in federal and state funding for centralized water-supply and sewage-disposal facilities has caused local governments to look to other sources of funding. Most communities have been unwilling to make up the shortfall by relying strictly on general funds. The resulting pressure on the public purse has had several consequences. Customers have seen utility rates rise, and developers have been charged more for tap and connection fees. An increasing portion of the cost of extending major trunk lines and providing additional treatment capacity is assigned to developers and indirectly to new residents.

Utilities that have expanded their facilities in advance of new growth and that enjoy excess capacity are now using cost-recovery systems and "buy-in" schedules that require developers to pay for a portion of a utility's infrastructure that is already in place. Utilities with systems that have relatively less capacity now are obliged to define carefully the areas they can serve efficiently. Those jurisdictions that have not adequately funded the upgrading and expansion of their wastewater treatment facilities now risk state-imposed sewer connection moratoria because treatment deficiencies prevent them from meeting surface-water discharge criteria.

Many suburban and rural subdivisions are located where utility service is not already provided. If connection to a central water or sewer system is available at or near the site to be subdivided, the local government typically requires the developer to provide local lines to serve individual lots; if it is empowered to do so, it may also require the developer to connect the local lines to the public system. Most utilities establish cost-sharing and reimbursement policies that apply when utility line extensions are some distance from the site. If the utility provider finances the extension itself, it may use tap fees and connection charges to recover at least a portion of the costs. If the developer is willing to finance the line extension, some utilities collect connection fees from property owners who will be served by the new extension and use those fees to reimburse the developer over a period of years. If a developer takes the initiative to provide the extension, and the service needs of the entire area dictate that oversized lines are required, the utility may provide immediate reimbursement for some or all of the cost of providing excess capacity.

A growing number of new technologies for disposing of wastewater now

---

Utilities extension policy

Policy I. Ordinary extensions. Developer pays the cost of utility line extension and receives prorated return as others connect. The cost of the utility line extension will be prorated on the basis of the gross land area to be served at the highest density that the projected zoning will allow. When any connection is made, this prorated cost shall be reimbursed through the City to the developer who paid the money.

Extensions that are considered for reimbursement shall include off-site utilities, major trunk lines, and lines where no service connections will be made.

Conditions of the extension shall be in the form of an extension agreement approved by resolution of the City Council. The City may also recover administrative and interest charges.

Policy II. Oversized lines. Utility line extensions installed for the purpose of providing a line larger than that

required of a developer for loop or trunk purposes will be paid for by the City and the developer, with the developer responsible for the cost of an 8-inch water line or 8-inch sewer line, as may apply, and the City paying the remainder of the cost.

Where the developer agrees to install the oversize line with City participation limited to the difference in cost of material beween the 8-inch line and the oversized line, the developer may install or contract for the installation.

Where the developer desires the City to participate in both cost of material and cost of labor for installation of the oversized line, the City must put the construction out for bid.

When the cost of oversizing is $10,000 or greater, the City may prorate the costs as outlined in Policy I for the purpose of recovering City funds.

Source: *Developer's Guide* (City of Las Cruces, N.M., 1985), 62.

compete with centralized, large-scale sewage-disposal systems.[27] Septic tanks can be placed in large mounds composed of fill materials placed above the grade of land that would not otherwise support such a system. Clusters of lines serving individual buildings may feed into a central tank or treatment facility for surface or subsurface disposal. An increasingly popular alternative is the package treatment plant, a small-scale, frequently prefabricated, secondary treatment facility. Although such units are easily installed and maintained, their long-term reliability remains unproven.

Alternative sewage disposal systems (as well as community water supply systems) pose two concerns for local governments. First, because individual and community sewage disposal systems are often subject to regulation by state agencies or regional authorities, the local plat approval agency may have little control over the location, extent, and maintenance of such systems or the quality of their effluent and its disposal. Second, the effectiveness of such systems depends largely on the quality of their operation and maintenance. A few local governments have found state-required arrangements for operation and maintenance unsatisfactory and now inspect, maintain, and even own such systems. A much more limited approach for local governments is simply to ensure that a properly organized property owners' association or other organization takes responsibility for ownership and maintenance of any proposed community systems.

The traditional septic tank is still an important sewage-disposal system in many parts of the country. If septic tanks are proposed for a subdivision (especially in conjunction with individual wells), the suitability of each proposed lot should be evaluated before even the preliminary plat is approved so that any redesign of proposed lots can be accomplished before lots are surveyed and recorded.

Street and street-related improvements

Sooner or later every jurisdiction enforcing subdivision regulations is forced to debate and defend its standards for streets and the improvements allowed within the street right-of-way. Despite the attention focused nationally on the relation between the costs of required infrastructure and the costs of housing, the standards for streets and related improvements remain deficient in many jurisdictions.[28] Some are deficient because they still reflect highway engineers' traditional emphasis on standards for higher-function streets and highways rather than for minor subdivision streets. Other standards, however, are deficient because they do not reflect gradations in function among the types of streets within a new residential subdivision. Worse, many standards in use have been carried over from the days of gridiron subdivisions and do not reflect the principles of good curvilinear or cluster design.

The major controversy often concerns local streets below "subcollector" in function, which typically carry an average daily traffic volume (ADT) of less than 200 or serve roughly 20 or fewer single-family detached houses.[29] The proper width of the cartway (the traveled portion of the right-of-way) of most local streets depends on the amount of traffic expected; but it also depends on whether on-street parking will be provided, whether curbs are desirable, and whether the cartway must serve as a storage area for snow.

On-street parking is an overlooked key to pavement width. If local streets serve lots about one-half acre or greater in size, parking needs can be satisfied on each lot, and on-street parking need not be provided. A cartway 16 to 18 feet wide can accommodate two moving lanes (18 or 20 feet if curbs are required to handle stormwater or to stabilize the road). If the lots are less than one-half acre but more than about one-tenth of an acre, the local government cannot assume that each lot can accommodate off-street parking needs. Streets serving lots of this sort should provide one moving lane and two lanes for on-street

Figure 8–12 Curbless roadway with properly designed stone shoulder.

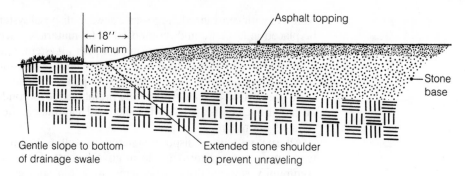

Gentle slope to bottom of drainage swale

Extended stone shoulder to prevent unraveling

parking, and the cartway should be at least 26 to 28 feet wide. Lots smaller than one-tenth of an acre generally appear in cluster developments where common off-street parking is provided. In such cases, on-street parking need not be provided, and cartway widths of about 20 feet are adequate. These standards are probably adequate even for short streets or cul-de-sacs with few houses. If snow storage areas are necessary or the terrain is hilly, the cartway width will need to be expanded.

Engineers and landscape architects have debated for years whether to curb or not to curb.[30] Engineers emphasize the advantages of curbs; landscape architects prefer streets with shoulders and swales and more natural methods of handling stormwater. Street curbing serves two general purposes: to channel stormwater and to stabilize the edges of a road. Curbs and gutters concentrate stormwater and dispose of it quickly, generally in storm sewer inlets and from there to the nearest stream. Vertical curbs (most favored by transportation engineers) prevent localized flooding and the accumulation of stagnant water. In addition, curbs stabilize roads by preventing the unraveling of the pavement edge, the seepage of water under it, and, where on-street parking is prevalent, the erosion of the shoulder area. Curbs may be necessary in steep terrain where natural drainage systems may not work. One disadvantage of a curb and gutter system is that it increases the velocity and flow of stormwater, making it difficult to control and reducing the chance that it can be returned to a natural drainage system without causing erosion and downstream flooding. Also, vertical curbs require that curb cuts be positioned prior to installation, which may constrain the location and orientation of the driveway, off-street parking, and the house itself. Curbs and gutters can also be more expensive to install and maintain than other good alternatives.

An alternative in many areas is a system of streets with shoulders constructed to slough water collected on the road surface into nearby swales (see Figure 8–12). Of course, a graveled road does not require curbs. Shoulders and swales can also function adequately where parking on road shoulders is infrequent or prohibited. For that matter, extending the base course of such streets beyond the edge of the pavement surface can improve the stability of the shoulder. Properly designed and installed swales can reduce stormwater runoff and the accompanying erosion and siltation, thereby reducing maintenance costs to the local government. Improperly designed and poorly maintained swales, however, can cause nuisance flooding and can even contribute to the erosion of the shoulder itself.

Although jurisdictions require curbs and gutters where lots are one-half acre or less in size, they may give little detailed review to the road drainage system when curbs are not required. Curbless streets should be allowed if the designer can show that soils, terrain, on-street parking needs, and overall site design warrant such an approach.

Many communities have reduced the right-of-way widths required in their regulations to allow developers to use their sites more intensively and reduce the per-unit price of housing.[31] If a good street classification system has been

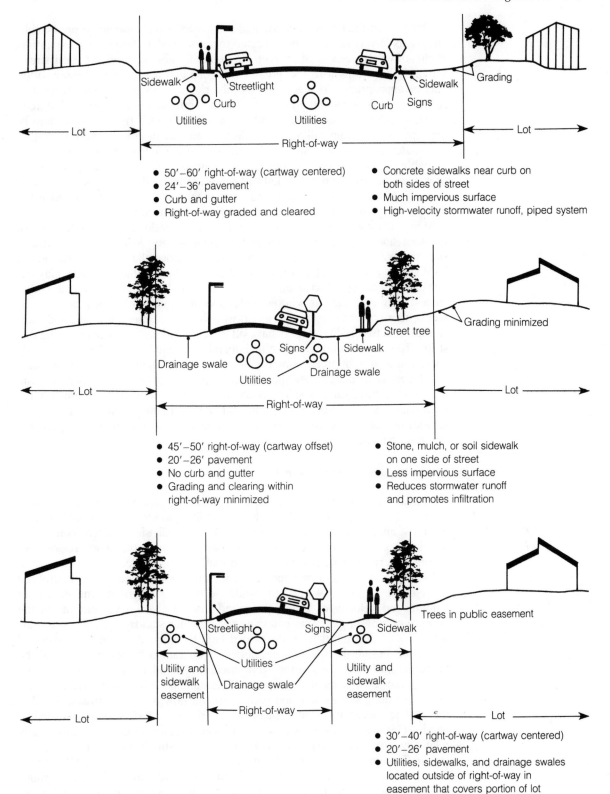

- 50′–60′ right-of-way (cartway centered)
- 24′–36′ pavement
- Curb and gutter
- Right-of-way graded and cleared

- Concrete sidewalks near curb on both sides of street
- Much impervious surface
- High-velocity stormwater runoff, piped system

- 45′–50′ right-of-way (cartway offset)
- 20′–26′ pavement
- No curb and gutter
- Grading and clearing within right-of-way minimized

- Stone, mulch, or soil sidewalk on one side of street
- Less impervious surface
- Reduces stormwater runoff and promotes infiltration

- 30′–40′ right-of-way (cartway centered)
- 20′–26′ pavement
- Utilities, sidewalks, and drainage swales located outside of right-of-way in easement that covers portion of lot

Figure 8–13   The three sections of this figure show variations in the design and use of the right-of-way. At the top is the traditional right-of-way alternative; in the center, an illustration of an emerging design alternative; and at the bottom, a special right-of-way variation.

established, traffic levels on residential subdivision streets should be predictable, and rights-of-way need not be expected to accommodate future road expansion. Rights-of-way in excess of 50 feet are generally not required for local streets serving subdivisions with lots greater than one-half acre in size. Lesser widths may be appropriate. As a general rule, the right-of-way of local streets must be sufficient to accommodate utility lines (both overhead and underground), street-lights, street trees, sidewalks, and traffic signs. Wider rights-of-way may be appropriate in terrain calling for moderate amounts of cross-section grading or in climates where plowed snow left at the side of the road does not melt quickly. Variable or "off-center" right-of-way alignments, which provide greater right-of-way on one side of the traveled surface, sometimes allow utilities to be placed in a strip along one side of the street rather than under it; similarly, sidewalks and bicycle paths can be located on one side but not on the other.

Many subdivision ordinances still require the developer to provide four- or five-foot sidewalks on both sides of all streets serving lots of one-half acre in size or less.[32] The emerging trend is to require sidewalks on only one side of local streets and none at all on short cul-de-sacs, but double sidewalks may still be necessary along collector and arterial streets or along streets leading to pedestrian-serving uses such as schools. Sidewalks are traditionally located about six feet or more from the curb with a parkway strip for planting, utilities, and snow storage in between. Developers have often been responsible for landscaping that strip. The other common design is an integral curb, gutter, and sidewalk, typically constructed of reinforced concrete. A new arrangement advocated by some developers is to place sidewalks within a special front-yard easement beyond the street right-of-way. A sidewalk located in this easement looks much like a traditional sidewalk located behind the parkway strip, but the easement is located in a lot owner's front yard, and the area counts toward meeting minimum lot-size requirements.

Stormwater and erosion control

Ordinance requirements that require or encourage storm sewers and related systems that use piping or channeling are still common.[33] Traditional systems are most appropriate in conventional small-lot subdivisions, where connection to a large, geographically comprehensive system is available or where soil conditions or terrain make natural drainage methods infeasible.

Ideally, a stormwater-management computer model based on a hydrologic analysis for an entire watershed would be used to determine the maximum amount and velocity of runoff permitted from a given development. In the absence of a basin plan, one emerging performance standard requires the characteristics of the runoff from developed land to be no different from those of the runoff before the site was developed. This standard, sometimes called the "natural runoff" standard or the "zero discharge" standard, allows the developer to determine how to meet the criterion. The standard favors more natural methods of handling stormwater and natural stream flow; its main attraction is that the facilities necessary to limit peak runoff (retention basins, detention basins, pervious infiltration areas, swales, and various varieties of drains) are generally relatively inexpensive, especially compared to after-the-fact remedies for downstream flooding. Furthermore, the quality of water retained on-site is often better than that of water carried off site. Natural drainage methods reduce water pollution and are less likely to require a discharge permit under federal water pollution legislation.

A number of facilities and techniques can control water velocities and prevent soil erosion and sedimentation. Strategically placed riprap, gabions, flumes, small check dams, and weirs can be used to dissipate water that has potentially eroding velocities and to stabilize swales and stream banks. (See Figure 8–14.)

Natural drainage methods do have their drawbacks. For example, basing a drainage system on the natural contours of the land may not be consistent with a street pattern that allows the most desirable subdivision of lots. Designing an optimal system may require detailed site data on soil types and permeability, precipitation, vegetation, surface-water flows, and existing drainage systems. Detention ponds and impoundment areas work best in large open space and park areas provided in cluster subdivisions. It is more difficult to distribute such areas among the individual lots of a conventional subdivision. If the water does not infiltrate or is not allowed to drain, such areas can stagnate, breed insects, and encourage the growth of algae. Large-scale basins and impoundment areas seem to attract children, which can create significant liability risks for the property owners' associations or local government that owns and maintains such areas.

Grassed drainage swales also require continuing maintenance to prevent siltation and erosion and to ensure that proper side slopes are retained (no less

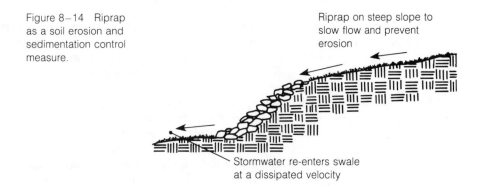

Figure 8–14 Riprap as a soil erosion and sedimentation control measure.

Riprap on steep slope to slow flow and prevent erosion

Stormwater re-enters swale at a dissipated velocity

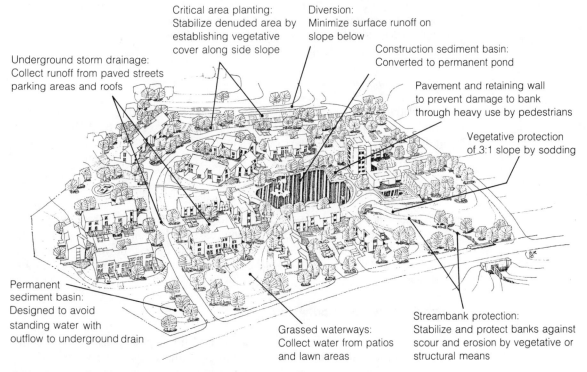

Critical area planting: Stabilize denuded area by establishing vegetative cover along side slope

Diversion: Minimize surface runoff on slope below

Construction sediment basin: Converted to permanent pond

Underground storm drainage: Collect runoff from paved streets parking areas and roofs

Pavement and retaining wall to prevent damage to bank through heavy use by pedestrians

Vegetative protection of 3:1 slope by sodding

Permanent sediment basin: Designed to avoid standing water with outflow to underground drain

Grassed waterways: Collect water from patios and lawn areas

Streambank protection: Stabilize and protect banks against scour and erosion by vegetative or structural means

Figure 8–15 Many temporary soil erosion and sedimentation control measures can be made permanent.

than 4:1). An unmaintained swale can degenerate into a ditch. Drainage swales do not lend themselves well to small-lot subdivisions. They are less compatible with sidewalks than are storm sewer systems, because the flat side slopes of swales take up more room within the right-of-way. Frequent use of culverts to carry stormwater under driveways can also substantially compromise the advantages of a system of swales.

Who should be entitled to design stormwater facilities is a matter for controversy in many areas. A number of jurisdictions require that stormwater management systems be designed and certified by a registered engineer. Other local governments allow stormwater systems, particularly natural drainage systems, to be designed by surveyors, landscape architects, and nonprofessionals. In some communities, the quality of the system depends largely on who is deemed qualified to design it.

Electricity, gas, telephone, and cable television

Most jurisdictions expect the subdivider to arrange for gas, electrical, telephone, and cable television service. It is now common to require the undergrounding of local gas and electricity lines and telephone and television cables, at least where soil, water tables, and terrain permit, and where lots are less than one acre in size.

The accepted practice for locating underground lines varies. Developers can save money by locating telephone, electricity, and cable television lines under the pavement in common trenches with sewer, water, and gas lines, if the utilities (particularly the power companies) are willing to cooperate. An alternative location for underground lines is along the side of the traveled portion of the street. Although the street pavement need not be disrupted when repairs are needed, this location can be unpopular with homeowners, especially when repairs disrupt landscaping, curbs, culverts, and driveways. Some communities locate lines along easements at the rear of lots, a practice that can be unpopular with the utility companies because they must contend with fences, sheds, and landscaping. The location and width of the easements may also make the lines inaccessible to their equipment.

Survey monuments

One of the oldest types of improvement requirements compels the developer to provide concrete or stone survey monuments at intersections of street lines and at the corners of the boundary of the subdivision. Typically, metal markers must be set at all lot corners.

Street signs and names

Many jurisdictions require subdividers to provide or assume the cost of new street signs. In some large metropolitan areas, subdivision streets originally laid out in grids may be assigned names. In many other areas, however, developers propose street names, and the local government merely checks for inappropriate duplication.

Special types of subdivisions

Cluster residential subdivisions, manufactured housing subdivisions, and commercial, office, and industrial park subdivisions have particular characteristics that need to be taken into account in the development of subdivision regulations. The three sections that follow examine these special types of subdivisions.

Conventional

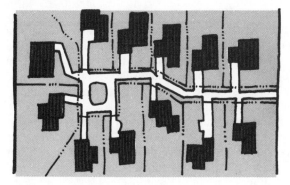

Gross density is two units per acre. Each lot has 20,000 square feet and there are no development constraints.

Cluster

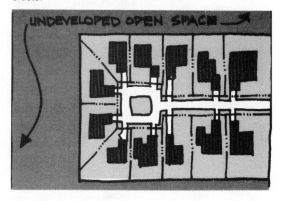

This illustration shows the same gross density, but with 10,000-square-foot lots. More than 120,000 square feet are available as public or community open space.

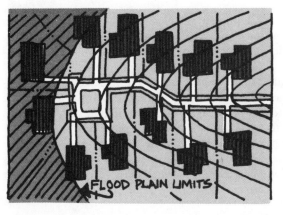

With conventional platting, a flood hazard zone precludes buildable sites on three or four lots.

Clustering allows the same number of lots outside the flood zone and permits natural areas to be preserved.

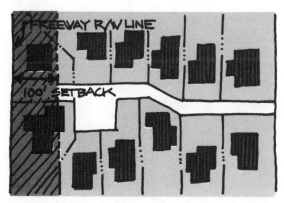

Required buffer or building setback from highway makes areas of several lots unbuildable.

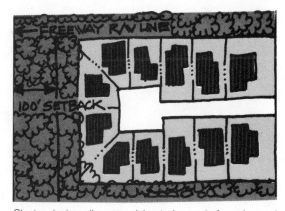

Cluster design allows provision to be made for noise and sight buffers.

Figure 8–16   Cluster development compared to conventional subdivision. In each case, the illustration shows a six-acre parcel divided into twelve lots. The development is residential and made up of single-family detached houses.

Cluster residential subdivisions[34]

In a cluster development, dwelling units are grouped on certain portions of a site, and other areas in common or single ownership remain open and free from development. In a cluster residential subdivision, which is a specific application of this concept, lots are smaller than in a conventional subdivision, the lots and units are clustered on those portions of the site best suited for development, and common or public open space is provided.

Clustering is an environmentally sound concept, because it allows development in the most appropriate areas and prevents development in inappropriate areas such as flood-prone corridors and areas of unstable soil or steep terrain. Cluster subdivisions take advantage of natural methods for handling stormwater and preserve open space and other important natural features.

Clustering is also economically sound, because it reduces infrastructure costs (the length of street and utility lines can be drastically reduced). The flexible location of buildings permits designs that save more energy than do conventional designs.

Although the cluster concept might seem to suggest that a cluster subdivision be developed to the same overall density as a conventional subdivision, only with a different pattern of development, many ordinances allow cluster subdivisions to include more units. The shape, size, and topographic limitations of the site prevent most conventional subdivision designs from achieving the maximum number of lots that theoretically could be platted. In most instances, the flexible open space of a cluster subdivision allows the maximum number of lots permissible under the ordinance, and most formulas assume no "inefficiency" in platting. Furthermore, some jurisdictions provide a bonus by ignoring the amount of land that would have been devoted to streets and other public areas had a conventional subdivision been designed, which may increase the number of units permitted in a cluster subdivision by 15 to 25 percent.

Figure 8–17 Zero-lot-line atrium housing with staggered or "z"-shaped lots.

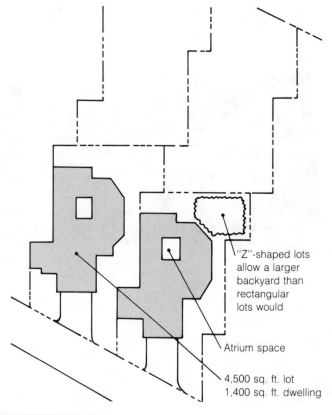

"Z"-shaped lots allow a larger backyard than rectangular lots would

Atrium space

4,500 sq. ft. lot
1,400 sq. ft. dwelling

There are several ways to compute the amount of common or public open space provided in a cluster subdivision. One approach requires open space to at least equal the sum total of the lot-size reductions allowed for each of the lots. Another approach simply requires some minimum percentage of the gross site area (e.g., 15 percent or 25 percent) to be devoted to open space, regardless of the lot-size reduction allowed.

Cluster subdivision design lends itself to both single-family detached and single-family attached housing. Single-family detached cluster subdivisions are generally organized around courts, cul-de-sacs, or short loop streets. In one variety, detached zero-lot-line houses are located to one side of each reduced-size lot. The second type of cluster subdivision is designed for single-family attached housing. (Some jurisdictions still classify *any* form of attached housing as multifamily, but this approach is nearly obsolete.) Because attached or semiattached housing units extend from lot line to lot line, the cluster concept is particularly appropriate for this type of housing. Town house or row house developments with six or eight units to a group are one of the most common forms of single-family attached units. Clusters of attached or semiattached units in pairs, triplets, or quads arranged around a private court or parking area are also increasingly common.

Many ordinances fail to make clear whether the cluster option is available for both detached and attached single-family housing in a particular zoning district or for detached single-family units only. Some ordinances allow single-family attached housing types (such as town houses) on smaller lots, with or without open space requirements, but do not characterize this as a cluster option.

Although the cluster concept is promising, cluster subdivisions are still not a common form of development in most communities. In some areas, developers are not interested in using the cluster design and providing common open space unless a significant density bonus is provided. In other areas, developers have used the affordable-housing argument to convince the governing board simply to rezone their properties to allow the development of smaller lots in conventional subdivisions.

Because clustering dwellings on different lots requires special design and architectural treatment, many planners believe that such a project (particularly involving single-family attached housing) deserves more careful scrutiny than a conventional project. As a result, application requirements and review procedures for cluster subdivisions may be more complex. In some cases, a site plan showing building locations and even building elevations may be required, and a special permit under the zoning ordinance may be involved. A small developer inexperienced in establishing homeowners' associations and in transferring control to them may try to avoid forms of development requiring common open space. Many housing consumers are wary of housing involving communal property ownership of any kind.

Many consumers, particularly in metropolitan areas, have found cluster housing satisfactory and more affordable than conventional alternatives, but the first choice of a majority of housing consumers is still apparently the large-lot–large-house combination of conventional subdivisions.

Manufactured-housing and related subdivisions

Despite the attention devoted to affordable housing, municipal zoning ordinances in many states still prohibit or restrict the placement of manufactured houses ("mobile homes") on individual lots in some or all residential zoning districts. This stance has discouraged the development of manufactured-housing subdivisions in which manufactured houses are sold on individual lots or in which lots suitable for manufactured houses are sold separately. Although manufactured-housing subdivisions are not yet common, neither are they particularly special. The streets, utility lines, fire protection facilities, and lot and street layout required for a single-family development of manufactured houses need not be any different from those of a subdivision with lots of the same size devoted to site-built housing. The arguments for reducing lot size, setback, and frontage requirements to encourage the development of inexpensive housing apply with equal force to subdivisions for manufactured housing and for site-built housing. Because new manufactured-housing units are unlikely to be moved after being sited, the emphasis on their mobility is misplaced. They should be viewed as a type of permanent housing.

Manufactured-housing subdivisions need to be distinguished from mobile home parks, planned residential communities in which spaces or lots for manufactured-housing units typically are leased and in which a housing unit may or may not also be furnished in addition to the space. Although some jurisdictions regulate mobile home parks the way they regulate mobile home subdivisions, mobile home parks are generally governed by site-development standards in the zoning code or in a separate mobile home parks ordinance, and not by the subdivision ordinance. The owner of a mobile home park generally retains title to the land; spaces are not permanently platted; and the owner may convert the park to another use if conditions warrant. Thus there may be good reason to allow mobile home parks to develop at a higher density than that permitted in a manufactured-housing or site-built-housing subdivision, where lots are unlikely ever to be reconsolidated.

Similar considerations suggest that property owners should not be allowed to plat and sell extraordinarily small lots in "campsite subdivisions" in recreational areas that are designed to accommodate overnight travelers using a recreational vehicle, camper, van, or tent. Such subdivisions should be prohibited, particularly if the lot is too small for, or is not provided with, services suitable for a residence.

Commercial, industrial, and office park subdivisions

Many industrial parks, shopping malls, and office parks are held in single ownership and are not subject to subdivision regulation. Sometimes only interior building spaces may be leased or sold; or if ground leases are to be offered, divisions to create leasehold interests may not fall within the scope of the subdivision ordinance.

Few subdivision ordinances make elaborate provision for commercial, industrial, or office park subdivisions. Such developments are often subject to site development standards of the zoning ordinance, and dedication and improvement requirements and design matters are specified in a site-plan-review process. Lots and setbacks in industrial, commercial, and office subdivisions need to be sized to accommodate off-street parking and loading space. Utilities and drainage facilities must accommodate greater demands than are created by residential subdivisions. Streets need to be able to endure more intense automobile traffic and, in some cases, greater truck traffic as well. Design details such as buffering and setbacks at the perimeter and at street connections demand special attention in developments such as these. Some of the development standards for single-family residential subdivisions (e.g., parkland dedication requirements) are clearly inapplicable, and the subdivision ordinance should make this clear.

Lots in industrial and business park subdivisions are often tailored to the needs of particular purchasers. Prior to plat approval, it may be difficult to design exact lot configurations that will conform to the needs of individual businesses purchasing such lots. The "building block" approach recognizes that revision of lot sizes and shapes is to be expected, and it permits approval of lots that are unusually narrow and deep. Purchasers can be encouraged to buy combinations of lots and then consolidate them to suit their preferences.

Lot subdivisions that are designed to accommodate attached units (strip commercial, industrial, and single-family residential) pose a different problem. If lot lines are defined in advance of building construction, it is almost impossible to ensure that the party wall between separately owned units is sited exactly on the surveyed property line. A better approach allows attached buildings to be constructed before the approval of the final plat, so that the recordable plat can be matched to the walls as built rather than the other way around. A second survey can thus be avoided.

Conclusion

For local governments, subdivision regulation is one of the principal means of guiding the direction, speed, and quality of land development. This chapter has summarized from several perspectives the practice of land subdivision regulation. First, what is the role of subdivision regulation in local government planning, and how does it complement other planning tools? Second, what powers do local governments enjoy in the regulation of land subdivision? Third, how should the subdivision review process be organized, and how should it be administered? Fourth, what design and improvement standards are appropriate for new subdivisions? Fifth, what costs of providing public facilities to serve new growth should be borne by developers?

Even though it receives less attention than zoning, land subdivision regulation is a critical ingredient in any local government planning program. Familiarity with its principles and applications is an essential part of a competent planner's expertise.

1   Donald Hagman, *Public Planning and Control of Urban and Land Development: Cases and Materials* (St. Paul, MN: West Publishing Co., 1973), 551.

2   See, for example, Alaska Stat. # 29.33.070 (1971 & Supp. 1984). (First- and second-class boroughs must regulate subdivisions on an areawide basis, although authority may be delegated to cities within boroughs).

3   Cities in Kansas may regulate three miles beyond their limits, certain cities in Oregon up to six miles beyond. Kan. Stat. Ann. # 12-705 (1982); Or. Rev. Stat. # 92.042 (1983).

4   See, for example, Tenn. Code Ann. # 13-3-402 (1980).

5   See, for example, Conn. Code Ann. # 8-25(a) (Supp. 1986).

6   See, for example, Ariz. Rev. Stat. Ann. ## 9-463.01H, 11-806.01B (1977).

7   See, for example, Utah Code Ann. # 10-9-25 (1977).

8   See, for example, Cal. Gov't Code # 66474(a) (West 1983).

9   N.J. Rev. Stat. # 40-55D-7 (Supp. 1986).

10 See, for example, Nev. Rev. Stat. # 278.320 (1981) (five or more lots).

11 See N.C. Gen. Stat. # 160A-376(4) (1982).

12 The discussion in this paragraph is abstracted largely from Institute of Transportation Engineers, *Recommended Guidelines for Subdivision Streets* (Washington, DC: 1984), 1–3.

13 See discussion and illustrations of this topic in Bucks County Planning Commission, *Performance Streets: A Concept and Model Standards for Residential Streets* (Doylestown, PA, 1980), 26–27, 38.

14 See discussion of this topic and illustration in ULI–the Urban Land Institute, *Residential Development Handbook* (Washington, DC, 1978), 183–184, and discussion of "marginal access roads" in Bucks County, *Performance Streets*, 27–28.

15 See Lynne B. Sagalyn and George Sternlieb, *Zon-*

ing and Housing Costs: The Impact of Land-Use Controls on Housing Price (New Brunswick, NJ: Rutgers University, Center for Urban Policy Research, 1973), and Stephen R. Seidel, *Housing Costs and Government Regulations: Confronting the Regulatory Maze* (New Brunswick, NJ: Rutgers University, Center for Urban Policy Research, 1978). Reduction in lot-size and lot-frontage requirements and increases in allowable single-family housing densities are also among the common ways that communities have changed their development regulations to make housing more affordable. This trend in regulatory reform is described in Welford Sanders and David Mosena, *Changing Development Standards for Affordable Housing*, Planning Advisory Service Report no. 371 (Chicago: American Planning Association, 1982) and in Welford Sanders, Judith Getzels, David Mosena, and JoAnn Butler, *Affordable Single-Family Housing: A Review of Development Standards*, Planning Advisory Report no. 385 (Chicago: American Planning Association, 1984).

16 See fuller discussion of panhandle lots in "New Ideas for a Controversial Topic: Zoning and Subdividing Flag Lots," in Charles Reed, ed., *The Zoning Report*, vol. 4, no. 1 (January 24, 1986): 1–8.

17 Discussion of impact fees abstracted in part from the following: Julian Juergensmeyer, "Funding Infrastructure: Paying the Costs of Growth through Impact Fees and Other Land Regulation Charges" (Paper delivered at the American Planning Association Joint Planning Conference, Montreal, April 1985); James Nicholas, "Florida's Experience with Impact Fees" (Paper delivered at the American Planning Association Conference, Montreal, April 1985); and Michael A. Stegman, "Development Fees for Infrastructure," *Urban Land* (May 1986), 2–3.

18 *Banberry Dev. Corp.* v. *South Jordan City*, 631 P.2d 899 (Utah 1981).

19 *Nollan* v. *California Coastal Commission*, 483 U.S.--97 L. Ed.2d 677, 107 S. Ct. 3141 (1987).

20 See discussion of adequate facilities ordinances in Jonathan Davidson, "Using Infrastructural Controls to Guide Development," *Zoning and Planning Law Report* (December 1985), 170–171.

21 *Golden* v. *Planning Board of the Town of Ramapo* 30 N.Y.2d 359, 285 N.E.2d 291, 334 N.Y.S.2d 138, *app. dism'd*, 409 U.S. 1003 (1972).

22 See discussion of reservation and use of official maps in Daniel R. Mandelker, *Land Use Law* (Charlottesville, VA: The Michie Co., 1982), 294–295.

23 Community associations are discussed in ULI, *Residential Development Handbook*, 281–291.

24 A substantial literature has developed concerning the need for and the means of streamlining the development review process. Fuller treatment can be found in John Vranicar, Welford Sanders, and David Mosena, *Streamlining Land Use Regulation: A Guidebook for Local Governments* (Chicago: American Planning Association, 1980); Stuart Hershey and Carolyn Garmise, *Streamlining Local Regulations: A Handbook for Reduced Housing and Development Costs*, Management Information Service Special Report, no. 11 (Washington, DC: International City Management Association, 1983); and Douglas R. Porter, *Streamlining Your Local Development Process*, Managing Design and Development Series Technical Bulletin no. 10 (Washington, DC: National League of Cities, 1981).

25 Vranicar et al., *Streamlining Land Use Regulations*, 3.

26 For a fuller discussion of performance guarantees, consult the following articles: Lane Kendig, "Performance Guarantees," *Land Use Law and Zoning Digest*, 35 (February 1983); 4–10, and Michael M. Schultz and Richard Kelley, "Subdivision Improvement Requirements and Guarantees: A Primer," *Washington University Journal of Urban & Contemporary Law* 28 (1985): 3–106.

27 Illustrations and brief descriptions of such systems may be found in *Small Wastewater Systems: Alternative Systems for Small Communities and Rural Areas* (Washington, DC: U.S. Environmental Protection Agency, Office of Water Program Operations January 1980).

28 A survey by the American Planning Association of 13 committees and 18 "affordable housing" projects indicated that communities were much more willing to change lot size, frontage, and setback and dimensional requirements than they were to change standards for infrastructural requirements such as streets. "Communities seldom modified their site improvement standards for streets and sidewalks, drainage, storm sewers, and other utilities to encourage affordable housing development." Sanders et al., *Affordable Single-Family Housing: A Review of Development Standards*, vii.

29 There is still an apparent difference of opinion between the design standards for pavement width for a local subdivision street suggested by transportation engineers and those recommended by land planners. Compare ITE, *Recommended Guidelines for Subdivision Streets*, 5–6 (22–27 foot minimum for a local street serving low-density development) with Bucks County, *Performance Streets*, 8–9 ("cartway" width geared to lot width; cartway width minimums of 16 and 18 feet recommended for subdivisions with larger lots). This discussion is abstracted from Bucks County, *Performance Streets*, ULI–the Urban Land Institute, *Residential Streets: Objectives, Principles, and Design Considerations* (Washington, DC: The Urban Land Institute, American Society of Civil Engineers, and National Association of Home Builders, 1975), 22–23, 30–33.

30 This discussion is abstracted from ULI, *Residential Development Handbook*, 163–165; ITE, *Recommended Guidelines for Subdivision Streets*, 7; "Elimination of Curbs," Project Development Update (Washington, DC: National Association of Home Builders, undated, unpaged); and Bucks County, *Performance Streets*, 9–10.

31 See ITE, *Recommended Guidelines for Subdivision Streets*, 5; Bucks County, *Performance Streets*, 33–35; "Right-of-Way Alternatives," Project Development Update (Washington, DC: National Association of Home Builders, undated, unpaged); and ULI, *Residential Development Handbook*, 159.

32 A good discussion of sidewalks and their location may be found in ITE, *Recommended Guidelines for Subdivision Streets*, 7–8; ULI, *Residential Development Handbook*, 163–165; and "Sidewalks in Subdivisions and Site Plans," in Charles Reed, ed., *The Zoning Report* vol. 4, no. 5 (May 23, 1986), 1–7.

33 The discussion in this subsection is abstracted from *Residential Storm Water Management: Objectives, Principles, and Design Considerations* (Washington, DC: Urban Land Institute, American Society of Civil Engineers, and National Association of Home Builders, 1975), 18–23; National Association of Home Builders, *Residential Development Handbook*, 54–56; and *Land Development 2*, (Washington, DC: 1981).

34 The discussion in this subsection is abstracted in part from the following: National Association of Home Builders, *Cost Effective Site Planning* (Washington, DC: 1982); National Association of Home Builders, *Density Development: Cost Effective and Affordable* (Washington, DC: May 1982), 12–22; "Cluster," Eighteenth Annual Land Use Report, *Builder*, 1 (7 August 1978), 23–38; and Welford Sanders, *The Cluster Subdivision: A Cost-Effective Approach*, Planning Advisory Service Report no. 356 (Chicago: American Planning Association, 1980).

9 Zoning

Zoning is the basic means of land use control employed by local governments in the United States today. Zoning divides the community into districts (zones) and imposes different land use controls on each district, specifying the allowed uses of land and buildings, the intensity or density of such uses, and the bulk of buildings on the land.

Traditional use regulations have separated land uses into four basic categories: residential, commercial, industrial, and agricultural. A small community may have only four zones, one for each use classification, while a large city may have dozens of different residential districts and a variety of commercial and industrial districts. Minimum lot sizes or a maximum number of dwelling units per acre are used to regulate density in residential zones. In commercial and light industrial areas, intensity is usually controlled by limiting the square feet of floor area that can be built for each square foot of land in the building lot, a measure that is called a floor area ratio. Bulk requirements include building height limitations, lot coverage requirements, building setback or yard requirements, and minimum lot sizes. Use and intensity controls actually set a threshold for land development patterns, whereas in most cases bulk controls simply establish design limitations. Later sections of this chapter contain a more detailed discussion of use, intensity, and bulk regulations in a zoning system.

Origins of zoning

Zoning as it is practiced today has a variety of historical roots, and an understanding of its origins is essential to an understanding of its limitations. Zoning originated in part as a means of protecting the health and safety of inhabitants of major cities. Many rooms in tenement houses lacked direct sunlight or air. Fire spread easily from one large adjacent building to another. Such conditions led to the adoption of early tenement house laws, which required that most rooms have direct access to light and air and imposed height and setback requirements designed to help contain fire and to allow light and air to filter among the buildings.

As large cities coped with the problems of tenement houses, smaller but growing communities faced conflicts between homeowners and neighboring industries over virtually unregulated industrial pollution. Some communities tried to control such conflicts by prohibiting industries likely to create pollution from locating in certain residential areas.

In New York and other large cities, proprietors of commercial establishments were concerned about preserving their neighborhoods as pleasant areas in which people would feel comfortable shopping. Although the economics of land use made substantial incursions by tenements or industries into prime commercial areas unlikely, early merchants felt threatened and sought local government protection of shopping districts.

Early zoning efforts were based in part on the health and safety concerns represented by the tenement house laws, in part on the economic concerns of homeowners and merchants. However, even the early zoning ordinances generally went beyond those basic issues and included land use patterns and bulk controls based partly on aesthetic concerns. One early planning document that influenced those first zoning efforts was called "The Laws of the Indies," which was promulgated by King Phillip II in 1573. The laws provided guidelines for the plaza-centered Spanish settlements in this country. Local government leaders who saw zoning as a way to make their communities beautiful as well as healthy were also influenced by more contemporary work, including Daniel Burnham's work for the 1893 World's Columbian Exposition and Ebenezer Howard's "garden cities" concept. (See chapter 2, "Historical Development of American City Planning," for a more complete account of the state of planning in America when zoning was first adopted.)

New York City adopted the first comprehensive zoning code for an entire city in 1916. Although the New York City model ultimately influenced local zoning controls throughout the country, the publication and adoption of the Standard State Zoning Enabling Act[1] and the Supreme Court decision in *Village of Euclid* v. *Ambler Realty Co.* (1926)[2] were the two events in the 1920s that provided the primary momentum for the zoning movement. It is important to note, however, that although the conceptual and legal basis for zoning was laid in the 1920s, the major impact of widespread local zoning was not really felt until the period of rapid building that followed World War II. Control of growth was not an issue during the Depression, and planning after the Depression was governed by the war effort.

The Standard State Zoning Enabling Act was drafted by a group of planning lawyers headed by Edward Basset, who had also directed the commission that developed the zoning code for New York City. The Act was published and distributed as an informational piece by the U.S. Department of Commerce in 1922 and again, in slightly revised form, in 1926. All fifty states ultimately adopted the model zoning act in basically its original form, which is a remarkable record for any model law. It remains in effect in the same form in all but half a dozen states, and even those that have changed the law have retained many key elements of the original.

The second major event encouraging the adoption of zoning was the 1926 Supreme Court decision *Village of Euclid* v. *Ambler Realty Co.*, which upheld the constitutionality of a comprehensive zoning system in Euclid, a suburb of Cleveland, Ohio. A landowner had challenged the ordinance, claiming that his property was worth $10,000 per acre as industrial ground but only $2,500 per acre as zoned by Euclid for residential purposes. What is important about the Court's decision is that it exemplified an attitude that was—and is—characteristic of traditional zoning (often called Euclidean zoning, after the village in the case). Like most early zoning, the plan in effect in Euclid was designed to protect neighborhoods of single-family detached houses. The Euclid decision upheld not only the plan but also its broader social and economic implications; the Court's opinion in the case describes a hypothetical apartment building in such a neighborhood as "a mere parasite, constructed in order to take advantage of the open spaces and attractive surroundings created by the residential character of the district."[3] The presumed superiority of the neighborhood of detached, single-family homes continues to provide a philosophical basis for much zoning law.

Another of the philosophical underpinnings of zoning is the notion that different land uses are incompatible and ought to be separated from each other. When zoning first originated, the now-pervasive system of federal and state regulation of industrial pollution was nonexistent, and the physical segregation of many industries was a practical health necessity. But the 1916 New York City zoning code went beyond what was necessary for health and safety, segregating different housing types from each other and from commercial areas. Many areas of New York had then and have now a healthy mixture of housing types and supporting commercial services, a pattern of development that was prevented in newer cities that grew up with zoning. *The Death and Life of Great American Cities*, published in 1961, challenged the wisdom of traditional zoning practices and stressed the importance of diversity to a vital neighborhood. Based on author Jane Jacobs's experiences in New York's Greenwich Village, the book provided part of the philosophical base for a broad movement toward controlled, mixed-use development.[4]

It is important to remember that the model zoning act, which still governs most zoning in the United States today, was based on an ordinance developed in the nation's largest city and was designed to respond to concerns about tenement housing and the location of industry. The New York City ordinance was also designed for a development pattern that occurred lot by lot—or, at most, block by block; it therefore incorporated detailed design and setback controls. Although traditional approaches to zoning continue to be of value, many issues facing local governments today differ from those facing New York City in 1916. Traditional zoning does not have adequate mechanisms for coping, for example, with flood plain regulation, sex businesses, large-scale residential development, industrial parks, shopping centers, or billboards, complex issues that require complex regulation. As later sections of this chapter show, such regulation may be a part of a traditional, comprehensive zoning system but must expand on that system. For example, regulations for a floodplain zone go beyond the traditional requirements for use, intensity, and bulk.

The zoning system today also does not operate in the way envisioned by the drafters of the model act. Early zoning experts saw the map and ordinance as fairly static; permits, variances, and special exceptions were expected to dominate zoning procedures but to occur within the parameters established in the ordinance. The designers of the model act apparently did not foresee the need or desire for frequent rezonings.

City officials who first implemented zoning in New York City and elsewhere determined initial zoning boundaries by considering existing neighborhood activities and selecting the dominant one as the appropriate use for each area. They simply had to reinforce existing land use patterns, not to predict future ones. In that context, their apparent assumption that a community could adopt a zoning map that would be basically "correct" and that could simply be administered by staff and the zoning board may have been accurate.

Today, however, rezonings are very common. Every local governing body is familiar with the jargon of rezonings. Agendas are often dominated by zoning matters, and campaigns for office are affected by them. A community with little growth may have a dozen or so requests for rezoning every month and a growing municipality may have that number every week.

The frequency of rezoning requests is created largely by the difficulty of predicting land uses. For example, a small city that has zoned a particular location for its only regional shopping center will probably approve a proposal by a responsible developer for a shopping center on a different site with good access. A city that has placed most industrial zoning along railroad tracks is not likely to turn down rezoning requests from electronics plants that prefer an attractive location along a highway and nowhere near rail. A growing city with predominantly single-family zoning can and must consider reasonable requests for rezonings for apartments, which are necessary to house part of the population in any area of significant size.

Because the drafters of the model act did not anticipate the need for rezoning, they did not create an effective mechanism for changing the map as necessary. Since the zoning ordinance is adopted as a local law, and the map is adopted by reference as part of the ordinance, the only way to change it is through an amendment to the ordinance, which is a legislative act. As is noted later in this chapter, the necessity for legislative review of individual development applications poses significant legal and procedural problems for local governments today.

Legal context of zoning

Zoning is a tool of the police power, which is the power of government to intervene in the lives of private citizens for the protection of public health, safety, and welfare. In the United States, the people are the supreme sovereign and retain all rights and powers not granted to government. In creating (constituting) state governments, the people gave those governments the police power; zoning is an instrument of the police power that is implemented at the local level.

Although the use of private land is subject to the police power, neither zoning nor any other tool of the police power can be exercised in any way not in furtherance of public health, safety, and welfare. It is worth noting, however, that the courts have defined health, safety, and welfare increasingly broadly in recent years. In practical terms, if it is possible to get enough votes to approve a new set of regulations, it is usually also possible to demonstrate that the regulations are within the scope of the police power. Most local government officials, influenced by the desires and concerns of their constituents, are simply more conservative than the courts in determining the extent to which government should limit private rights in the exercise of the police power. However, in adopting a new regulation, the local government should ensure that it documents the necessity of intervening under the police power.

In determining the scope of local zoning authority, the limitations on the power of local governments are of considerably more significance than limitations on the police power. All local governments are literally created by the state government, in part by the state constitution and in part by state statutes. Because cities, towns, townships, villages, and counties are creatures of the state, they have no inherent, independent existence or powers; their scope of existence and powers are determined by the state. In general, most power is granted to local governments by enabling legislation, which permits local governments to execute specific powers. Some states have one or more categories of local government whose powers go somewhat beyond those provided in the enabling legislation; such local governments are often called "home-rule" governments. Even in home-rule cities or counties, however, state enabling legislation frequently provides guidelines if not absolute parameters for the scope of power. Enabling legislation authorizes local governments to carry out zoning as it authorizes them to execute other powers.

As noted earlier, the Standard State Zoning Enabling Act remains in effect in all but a handful of states and is a model for much of the legislation even in those states that have departed from it somewhat. That model law gives most local governments the authority to zone. In the rest of this chapter, common variations from the model are noted as appropriate; specific variations can be found by checking state statutes.

Implementing zoning

Zoning requirements are laid out in two documents: the zoning map and the zoning ordinance. The requirements are then executed through the work of four groups: the governing body, the planning commission, the board of appeals, and the staff (see Figure 9–1). The five sections that follow describe the documents and explain the work of the entities that oversee their implementation.

Body	Role or responsibility
Governing body	Adopts zoning law (ordinance), including map. Has final authority on any changes to ordinance or map. *Final authority on most zoning matters.*
Planning commission	Recommends boundaries of districts for original zoning map. Reviews and makes recommendations on all changes to ordinance or map. *Advisory only on zoning matters.* In some jurisdictions, has final authority to adopt master plan.
Board of appeals/ adjustment	Considers applications for variances. Considers applications for special exceptions, also called special licenses or special permits. In some jurisdictions, considers appeals or interprets unclear ordinance provisions and lines on map.
Staff	Administers zoning ordinance. Enforces zoning ordinance. Assists governing body, planning commission, and board of appeals or adjustment by providing project reviews and other information.

Figure 9–1   Distribution of authority and responsibility for zoning decisions.

Zoning map and zoning ordinance

The zoning map simply shows the boundaries and labels of the zones into which the community has been divided. Legally it is adopted as a supplement to the local zoning ordinance. Local government staff and officials, landowners, community residents, and developers all refer to the map to determine how a particular piece of land is zoned. To maintain an accurate map despite frequent changes, many communities now prepare the map in a form that can be quickly and cheaply reproduced, enabling interested persons to obtain weekly or monthly updates at a reasonable cost. The zoning ordinance, as that term is commonly used, refers to the local law containing the zoning requirements of the jurisdiction. A local law may be called an ordinance, a resolution, or a set of zoning regulations; the terminology does not affect the substance of zoning controls, although it may be of some local significance. The important point is that the zoning controls imposed by a local government are invariably contained in a local law adopted by the local governing body.

Governing body

In this chapter, the term *governing body* refers to the legislative branch of local government. That body may be purely legislative or both legislative and administrative, as in the commission form of government. It may be called the city council, board of county commissioners, board of supervisors, town board, or board of freeholders. Regardless of the name, the governing body has most of the power and responsibility for zoning decisions.

The creators of the model act conceived of zoning as a local law that would be passed by the local legislative body, administered by the staff, and interpreted by the board of adjustment or appeals. Only changes in the law would then come back to the governing body and the advisory planning commission. As noted earlier, the designers of the model act did not anticipate the eventual importance of rezoning. In many communities, virtually every significant development proposal begins with a request for rezoning. A rezoning, however, is not a simple administrative application, like a subdivision plat submittal but is a request for a change in the law, which must therefore go before the local governing body.

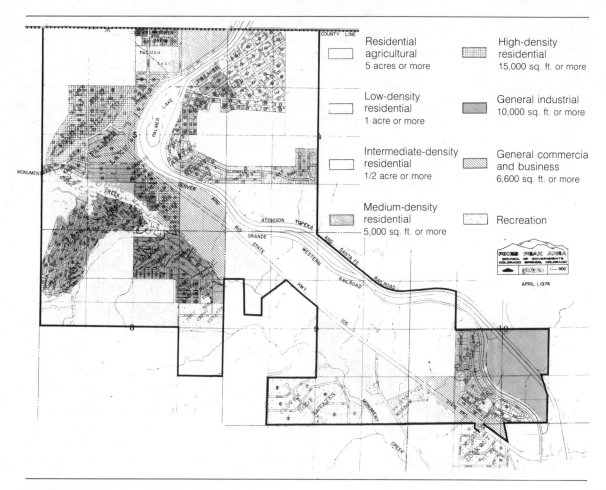

Figure 9–2   Zoning map of Palmer Lake, Colorado.

Planning commission

The Standard State Zoning Enabling Act provided for the creation of a zoning commission, but it also noted that "where a city planning commission already exists, it may be appointed as the zoning commission."[5] Most local governments today have a planning and zoning commission or simply a planning commission that functions under the zoning laws as well as under planning and other acts. Although state statutes typically give the planning commission direct, and in some cases final, authority in the adoption of master plans and the review of subdivisions, on zoning matters the commission is advisory only.

The form of the planning commission is usually governed by a state planning act or, in some circumstances, by local government charter. A membership of five, seven, or nine members is typical. In some jurisdictions the membership includes an *ex officio* representative from the governing body. In most jurisdictions the planning commission is appointed by the local governing body, although in some cities a mayor may have that power.

The original purpose of the commission, one which continues in the law, was to "recommend the boundaries of the various original districts . . . and hold public hearings thereon." Through a combination of its separate planning function and its role of recommending boundaries, the commission clearly should originate or review any comprehensive revisions to plans and zoning maps. Most local governments also submit rezonings of individual parcels of land to the planning commission for review. As a result, a typical planning commission devotes most of its time to reviewing specific development proposals and a relatively small portion of its time truly planning.

Board of adjustment or appeals

The most common and best-known function of the zoning board is the consideration of requests for variances, an issue on which it is the final authority in most jurisdictions. The model act gave the board the power to grant special exceptions to the terms of the zoning ordinance. (Special exceptions are called special licenses or special permits in some communities.) Variances generally involve minor deviations from specific rules in a zoning district—for example, reducing a 25-foot setback to 15 feet in a particular case. Special exceptions generally involve permitting a use that would otherwise not be allowed in the district; allowable uses by special exception are often contained in a list in the zoning ordinance. Variances and special exceptions are explained in more detail later in the chapter.

There are variations in how different states implement the section of the Standard State Zoning Enabling Act dealing with the zoning board, including two versions of the name: board of adjustment and board of appeals. In some states, the zoning board has the power and responsibility to consider appeals from actions of administrative officers, such as denial of a building permit for a reason related to zoning. In some states it has the power to interpret unclear provisions of the zoning ordinance, including the specific location of boundary lines.

Staff

Most local governments have staff to support the planning commission, zoning board, and governing body in their zoning functions. The staff basically has three roles. First, the staff administers the zoning ordinance. If an applicant intends to make a use of land that meets all of the requirements of the zoning ordinance, that person simply needs a permit reflecting compliance; the staff can issue such a permit without review by any other entity. Second, the staff enforces the ordinance. Although in some jurisdictions, the governing body must review an enforcement action, in every case the staff carries most of the burden of ensuring that an activity in conflict with the zoning ordinance is stopped. Third, the staff performs project reviews for the governing body, planning commission, and zoning board. The zoning board and planning commission are usually composed of volunteer citizens. Governing body members, whether paid or not, have numerous responsibilities besides zoning matters. Thus, all three bodies depend on the staff to provide accurate and complete information on which to base their decisions. Although the staff cannot directly control the response of the governing body to the project review, its indirect power can be substantial. An incomplete or inaccurate review by staff can lead to approval of a bad project or rejection of a good one.

Zoning in operation

The implementation of the zoning ordinance gives rise to three principal activities: rezoning; the review of variances, appeals, and special exceptions; and enforcement. The sections that follow consider each of these areas in detail.

Rezoning

The most important and most common zoning action of any local government is the map amendment or rezoning of land. Given the strong legal, cultural, and economic heritage of private property rights in this country, it is virtually impossible for any public body to "plan"—and then to implement through zoning—a specific future use for a piece of undeveloped land. Although most people will accept the notion that a local government can and should prohibit feedlots and steel mills in residential neighborhoods, it is difficult to persuade the average landowner (or member of a governing body) that property planned and zoned for a warehouse should not be used as a lumberyard if the location and access are suitable, as they well may be. A landowner whose property is zoned for industrial use but who has an immediate opportunity to sell for commercial use will urge, correctly, that the commercial use will have less impact on the neighborhood than industry might. Furthermore, not all of the arguments for granting rezoning favor the landowner. A community seeking its first shopping center, new industry, or variation in its housing types has ample motivation to accept, if not encourage, particular rezoning proposals.

As noted earlier, however, the model zoning act provides no effective administrative mechanism for map amendment. The map is changed the same way that it is adopted, which is the same way that a new zoning ordinance would be adopted. The steps in the formal review process typically include

1. Submission of application
2. Staff review
3. Notice of planning commission hearing
4. Preparation of staff report
5. Planning commission hearing
6. Planning commission action
7. Initial governing body action, including setting for hearing
8. Notice of governing body hearing
9. Governing body hearing
10. Governing body action.

That a map amendment, or rezoning, is a legislative act raises troublesome issues. The rezoning applicant and interested neighbors view the rezoning application as similar to subdivision or liquor license applications, which are reviewed in accordance with established standards and approved or disapproved on an objective basis. But the rezoning "application" is a request to change the law, and in changing the law the governing body can do what it likes, subject only to broad constitutional and state legislative limitations. Because the granting or denial of rezonings is generally performed without reference to significant standards, it is often unpredictable and can be unfair.

Zoning law is a remarkable anomaly in this respect: In no other area of American administrative law are requests for amendments to the law so frequent that there are specific application forms and fee schedules for requesting the amendments. At every level of government, most administrative laws set out standards for approving or disapproving applications and leave to staff or to an administrative board the task of acting on the applications—guided, of course, by the standards.

Some efforts have been made to limit the relatively unfettered legislative discretion of local governments in acting on rezonings. A small minority of states, led by California, Oregon, and Florida, changed the law to mandate that rezonings follow a predetermined local plan, which ideally provides standards that make rezoning decisions nearly administrative acts. In a handful of other states, the courts have determined that the rezoning of a parcel at the request of the landowner is a quasi-judicial action that must be based on express facts determined from the record. Other judicial doctrines, such as the prohibition of "spot zoning" and the "change or mistake" rule, both covered later in this chapter, are too vague to be of use in the administration of zoning.

Outside of the ten or so states with clear-cut legislative or judicial rules on the subject, the only real limitations on rezonings are procedural. Prior review by the planning commission is mandatory. Most jurisdictions require public hearings before both the planning commission and the governing body. The applicant and other affected parties must receive notice of the hearings, often in accordance with detailed requirements in the ordinance or in state law. Those requirements often include published notice and notification by certified mail to owners of property within a specified distance of the affected parcel.

Variances

The second most common zoning operation is the consideration of applications for variances. A variance allows the applicant to depart from the standard rules. Variances were included in the model act to alleviate "unnecessary hardship," which typically refers to hardship inherent in the physical characteristics of the land. For example, a preexisting lot of 9,500 square feet in a zone requiring a 10,000-square-foot minimum lot size would be a good candidate for a variance. A strangely shaped lot on which the enforcement of normal setback requirements might preclude building a rectangular house would also justify a variance.

There are two common misconceptions about variances: the first is that financial hardship justifies a variance. As noted above, the variance is supposed to alleviate a hardship that is inherent in the piece of land, not a hardship created by the owner's error in paying too much for the parcel. Financial hardship should rarely be a consideration in variance review unless it relates to the physical characteristics of the land. For example, let us say that a landowner applies for a setback variance because the applicable 25-foot setback would force the rear 5 feet of a normal-sized house for the district into a flood fringe area; by varying the setback to 20 feet, the zoning board can alleviate the topographic problem without requiring the landowner to build dikes or otherwise reengineer the floodplain. In such a case, the variance may save the landowner money, but the variance is granted basically because of a topographic problem.

The second misconception, a corollary of the first, is that financial hardship justifies *use* variances. The physical characteristics of a piece of land may dictate variances in bulk requirements such as setbacks and lot size but will rarely dictate one building type rather than another. Outside of the few jurisdictions with special provisions for them, use variances should not be granted.

Many requests for variances are for minor bulk variances in existing neighborhoods: for example, expansions of patios or carports one or two feet into designated side-yard setbacks. On such matters the zoning board becomes a sort of neighborhood arbitration board, dealing with physical hardships. Although these hardships are rarely great, this should be weighed against the extent of the public sector's stake in the somewhat arbitrary determination that a 10-foot side yard is superior to a 9-foot one.

Appeals

Under the model act, one of the powers of the zoning board is "to hear and decide appeals where it is alleged there is error in any order, requirement, decision or determination made by an administrative official in the enforcement of this act or of any ordinance adopted pursuant thereto."[6] Some communities use the appeal function of the zoning board to protect staff members from having to make judgment calls in difficult situations. For example, the zoning board would interpret ambiguous provisions of the ordinance or determine the exact location of disputed zone district boundary lines. The role of arbiter is a useful and appropriate one for the zoning board, although not all communities use it that way.

In some states the zoning board plays an even more critical role. Under a requirement for the "exhaustion of administrative remedies" before a case can be allowed in court, a landowner's challenge to the zoning of a parcel of land cannot be considered until the landowner applies for a building permit for the desired use. Although such an effort is often futile—the permit must be denied because it is inconsistent with the zoning—it is required by the courts. Most of those courts then also require that a landowner denied a building permit appeal to the zoning board before taking the case to court. The appeal may be somewhat

---

The case of the adjoining non-conforming lots Suppose that the ordinance provides that on single lots whose area or width is below that required in the district a single-family residence may be built, provided yard requirements are met. If they cannot be met, a variance is required.

However, where two or more lots adjoin in continuous frontage and ownership, and all or part of them do not meet the ordinance requirements for width and area, the land must be considered an undivided parcel. No portion may be used or sold in a way that diminishes compliance with the ordinance or that creates a lot width or area less than required.

Comes now Attorney Glibwise for a variance. He represents Mrs. Smith, the widow of the late Hector Smith. Mrs. Smith, Glibwise notes, is in frail health and precarious financial circumstances. Prior to enactment of the zoning ordinance, he continues, the late Mr. Smith purchased three adjoining lots facing on Pine Street. A residence was erected in the center of this property, leaving two vacant lots at the sides. . . . Mrs. Smith . . . would like to sell them. Mr. Smith had always anticipated building on them for rental property but was unable to do so before his death. Mrs. Smith, Glibwise points out, is virtually destitute as a result of the medical bills and is herself in need of a series of operations.

In addition to humanitarian reasons for granting the variance (or variances if the board elects to handle each lot individually), there is an injustice to be corrected here, Glibwise says. The ordinance calls for a 60-foot minimum width, but the lots are only 50 feet

wide. Because of the location of the house, strict application of the regulations requires Mrs. Smith to maintain 150 feet of frontage—two and a half times the minimum for the district. To prohibit the sale of the two vacant lots, or their use for construction, says Glibwise, is obviously confiscatory, since no use allowable in the district can be made of the individual lots. No court in the land would uphold denial of the variance, he says, citing a number of cases that are superficially similar in support of his position. Surely, Glibwise adds, the board can see the unfairness of subjecting Mrs. Smith (in her straitened circumstances) to the added expense of an appeal.

A report from the city's planning department is considered at this point. In the general area involved, the report says, subdivision took place in the 1920s, and most of the lots are 50 feet wide. The area is fairly well built up, with a significant proportion of residences being built on two- or three-lot combinations, some on the pattern of Mrs. Smith's, with the dwelling on a single lot and a vacant lot on one or both sides.

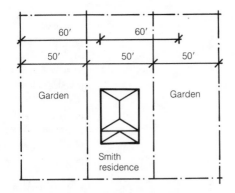

less futile than the original application, because the zoning board will presumably resolve some cases by granting variances or special exceptions.

Although some local governments have a separate appeal process by which decisions of the zoning board can be appealed to the governing body, such a provision is not included in the model act and does not exist in the majority of communities.

In short, the use and importance of appeals vary greatly from one local government to another.

The 60-foot minimum applies generally within the R-2 district in which the property is located. The planning report notes that this minimum is desirable because most of the land lying within R-2 districts *is* platted in 60-foot lots, and a considerable area remains unsubdivided. The future pattern of these tracts should involve the 60-foot minimum width. Finally, several neighbors voice opinions that are generally favorable to Mrs. Smith's case.

Given this scenario, what action should the board take?

Personal and financial hardships (and even nostalgia) should be played down. There is a hardship and it is not self-inflicted. It is also difficult to believe that it could be construed as a *necessary* hardship, considering the purposes of the ordinance. Thus, it seems a rank injustice to require Mrs. Smith to maintain a frontage two and a half times the minimum for the district, and it seems clearly confiscatory to prohibit building on two of the three vacant lots. Under the ordinance, however, they are not to be construed as three lots, but as one parcel, and for that parcel there already exists a reasonable use.

The planning department's report indicates that the problem, while not general, also is not uncommon in the area. And the opinion of the neighbors, while it may be considered, should not be a weighty element in reaching a decision. When boards give undue weight to such opinions, getting a variance depends on the kind of neighbors the appellant has, rather than on the equities involved. In any event, the character of the neighborhood would not be adversely affected either way by the decision in this case. As indicated by the planning department's report, most lots in the area are 50 feet wide and are occupied by single-family houses.

Given this array of considerations, the board should *not* grant the variance. This course, if matters stop there, will send the board members home feeling righteous and miserable. If they grant the variance, on the other hand, they will feel guilty and warm, having dispensed mercy rather than justice. But matters need not stop there. The board can set in motion a remedial action that will solve Mrs. Smith's problem without granting her a variance, and help a lot of other people as well (including the board, by reducing its future work load).

It seems fairly obvious that it is the ordinance that needs adjustment, and, since the board discovered the deficiency, the board should suggest it. This is not a duty assigned by law but an action dictated by common sense.

The board should ask itself: Why was an extensive built-up area with a 50-foot pattern zoned for 60-foot lot widths in the first place? Character was established and is unlikely to be changed by the greater width requirement. An easy and fairly simple solution might be to suggest surrounding such enclaves with their own boundaries and making them R-2A districts, with the same general regulations as for R-2 except for a minimum lot width of 50 feet, rather than 60.

Source: Frederick H. Bair, Jr., "Variances and the Zoning Board," *Planning* (July 1984), 20–21.

Special exceptions

Early zoning regulations assumed that an application for a use conforming to the zoning ought to require only that the staff issue a permit, without any sort of discretionary review. Although this approach was probably workable in some circumstances for individual houses and stores, even the drafters of the model act recognized that blanket permission would not be appropriate for all uses. For example, although an electric-utility transformer or substation might be needed somewhere in a residential neighborhood, the local government could hardly be expected to give blanket permission to place such a facility in a residential zone. On the other hand, rezoning the property for an industrial use (a typical classification for major electrical facilities) would be inconsistent with the comprehensive plan and would allow undesirable and unnecessary uses into the neighborhood. Thus, the drafters of the model act created a category of uses by "special exception"—a list of otherwise nonconforming uses that would be allowed in residential zones after a special review. The list of allowed special-exception uses is generally contained in the zoning ordinance under each zone classification to which it applies.

Uses that require a review are called uses by special exception (or special license, or special permit) and are usually spelled out in a list of "uses by review" for each district. The zoning board traditionally performs the reviews.

The emphasis on special exceptions and special permits varies enormously from one community to another. Most communities now impose a detailed review requirement on any development of significant size. Planned unit development reviews, site plan reviews, and other techniques cover such developments. Some communities integrate these reviews into the traditional special exception system, giving the zoning board an important role in reviewing large-scale projects. A greater number of communities have established a review system in which the planning commission, governing body, or both, perform most of the discretionary reviews, which makes the traditional role of the zoning board— the review of special exceptions—insignificant, except for small decisions in established neighborhoods.

Enforcement

Control of building permits is the primary form of zoning enforcement. In some communities, the chief building official is also the zoning enforcement officer. In others, the chief building official must obtain a certificate from the zoning enforcement officer or planning director before issuing a building permit. In all communities with building codes and zoning ordinances, every proposed structure is reviewed by staff before a building permit can be issued, to ensure that the structure complies with all zoning requirements. The building inspection staff then verifies that the structure that is built is substantially the same as the structure proposed on the permit application. Since most land use proposals include requests to build structures, and since building permits are required for most structures, and since most people comply with the building permit requirement, this system of enforcement usually works well.

Communities must occasionally use other enforcement techniques. If, for example, construction is begun without a building permit, or if a structure is built or located differently than the approved plans showed, the building department will generally issue a "stop-work" order. In some communities, stop-work orders are almost self-enforcing; in others, the local government must seek an order from the municipal or lower state court to enforce the stop-work order. The stop-work order is usually effective, because it compels the builder or developer to choose between complying with the ordinance and walking away from the investment in land and partial construction.

Some land use problems are unrelated to the building department. The most common is the accumulation of vehicles on private property. The accumulations may be junk, or a resident may be starting a repair shop or used-car lot on property not zoned for that purpose. Businesses—a beauty salon or a ceramics shop, for example—are sometimes set up in residential-only neighborhoods.

A letter or notice from the local government is the first step in enforcing the law against such violations. If the property owner is simply not aware of the law, there is a reasonable chance of voluntary compliance. If a letter or formal notice does not result in cooperation, then the local government must bring an enforcement action in court. Typically the enforcement action will request a fine and an injunction against continuing the violation; in most cases, the court is likely only to serve an injunction.

"Nonconforming" uses pose a peculiar enforcement problem. Nonconforming uses exist because in many instances, zoning regulations were imposed on areas that already had a mix of uses: the combination of residential and retail structures in cities is a familiar example. Those uses that became "nonconforming" after the enactment of the zoning ordinance were often permitted to remain, but only as long as the structures lasted. What seems like a simple enough proposition can, however, become a source of dispute. The owner may, for example, apply to remodel the structure or to rebuild it after partial destruction by fire or other casualty. If the local government consents to the rebuilding or remodeling, it perpetuates a use that is inconsistent with the current zoning of the neighborhood. On the other hand, if the permit for rebuilding or remodeling is denied, the property will probably remain or become an eyesore. If the building cannot be remodeled to serve current needs, the owner loses economic and psychological motivation to maintain it. Decisions about nonconforming uses are strictly judgment calls.

Local governments must enforce zoning to make it effective. Good enforcement must be prompt, consistent, predictable, and firm. Promptness is essential for several reasons: delay in enforcing requirements for a structure may allow the builder to obtain legally vested rights that prevent the local government from enforcing its own ordinances. Furthermore, an enforcement action that is brought promptly after the local government has learned of the problem is generally better received by the violator and by the courts that must enforce it.

Deterrence of future violations is a major purpose of a zoning enforcement action; but enforcement is not a deterrent unless it is consistent and predictable. In addition, inconsistency may give rise to a "denial of equal protection" defense by an individual accused of violating the ordinance.

The need for firmness in enforcement is related to the need for predictability. If a local government is known for negotiating solutions to zoning violations rather than enforcing the terms of the ordinance, the public will hold little regard for the ordinance, and the level of voluntary compliance will be low. If local government officials are reluctant to enforce a particular provision of the local zoning ordinance, that provision should be considered for amendment rather than simply neglected.

Zoning and other controls

Municipalities implement the zoning ordinance alongside a number of other controls: the comprehensive plan, subdivision regulations, aesthetic and architectural controls, off-street parking requirements, building codes, and covenants or deed restrictions. The sections that follow describe the relationship between zoning and these other forms of land use and design control.

Comprehensive or master plan

Although the terms *comprehensive plan* and *master plan* are used almost interchangeably by many local officials, they are not synonymous in zoning law. Section 3 of the Standard State Zoning Enabling Act provides in part that zoning "regulations shall be made in accordance with a comprehensive plan," but the term is not defined anywhere. In contrast, Section 6 of the Standard City Planning Enabling Act defines a master plan in great detail (see sidebar). That act, a 1927 document prepared by the same team that prepared the model zoning act, has not achieved the universal acceptance accorded the zoning act, but the sections that establish the planning commission and define the master plan have been widely adopted

Two questions have arisen frequently in the courts. First, must a community have a master plan to have zoning? Second, if a community has a master plan, must the zoning follow it exactly? The almost universal answers have been that

---

A master plan

General powers and duties It shall be the function and duty of the commission to make and adopt a master plan for the physical development of the municipality, including any areas outside of its boundaries which, in the commission's judgment, bear relation to the planning of such municipality. Such plan, with the accompanying maps, plats, charts and descriptive matter shall show the commission's recommendations for the development in said territory, including, among other things, the general location, character and extent of streets, viaducts, subways, bridges, waterways, water fronts boulevards, parkways, playgrounds, squares, parks, aviation fields and other public ways, grounds and open spaces, the general location of public buildings and other public property, and the general location and extent of public utilities and terminals, whether publicly or privately owned or operated, for water, light, sanitation, transportation, communication, power, and other purposes; also the removal, relocation, widening, narrowing, vacating, abandonment, change of use or extension of any of the foregoing ways, grounds, open spaces, buildings, property, utilities or terminals; as well as a zoning plan for the control of the height, area, bulk, location, and use of buildings and premises. As the work of making the whole master plan progresses, the commission may from time

to time adopt and publish a part or parts thereof, any such part to cover one or more major sections or divisions of the municipality or one or more of the aforesaid or other functional matters to be included in the plan. The commission may from time to time amend, extend, or add to the plan.

Purposes in view In the preparation of such plan the commission shall make careful and comprehensive surveys and studies of present conditions and future growth of the municipality and with due regard to its relation to neighboring territory. The plan shall be made with the general purpose of guiding and accomplishing a coordinated, adjusted, and harmonious development of the municipality and its environs which will . . . best promote health, safety, morals, order, convenience, prosperity, and general welfare, as well as efficiency and economy in the process of development; including, among other things, adequate provision for traffic, the promotion of safety from fire and other dangers, adequate provision for light and air, the promotion of the healthful and convenient distribution of population, the promotion of good civic design and arrangement, wise and efficient expenditures of public funds, and the adequate provision of public utilities and other public requirements.

Source: Sections 6 and 7, Standard City Planning Enabling Act, U.S. Department of Commerce, 1927.

no elaborate plan is required and that, in most circumstances, the plan is advisory and that deviations from it in zoning decisions are acceptable. Exceptions exist in a handful of states (led by California, Florida, and Oregon) that have, since 1970, amended their state statutes to require that local land use controls follow a plan that meets certain state guidelines. In any state with such legislation, the plan must conform to state law, and the zoning must then follow the plan.

In most other states, local governments may view a master plan as a document that is legally both optional and advisory. However, in reaching that state of the law, the courts have not ignored entirely the requirement that zoning be "in accordance with a comprehensive plan." The "change or mistake" rule, now dying in many jurisdictions, and the common rule against "spot-zoning" are two doctrines developed by the courts to implement and interpret the comprehensive plan requirement of the model zoning act.

The "change or mistake" rule gives the zoning map itself the status of a "comprehensive plan." According to the change or mistake rule, the zoning map can be amended only to correct a mistake in the creation of the map or to respond to a change in a neighborhood. The rule rarely is strictly followed now. It quickly became meaningless in growing areas, because of the ease of demonstrating change in the community. When the rule did function, it was most likely to affect rezonings of small parcels in established neighborhoods, a type of rezoning that usually has little effect on the community as a whole but that may be controversial within the neighborhood. In such cases, the rezoning would be allowed if there were a mistake in the map or if there were a demonstrated change in the neighborhood.

Courts have commonly used the rule against spot-zoning to overturn rezonings of small "spots" of commercial uses in residential areas, claiming that the commercial use is inconsistent with the comprehensive plan—as expressed by the combination of existing neighborhood conditions and the existing zoning map. Many courts have lost sight of the fact that the rule against spot-zoning originated in the requirement for a comprehensive plan; they therefore feel free to strike down spot-zoning whenever they think they see it—without regard to the actual comprehensive plan, which may permit spot-zoning under some circumstances. That attitude is unfortunate; most planners recognize the desirability of well-planned neighborhood shopping centers in residential areas. A good comprehensive plan spells out the need for commercial services in residential areas, ensuring that a new neighborhood shopping center will not violate the plan.

Although in most states and in most circumstances the comprehensive or master plan is viewed as advisory and not binding on zoning decisions, local governments can benefit from developing, adopting, and following a good master plan. Such a plan coordinates future zoning and capital improvement budgeting so that new public improvements are placed in the areas most likely to develop. The master plan can guide public officials through tough zoning decisions with a good developer on one side and nervous neighbors on the other. The plan can provide invaluable support if zoning decisions are challenged in court; even though courts do not require adherence to a plan, a community can nevertheless use adherence to the plan to defend its actions. Furthermore, a good master-planning process collects data about the community's present and future capacities and demands, which the planning commission and governing body can then use to make zoning decisions.

As the plan is developed, however, the limitations on a local government's ability to predict or plan the future use of private land should be kept in mind. Highly specific, rigid designations of future uses for undeveloped land may prove inaccurate at best and may be used against the local government at worst. If, for example, a community designates an area for future industrial use and then changes the zoning to residential or agricultural when a planned sewer extension does not materialize, a local landowner could use the local government's original plan in court to attempt to obtain industrial zoning for the property. Certainly the local government can amend the land use plan every time a zoning change is made, but that process is cumbersome and makes the plan less credible. A better practice is to design a land use plan that delineates land use areas only very generally and also designates broad categories of possible uses within each area.

The most valuable parts of the plan set forth the goals and policies of the local government. Those goals and policies can guide land use, capital expenditures, and other decisions and can serve the local government long after a future land use plan has been forgotten or superseded by changing development patterns.

Subdivision regulation

Along with zoning, subdivision regulation is the other principal tool of the police power that controls the development and use of land in the United States. Chapter 8 is devoted to the subject of subdivision control; this section is limited to a discussion of the relationship between zoning and subdivision regulation.

Subdivision controls regulate the division of larger parcels of land into individual building lots. In most communities, subdivision regulations deal with all aspects of subdivision design, including lot size and shape and street width and layout. Construction standards for improvements such as streets, sewers, water mains, and sidewalks are also incorporated into subdivision controls, and the regulations frequently contain requirements for dedications for parks and other public lands. Zoning, in contrast, prescribes allowed uses of land and buildings and specifies relationships between the amount of land and the size and placement of buildings on it.

In most communities, the zoning and subdivision control systems function almost independently, although both involve planning-commission review and are typically administered by the same planning staff. The disadvantage of separating zoning and subdivision control is that there are many respects in which they overlap. For example, subdivision design is theoretically determined by subdivision controls, but zoning requirements for lot size and shape and building setbacks greatly influence subdivision design. The use of land (regulated by zoning) and site design (regulated by subdivision controls) are critically interrelated in all but the simplest development projects. No responsible site planner would attempt to determine the location of the community shopping center in a large new project without first determining utility and traffic patterns. But a local government that grants a zoning request without knowing what the site plan will be is doing just that.

Because many developers recognize the interrelationship between zoning and subdivision control, they often present tentative or conceptual site plans along with rezoning proposals. However, traditional systems of zoning and subdivision control do not include a mechanism for ensuring that the site plan presented with the rezoning request will be the one submitted in the subdivision plan and actually built.

Through more modern regulatory systems, principally planned unit development controls, local governments have attempted to tie the use and design decisions more closely together in the development approval process. In most communities, however, a large number of projects still proceed through a rezoning followed simply by a subdivision review; it is therefore important to understand the problems that this system presents.

There are two reasons that an application for rezoning almost always precedes the application for subdivision review. First, most local subdivision controls allow the approval of a subdivision only if it conforms to the zoning for the area. Second, although the zoning application is more likely to be controversial, the subdivision application is far more expensive because of the engineering work required. Many developers and landowners defer the cost of preparing the subdivision application until zoning has been approved for the project.

Aesthetic and architectural controls

Although sometimes included in a separate "appearance code," most aesthetic or architectural controls are actually included in the zoning ordinance. Furthermore, many traditional zoning controls are basically aesthetic: most limitations on building height and many setback requirements are based on aesthetic judgments rather than on scientific determinations of health or safety needs.

Some communities have special districts in which architectural or aesthetic control is imposed. Historic districts, for example, require architectural compatibility with historic structures. The French Quarter in New Orleans and the Plaza area in Santa Fe are examples of districts with rigid architectural controls. Some communities impose height limitations related to local landmarks or views. Until recently, building heights in Philadelphia were limited to the height of William Penn's hat on a statue on top of City Hall. Figure 9–3 shows an example of an aesthetic control.

The zoning ordinance is the logical place for architectural and other aesthetic controls. First, it already contains certain such controls. Second, it is sometimes desirable to limit the effect of such controls to a particular area of the community. Third, separate enabling legislation for architectural controls rarely exists, and the zoning law is the most logical source of legal authority for such controls.

Off-street parking requirements

Off-street parking requirements are typically part of the zoning ordinance, although they are sometimes contained in a separate section of it and are often adopted and amended separately from zoning regulations. Off-street parking requirements are included in zoning controls because the provision of off-street parking is closely related to land use and intensity of development, both of which zoning was designed to regulate.

Figure 9–3   Aesthetic controls in Santa Fe, New Mexico, require that newer buildings match the design, scale, materials (adobe or adobe-look stucco), and details of the many mission-era buildings remaining in the area. This photo shows a mixture of old construction and new.

Building codes

Building codes control the design and construction of buildings. Although local ordinances typically require that proposed buildings comply with all zoning requirements before building permits can be issued under the building codes, there is rarely a direct relationship between building codes and zoning.

Covenants or deed restrictions

Restrictive covenants, also called simply "covenants" or "deed restrictions" are private land use controls included in the chain of title of property. A valid covenant restricts the use of the property against which it is recorded and is enforceable by a limited group of persons—usually landowners in the same subdivision and with similar restrictions on their properties. Early covenants were commonly short and simple and dealt with a single issue, for example, prohibiting the sale of alcoholic beverages on the premises. In many large development projects built since 1960, however, lengthy covenants set out complex systems of land use and architectural control.

It is very important to understand that covenants have *no effect whatever* on zoning and that zoning has *no effect whatever* on covenants. Since both are land use controls, as a practical matter the more restrictive takes precedence. For example, if the zoning allows residential uses and a covenant limits the property to single-family residential uses, the covenant will effectively control. If the two are in conflict—for example, if industrial property is burdened by a "residential only" covenant—then the landowner must get one or the other changed. But the conflict creates no obligation for the local government to amend the zoning; any request for rezoning should simply be considered on its merits, without regard for the covenant.

Another issue that arises involves requests by residents that zoning officials enforce covenants. In general, a local government has no power to enforce covenants and should not intervene in covenant enforcement any more than it would intervene in any other private contract. There are exceptions, but they are both rare and clear. Two exceptions would be (1) to preserve open space or some other quasi-public amenity in a planned unit development, if the local government had relied on that open space as part of its reason for approving the project; and (2) to enforce covenants in Texas cities that do not have zoning and where the local governments are specifically authorized by state law to enforce private covenants.

Substance of zoning: Use regulations

Land uses are traditionally divided into four basic categories: residential, commercial, industrial, and agricultural. A small community may have only these four zones, while a large city may have many subcategories.

The zoning ordinance imposes different use, intensity, and bulk regulations for each district. Under use regulations, there are typically three categories of allowed uses: principal uses, which are generally "uses by right"—allowed in the zone without further review and without any limitation other than the bulk and intensity requirements of the zone; accessory uses, such as garages and outbuildings, which are allowed only as uses incidental to the principal use; uses that are allowed by special exception or some other form of special review.

Residential

Residential use districts in a typical community are generally distinguished from one another by the intensity of the use. The "highest" residential district in a

Pyramid zoning Some communities use a "cumulative" or "pyramid" form of zoning. Pyramid zoning is based on the idea that a hierarchy of land uses (the pyramid) can be designed according to the relative desirability of each use. Under cumulative zoning, only uses that are less desirable than the designated use are excluded from any zone; more desirable uses are allowed. The pyramid places single-family detached residential uses at the top, followed by other types of residential uses in reverse order of density, followed by commercial uses in order of increasing intensity of use, followed by light industrial and, finally, by heavy industrial uses. In such a system, only single-family residential uses would be allowed in the top zone, but all residential uses would be allowed in any commercial zone and any use at all would be allowed in a heavy industrial zone.

Because residents tend to object to certain industrial activities near their homes, many communities now bar residences from industrial zones. For similar reasons, some communities prohibit residences in some or all commercial zones. Thus, complete cumulative zoning is not as common as it once was. However, most communities still have cumulative provisions *within* their residential, commercial, and industrial districts, respectively.

community requires the largest minimum lot size; the districts below it allow progressively smaller minimum lot sizes until a level has been reached that allows townhouses or duplexes; districts below that allow increasingly intense use for multifamily housing. Setback and other bulk requirements vary somewhat as the intensity of use is allowed to increase.

Uses within residential districts are almost always cumulative; that is, a single-family detached house would be allowed in any residential district, and a duplex would be allowed in a district zoned for multifamily housing (see sidebar). The most important aspect of use control in residential districts is the exclusion of commercial and industrial uses. As noted earlier, the zoning system presumes the superiority of the single-family detached home.

The three basic classifications of residential uses are single-family detached; single-family attached; and multifamily. Many local ordinances also refer to duplexes, triplexes, and four-plexes, which are small multifamily dwelling units. In administering zoning, a local government should not be concerned with whether a particular building is a condominium, a row of town houses, or an apartment building, but with which of the three basic use types defines the building and whether the use is allowed in the zone for which it is proposed. Note that for purposes of regulation, condominiums and apartments are designations of different types of *ownership*, not different types of land use.

In some communities, the definition of "single-family" is an issue associated with one of two uses: boarding houses, including student housing, such as fraternity houses; and group homes for persons with disabilities. Some communities use traditional definitions of the word "family" to prohibit both from single-family zones. Although a 1974 Supreme Court decision upheld a local ordinance prohibiting boarding houses in a single-family zone,[7] many state legislatures have eliminated local authority on the issue of group homes and simply defined such homes as "single-family dwellings" under state law. Chapter 11, "Social Aspects of Physical Planning," includes additional discussion of group homes.

Commercial

In communities with multiple commercial zones, distinctions among the zones usually rest on the perceived impact of the use on the surrounding neighborhood. A community may have a neighborhood business zone of small stores and professional offices; a community business zone of large stores, banks, and office buildings; and a general business zone that allows such high-impact commercial uses as auto dealerships and lumberyards, as well as all other commercial uses. Like residential zoning, commercial zoning is almost always cumulative from one commercial district to another.

Some communities have more specialized commercial zones, such as a highway commercial zone for businesses like motels and fast-food restaurants. (It should be noted that the imposition of such a zone along a highway is likely to reinforce the development of a strip commercial area that may become a land use and traffic problem.) Communities with special recreation facilities such as marinas, ski areas, and casinos often create special commercial zones for those facilities.

Some communities create a restrictive commercial district in the downtown area to encourage stores and office buildings designed for pedestrian access and to discourage automobile dealerships, lumberyards, and other commercial uses that require large land areas and attract little walk-in traffic. Such a district may include regulations that severely limit off-street parking so that merchants and office tenants will have to depend on public parking in the downtown area.

In a community with several commercial districts, the districts should, in general, be distinguished from one another by explicit, objective standards, including store and building size, building height, parking requirements, land coverage, floor-area ratio, and projected traffic generation. Only general use categories should be specified. Some communities that have tried to list all allowed uses in each commercial district now find themselves with adequate provisions for saddleries and tallow works but without zones that permit ski shops or video rental outlets.

Industrial

One of the original purposes of zoning was to separate noxious industrial uses from residential areas (see Figure 9–4). That continues as a purpose of zoning, and heavy industry is excluded from most efforts at mixed-use development. Furthermore, many communities have ceased to permit dwellings in industrial areas, a step that allows for a planned approach to industrial zoning, protects industries from potential complaints from neighbors, and protects residents from the effects of industrial uses.

Traditionally, industrial zones have been either "light industrial" or "heavy industrial" districts. Light industrial districts generally include uses such as ware-houses and light assembly plants, which have little impact on the surrounding neighborhood other than truck traffic and visual impact. Heavy industrial uses include steel mills and manufacturing facilities likely to create noise, odors, or smoke that can affect surrounding areas.

Early zoning ordinances listed uses that fell in each category, but these were rapidly outdated. Many communities now use performance standards to distinguish among types of industrial use. Typically, the light industrial zone allows uses that can meet a zero-impact or other specified criterion at the property line for smoke, odors, noise, vibration, and glare. The vigorous enforcement of federal laws concerning air pollution and job safety has greatly reduced the output of smoke, odors, noise, and vibration from most industry. Glare is easily controlled through proper site and architectural design. Thus, more and more businesses can meet the criteria for the light industrial zones. Further, electronics plants, which are the majority of new plants built today, generate little neighborhood impact other than traffic.

The growth of low-impact industries and of service and information industries has led to a relatively new type of development, the landscaped industrial park. Older zoning ordinances need to be amended to allow and protect such areas: no company will build an architecturally attractive, landscaped plant if local

Figure 9–4 Zoning generally separates incompatible uses, such as residential and industrial uses. Here a home is nestled next to a major trainyard.

zoning allows a fully paved pipe-storage yard to be built next door. Zoning for industrial parks should limit buildings, paving, and other impervious cover to a specified portion of the lot; allow only industries with little or no external impact; and include basic landscaping and aesthetic controls. Some modern industrial parks include on-site recreational facilities, ranging from tennis courts to jogging trails and golf courses; the zoning needs to be flexible enough to allow such facilities.

Just as American industry has changed, so has the zoning to accommodate it. The smokestack industries that remain in many communities must be allowed in the appropriate zoning district. As new industries seek locations away from rail and from old industries, however, new industrial zoning categories must be developed to supplement the traditional ones.

Agricultural

Local governments today use three types of agricultural zoning: truly agricultural zoning in rural areas without development pressure; agricultural zoning that is really a temporary or holding zone where development pressure is increasing; and agricultural zoning that is designed to preserve agricultural land in a developing area.

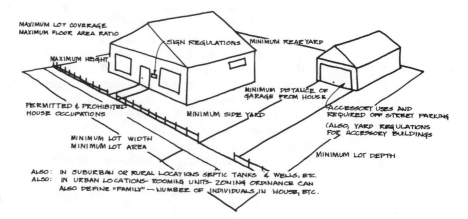

Figure 9–5 Single-family house as perceived by the zoning inspector.

In general, agricultural rural zoning simply restates the obvious, giving land an agricultural designation when it is unlikely to be used for anything else. Such zoning can be valuable, however, in discouraging scattered rural residential development. Such development can prevent nearby farmers from using aerial spraying and can bring children, domestic dogs, and pollens from domestic yard plants into the area, all of which may be incompatible with efficient agricultural production.

"Agricultural" zoning in an area likely to develop in the future is a misnomer that illustrates the difficulty of predicting future uses of undeveloped land. Some communities more accurately term such zones "holding" or "open" zones. Used in isolation, agricultural zoning as a means of preserving undeveloped areas is doomed to failure. Although tying such zoning to a system of compensation or development rights purchases can be effective, requiring a landowner to maintain developable land in an agriculturally inefficient minimum lot size of 160 or even 40 acres would almost undoubtedly be found to be a taking and be struck down by the courts.

In short, agricultural zoning is extremely important in rural areas, including rural areas that happen to be near urban areas, but in developing suburban and exurban areas, agricultural zoning is not a particularly useful tool.

Special uses

Certain unusual land uses require special controls. A discussion of a number of those uses and the related controls follows.

Land use around airports is a major concern in many communities, both because of the noise of aircraft operations and because of the increased risk of crashes in certain areas adjacent to airports. Many communities use zoning to eliminate the land use conflicts, usually by limiting the height of buildings in the flight path and prohibiting schools, institutions, and other high-intensity land uses in "critical areas." Zoning regulations may also limit the density of residential development in critical areas and in the noisiest areas.

Such efforts can work, as long as the zoning is basically consistent with development patterns around the airport. If, however, there is economic pressure for more intense use than the airport zoning allows, the zoning is likely to fail, either politically or legally. In general, where the zoning has caused a significant economic loss to the landowner, the courts have been unwilling to sustain zoning to protect an airport.

Communities sometimes promote "airport zoning" as a way to protect the public. In reality, airport zoning protects the airport by limiting incompatible land uses on land that is so close to the airport that it is almost a part of airport operations. Airport managers cannot handle the risk of an apartment building or a school in a hazard area, but they may tolerate the lesser (political and financial) risk of having a few houses on the same site, as an alternative to having to buy the property. Properly located airports that own adequate amounts of land do not need the protection of airport zoning.

Zoning control of *sex businesses* has been held by the Supreme Court to be within the scope of permissible regulation.[8] Although the Court's first decision on the subject in 1976 upheld an ordinance that prohibited only the aggregation of several sex businesses in one area, it was broad enough to sustain local ordinances limiting them to specific districts or requiring the aggregation of such uses—an approach used in some large cities. In its second decision, a 1986 case involving the city of Renton, Washington, the Court upheld a local ordinance that prohibited adult theaters within one thousand feet of any residential area, school, or church. That ordinance left one 520-acre area of the city available for such uses, although the theater chain challenging the ordinance claimed that there were no theaters in the area and no "commercially viable" land for sale in it. In spite of the claims of the theater chain, neither of the Court's decisions is broad enough to sustain the complete exclusion of such businesses from a community, a form of regulation that would raise First Amendment issues.

In the regulation of *signs*, land use controls directly confront the First Amendment's freedom of speech provisions. In attempting to restrict or ban billboards, many communities adopted sign controls that allowed a business to have identification signs on the premises but that limited the use of signs to advertise off-premises. The U.S. Supreme Court struck down such an ordinance on the grounds that it limited noncommercial (i.e., political) speech more than it limited commercial speech, since noncommercial speech rarely has a "premises" on which to place signs.[9] Although the decision dates from 1981, many communities remain unaware of either its existence or its significance and have sign regulations in effect that do not meet the Court's requirements. Under the Court's opinion, only sign regulations that are content neutral and that deal with the size, material, color, and lighting of signs, and with their location in relation to traffic or adjacent uses, are fully protected.

Churches and *schools* have long posed problems for zoning officials. Such institutions clearly serve residents of an area and have been allowed as uses by right in many residential areas. However, the traffic and parking problems associated with churches and schools have made them somewhat less than desirable neighbors, and many communities now allow them in residential areas as uses by special exception or special permit, a type of review covered earlier in the chapter.

Even more unpopular as neighbors than churches and schools are *waste disposal sites*. No longer simple "dumps," waste disposal sites fall into two categories: domestic disposal sites, which are usually sanitary landfills, and industrial disposal sites, which, by federal law, must be called "hazardous waste" sites and which are disposal sites for bulk liquid waste as well as for more toxic solid wastes. Although such sites are exempt from zoning in some states, particularly if located on public land, in many states local zoning approval is required even for a facility operated by a local government. Wide publicity about the past mismanagement of unregulated chemical dumps has made neighborhood opposition to even the safest of operations likely, and pragmatic public officials may view the "best" solution as the one that requires the least public participation and review—because that is the solution with the greatest chance of success.

As noted earlier, zoning has long been used to preserve such famous *historic districts* as the French Quarter in New Orleans and the Plaza area in Santa Fe. The designation of a historic district and the imposition of special architectural controls in that district are easy ways to integrate historic-preservation controls into a zoning ordinance. It is important that architectural controls in a historic district be based on carefully determined standards and not on the mood of the review board on the night of the hearing. Model ordinances are a good source for standards dealing with such matters as building materials, roof treatment, facade proportions, porch and entry design, ratios of solids to voids, and rhythms of solids to voids.

As a control technique for *floodplains* and other *environmentally sensitive lands,* zoning is not particularly effective. To draw boundaries around a district, it is essential to know where the district is. Drawing hard lines around environmental features is difficult under any circumstances, but the difficulty is compounded in an area such as a floodplain in a developing area, where the boundary changes as increased development causes increased runoff. Performance standards, discussed later in the chapter, are a more effective approach to zoning than is the designation of districts. Although performance standards can be imposed specifically in a floodplain or other environmentally sensitive zone, it is usually simpler and more effective to avoid designating zones at all and simply to make the performance standards apply wherever lands meeting the definition of, for example, "floodplain" occur.

Substance of zoning: Intensity and bulk controls

In addition to regulating land use, zoning determines the size and placement of buildings. Intensity or density of development is generally controlled by linking permitted building size to land area. Bulk requirements include building height limitations, lot coverage requirements, building setback or yard requirements, and minimum lot sizes. The two sections that follow consider intensity and bulk controls in detail.

Intensity or density

The specification of minimum lot sizes for single-family homes was the most common early form of regulation of intensity or density of development. One zone might require one-acre lots, the next one-half acre, and the next one-fourth. Such requirements are still common in most single-family zones.

Multifamily, planned unit development, and mixed-use zones usually specify the intensity of residential development as a number of dwelling units per acre, sometimes abbreviated "DU/acre." A 4 DU/acre requirement is not the same as a requirement for quarter-acre minimum lot size, because the 4 DU/acre requirement might result in two homes on 14,000-square-foot lots and two on 9,000-square-foot lots, or in four homes on 7,000-square-foot lots with the remaining land retained as open space. Density requirements specified in DU/acre are usually supplemented by a minimum lot-size requirement, but in that context the minimum lot size is more a bulk control than an intensity control.

The intensity of commercial development in early ordinances was governed somewhat indirectly by the combination of minimum lot-size requirements and height and lot coverage requirements, which are basically bulk controls. If, for example, a particular zone requires a 10,000-square-foot commercial lot and allows nothing higher than 35 feet and no more impervious coverage than 50 percent of the lot, land use intensity is definitely limited, however indirectly. On a 10,000-square-foot lot, 50-percent coverage allows building on 5,000 square feet. The height limit of 35 feet allows room for 3 stories. Thus, the largest building that can be built on the lot is 15,000 square feet, plus a basement. In a retail zone, the desire of most retailers to be on ground level creates a further effective limit on land use intensity.

More sophisticated commercial zoning requirements use a floor-area ratio (FAR) to impose limits on commercial development intensity. An FAR of 1 allows one square foot of building for each square foot of land area, while an FAR of 4 allows four square feet of building for each square foot of land area. A commercial zone with FAR requirements may also have bulk requirements, such as a 50-percent limit on lot coverage, which would mean that a building in a zone with an FAR of 1 may be a two-story building on half the lot.

Warehouse and light industrial zones usually contain intensity limitations similar to those in commercial districts. Intensity of development is rarely a major issue in heavy industrial zones; performance standards and buffer, or setback, requirements (discussed later in this chapter) are usually far more important tools for regulating heavy industrial development than are intensity controls.

Note that DU/acre or FAR requirements for large developments should specify whether the limitations apply to "net" or "gross" land area. Gross land area includes the entire site or that portion of it to be devoted to a particular use. Net land area includes the entire site less specified undevelopable land, such as streets and parks. With a typical land loss in residential areas of 8 percent for streets alone, a 5 DU/acre requirement applied to the *gross* area of the development will actually allow 5.43 DU/acre of developable land.

Bulk

From the perspective of the community as a whole, bulk requirements are far less important than use and intensity controls, but from the perspective of immediate neighbors, bulk requirements are very important indeed. For example, if the local government knows that there will be twenty dwelling units on a parcel of land, that is really all the information necessary to plan sewer and water systems and predict tax revenues; the government does not have a big stake in how the houses are placed on the property. On the other hand, the impact of those twenty houses on adjacent lots will vary greatly depending on whether the houses are three-story structures set back 5 feet from the property line or one-story houses set back 15 feet from the property line.

Bulk requirements are design requirements. Traditional bulk requirements, specifying the shape of the lot and a three-dimensional area into which any building must fit, were created in part to give predictability to development, enabling the first person to build a house on a new block to know where nearby homes would eventually be located. Such zoning specified a front-yard setback, a rear-yard setback, sideyard setbacks, and building height limits (see Figure 9–5).

In the larger-scale developments typical of building patterns in the United States today, all homes are built at about the same time, often by the same builder. The builder controls the predictability of building location, and there is less need for zoning to include specific design requirements. In zones used for larger developments (such as planned unit development and cluster zones, discussed later in this chapter), many communities today allow a good deal of flexibility in bulk requirements.

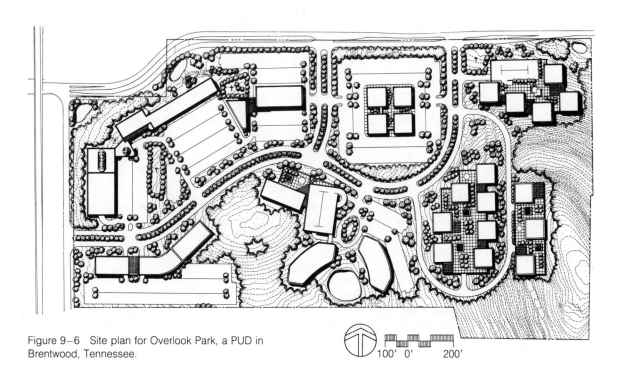

Figure 9–6 Site plan for Overlook Park, a PUD in Brentwood, Tennessee.

100' 0' 200'

Beyond traditional zoning: Other approaches to land use control

As the assumptions that once guided zoning have changed, a number of approaches to land use control have evolved that reflect—and encourage—shifts in development patterns. These include planned unit developments, the use of performance (rather than design) standards, phased development controls, and growth management systems. The next four sections consider each of these approaches in detail.

Planned unit development controls

A planned unit development—or PUD—involves a mixture of single-family residences, town houses, apartments, some commercial and institutional uses and, occasionally, some industry. Such a mixture flies in the face of zoning's traditional assumptions about the superiority of the single-family home. Planned unit development controls were developed largely by the private sector to provide the public sector with an effective means of regulating such developments, a concept which did not fit comfortably under traditional zoning district regulation. Planned unit development controls can be viewed as an attempt to merge the zoning and subdivision procedures into a single, sequential development review process.

Early advocates of PUD were trying to escape the use-segregation requirements of zoning as well as to find relief from the detailed, lot-by-lot design requirements imposed by traditional bulk regulations. Such requirements often encouraged developers to bulldoze the landscape in order to make it fit the gridiron development pattern that optimizes land use under traditional zoning design requirements. Supporters of PUD pointed out that varied lot sizes and clustered homes would preserve open space without increasing density and without increasing the effective impact on the community. Implemented responsibly, the greater flexibility of PUD allowed for site design that was more creative and responsive to environmental considerations.

Zoning by negotiation Simplicity and clarity are major advantages of traditional zoning over many other systems of regulation. In most cases, a quick review by a junior staff member will determine whether a proposed structure complies with zoning requirements. On the basis of that determination, the structure is either approved or disapproved. Simple.

Reviewing applications for complex development projects that may cover dozens, or even hundreds, of acres and be built over many years is far more complicated. Even after detailed technical review, it is often difficult to determine whether the project complies with all applicable standards. The issue is made more complex when the local government has adopted a more flexible and, at times, "standardless" form of regulation.

Too much flexibility in standards can create a system of "zoning by negotiation," whether by accident or by design. The negotiation may cover the ultimate density of the project, or the developer may be encouraged to "donate" certain additional amenities to the local government in consideration for development approval. The practice at times smacks of what once was called "contract zoning," a practice frowned upon by the courts as a bartering of the police power. However, when such requirements are imposed as conditions for approval of a complex development, rather than being tied up in a traditional contract, they may be hard to detect as such.

In a 1987 decision (*Nollan* v. *California Coastal Commission*, 1987), the Supreme Court found a particular negotiated land use decision to be

---

Part of the appeal of PUD lies in the emphasis on *planning*. As noted earlier, traditional zoning bulk controls were designed to regulate development lot-by-lot, but the flexibility built into PUD controls can be achieved only if a larger tract is planned and developed *as a unit*. Planning larger tracts offers developers both the opportunity and the incentive for better planning. Since the developer owns all the land in the project, a major error in site design or in locating adjacent land uses will create difficulty in selling the land.

Planned unit development controls were gradually accepted in the 1960s and early 1970s and are now a common form of land use control in most states. Planned unit development controls are usually implemented as part of a zoning ordinance containing one or more PUD zones. Such zones may be "overlays," which are effective in addition to the basic zoning for a parcel of land. In other cases, the implementation of PUD regulations is triggered by a request for rezoning to a PUD zone.

Not all planned unit developments include nonresidential uses, nor do all planned unit developments contain clustered housing with common open space, although most do. Some ordinances provide only for clustering, with minimal variations from basic bulk regulations; such provisions are sometimes called "cluster zoning" rather than PUD. All PUD or cluster regulations do involve variations from bulk controls. The most common variations are the use of density rather than minimum lot size to measure intensity and the reduction of yard setback requirements.

One problem with planned unit development controls is that some communities have eliminated traditional zoning standards without replacing them with other guidelines—standards for maximum density and general performance, for example. If the PUD classification simply creates an open, "standard-free" zone, the community risks "zoning by negotiation." (See sidebar.)

Planned unit development controls are an effective modern regulatory technique if properly implemented. However, like any other form of regulation, they can be mismanaged by intent or by neglect. Because planned unit development controls are more flexible and thus more complex than traditional zoning

---

unconstitutional and held that the governmental entity involved should pay damages for a "taking" of private property. In the case, a special state coastal commission had approved the issuance of a building permit for a beachfront house, but it made the approval subject to the condition that the owner provide public access along the beach. The Court held that there must be a "nexus" (logical connection) between the approval granted and the condition imposed and found such a nexus missing in the case. The decision of the Supreme Court in that case points out the legal hazards of land use regulation by negotiation. It is much easier to demonstrate a nexus between a proposed development and a standard included in an ordinance and supported by planning studies than it is to show a nexus between a development project and a permit condition

negotiated or imposed in the review process without advanced study.

The practical problem with zoning by negotiation, whatever the motives, is that it represents decision making in a policy vacuum. Lawyers have a saying that "hard cases make bad law." Planners could say "hard cases make a bad plan." The hard cases are those that are not clearly guided by established standards and policies. They result in bad plans because it is impossible for the governing body to set good policy in a public meeting room with an eager developer on one side, unhappy neighbors on the other, and a specific piece of land in the middle. Good policy must be established in the abstract, away from such particular pressures and concerns, and then enforced in the review of individual applications.

requirements, mismanagement is more likely to occur and harder to detect. Most communities need some form of planned unit development controls, but those controls must be carefully implemented.

Performance standards

Performance standards offer an alternative to traditional design or use standards. Performance standards in a zoning ordinance set out a minimum requirement or maximum limit on the effects or characteristics of a use. For example, rather than specify a traditional list of uses, a zoning ordinance that incorporates performance standards might describe the allowable amount of smoke, odor, noise, heat, vibration, glare, traffic generation, and visual impact of uses permitted in the zone. This approach defines precisely what the community wants as an end result but allows the developer choice in the means used to achieve that result.

Performance standards, which are also used in subdivision ordinances and building codes, depend on the technical possibility of quantifying effects and measuring them to ensure that they meet ordinance requirements. The most advanced work in performance standards has been in the area of industrial emissions. (Local requirements in many fields, especially pollution control, have now been superseded by federal or state regulations.) Because such measures require technical skill and often some expensive equipment, small communities tend to prefer the more traditional approach of specification standards, which substitute clear statements of purpose or intent for precise, measurable standards.

Phased development controls

Phased development controls require or encourage development to be staged in a way that is consistent with the patterns of expansion of public facilities.

The most common form of development phasing is the establishment of an urban growth zone with an outer boundary beyond which no development will be approved for a specified period of years. This effort to match development to the availability of public facilities has faced two sets of problems. First, the outer boundary essentially proscribes development on land outside the boundary and gives a stamp of public approval to land inside the boundary. Second, by limiting the supply of apparently developable land, the local government effectively allows landowners inside the boundary to raise land prices, resulting in increased housing prices and commercial occupancy costs.

Such systems have not fared particularly well in the courts. Partly because of the arbitrariness of most boundary lines, and partly because most courts believe that local governments should expand their public services to meet demand, challenges to urban growth zones by landowners outside the boundary lines have been relatively successful.

Other communities have used an approach to phased development that is a hybrid of performance standards and phased development requirements. Ramapo, New York, a pioneer in this area, required any new development to obtain a permit; eligibility for the permit was based on a point system, with points based on the availability of various public facilities. Although such a system allows development to occur first in areas served by the most public facilities, it is not really based on performance standards, because a developer may achieve the requisite number of points without having all services available. Although its system strongly influenced other communities, Ramapo itself abandoned the system after approximately fifteen years of use.

Requiring developers to meet performance standards to obtain access to major arterials and sewer and water service has much the same effect as a phased development system, because it encourages the development of land closest to major facilities first. However, it avoids the problems of a strict phased development system. First, the absence of an arbitrary mapped boundary line avoids many legal and political disputes. Second, there is no distortion of the land market, because a developer who is asked to pay an outrageous price for the most developable parcel can still purchase the next parcel out and simply extend services to it; thus, the most valuable parcel of land in the community is worth only the price of the next parcel out plus the costs of extending equal services to that parcel.

Growth management systems

A small number of communities now take a more direct approach to the issue of community growth. Instead of simply changing zoning and subdivision controls to respond to growth, those communities use a variety of techniques to limit or manage growth.

In 1972 Boca Raton, Florida, adopted a limit on the total number of dwelling units to be allowed in the community, a limit that was ultimately struck down in the courts. In 1972 Petaluma, California, established a fixed annual limit on the number of building permits to be issued. In 1976 Boulder, Colorado, adopted a variation of the Petaluma system, basing the annual limit on a percentage growth rate. Both Boulder and Petaluma based awards of the limited number of building permits on a competitive application process that ranked applicants against one another and against municipal development standards.

Other communities avoid arbitrary and fixed limits on annual or total development but still try to balance the growth rate and the availability of services. In 1977 Westminster, Colorado, adopted a long-term growth management program that limits the number of units for which building permits can be obtained to the number of "service commitments" held by the developer; one service commitment represents the immediate availability of water and sewer service for one single-family dwelling unit. The number of new service commitments issued each year varies widely, depending on the availability of sewer and water capacity. In times of capacity shortages, the system gives priority to the orderly completion of projects already underway, but it also allows for the initiation of new projects each year. (The charter provision for Westminster's growth management program is shown in the accompanying sidebar.)

Growth management charter provision, Westminster, Colorado By ordinance, the Council may regulate the use, division and development of land; and use, construction, alteration and removal of structures; and the pattern, location and rate of growth of the community, all for the general purpose of protecting the public health, safety and welfare. As used in this section, "public health, safety and welfare" shall mean, but not be limited to:

1. The preservation of sound fiscal balance for the City in providing municipal services within the City limits;
2. The maintenance of a sound balance between available public resources, facilities and services and the demands for such services;
3. The preservation of a safe, healthy, and sound natural environment within the City.

The Council may amend, repeal or revoke any ordinance or other action taken by it under this section, by following the same procedures used for the adoption of the ordinance or approval of any other section.

Source: Westminster City Charter, Section 4.16, Westminster, Colorado (1980 Amendment).

Zoning and the courts

Several multiple-volume works have been published on legal aspects of zoning, two of which are cited in the selected bibliography for this chapter. The material in this section is intended not to be a comprehensive legal analysis but to identify major legal issues frequently encountered in the implementation and administration of a zoning system and to provide some guidelines for approaching those issues.

Due process

The basic meaning of due process is fairly simple: an individual whose rights are being determined or directly affected by a governmental action ought to be notified of that action and to be given the opportunity for a fair hearing before an impartial tribunal. Although the hearing and notice requirements set out in the Standard State Zoning Enabling Act and in most local zoning ordinances provide for the minimum elements of due process, a local government can take additional steps to ensure that its zoning procedures are not subject to a successful due-process challenge.

First, the notice procedure should be effective. Published legal notices that comply with minimum statutory requirements may not be effective notice to many neighbors. A sign on the site with large lettering is often the most effective form of actual notice to neighbors. Some communities place small display advertisements in the local newspaper with maps showing the specific locations of development proposals. Although most applicants are careful about checking the hearing schedules, local review processes should include some form of direct notice to the applicant.

Second, the tribunal should be impartial. Although individual members of the planning commission or governing body may come into the hearing with opinions, everyone involved should take all necessary steps to ensure that there is no tacit or expressed group position on the issue prior to the hearing. Furthermore, any opinions held by individuals on the planning commission or governing body should not be expressed before the hearing; any such expression casts doubt on the fairness of the process. For that reason, pending zoning applications are poor subjects for campaign platforms or for service club speeches.

Third, the hearing must be fair to the applicant and to those opposed to the application. Fairness requires a thorough hearing of all points of view. It does not, however, require that the hearing body listen to endless or redundant testimony. The hearing body can impose total time limits and time limits for individual speakers as long as care is taken to allot time equitably. In general, a process that gives approximately equal time to the applicant and to opponents is more fair than one that allocates equal time to each individual speaker. Staff reports should not be counted toward the time of either point of view.

Fourth, the decision should be based on the hearing and on all other information available to the hearing body. Ideally, the decision should contain explicit findings of fact to support it; those findings should deal not only with facts favorable to the decision but also with major negative points raised in the hearing. For example, if neighbors are concerned about traffic and the governing body is convinced that traffic will not be a problem, the findings of fact might note specifically that the traffic issue had been considered but that the governing body found that existing roads would handle the increased traffic.

Findings of fact need not be elaborate, and they need not be drafted by attorneys. An effective motion containing findings of fact can be made from the floor. For example:

I move that we approve this rezoning to commercial because the adjacent properties are already commercial, because the property in question fronts on a commercial street, and because additional shopping is needed in the area; furthermore, the evidence from our traffic department shows that with the curbcut limitations contained in our ordinances, the existing street system can handle the increased traffic.

This motion contains the proposed action, adequate findings to support it, and a direct response to the major concern raised in the hearing.

Although it is sometimes necessary to defer action on an application for further review, any delay between the hearing and the initial action risks being viewed as a sign that back-room considerations are controlling the decision-making process and that the hearing was somehow irrelevant. To the extent that local practice can accommodate it, prompt action after the hearing is desirable.

The "taking" issue

The Fifth Amendment to the Constitution provides in part that private property shall not be taken for public use without just compensation. The Fourteenth Amendment makes that provision applicable to states and their instrumentalities, and most state constitutions contain similar provisions.

The constitutional requirement for compensation for takings applies primarily to government seizures of land and other property for public use, which normally takes place through eminent domain proceedings. Courts have found, however, that zoning or other regulatory acts may amount to an unconstitutional taking. Although the legal reasoning behind the decisions is complex, the basic economic theory is not. If a governmental entity condemns private property to be used for a wildlife refuge, the private owner loses the ownership and use of the property but receives compensation for it. However, if that same governmental entity zones the property for use only as a wildlife refuge and prohibits the owner from making any other use of it, the governmental entity has accomplished its purpose and the owner has still lost the use of the property. Moreover, in the second instance, the owner not only receives no compensation for the land but also retains the burden of paying taxes on the property. Clearly, it is unfair to let the government achieve without cost through zoning what it should have gained through eminent domain. A court faced with the second set of circumstances would be likely to find that the zoning was an unconstitutional taking of private property.

Although courts generally agree on the legal principle that certain regulatory actions may amount to an unconstitutional taking of private property, the dividing line between constitutional regulation and unconstitutional taking is not well defined. Clearly, for a court to find an unconstitutional regulatory taking, there must be some actual economic harm to the landowner. For example, zoning property for agricultural uses with a large minimum lot size in a rural area in Kansas is unlikely to have any effect on the economic value of the property and thus does not even raise the issue; on the other hand, imposing the same zoning requirement in a Chicago suburb will adversely affect the economic value of the property and thus at least raise the taking issue, whether or not a taking is ultimately found.

The clearest cases of takings are those in which the government actually substitutes regulation for the use of eminent domain, as in the wildlife refuge case just cited; another example is nondevelopment zoning close to airports. In both cases, the appropriate governmental action is the purchase of additional ground.

The government is most clearly innocent of taking when it simply resolves a conflict in the private sector, as, for example, when a municipality limits industrial development near residential areas. In such cases, the government's goal is clearly unrelated to any purpose for which eminent domain would normally be used, and the courts have generally deferred to the governmental entities involved.

There are no easy rules to guide a governmental entity in dealing with the less clear-cut cases. Although the cases in which the issue of taking is most likely to arise are those in which the zoning or other regulation has a substantial negative economic effect on property values, such an effect is not in itself unconstitutional: for example, under certain circumstances, courts have upheld as constitutional regulations that deprived an owner of 90 percent or more of the value of property. Potentially problematic cases should be reviewed by the local government's land use attorney in light of state court decisions.

Courts that have found specific regulations to amount to unconstitutional takings have generally struck down the regulations, leaving the local government to rewrite them. Although in the early 1980s some courts began to award monetary damages in regulatory takings cases, damages in land use cases are fairly rare and tend to be awarded only in extreme or unusual circumstances. The remedy of striking down the regulations remains far more common than damage awards.

In 1987 the U.S. Supreme Court held that where land use (or other regulation) has accomplished "a taking of all use of property," the government adopting the regulation must pay compensation for the use taken for the length of time for which it is taken.[10] Thus, when a zoning provision is declared unconstitutional, a local government can either repeal the offending provision and pay compensation only for the loss of use while it was in effect or leave the zoning in effect and buy the property. The "taking of all use" language in the case, which involved a floodplain ordinance, suggests that zoning provisions that prohibit essentially all human uses of the property (like many floodplain ordinances) are most vulnerable to challenge as "takings."

Shortly after handing down that decision, the Supreme Court found a land use regulation to be a taking requiring compensation.[11] That case involved a permit condition that, the Court felt, lacked a required "nexus," or logical connection, to the permit sought. That decision has broad implications for such requirements as land dedications and impact fees—typically found at the subdivision review stage—and other permit conditions that go beyond simple land use regulation.

Local officials should be aware of the taking issue as it affects zoning but should not be intimidated by it. The courts are not asking local governments to abandon land use regulations in the name of constitutional protection. What they are demanding is that local governments be cognizant of the basic constitutional rights of landowners and others affected by their actions. As Mr. Justice Blackmun of the Supreme Court said in one case: "After all, if a policeman must know the Constitution, why not a planner?"[12]

Exclusionary zoning

Exclusionary zoning is a doctrine defined by state courts, primarily in Pennsylvania and New Jersey. In those states and a few others, courts have struck down local zoning schemes found to be exclusionary of specific groups of people, generally groups with larger families, lower incomes, or both.

Techniques used for exclusionary purposes include overly large minimum lot-size requirements (often 1 acre or more), bans or severe limitations on apartments, expensive amenity and site-improvement requirements, and other techniques that directly or indirectly increase the cost or decrease the feasibility of housing development. Although in early decisions the courts simply struck down the troublesome regulations and allowed local governments to rewrite them, by the 1980s the courts became more aggressive and in some cases went so far as to supervise the rewriting of the regulations by court-selected experts. In New Jersey there is now an affirmative obligation for communities to absorb their "fair share" of regional growth.

Although the problems created by exclusionary zoning have been much publicized throughout the country, prohibitions against such zoning have not been adopted by the federal courts and have been adopted by only a few state courts. The legal doctrines supporting the strong antiexclusionary zoning policies in New Jersey and Pennsylvania are basically legal rationalizations for policy judgments by the courts and are not likely to be followed blindly by other states. In most states, prohibitions against exclusionary zoning are not likely to affect local decisionmakers.

It should be noted that racially exclusionary zoning was struck down as unconstitutional by the Supreme Court in 1917.[13] Any zoning or other regulatory system that excluded groups based on race, creed, or national origin would be struck down by federal courts anywhere in the country.

Antitrust issues

A 1984 amendment to the federal antitrust laws eliminated much of the concern of local governments with antitrust issues, because it eliminated the award of damages against local governments in antitrust actions. However, injunctions can still be granted against local governments, and the prevailing parties can be awarded costs and attorneys' fees, which can be substantial in antitrust cases. Furthermore, remedies under many state antitrust laws remain intact.

Shopping centers and redevelopment projects are the two primary areas in which the antitrust laws might affect local government land use decisions. A community has a stake in protecting a vital downtown area, a major shopping mall, or businesses in a redevelopment project, and the local government can take reasonable action to protect all such businesses. What a local government should not do is enter into any agreement, express or tacit, to use its zoning power to keep competitors of such businesses out of the community. Such action could amount to an illegal conspiracy in restraint of trade. Positive steps taken to encourage the type of downtown area or redevelopment area that a local government wants are not likely to run afoul of the antitrust laws, but negative actions taken to prevent competition within such areas may pose antitrust problems.

Uses and limitations of zoning

Zoning is a useful tool of the police power. Properly used, it can play an important part in helping local governments guide community growth and development. However, local officials should not undertake zoning with the impression that it can be used to fashion ideal development patterns on private land. No matter how good or how effective the zoning in a particular community may be, landowners, developers, and individual citizens still make a variety of decisions that heavily influence, if not determine, the final land use patterns of the community.

A basic development pattern typifies most communities in this country, whether they have grown up with or without zoning. The major differences among communities occur in variations on that basic pattern, not in departures from it.

A community of any size generally has a commercial core with retail shops, financial institutions, and offices in an area that is more intensely developed than the rest of the community. In most communities, residences are mixed into that commercial core; in small and medium-sized communities, those residences may be modest walk-up apartments over the stores and offices. The commercial core is usually surrounded by an area of mixed institutional, light commercial, and multifamily residential uses. Government offices are sometimes located in the commercial core and often in the area immediately surrounding it. Beyond the mixed-use ring lies most of the single-family detached housing. Schools, hospitals, and churches are scattered, usually along major roads but in residential areas. Industrial areas, now often surrounded by other uses, generally fall along the railroad tracks and outside the original commercial core. Smaller commercial centers are scattered throughout the community. In older commuter suburbs, the entire development pattern centers around the railroad station. Major parks, greenbelts, parkways, public institutions, transit systems and other public investments have varied and improved upon this development pattern in many communities, but the basic pattern remains.

Zoning will not substantially change the way that communities are built. The history of communities built under zoning shows that they differ little from communities built without zoning, with two major exceptions: the service-free residential area and the strip commercial area. Residential areas built without zoning generally have a scattering of neighborhood shopping centers. In contrast, some residential areas built under zoning have vast land areas with no services whatever. The strip commercial area exists under zoning for two reasons. First, zoning wisdom for many years called for a commercial strip one block wide and centered on a major arterial, partly on the theory that the traffic would prevent the property from being used for much else. Second, all the inhabitants of service-free residential areas had to shop somewhere, and the first major arterial outside the neighborhood was a logical location for retail stores.

Zoning is not a particularly effective way to change the overall development pattern in a community. Public investments in sewer and water lines and in amenities such as parks can have far more influence than zoning, and effective planning agencies study and plan those systems because of this. What zoning can do is reinforce the basic pattern of community development in ways that are most consistent with public health, safety, and welfare and with local goals and policies. For example, zoning can keep heavy industry out of the commercial core, large shopping areas out of primarily residential areas, and apartment houses out of areas with inadequate services. What zoning cannot possibly do is create any sort of ideal land use pattern. There is far more industrial zoning in the country than will be used in the next century because eager communities have hoped that zoning land for industry would make industry appear. A community may become frustrated when it zones a site for a future shopping center, only to have a developer propose the first shopping center on another site, which may be equally good but is not commercially zoned. Such events are predictable, however, because the commercial zoning on the first parcel may cause the owner to ask an unrealistic price for it, while other, similarly situated land without commercial zoning remains reasonably priced. Many communities become frustrated when prime development land adjacent to existing development remains agricultural because the owner does not want to sell; no zoning action can change the owner's decision.

Zoning is a useful and powerful tool, but it must be exercised in the context of the social, economic, and political forces that shape a community. It cannot eliminate or overwhelm those forces.

1 Standard State Zoning Enabling Act, rev. ed. (U.S. Department of Commerce, 1926).

2 *Village of Euclid* v. *Ambler Realty Co.*, 272 U.S. 365, 47 S.Ct. 114, 71 L.Ed. 303 (1926).

3 *Id.*, 272 U.S. at 397.

4 Jane Jacobs, *The Death and Life of Great American Cities* (New York: Vintage College Books, 1961).

5 Standard State Zoning Enabling Act, Section 6.

6 *Id.*, Section 7.

7 *Village of Belle Terre* v. *Boraas*, 416 U.S. 1, 94 S.Ct. 1536, 39 L.Ed.2d 797 (1974).

8 *Young* v. *American Mini Theatres, Inc.*, 427 U.S. 50, 96 S.Ct. 2440, 49 L.Ed.2d 310 (1976), rehearing denied, 429 U.S. 873, and *City of Renton* v. *Playtime Theatres*, 47 U.S. 41, 106 S.Ct. 925 (1986).

9 *Metromedia, Inc.*, v. *City of San Diego*, 453 U.S. 490, 101 S.Ct. 2882, 69 L.Ed.2d 800 (1981).

10 *First English Evangelical Lutheran Church of Glendale* v. *County of Los Angeles*, 107 S.Ct. 2378, 55 U.S.L.W. 4781 (1987).

11 *Nollan* v. *California Coastal Commission*, 107 S.Ct. 3141, 55 U.S.L.W. 5145 (1987).

12 *San Diego Gas & Electric Co.* v. *City of San Diego*, 450 U.S. 621, 101 S.Ct. 1287, 67 L.Ed.2d 551, at note 26, 67 L.Ed.2d, 578 (1981).

13 *Buchanan* v. *Warley*, 245 U.S. 60, 38 S.Ct. 16, 62 L.Ed. 149 (1917).

Part four: Economic and social planning

10 Economic development

Economic development is the process of creating wealth by mobilizing human, physical, natural, and capital resources to produce marketable goods and services.

At one time, economic development was principally the province of the private sector, including utilities, railroads, banks, and business organizations such as chambers of commerce. It was associated with distressed or underdeveloped areas of the country. In the past ten years, economic development has become a critical function of local government in every region of the country and in every phase of development.

The role of the public economic developer is to foster the growth and retention of business activity and, through a healthy local economy, provide employment opportunities and a strong tax base. Economic development programs typically are concerned with

Retaining existing business and industry

Attracting business (manufacturing, service, or nonlocal government)

Nurturing small and start-up businesses

Developing and financing facilities that help capture business or recycle local funds

Counties, cities, and other units of government either employ economic development professionals directly or contribute to a public-private cooperative economic development organization. Over forty percent of the chambers of commerce and other business organizations involved in economic development receive over half of their budget from the public sector.

Planners can play a critical role in economic development. People trained as planners are often the leaders in economic development, having perceived that the future development of their communities depends on maintaining and enhancing the economy. Planners who place stronger emphasis on physical development must nevertheless understand the importance of a strong economy, familiarize themselves with approaches to enhancing community growth, and be aware of the impact of physical development on community economic health. In many smaller cities, the planner is the sole professional concerned with both physical and economic development of the community.

This chapter is written to familiarize the practicing planner with the important issues of economic development at the local government level. Planners need a basic understanding of the concepts, tools, and programs of economic development planning and action. The chapter should prepare the planner to participate constructively and help lead the public-private partnership that is critical to effective economic development.

The context of local economic development

Local economic development has evolved into a complex and sophisticated profession. Rapid and fundamental structural changes in the national economic environment threaten the economic base of many communities and make it difficult to identify opportunities for growth and development. Competition for those opportunities has become intense as jobs and new investment have become priorities for virtually every American community. Understanding the impact of emerging economic trends has become a significant challenge to economic developers and, in many ways, a prerequisite to designing and implementing an effective economic development program. The rest of this section covers the context of economic development from four different perspectives: the globalization of the U.S. economy, economic restructuring, geographic shifts in economic activity, and changing public policy. Consideration of these topics will provide a basic understanding of the emerging economic, demographic, and political trends that will shape local economic development in the coming decade.

Globalization of the U.S. economy

The U.S. economy has changed dramatically during the past two decades. The unchallenged economic leadership of the United States in the period after World War II has given way to a global economy in which the American economy is closely intertwined with the economies of our trading partners. The report of the President's Commission on Industrial Competitiveness offers the following statistics as evidence of the globalization of the U.S. economy:

Imports and exports have doubled as a percentage of the U.S. gross national product in the past 20 years;

Seventy percent of the goods produced by U.S. economy compete with goods from abroad;

The dollar volume of world trade has increased sevenfold since 1970; and

Almost 20% of the U.S. industrial production is exported.[1]

This new economic scenario brings both challenge and opportunity to local economic developers. Competitive foreign manufactured goods are challenging the viability of many U.S. manufacturing industries, although foreign investment and growing international trade represent new economic opportunities.

Foreign competition The United States has been running a trade deficit since the mid-1970s. Imports have strengthened their position in a diverse range of industries, while the U.S. share of world markets slipped from 15 percent in 1962 to 12 percent in 1982.[2] In the future, Third World nations are expected to increase their share of all manufacturing production by capitalizing on a growing labor force and low wages. Japan and the Western European nations are expected to continue to carve out specialized market niches.

The response of most U.S. manufacturers to foreign competition will be to invest in more efficient plant and equipment, increase research and development, and improve quality, according to a survey published in *Business Week*.[3] In addition, the impact of management techniques—for example, those used in the General Motors-Toyota joint venture at Freemont, California—is expected to be important. The future of the "Made in U.S.A." label may depend on the ability of manufacturing companies to adopt new production technologies, aggressive research and development programs, and improved management techniques to lower costs and improve quality.

Foreign reverse investment in the United States Foreign investment in the United States is now as pervasive as American investment in Europe was in the 1950s and 1960s. The attractiveness of the American market for foreign interests rests in its size, stability, and favorable growth prospects. Japanese, European, Canadian, Middle Eastern, and other foreign investors are active in a wide range of businesses including manufacturing, real estate, and banking. The Japanese are investing heavily in American manufacturing capability by acquiring existing American companies, forming joint ventures, and establishing branch plants. Canadian real estate developers have become significant players in major American real estate markets. Other strategies for entering the U.S. market include joint ventures, acquisitions, and mergers.

The globalization of the U.S. economy will have continuing, complex implications for local economic development efforts. Although foreign competition has contributed to employment declines in many of America's basic industries, such as steel, machinery, and textiles, states such as California, Oregon, and Washington have benefited from reverse investment and trade with Pacific-rim countries. Communities along the United States-Mexico border have attracted new investment with the twin plant concept. Even in the Midwest, investments by foreign auto assembly operations and parts manufacturers have helped spur the recovery of the region since the recession of the early 1980s.

New to the economic development profession are programs to help local firms seek out opportunities in export markets and become more productive to meet foreign competition. Marketing and development on an international scale are complex and expensive undertakings that will force many communities to rely on their allies, some of which are familiar (utilities, state departments of commerce, etc.) and some of which are not (foreign banks and consultants). Local governments must take a broader view of economic development. Decisions made in Tokyo and other foreign capitals can affect local economic development by closing or expanding facilities. Competition for labor-intensive manufacturing and service operations may include overseas locations. Global interdependence is a reality and must be accounted for in local economic development planning.

Economic restructuring

The U.S. economy has undergone a dramatic transformation since the early 1970s. It has changed from a predominantly industrial economy to one that is information- and knowledge-based. Emphasis has shifted from goods production to services. The introduction of computer technology to all areas of business also has transformed the economic landscape.

The most dramatic implication of these transformations for local economic developers is that the sources of new jobs have changed and will continue to change through the 1990s. From 1969 to 1984, manufacturing employment declined by almost 700,000 net jobs, while the service sector alone added 10.6 million new jobs.[4] Job growth is expected to be concentrated in a variety of service and information-processing occupations rather than in blue-collar, production-related jobs. Most economic development organizations, however, have traditionally focused almost entirely on attracting and retaining blue-collar manufacturing activities.

Manufacturing activity is not, however, disappearing in the United States; it is only employment growth that has slowed. Manufacturing output has increased regularly in virtually all sectors in the past decade. Improved productivity—through automation, mechanization, and efficient management—has boosted output without corresponding increases in employment. For example, in 1984 basic industries spent two-thirds of their capital expenditures on automation, computers, and telecommunications, up from one-quarter in 1972. Expenditures for factory automation are expected to more than double between 1985 and 1990, from $15.3 million to $32.3 million.[5]

The automation of manufacturing processes is changing the factors that influence new facility locations. Manufacturers are placing increasing emphasis on the availability of skilled labor, vocational educational services, financial assistance for job training, and the availability and reliability of utilities, especially electric power. Because facilities will tend to be smaller and employ fewer people, automated manufacturing processes will produce a smaller payoff for business attraction efforts.

High technology—from electronics to plastics to biotechnology—is one growing sector of the manufacturing industry. Communities and states alike are courting companies in this sector with an array of incentives and giveaways. Although only a limited number of locations have the critical mass of business services, educational resources, living conditions, and other requirements to support high-technology manufacturing operations, the companies' emphasis on these factors in the site-selection process has made clear to economic developers how important they are to a community's economic growth potential.

The increasing economic importance of technology and technological change has brought a new partner to local economic development: the university. "Growing your own" high-technology industrial base is proving to be an effective strategy for some communities. Economic developers must now seek ways to encourage the commercialization of new technologies, products, and services as a means of stimulating job growth and new investment. Eighty-nine percent of the new private-sector jobs created in the United States between 1977 and 1985 were in firms with less than one hundred employees.[6]

In response to these economic trends, local economic development organizations have begun to expand their horizons, focusing less on attracting business and placing more emphasis on retaining existing business, promoting entrepreneurial and small businesses, and building the service sector. The heyday of "smokestack chasing" that dominated economic development in the 1970s appears to be over.

Geographic shifts in economic activity

Major shifts of population and economic activity since World War II have brought prosperity to some communities and decline to others. These shifts have three dimensions: movement from the older industrialized areas of the nation to the rapidly growing Sun Belt, from the nation's major urban cores to the suburban and exurban periphery, and from the larger metropolitan areas to nonmetropolitan communities.

Regional shifts   Although the "rise of the Sun Belt" (southeast, central, and west) and the "decline of the Rustbelt" have perhaps been exaggerated by the media, significant economic change *has* occurred among the regions of the United States, as Table 10–1 illustrates. The Northeast and North-Central (the "Rust Belt") states employed almost three-fifths of the nation's workers in 1960; by 1975 this share had dropped to a little over one-half. Much of the decline in employment share in the northern states is due to losses in manufacturing. Between 1960 and 1982, New England lost 20,000 manufacturing jobs, the

Table 10–1   Regional share of total U.S. nonagricultural employment—1960 to 1984.

Region	Percentage of total U.S. employment			
	1960	1975	1982	1984
Northeast	29.2	24.1	22.7	22.6
North-Central	29.4	27.4	25.0	24.6
South	26.5	30.7	32.8	33.1
West	14.9	17.9	19.5	19.8
U.S. total	100.0	100.0	100.0	100.0

Middle Atlantic states 590,000 jobs, and the East North-Central states 460,000 jobs. During this same period, the South gained over 2 million jobs in manufacturing.[7]

The Sun Belt has grown for a number of reasons. First, the population growth and growth in manufacturing have been closely intertwined. Although the development of air conditioning and the attraction of warmer winters certainly fostered the immigration of northern residents, this trend would not have continued without the availability of employment. Second, many of the Sun Belt states undertook aggressive economic development programs, including innovative vocational training, tax incentives, and courting of defense plants and military installations. Third, the development of the nation's interstate highway system and commercial air service, as well as the restructuring of rail tariffs to remove biases against certain regions, gave the Sun Belt access to national markets. Fourth, as manufacturing shifted from heavy durable goods to lighter consumer products, and population continued to shift, the relative cost of transportation no longer prevented southern locations from serving national markets. Finally, the general absence of unions, and the consequent lower wage costs, sparked the interest of many industrial firms that were once located in the nation's older industrialized cities.

The continued growth of the Sun Belt is not being driven by manufacturing alone; several major metropolitan areas in the Sun Belt have become leading financial, service, and trade centers, in part because of the natural maturation of the regional economy and in part because advances in telecommunications and electronic data-processing technology have allowed office functions to decentralize from large metropolitan centers. Faced with rising operating costs, congestion, and an increasingly expensive living environment for executives, some companies even relocated headquarters and administrative functions to the Sun Belt. In addition, a variety of office functions from corporate headquarters to regional insurance claims offices have been established in the Sun Belt.

In spite of their economic problems, the Northeast and North-Central regions of the nation continue to have significant economic potential. For example, in the 1980s New England experienced a dramatic economic development renaissance based on an evolving high-technology industrial base that is an outgrowth of the region's academic and research institutions. Unemployment levels in this region are among the lowest in the nation, a stark contrast to circumstances twenty to thirty years ago, when textiles, the traditional industrial base of New England, shifted to the Southeast.

Urban-suburban shifts The movement of population out of the nation's central cities to the suburban periphery began more than a half-century ago and was followed rapidly by retail trade and personal service activities. Increasingly, economic growth has also taken place in suburban areas in a wide range of basic manufacturing and business service activities. Modern suburban industrial, business, and office parks offer attractive work environments and excellent access. Many blue-collar workers commute from the central cities to jobs in the suburbs. Although the suburb-to-city commute remains typical for white-collar workers, an increasing number of metropolitan areas are multinucleated, with multiple major employment centers and large reverse commuting populations. This pattern is occurring both in major cities with strong downtown cores and in smaller cities.

The restructuring of metropolitan areas has resulted in significant problems for many central cities and older suburban areas. Growth has stagnated because of a stable or declining employment base and lack of land. The level and quality of services have declined, particularly public education and infrastructure maintenance. Both emerged as major local government policy issues of the mid-1980s.

These various urban-suburban shifts are not necessarily negative. The emergence of the suburban high-tech environment may well capture for the northern metropolitan areas a generation of economic growth that might otherwise have been lost. Multiple employment centers promise to reduce commuting and disperse congestion in the long run. Because urban-suburban shifts have different implications for different areas, economic development agendas vary for central cities, downtowns, neighborhoods, older suburbs, and new suburbs.

Rural renaissance and decline   On the strength of rising commodity prices and improved highway systems, nonmetropolitan areas experienced rapid population and employment growth in the 1970s. The 1980s have seen a dramatic reversal of this trend. Disflation and declining commodity prices have decimated agriculture, mining, and other resource industries. Increasing use of automated manufacturing techniques has lessened the importance of the low-cost, unskilled labor that is readily available in rural areas. As a result, many states as diverse as Colorado, Illinois, and South Carolina have instituted specific economic development programs aimed at improving rural economic health. These programs

Figure 10–1   Tyson's Corner, Virginia, in 1962 and 1986, one of the prime examples of rapid—and massive—suburban growth.

are the beginning of a broader trend toward helping rural areas, as states, utilities, and other regional development agencies seek to reverse the severe and sudden economic decline of rural America.

Changing public policy

From the early 1960s to 1980, the federal and state governments increasingly set the context for local economic development planning and action. The various urban renewal programs, parts of the Community Development Block Grant (CDBG) program, the manpower and training programs, and the Economic Development Administration all presented specific program opportunities and an array of higher-level governmental requirements. These dominated the practice of economic development in many communities.

The Reagan administration made major changes in the federal and state roles in economic development. The Economic Development Administration was cut back and nearly abolished, although the Urban Development Action Grants (UDAG) of HUD survived numerous challenges. Federal emphasis shifted to general economic policy (fiscal, monetary, and tax policy) and a proposal for Enterprise Zones (not adopted by 1987). State governments have become active in economic development, and several states have adopted grant and loan programs that use CDBG or their own funds and are patterned after the UDAG program. Figure 10–2 summarizes the major programs and types of programs available from federal and state governments as of mid-1986. Because these programs vary from state to state and over time, economic development planners

Figure 10–2 Federal and state economic development assistance programs.

Federal level

Department of Commerce
Economic Development Administration
 Grants for infrastructure development and
  planning
 Loan guarantees
International trade and reverse investment
Information

Small Business Administration (SBA)
Loan guarantees (SBA 7(a))
Direct loans (SBA 503/504)
Equity—Small Business Investment
 Corporation (SBIC)
Technical and educational assistance—
 Service Corps of Retired Executives
  (SCORE)

Department of Housing and Urban
Development
Community Development Block Grants
Urban Development Action Grants
Section 312 Rehabilitation Loans

Environmental Protection Agency
Planning and Construction Grants

Department of Labor
Job Training Partnership Act

State level

Financial incentives
Grants
Direct loans
Leasing
Equity and venture capital
Interest subsidies
 Direct subsidies
 Loan guarantees
 Industrial revenue bonds
 Umbrella bonds
Tax increment financing

Tax incentives
Job credits
Investment credits
Research and development credits
Sales tax abatements
Enterprise zones

Infrastructure development
Grants (matching)
Direct loans
Interest subsidies
Development of land and buildings

Nonfinancial assistance
Business consulting
Site selection
Export seminars
Job training
Technology transfer and development
Licensing regulation and permitting
Business procurement assistance
Local technical assistance

must work closely with state and federal officials to be knowledgeable about current specific tools and resources.

As important as specific programs are, the broader policy issues addressed at the federal and state levels often have far greater effects on development than do specific funding programs. The key issues are business climate, basic services and infrastructure, marketing, and changing financing and tax climate.

Business climate   Business climate is the economic environment in which a company operates. Business climate depends on a number of factors, some of which can be influenced at least somewhat by local and state governments. Key elements of business climate include state and local taxes (both corporate and individual), wage rates and unionization, workers' compensation, unemployment insurance, environmental regulation, educational funding, financing attitudes of local bankers, and incentives for new business. As it has received more emphasis from corporate site seekers, business climate has become increasingly important to economic developers. First, the impact of the recession in the early 1980s

Table 10–2   State business climate.

Regions and states	National ranking		National score	
	1985	1984	1985	1984
Southwestern				
Utah	2	5	74.8	70.5
Arizona	4	12	71.8	65.6
Colorado	14	15	63.2	61.6
Nevada	17	17	60.6	60.2
New Mexico	21	29	51.8	47.5
Regional average	12	16	64.5	61.1
Southeastern				
Florida	6	3	70.8	75.0
North Carolina	7	8	70.4	70.2
Georgia	8	9	70.0	67.6
Mississippi	10	6	64.6	70.2
South Carolina	11	14	64.5	64.7
Virginia	12	11	64.3	65.7
Tennessee	13	10	63.6	66.7
Alabama	29	19	49.0	56.0
Kentucky	30	21	45.4	52.7
Regional average	14	11	62.5	65.4
North-Central				
South Dakota	1	1	89.1	94.9
Nebraska	3	4	74.0	74.3
North Dakota	5	2	71.1	75.4
Kansas	9	13	77.3	65.6
Missouri	16	20	60.7	56.0
Idaho	19	18	57.1	59.6
Iowa	22	26	51.5	48.6
Wyoming	41	43	30.3	26.6
Montana	46	34	21.2	37.0
Regional average	18	18	58.0	59.8
South-Central				
Arkansas	15	7	60.8	70.2
Texas	18	16	58.9	61.2
Oklahoma	25	23	51.0	50.2
Louisiana	39	40	31.1	32.7
Regional average	24	22	50.5	53.6

varied considerably from state to state, highlighting differences in tax structures and rates. Second, high-technology companies are "footloose" and tend to focus on business climate in the site selection process. Finally, heated competition among states for new jobs has led to a high-stakes game of who can offer the best deal.

The accounting firm of Grant Thornton annually publishes a study of the business climates of the forty-eight contiguous states. The latest rankings of the state business climate are shown in Table 10–2. An alternative business climate ranking by SRI/AmeriTrust attempts to measure economic capacity as a function of the factors listed in Figure 10–3. Although no overall ranking is provided, the Mid-Atlantic, Pacific, New England, and Great Lakes regions receive high ratings. These four regions are rated least favorable in the Grant Thornton study.

There has been substantial debate about the relative impact of state business climate on economic growth and development in comparison with other factors such as natural resources, infrastructure, quality of life, and access to markets.

Table 10–2 *continued.*

Regions and states	National ranking		National score	
	1985	1984	1985	1984
New England				
Vermont	20	33	52.2	40.8
New Hampshire	24	27	51.2	48.2
Massachusetts	27	28	50.1	47.6
Connecticut	33	36	40.7	36.6
Rhode Island	37	47	36.5	17.2
Maine	47	46	19.0	20.9
Regional average	31	36	41.6	35.2
Mid-Eastern				
New Jersey	23	24	51.4	49.8
Delaware	31	32	44.0	42.4
Maryland	32	30	44.0	43.7
Pennsylvania	40	39	30.6	33.5
New York	42	38	30.3	33.7
West Virginia	45	45	26.0	23.2
Regional average	36	35	37.7	37.7
Western				
California	26	25	50.9	48.8
Washington	38	37	34.9	36.2
Oregon	44	44	26.1	25.9
Regional average	36	35	37.3	37.0
Great Lakes				
Indiana	28	22	49.4	51.9
Illinois	34	42	40.5	29.8
Wisconsin	35	31	39.0	42.6
Minnesota	36	35	38.9	37.0
Ohio	43	41	29.0	32.7
Michigan	48	48	6.2	11.1
Regional average	37	37	33.8	34.2

Some scores based on 22 measurement factors viewed by manufacturers as important to business success. Factors are oriented toward cost of doing business and availability of resources.

The planning profession has generally taken the view that these broader locational factors and economic resources are the most critical, a view that is only partly correct. When states and communities with otherwise similar locations have different business climates, their competitive advantages differ significantly. Moreover, the state legislative and regulatory environment, which is one aspect of its overall business climate, can seriously affect the cost of doing business in that state.

For example, when Oregon repealed unitary taxation of corporate income, it received a flood of new facilities from Japanese and other foreign investors. Prior to the change, foreign companies viewed Oregon with disfavor, because the state taxed corporations on the basis of their worldwide income. In another example, when South Dakota removed its usury law restricting interest rates charged by financial institutions, it attracted a Citicorp credit card processing center. Although it is certainly true that broad shifts in the location of business activity reflect changes in the underlying economic structure of the United States, individual states can affect their development potential by altering the legislative and regulatory environment for business.

The power of the local practitioner to affect these issues is limited, although it exists. Restricting the local tax burden can offset high state taxes to a certain extent. Collective lobbying action at the state level by economic developers in cooperation with other business organizations can help build and maintain a favorable legislative climate for business. As economic development issues are integrated into the public arena, economic developers will have to become accustomed to functioning in a political environment.

Basic services and infrastructure   Basic services and facilities such as schools and infrastructure are necessary for a community to enter the competitive arena for new investment. In part the renewed concern with basic services simply reflects the aging of our infrastructure. Much of the highway system, for example, was built in the 1950s or, in some cases, the 1930s. In both 1983 and 1984, the U.S. Conference of Mayors identified our aging infrastructure as a pressing issue. A

Figure 10–3 State economic capacity indicators.

Accessible technology	Skilled and adaptable labor	Capital availability
Quality of science and engineering faculty	Percentage of population over 25 with various educational attainments	Total equity capital in commercial banks ($1,000s per capita)
Research articles per faculty	Grade 8 or less	Size of venture capital fund ($ per capita)
Science and engineering Ph.D graduates ($1,000s per capita)	At least 4 years high school	No interest rate ceiling
Total R & D in universities ($ per capita)	At least 4 years college	Branch banking allowed
Industry R & D in universities ($ per capita)	Number attending various institutions as percentage of those 16 to 24 years old	State equity and venture capital funds
State and local R & D in universities ($ per capita)	Noncollege vocational training	State loan-guarantee program
Industry's own R & D ($ per capita)	2-year college	State-sponsored business incubators
Number of patents issued (per capita)	4-year college or university	
University-industry initiatives	Expenditure per pupil (K–12)	
	State and local educational expenditure ($ per capita)	
	Average SAT score	
	Average ACT score	
	Percentage of state's college students attending within the state	

number of states have undertaken massive programs of rebuilding infrastructure and making new investments that, it is hoped, will at least lay the groundwork for economic development. For the local economic development practitioner, it is important to ensure that local and state efforts are undertaken to provide key infrastructure and that basic services—including public schools and community college systems—are working effectively to meet the needs of businesses in the community.

Marketing　The 1960s and early 1970s were times of direct grants-in-aid for economic development; the 1980s have become the decade of hyperbole. Whatever the status of the business climate or basic infrastructure, virtually every state has undertaken a marketing effort for economic development. These efforts typically include a number of elements: promotion of a general image, development of tourism, use of direct domestic calling programs, advertisement of economic advantages, participation in international trade missions, and creation of financial incentives packages.

Although many of these programs have catchy slogans such as "I Love New York" or "the Magnificent Miles of Illinois," the programs also involve major efforts at state and local cooperation. In most cases, the policy is to promote the state as a whole and attempt to provide impartial information and assistance regarding available sites and facilities. Hence, local marketing efforts are often linked to state campaigns.

In addition to marketing, the states also provide creative leadership in framing specific industrial development projects. States often spearhead efforts to attract a major firm, working with localities to design an incentive package of financing assistance, sites, tax abatement, job-training programs, and similar assistance. A number of states also provide assistance to smaller localities by creating development bond banks and similar vehicles to raise funds and to help reduce the difficulty smaller communities have in using industrial development revenue bonds (which remain available for industrial plants through 1989).

Additional regional partners in economic development are utility companies, railroads, and financial institutions. For these private-sector organizations, economic growth increases business within a fixed market area, and economic development is usually one aspect of a general marketing plan. Overall business conditions tend to dictate the level of involvement of these organizations in economic development. For example, gas and power shortages and antigrowth campaigns led to the dismantling of highly effective area development programs that had been conducted by utilities from the mid-1970s to the early 1980s. The current excess capacity has renewed and expanded interest in economic development in the utility industry. For the local practitioner, these private-sector agencies can be effective partners in all aspects of a comprehensive economic development program.

Changing financing and tax climate　Almost all significant private development efforts involve one of two types of financing: commercial/corporate or real estate. Commercial/corporate financing is required to support the ongoing activities of businesses; it is used, for example, to obtain working capital, and to finance machinery and equipment, receivables, and so on. Real estate financing generally involves longer-term commitments of debt and equity for real property used by businesses or rented to them (e.g., office space). Both types of financing include debt and equity components. Real estate financing in particular historically has been sensitive to the federal income tax.

On the public-sector side, economic development projects require the support of infrastructure such as roads, sewers, and water systems or, in the case of redevelopment, land assembly and write-down (land resale at a lower price).

Historically, these costs have been supported by the bonding authority of local governments and by such vehicles as tax increment financing and special service areas, among others.

The federal tax code has governed and influenced many of these public-sector vehicles in economic development. With the Tax Reform Act of 1986 and the extensive changes effective beginning in 1987, one era of development finance ended and a new one began. Prior to 1986, federal law provided for the issuance of tax-exempt revenue bonds for a wide variety of private developments including hotels, office buildings, industrial parks, and sports arenas, as well as for entirely public facilities such as airports. For infrastructure and land assembly, tax-exempt bonds could be used with relatively few limitations as long as they were not primarily for the benefit of a single private party. The 1986 tax act changed these provisions substantially. Tax-exempt revenue bonds for private purposes (that is, not basic public purposes such as streets, sewers, etc.) are now severely limited. Virtually all private uses for these bonds such as hotels, office buildings, or retail centers have been eliminated. Industrial buildings are permissible uses until 1989. Tax-exempt bonds for *redevelopment* must meet certain requirements and be issued as "Qualified Redevelopment Bonds."

The 1986 Tax Reform Act also dramatically affects real estate and drastically reduces its investment attractiveness. Useful lives of property for depreciation purposes have been extended. Taxable income losses for real estate are now classified as a new type of income—passive income—and losses can be deducted only against passive income, not salary income. As a result, real estate projects with poor cash returns—as is the case for many economic development projects—may no longer generate tax benefits sufficient to attract equity financing.

As a result of these changes, financing both the public and the private portions of economic development will require greater sophistication than in the past. In both cases, development personnel must work more closely with the public finance and general finance communities to move economic development finance into the mainstream. Among those resources and tools that will become increasingly important are the following:

Public
1. Capital budgeting process
2. Taxable bonds for private projects
3. Tax increment financing
4. State government financing pools for infrastructure or remaining projects under federal programs such as UDAG.

Private
1. Mortgage bankers
2. Venture capital firms
3. Commercial loan departments of banks
4. Investment bankers (for public or private offerings)
5. Real estate syndication or investment firms.

The financing and tax climate is in continuous change, and it is now critical to develop a network of advisors and contacts who can bring the latest in development finance to bear on each year's economic development program.

In the context of state marketing efforts and more complex financing tools, local economic development efforts have become more proactive and more focused on the private sector than ever before. A number of local public efforts are critical to effective economic development. These include

1. Providing a community that is a fundamentally attractive place to live and to do business

2. Governmental responsiveness to the needs and perspective of business, including sensible and consistent regulation
3. An understanding of the business point of view and an ability to create development packages that are good for the community and the business involved.

The creation of successful economic development packages requires a clear strategic plan, a working partnership between public and private sectors, the ability to spot and act quickly on a good opportunity, and wise use of the numerous tools and programs that, despite reduced direct federal involvement, are available to the local planning practitioner.

Creating a strategy for economic development

This section is an introduction to the economic development planning process and to the major analytical tools used by economic development practitioners to create an implementable economic development strategy.

The planning process

The planning process for economic development resembles the strategic planning process used by business. It consists of four basic steps, each of which is discussed briefly in the following sections.

1. Organizing for planning
2. Identifying development opportunities
3. Developing action plans
4. Organizing for implementation.

Organizing for planning Organizing the planning process for economic development focuses on two key tasks: determining the participants and establishing the overall work plan and time lines.

Typically, a steering committee is established that includes key leaders from the private and public sectors in the relevant geographic area. If an entire community is to be the focus of economic development, the following might be included:

City manager/administrator/mayor

Finance director

Chamber of commerce representatives

Representatives from the principal local banks

Representatives of the largest businesses (manufacturing and nonmanufacturing)

Utility company representatives

Railroad representatives

Airport manager

Real estate developers and brokers

Representatives of the school district

Representatives from the local community college and university/four-year college

Representatives from the job training council

Citizens/neighborhood representatives

One of the purposes of the steering committee is to build the basis for a strong public-private partnership throughout the planning process. In all likelihood, both the public and private sectors will be required to implement the plan; the membership of the steering group should therefore reflect this. While broad representation is important, it is also critical that balance be maintained. If, for example, the principal purpose is citywide economic development, then neighborhood groups should not be overrepresented. If neighborhood business district improvement is the focus, neighborhood businesses should dominate. Through initial discussion, planning staff can refine the purpose of the planning process and determine the membership and structure of the steering group.

Staff would then work with the steering group to develop a work plan and decision-making framework for the planning process. The goals of this initial work plan are to

1. Identify the focus of effort (e.g., citywide, downtown, or neighborhoods)
2. List work plan elements (economic analysis, physical inventories, research of development tools, etc.)
3. Assign initial responsibilities
4. Outline time frames for completion.

It is important to understand that economic development planning is both a management and an analytical process, requiring the mobilization of community residents as much as the analytical work of the planning department. The analytical aspect of the planning process helps define a direction for local development efforts, but it is the management of people and resources that sets the framework for implementation. Without that management, there is little point in identifying development opportunities.

Identifying development opportunities   The identification of opportunities is crucial to a successful economic development program. This identification is based

---

Organizing for action: Recommended plan for a downtown development effort in Champaign, Illinois

1. Formulate and adopt a master plan that outlines the desired scale, timing, and locational pattern for development. The plan should express a vision of a revitalized downtown as well as provide an overall framework to guide public and private investment.
2. Establish a private, not-for-profit downtown development corporation to lead downtown development efforts. The corporation will also be an important vehicle for building joint public and private support and action.
3. Build and maintain a data base on real estate market conditions and development patterns in downtown

and the whole metropolitan area. The data base will be an important tool for identifying and tracking development opportunities in the downtown and will include a building, tenant, and lease inventory; a listing of available building space; an inventory of vacant land; records of sales and lease activity; and demographic and economic data (e.g., population, income, retail sales, assessed value).

4. Initiate a marketing effort to identify and attract commercial and office tenants to downtown.
5. Recruit qualified real estate developers to undertake projects that have been identified for downtown, including multifamily housing, a small-business incubator, a specialty retail center/community theatre, and an office building.

on both intuition and analysis. Often it is more important that someone is motivated to do something than that economic forces are in the community's favor. Nevertheless, a careful analysis of the economic situation is crucial to determining what the development opportunities are.

Developing action plans   Once opportunities have been identified, planning staff should determine and pursue the action steps needed to take advantage of those opportunities. Specific responsibilities for implementing the action steps should be assigned to organizations in the community on the basis of their experience, resources, and capabilities. A clear division of responsibilities helps to avoid "turf battles" and other conflicts.

The implementation steps will vary depending on the specific opportunity under consideration. The sidebars on Champaign, Illinois, and Wichita Falls, Texas, present a sample action plan for downtown development and the goals and objectives of a target industry marketing program.

Organizing for implementation: The public-private partnership   Effective implementation of an economic development strategy depends on the involvement and commitment of local public and private sector leaders. Who are the key individuals? In every community, a relatively few people have both the access to resources and the respect necessary to motivate people to act. It is essential that the planning staff identify the leading individuals and create a vehicle for their involvement. The list of key individuals typically includes those tapped for

---

Goals and objectives for a target industry marketing campaign: Wichita Falls, Texas, Board of Commerce and Industry

Goals

1. Build a general awareness of the locational opportunities within the Wichita Falls area through advertising and general promotional activities.
2. Develop specific prospects within the target industries recommended.
3. Reinforce the Board of Commerce and Industry's interest in overall community development, economic growth, and the expansion and success of existing local industry.

Objectives

1. Develop adequate research and library resources to monitor trends in target industries, evaluate prospects, and develop direct mail lists.
2. Prepare printed promotional materials that highlight the general locational advantages of Wichita Falls, including an "executive-level" brochure, community profile, direc-

tory of manufacturers, and wage and fringe-benefit survey.
3. Organize a direct-mail campaign to 2,500 prospects in nine target industries.
4. Conduct a telemarketing campaign to improve response rate on the direct-mail program.
5. Plan opportunities to make personal contact with prospects through nationwide marketing trips and at trade and business conferences.
6. Prepare an audiovisual presentation of the metropolitan area for prospect briefings and visits.
7. Maintain regular contact with industrial allies.
8. Implement a media advertising campaign for placement in trade publications.
9. With a professional consultant, develop an aggressive public relations campaign to emphasize positive aspects of the area.
10. Plan a strong retention program that focuses on the needs of local business and includes programs for industry appreciation, education, and networking.

Figure 10–4   Common
distribution of economic
development functions.

Business attraction   Areawide chamber of commerce or economic development council in cooperation with regional and state agencies.
Business retention   Local government or economic development council.
Small-business assistance   Chamber of commerce and community college or local university.
Financing   Local government, certified development corporation, for-profit economic development corporation.
Land development   Local government or economic development corporation.
Job training   Community colleges, vocational and technical schools, private industry councils.
Tourism and conventions   Convention and visitors' bureau.
International trade   Port authority.

the planning process along with the top management of the largest local employers.

In most communities, a number of groups concerned with economic development will already have been organized, such as chambers of commerce, business roundtables and committees of 100, a county economic development council, regional planning agencies (which once may have been Economic Development Administration grantees), private industry councils, economic development corporations, community colleges, railroads, utilities, and various convention and tourism agencies.

The various economic development agencies in a community can be organized in a number of ways. However, the trend toward consolidation on reflects the increasing complexity of local development efforts and growing competition for new investment. A professional, comprehensive local economic development effort cannot afford to waste time and energy by allowing "turf battles" among local development agencies; nor can it afford to permit duplicative efforts to dissipate resources. Figure 10–4 shows typical distribution of economic development functions.

Analyzing growth opportunities and constraints

Current economic conditions defy traditional approaches to economic development and have spawned a virtually limitless range of economic activities that are being pursued under the banner of job creation. Despite this diversity, a common thread among effective local economic development programs is the establishment of priorities and the concentration of available resources on specific opportunities. The priorities should reflect a comprehensive analysis of a community's growth opportunities and constraints in relation to national and regional economic trends. This outward-looking perspective is necessary to assess objectively a community's competitive position for new jobs and investment.

Many of the traditional economic sectors can be divided into two broad categories. The first category includes the facilities and activities that are typically the focus of local business attraction and retention efforts: manufacturing plants; wholesale trade and distribution facilities; and corporate offices, including headquarters, administrative offices, information processing, and research and development. These businesses and industries provide goods and services to multi-state, national, and international markets. The choice of sites for individual facilities is based on access to these markets, the location of other company facilities, and specific operating requirements. A community's potential to attract or retain such facilities depends primarily on its competitive position with regard to the factors typically analyzed by corporate site seekers, such as labor market conditions, access to raw materials and markets, and utility services.

The second category of activities includes key elements of the growing nonmanufacturing sector of the economy: retail trade, services (business and personal), health care, and tourism. The growth of these activities is driven by market opportunities within a multicounty area, which in turn depend on existing and expected demand and supply patterns for specific goods and services. Historically, developers have been passive in relation to the nonmanufacturing sector, although the shift in job growth from manufacturing to nonmanufacturing industries has heightened interest in market-driven activities.

From the perspective of a local economic development program, there is one particularly important distinction between these two categories of economic activity. Business attraction and retention activities are aimed directly at the corporate executive. Economic development that is focused on market-driven activities, on the other hand, is encouraged indirectly through the real estate development process. The economic developer's task is to create a feasible development project by attracting a developer to a community. The developer is then responsible for marketing the project to the end user, which might be a national hotel chain, a small retail store, or a business.

This distinction is relevant to the analysis of growth opportunities and constraints. The business attraction and retention activities in a community should reflect that community's ability to compete on a national and regional scale for new corporate investment or facilities. To determine growth opportunities and constraints, all the economic resources of a community must be evaluated in relation to (1) decision-making criteria for corporate site selections and (2) available resources in competing communities. In contrast, the potential for market-driven activities reflects local or regional real estate market conditions and trends as a function of present and future supply and demand patterns.

A comprehensive analysis of growth opportunities and constraints in a community combines both types of economic activities and includes the following components:

1. An assessment of overall economic base and growth trends
2. An analysis of competitive business profile and identification of target industries
3. An analysis of the opportunities for, and feasibility of, real estate development projects.

Each of these areas of analysis is discussed briefly in the three sections that follow.

Economic base and trend analysis   The future challenges facing local economic development efforts will reflect the evolution of the local economy. An analysis of local economic development conditions to determine future development options should include three elements:

1. An assessment of local economic growth potential in relation to evolving regional, national, and international economic and demographic trends
2. An inventory of existing real estate market conditions
3. A projection of future trends in job growth, personal income, and other relevant economic variables.

Assessment of growth potential   The current structure of the local economy and the historical growth patterns that have created this structure should be analyzed in relation to the emerging national and regional economic trends outlined in the first section of this chapter, "The Context of Local Economic Development." The comparison of global trends with local trends will provide an initial indication of strength and weakness in the local economy. The ability of local industries to adapt to the changing global economic environment will determine the magnitude and rate of economic adjustment that must be managed by the local development effort.

The structure of a local economy can be described in terms of the following characteristics:

1. *Major employers.* The largest manufacturing and nonmanufacturing employers should be inventoried with regard to their size, expansion plans, level of commitment to the community, and links to the local economy.
2. *Employment growth trends.* A comparison of local employment growth trends with state, regional, and national patterns can reveal important information about the relative level of strength and specialization in the local economy. In addition to attending to the industrial sectors of the economy, the analysis should identify occupational growth in nonindustrial sectors.
3. *Demographic growth trends.* Local demographic trends should be compared with national and regional trends in population (size, growth rate, density); income levels; educational attainment; and labor force characteristics (age structure, unemployment rate, and participation rate).
4. *Business conditions.* Major business openings and closings should be documented; the information should include the industrial sector, age, location, ownership, and size of the facility. Standard economic development multipliers should be used to assess gain (or loss) of direct and indirect jobs, retail sales, and so forth.

Economic development information sources

Private data services and trade associations

Grant Thornton Chicago, IL 60601	*A Study of the Manufacturing Business Climate in the Forty-Eight Contiguous States* (annual)
American Association of Engineering Societies New York, NY 10017	*Engineering and Technology Enrollments* (annual) Vol. I—Engineering Vol. II—Technology
American Chamber of Commerce Researchers Association Washington, DC 20005	*Inter-City Cost of Living Indicators* (quarterly)
Bill Publications New York, NY 10017	*Sales and Marketing Management, Annual Survey of Buying Power* (Consumer and Industrial)
Chamber of Commerce of the United States Washington, DC 20062	*Employee Benefits*
Conway Publications Atlanta, GA 30341	*Site Selection Handbook*
Dun & Bradstreet New York, NY 10007	*Middle Market Directory* (annual)
Dun's Marketing Services Parsippany, NJ 07054	*Million Dollar Directory*
Edison Electric Institute Washington, DC 20036	*Typical Residential, Commercial and Industrial Bills—Investor-Owned Utilities*
Executive Compensation Service The Wyatt Company Fort Lee, NJ 07024	*Office Personnel Salary Report* (annual)

Potential information sources to support this analysis include federal government publications and private data services and trade associations. In addition, each state has its own unique sources of economic information. Universities, state budget departments, regional planning commissions, and employment security bureaus are all potential sources of valuable economic information.

Inventory of real estate market conditions The real estate market is an excellent barometer of local economic conditions. The status of the real estate market reflects the current state of the local economy, and the level of planned and proposed development is a good indicator of investor confidence in the future of the community. Economic developers are concerned primarily with commercial real estate—office, industrial, hotels, and retail. Major areas of commercial development should be identified for each land use and then inventoried according to location, size (square feet, acres), age, occupancy, sales/lease price, and expansion plans. The planner should be aware, however, that this information is rarely readily available. Although real estate brokers, developers, and facility managers are good sources, they rarely have comprehensive, marketwide data. The economic developer usually must collect this information from primary sources. Such data are relatively easy to maintain, however, once the initial inventory is completed.

Projection of future economic trends It is important to have a baseline forecast

Marshall and Swift Publications Los Angeles, CA 90002	*Marshall Valuation Service* (loose-leaf with monthly updates)
Official Airline Guide, Inc. Oak Brook, IL 60521	*Official Airline Guides: North American Edition* (monthly)
Reggio and Associates Chicago, IL 60606	*Area Salary Differentials* (annual)

Federal government publications

(All publications listed below are sold by the Superintendent of Documents, Washington, DC 20402.)

U.S. Department of Commerce, Bureau of the Census	*County Business Patterns* (annual; includes individual state volumes, a U.S. summary volume and an especially useful comparative volume for Standard Metropolitan Statistical Areas) *County and City Data Book* *Statistical Abstracts of the United States*
U.S. Department of Commerce, Industry and Trade Administration	*U.S. Industrial Outlook* (annual)
U.S. Department of Labor, Bureau of Labor Statistics	*Analysis of Work Stoppages* (annual) *Area Wage Surveys: Selected Metropolitan Areas* (annual compilation of individual surveys) *BLS Handbook of Methods* *Employment and Earnings* (monthly) *Handbook of Labor Statistics* (annual)
Federal Bureau of Investigation	*Crime in the United States Uniform Crime Reports* (annual)

of future growth in the local economy. This forecast should reflect both historical trends and future expectations; furthermore, it should take account of the impact on the local economy of regional and national growth trends *in the absence of* an effective local economic development effort. In other words, the forecast is a clear statement of the economic challenges and opportunities facing local leadership. The variables included in the forecast are employment and population growth, personal income, retail sales, and so on—variables that are relevant to local decisionmakers and goals for economic development.

The wide range of techniques for developing forecasts of local economic performance varies considerably in sophistication, accuracy, and relevance. Local economic development efforts are usually limited by time and resources from creating independent economic forecasts. A more practical approach is to express local economic conditions as a share of the performance of some broader region for which a forecast has been prepared. This share can reflect a community's existing economic conditions and historical performance and can be altered to reflect public policy options that allocate varying levels of resources to economic development. The advantage of this approach is that through the forecast of regional employment growth, it incorporates the broader structural shifts in the national economy, and it places the local economy in the context of its competitive environment.

Typical sources of state or regional economic forecasts include the Bureau of the Census, the Bureau of Labor Statistics, the Office of the Bureau of Economic Research, the Bureau of Economic Analysis, the National Planning Association, state universities, and regional planning commissions. A variety of private forecasts are available as well, including those from Chase Econometrics and Data Resources, Inc. Often, the state budget office will contract with a private service to forecast long-term growth patterns. These forecasts are available to local economic developers.

Business location profile and target industry identification   The economic base and trend analysis identifies the underlying forces influencing local economic growth patterns but stops short of defining specific targets for concentrated development efforts. The success of such efforts depends on identifying target industries and businesses that are likely to be investing in new facilities that could profitably be located in a specific community. The identification of target industries and businesses requires a phased process of elimination to achieve as close a match as possible between local economic resources and business locational needs.

As a first step, the community's ability to meet key requirements of corporate site seekers should be assessed. Second, industry growth trends, locational preferences, and investment patterns are analyzed to determine which industries are growing and whose locational requirements match local resources.

Business location profile   A business location profile identifies the strengths and weaknesses of a community as a corporate facility location according to the factors corporate site seekers use to assess potential facility locations and in relation to national trends in facility location. (Figure 10–5 lists the major elements of business investment decisions.) The importance of these factors varies by industry and business group. For example, access to markets is a threshold consideration for a manufacturing plant or distribution center but is of little or no concern in the location of administrative offices in the insurance and financial services industry. However, since any or all of these factors may be important in any given locational decision, it is necesssary to develop a generalized community business profile.

Each locational factor should, therefore, be investigated thoroughly in relation to the full range of corporate facilities—manufacturing plants, distribution facilities, corporate offices, research and development centers, and so on. Comparisons should be made with other communities that are potential competition for new investment, in terms of the standards used by corporate investors to weigh business opportunities.

Target industry identification   The target industry identification not only selects the final target industries but also can be used to define the type of corporate facility best suited to the community. An industry or business group targeted for an economic development program should meet the following five criteria:

1. It should be compatible with local goals and objectives for economic development.
2. The primary advantages of the community should correspond to the major factors the industry uses to make decisions concerning facility location and investment.
3. Economic and locational factors for which the local area is not strongly competitive should not be significant to facility location and investment decisions.
4. Economic growth must be expected at both the national and the regional level.
5. The industries and business groups must be large enough to be worthy of a concentrated development effort.

The target industry screening process usually involves at least the following four steps:

1. *Analysis of national and regional growth and investment trends by industry in terms of employment, value of shipments or sales, and size and number of establishments*. Strong growth performance, past and projected, is a desirable indication that an industry will invest in new facilities. Because of improved productivity in the manufacturing sector, value of shipments is a better indicator of growth than is employment, which has declined over the past decade.
2. *Analysis of general industry characteristics to ensure that each industry or business group is suitable for a concentrated marketing effort*. Industries vary considerably in size, number of companies, financial resources, tendency to establish decentralized facilities, and other variables that are

Figure 10–5   Primary factors in business investment decisions.

Labor
Short- and long-term availability
Wage levels
Quality and productivity
Labor-management relations
Training and educational resources

Transportation (air, truck, rail, water)
Market access
Resource availability and access
Availability and quality of service

Utilities (electric power, natural gas, water, sewer, telephone)
Cost
Availability and reliability

Land and buildings
Sales or lease price
Availability and suitability

Financial resources for business
Private
Public

State and local business climate
Tax burden
Legislation and regulation
Community cooperation
Organizational structure and approach to economic development

Quality of life
Housing
Education
Recreation and culture
Temporary lodging
Health services

relevant to the marketing process. For example, a community with a population under 25,000 should not target industries that average over 600 employees.

3. *Identification of regional market opportunities that present strong reasons for companies within an industry to consider the region for a new facility.* Some of this information would usually be obtained from the economic base and trend analysis described earlier. Key opportunities are usually defined in relation to linkages with existing suppliers and industries; regional market orientation and access; local resource base; and corporate distribution patterns and facility location trends.

4. *Evaluation of the fit between industry location requirements and the local business environment as defined in the business location profile.* Key factors in determining such a fit are usually wage rate structure, utility costs and service capability, transportation services (e.g., the availability of mail service), and local property tax burden.

The target industry screening process begins with over 750 industries. Information on these industries is organized by the Standard Industrial Classification (SIC) code, which classifies industries according to similarities in products, services, and production and delivery systems. The code organizes information at increasing levels of detail ranging from general economic sectors (e.g., manufacturing versus trade) to specific industry segments.

Most communities identify five to ten industry or business groups for intensive development efforts. Data for the target industry screening is obtained from publicly available sources, such as the U.S. Census of Wholesale Trade, Services and Manufacturers; the Bureau of Labor Statistics; U.S. Industrial Outlook; and the Annual Survey of Manufacturers. Private-sector sources include business and trade journals, interviews with industry executives, and industry trade sources.

The SIC code has two important drawbacks for economic developers. First, because the code does not classify information on activities performed at a given location, the information can be misleading to economic developers. For example, J. I. Case in Racine, Wisconsin, maintains one of the largest computer- and data-processing centers in the state, but the SIC code classifies all the employment at J. I. Case as manufacturing because that is the company's primary business. In other words, the SIC code is a poor source of information on such growing employment opportunities as data processing and other administrative office functions within such a firm. Second, the Bureau of Census only recently has revamped the SIC code to reflect the evolution of growing industries such as robotics, computer-integrated manufacturing and ceramics; and the collection and classification of information on these growth opportunities has just begun.

Despite the inadequacies of the SIC code, it remains the most effective framework for target industry analysis. Most information on the U.S. economy is classified by the SIC code. Moreover, the code is used to organize mailing lists and other information that can be used to identify companies for business attraction and retention efforts.

Analysis of real estate development opportunities For an individual community, a major portion of growth comes from capturing a share of regional economic growth and translating it into local development. By proactively assessing its realistic development opportunities on an area- and site-specific basis, a community can influence the share of growth captured or the location within the community at which development occurs. The community can then formulate realistic and profitable development projects and work with the private sector to implement them.

This section will focus on the analysis of development opportunities that grow out of the regional economy. This location-specific analysis brings together economic growth and particular local characteristics to identify opportunities to develop real estate for various land uses. (Note that this is an important intersection between economic development and traditional physical planning.) The analysis moves through a series of phases:

1. Site and area location assessment
2. Market analysis for each land use
3. Assessment of projected absorption potential and attainable prices
4. Development of preliminary site-specific use opportunities and concepts
5. Initial financial analysis
6. Creation of a development program
7. Financial feasibility and investment analysis
8. Development of an implementation action plan

Each of these elements is discussed in the eight sections that follow.

Site and area assessment   The area to be studied for development potential must be determined; or if a development potential has been identified, the proper location for it must be sought. (On occasion, a franchise operator or industrial user looking for sites will approach a city; this discussion, however, considers the creation of development projects from the perspective of a community trying to revitalize an area, since that is more common.) Once an area has been targeted for development, the existing land use patterns must be inventoried and studied. A parcel-by-parcel, building-by-building inventory should be compiled listing as much of the following information as possible:

1. Parcel square footage
2. Building square footage and stories
3. Specific use (e.g., women's apparel, jewelry, adult books)
4. General condition
5. Occupancy
6. Rent
7. Ownership
8. Retail sales volume
9. Number of employees
10. Market base of customers
11. Apparent business health

Some of this information may require a personal interview. Information on office buildings and retail malls with multiple tenants should be as specific as possible, including the specific types of businesses in the office space. Separate inventories (including peak-hour occupancy levels) should be prepared for existing parking lots and structures.

The information gathered through the inventory should be delineated in detail on a map that includes streets and traffic flow. The map should then be reviewed in conjunction with a field inspection by senior planning and real estate personnel. The map review and site inspection are the basis for understanding the physical conditions in the area—identifying potential use conflicts and complementarities and vacant and underutilized sites, and evaluating accessibility and visibility. The goal is to determine whether favorable physical conditions exist for various types of development. Land uses for which there appears to be physical potential are then listed and used as the basis of the next phase.

Market analysis   The market analyses that must be conducted for each land use are based on a much larger area than the site and area location assessment, because each land use draws on a somewhat different territory for its market support, depending upon the nature of the use and the competition in the area or region. For example, major multitenant office uses may draw on tenants currently located either in the local area or elsewhere. Professional offices generally will be supported by the neighborhood population. A regional shopping center can draw from a ten- to twenty-mile trade area or larger, depending on population and competition. A grocery/drugstore-based center will typically draw on a one- to three-mile trade area. Housing demand may come from regional demographic shifts that occur as the population ages and "empty nesters" select an apartment downtown or as young professionals enter the work force.

Because specific markets and targets of opportunity vary greatly from one situation to another, a specialist usually conducts this phase of analysis. The concepts underlying market analysis are relatively simple, however; they focus on the question "Who might like to engage in some activity at this location, and why?" The "who" helps to define the geographic and demographic parameters of the potential market area. The "why" helps to focus inquiry on the motivational and qualitative factors that influence the choices of people using facilities. The product of a market analysis is a profile of the type of land use, its market niche, target demand, and price point, and the magnitude of capturable demand. The analysis involves the following five research steps.

1. *Delineate market areas and potential target markets for each land use.* This determination is based on general knowledge of each use and of demographic and economic trends.
2. *Prepare inventories of existing and planned competitive developments for each land use.* These inventories will cover the potential trade or market areas for each land use and will include the following types of information, tailored to the specifics of each use: name; location; date of opening; size (number of units, etc.); prices and rents; sales volume; occupancy; initial sellout or leasing period; amenities (parking, etc.); and tenant or user profile. Some of the data developed in preparing the inventory of real estate market conditions (part of the economic base and trend analysis) can be used to prepare these inventories. Historical patterns of market area prices and absorption and utilization of space can be calculated and analyzed on the basis of these inventories.
3. *Research underlying demographic and economic trends.* This research includes assembling data on employment growth, population and age, income, and household status. Sources for the data include the Census and various government reporting agencies.
4. *Analyze demand for each land use.* Each use responds to different underlying economic and demographic factors and must be analyzed accordingly. Typically, demand analysis focuses on the relationship between the absorption of space in the past and the relevant underlying factors. Although sophisticated techniques such as multiple stepwise regression analysis can be used, data limitations almost always dictate that simpler ratio analyses be used instead; for example, the number of square feet of office space absorbed might be compared with employment growth in the areas of finance, insurance, real estate, and services. Often, two or three alternative ways of measuring demand are constructed; similar results give the analyst a higher degree of confidence in the conclusions. Figure 10–6 profiles the key factors underlying demand for each major land use.
5. *Assess competition and capture potential for each use.* On the basis of the inventory of regional competition, a supply-demand analysis is conducted to determine market opportunities and specific niche for the site or project. A portion of this analysis is quantitative—for example, comparing the total supportable retail square footage with the existing supply. Two key concepts involving both quantitative and judgmental factors provide the core of the supply-demand and competitive capture

Figure 10–6 Factors
underlying land use
demand.

Retail
Population
Household growth
Real income growth
Sales (goods purchased per capita)
Sales required per square foot of selling
  space
New retail concepts

Office
Employment growth in finance, insurance,
  and real estate and services
Specific plans of major space users
Lease expiration dates/turnover
Absorption per added employee

Residential
Household formation by selected age
  groups
Income levels
Housing preferences and needs
Losses to housing stock

Elderly/congregate housing
"Income-eligible" elderly
Housing choice selection factors

**Hotels, convention centers, and
conference centers**
Growth in occupied room-nights
Projected economic growth
Special use potential (e.g., function related
  to a university, hospital, or research
  center)
Business and R & D meetings in region
Statewide/national conventions/meetings

analysis: market niche and penetration. A market niche is a specific type of demand (e.g., "yuppie") or facility, such as a strip shopping center, enclosed mall, or specialty retail enterprise. Penetration refers to the portion of the market that can be captured at a site.

The assessment of the competitive environment considers specific target markets in relation to economic, demographic, and facilities concepts that do not currently exist in the area. For example, there may be no first-class multitenant office space available in an area that meets all the right criteria for such space. Or there may be an excess of hotel rooms but no all-suite hotels in an area where technicians and sales representatives make many multinight stays.

Following the identification of the specific market (for example, specialty retail), total demand and supply for that use are estimated quantitatively; the site or area's potential penetration of that market is then estimated. This estimate may be based on such concepts as "fair share," competitive advantage, or queuing theory. Alternatively, the market share required to support a potential land use may be determined; that amount of demand can then be compared to total estimated demand to determine the reasonableness of the necessary market share—in terms of either established norms or "common sense." For example, it is not reasonable to capture a large percentage of demand to one project if there is a lot of competition, or to capture all demand even if there is only one project. If existing facilities have high vacancies, there should be a specific, identifiable source of demand for the new space.

Absorption potential and attainable prices The determination of projected absorption potential and attainable prices is a refinement of the market assessment. This analysis includes the timing of demand and competing supply, the potential timing of delivery of the real estate product, the dynamics of the marketing and acceptance of the product, and the detailed price structure of the competition. For example, hotels start at lower occupancy the first year, then build over time to a stabilized level. The initiation of a project may be delayed to allow an excess of supply to be absorbed. The price level reflects current market prices, discounts, and other marketing factors.

Preliminary use opportunities and concepts   Once the absorption potentials and price points have been determined (there may be several uses and price levels), the demand and sites must be examined together so that the most advantageous uses and opportunities can be selected. This involves a preliminary determination of site capacities for the various land uses. Economic factors are important in determining project size. For example, the amount of office space would reflect the length of time required to absorb the space. Typically, not more than one to two years' space requirement would be incorporated in a single building because of the cost of carrying vacant space. The minimum size of a hotel would be determined on the basis of operating efficiencies. For example, 150 to 200 rooms are typically required to support such services as restaurant facilities and a twenty-four-hour desk. (Additional factors included in determining site potentials are access, parking, visibility, and pedestrian linkages.) This step involves careful, often multidisciplinary thinking about a wide range of engineering, marketing, human behavior, and architectural issues. On the basis of these assessments, specific land uses, concepts, size, and target markets are identified for each available site.

Some sites may already be developed and may appear ripe for a new use. At this stage, the possibility of converting a developed site to a new use may be considered, but this hypothesis should be tested through subsequent stages of financial analysis.

Initial financial analysis   Financial analysis, coupled with physical design disciplines, is used to refine the development concepts and ensure their feasibility. Financial analysis progresses through several stages, the first three of which require preparation of operating projections, estimation of construction costs (hard and soft), and determination of potential returns. Most financial analyses are now performed with the use of computers, computerized spreadsheets, or preformatted programs.

1. *Operating projections.* Operating projections provide estimates of revenues and expenses from the opening date through lease-up and through the initial years of operation, usually five or ten years in total. (The public accounting field now calls these "prospective financial analyses," although most real estate and finance professionals still use the terms *projections* or *forecasts*.) The goal of operating projections is to determine "net operating income." To prepare such projections, the building must be conceived to the point of specifying the size in rooms, square feet, and units; type of utilities; opening year; levels of service to be provided, and so on. Virtually any of these estimates can materially affect the outcome. Expenses are based on industry data on similar buildings, compiled by the analyst and in some cases drawn from industry data bases. (Published data are often misleading because they tend to mix dissimilar buildings.)

2. *Construction cost estimates.* Both hard and soft costs (for example, financing fees, developer fees, and construction-period interest) are estimated on the basis of either architects' figures or industry sources on construction costs. Soft-cost estimates are based on market conditions for developer fees, interest rates, and so forth. These estimates are often spread over the construction period to reflect actual conditions more precisely.

3. *Determination of potential returns.* There are many different ways to

make preliminary determinations of returns. At this stage, the purpose is to determine whether the development costs are likely to be sustained. The analysis can be done before any financing or can be based on the assumption of sufficient cash to cover a certain level of financing at a certain interest rate. The initial test of feasibility may vary depending on the analyst and the situation. Some analysts actually skip most of the initial feasibility assessment if the site and other conditions are favorable, rents are at market, and others are building currently to lease at the same rents. In most situations involving the public sector, however, land and site infrastructure costs are such that formal analysis is needed. The simplest test is to calculate the amount that can be capitalized on the basis of the stabilized cash flow (typically third or fourth year) and a desired return rate. However, this technique may underestimate the supportable capital costs, particularly if future growth in rents is expected in real terms. A better method is to calculate the return on assets by using a discounted cash flow analysis of the net operating income and assumed capitalized value of the property at the end of the projection period. Both discount rates and capitalization rates must be selected for this analysis, and they should reflect those being used by real estate appraisers and other professionals and the actual values being attained in the market. This analysis indicates whether the value being created is greater or less than the costs of creating it. (Note that if financing that is below market rate is likely to be used, this analysis must be modified.)

Development program The initial financial analysis is used to test alternative physical configurations, levels of quality, expenses for land or infrastructure, and so on. These iterations permit the development program to be refined; they also permit a number of factors to be determined that are relevant to both the public and private planning process, such as the affordable price for land, supportable infrastructure costs, and tax flow supporting tax increment financing. This analysis can also be done on an after-debt basis if preferred, depending on the needs of the locality and of the potential developers.

Financial feasibility and investment analysis After the development program is refined, a more detailed financial analysis is performed. This analysis typically makes some further assumptions regarding the financial structure of the project and can reflect public assistance such as a UDAG-based mortgage, public land write-down, publicly paid infrastructure costs, and the like. Once public assistance has been taken into account, private equity and debt requirements can be determined and the returns on investment calculated. In the past, investment returns would generally have been measured as after-tax returns, and complex analyses of depreciation, tax credits, and other tax factors would have been undertaken. The Tax Reform Act of 1986 has rendered such analyses less relevant for most developments. Through research, an appropriate pre-tax-return level can be determined and the development evaluated on the basis of pre-tax, after-debt return. In the case of historic properties, however, tax credits are still available and should be included in total returns.

Investment results should be looked at from several different perspectives to determine whether the project and the deal are practicable. These perspectives include cash-on-cash returns on equity (actual cash profit each year/total equity), total equity amount and percentage of total costs, internal pre-tax rate of return on equity, and internal after-tax rate of return on equity. The required return levels will vary over time depending on the rates of return obtainable on alternative investments that are available to the various players in the development marketplace.

Implementation action plan   A wide variety of other factors besides financial feasibility and market support are critical to a development project's proving "doable." Some are tangible and some are intangible. Among the more common issues are site control, project size, image, and responsibility.

1. *Site control*. Developers often cannot help to gain site control, and unless the locality can assemble and deliver the site, it will be unable to attract a developer to help implement the project.
2. *Project size*. The fee for a developer's time and effort is rarely greater than 5 percent of total project costs, plus reimbursables. A small project is therefore of little interest to an out-of-town developer, and it may be of little interest to a local developer if the project is too difficult to carry out. (Occasionally, developers are paid for their time even if a project does not proceed. Usually this is not the case, and it is rarely viewed by developers as a sufficient return on their efforts.)
3. *Image*. A locality that has a weak market image may need to do a great deal of marketing to developers, even if a properly done analysis shows potential. Similarly, area developers are not likely to have confidence in a local government with which they have had difficulty working in the past.
4. *Responsibility*. The final critical factor often comes down to an individual with enough personal interest and sense of ownership to ensure that the desired, otherwise feasible project is undertaken. Unless someone from the local government or other power structure takes charge, most developments that need public-sector help in the first place simply will not happen. Innumerable particulars can go wrong in development. The developer, local or not, needs a local partner who can cooperate in good faith to solve problems. The private developer should offer a similar level of commitment and support to carry out the project.

Economic development programs and tools

This section briefly outlines several specific programs for economic development. The intent is to provide an overview of the key implementation elements and of the tools to carry out an economic development action plan.

Development finance tools

The tools and vehicles to be used depend on what is to be financed. As shown in Figure 10–7, tools and sources vary for different purposes. The five sections that follow profile tax increment financing, the capital budgeting process, taxable development bonds, local equity funds, and private capital.

Tax increment financing   With the reduction of federal involvement in development, tax increment financing (TIF) has become the single most important source of funds for development. Widely cited as a "bootstrap technique," TIF is available to localities in almost every state. To use TIF, a locality begins by establishing a TIF district under state redevelopment law. The district must meet established criteria (which vary by state) for blight or underdevelopment, and a redevelopment plan must be formulated. Once adopted, the increase in property tax revenues generated within the district is available to the municipality to retire debt or pay for costs incurred under the redevelopment plan. This increase includes revenues that ordinarily would go to the school district, county, or other jurisdictions that tax the property in the district. In some states other revenues such as sales taxes also are tapped.

TIF revenues can be applied to uses such as infrastructure, land assembly, and parking, as provided by state redevelopment law. Under the 1986 Tax Reform Act, however, bonds for some of these purposes may not be tax-exempt. The act does not limit the use of TIF funds to support these purposes, as long as they still meet the requirements of state law. Bonds would simply have to be taxable rather than tax-exempt, and the interest rate would therefore be higher.

Capital budgeting process   Although TIF and the public grants that remain, such as UDAG, can theoretically operate as separate programs, the major public role in economic development is to provide the infrastructure to support private activity, including sewer and water systems, streets and highways, parking, and, on some occasions, specialized equipment. In some states, for "greenfield" development projects (such as an industrial park in a previously undeveloped area), TIF cannot even be used. In most cases, TIF alone is neither sufficient nor sensible; the local capital budget is therefore critical to economic development.

Most municipalities have a fairly organized process by which the capital requirements of various departments are gathered and incorporated into an annual capital budget. The finance department then develops a program of borrowing or appropriation to meet some or all of these needs. Near- to medium-term needs to support economic growth should be similarly identified and incorporated into annual budget requests. If available, TIF becomes one means that the finance department can use to pay back debt or pay for capital items, in addition to other sources such as categorical grants, departmental revenues (e.g., sewer and water fees), and the debt service appropriation in the operating budget. It may be desirable also to maintain a contingency account so that a particular opportunity to attract development can be seized.

Taxable development bonds   The loss of the federal tax exemption for interest on private-purpose bonds created a gap in the local financing arsenal. Long-term real estate loans are not always readily available, particularly for smaller projects and in secondary markets far from major mortgage lending sources. Tax-exempt bonds met these needs by attracting the interest of investment bankers and other financial institutions that would not have been interested in certain communities or projects were it not for the high after-tax effective interest rates.

The attraction of capital to replace this source will now require the establishment of taxable bond programs. In most states, local governments can still issue

Figure 10–7   Sources of development capital.

Infrastructure
General obligation (GO) bonds
Revenue bonds
Tax increment financing bonds or dedicated
  revenue (tax-exempt)

Redevelopment land assembly
Qualified redevelopment bonds
  (tax-exempt)
Taxable GO bonds
Tax increment financing bonds (taxable)

Private-use buildings
Equity
  Local equity fund
  Syndicators
  Pension funds
Debt
  Life insurance companies
  Pension funds
  Taxable development bonds (pool or
    individual)
  Urban Development Action Grants
Construction
  Commercial bank
  Bond proceeds
  Community Development Block Grants

Figure 10–8 Financing sources for a real estate development project. The project is a 100,000- to 125,000-square-foot office building expected to cost $16,000,000.

Use	Amount	Source
Front money (risk)	$250,000 for studies and options; $3,000,000 for land	Developer's capital
Construction loan (rate: percent over prime)	$12,000,000 loan	Commercial bank Savings and loan association Proceeds from bond sale
Equity (risk; possible preferred return to limited partners)	$2,000,000–$4,000,000	Developer's capital Syndicator-Master Limited Partnership (MLP) Real Estate Investment Trust (REIT) Real Estate Separate Account (pension fund) Insurance company joint venture Developer capital followed by equity sale
Permanent debt (fixed or variable rates, contingent interest; kickers)	$12,000,000–14,000,000	Life insurance companies Savings and loan associations Syndicators Collateralized Mortgage Obligations (CMO) (investment bankers) Bonds (now mostly taxable)

industrial development revenue bonds, except that the tax exemption is no longer available. Because there are bond buyers interested in fixed-rate, long-term obligations, and because the investment bankers earn fees from the process, there are still investment bankers and underwriters interested in placing financing and selling bonds. The rate may be close to general mortgage rates, but the bonds are an alternative way to reach these sources. Such revenue bonds are a way to help bring capital to a community that is outside the capital mainstream and that deals with local developers who have limited access to outside capital.

The bond program can be focused on a single project or on a pool of projects. Projects worth $50 million to $100 million over three years are likely to be needed to attract an underwriter's interest. Under certain market conditions, bonds can be sold without a specific project and invested in short-term obligations until the money is lent to projects. Any bond program requires a stringent system of local bank risk sharing (letters of credit) and/or outside credit enhancement. Once established, however, long-term (ten-year) capital is available to development projects in a community that individually would not have had access to this quality of financing in terms of interest rates or amortization and term-of-loan provisions.

Local equity funds   Often there are local development projects for which the equity portion of the private financing is unavailable, a circumstance that is likely to be exacerbated by the 1986 Tax Reform Act. Many municipalities have established development funds to undertake such projects as land assembly and land holding. This concept can be extended to equity, and the equity fund can complement the taxable bond program described in the preceding section. In such an effort, a private economic development group would establish an equity investment fund to invest in local projects. A local investment banker or local office of a regional brokerage firm might act as the sponsor to establish the pool.

Investment standards would be established, and proposed investments would be screened to ensure that they meet the standards—as well as meeting the objective of the fund, which is to support local projects that the private sector cannot or will not fund on its own. Sometimes local governments participate in such a fund.

Private capital   Obtaining private capital to support the real estate development and corporate needs of local firms is increasingly important to local development as a result of tax changes and cutbacks in categorical federal programs. Just as participation in the mainstream of capital budgeting is increasingly critical for infrastructure finance, so too is access to the mainstream of private capital. It is of crucial importance to understand and become acquainted with key organizations and individuals in the private sector finance community, such as venture capital firms, commercial loan departments at commercial banks, investment bankers or brokerage firms, real estate syndicators, and mortgage bankers. It may be worthwhile also to establish a development finance advisory committee.

The multiplicity of players in the complex world of private finance is perhaps best illustrated by Figure 10–8, which shows the structure of financing and the players in a midsize real estate development project. A similar chart for the capitalization of a growing company is shown in Figure 10–9.

Business retention and expansion

The loss of jobs in any community is a natural process. Outmoded facilities close, cycles in demand result in layoffs, and automation reduces job opportunities for the less skilled. The economically healthy community, unlike the distressed community, experiences a net gain in employment through a high rate of new job creation, accomplished largely by firms already located in the community. The existing business and industry base of a community accounts for the majority of employment growth in most communities.

Business retention and expansion programs address the issues that might affect decisions by established businesses and industries to remain or expand. Such issues might include property taxes, water or sewer service, street access or

| | Investment bankers | | | | | | Commer- | |
| | | Con- | | | Issuance of stock | | cial | Venture |
Uses	Bonds	vertible bonds	Junk bonds	Deben- tures	Common	Preferred	banks	capital
Working capital	X	X		X			X	
Capital spending and expansion	X	X	X	X	X	X		
Retirement of debt	X	X	X	X	X	X		
Corporate financial restructuring	X	X	X	X	X	X		
Leveraged buyout	X	X	X					X
Acquisition	X	X	X	X	X	X		X

Figure 10–9   Business financing sources.

maintenance, traffic flow, police and fire protection, zoning, obtaining permits, financing sources, labor training programs, technology transfer, government procurement, and export assistance. Any of these issues or numerous others could restrict or damage the operation of a particular firm to such an extent that the firm would consider moving or expanding elsewhere.

A successful business retention and expansion program consists of three key elements: inventory, visitation, and follow-up.

Inventory   Existing businesses should be listed and classified by type. Of greatest importance for the business retention and expansion program are those that serve regional, national, or international markets, that is, "basic" industries. These firms do not depend on the local market and can more readily move or expand elsewhere, as well as bring dollars into the community from outside. With the use of information from the chamber of commerce or electronic data bases such as *Dun's Market Identifiers*, each business should be profiled in terms of industry and type, size, number of employees, facilities, location, and key executives. The contact person should be identified and the appropriate level of public official selected to make the contact.

Visitation   Each identified firm should be visited. Depending on the firm, an official as high as the mayor may make the visit. The visit indicates that the community cares about existing businesses and appreciates their contributions to the local economy. It also affords the opportunity to discuss with local firms the types of economic development assistance available to them. Furthermore, it enables the economic development staff to obtain an early warning of future needs or potential problems and to communicate this information to the appropriate local government agency for further action.

It is vital that any economic development professional involved in the visits be well trained in listening techniques. The specific problems and needs of the local firm should be carefully elicited in such areas as finance, facilities expansion, technology development, and human resource development. Early identification of any problems provides the opportunity for community officials to respond in a timely and effective fashion.

Follow-up   Unless it is clearly demonstrated that responses to problems can be implemented quickly and correctly, the credibility of the program will be undermined. The economic development professional should monitor the follow-up and may have to serve as "ombudsman," mediating between the private sector and the appropriate public agencies.

Public relations is another important aspect of follow-up in the business retention program. Newsletters sent to established firms serve as constant reminders of available local programs for industry assistance. These newsletters should contain usable information related to industry operations, for example, information on taxes, financing mechanisms, laws and regulations, market opportunities, marketing strategies, and new technological developments. They should also highlight the activities of local business and industry. Public relations efforts also should include expressions of the community's appreciation of local firms, such as luncheons, dinners, tours, and media stories.

Small business assistance

The 1980s have become the decade of small business. The economic development spotlight has turned from the large, new manufacturing facilities (with some notable exceptions) and is now focusing on the small business and the entrepreneur. Expanding new, small operations become important occupants of vacant industrial space, often space abandoned by older companies. Unlike many larger companies today, smaller firms tend to be locally owned, which usually translates to a greater interest in community affairs.

Although small business activity is now the most dynamic element of the economy—particularly the "young" firms—there are drawbacks. For example, small firms tend to pay less well, be more unstable, and provide fewer benefits to employees. Furthermore, small manufacturing firms often face serious barriers in obtaining equity and long-term debt, and public-sector involvement in the capital market problems of small businesses does involve definite risk. Local government, through its own efforts and through cooperation with chambers of commerce and other organizations, can become a catalyst for small business growth. Assistance typically focuses on management, technical needs, marketing, and financing.

Management assistance   Because the success of a small business depends largely on sound management, the improvement of management capability decidedly influences the survival and growth of small firms. Local government can organize resources for management assistance. Now faculty and graduate students of state universities offer counseling and assistance with a wide range of managerial functions, such as accounting, engineering, marketing, financial analysis, and business planning. The Service Corps of Retired Executives (SCORE) is another source of this type of assistance. In some communities, locally funded and staffed organizations made up of small firms can provide educational programs, professional resources, and coordination of locally available services.

Technical assistance   The technical assistance needs of small business cover a wide range, including production processes, plant layout, materials handling, computerization, product design and packaging, and energy conservation. Here again, a variety of resources may be available through university cooperative extension services, technical societies, and other local firms.

Marketing assistance   The successful small firm has to do more than produce a good product or service; it also has to sell it. A local economic development program can facilitate business sales in a number of ways. One approach is to compile and produce a directory of local manufacturers and businesses, which can serve as a listing of potential suppliers as well as potential customers. Also, when local suppliers are competitive with out-of-town suppliers in terms of both price and quality, the local government may make an effort to purchase from local suppliers. A number of communities have set up programs to assist local businesses to establish exports and to bid for federal and state government business. Assistance in creating such programs typically is available from state and federal agencies.

Financial assistance   Almost all new businesses obtain their start-up funds from personal savings or "business angels," that is, relatives, close friends, and wealthy individuals. It is estimated that there are over 200,000 business angels in the United States who provide $50 billion of venture capital per year, over twice the amount invested by venture capitalists.[8]

Businesses are financed through a combination of equity and debt. Equity, or owner/investor capital, typically comes from the founder, from a small group of investors, from a public stock offering, or from a venture capital firm. Debt or working capital for operating a business (as opposed to real estate) comes from commercial banks, bond issues, commercial credit companies, and similar sources.

Government agencies have tried to enhance the availability of financing for small businesses for many years. Most emphasis has been on the debt side, through the widely available programs of the Small Business Administration.

Local and state governments have devised a sizable array of approaches to financing.

The local economic development agency can provide two major services: first, to make available current research on the existing programs in a particular state; and second, to organize a local financing group that would ask the banking community to increase its awareness of the programs and of the need for financing. The financing group would also encourage the banking community to increase its involvement with small businesses.

Incubator facilities

The business incubator facility, a nurturing center for small business, is an attractive and well-publicized approach to encouraging entrepreneurial activity. The incubator is a multitenant building that offers space at below-market rents; inexpensive support services, such as secretarial help and copying equipment; and sometimes technical assistance with concerns such as accounting, personnel, management, insurance, legal issues, and employee training. Frequently, the business incubator either provides for financing or arranges access to the financing required by the fledgling firm. Finally, a conscious effort often is made to encourage the firms in the incubator to provide complementary services to one another—the premise being that the low overhead frees money that can be used to expand the enterprises.

In 1985 approximately 115 incubators were operating in the United States, and many more are in the planning stage. Successful centers have been set up in Chicago, Akron, Ohio, and Bennington, Vermont. Control Data, based in Minneapolis, operates a number of incubators in cities across the country, as do a number of other private-sector developers.

Incubators frequently are housed in old, renovated buildings and get started with financial help from federal, state, local, university, and corporate sponsors. Nearly all existing incubators have been financed with a combination of public and private funds. All the sponsors hope that incubators will spur job growth, and, of course, the corporate sponsors hope to make a profit.

About 10 percent of all incubators are currently associated with universities. Universities can offer a wide range of business assistance: the business faculty for business and financial plans and market research studies; the engineering faculty for technical problems; and graduate students for relatively inexpensive and highly trained labor. Among the more well-known university incubators are the one sponsored by the Rensselaer Polytechnic Institute in Troy, New York; one shared by Carnegie-Mellon and the University of Pittsburgh in Pittsburgh, Pennsylvania; and Yale University's Science Park in New Haven, Connecticut.

Figure 10–10   This incubator facility in Minneapolis, Minnesota, is a renovated high school that houses a range of companies, organizations, and services including advanced research and development, light manufacturing, computer-related hardware and software, publishing, and consulting.

Not only do these university-affiliated incubators provide work and business opportunities for students and faculty, but they also offer the hope of generating a successful enterprise that could produce additional sources of income for the school.

When a business incubator facility is being established, there are a number of important questions to consider, including the following:

1. Is there a need to create a low-cost facility, or is sufficient low-price space already available?
2. What services are needed (e.g., legal, financial, training), and how can they be linked to other small-business assistance programs?
3. How will financing (both capital and operating) be obtained for the incubator itself and to cover lease-up and turnover?
4. What are the roles of various economic development players, such as the university or community college?

Industrial, business, research, and office parks

In communities of all sizes, the nature and availability of sites for new or expanding facilities constitute two key economic development issues. The community may meet all of the basic locational requirements for a new facility, but if no suitable site exists, all other advantages are of little value.

In response, communities and private developers have created planned business centers that cater to the site, access, and infrastructure needs of businesses. Conceptually similar to the residential subdivision, planned business parks provide land with developed roadway, sewer, water, and other facilities and services (for example, rail). The rapid changes in the economy have resulted in three variations on this essential idea: industrial-business-warehouse parks, research and development centers, and office or office/distribution parks.

The role of local planning and economic development agencies varies widely in the establishment of industrial and business parks. In economically strong communities, the private sector may provide the impetus for the establishment of such parks, and the locality may do little more than provide the usual public services. If the economy is relatively weak, or analysis shows an unmet opportunity, then the municipality may become the developer. Finally, and most commonly, when the community's economic analysis shows the need for a park, the most effective strategy may be to seek an outside developer and negotiate for the provision of the appropriate development. This offers many advantages, including shared risk and the opportunity to tap the effort of the private sector on the community's behalf.

Industrial and business parks   Before 1950, probably fewer than one hundred industrial parks existed in the nation; the number is now well over four thousand. The "lighter" and cleaner industries of today prefer the planned environment of the industrial park over a freestanding site. Only the occasional large manufacturing operation will seek a large site set apart from other industrial development. Much of the nation's new industrial growth is occurring in campus-like industrial parks that are complexes master planned and environmentally balanced. The desired elements of these developments include

1. Proper industrial zoning and protective covenants to ensure compatibility with surrounding land uses and the protection of land value
2. Sufficient scale (100 to 1000 acres)
3. All utility services in place
4. Access to major highways and railroads (optional, depending on the nature of the industrial base), as well as an efficient local road network

5. Preliminary grading and clearing
6. Satisfactory topography, drainage, and soil load-bearing capacity
7. Controlled ownership and an established sales price and sales terms
8. Attractive landscaping
9. Professional management

In a number of smaller or midsized cities, the local industrial market is not large enough to attract a private developer or investor. Often this has led to ownership and development of industrial parks by local government or a designated nonprofit economic development organization.

The relative decline of manufacturing and the rapid expansion of the service sector have created a need for a campus-like environment to house functions such as distribution, sales and service, business services, "back-office" operations (labor-intensive office operations related to information processing), small light manufacturing, laboratory work, and research and development. Many of the larger business parks increase their attractiveness by incorporating space for uses such as restaurants, lodging, banking, small retail centers, and recreational facilities.

Business parks tend to be located near major highways and near the urban sectors in which the professional and managerial work force resides. The higher cost of development of the typical business park reflects a greater emphasis on landscaping and other amenities in response to market demand for a better working environment. Also, building space is more likely to be leased by the developer rather than owned by the occupant, and the business park developer is usually involved also in the construction of speculative space in multitenant facilities.

Research and development parks   A considerable amount of attention has been focused in recent years on research and development parks. The first such park was the Stanford Research Park, developed in Menlo Park, California, in 1948. Research-generated products associated with activity at Stanford University led to a rapid concentration of high-technology activity in this area. Another early high-technology park, started in the early 1960s, was the Research Triangle Park in Raleigh-Durham, North Carolina. It is generally agreed that high-tech industries include electronics, computers, telecommunications, biomedical products, robotics, and aerospace. Because of its technical nature, the locational requirements for high tech are rather stringent. They include a highly skilled work force, access to specialized business services, the presence of academic institutions with noted science or engineering programs, an attractive living environment, and access to venture capital. These characteristics are particularly important to high-tech firms at the start-up phase of development. Research and development often depend on the cross-fertilization of ideas typical of the academic environment.

Because high-tech firms move through various stages of development, a variety of research and development (R & D) parks exist. A "science" park is clearly oriented toward the earliest stages of high-technology product development. Most of these parks, in fact, restrict the amount of manufacturing and assembly that can occur in the facility. The majority of the work force consists of professional and technical personnel. Many science parks are closely affiliated with a major university. Except for the research facilities of large corporations or federal agencies, most science park tenants are likely to have very small operations.

At the latter stages in the development of a growing firm, when product assembly dominates the operation, the importance of certain locational characteristics diminishes and others take on more value. For production-oriented high-tech facilities, the typical requirements include reasonable labor costs, lower land costs and taxes, good transportation systems, and an attractive industrial environment.

The "technology" park caters to this type of firm. Basically it is a high-quality real estate development that houses a wide range of activities in an attractive work environment with appropriate amenities. Although R & D firms may be located in such a park, the park may also contain light manufacturing, corporate office and administrative functions, and a number of services. A technology park is often very similar to a business park. Because of the specific locational requirements of R & D and high-tech facilities, most urban areas are unlikely to attract them. Unless the community has a major university, an entrepreneurial climate, and good transportation, it would be inappropriate to develop a marketing program oriented toward high-tech activity.

Office parks   In a number of metropolitan areas, office employers have located new facilities in suburban areas in a campus-like atmosphere. Emphasis on improving the work environment to attract and retain office workers has created the office park, a real estate development that restricts itself to office functions and selected amenities. Office parks can vary from low-rise, campus-like settings with considerable open space, to high-rise, high-density developments.

The following are among the factors that make an office park attractive to tenants:

1. Availability of prebuilt office facilities or fully developed sites
2. Attractively landscaped setting
3. Location on or near a major highway
4. Access to an adequate clerical work force
5. Proximity to managerial and executive residential areas
6. Proximity to restaurants, lodging, health club and recreational facilities, and other amenities
7. Master planning and high-quality design
8. Adequate on-site parking and good local traffic flow
9. Restrictive covenants
10. Professional management and good maintenance.

Marketing and promotion

Communities across the nation are aware that, often, a good economic development program is just not enough. If the corporate world is not alerted to the locational advantages of a community, or if the small business owners are unaware of local programs to assist them, potential business investments may be lost.

Some communities do a conspicuously better job than others of attracting new jobs and business investment; this is not just the luck of the draw. These communities have more than desirable geographical locations, adequate funding for economic development and marketing, and strong leadership; they have made decisions about priorities in their economic development programs. They have become focused on opportunities. Because these communities know what they have to sell, they have a firm foundation for their marketing programs.

The competition among metropolitan areas for new jobs and investment continues to increase. Although no comprehensive list exists, it is generally believed that eight to ten thousand organizations are currently promoting their communities to attract new business and industry. Budgets for these marketing efforts are growing rapidly, and both new and traditional funding sources are being aggressively tapped. Sophisticated media and audiovisual presentations are being developed, and annual salaries for leading economic development and marketing professionals have risen to over $100,000. Even the smaller communities are hiring advertising, public relations, and consulting firms to enable them to present a more professional face to the business world. In this environment, the local economic development organization has to learn to be more competitive and more competent in its marketing efforts.

The question often arises of which agency should be responsible for marketing. In many urban areas, this task has fallen to the local chamber of commerce or some comparable not-for-profit economic development organization. In some cities, but not many, the department of economic development, the planning department, or the mayor's office takes on the marketing responsibility. In a number of communities, no one does any marketing.

It is difficult to generalize about who should handle the promotion and marketing for new business and industry. Community leaders should make a decision based on the following criteria:

1.   Which agency is best positioned to raise funds for the marketing effort?
2.   Who has the staff with the strongest marketing skills?
3.   Who has been most effective in the community's past marketing efforts?
4.   Who has the greatest credibility locally in dealing with business prospects?
5.   What should be the relationship between local marketing efforts and those of regional and state agencies?

Once the agency responsible for industrial marketing has been chosen, the marketing approach must be determined. This approach should be based on an understanding of the economic development goals of the community, which will enable the marketing team to address key marketing questions such as

1.   What types of employers are we trying to attract to our community?
2.   What are our major competitive advantages in attracting them?
3.   How much time and money should be spent on marketing?
4.   How realistic are our marketing expectations?

Most marketing programs include some common elements, although the emphasis on particular elements varies from community to community. To achieve a cost-effective program, coordination with the now ubiquitous state-level efforts is critical as well.

Downtown revitalization

Business retention and expansion and industrial park development are key economic development strategies for many communities, particularly those with land available for development. For many communities, revitalizing downtown areas is just as critical.

One of the fundamental shifts that has occurred in the 1970s and 1980s is the rapid expansion of business and financial services. Because these employment sectors drive the demand for office space, the ability of a community to provide an appropriate office environment—and to do so in a downtown area—are key both to the physical revitalization of downtown and to the capturing of this element of economic expansion.

The provision of downtown housing is a second key element of downtown revitalization. In many cities, the expansion of downtown office space and the consequent increase in the number of employees, along with provision of convention centers and convention hotels, have added to the downtown base of recreation and entertainment. As a result, downtown has once again become the single most exciting place to live, creating the opportunity for the development of downtown housing.

A third key element of downtown revitalization is the revival of downtown retailing. In most communities, downtown retailing declined as the affluent

Figure 10–11
Downtown Burlington, Vermont, before and after the development the Church Street Marketplace, a revitalization effort.

retailing. In most communities, downtown retailing declined as the affluent population moved to newer residential areas where there were shopping centers with easy access and parking. Building on a base of downtown workers and a number of remaining specialty stores (often clientele-based apparel or jewelry stores), many downtowns have been able to rebuild retailing by featuring restaurants, specialty stores, and shops geared to office needs. In some communities, festival marketplaces and enclosed downtown shopping centers have been successful.

The specific development opportunities will vary in each downtown and at each stage of development and revitalization. In some suburban areas, there is no downtown and the desire is to create one. In the downtown area of some midsized cities, there may be an opportunity to establish the best office environment in the region and capture virtually all of the growth in service employment. Focus on the downtown is an important element of an overall economic development program and is an ongoing process. Periodically, say every five years, current opportunities for development should be reviewed and specific strategic implementation plans set.

Development opportunities assessment   A detailed market assessment and inventory of land uses and physical conditions in the downtown area should be undertaken, as was discussed in more detail in an earlier section. Existing demand, prices/rental rates, and occupancy/vacancy should be analyzed for each major land use in the downtown area, including office space, hotel and meeting space, retail space, housing (including elderly/congregate), and parking.

Figures on historical and projected absorption rates should be prepared and the time at which additional space can be accommodated should be determined. The projections should take into account regional demand and supply and the relative competitive position of the downtown. The physical inventory should include vacant sites, underutilization, traffic flow, access, and parking locations and capacities. Land ownership patterns of key sites should be researched and land prices determined. On the basis of these assessments, specific development opportunities for individual sites can be determined.

Strategic action plans   Because each development opportunity will require different steps for implementation, it is important to detail the necessary steps and to take advantage of the opportunity. These may include a land assembly strategy and plan, site development programs, a public infrastructure plan, a traffic and parking plan, financing plans, and developer recruitment.

Devising a downtown development strategy requires leadership and the establishment of an interdisciplinary planning and implementation team. Key disciplines include development economics, traffic and parking, urban design, site planning, and architecture. The team may require consultants, since few localities employ all the necessary professionals. The inclusion of energetic firms with good contacts in the development and finance worlds can greatly aid implementation.

Working with developers

A number of economic development strategies require that a private development company be attracted to carry out a development project or negotiated with to arrive at a satisfactory development agreement. For a community and its planning professionals, the task of attracting and working with developers is very different from the more common role of regulating development. The community has specific objectives to achieve; the developer is a private entity with business interests that are difficult to protect in a fully public process; and the citizenry is often inherently suspicious of the developer and the profits that will accrue to the development company.

Working effectively with a developer requires a careful process to protect the public interest and attract the best developer. State law may also proscribe certain activities. A number of steps should be followed, which are described in the five sections that follow.

Defining the development project The locality should undertake an initial project-planning effort to define the desired development relatively specifically. For example, one community and its planner designated a one-mile shoreline area as multi-use and defined its major traffic spine. This general concept was then turned over to a developer. In some cases, the uses will be relatively obvious and their economical feasibility will be agreed upon by all. In other cases, as in many existing downtowns, the uses will not be obvious, and the locality will need to undertake preliminary planning and economic feasibility studies to define a practicable project that can be refined by the developer. The local government may need to work with development consultants to create preliminary cost estimates; assess market absorption potential, site capacity, site plan and development concepts, and financial feasibility; and conduct investment analysis.

Recruiting a developer By their very nature, few projects sponsored by the public sector are highly attractive to large numbers of developers. (There are a few exceptions, such as large redevelopment projects in major cities like Chicago's North Loop or Cincinnati's Fountain Square West). The complexity of working with local officials in an open decision-making forum is enough to drive away many developers, particularly if they have private project opportunities of a similar scale in the suburbs, which will present inherently fewer problems. Developer recruitment should therefore respect the time and financial requirements of a business person and avoid wide-open competition if possible. To the extent permitted by state law, the following is a suggested procedure:

1. Prepare a briefing packet for developers.
2. Using industry sources and consultants, identify up to twenty potential developers.
3. Make telephone contact to describe the project and determine initial interest.
4. Exchange information on the project and the firm, including references if possible.
5. Assemble background information on firms including Dun & Bradstreet reports or similar financial status reports. Use local bankers to help assemble such information.
6. Review firms and select three to five for interviews.
7. Request selected firms to make a presentation describing their approach to the project.
8. Select a firm to recommend for preferred developer status. A "preferred" developer is one who is given the exclusive right to try to put together a project for a set period of time. Preferred status does not bind the developer to complete a project, but the locality is committed to working with only this developer.

If a public bidding process is mandated, every effort should be made to limit the public bidding to a request for qualifications, which minimizes a developer's initial investment and maximizes the locality's chance of attracting a busy, high-quality, development firm.

Negotiating a preferred developer agreement After the selection of the preferred developer, an agreement should be negotiated that delineates the specific performance expected of the developer during a preplanning period. The agreement should include the following:

1. Time frame and performance dates
2. Elements to be accomplished; for example, site plan, detailed feasibility study, architectural plans, or grant applications
3. Outline of economic structure; for example, land lease or sale, and public obligations such as parking
4. Cost responsibility for planning. (The public may share certain hard costs like engineering and architectural fees if it will own the outcome. The developer should "spec" the development firm's time but not necessarily "hard" expenses, such as architectural, legal, and consulting fees.)

Negotiating the final development agreement   The final agreement is negotiated upon satisfactory completion of the items in the preferred developer agreement. This includes economic terms, specific performance terms, and so on. From a policy perspective, the final agreement is difficult because it occurs at a time when the process is neither open nor competitive. To achieve fair economic terms, including the costs of public infrastructure and incentives, the local government cannot rely on comparing bids. Instead, the public sector needs to develop its own analyses of the economics of the project—both from the developer's point of view and from that of the community's costs and benefits. The analysis of the developer's returns includes fees, cash returns, and tax benefits. The benefits to the locality include taxes and possibly indirect benefits. Costs are the costs for infrastructure or other assistance to the project. The analysis of the developer's economics permits the "deal" to be evaluated against return requirements in the investment/development marketplace. (Return requirements can be determined independently through appraisers, investment bankers, and development consultants.) The assessment of the locality's cost and benefits permits the community to assess whether its contribution is worth the cost and whether the deal is a reasonable investment for the developer.

Once the economic terms are agreed on, a wide array of specific performance and other business terms must be developed. This part of the process will involve advice from legal counsel and accounting and tax professionals as well as planning and economic development officials.

Final approvals   Ultimately the development agreement must be ratified by the local governing body. The governing body and the public have a reasonable right to know the terms of the deal and the economic ability of the developer to perform. The developer has a right to some degree of privacy regarding the details of both firm and personal finance. Each community must work out its own method of balancing disclosure and privacy.

Each locality and state will have different requirements for selecting developers. To the extent possible, however, the key to the process is for the public sector to shoulder a reasonable share of the up-front costs, recouping them when the development goes forward, and to create a fair, efficient process that strikes a balance between accountability and the reasonable business practices of a private developer.

Conclusion

Economic development is a proactive process for and by government and the private sector. Planning is preparation for action. Planning is strategic; it takes into account the forces shaping the local economy and the ability of local communities to reshape their economies. Where economic development is successful, planning and implementation go hand in hand.

The local government has a key role in facilitating economic development on the industrial fringe, in the downtown area, and in older neighborhoods. The field is complex and requires the establishment of a true private-public partnership that preserves the public interest.

1   *The Report of the President's Commission on Industrial Competitiveness, vol. 2, Global Competition: The New Reality.* (Washington, DC: U.S. Government Printing Office, January 1985).

2   Ibid., 37.

3   *Business Week*, 26 August, 1985, 68.

4   *Employment Projections for 1995: Data and Methods* (Washington, DC: U.S. Department of Labor, Bureau of Labor Statistics, April 1986), Table 1, p. 27.

5   *Business Week*, "High Tech to the Rescue." Special Report, 16 June 1986, 102.

6   David L. Birch, "Yankee Doodle Dandy," *INC.* (July 1987), 33.

7   U.S. Department of Commerce, Bureau of the Census, Table: "Employees in Nonagricultural Establishments, by State." *Statistical Abstract of the United States, 1962, 1986.* (Washington, DC: U.S. Government Printing Office).

8   *Economic and Industrial Development News*, 6 April 1987, 6.

11 Social aspects of physical planning

Most local planners deal primarily with land use and economic development. They think of social planning as something done by other people with whom they have little contact—health planning agencies, area agencies on aging, city or county departments of social services, and maybe United Way organizations.

Because local communities, even small ones, are diverse places, planners must serve many constituencies. Understanding social diversity and responding to social change are keys to effective physical planning. Although social and physical planning are professionally and institutionally quite separate, it can be argued that planning at its best takes account of the social implications of land use and economic development decisions.

The purpose of this chapter is to clarify the relationship between social factors and land use planning. The chapter first considers examples of social problems created by physical problems; it then explores current planning techniques that can prevent or relieve such problems.

What is a social perspective?

A social perspective focuses primarily on the diversity of needs within a community and is concerned particularly with the equity or distributional implications of planning. The purpose of social planning is not simply to discover the likely distributional impacts of decisions but to reduce impacts that place particular groups at a disadvantage and to achieve greater equality among social groups. In other words, social planning is not neutral but openly and inherently normative.

Because they are concerned with equity, social planners tend to focus on two overlapping groups: The first consists of those who are to some extent dependent on others—children and poor, unemployed, handicapped, or elderly members of the community. The second consists of those who have been systematically discriminated against by social and political systems—minorities, women, and elderly and handicapped people. These groups of potentially and actually dependent or disadvantaged people include a substantial majority of the population.

Although many individuals in these groups are not, in fact, dependent and would reject the idea that they are disadvantaged, social and economic forces, ranging from deliberate discrimination to the normal operation of the business cycle, can place them particularly at risk. In recognition of the potential for risk, social policy has been developed to provide assistance when it is needed.

The primary concern of traditional social planning has been to provide income and social services to these vulnerable groups. Services for the various groups are usually administered by separate, service-providing bureaucracies at the federal, state, and local levels. Because many of the services are actually provided by contract with local, voluntary, nonprofit agencies, planning for social services is carried out by a number of independent organizations, such as health planning agencies, area agencies on aging, developmental disabilities councils, and local departments of social services. Not only is most social service planning fragmented in itself, it also bears little or no relation to local land use planning, although some communities have tried to incorporate some social services planning into their comprehensive plans.

The traditional organization of planning work tends to deflect attention from the needs of individual groups, because work is usually divided along functional or geographical lines: for example, planning for transportation or housing or planning at the regional or neighborhood scale. The categories that a department uses for analysis will significantly influence its understanding of issues and the plans and policy recommendations it makes.[1] In practice, most local planning agencies deal only with explicitly "social" issues when physical or economic development will create obvious social side effects.

In some instances, planners may be insensitive to inequities because disadvantaged or dependent people do not have a voice in the planning process. Children and mentally handicapped individuals generally cannot speak for themselves; other groups, such as minorities and poor, handicapped, and elderly citizens, historically have not been organized or politically potent, although since the 1960s this has changed considerably.

At the local level the politics of physical planning are largely dominated by

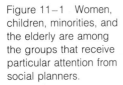

Figure 11–1 Women, children, minorities, and the elderly are among the groups that receive particular attention from social planners.

the interests of powerful economic groups—landholders, from owners of single-family homes to large-scale developers; businesspeople; and industrialists. Some planners are troubled by the inequities of the planning process and make an effort to identify distributional impacts of proposed policies.

In addition to understanding how physical plans affect various groups in the population, planners need to comprehend the effects of social trends on physical planning. As a result of demographic trends, constituencies with new needs emerge or grow, while others change in ways that must be taken into account by physical planners.

Demographic diversity

Planners need to understand the implications of the demographic composition of their communities. Different population groups have different needs that can affect land use, housing, or transportation patterns. In addition, demographic change may create new groups with new needs. This section will look briefly at demographic diversity and change in relation to the baby boom generation, women, and elderly citizens.

The baby boom generation

The so-called baby boom was created by the increased fertility rate of the 1940s and 1950s. (Since the 1960s, the fertility rate has returned to the overall, long-term decline that began before 1900.) That portion of the population born in the forties and fifties has had and will continue to have a pervasive influence on planning, just as it has had on marketing. This demographic "bulge" represents a market not only for private goods and services but for public ones as well.

Simply in terms of numbers, the generation born in the 1940s and 1950s has had a substantial impact. For example, elementary and secondary school enrollments grew steadily through the 1950s and 1960s, peaked in 1970, and then began to decline. In individual neighborhoods or communities, this decline might have been heightened or dampened by migration; in any case, in many school districts school construction was replaced by school closings.

Communities now must decide what to do with the empty school buildings and must gauge the effect of school closings on central-city revitalization efforts. The complexity of both issues is compounded by a ripple effect: the children of the earlier generation have now begun to enter school themselves, which suggests that facilities may again be needed. However, predicting enrollments for this group is more difficult, because more women may delay having children, have fewer children, or remain childless.

Along with influencing school enrollments, the population bulge affects the housing market. Between 1955 and 1975, central cities declined in part because a smaller than average number of people each year reached the age at which they would enter the housing market.[2] However, since 1975 this pattern has reversed. Thus, the number of people reaching age 30—the time for entering the housing market—is expected to peak about 1990 and then to tail off gradually until about 2000. The effect of this population surge has been magnified because household size has been dropping (from 3.33 people in 1960 to 2.67 in 1986),[3] and growth in household formation until 1980 was more rapid than growth in the population as a whole. These demographic changes have increased the demand for housing. Meanwhile, the cost of housing has been rising, due in part to demand and in part to restrictions on supply and higher production costs. Thus, many of the new single-person households or single-parent families cannot afford traditional single-family housing or, in some markets, virtually any of the housing available.[4]

Many of this generation have been settling in the suburbs just as their parents did, although others have been investing in and gentrifying older city neighborhoods.[5] Those who are moving into cities are drawn in part by good housing buys and in part by a new set of values. Many reject the suburban life in which they grew up. As well-educated, two-earner, professional families, they want to be close to work and to the cultural attractions the city can provide. Frequently they have no children or expect to have only small families, so that suburban amenities for children may be less critical than ease of access to such services as day care.

In effect, population pressure and the private market have accomplished what planners have been struggling to achieve for thirty years: upgrading some central-city neighborhoods. The impact has not been as great as some media accounts suggest; these new neighborhoods are still "islands of renewal in seas of decay,"[6] and it is difficult to predict whether this is a temporary or a permanent phenomenon. Moreover, upgrading does not occur without creating other planning problems, the most significant being displacement of low-income residents. In addition, middle-class residents moving into and renovating older city neighborhoods may increase demands for upgrading city services and facilities such as parks and schools. The new residents are also less likely to accept the mixture of land uses often found in older neighborhoods.[7]

Changes in the traditional family

The "traditional" family of working husband, housewife, and several children is rapidly being overtaken by single-parent families (headed by either men or women), unmarried couples, and single individuals living alone. The proportion of traditional families fell from 74 percent in 1960 to 57 percent in 1986.[8] These new family patterns pose a variety of issues for planners. Land use and housing patterns that worked for the traditional nuclear family may not serve new families as well, and changes may be required in zoning, in the provision of services, and in housing programs.[9]

Women in suburbia provide a good example of the way in which demographic change can create new planning needs for a specific group. The present patterns of suburban land use and transportation modes were set primarily in the period just after World War II, when suburban residents generally *did* fit the image of the traditional middle-class nuclear family. Low-density residential suburbs were seen as a semirural refuge from the husband's work and as ideal places for raising children. Transportation was provided primarily by that apotheosis of Americanism, the private car.

Figure 11–2 The "traditional" family, which continues to be the basis for many current patterns of land use and transportation planning: Mom, Dad, the kids, and the family car.

Funding child care with developer fees   The City of Concord, California, has found a way to ensure the availability and affordability of quality child care for an expanding workforce in a community experiencing dynamic economic growth. Enacting an ordinance imposing a fee on new developments for child care . . . [is] part of this city's solution to the increased demand. . . .

The ordinance requires developers of nonresidential projects to pay a fee equal to one-half of one percent of the development costs of the project. The fee applies to commercial, office or industrial projects citywide. The assessment of development costs is made by the public works department and is determined by the project's value on the city-issued building permit. The fee is collected when a certificate of occupancy is issued on the project.

The ordinance stipulates that the fee shall be placed in a special account and used to fund activities of the Concord child care program. These activities include support for the operations of the nonprofit child care agency, direct support for child care programs, and provisions for city-built and owned child care facilities.

Because of the cyclical nature of development revenues, the council has discussed establishing a trust fund with a portion of the fees received, distributing only the interest earnings each year. This would sustain a consistent level of funding and buffer funded activities from downturns in the pace of development and the eventual effects of build-out.

Residential development, projects of less than $40,000 value, construction of child care facilities themselves, proj-

---

By the mid-1980s, however, as a result of general changes in family patterns, the suburbs had become more diverse in terms of age, marital status, and employment patterns. The low-density and automobile-centered land use and transportation patterns that worked fairly well in the 1950s are now a source of significant problems, especially for women.

For example, despite the popular image of the suburban mom and her station wagon, women in suburbia have significantly less access to cars than do men. In a study of a suburban Toronto community,[10] car ownership and ability to drive ranged from 17 percent and 58 percent, respectively, for nonworking women, to 42 percent and 83 percent for working women, and to 100 percent for both for men. Limited mobility affects a wide variety of activities. Many women who wish to work or must work are restricted to jobs that are accessible by public transportation, which is often inadequate. Even married women with cars are often restricted in the length of their commute if they expect to do housework or take a child to day care. Housewives who do not have access to cars have an even more difficult time. They must struggle to do even the most routine shopping, and they inevitably spend considerable time isolated at home.

Because suburban women are a fairly nonmobile, captive labor force, they have often had to accept lower wages or take only part-time work, and they frequently work closer to home than do men. The recent movement of businesses to the suburbs should help these women, but low-density development patterns and lack of adequate public transit may make the new jobs inaccessible to many.[11]

The restrictiveness of American suburban land use and transportation patterns can be illustrated by comparison with Sweden, where suburban development is oriented to public transit.[12] A study released in 1980 showed that a larger proportion of Swedish women than American women worked (three-quarters versus half), in part because public transit gave them considerably greater access to jobs. In addition, they had better access to services such as day care and shopping, and housing units were generally smaller and easier to maintain.

ects constructed by a public agency, and projects which can demonstrate that they create no greater demand for child care than that of a previously approved project on the same site are exempt from the fee requirement. A determination of exemption is made as part of the initial environmental impact analysis during the planning approval stages of a project.

The program also provides for exceptions and credits to the fee. These may be granted if a developer will provide or arrange to provide a child care facility and program. The developer must enter into a contract with the city to conduct a study performed by a consultant selected by the city. The study determines the data necessary to ensure that the child care needs of the project will be met by the proposed facility and program. If the developer can show that occupants of the project

will offer a child care benefit to employees housed in the building, a credit will be granted. The benefit program must eliminate, subsidize or reduce the need for local child care facilities. Again, the developer is required to pay for a study evaluating the employee child care benefit.

Another method of obtaining an exception or credit is for the developer to provide funding to off-site child care facilities or programs, excluding information and referral services. The determination to grant an exception or credit is made when the developer applies for the first discretionary action by the city on project approval. . . .

Source: Adapted from Colleen Coll and Diane Longshore, ''Funding Child Care with Developer Fees,'' *Western City* (July 1986), 13–14.

American women, despite the women's movement, have not been particularly vocal in raising the issues presented here. Many still take for granted the roles to which they are restricted by typical suburban land use patterns, even though divorce and economic pressures have made those roles increasingly obsolete. Many women may accept these restrictions as normal and inevitable, having had little experience of anything else. However, it is interesting to note that in surveys asking about satisfaction with suburban living, men consistently rate it higher than do women.[13]

Although planners need not consider these patterns inevitable, they generally do. Transportation planners, for example, basically work with models developed with data collected in the mid-1960s, although they can modify their traffic forecasts to take into account demographic changes, such as smaller families or more elderly people, that affect numbers of trips per household. However, transportation planners take as given the low-density land use patterns and do not consider how much that pattern is itself shaped by the transportation system or whether land use patterns and transportation together place some groups— such as women—at a systematic disadvantage.[14] By contrast, many physical planners have long advocated greater density, more mixed-use development, and more mass transit, all of which would help women.

Some of the diversity in suburban needs stems from the substantial growth in the number of single-parent families. Such families increased from 8.3 percent of all households in 1960 to 11.5 percent in 1986.[15] Among children born around 1970, about 40 percent are expected to live in single-parent families before they reach 18. Whether these families live in the suburbs or in central cities, they pose a challenge to physical planners. There is no one type of single-parent family. In 1985, such families—87 percent—were headed by women.[16] Minorities were disproportionately represented, but a large majority were white. In 1985, even though 62 percent of female heads of families worked, female-headed households were often poor. Just over one-third of persons in female-headed families (both white and black) had incomes below the poverty level. Median 1984 after-tax income for female-headed single-parent families was only 46 percent of that for married couples with children.[17] Moreover, in 1981, 54 percent of female-headed households occupied physically inadequate, overcrowded, or excessively expensive housing.[18] These facts illustrate what has been called the "feminization of poverty."

In part, the central policy problem posed by single-parent families is poverty, an issue that local planners have little capacity to affect. However, single-parent families also present zoning and housing problems, where planning can be of some assistance. For example, changing the definition of "family" in local zoning ordinances to allow a single-parent family to rent rooms or to share living quarters with another single-parent family in single-family districts is one possible change, albeit one that may be controversial. Forbidding discrimination against renters with children in the household is another possible legislative step. Encouraging the construction of low- to moderate-income family housing, perhaps in the form

Figure 11–3   Planning needs to take account of demographic diversity: nonfamily households, single-parent households, and people living alone.

of cooperatives, is still another strategy. Conveniently located and affordable services such as day care would have to be built into such projects.[19]

This consideration of the needs of single-parent families leads naturally to the needs of elderly people, many of whom are also women and many of whom are also poor. Planning issues and solutions for single-parent families and elderly people overlap considerably.

Elderly people are a rapidly growing segment of the population. In 1900 the proportion of the population over 65 was 4.1 percent, by 1985 it was 11.9 percent, and by the year 2050 it may be as high as 16 percent. Since women generally live longer than men, 76 percent of women over age 75 have no spouse, and 41 percent of women over age 65 live alone. Although social security has increased their ability to live independently, in 1984 the median income of women over 65 was only $6,020.[20] Like female heads of households, elderly women are also part of the feminization of poverty.

In some communities, elderly people will constitute an even larger proportion of the population than the national average. Areas with many amenities, for example, will draw retired people. In suburban areas developed in the 1950s and 1960s, a whole generation is likely to reach age 65 more or less simultaneously between the 1980s and the year 2000. These future elderly persons may be more likely to be homeowners than present elderly people; and since mobility rates for elderly people are half those for younger people, elderly citizens are likely to age in one place.

Although older residents are often strongly attached to their houses and neighborhoods, they may develop health problems that make independent living difficult. In addition, fixed or reduced incomes make elderly persons more likely to suffer from increases in housing costs such as maintenance and taxes. Increasingly, public policy is designed to help elderly residents remain in their homes, particularly as the rapidly growing cost of publicly funded nursing-home care has made home care more financially attractive to policymakers.

On the other hand, between 35 percent and 50 percent of older people live in houses that are larger than they need.[21] In communities where housing is in short supply or very expensive, this underutilized housing represents an untapped resource. Housing patterns such as homesharing and accessory apartments would allow elderly persons to remain independent and make available more moderate-cost housing. However, taking advantage of these opportunities can require zoning changes as well as additional social services to help elderly people in their homes.

In homesharing, perhaps the easier of the two options, a homeowner—often an older person, but sometimes a single parent—rents a room, in exchange for either money or services such as cleaning, cooking, or driving. The house need not be modified. In communities that allow roomers in single-family homes, this practice is an old one; it is now simply being done more systematically, through programs that arrange homesharing matches.[22] However, where zoning ordinances restrict the sharing of houses by unrelated individuals, possibilities for this housing option are limited.

Accessory apartments, sometimes known as mother-in-law apartments or granny flats, are separate apartments in single-family houses. Many such conversions occur illegally. Because of fears that legalizing accessory apartments will change the nature of single-family neighborhoods, ordinances permitting conversions often restrict them to a certain size, to houses with owner-occupants, to elderly owners or renters, or to occupancy only by other family members.[23]

Zoning can be used to encourage housing construction for elderly people. Zoning options range from allowing higher densities and reduced numbers of parking spaces to constructing "echo housing" units—temporary houses for elderly parents that can be placed on the adult children's single-family lot.[24]

These examples indicate that changes in demographic patterns and in values are requiring planners to be more inventive about meeting the housing, employment, transportation, and service needs of diverse groups. Most planning departments do some demographic analyses, although their level of complexity may vary a good deal. The surveys of the needs of children, single-parent families, and elderly people done by the Human Resources Division of the New York City Planning Department for the 1982 long-range capital needs study are good examples of detailed analysis and recommendations. This same kind of analysis and inventiveness will be needed to meet the needs of many groups, in the population besides those discussed here.

Effects of economic decline

When a planning department must propose policy measures to deal with the problems of a particular group, it may first conduct an assessment of their needs. This section will look at a particular needs assessment undertaken in Madison, Wisconsin, examining both its methods and how it fit into a broader planning framework.

Needs assessment

Economic decline has social effects at both the community and individual levels, and effective policy must address both. In the community, out-migration of jobs and population can lead to what has been called "functional decline," which reduces the capacity of the community to perform its necessary functions.[25] These functions include the provision of adequate physical and social services as well as economic functions such as employment, income, and economic innovation.

In areas suffering economic decline, unemployment is the most common impact at the individual level. Because ours is a work-oriented society, an individual's work is often central to his or her identity. The importance accorded work is related in part to skills, status, and satisfaction and in part to the ability to earn

---

Accessory apartments: one approach to creating affordable housing   For towns unwilling to accept governmental funds, accessory apartment regulations offer a means of providing housing without subsidies. For residential communities wishing to preserve existing lifestyles, they offer an alternative to apartment complexes, which the communities may perceive as antithetical to their way of life. . . . There is a great need for smaller housing. The average household size in 1970 was 3.11 persons. In 1980, it was 2.75. The elderly population is steadily increasing, as is the number of single parents, and, in particular, the number of households headed by single women. An important component of this latter group is the "nouveau poor"—middle-income women who are "house rich and income poor." They own their own homes but have experienced a dramatic decrease in income

on account of divorce, widowhood, or abandonment. And then there are the young, professional couples who cannot afford a "starter home" but would prefer to live in single-family residential neighborhoods. Accessory apartments would fit their needs. . . .

Accessory apartments typically cost 25 to 40 percent less than newly built apartments of equivalent size. Because construction costs are lower and because the owner often occupies one of the units, the rents for accessory apartments are often lower than those for comparable nonaccessory apartments.

Coupled with the dramatic demand for affordable housing is the demand for housing that is appropriate to meet the needs of today's family. The Honolulu accessory apartment program is designed to achieve "Ohana" housing.

Figure 11-4 Amish "grossdawdy" houses in Lancaster County, Pennsylvania, have accessory apartments for elderly relatives. The "Elder Cottage" is an innovation of the Lancaster County Office of the Aging. The units are removable, low in energy costs, and designed specifically to meet the needs of elderly residents.

Ohana, a Hawaiian term for family, encompasses the intergenerational concept of the extended family. This kind of program would allow an elderly person to rent an apartment in her* home to a young couple, or to move into the apartment herself and to rent the principal unit to the young couple, resulting in a new source of income for the elderly homeowner, as well as the potential for additional companionship. Informal or contractual arrangements could be made whereby the young couple would do chores such as shopping and gardening in exchange for a reduction in rent. A mother with small children might rent an attached apartment to an elderly couple with whom she could make a babysitting arrangement. Thus, housing can become not only affordable but also appropriate in terms of meeting the social needs of families. Accessory housing also helps to diversify the population of a commu-

nity; it prevents the homogeneity of age groups created by age-restrictive zoning regulations and covenants.

Renting an accessory apartment may provide homeowners with the income they need to remain in their homes. In this way, accessory apartment regulations promote neighborhood stability. They also encourage the maintenance of the existing housing stock: homeowners can apply the income received from the rental units to the upkeep of the house. For the large, older home that is difficult to sell because it is expensive to maintain and too large for today's family, the opportunity to convert part of it into an accessory apartment may save the house from demolition.

Source: Adapted from Edith M. Netter, "Accommodating Accessory Apartments," *Urban Land* (April 1984), 34–35.

money, to be self-sufficient, and to support a family. Unemployment—and its associated social and psychological effects—tends to bear most heavily on certain segments of the population—older workers, women, minorities, and the poor.

Studies at different times—the 1930s, the 1960s, and the 1980s—and in different cities—New Haven, New York, Detroit, and Madison, Wisconsin—produced similar findings about the impact of unemployment.[26] Unemployed people often become more isolated socially, in part because they are cut off from social contacts at work. But beyond that, feelings of shame or loss of status, as well as reduced financial resources, tend to restrict social contacts, and activities. Within the family, the roles of husband and wife may change, particularly if the man is unemployed and the woman works. This period of change may ultimately strengthen a marriage, or it may further weaken a marriage that is subject to problems.

Psychologically, unemployed workers may feel anxious, depressed, and irritable. Financial hardships such as increased debt and going without essentials such as food, clothing, or transportation are severe problems in themselves that add to emotional distress.

Because both social and pychological effects are likely to be more severe as the period of unemployment lengthens, it is logical to ask which workers are likely to have the most trouble finding new work. Several studies have found that blacks, women, and older workers were unemployed for longer periods of time. In addition, workers who were less skilled and less educated had more trouble finding work, a problem that was somewhat confirmed in the Madison needs assessment (to be discussed later in this section), in which workers perceived that employers were more reluctant to hire older workers, those with poor literacy skills, and those whose previous skills were not adaptable or relevant to the new job.

Moreover, even when unemployed persons can find work, the work may be quite different and is often less well paid and less satisfying than what they had before. In Madison, women reported more problems with lower wages in their job searches than did men. Some workers, particularly the less skilled, may have to shift occupations. For example, in Madison less than half of the workers laid off from jobs in manufacturing found new jobs in manufacturing. The shift into service occupations such as maintenance or janitorial work is particularly striking.

Methods of needs assessment

The kind of detailed knowledge of workers' needs that is required for planning cannot simply be inferred from existing studies. Workers' skills, available jobs, the kinds of new skills workers need, and the kinds of assistance they are willing to accept vary from one community to another. A needs assessment must therefore be undertaken at the local level.

Needs assessments can be done in any of several ways, each of which has advantages and disadvantages. The three most common types of data-gathering methods are participatory methods, surveys, and the use of social indicators.[27]

Participatory methods are based on meetings at which affected groups can present their needs directly to staff and policymakers. One common format is a public hearing in which each person or group has its say, with minimal opportunity for exchange or discussion. An increasingly popular format is the structured group meeting—for example, the Nominal Group Technique—which allows for discussion time as well as an opportunity to rank problems or needs that have been identified.[28]

The advantage of participatory methods is exactly that—they are participatory. Participants have a chance to present their ideas directly to decision makers. In the case of the structured group process, it may also be possible to reach consensus on the priorities of problems or needs, although in some cases such a consensus may be more mathematical than real. The primary disadvantage of participatory mechanisms for identifying needs is that some kinds of people are less likely to participate than others. People who are not politically aware or organized, often those who have low social or economic status or who are members of minority groups, or people who are ashamed of their problems, are all likely to stay home. With an issue such as unemployment, these may be some of the people whose voices most need to be heard.

Surveys, and, to a lesser extent, social indicators, present a virtual mirror image of the advantages and disadvantages of participatory methods. Although neither approach gives the public an opportunity to participate directly in developing a consensus on the importance of various needs, surveys and social indicators do provide information about the needs of people who might not be represented in a participatory process.

Surveys use a predetermined questionnaire to ask respondents directly about their needs. A survey can be designed to obtain specific information on topics for which other data is not available. Social indicators, on the other hand, use data collected routinely by government or private groups. For example, a needs assessment can be based on detailed analysis of census data. The primary disadvantage of indicators is that, in many cases, there is no suitable indicator for the particular need or policy outcome that the planner needs to know about. On the other hand, if suitable indicators do exist, they have the advantage of being collected over time and sometimes for small geographic units such as census tracts. This makes it possible to analyze changes over time, for example in monitoring the outcomes of a particular policy, or to look at the incidence of problems in different areas of a city.

A needs assessment in Madison, Wisconsin

Madison, a city of 175,000, has generally held its own in a growing metropolitan area. As a state capital and a university town, it has had a strong economy resistant to cyclical fluctuations. However, its manufacturing sector, while stable in numbers of jobs, has changed in composition in response to changes in the national economy. Locally owned companies have been bought up by outside firms, several plants have closed, and others have laid off workers.

Madison's needs assessment was commissioned by the Economic Development Commission's Blue Collar Task Force[29] as part of a larger effort to plan for possible plant closings or layoffs. Because research on national economic trends and plant closings in other communities was not able to provide sufficient information on the needs of Madison's unemployed population, the needs assessment included a survey of laid-off workers. The survey was designed to explore a number of areas: characteristics of the job the respondent was laid off from and the current job, if any; job skills; the problems workers had finding new jobs; the stresses of unemployment; and the kinds, of services and retraining that would be most helpful.

The study led to recommendations to establish a center for laid-off workers that would help them to identify their skills and find either jobs or retraining programs. The center could also refer workers to agencies providing financial, health, and counseling assistance.

The center was to be only one element in a developing plan that would address unemployment at both the individual and the structural levels. At the structural level, the study concluded that the city should make a particular effort to attract and retain manufacturing jobs, despite the dominance of white-collar service jobs in its economy. Helping an industry such as computerized, small-lot machining, for example, would create jobs that would be a more modern form of the kinds of jobs the city had been losing.

The assessment also reinforced the need for a mechanism to deal with layoffs and plant closings, such as an "action team" that could identify plants likely to face major layoffs or closings and either work toward keeping them open or plan in advance for finding laid-off workers new jobs.

Finally, the study indicated the importance of coordinated job training and job creation targeted at the kinds of people being laid off. The city currently has a program for older displaced workers, and the local vocational school has been developing programs aimed at younger workers as well. The planning department has made efforts to ensure that city subsidies are used to create jobs. For example, the city has created a voluntary "first source" program in which businesses that receive subsidies from the city, such as tax increment financing, agree to place welfare clients in entry-level jobs.[30]

If planners are to develop appropriate housing, transportation, and other facilities, accurate assessment of community needs is essential. The Madison study illustrates, for example, that unemployed people require a wide range of human services. Thoughtful planning for economic development and job training can help to ensure that workers do not become welfare recipients or homeless persons. Such planning, however, rests on careful determination of community needs—whether the target group is unemployed people, single-parent families, suburban women, or elderly residents.

Location of facilities for mentally handicapped people

Sometimes physical planning problems are created by shifts in social policy. One example of this in recent years is deinstitutionalization,[31] as a result of which many mentally retarded, mentally ill (collectively referred to as "mentally handicapped" or "mentally disabled"), and elderly people who lived in large institutions have been released into local communities. For example, between 1955 and 1985, the population of public mental hospitals was reduced from about 559,000 to about 120,000 patients. It is worth noting, however, that 40 percent of deinstitutionalized mentally handicapped persons return to their families, and about 11 percent live in foster homes, where they are cared for by families that receive a small stipend in return.[32] Deinstitutionalization has nevertheless created substantial numbers of handicapped individuals who require housing and various supportive services.

From a physical planning standpoint, the problem of dealing with deinstitutionalization is made more difficult by a drop in the number of inexpensive, single-room residential units, which number only one million units nationwide, or about half the number of units that existed in 1970. At the same time, federal assistance for low-income housing dropped from $26 billion in 1981 to $11 billion in 1987.[33] With more unemployed, deinstitutionalized, and simply destitute people and fewer places for them to live, homelessness has become a growing problem in many cities.

The focus in this section will not be on homelessness per se but on the related problem of accommodating deinstitutionalized mentally handicapped people in the community. This problem requires communities not only to increase emergency facilities for the homeless but also to help create suitable permanent housing and support facilities for a dependent population.

Communities often reject people who are "different," for example, relegating the disadvantaged groups to certain parts of the city, usually slum areas. The practice of separating some groups from the rest of the population has been aided by social policy, which, until recently, placed members of dependent groups—handicapped, mentally ill, and some elderly people—in institutions, thus removing them from the community altogether. As social policy has shifted away from institutionalization and toward integration into community life, various segments of the community have resisted the change. Businesses, for example, do not want facilities serving mentally handicapped individuals to be located in commercial areas because of fears that customers will be, or at least will feel, threatened. Residential neighborhood groups resist facilities such as group homes because they fear the mentally handicapped themselves and are concerned also that the proximity of such facilities will increase traffic and crime and lower property values.

Research on responses to mentally handicapped persons has found that three factors are likely to affect neighborhood acceptance of facilities for mentally handicapped people: the nature of the proposed facility, the nature of the population to be served, and the nature of the community that will be affected.[34] Facilities for the mentally handicapped differ considerably in purpose and size. Many are purely residential. Because service providers are committed to integrating mentally handicapped persons into the community, they make an effort to locate facilities in "normal" residential neighborhoods.

Nature of the facility

Neighborhood concern is generally limited to larger facilities such as group homes, halfway houses, and boarding homes. Many though by no means a majority of facilities face neighborhood opposition. A 1974 study of reasons for denial of requests for zoning variances for such facilities in forty-one cities indicated that 44 percent had been denied because of prejudice toward retarded persons by decisionmakers or opposition from nearby landowners.[35]

The most common legal basis for opposing such facilities is the definition of a "family" often used in local zoning ordinances, which limits occupancy of residences in certain zoning districts to those related by blood, marriage, or adoption. This practice was upheld by the U.S. Supreme Court in *Village of Belle Terre* v. *Boraas* (1974).[36] However, several state courts have found that small group homes for retarded persons do in fact function like traditional families and so should be considered to be families for the purposes of zoning.[37]

These cases point up how important the size of a facility is to its acceptability. Almost by definition, a larger facility is likely to create more external effects, such as traffic and parking. Only small group homes have been successfully argued to be like families from the standpoint of zoning. Thirty states have passed laws that permit such groups homes for mentally disabled people, or that at least allow conditional uses in single-family residential areas. However, about twenty of these states allow only homes with six or fewer or eight or fewer residents. Group homes serving up to sixteen residents are allowed in several states, but only in districts with a large component of multifamily housing.[38]

Larger facilities, such as emergency shelters, where residents are transient, and those that lack professional staff to supervise and help the residents, are more problematic. Their impact will be greater and their presence more obvious. No residential neighborhood wants such facilities, although some low-income inner-city neighborhoods may not be organized enough to reject them.

To ensure successful reintegration of formerly institutionalized people into the community, nonresidential facilities are also necessary, such as mental health clinics, day care facilities, and sheltered workshops.

Although such facilities may be suitably located in commercial areas, it is not uncommon for businesses to object to the establishment of an outpatient or drop-in facility because of the obvious presence of mentally disabled persons. Facilities with organized and supervised day-long activity programs are less likely to have clients simply "hanging out" than are unstructured, drop-in facilities.

Population to be served

The size and purpose of a facility are not the only factors that affect acceptability. Objections of neighbors, whether residential or commercial, depend also on the

Homelessness: demographics, causes, and cures   Estimates of the number of homeless people in the United States range from 250,000 to 4 million. Luckily, since we are obviously without one, an exact count of the homeless is not important; what is important is a recognition that their number is growing. . . .

This epidemic of homelessness is comparable to the one that occurred during the Great Depression. The 1980s feel like the 1930s because of a similarity in the demographics of the homeless population. Then, as now, those without shelter represent a broad cross-section of American society—the young and old, single people and families, the (mentally and physically) disabled and the able-bodied. In the 1950s and 1960s the majority of homeless persons were typical skid row residents—male, white, addicted to alcohol or drugs. Beginning in the early 1970s and

accelerating by the end of the decade, the homeless population began to diversify. . . .

Perhaps the most visible change in the homeless population in the last five years is a drastic increase in the number of women, children, and young men. A widely reported estimate of the average age of the homeless is 34 years. . . .

Besides being diverse demographically, the homeless population varies significantly in duration of homelessness: *the chronic*, who are homeless for more than thirty continuous days (most chronic homeless have been in that state for months or years); *the episodic*, who tend to alternate for varying periods of time between being and not being domiciled; and *the situational*, for whom homelessness is the temporary result of an acute life crisis. . . .

nature of the population to be served. Elderly people are not viewed as negatively as retarded people, who, in turn, are regarded in a better light than those who are mentally ill.

The tendency to make distinctions among various groups of mentally handicapped persons may be connected to the ways in which these groups have been viewed historically. For example, both the law and the general public tend to regard retarded persons as permanently disabled and needing consistent, continued care, whether in institutions or in the community. In other words, retarded citizens tend to be either segregated from the rest of the community or closely supervised within it. Mentally ill persons, on the other hand, who can move back and forth between mental competence and incompetence, are more likely to be on their own in the community. Because the legal history of deinstitutionalization of the mentally ill has led to the development of the right to reject treatment, it is not uncommon for a mentally ill person to be released into the community while on medication, then to refuse treatment, and then to be reinstitutionalized temporarily following a period of deterioration.[39]

Other service-dependent groups such as drug addicts and ex-offenders are even less acceptable to the public. Table 11–1 shows the results of a study in which respondents were asked to rate various kinds of facilities for their perceived effects on a neighborhood.[40]

State laws reflect the distinctions commonly made among populations to be served. Among states that allow group homes for the mentally disabled in low-density residential areas, over half permit homes for retarded and physically handicapped people but not for mentally ill people or any of the less "acceptable" groups.

Nature of the community

Although fears that facilities for mentally handicapped people will adversely affect neighborhoods may be widespread, there is considerable evidence that

The most widely accepted approach to housing the homeless is a three-tier system, beginning with emergency shelters and moving through transitional accommodations to long-term housing. Commonly, projects to provide shelters for the homeless involve the rehabilitation of old buildings and are minimally funded. In the view of some observers, one solution to the homeless problem is to make the renovation of buildings for low-income housing attractive, that is, profitable, for developers or investors. . . .

A New York state program provides state funding to rehabilitate buildings in which the developer agrees to set aside for five to ten years a certain number of units for the homeless. When the set-aside period is finished, the temporary shelter units are converted to low-rent apartments. Projects that mix emergency shelter units with long-term rental units may also take advantage of city funds used to pay for emergency shelter. In one such project in New York City, a nonprofit developer acquired two vacant, city-owned, six-story walkups, promising to use one to house families and children on an emergency basis. Rehabilitation financing was provided by a low-interest loan from the city, and the per diem rate paid by the city to the homeless families using the emergency shelter building is being used to amortize the rehabilitation costs of the second building. Moreover, after eleven years, the emergency housing will be converted to permanent housing for low-income households. . . .

Source: Adapted from Nora Richter Greer, "Homelessness: Demographics, Causes, and Cures in a Nutshell," *Urban Land* (May 1986), 32–33.

---

such fears are exaggerated. In New York and Montreal, studies were undertaken to examine the perceived effects on neighborhoods of facilities for the mentally ill. Both studies compared responses of residents living close to a facility to responses of residents in a closely matched control area without a facility. The curious finding in both cases was the high proportion of people who lived near a facility—on the same street or block—who were unaware of the facility's existence. In the New York City study, 77 percent of the noncontrol respondents were unaware that a facility was nearby. In Toronto, a striking 91 percent were unaware.[41]

Another study attempted to identify neighborhood demographic characteristics that would influence acceptance or rejection of facilities. This study showed that acceptance is more likely to occur in neighborhoods of mixed land uses, fairly high population density, and fairly high transience. In addition, the accepting residents are likely to have fewer children, to be well educated, and to be English speaking.[42] This collection of characteristics certainly suggests that middle-class neighborhoods in or near the inner city are likely to be more accepting. Although such findings should be interpreted cautiously, they correspond to what is in many cities the existing pattern for the location of facilities for the mentally handicapped. Such facilities cluster in neighborhoods in the inner city, sometimes forming "service-dependent ghettos."

One would expect more opposition from single-family residential neighborhoods, where fear about declining property values, for example, might create resistance to proposed facilities for mentally handicapped people. But how realistic is the argument that such facilities will lower neighborhood property values? Research shows these fears to be groundless. Two studies, one covering ten cities in New York State, and the other in metropolitan Toronto, used matched impact and control areas to examine this issue. Both concluded that the location of a mental health facility did not lower the selling price of nearby homes. In addition, rate of turnover was not significantly higher for properties near the facilities, nor were sales depressed by their proximity.[43]

Table 11–1   Attitudes toward social service facilities.

Facility	Percentage of respondents who perceived the facility as having a bad effect on a neighborhood
Methadone-maintenance program	66
Home for former mental patients	46
Psychiatric clinic	35
Home for mentally retarded persons	30
Recreation center for teenagers	9
Home for elderly residents	3

Research on the location of facilities for mentally ill and handicapped people suggests a number of conclusions. Different kinds of facilities are likely to be accepted in different kinds of areas. Facilities designed to house small numbers of people in a family-like setting are not, for example, generally perceived as a threat to social or property values. Because some groups of mentally handicapped people are viewed more favorably than others, in a fearful neighborhood it is easier to locate a facility for a more accepted group. Moreover, neighborhoods that are more accepting of facilities for mentally handicapped people may become the location of a number of facilities. Finally, some facilities, due to their size, function, or clientele, may not be acceptable to any neighborhood without careful planning and buffering.

Planning strategies

Despite considerable information about the likely effects of facilities, it is not possible to spell out a definitively successful strategy for determining their loca-

Figure 11–5   One of the goals of group homes is to integrate residents into the life of the community.

tion. The issue can become extremely politicized and bitter, especially when facilities are large and the inhabitants have serious disabilities.

Sometimes facilities that open quietly, without any previous notice or fanfare, are largely unnoticed and unopposed. In other cases, neighbors feel betrayed for not having been involved in the decision-making process. In still other cases, an open, participatory strategy with neighborhood groups may only increase opposition rather than diffuse it.

Of course, where group homes and other facilities are not permitted uses, notice must be given and hearings held. How much negotiation occurs between the project sponsor and the neighborhood depends substantially on the nature of the proposed facility and on accepted local practice. It is interesting to note, however, that in a national study of 611 community residential facilities for retarded people, managers of 89 percent of the facilities indicated that opposition decreased after the facility opened, primarily because no problems materialized.[44] In the case of a facility likely to meet strong opposition, such as a large emergency shelter for the homeless, it is essential to develop a participatory process that provides a balance between neighborhood groups, client advocates, agencies involved in providing housing and related services, and planners or decisionmakers with a concern for the interests of the community as a whole.

The most difficult decision planners face is whether to fight for the dispersal of facilities. The easiest course is to accept the status quo, which means that facilities for mentally and physically handicapped people are most likely to be located in inner-city neighborhoods rather than in outlying residential areas. However, allowing the development of large concentrations of disabled residents in inner-city neighborhoods may deter planning-department efforts to revitalize the central city. If pressures for gentrification are strong enough to displace these service-dependent groups,[45] a systematic effort must be made to locate facilities in outlying areas.

Several strategies have been suggested for dealing with the problem of the concentration of group homes for mentally handicapped people. For example, a community can enact regulations to prevent facilities from clustering in a single neighborhood. One approach limits the proportion of people living in group homes to, for example, 3 percent of the population within a half-mile radius. Another approach requires a given distance between facilities.[46]

More generally, it has been suggested that physical planners work with social welfare agencies at both the state and local levels to plan systematically for the location of facilities.[47] Such planning would have to overcome the traditional separation between physical and social planning as well as the fragmentation within the social services system. However, without committed and coordinated planning, development of a housing and service system that works both for handicapped citizens and for the community at large will be largely a matter of chance.

Social impacts of physical and economic development

Changes that result from economic and physical development appear inevitably to benefit some populations while causing harm to others. Planners must be aware of such negative effects and try to forestall them as much as possible. Two particularly clear examples of this problem have developed in recent years. One is the social impact of rapid economic development on small, rural communities—the problem of boomtowns. The other is the social impact of gentrification in central cities, particularly the displacement of low-income residents. The primary technique that has been developed for defining the needs of people affected by these kinds of changes is social impact assessment.

Origins of social impact assessment

Planners became acutely aware of the social impacts of development during the 1950s, the heyday of urban renewal and highway construction. Both programs reflected national policy that was designed to promote economic development, and both required land to be cleared in densely populated central cities. The neighborhoods most affected were those of low-income, often minority people who had the least capacity to resist.

Initially, no notice was taken of the effects of such programs on the residents of these neighborhoods. The inexpensive housing they had lived in was replaced by highways or often by offices, commercial space, or luxury and middle-income housing. The original 1949 Housing Act establishing the Urban Renewal program stated that displaced residents should be relocated in "safe, decent and sanitary housing," but neither assistance nor monitoring was provided to ensure that this occurred.

However, beginning in the mid-1950s, a rising tide of neighborhood opposition and the findings of studies by planners on the social impacts of urban renewal began to convince both planners and policymakers that the negative social effects of urban development could not be ignored. Herbert Gans's study of urban renewal in Boston's West End showed that "renewal" had destroyed not a disorganized slum but a healthy, well-established, working-class neighborhood.[48] Complex social networks tied to the neighborhood were broken up by the forced relocation. In "Grieving for a Lost Home," Marc Fried noted that 46 percent of the women and 38 percent of the men relocated from the West End still showed symptoms of fairly severe grief two years after the move.[49] Many small businesses displaced by public projects shut down entirely.

Not all neighborhoods torn down for renewal or highway construction were as socially cohesive as the West End, and many, but by no means all, of the residents who were relocated found adequate or better housing than they had had before.[50] However, both research findings and the opposition of target neighborhoods did lead to gradual changes in the renewal and highway programs, requiring more adequate relocation assistance and a larger role for residents in project planning.

Since the 1960s, because of the obvious connection between local opposition to projects and negative social effects, the logic of considering these effects and of requiring participation by affected people has spread to other areas of federal activity and to much large-scale private development. The National Environmental Policy Act, passed in 1969, required both more open citizen participation and the preparation of environmental impact statements (EISs). State legislation extended the EIS requirements to state and local actions. Beginning in 1971, courts began to require assessment of social and economic impacts as well as environmental ones.[51] Today, EISs, including social impact statements, are required for all kinds of large federal projects and for large renewal projects in many cities. A recent study of facility siting decisions by utilities indicated that during the 1970s, instances of structured citizen participation increased, as did instances of socioeconomic impact assessments of projects.[52]

Social impact assessment

In the United States, social impact assessment (SIA) is the primary mechanism that has been developed to plan in advance for the social effects of development. SIA is usually an aspect of a broader socioeconomic impact assessment, which is tied, in turn, to an environmental impact statement. These studies, commonly prepared by consultants working for the developer of the project—an oil company, a utility, or a government agency—are ultimately submitted to the state or federal agency that must approve the project. The role of the local government that will be affected by the project is usually not formal and depends largely on its political ability to make its voice heard.

The techniques for conducting an SIA are varied, with little consensus on any single best method. Generally the social assessment is done in conjunction with the assessment of economic, demographic, service, and fiscal impacts, to which it is obviously closely related. Because of the intangible nature of many of the variables, however, the techniques for social assessments are quite different from those used in the more quantifiable economic and demographic areas.

Besides the technical issues involved in the choice of a methodology, two other, more basic issues must also be addressed when an SIA is being designed. First, are impacts projected in the aggregate, for the community as a whole, or are separate projections made for different groups, such as elderly people, women, or newcomers? Second, what is the extent of community involvement in the assessment?

Methods of social impact assessment Computerized socioeconomic assessment models are now commonly used to assess economic and demographic impacts of a project. A substantial number of these models, with names like ATOM 3 and BOOM 1, have been developed.[53] Each model usually consists of several submodels. For example, one type starts with an economic module using input-output or export base analysis to project business volume and employment by sector, along with a demographic projection (generally based on cohort survival) to project the labor force and total populations. These two sets of projections are then combined to produce an estimate of net migration. On the basis of net migration, a residential allocation module estimates housing needs; a service requirement module estimates the need for services and infrastructure such as schools, water supply, and sewage disposal; and a fiscal impact module estimates costs of the various services and revenues to cover them.

The model is used to describe the community at a baseline period before development occurs and then to project changes in the variables assuming (1) that no development occurs, and (2) that the project is built. The difference is the impact attributed to the project.

These computer models can show decisionmakers the nature and magnitude of economic and social impacts of a project. For social planning, they yield estimates of increased needs for various kinds of facilities and services. Housing can be estimated by amount, by type—temporary or permanent, single- or multifamily—and sometimes even by location. For services such as education, health, libraries, and recreation, needs for staff and for physical facilities can be projected—on the basis of a rate of service usage per unit of projected population.[54]

As useful as these computerized models are they cannot estimate more subtle personal and social impacts or project needs for "softer" services such as mental health and welfare services; such analyses are usually made as a separate element of the EIS. A wide variety of methods have been proposed to assess the less quantifiable effects of change.

Techniques for developing a profile of the community and projecting impacts of a project can generally be used whether the analysis is done in the aggregate or broken down to examine impacts on particular groups. Most SIAs focus on aggregate analysis, but the arguments for disaggregation are strong. Although a project may produce beneficial impacts in the aggregate—higher incomes, a higher rate of employment, and better and more varied services—some groups, such as elderly residents or women, may suffer most from the negative effects that do materialize. Although it may be possible to mitigate some of these problems, thus increasing the aggregate benefits of the project, without an analysis focusing on groups that are potentially at risk, such problems may not be identified.

The politics of social impact assessment   Despite all its technical trappings, social impact assessment is only one element in a highly political decision-making process. SIAs prepared for developers tend to use aggregate analyses and stress economic impacts because aggregate economic impacts—such as new jobs and income—are the most significant local benefits of any project. It is not surprising that the developer would wish to downplay, to licensing bodies and local residents alike, the often less tangible, but also more negative, social impacts of the project.[55]

The role of community residents, in the development of the SIA document, and in the overall decision-making process points up the complexity of SIA. Ideally, residents should be fully involved in defining, evaluating, and mitigating project impacts, but in many cases, the community has little power relative to other participants in the decision-making process. Local residents have little expertise or planning capacity. They want the jobs the project has to offer and may be willing not to look too closely at possible social dislocations. The developer of the project, on the other hand, is often a multinational corporation with large financial and legal resources. If the project is a high national priority, as energy development was in the 1970s, the community may have even less leverage.

Because many SIAs are undertaken for project developers, there has been little incentive to invite residents to participate other than by responding to surveys or reacting at legally required public hearings once the draft EIS has been prepared. A study of participation in power-plant-siting decisions indicated that where participation focused on socioeconomic impacts, it was limited 95 percent of the time to the late, review, and implementation stages of the process,[56] a pattern that can create a sense of fatalism among community residents.[57]

In some cases, communities with a will and some source of political leverage have become an integral part of the SIA and the larger decision-making processes. For example, Native Americans are among those who have consistently and actively asserted their right to participate. In five western states, Native American tribes are estimated to own 13 percent of the coal lands as well as substantial holdings of oil, gas, and uranium. These lands have been actively sought by energy development companies. In the 1950s and 1960s, the Federal Bureau of Indian Affairs negotiated mining leases at terms that were quite advantageous to the energy companies. Beginning in the mid 1960s, however, with Peabody Coal's Black Mesa strip mine on the Hopi and Navajo reservations, Native Americans began to demand and gradually to get a more central role in negotiating leases for extraction of resources from their reservations.

Native Americans have made particular use of the requirement that EISs evaluate social impacts. In fact, 1978 amendments to the National Environmental Policy Act (NEPA) regulations required that Native American tribes have early knowledge of projects and participate in research related to impacts as well as being able to comment on the draft EIS. In addition, their leverage was strengthened by the American Indian Religious Freedom Act of the same year, which guarantees Native Americans access to and use of sacred sites and resources.[58]

Because of federal and state regulatory requirements, the social elements of EIS have been particularly well developed in relation to large-scale energy or public works projects in small, rural communities. Ironically, however, SIA and the mitigation of negative impacts have been required less often in neighborhoods undergoing the current equivalent of urban renewal—gentrification.

Boomtowns

EISs typically are required for the development or expansion of large physical projects such as mines, dams, power plants, highways, or airports in or near a small community. The communities in question are often rural towns that have been losing population, especially younger people. Residents are usually pleased to have the new development because of the promise of jobs and renewed economic vitality.

The image of boomtowns portrays them as subject to a self-reinforcing spiral of problems.[59] As new residents flood into the community, services rapidly prove inadequate. Schools go on double or even triple shifts. Local health services, if they exist at all, are quickly overwhelmed. Housing is a particular problem because the price of the existing supply is bid up dramatically. Increases in supply cannot keep pace, partly because population growth is too rapid, and partly because construction wages are generally better in the mine or the power plant than in housing construction. Many people live in inadequately serviced mobile homes and in other buildings not intended for housing at all.

The problems created by inadequate physical infrastructure and inappropriate land use are made worse by lack of planning. Until the advent of a large project, rural towns do not perceive themselves as needing planning. Tax revenues and bonding capacity are often inadequate to finance needed infrastructure, and the original residents must bear most of these costs if expansion is to precede development. A large new installation pays few taxes until it is in operation, and may pay none if it is located in a separate jurisdiction.

Predicting how much expansion of services may be needed is difficult in the face of uncertainty about how much development will actually occur. Often, the company or agency in charge of the development is initially unsure of its scale and timing. Because many large facilities require only a small work force once they are in operation, there may be only a temporary boom during the construction period. Questions about whether other industries or facilities will come in with the new development. Uncertainty about the amount of development to be expected has sometimes led optimistic communities to overbuild, creating a tax burden that could be sustained only with difficulty. Other communities have done nothing and have been overwhelmed by infrastructure and service demands.

The social problems commonly attributed to boomtowns often sound like a litany of demoralization and vice. For the newcomers, the long work hours and inadequate housing, schools, recreation facilities, amenities, or jobs for women all contribute to stress at home and to absenteeism, high turnover, and low productivity on the job. Employment problems create a need for an even larger work force, thereby overloading the town's facilities even more.

Meanwhile, the town's original residents see their old way of life eroded. The pace quickens; the larger scale makes relationships more impersonal. Greater affluence and the breakdown of traditional informal social controls lead to new problems with alcoholism and juvenile delinquency, for example. Business demand expands rapidly, but traditional shopkeepers who cannot adjust to the more aggressive environment and the larger scale may go under in the competition with new businesses. Labor is bid away from local employers by the high wages of the new project. Prices rise, a particular problem for elderly people on fixed incomes.

Newcomers and old-timers may be in conflict over style of life as well as over development issues. Original residents may pay most of the property taxes, since newcomers are more likely to rent than to buy housing. Disagreements arise over the expansion of local services. Social and political status and influence patterns may change as old elites lose power to those who can deal with the new industry and the new population. New residents, especially temporary ones, may have little involvement in the social or political life of the community. Even without their participation, the changes brought by development and by the original residents' responses to change lead to new political issues and cleavages.

Although some empirical studies have questioned the uniformly negative character of this portrait of a boomtown, the findings are mixed: they suggest that

Downtown housing for minimum-wage workers   Unable to secure federal funding for a low-income housing project, the city of St. Paul, Minnesota, assembled a group of business leaders, local foundations, and city agencies to finance and manage a 56-unit rooming house for downtown minimum-wage workers. At a cost of nearly $2 million, the historic American Beauty Macaroni Company Building, located in the city's Lowertown district, was converted into affordable, single-room occupancy housing for some of the city's hardest-to-house. (Lowertown is the old warehouse district and a part of St. Paul's CBD.)

"I'm glad to report that the city has found a means to deal with the dark side of successful downtown development—housing for minimum-wage workers who have moved out of the downtown because of high rents in the building boom," said Mayor George

Latimer. "These are the people who maintain our downtown office buildings, who work behind the scenes at our finest hotels and restaurants, who work in some of this city's most stable and steadfast businesses," he added.

The five-story American Beauty Building at Wacouta and Fourth Streets was recently placed on the National Register of Historic Places. . . . The top four floors of the building were renovated to include 56 furnished rooming units. Each unit will include a bed, dresser, chair, and lamp. There will be one large, shared kitchen, an eating area, a lounge, and four shared bathrooms on each floor. Room rents are set at $175 per month, with the project targeted to single men earning from $3,000 to $10,000 a year. The Wilder Foundation (a local foundation that has been active in providing housing for the elderly, day care, and social services for the mentally ill) will manage the housing

---

services clearly are disrupted by rapid growth and that psychological well-being or community integration may be reduced in some cases but not in others.[60]

Moreover, the degree to which problems materialize appears to depend somewhat on how well they have been anticipated and planned for. Planners have not been able to deal very well with the pervasive uncertainty mentioned earlier, but an active response to growth management has still been more effective than a passive one.

Even where planning has worked fairly well and negative effects have not been severe overall, the burden of the impact may be greater on some groups than on others. Current knowledge of these differential impacts is only rudimentary. However, newcomers, women, single-parent families, elderly people, and minorities all are groups whose experiences might differ from those of the working-age, white males who are most likely to be attracted to and employed by the kinds of projects coming into a boomtown.

Planning responses have to go beyond the provision of adequate housing and community services. In the case of women, for example, job training and employment opportunities equal to those available to men would be one obvious response. Day care services and the establishment of organizations that would rely on women to deal with community problems would provide independence and reduce feelings of fatalism. The professionalization of social services that is likely to occur in a growing community should not be allowed to foster dependence or the idea that individuals facing stresses related to growth are somehow personally at fault. Finally, the better the information is about the effect of boom conditions on particular groups, the more appropriate the planning response can be.

The social impacts of gentrification

In large cities in recent years, the most obvious social side effect of development has been the displacement of residents by gentrification and downtown rede-

complex and is responsible for compiling a list of those interested in renting rooms. One floor will be reserved for women if there are enough requests for space; if the number of interested women is small, a half-floor will be reserved. The street level will be leased to a commercial restaurateur. . . .

The Wilder Foundation . . . also will fund any operating shortfalls not covered by the tightly controlled rent ceiling. "Housing low-income people is a pressing community need and a new direction for the Wilder Foundation," said Leonard Wilkening, chairman of the foundation. "We are pleased to be part of this creative and lasting solution to a difficult human problem."

Speaking as an entrepreneur involved in the project, Brian Nelson, president of Asset Development Services, explained his reason for taking on such an unusual venture. "Asset stands to

be a big winner in Lowertown through our successful commercial development of Union Depot Place, market-rate housing in the James J. Hill buildings, and proposed riverfront developments like Water Street Plaza and KRCA's Minnesota TeleCenter. As we've stated in the past," he continued, "we feel we've been part of the problem [the overall displacement of residents from downtown rooming houses through the combined effect of local redevelopment efforts] and we want to be part of the solution. . . . The American Beauty Macaroni Building gives us a chance to build a healthy, diverse downtown community to support all our projects— and it gives us a chance to give something of real value back to the city. . . ."

Source: Adapted from "Downtown Housing for Minimum-Wage Workers: St. Paul Fashions One Solution," *Urban Land* (May 1986), 26–27.

---

velopment. As was the case with urban renewal in the 1950s and 1960s, planners have an ambivalent response to this issue. On the one hand, when middle-class people have moved into and refurbished dilapidated inner-city neighborhoods, they have accomplished some of the urban revitalization that planners have been struggling to generate for thirty years. The city tax base is increased, the multiplier effect of more affluent households improves the economic condition of the city, and the demand for some kinds of welfare-related services goes down. On the other hand, the withdrawal of these upgraded housing units from the stock of low-income housing and the increase in property values mean that low-income residents who can no longer afford to live in these neighborhoods must go somewhere. Clearly, planners would feel more comfortable about the benefits of gentrification if they also felt that the costs being borne by displaced residents were not heavy. Unlike urban renewal, gentrification has been largely a private-market phenomenon, accomplished house by house by middle-class "pioneers" who buy and renovate their own houses or by speculative developers who do it for them. Although public inducements may be granted to gentrifiers through local tax exemption, landmark designation, and federal tax deductions for historic preservation, gentrified neighborhoods are not the kind of large-scale planned and publicly subsidized developments that are subject to public decision making and relocation assistance. As a result, the costs to displaced residents generally are not the subject of planning analysis; nor are they often mitigated by public action.

What are the social impacts of gentrification? How many persons are displaced, who are they, and what happens to them? The answers depend on what kind of neighborhood is being renovated. The most common image of the gentrified neighborhood is of single-family dwellings or row houses built during the nineteenth century. The neighborhoods may be working-class areas where housing is largely owner occupied, or the housing may have been converted to apartments and rooming houses serving lower-class residents. (Conversion of apartment buildings to condominiums can be another form of gentrification.)

Research on displacement is difficult, because most of the subjects have moved. The research has often focused on single neighborhoods or cities or on particular groups within the larger set of displaced residents.[61] Perhaps the most definitive study to date is Michael Schill and Richard Nathan's study of voluntary (unrelated to gentrification) and involuntary moves among renters in nine gentrifying neighborhoods in five cities.[62] (On the assumption that renters were most likely to be negatively affected, Schill and Nathan eliminated from their analysis both homeowners and residents of halfway houses.)

Given the common expectation, based on previous research and media coverage, that displacement causes considerable hardship, some of Schill and Nathan's findings were unexpected. The rate of displacement in the neighborhoods was generally around 20 percent, but ranged from 8 percent to 40 percent. Elderly and black people were not disproportionately represented among the group that moved involuntarily compared with voluntary movers. However, displaced households had lower incomes, less education, and, because of the 40-percent displacement in one particular neighborhood, were more likely to be Hispanic. Female-headed households, single-person households, and households with an unemployed member were also more likely to have to move involuntarily.

Especially surprising was the finding that fully two-thirds of displaced households felt that their new home was better than their previous one, although involuntary movers were significantly less satisfied than voluntary movers. That involuntary movers took longer to find new homes and had to pay somewhat more rent suggests that the moves had their drawbacks. In addition, as many as 70 percent of the displaced households moved to another part of the same neighborhood or to a nearby area, which enabled them to retain social ties with the old neighborhood but also increased the likelihood that they might have to move again if gentrification spread. The only groups that were dissatisfied after the move were households with an unemployed member and those that were particularly transient, making five or more moves in ten years.

These findings suggest that the negative effects of displacement are not as great as might be expected. In the Schill and Nathan study, the neighborhoods from which residents were displaced were apparently not cohesive ethnic communities like Boston's West End. Alternative affordable housing was available, and the gradual pace of gentrification allowed low-income movers to relocate before the price of the housing to which they moved was bidded up.

While Schill and Nathan's study does indicate that concern about the impact of gentrification on renters may be exaggerated, it is clear that vulnerable groups such as unemployed people, transient people, and nontraditional households (including those headed by women) do have problems.

Another study that included both homeowners and renters found that elderly residents may be more likely to move out of gentrifying neighborhoods than either female-headed or blue-collar households.[63] This may be a matter for some concern, given that elderly people are, overall, less likely than other groups to move, in part because they have fewer physical, psychological, and financial resources for adapting to a new place. Some elderly persons may move voluntarily in response to good offers for their houses, but others may be encouraged or forced to move by speculators, higher taxes or costs of living, or incompatibility with incoming residents.

Condominium and other types of multifamily housing conversions appear in some respects to have created greater problems than has gentrification of lower-density areas. Elderly residents living on fixed incomes are often unable to buy an apartment and must move. Residential facilities for service-dependent groups are often seen as incompatible with the middle-class character of gentrified neighborhoods and may be forced out. Low-income residents of boarding houses and residence hotels—whether on Manhattan's West Side or in San Francisco's South of Market—have had fewer and fewer housing alternatives. Some of these people are also mentally handicapped, alcoholics, or addicts who are not necessarily welcome in other neighborhoods. Many, however, are low-income single elderly people with no place to go that they can afford. New York City estimates that 13 percent of its homeless people formerly lived in single-room occupancy (SRO) hotels.

Gentrification has become a divisive issue within the planning profession because it pits planners' desires to revitalize the central city against their obligation to be responsive to the needs of particularly vulnerable groups. How a planner sees the balance of costs and benefits is due as much to ideology or values as it is to the "facts" concerning the impacts of gentrification.[64]

If gentrification is viewed as a zero-sum game, then a choice must be made. The challenge to planners is to try to prevent gentrification from being a zero-sum game. In some instances where public sponsorship of a project is involved, social impact assessment can identify the needs of people likely to be displaced, although in many places it is not legally required. In public projects requesting SIA, relocation assistance is also required.

Social impact assessment has been used in planning for a few large-scale developments, for example, in New York City. Critics argue that such studies have not been very thorough because project sponsors were anxious not to encourage political challenge, and potentially affected groups were not sufficiently organized to counter with their own analyses. Because they recognized the dependence created by developer-sponsored SIAs, the New York City Planning Department and Board of Estimate decided in 1985 to allocate $2 million to the Planning Department to do its own impact assessments of selected projects.

Social impact assessment could certainly be used more than it has been to mitigate social impacts of both large and small urban projects. Although methods somewhat simpler than the elaborate modeling efforts used in western boomtowns and more appropriate to urban projects do exist, the key appears to be a political demand for such analysis.[65]

Beyond analyzing the needs of people vulnerable to displacement, local governments have tried a variety of both short- and long-term policy initiatives to control displacement or to mitigate its negative effects. Short-term responses to immediate political pressures generally consist of moratoria on condominium or SRO conversions, for example. Longer-range efforts to limit increases in housing costs have also been tried. Rent control is one broad approach to this problem. Tax relief for elderly or low-income homeowners is designed to reduce increases in the cost of housing for particularly vulnerable groups. Focusing more specifically on gentrification, Washington D.C., after considerable controversy, passed a weakened version of a speculation tax on the sale of any housing that had code violations and that had been held for less than three years. Local governments have attempted also to encourage neighborhood upgrading without displacement. For example, Community Development Block Grants (CDBG) or local government monies have been used to provide infrastructure in basically stable but somewhat run-down neighborhoods.

The need for low-income housing is central to the problem of displacement and to its solution. The low-income involuntary movers studied by Schill and Nathan were cushioned from the negative effects of displacement because an adequate supply of affordable housing existed in their cities. However, if gentrification and condominium conversions are accompanied by housing disinvestment and abandonment, the supply of low-income housing can be dangerously reduced. With federal funds for low- and moderate-income housing dramatically reduced, most communities have few options and are faced with increases in the number of homeless persons.

Some communities have begun to save and rehabilitate SRO hotels.[66] In other areas, where development has created housing shortages and high prices, innovative efforts are being made to turn development into a source of more housing,

Figure 11–6   A room in a remodeled SRO in Portland, Oregon.

especially for low- and moderate-income residents. Boston, San Francisco, and a number of smaller California cities are requiring builders of new office space either to build housing themselves or to contribute to a trust fund for housing construction. The argument used by these cities is that many of the office workers drawn by the new development will live in the city, thus placing even more pressure on an already tight housing market.

Variants of the same strategy have been tried in other cities. Atlantic City, where casino development has displaced low- and moderate-income residents, taxes casino revenues for a somewhat similar but broader trust fund. A trust fund in Montgomery County, Maryland, is financed by a tax on condominium sales. Of course, such trust funds are possible only in areas where there is strong development pressure. Moreover, the trust funds are not large enough to make up for the loss of federal housing assistance.[67]

Planners and policymakers have been trying to develop a variety of policies to prevent gentrification from becoming a zero-sum game. However, planning *for* groups that may be displaced is likely to produce less responsive solutions than planning *with* them. The experience with urban renewal in the 1950s and planning for energy development in the West indicate that planners and project sponsors are most responsive when the affected groups are organized and active on their own behalf. It is important that planners with a social perspective not allow the use of techniques such as SIA to curtail the involvement of affected population in decision making.

Social elements in comprehensive plans

Social considerations are sometimes included in comprehensive plans, although this is not the same as developing a plan that systematically takes a social perspective throughout. Cleveland under Planning Director Norman Krumholz is the only city in the country to have developed a comprehensive plan based on a social perspective. (This plan will be discussed in a subsequent section.) Traditionally, housing and community facility elements of comprehensive plans have dealt at least to some degree with social issues or with physical facilities for social programs. Although a few planning departments around the country have some social planning staff, California is perhaps the only state that encourages the development of social elements in comprehensive plans by including them in state legislation as an option for localities. However, even with the encouragement of the California League of Cities, in 1985 only 22 of 433 cities had developed a social element.[68] Like social planning activities in other cities, these social elements generally deal with traditional social planning concerns related to the provision of human services. The plans are not designed to consider the implications of physical planning on various possibly disadvantaged groups in the community.

Obstacles to the development of social plans

The institutional separation between physical planning and social services is probably the greatest block to the inclusion of a social services element in a comprehensive plan.[69] Some of the separation is due simply to traditional attitudes—planning departments and planning commissions deal primarily with physical issues. But the separation is structural as well. In many jurisdictions, income maintenance and many social services programs are provided at the county rather than at the city level. Cities may provide some additional services, such as senior citizen centers or centers for teenagers, both of which are extensions of recreation programming. Moreover, many services may be provided in the community by local voluntary organizations—churches, religiously affiliated social service agencies, and grass-roots, single-purpose service agencies—with funds from county, state, or federal agencies or from private sources such as the United Way. Although these programs serve local residents, the local government may have little or no formal relationship with them.

Fragmentation of services is the rule, not only between governmental levels, but also at any single level. In many cases separate bureaucracies exist at the federal, state, and county levels for different service populations—low-income, developmentally disabled, mentally ill, and elderly. Coordination of services has been one of the major planning issues in the social service system during the past fifteen years, but success in achieving it has been mixed at best. Social service elements in comprehensive plans might be one mechanism for such coordination, but they have not generally been linked strongly enough to the human services system that provides the services.

Only where a social planning effort is formally connected to the service network is it likely to be effective. In a few cities where social elements of comprehensive plans have been developed in conjunction with the city's human services agencies, coordination between agencies has increased. In Monterey California, for example, the plan guides the city in allocating revenue-sharing funds to social service agencies and has resulted in some rearrangement of service responsibilities among agencies. Baltimore has the same legal status as a county and provides many human services. Since there is no single, overarching human services agency, the mayor established an Office of Human Development to inventory the city's services and to identify service gaps and duplication. The staff work for this office has been done by the city planning department. In many other large cities that have substantial human service programs, however, social planning of this type is largely the domain of human services agencies.

Equity issues and social plans

As noted at the outset of this chapter, planning from a social perspective takes account of the equity or distributional implications of physical planning. For equity issues to be dealt with by local planning departments, they have to be shown to have implications for land use and economic development; it is then that physical planners are likely to develop a genuine interest in them. Interestingly, relegating equity issues to a separate "social element" may actually have a negative effect, by legitimizing their neglect by the planning commission and staff. Santa Rosa, California, which adopted a social element in its 1978 plan, eliminated it in the 1984 revision, distributing many of the goals that had been in the social element throughout other, more traditional, plan elements.

In fact, some traditional elements in comprehensive plans have always dealt with social service and equity issues. Housing is one example. Joint planning between social service agencies and planning departments on the nature and location of physical facilities is probably the most well developed form of cooperative social planning, although the experience with the location of facilities for mentally handicapped people suggests that major improvements must still be made. Initially, Baltimore's social planning program grew out of an effort to develop a plan for multiservice centers located throughout the city. The planning departments in Baltimore and in New York have been involved in assessing the need for day care facilities. Although a community may appear to have a sufficient number of day care facilities, they may not be located where they are most needed. When developers of such facilities request zoning changes, the staff can either work with them or give advice about location.

Successful facility planning requires (1) ties to the service system that actually provides the services and (2) good information about the needs of the group to be served. Finally, it requires a commitment to ensuring that the group—whether the children of single parents, handicapped people, or whatever—does have its needs met even if this raises some political hackles.

The Cleveland example

What may be needed for successful social planning is, a reorientation of the whole concept of the comprehensive plan that would place equity at its heart. The Cleveland Policy Planning Report[70] is probably the only example of a plan and a planning department that tried to achieve such a reorientation. In 1970 when the country's first black mayor, Carl Stokes, took office, Cleveland was struggling with the problems of inner city poverty: In 1969, half of its families were in the bottom third of all families in the Standard Metropolitan Statistical Area (SMSA) in terms of income; about 25 percent received some form of public assistance. The plan, published in 1975, explicitly stated its central theme:

In a context of limited resources . . . equity requires that locally-responsible government institutions give priority attention to the goal of promoting a wider range of choices for those Cleveland residents who have few, if any, choices.[71]

Although the plan recognized the limited capacity of local planning to deal with the problems of poverty, members of the planning staff did try to view from an equity standpoint the land use, transportation, and economic development issues that fell within their jursidiction. In negotiations with the regional transportation planning agencies, the city advocated lower fares and better, more flexible transit service for Cleveland's transit-dependent residents. The city opposed plans for a new rail system and sued to prevent the construction of a freeway through several city neighborhoods. It also opposed the provision of a city subsidy for downtown office development in favor of support for neighborhood rehabilitation.

Cleveland's planners were not shy about taking part in the political conflicts that the emphasis on equity inevitably produced. They tried to avoid unnecessary confrontation, worked to develop coalitions, and used their technical skills in the protracted negotiations characteristic of an incremental decision-making process. Because of the magnitude of the shift in orientation the planners were proposing, they lost on some issues but were able to revise policy somewhat on others.

Although the Cleveland plan was an innovative effort praised by some, it was criticized by others for not going far enough, particularly for not organizing poor residents to advocate their own interests.[72] The Cleveland model has never been copied. Despite its moderation, the plan was too great a departure from the accepted style of local planning, which has traditionally been less overtly political and has primarily served propertied groups within the population. The Cleveland plan does, however, represent the fundamental "social" planning envisioned in this chapter.

Conclusion

In meeting the diverse needs of a heterogeneous population, planners with a social perspective continue the planning traditions set in the 1960s by Paul Davidoff's advocacy planning and the equity-oriented planning of Norman Krumholz in Cleveland.[73] The rhetoric of the sixties and early seventies may be gone, and so may some of the political activism, but the needs that generated the activism are more pressing than ever.

A more conservative national mood influences social policy from the federal to the local levels of government. Current rhetoric stresses maintaining the social "safety net" while eliminating expenditures for individuals who are not considered truly needy. Many communities, however, have found the safety net inadequate to deal with recession and long-term, structural unemployment. Meanwhile, in the ghettos that saw racial riots in the 1960s, conditions have improved little and in some ways have worsened. The social programs of the 1960s did not solve the problems of the inner cities, although explanations of why they did not differ as much as ideas about what should be done now.

Problems of poverty and the distribution of income lie largely beyond the scope of local planning. However, neighborhood revitalization and economic development are both concerns of local planners. It is important for planners to resist the argument that any revitalization or development benefits everyone. Some kinds of revitalization benefit some residents at the expense of others; for example, certain forms of economic development may leave behind the laid-off workers of defunct industries. Planners can play a significant role in the decision-making process by looking carefully at who gains and who loses. Beyond such an analysis, planners have a professional obligation under American Planning Association policy and under the 1981 American Institute of Certified Planners' Code of Professional Ethics

[to] strive to expand choice and opportunity for all persons, recognizing a special responsibility to plan for the needs of disadvantaged groups and persons, and must urge the alteration of policies, institutions and decisions which oppose such needs.[74]

The effectiveness of this socially responsive role rests first and foremost on careful and thorough technical analysis of the needs of different groups or the effects of a proposed project. Because social equity can be a politically divisive issue, this role means that planners must develop political as well as technical skills. Taking a more political stance need not mean generating conflict; more often, it will require that the planner build and mobilize support and try to deal realistically with the fears and concerns of opponents. This role requires skill and a continuing commitment to ensuring that the results of planning are fair to all groups in the community regardless of their political or social power.

More fundamentally, the social orientation advocated here is a traditional liberal perspective. It is closely associated with the idea that government should commit itself to helping those defined as being in need, while avoiding a paternalistic or bureaucratic approach. It is essential that planners recognize the need for a broad social perspective. Planning schools can cultivate this perspective. Planning work can be reorganized so that analysis of issues from the viewpoint of affected groups is added to functional and geographical assessments. New political skills will be required—skills that should be used for responsive and democratic ends. Rather than act on behalf of various groups, planners should help to empower members of the public, especially disadvantaged or dependent groups, to understand planning and to act for themselves in the planning process.[75] This approach includes the responsibility—required in APA's Social Responsibility policy and in the Code of Ethics—to ensure participation by affected citizens in the planning process. But it must also involve the provision of clear technical information, the exploration of policy alternatives, and a conscious effort not to depoliticize legitimately political issues.

1   Jerome Kaufman, "An Approach to Planning for Women," in Karen Hapgood and Judith Getzels, eds., *Planning, Women, and Change*, Planning Advisory Service Report no. 301 (Chicago: American Society for Planning Officials, 1974), 73–78.

2   Rolf Goetze and Kent W. Colton, "The Dynamics of Neighborhoods," *Journal of the American Planning Association* 46 (April 1980): 184–194.

3   U.S. Department of Commerce, Bureau of the Census, *Statistical Abstract of the United States: 1987* (Washington, DC: U.S. Government Printing Office, 1986).

4   George Sternlieb and James Hughes, "Less Space, More Demand," *Planning* 50 (January 1984): 4–8.

5   Dennis E. Gale, "Middle Class Resettlement in Older Urban Neighborhoods," *Journal of the American Planning Association* 45 (July 1979): 293–304, and John L. Goodman, Jr., "Reasons for Moves out of and into Large Cities," *Journal of the American Planning Association* 45 (October 1979): 407–416.

6   Brian Berry, "Islands of Renewal in Seas of Decay," in Paul E. Peterson, ed., *The New Urban Reality* (Washington DC: The Brookings Institution, 1985).

7   Shirley Bradway Laska and Daphne Spain, "Urban Policy and Planning in the Wake of Gentrification," *Journal of the American Planning Association* 45 (October 1979): 523–531.

8   Ibid., Table 55.

9   An extended treatment of planning issues growing out of these new demographic patterns that particularly affect women can be found in Eugenie Ladner Birch, ed., *The Unsheltered Woman: Women and Housing in the 80's* (New Brunswick, NJ: Rutgers University, Center for Urban Policy Research, 1985).

10 Mary Cichocki, "Women's Travel Patterns in a Suburban Development," in Gerda R. Wekerle, R. Peterson, and D. Morley, eds., *New Space for Women* (Boulder, Co: Westview Press, 1980), 151–163. See also Mary Ellen Mazey and David Lee, *Her Space, Her Place: A Geography of Women* (Washington DC: Association of American Geographers, 1983), 23.

11 Phyllis Kaniss and Barbara Robins, "The Transportation Needs of Women," in Karen Hapgood and Judith Getzels, eds., *Planning, Women, and Change,* Planning Advisory Service Report no. 301 (Chicago: American Society of Planning Officials, 1974), 66, and Marion B. Fox, "Working Women and Travel," *Journal of the American Planning Association* 49 (Spring 1983): 156–170.

12 David Popenoe, "Women in the Suburban Environment: A U.S.–Sweden Comparison," in Wekerle et al., *New Space for Women*, 165–173.

13 Popenoe, "Women in the Suburban Environment," 170.

14 Frank Spielberg and Stephen Andrle, "The Implications of Demographic Changes on Transportation Policy," *Journal of the American Planning Association* 48 (Summer 1982): 301–308.

15 Ibid.

16 Ibid., Table 61.

17 Ibid., Tables 751 and 446.

18 Birch, *The Unsheltered Woman*, Table 2.18.

19 Edith M. Netter and Ruth G. Price, "Zoning and the Nouveau Poor," *Journal of the American Planning Association* 49 (Spring 1983): 171–181.

20 *Statistical Abstract*, Tables 13, 38, 46, and 724.

21 Terry Saunders Lane and Judith Feins, "Are the Elderly Overhoused? Definitions of Space Utilization and Policy Implications," *The Gerontologist* 25 (June 1985): 243–250.

22 Elizabeth Howe, "Homesharing for the Elderly," *Journal of Planning Education and Research.* 4 (April 1985): 185–194.

23 Patrick H. Hare, "Carving Up the American Dream," *Planning* 47 (July 1981): 14–17, and Patrick H. Hare with Susan Conner and Dwight Merriam, *Accessory Apartments: Using Surplus Space in Single-Family Houses*, Planning Advisory Service Report no. 365 (Chicago: American Planning Association, 1981).

24 Carole R. Shifman, *Increasing Housing Opportunities for the Elderly,* Planning Advisory Service Report no. 381 (Chicago: American Planning Association, 1983).

25 Katharine Bradbury, Anthony Downs, and Kenneth Small, *Urban Decline and the Future of American Cities* (Washington, DC: The Brookings Institution, 1982).

26 Research on the unemployed includes Michael Aiken et al., *Economic Failure, Alienation and Extremism* (Ann Arbor: University of Michigan Press, 1968); E. Wight Bakke, *The Unemployed Worker* (New Haven: Yale University Press, 1940); E. Wight Bakke, *Citizens without Work* (New Haven: Yale University Press, 1940); Katherine Naherny, *Laid-off Industrial Workers in the Madison Area: The Patterns and Quality of Their Re-employment Experiences* (Madison, WI: Madison Department of Planning and Development, May 1985); and Richard C. Wilcock and Walter H. Franke, *Unwanted Workers* (New York: Free Press, 1963; Hippocrene Books, 1979).

27 Robert M. Moroney, "Needs Assessment for Human Services," in Wayne F. Anderson, Bernard J. Frieden, and Michael J. Murphy, eds., *Managing Human Services* (Washington, DC: International City Management Association, 1977).

28 Andre Delbecq, Andrew Van de Ven, and David Gustafson, *Group Techniques for Program Planning* (Glenview, IL: Scott, Foresman & Co., 1975).

29 Madison Economic Development Commission, *Enhancing the Madison Advantage* (Madison, WI, September 1983), 42.

30 James Peters, "Job Targeting: What Planners Can Do," *Planning* 49 (October 1983): 26–30.

31 A good survey of issues related to deinstitutionalization is Leona Bachrach, ed., *New Directions in Mental Health Services, vol. 17, Deinstitutionalization* (San Francisco: Jossey-Bass, March 1983).

32 Personal communication from Jerry Diamond,

Division of Care and Treatment Facilities, National Institute of Mental Health, August 1985.

33 "Public Housing Bill Approved by House," *New York Times* (12 June 1987), A16.

34 Bachrach, *New Directions in Mental Health Services.*

35 Daniel Lauber with Frank S. Bangs, Jr., *Zoning for Family and Group Care Facilities,* Planning Advisory Service Report no. 300 (Chicago: American Society of Planning Officials, 1974) 9. See also G. O'Connor, *Home Is a Place: A National Perspective on Community Residential Facilities for Developmentally Disabled Persons,* Monograph no. 2 (Washington, DC: American Association on Mental Deficiency, 1976).

36 *Village of Belle Terre* v. *Boraas,* 416 U.S. 1, 94 S.Ct. 1536, 39 L.Ed. 2d 797 (1974).

37 *Driscoll* v. *Austin Town,* 328 N.E. 2d 395 (1974), 42 Ohio 2d (1975); (1974). *White Plains* v. *Ferraioli,* 34 N.Y. 2d 300, 313 N.E. 2d 756 (1974); reversing 339 N.Y. 2d 27 (1972); and *Little Neck Community Association* v. *Working Organization for Retarded Children,* N. Y. S.Ct. 2d 364, 52AD 2d 90 (1976).

38 National Association of State Mental Retardation Program Directors, Inc., *Housing for Developmentally Disabled Citizens* (Washington, DC: U.S. Department of Health, Education and Welfare, November 1978), 146–147.

39 Clarence Sundram, "The Mentally Retarded and the Mentally Ill: Different Challenges for Community Care," *New England Journal of Human Services* 5 (Spring 1985): 14–16.

40 Judith G. Rabkin, Gregory Muhlin, and Patricia W. Cohen, "What the Neighbors Think: Community Attitudes Toward Local Psychiatric Facilities," *Community Mental Health Journal* 20 (Winter 1984): 309.

41 Rabkin et al., "What the Neighbors Think," and Dear and Taylor, *Not on Our Street,* 99.

42 Dear and Taylor, *Not on Our Street,* and S. M. Taylor et al., "Predicting Community Reaction to Mental Health Facilities," *Journal of the American Planning Association* 50 (Winter 1984): 36–47. See also Francis Moreau, Angela Novak, and Carol Sigelman, "Physical and Social Integration of Developmentally Disabled Individuals into the Community," in A. Novak and L. Heal, eds., *Integration of Developmentally Disabled Individuals into the Community* (Baltimore: Paul H. Brookes Publishers, 1980), 98.

43 Julian Wolpert, *Group Homes for the Mentally Retarded: An Investigation of Neighborhood Property Impacts* (Albany: New York State Office of Mental Retardation and Developmental Disabilities, August 1978), and Dear and Taylor, *Not on Our Street,* Chap. 9.

44 O'Connor, *Home Is a Place.*

45 Jennifer R. Wolch and Stuart A. Gabriel, "Dismantling the Community-Based Human Service System," *Journal of the American Planning Association* 51 (Winter 1985): 53–62.

46 Richard Babcock and Marlin Smith, "Zoning By the Numbers," *Planning* 51 (June 1985): 12–16.

47 Wolch and Gabriel, "Dismantling the Community-Based Human Service System."

48 Herbert Gans, *The Urban Villagers* (New York: The Free Press of Glencoe, 1963).

49 Marc Fried, "Grieving for a Lost Home: Psychological Costs of Relocation," in Leonard Duhl, ed., *The Urban Condition* (New York: Basic Books, 1963).

50 Chester Hartman, "The Housing of Relocated Families," *Journal of the American Institute of Planners* 30 (November 1964): 266–286 and U.S. Housing and Home Finance Agency, *The Housing of Relocated Families: Summary of a Census Bureau Survey* (Washington, DC., 1965).

51 Kenneth Watson, "Measuring and Mitigating Socio-Economic Environmental Impacts of Constructing Energy Projects: An Emerging Regulatory Issue," *Natural Resources Lawyer* 10 (1977): 397.

52 Dennis W. Ducsik, "Power Plants and People: A Profile of Electric Utility Initiatives in Cooperative Planning," *Journal of the American Planning Association* 50 (Spring 1984): 162–174.

53 Steve H. Murdock and F. Larry Leistritz, "Selecting Socioeconomic Assessment Models: A Discussion of Criteria and Selected Models," *Journal of Environmental Management* 10 (May 1980): 241–252.

54 The use of standards for projecting rate of service usage is always somewhat problematical. Such standards may be based either on previous local service levels or on nationally used, professionally derived standards. They may not correspond closely to the actual needs or demands that develop in the community during development. More fundamentally, there is not necessarily a clear relationship between the inputs measured by the standards— for example, square feet of space or staff-to-client ratios—and the actual outputs of the service. It is possible to have a school of "adequate" size with a staff that does not provide "adequate" education. See Herbert Gans, "Supplier-Oriented and User-Oriented Planning for the Public Library," in Herbert J. Gans, ed., *People and Plans: Essays on Urban Problems and Solutions* (New York: Basic Books, 1968), 98.

55 James Boggs, "Adversarial Politics and Indian Tribal Involvement in NEPA: A Case Study," in C. Geisler et al., eds., *Indian SIA: The Social Impact Assessment of Rapid Resource Development on Native Peoples,* Monograph no. 3 (Ann Arbor: University of Michigan Natural Resources Sociology Research Lab, 1982), 65–71.

56 Ducsik, "Power Plants and People."

57 Robert Moore, *The Social Impact of Oil: The Case of Peterhead* (London: Routledge & Kegan Paul, 1982), 48, and Elizabeth Moen et al., *Women and the Social Costs of Economic Development: Two Colorado Case Studies* (Boulder, CO: Westview Press, 1981).

58 Geisler et. al., *Indian SIA,* and Joseph Jorgensen et al., *Native Americans and Energy Development* (Cambridge, MA: Anthropology Research Center, 1978).

59 John Gilmore, "Boomtowns May Hinder Energy Resource Development," *Science* 191 (13 February 1976): 535–540; Steve H. Murdock and F. Larry Leistritz, *Energy Development in the Western United States* (New York: Praeger, 1979), Chaps. 8 and 9; Kurt Finsterbusch, *Understanding Social Impacts: Assessing the Effects of Public Projects,* Monograph no. 110 (Beverly Hills, CA: Sage Library of Social Research, 1980), Chap. 6; and Gary W. Malamud, *Boomtown Communities.* (New York: Van Nostrand Reinhold, 1984).

60 William R. Freudenburg, "Women and Men in an Energy Boomtown: Adjustment, Alienation, and Adaptation," *Rural Sociology* 46 (Summer 1981): 220–244; Lynn England and Stan Albrecht, "Boomtowns and Social Disruption," *Rural Sociology* 49 (Summer 1984): 230–246; and Richard

Krannich and Thomas Greider, "Personal Well-Being in Rapid-Growth and Stable Communities: Multiple Indicators and Contrasting Results," *Rural Sociology* 49 (Winter 1984): 541–552.

61 Howard J. Sumka, "Neighborhood Revitalization and Displacement: A Review of the Evidence," *Journal of the American Planning Association* 45 (October 1979): 480–487.

62 Michael Schill and Richard Nathan, *Revitalizing America's Cities: Neighborhood Reinvestment and Displacement* (Albany: State University of New York Press, 1983).

63 Jeffrey Henig, "Gentrification and Displacement of the Elderly: An Empirical Analysis," *The Gerontologist* 21 (February 1981): 67–75.

64 For a good example of the ideological debate, see the exchange between Howard J. Sumka and Chester Hartman in the *Journal of the American Planning Association's* special issue on neighborhood revitalization: Howard J. Sumka, "Neighborhood Revitalization and Displacement," and Chester Hartman, "Comment on 'Neighborhod Revitalization and Displacement: A Review of the Evidence,' " *JAPA* 45 (October 1979): 480–491.

65 Kathleen Christensen, *Social Impacts of Land Development: An Initial Approach for Estimating Impacts on Neighborhood Usages and Perceptions* (Washington DC: The Urban Institute, 1976), and Dean Runyan, "Tools for Community-Managed Impact Assessment," *Journal of the American Institute of Planners* 43 (April 1977): 125–135.

66 William Fulton, "A Room of One's Own," *Planning* 51 (September 1985): 18–22.

67 Joel Werth, "Tapping Developers," *Planning* 50 (January 1984): 21–23; Douglas R. Porter, "Boston's Linkage Program: Sharing or Shackling Downtown Development?" *Urban Land* (January 1985): 34–35; and "Building Housing Trust Funds," *Zoning News* (July 1985): 1–3.

68 Governor's Office of Planning and Research, *California Planner's Book of Lists* (Sacramento, CA, August 1985); League of California Cities, *Handbook: Assessing Human Needs* (Berkeley, CA: August 1975); and League of California Cities, *Social Element Planning in California* (Sacramento, CA: January 1977).

69 Wolch and Gabriel, "Dismantling the Community-Based Human Service System."

70 Cleveland City Planning Commission, *Cleveland Policy Planning Report, vol. 1* (Cleveland, 1975), and Norman Krumholz, Janice M. Cogger, and John H. Linner, "The Cleveland Policy Planning Report," *Journal of the American Institute of Planners* 41 (September 1975) 298–304.

71 Cleveland City Planning Commission, *Cleveland Policy Planning Report*, 9.

72 Norman Krumholz, "A Retrospective View of Equity Planning: Cleveland 1969–1979"; Jerome L. Kaufman, "Comment"; Paul Davidoff, "Comment"; and Lawrence Susskind, "Comment," *Journal of the American Planning Association* 48 (Spring 1982): 163–183.

73 Paul Davidoff, "Advocacy and Pluralism in Planning," *Journal of the American Institute of Planners* 31 (November 1965): 331–338 and Krumholz et al., "The Cleveland Policy Planning Report."

74 American Institute of Certified Planners, *Code of Ethics and Professional Conduct* (Washington, DC: American Planning Association, September 1981), (A)(5), and American Institute of Planners, *The Social Responsibility of the Planner* Washington, DC, 1973), 2.

75 For a similar argument, see John Forester, "Critical Theory and Planning Practice," *Journal of the American Planning Association* 46 (July 1980): 275–286; John Forester, "Planning in the Face of Power," *Journal of the American Planning Association* 48 (Winter 1982): 67–80; and Howell S. Baum, *Planners and Public Expectations* (Cambridge, MA: Schenkman Books, Inc., 1983), Chap. 8.

12 Planning for housing

Physically, socially, and economically, housing is one of the most important elements in our lives. Housing begins as shelter; unsafe, unsanitary, and inadequate housing can affect our physical and mental health, privacy, and security. The physical condition of housing is a matter of public health, and the regulation of housing through zoning, subdivision controls, building and housing codes, and sanitation ordinances has been an accepted part of local government activities for many years.

The location of housing as well as its physical condition affects the quality of community living. Location determines access to community facilities, transportation, shopping, jobs, and schools. Location also provides social contacts, friendships, and a sense of belonging.

Economically, housing has important impacts. Housing-related expenses constitute a major portion of personal budgets of households (about 25 percent, not including furnishings). Furthermore, a home is the largest investment and principal savings vehicle for most households.

Residential development is usually the overwhelmingly predominant user of urban land and thus has considerable impact on local government. Property taxes on housing are a principal source of local government income, and services to housing and households are a major local government expenditure. In suburban areas, infrastructure serves largely residential uses.

Housing is also a major component of the national economy. In 1984 residential construction represented almost 47 percent of the value of construction put in place.[1] In addition, there was construction for utilities, streets, schools, and community facilities to support housing. As already noted, almost 25 percent of personal income expenditures are for housing services.[2]

This chapter presents a framework for addressing the role of local government in housing. First the governmental roles in housing are examined. Next a description of the various components of the housing industry are presented. Then goals and standards for housing are discussed to identify directions for local government action. Finally an outline for housing planning is presented. Housing is no longer a simple problem of physical planning, zoning, and code enforcement.

Governmental roles in housing

Housing is today, and has always been, primarily a function of private industry and private ownership in the United States. Although the land use powers of local government have always been a critical factor, the role of local government has been limited largely to regulation and provision of services: Local governments zone the land, impose standards on construction, and provide physical support—water, sewer, and roads—and protective functions—police and fire.

Apart from regulation of the private market, government intervention in housing has usually been limited to areas in which the private sector is deficient. Until recently, most government intervention originated at the federal level. The federal government provided the funds, the programs, and the rules to eliminate slums, to build housing for the poor, and to fight racial segregation. Although these programs have been implemented locally, for the most part the federal government has been looked to as the source of solutions to housing problems.

In recent years, however, the federal government has reduced its involvement in housing. In its 1982 report, the President's Commission on Housing advocated a transfer of housing responsibilities to state and local government, a reliance on housing allowances instead of construction subsidies, and a focus on financing and regulatory problems in housing, primarily at the state and local levels.

People live in places, and land is intrinsically local, its uses controlled by local regulation. The legal order and legislative atmosphere needed for housing to thrive in this society must be created by States and localities.[3]

At the same time that the federal government has withdrawn from many housing subsidy programs, federal deregulation of financial institutions has disrupted traditional sources of funding for housing. New priorities, particularly tax reform and the reduction of the federal deficit, also are affecting support for housing.

While the federal role has diminished, the segment of the population affected by housing problems has broadened. Housing affordability was once a problem primarily for the poor in declining central cities. By the early eighties, affordability had become a concern for middle-income families in suburban areas. In the late 1970s and early 1980s, inflation increased, the availability of housing credit declined, housing prices and interest rates soared, and access to home ownership for many households, particularly young ones, became an impossible dream. Changing demographics and limited funds for infrastructure presented additional challenges to local government managers and housing planners.

Planning for housing at the local level is becoming more important. States are

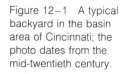

Figure 12–1   A typical backyard in the basin area of Cincinnati; the photo dates from the mid-twentieth century.

now assuming more responsibility and providing more financial support for housing, replacing the federal government as the policy and program provider. Both local and state governments will need to develop a better understanding of the dimensions and dynamics of housing. Government attention to housing began with concern for the effects of slums on health. By the latter part of the nineteenth century, industrialization, large-scale immigration, and migration into cities had created appalling housing conditions in crowded urban areas. Crime and poor mental and physical health were associated problems.[4] Crusades for better housing and for the elimination of slums were among the earliest movements leading to establishing city planning in the United States.[5] Concern for the health and safety of residents led to the adoption of laws regulating land use and construction in urban areas, including building codes, sanitation ordinances, safety regulations, and zoning and subdivision controls.

One observer has written that "progress in housing legislation has generally been a response to crisis conditions."[6] Development of housing programs has followed identifiable crises or periods of major change.

The changing federal role

The federal government is involved in housing in a number of ways. First, it provides housing subsidies and community development grants. Second, it regulates private financial institutions and has established federal instruments that provide insurance, liquidity, and credit for housing. Third, federal tax policies are a major influence on housing. Fourth, civil rights legislation is the major means of addressing discrimination in housing.

Development and effects of federal programs[7]   The major federal housing programs began evolving during the Depression. One set of programs affected housing finance; the other established housing programs for the poor.

During the Depression, large numbers of housing mortgages were defaulted, and owners lost their homes. Banks were reluctant to lend money and savers reluctant to deposit in banks. The Housing Act of 1934 created new credit instruments to guarantee depositors' money in banks and to insure mortgages. The creation of the Federal Housing Administration (FHA) in 1934 revolutionized housing finance. The FHA did not lend money but rather insured mortgages. If a borrower defaulted on an FHA mortgage, the FHA assumed financial responsibility. This encouraged banks to resume lending. But beyond eliminating risk for lenders, the FHA changed the practices of mortgage lending by insuring longer-term loans, establishing greater loan-to-value ratios, and providing for uniform, self-amortizing payments over the life of the loan.

Although World War II slowed these activities, a major housing tool was added at the end of the war when the Veterans Administration (VA) home loan program was established. This program provided loan guarantees for low-interest, long-term mortgages requiring low down payments.

Following the war, FHA- and VA-insured mortgages fueled a period of unparalleled suburban housing development and a rapid growth in homeownership, from less than 45 percent of occupied housing in 1940 to more than 60 percent by 1960. Although FHA and VA programs now insure a small proportion of home mortgages and have been replaced largely by private mortgage insurance, they established a pattern in mortgage lending that has made homeownership the norm in the United States. By 1983, 64.7 percent of occupied year-round units were owner occupied.

The provision of housing for the poor was less successful. Public housing was established by the Housing Act of 1937. This program financed housing for the poor by giving funds to local public housing authorities who built, owned, and operated the housing. The program was linked to slum clearance because it initially required the demolition of a slum housing unit for each public housing unit built.

After World War II, the slum clearance aspect of the program was established independently of the provision of public housing. The Housing Act of 1949 created the Urban Renewal program, which provided funds to local urban renewal agencies to acquire land, clear it where necessary, plan, and resell the land to private developers at market rates. The federal funds, together with local funds, provided the difference between acquisition and preparation costs and the eventual sale price. Unlike the Housing Act of 1937, which focused on public housing, the Urban Renewal program was initially concerned with redevelopment of residential slums. However, the desirability of using federal funds to replace deteriorating central-city areas led to the expansion of urban renewal to include commercial, industrial, and institutional redevelopment. Although federal support for public housing continued, it was overshadowed by broader redevelopment objectives and was never the most favored federal subsidy available to local governments.

In the 1950s and 1960s, a succession of federal housing acts modified the basic public housing, urban renewal, and FHA programs. Many of the modifications initially were made to accommodate the needs of urban renewal. The federal government extended the range of activities included in urban renewal and added grants for community facilities. FHA insurance was modified to insure special housing categories by providing liberalized terms, covering riskier investments, and encouraging developers to enter more questionable markets. Direct federal lending and subsidized interest rates, originally limited to public housing for very low-income people, were extended to privately owned housing for certain moderate-income elderly and handicapped persons and those displaced by government actions. Through insurance and direct spending, the federal government then began providing much broader housing assistance. Usually, the housing providers were nonprofit or limited-dividend corporations.[8]

During the years of growth in the scope and scale of federal government programs, most private housing activity took the form of suburban expansion and "white flight," or exodus from central cities. Dissatisfaction with the conditions in central cities contributed to a series of riots by blacks left behind in the late sixties. These riots encouraged a new look at federal policies.

Two national study groups in 1968 investigated the nation's housing, and their reports are still among the most comprehensive housing evaluations available. The President's Committee on Urban Housing (the Kaiser Committee)[9] and the National Commission on Urban Problems (the Douglas Commission)[10] established the first, and only, federal quantitative housing goals—26 million new or rehabilitated housing units in ten years (including 6 million units for low- and moderate-income families)—and they recommended new federal subsidy programs that would help the nation reach this goal. In the 1968 Housing Act, Congress adopted the goal and the programs,[11] but almost twenty years later the goal for publicly assisted housing is still unmet. There has always been the need but never the demand. Publicly assisted housing for low-income persons has never been the top priority of local governments for development or redevelopment, and federal support has never been sufficient to accomplish the goal.

In the late 1960s and early 1970s, federal subsidy and development programs shifted again. The War on Poverty and other programs had produced hundreds of categorical grants for local (and sometimes state) governments. In 1974 urban renewal as a separate program was ended and was combined with other development grants in the Community Development Block Grant (CDBG) program. The CDBG program was designed to simplify federal aid and increase local discretion in the use of funds. The 1974 legislation also established the Section 8 rent supplement, which broadened the way private housing could be subsidized.

Under Section 8, all or part of the units in a rental structure could be subsidized. The units could be new, rehabilitated, or existing.

In 1977 the Urban Development Action Grant (UDAG) was created to supplement private investment. The UDAG provides federal grants to leverage private capital for development projects—including housing—that would not be feasible without a subsidy. Both the CDBG and the UDAG have remained through the 1980s, at reduced funding levels. Although they are primarily intended to aid lower-income persons and can be used for housing, they also are used for other development. The CDBG program is locally allocated. The UDAG grants are awarded at the central HUD office by national competition. In 1983 the Housing Development Grant (HoDAG) was established to make grants specifically to housing projects, again by national competition.

In the early and middle 1980s, concerns with the federal deficit led to curtailments of aid to state and local governments, cutbacks in existing programs, and reductions in new authorizations for housing construction subsidies.

In 1982 a third presidential study group reported on housing and arrived at a view of the housing problem and its solutions that was quite different from the views of the Kaiser and Douglas groups. The President's Commission on Housing concluded that housing was basically a state and local responsibility. It advocated concentrating on federal housing allowances for individuals rather than on construction subsidies. It also recommended less federal intervention in housing finance, more concentration on land use regulatory reform, primarily at the state and local levels, and elimination of tax policies that subsidized housing through federal tax deductions.[12] The report declined to project any housing need. The commission's report reflects a concern for the federal deficit and a perceived need to reduce social spending.

As the decade of the eighties moves beyond the midpoint, the federal government continues to withdraw from its fifty years of support for housing. After years of federal subsidies for housing programs, one might expect that there would be large stocks of assisted housing. In reality, federally assisted housing represents a very small part of the housing supply. In 1983, when there were about 93.5 million housing units in the United States, only 1.48 million were public housing—1.6 percent of housing stock. All assisted housing in the United States (including housing for the elderly and Section 8) totaled 3.7 million units, constituting about 4 percent of supply.[13] As one noted observer commented, "There has developed over the years a substantial national housing policy and national housing program. Yet the absolute accomplishment[s] of these efforts in meeting the housing crisis are amazingly small when measured against the dimensions of need."[14]

The federal government and housing finance   FHA and VA insurance are only a part of the federal government's role in housing finance and investment.[15] Federal regulation of financial institutions helps protect a line of credit for housing. The Federal Reserve System regulates and provides credit to federally chartered member banks. The Federal Home Loan Bank system provides credit and regulates federal savings and loan associations, which have been the principal source of mortgage credit. The Federal Deposit Insurance Corporation and Federal Savings and Loan Insurance Corporation insure deposits in federally chartered institutions, safeguarding depositor's savings against possible bank failure.

Federal, quasi-public agencies are the major secondary market for mortgages in the United States. The secondary mortgage market provides liquidity to the mortgage market by enabling the originators of mortgages to sell them to other investors rather than holding them. The Government National Mortgage Association (GNMA) buys mortgages backed by FHA and VA insurance, pools them, and issues securities based on those mortgages. The Federal National

Mortgage Association (FNMA) buys and holds mortgages, including conventional ones. The Federal Home Loan Mortgage Corporation (FHLMC) packages mortgages from its member institutions and sells securities. Securities backed by pooled mortgages and sold to investors are termed "pass-through" securities. When they are backed by federal insurance, they can be attractive investments. Private pass-through securities backed by mortgages have not yet developed as a major private investment vehicle. Another important source of funds for housing is rural credit, which has long been supplied by the Farmers Home Administration (FmHA) through direct loans for rural housing and community development.

Income tax provisions may be among the most important federal financial policies affecting housing. For example, the fact that apartment owners have been able to take depreciation on their rental properties has attracted investors seeking a tax shelter. Tax credits for rehabilitation of rental property have encouraged conversions and redevelopment in urban areas. But the most important income tax provision has been the deduction allowed to homeowners for payment of mortgage interest and property taxes. While housing advocates have sought subsidies to aid low-income families, tax laws have, in effect, made homeowners the major recipients of housing subsidy. The deductions granted homeowners each year are estimated to be worth far more than all expenditures for low- and moderate-income housing.[16]

Changes in federal tax policies, whatever form they take, inevitably affect housing practices. The federal deficit, concerns over the need for tax simplification, and increasing taxes have contributed to the impetus for tax reform. The Tax Reform Act of 1986 affects housing negatively in several ways. It has made rental housing less attractive as an investment and reduced the use of tax-exempt revenue bonds for financing housing. Reduced tax rates make all deductions, credits, and tax shelters less valuable. Investment in real estate is now less attractive because depreciation allowances are reduced, capital gains are taxed as ordinary income, and losses from passive investments are limited. Rental housing investments, particularly for low-income housing, often depended on tax deductions and credits to make them financially attractive. Tax-exempt revenue bonds are now "capped," that is, there are limits on the total amounts states can issue. In addition, there are stringent requirements on the kinds of projects revenue bonds can finance. Rental projects using revenue bonds must serve more low-income residents than was previously required. The use of tax-exempt revenue bonds for single-family mortgages is slated for elimination. The interest deduction for homeowners remains, however.

Civil rights   One of the aims of federal civil rights legislation has been the provision of equal housing opportunity. Legislation prohibits discrimination in any federally assisted housing, bars discrimination in the sale, rental, or financing of most housing, and requires federal agencies to incorporate affirmative action into the administration of their programs. Federal civil rights legislation is aimed at more than the elimination of discrimination; it actively promotes integration.[17]

The emerging state role

States are playing an increasingly important role in the financing, provision, support, and regulation of housing.[18] Almost all states have housing finance agencies that provide tax-exempt mortgage financing for housing. In addition, many states have other forms of financial subsidies for selected housing or households. States provide a variety of community development assistance and infrastructure assistance. The regulation of housing takes many forms, some protecting consumers and others restricting development. Finally, many states have consumer protection and antidiscrimination laws.

Financial assistance   In some forty-six states, housing finance agencies administer state-sponsored housing programs.[19] After World War II, several states initiated home loan programs for veterans and issued tax-exempt bonds to underwrite the mortgages. During the 1970s, as federal government programs expanded, states began to develop additional finance programs to complement the federal programs. Often they facilitated federal programs; states might, for example, provide tax-exempt construction loans as well as permanent financing for housing construction receiving federal rent subsidies.

State housing programs are sometimes funded with general obligation bonds but more often with revenue bonds. Revenue bonds were initially issued only for multifamily housing, but beginning in 1975, states started to issue tax-exempt revenue bonds for single-family housing. The tax-exempt bonds carry below-market interest rates and can therefore be reloaned to builders and homeowners as mortgages with interest rates below conventional mortgage rates. Although this is a popular way to reduce the cost of housing, the federal treasury "pays" for the cost of the lower interest rate with forgone income taxes. By 1980 tax-exempt financing for housing had become so popular that it represented about 30 percent of all municipal bonds.[20] Amid concern for the rising federal deficit and widespread interest in tax reform, tax-exempt financing, particularly revenue bonds, eventually came under fire. In 1980 the Mortgage Subsidy Bond Tax Act first proposed to phase out tax-exempt revenue bonds for single-family housing and put limits on other revenue bonds. The Tax Reform Act of 1986, as noted, has limited the use of tax-exempt revenue bonds for housing, severely restricting a major tool for states.

In addition to tax-exempt bonds, many states have provided other subsidies to housing. These include property tax abatement and direct assistance to special groups. Property tax abatement reduces the operating costs of housing and has been provided to developers to encourage construction of certain kinds of housing. In some states, property tax abatement or rebates are given to certain elderly or low-income households.

Direct assistance is also provided for the special housing needs of elderly persons and of mentally or physically handicapped individuals. State movements to deinstitutionalize mentally ill or retarded persons have created a need for alternative housing. Many states provide financing for group homes for developmentally disadvantaged or disabled residents. The regulation and licensing of congregate housing is an increasing state responsibility; for example, states regulate life-care communities and domiciliary and nursing homes. Some states have begun programs to provide emergency shelters for the homeless and for abused spouses.

State governments have traditionally provided assistance for infrastructure. The demand for this assistance appears to be increasing, perhaps in part because federal funding is being reduced. States provide loans, direct grants, or tax sharing for transportation, water and sewer facilities, and schools. Newer approaches to providing support for housing include making state-owned land available at little or no cost.[21]

State regulations   State housing regulations are probably more important than either federal or local ones.[22] Statewide building and housing codes have been recommended as a means of overcoming restrictive and diverse local codes and of standardizing construction requirements. However, few statewide codes actually exist. Some states *have* preempted regulation of manufactured housing.

Environmental regulations, which have been increasing in recent years, have both favorable and unfavorable effects on housing production. The disposal of hazardous wastes and toxic chemicals and the safeguarding of old landfills are receiving increased attention as polluted groundwater affects communities. Stormwater management, conservation of wetlands, flood protection, and sediment control are areas where states are developing additional programs to safeguard natural resources. Although the protection of resources is important, it can burden builders. State regulations are frequently cited as contributing to the rising cost of housing, as the growing number of permits and inspections required increases the time and costs involved in development.

Civil and consumer rights   While the federal government has provided leadership in eliminating discrimination, states have also been active supporters of civil and consumer rights. States promote the construction of low- and moderate-income housing by establishing target levels for such construction and by withholding state discretionary grants from communities that fail to provide specified levels of low- and moderate-income housing.[23]

In the area of consumer rights, states have passed legislation to define landlord-tenant rights, to protect buyers of new homes from poor construction, and to establish procedures for converting apartments to condominiums.

The variety of housing programs originating at the state level is almost endless, and new and innovative programs are constantly being developed. Housing advocates today are focusing their energy and attention on the states.

The local housing agenda

Although the federal and state governments are responsible for financial and regulatory functions that affect housing, local government plays the major governmental role. For example, neither the federal nor the state government builds housing; it is at the local level that housing is actually provided. Local government bears the major responsibility for accommodating, supporting, and regulating housing; virtually no housing is possible without some local approval. As housing issues broaden from housing the poor to include affordability by middle-income persons, housing the elderly, providing consumer protection, and other concerns, more local governments are undertaking housing programs. Previously, housing was of concern primarily to central cities. Today, many suburban areas have housing programs of one kind or another.

Directly or indirectly, almost every local government activity is linked to housing. Local government has always provided the land use controls, subdivision regulations, and building and housing codes that affect housing. Local government provides the services that people require and that determine the quality of life in residential communities. It provides the infrastructure and builds the streets, sewer and water lines, and schools. It also collects garbage and provides police and fire protection, recreation, and health and social services.

Financial support   Most local financial support to housing is derived from federal or state subsidy programs. Although reductions in federal aid have made less assistance available, the CDBG, UDAG, and HoDAG programs do give local governments more discretion in how assistance is used. These programs also require local government concurrence; in the past, some federally subsidized housing could be developed without local participation.

While overall federal subsidies are decreasing, state subsidy programs are growing. Because local governments have considerable influence on state legislatures and agencies, state funding programs are often more responsive to local needs than are federal ones. Some local governments do finance their own housing subsidies by issuing bonds or making appropriations for assistance. In addition, many local governments have adopted forms of tax abatement as part of public policy. Whether assistance originates at the federal, state, or local level, it is the local government that determines where and how it will be applied.

Development programs The provision of infrastructure and the determination of land use are two traditional local government functions that affect housing. In recent years, local governments have begun to approach—and use—these functions in new ways. For example, to ensure that infrastructure is provided and financed in an orderly way, local governments are turning to growth management, impact fees, and other techniques, such as adequate public facilities ordinances. Much infrastructure cost at the local level is beginning to be carried by new development.

Local governments are routinely examining land use and other regulations to assess their impact on housing and housing costs. Efforts to provide affordable housing are increasing. Local governments are also modernizing building codes, which are frequently outdated, raise housing costs by prohibiting the use of newer materials, and restrict experimentation in construction.

Social programs Consumer protection regulations, antidiscrimination ordinances, and other social programs have long been implemented at the local level, where problems often become apparent long before they reach state or federal agendas. Emergency shelter for homeless or abused people first appeared at the local level. Concern about deinstitutionalized mentally ill or retarded individuals was also first apparent at the local level. Local measures affecting housing include rent control, affirmative action in real estate marketing, fair housing legislation, and landlord-tenant legislation.

It is appropriate that planning for housing occur at the local level, because it is there that housing is built, serviced, and regulated. Although many housing programs are developed at the federal or state level, it is only at the local level that they can be implemented.

The dynamics of housing

Housing can be understood as having three interrelated components: supply, demand, and finance. Government can be viewed as intervening to alter the relationship among these components. Housing planning identifies and defines the nature of that intervention.

Housing supply includes all existing housing stock; new construction; and the labor, industry, and services required to maintain the supply. Housing demand is determined by the number and characteristics of consumers of housing services, ownership patterns, and market behavior. Supply and demand are greatly influenced by financial institutions and their operations.

Housing supply

Characteristics of housing supply Housing supply in the United States has two principal characteristics. First, the vast majority of housing is provided by the private sector; this is in marked contrast to the situation in other industrialized countries, where government is a major producer of housing. Second, private ownership is widely dispersed. The United States is a nation of homeowners: almost 65 percent of all units are owner occupied. Ownership of rental housing is very broadly based.

The basic unit of measurement for housing supply is the housing unit, which may be a single-family house, apartment, or condominium. As of 1983, the United States had 93.5 million housing units, not including group quarters or transient facilities.

The U.S. Census classifies housing units by characteristics that include tenure, housing type, size, and cost. Tenure refers to whether the occupant is a renter or an owner. Type refers to building structure (single-family, attached or detached; multifamily, low-, medium-, or high-rise). There are also specialty terms such

Figure 12–2 Housing types include single-family, attached or detached, multifamily, and low-, medium-, or high-rise.

374 The Practice of Local Government Planning

as duplex, quadriplex, or town house. The most important measure of size is the number of bedrooms, which indicates the number of people who can live in the unit. Square feet of floor area also indicates size. Cost is measured by rent or sale price. Gross rent, as contrasted with shelter rent, includes utilities. Contract rent, the payment from the lessee to the lessor, can be either gross or shelter. Other characteristics tracked by the Census include year the structure was built, availability of plumbing, number of units in a structure, and condition.

Additions to housing supply   The fluctuation in housing production from year to year has a major influence on the national economy, and it is not unusual for housing construction to rise and fall dramatically. A drop in new housing starts can cause unemployment in the construction industry and financial problems for builders. Between 1970 and 1985 (Table 12–1), housing production varied from a low of 1.072 million units in 1982 to a high of 2.379 in 1972. Production in 1972 was 220 percent of the 1982 level. Despite the attention it receives as an economic indicator, new housing constitutes a small portion of housing stock, usually between 2 and 3 percent. In 1983 the 1.7 million units added were less than 2 percent of total supply.

Changing patterns in housing production   The types of housing produced reflect factors such as demographic change, consumer preference, and cost. In 1971, 1972, and 1973, new housing production was high—more than 2 million units started each year—and a large proportion of that (44–45 percent) was multi-family housing. By the mid and late seventies, however, both the number and the percentage of multifamily housing declined.

One of the most significant changes in new housing is the continuing increase in cost. In 1970 the median selling price of a new one-family home was $23,400. By 1984 this figure had risen to $79,900. As housing prices have risen, significantly more attached single-family units have been started. As rental property has become less attractive for investment, almost one-third of all multifamily units constructed have been condominiums. Mobile homes represent a continuing source of lower-income housing.

The development process   Housing development is a complex process involving financing, planning, building, and marketing. Before building, a developer must acquire land; secure zoning and other government permits; and prepare site plans, building plans, and specifications. Before a site is buildable, it requires access to community facilities including roads, utilities, sewers, and water.

Construction includes two phases: site preparation and building construction. Site preparation requires grading and building streets and extending water, sewerage, and other utilities to the building sites. Building construction is a combination of on-site and off-site work with various components of material and labor.

Industrialized housing, or the factory production of housing, has frequently been proposed as a solution to high housing costs. Many who regard the home-building industry as inefficient—composed of small, local builders who lack stability and continuity—view factory production as a way to increase production, reduce costs, promote efficiency, and stabilize employment in the construction industry. Until recently, however, efforts to industrialize housing have met with greatest success in the growing use of factory-built components.

Housing demand

The demand for housing can be aggregated into a total housing market demand with many submarkets.[24] The major market is divided between renters and owners, and, as was mentioned earlier, the majority of households own in this country. Government encourages ownership, believing that owners represent

Table 12–1 New housing units started, United States, 1970–1985 (thousands).

| | | | Private starts only | | | | |
| | | | Single-family | | Multifamily | | |
Year	Total	Total private	Number	Percentage	Number	Percentage	Mobile-home shipments
1970	1,469	1,434	813	56.7	621	43.3	401
1971	2,085	2,052	1,151	56.1	901	43.9	497
1972	2,379	2,357	1,309	55.5	1,048	44.5	576
1973	2,057	2,045	1,132	55.4	913	44.6	567
1974	1,353	1,338	888	66.4	450	33.6	329
1975	1,171	1,160	892	76.9	268	23.1	213
1976	1,548	1,538	1,162	75.6	376	24.4	246
1977	2,002	1,987	1,451	73.0	536	27.0	277
1978	2,036	2,020	1,433	70.9	587	29.1	276
1979	1,760	1,745	1,194	68.4	551	31.6	277
1980	1,313	1,292	852	65.9	440	34.1	222
1981	1,100	1,084	705	65.0	379	35.0	241
1982	1,072	1,062	662	62.3	400	37.7	240
1983	1,712	1,703	1,068	62.7	635	37.3	296
1984	1,756	1,749	1,084	62.0	665	38.0	296
1985	1,745	1,742	1,072	61.5	670	38.5	284

Figure 12–3 Mobile homes are one source of housing for lower-income households.

better managers of housing, contribute more taxes, make a greater contribution to the community, and have a bigger stake in the future.

The forms of ownership include cooperatives and condominiums, which combine the financial benefits of ownership with the service benefits of renting. In recent years, the attractiveness of rental property as an investment has declined, and many rental buildings have been converted to condominiums.[25] This has spurred legislation to protect renters who occupy buildings undergoing conversion.

Housing choice   The basic unit of housing consumption is the household. The demand of households determines in large measure where housing units will be located in relation to population. Demand, in turn, is influenced by two factors, both of which are weighed by consumers in their choice of housing: location and cost. In addition to seeking a specific housing type, households consider amenities and the nature of the community. The same house will bring different prices in different neighborhoods, because in addition to buying housing, consumers also buy access to employment, transportation, community facilities, schools, recreation, open space, and types of neighbors. In making a housing choice, households weigh location against what they are willing and able to pay. Because the bulk of the housing stock is supplied by the private sector, income is a major determinant of choice. Lower-income households have always had fewer selections to choose from. As housing costs rise, fewer households are able to occupy new housing, and more must pay a greater share of their incomes for housing.

One of the goals of housing planning is to ensure that the needs of households can be matched appropriately to housing—in other words, to enlarge choice. Major changes in population characteristics, such as the aging of the population, the increase in the number of smaller households, and the decrease in the number of children, need to be taken into account in planning for housing.

Vacancy   Vacancy is an important housing indicator because it indicates the degree of choice available. Too high a vacancy rate can be disastrous for owners

---

Opening up the suburbs to multi-family housing development   In 1976, the geographic distribution of low-income housing in the Minneapolis/St. Paul metropolitan area was, to say the least, lopsided: 90 percent of it was located in the two central cities, which together account for only 30 percent of the region's total population. Suburban land zoned for housing and already serviced by regional sewer and highway systems was in abundant supply, but low- and moderate-income housing was not being developed. The reason: restrictive approval processes. . . .

By 1986, the situation had changed. The suburban share of low-income housing in the region had climbed to 40 percent. . . . The number of suburban multifamily units approved from 1983 to 1985 was more than 100 times the number approved from 1973 to 1975. . . .

This dramatic turnaround has resulted in large part from the Minnesota Land Planning Act and the Twin Cities Metropolitan Council plans and policies enacted in the mid-1970s. The legislation has protected the review process from much of the local opposition and

dramatically decreased the amount of political controversy previously associated with multifamily housing approvals. . . .

In 1976, the council adopted a growth guidance system for the area, known as the Development Framework. It also persuaded the Minnesota legislature to include in the Minnesota Land Planning Act a requirement that each local governmental unit within the Twin Cities metropolitan area prepare a comprehensive plan and that each plan contain a housing element. . . . to meet existing and projected local and regional housing needs, including but not limited to the use of official controls and land use planning to promote the availability of land for the development of low- and moderate-income housing.

It also mandated a *Mount Laurel*-type regional fair-share obligation. . . .

These comprehensive plan provisions were enforced, in turn, through two consistency requirements that prohibited a municipality from adopting any official control (zoning, subdivision, and so on) or fiscal device that conflicted with its comprehensive plan, and

trying to sell or rent. Too low a vacancy rate can force prices up. Vacancies between 4 and 5 percent are usually considered healthy.

The Census reports several categories of vacancies. A portion of units are vacant because they are used seasonally or by migrant workers. The rest are year-round vacancies and include those for sale or rent. Within this category, however, some units are second homes held for occasional use, some are awaiting occupancy after being sold or rented, and some are pending settlement of an estate.

Mobility and filtering   Mobility, another important factor in the housing market, reflects both supply and demand. Mobility allows people to alter their housing as their economic or social circumstances change. About 17 percent of the U.S. population moves annually, primarily to a different housing unit within the same area. About 60 percent of all movers stay in the same county, and almost 80 percent stay within the same state.

A move by one household means that its former unit becomes available. This sets up a chain of additional moves, until a unit is vacated that is then removed from the housing supply or until a new household is formed without a unit being vacated.

The term *filtering* refers to the process involving a chain of moves. Housing *trickles down* if it becomes available to a lower-income family; it *trickles up* if it is occupied by a higher-income family. In a well-functioning housing market, new housing supply will improve housing choice by beginning a series of moves

---

required each city to amend its zoning ordinances and other official controls to conform to its comprehensive plan. . . .

Each municipality's housing plans were required to contain a detailed description of existing housing stock by type, size, and age, including vacancy rates for nonowner-occupied units, a set of local policies detailing future municipal goals for all forms of housing, and an implementation program identifying specific measures (lot-size reduction, tax increment and bonding programs, housing authority programs, and so on) that would be instituted to achieve the numerical goals. Communities were encouraged to specify in their comprehensive plans urbanized areas that were the most desirable locations for multifamily housing. . . .

Previously, Twin Cities communities had evaluated multifamily housing proposals on an ad hoc basis. Their decisions were based on regulations designed primarily to control the "nature" of a development. Such regulations could be interpreted subjectively to keep out the "wrong" kind of development or the "wrong" kind of people, and decisionmakers were eas-

ily pressured to do just that. Requests for rezoning to higher density were easily denied, because no overall housing plan existed, supported by maps, to prove rational basis. . . .

The comprehensive plan system now in effect has provided the necessary backbone with which local elected officials can make politically tough decisions. Municipalities and developers now use the same information to determine the need for and location of multifamily housing. Each community is required to act upon each application in a manner consistent with its comprehensive plan and housing element. City council members now have the tools to withstand neighborhood objections. They can base their approvals of higher-density, multifamily housing on a foundation that is legally, factually, and politically sound. . . .

Source: Adapted from Robert L. Hoffman and Forrest D. Nowlin, "Opening Up the Suburbs to Multifamily Housing Development," *Urban Land* (April 1986), 34–35.

Figure 12–4   Housing today needs to serve a wide variety of people and ways of living— young singles, older people, families with children, young couples, and groups of many kinds.

that will eventually allow the worst housing to be vacated and then eliminated. Filtering is sometimes put forth as a means of providing better housing for the poor by providing additional housing for middle- and upper-income families. In fact, a significant amount of new housing does replace housing removed from supply each year. Almost one-third of annual housing production replaces existing inventory.

Gentrification   Gentrification is a process in which demand created by middle- and upper-income households acts to change traditionally poorer urban neighborhoods. As more affluent households move into these neighborhoods, they rehabilitate houses and displace the original occupants. Rehabilitation increases property values and therefore rents and taxes, encouraging current residents to leave. Although outright eviction or displacement seldom occurs, gentrification is nevertheless a problem in some changing urban neighborhoods.

Discrimination   Some households are excluded from housing by deliberate marketing practices. Although blacks and other racial minorities have suffered the most, other groups may also meet with discrimination—for example, homosexual or handicapped people, and welfare recipients.

Overt discrimination is rare, but since minorities also frequently have low incomes, the simple failure to provide housing for low-income households excludes them. These exclusionary policies, particularly in suburban areas, have kept blacks and other racial and ethnic minorities from the suburbs. The 1980 Census reported that about 73 percent of all blacks and 60 percent of Hispanic people were in the central-city portion of metropolitan areas. By contrast, only 36 percent of metropolitan whites still lived in central cities.

The housing market area   To the local planner analyzing supply and demand, the housing market area is an important concept. The term is used to designate the region within which housing is generally competitive.

A housing market area is the physical area within which all dwelling units are linked together in a chain of substitution. . . . In a broad sense, every dwelling unit within a local housing market may be considered a substitute for every other unit. Hence all dwelling units may be said to form a single market, characterized by interactions of occupancy, prices, and rents.[26]

The housing market area is the physical area in which daily economic, geographic, and social interdependencies exist. The major factors in defining a housing market area are its interdependent economic and employment structures, but additional factors include shared institutions, transportation systems, educational and health facilities, wholesale and retail trade centers, and communication networks. Geographical features, such as rivers, mountains, or forests, may define the physical boundaries of a market area. People are tied to particular locations because of jobs, family, or other personal relationships, and they seek housing in areas where they have reasons to live. They rarely move to a new region merely because of the availability of housing.

Financial aspects of housing

The United States has a complex and complete housing finance system that operates, in general, to make us a well-housed society. Although financing is critical to the operation of the housing market,[27] the financing of housing is often taken for granted because it is well developed and operates smoothly.

Housing, whether purchased by a resident owner or by an investor, is almost always a highly leveraged commodity. Few people can or will buy a residential property without a mortgage, and traditionally, the ratio of the loan to value is high, frequently 80 to 90 percent of value. Therefore, an owner's equity, or personal investment, is low. Because housing investment is highly leveraged, the cost and availability of money have a significant impact on housing markets and on housing construction.

The overall financing of housing includes (1) short-term loans for construction of new housing, (2) long-term mortgages for completed and existing housing, (3) mortgage insurance protecting the loans, and (4) secondary mortgage markets providing liquidity and investment opportunities. As already discussed, the federal government plays a major role in financing housing: It has set the standards for mortgage practices; it provides insurance and secondary mortgage vehicles; it regulates financial institutions and, through the tax code, influences the attractiveness of housing investment. It also protects savings deposited in federal institutions.

Every phase of housing finance is essential. If construction financing is not available, builders cannot operate. If mortgage credit is not available, owners and investors will not buy housing. If secondary mortgage markets are not readily available, lending institutions may be unable to make additional commitments.

The fluctuations in housing construction are largely attributable to fluctuations in financial markets. Housing is said to be countercyclical: When the economy is booming, housing construction tends to decline; when the economy is in decline, housing construction is likely to increase before other areas of economic activity do so.

Because the demand for money for housing must compete with other demands for money in our economy, the availability and cost of money for housing loans are determined by factors outside of housing. Housing is financed by savings and loan associations, commercial banks, insurance companies, mutual savings banks, and other financial institutions. Savings and loan associations hold about 50 percent of all residential mortgage loans. When the economy is booming, the demand for money increases, interest rates rise, and money flows from savings and loans into more profitable investments. Hence, less is likely to be available for home mortgages. (Like savings and loans, other financial institutions choose more profitable investments and put less money into housing when interest rates rise.) When the economy is in decline, there is less demand for money, interest rates fall, other investment opportunities decline, and more money flows into savings and loans and banks. It is then available for mortgages.

Recent steps toward deregulation have attempted to provide more flexibility to financial institutions and to align housing finance with other credit markets.[28] Deregulation of financial institutions and rising interest rates can reduce the flow of savings into mortgages. Deregulation has also affected the stability of some savings and loan institutions. Mortgages provided by savings and loans are usually fixed rate and long term, perhaps twenty to thirty years. When interest rates rise, savers withdraw their money or seek higher interest rates, leaving the savings and loans with low-paying securities (i.e., mortgages) and depositors demanding higher rates. Deregulation has allowed these institutions to enter other fields of lending and pay higher interest rates, but it has also allowed more risky investments.

Newer financial instruments   Difficulties with long-term, fixed rate mortgages and higher interest rates have led lenders to develop new mortgage forms, including the adjustable rate mortgage (ARM), the variable rate mortgage (VRM), and the graduated payment mortgage (GPM). All these types of mortgage have flexible payment plans. The interest rate may go up or down (perhaps within defined limits) with changes in the interest market. The payment may increase in later years. Sometimes these mortgages will not increase monthly payments but will add increased costs to the mortgage balance and extend the life of the mortgage.

In addition to newer mortgage forms, other sources of credit for mortgages are being developed. These include additional pass-through instruments, which package mortgages, issue securities, and pass through mortgage payments to the holders of these securities. This is the way the Government National Mortgage Association (GNMA) works. Pass-through securities are also starting to be developed by the private market.

Pension funds, particularly government ones, are now seen as a source of credit for housing and as potential buyers of or investors in mortgage-backed securities. Although it would be possible for pension funds to issue mortgages directly, it is not likely that many would do so.[29]

All of these securities are protected when the base mortgages are insured. At one time, FHA and VA insured the bulk of mortgages, but today, private mortgage insurance has replaced most government insurance. As a result, insurance has become easier to obtain but is perhaps riskier for the mortgage holder, because private insurance is not always completely safe.

In the view of the 1968 President's Committee on Urban Housing, one of the most important steps public officials could take in support of housing was to increase their consideration of fiscal and monetary matters and avoid policies that severely restrict the funds available to housing.[30] The potential effects of tax reform, mentioned earlier, are a clear example of the power of fiscal policy to affect housing. Although the impact on housing was not a major concern of tax reformers, tax reform will have a significant impact on housing investment.

Housing goals and standards

A goal is a general good to be achieved. A standard sets a measure or quantifiable target of adequacy. Housing goals are seldom stated explicitly, and when stated they are often general and platitudinous. It has been said that the major implicit housing goal in the United States is that people should own their homes. This goal is being reached, as almost two-thirds of households own. Our major public programs, tax policies, and subsidies support homeownership.

Explicit goals usually refer to meeting the needs of low-income households and eliminating inadequate housing. The Housing Act of 1937 was designed to provide federal assistance "for the elimination of unsafe and unsanitary housing conditions, for the eradication of slums, for the provision of decent, safe and sanitary dwellings for families of low income and for the stimulation of business activity." It was our first major federal commitment to providing better housing for the poor. The U.S. Housing Act of 1949, another landmark act, introduced urban redevelopment, which later became urban renewal. This act called for "the realization as soon as feasible of the goal of a decent home and a suitable living environment for every American family." Every housing act since then has reaffirmed that goal, but the problems of inadequate housing have yet to be eliminated in our society.

This section describes the general intent of governmental housing goals, sets forth housing standards, and then discusses the magnitude of the housing problem.

Despite failure to meet our explicit goals for the poor, overall we are probably the best-housed people in the world. As the Kaiser Commission report stated:

Despite the grim statistics . . . the United States is a world leader in the quality and relative quantity of housing. . . . It is fair to conclude that the U.S. population, at least on the average, enjoys a combination of amenities and space per capita unequaled by any other country.[31]

The 1982 President's Commission on Housing pointed out that there have been enormous improvements to housing since 1949, when urban renewal began. Inadequate units—those that lack plumbing, are dilapidated or in need of major repairs, or are crowded—have been virtually eliminated.[32]

Housing goals

Implicit in most government housing programs are goals for housing in four general areas: community life; social and equity concerns; stability of production; and design and environmental quality.

Community life *From a community perspective, the objective of housing policy is the provision and maintenance of safe, sanitary, and satisfactory housing together with efficiently and economically organized community facilities to support it.* Housing should protect occupants from fire, hazards, weather, and crime.

Effective management of local government services requires that housing be coordinated with both capital and operating expenditures. New housing developments should be planned in concert with community facilities and public services, and existing housing should be provided with adequate services. Furthermore, communities should encourage sufficient upgrading of property to prevent loss of tax revenues.

Although these policies may not always be articulated, they are implicit in most local government operations. Zoning, subdivision control, and building and housing codes are means of managing housing and its development. The usual local facilities, including schools, fire and police stations, parks, and roads, are generally designed and coordinated to meet housing needs.

Social and equity concerns Social goals may receive more explicit definition than community goals, but they often receive less attention. The aim of social goals is to eliminate housing inadequacies affecting the poor, those unable to find suitable housing, and those discriminated against.

Housing the poor who are not poor Early in 1983, the New Jersey Supreme Court ruled in *Mount Laurel II* that the state's municipalities had an affirmative obligation to provide realistic development opportunities for low- and moderate-income housing. In February 1985, new homebuyers began moving into Village Green, the 260-unit condominium project in Bedminster Township that was, according to the *Philadelphia Inquirer,* the first to satisfy the *Mount Laurel II* decision. These condominiums range in price from $27,000 to $60,000—an unusual price category in this traditionally large-lot, expensive community 30 miles west of Newark. The condominiums form part of a larger town house project that runs to luxurious $200,000 units.

But, reports the *Inquirer,* the first buyers are not the "poor" in the generally understood sense of the word. They include in their number policemen, secretaries, bus drivers, and deli managers; they are in their twenties; many have graduated from college; many are single; and they are white. Generally, they are only "poor" because they are just starting out. In the words of one critic, Peter J. O'Conner, executive director of the nonprofit Fair Share Housing Center in Cherry Hill, these homebuyers are "lower-middle-class people who are upwardly mobile and will eventually become middle-class."

William T. Eldred, Jr., a planner who has reacted enthusiastically to the project, compares Village Green homebuyers to the couples who struggled to buy their first homes in the suburbs in the 1950s. He says that, ironically, the profile of the Village Green purchaser resembles neither the community-feared buyer of low-cost housing nor the intended beneficiary of the state supreme court's decision. Eldred says he doubts that the judges in this case realized that this reservoir of "poor" but upwardly mobile people existed.

Source: "Housing the Poor Who Are Not Poor," *Urban Land* (May 1985), 26–27.

Every community should provide safe, satisfactory housing opportunities to all households, at costs they can afford, without regard to income, race, religion, national origin, family structure, or disability.

Communities differ in their response to social and equity goals. Older urban communities are more likely to address them than are suburban governments. Although every responsible local government wants safe housing, well-serviced communities, and sound housing stock, not every government assumes a responsibility to accept low-income residents, those who are disadvantaged in the housing market, and minorities. Although a community may not engage in overt discrimination, simply not allowing housing that would serve the needs of low-income or minority residents is a way of effecting discrimination. One approach to ending discrimination is to create more housing opportunities in the suburbs. This would mean ending exclusionary zoning that precludes multifamily housing, mobile homes, or other housing for lower-income groups. It would also mean encouraging housing development for lower-income families.

Stability of production　Housing is a factor in the national economy, and housing goals should reflect its importance. As noted earlier, the cyclical quality of housing creates uncertainties for investment, labor, and builders. Although local and state governments have attempted, in modest ways, to encourage housing production by providing financial incentives, housing production and investment are primarily determined by federal policies dealing with money supply, interest rates, tax codes, and regulation of financial institutions.

Housing production should be stabilized to reduce fluctuations in construction, ensure a predictable supply of new units, provide steady employment, reduce inflationary trends, and direct a reliable flow of credit into the industry.

Design and environmental quality　Where housing is located and how it is designed affect the natural environment and the quality of life of the housing's occupants.[33] *Housing should be designed to accommodate household needs, optimize the qual-*

Figure 12–5　The cyclical nature of housing construction has a strong influence on the national economy.

ity of life, use land and resources efficiently, and create minimal adverse impact on the natural environment.

The design of housing includes both site planning and design of the unit. Site planning ensures that the housing is related to its environment. The design of the unit should meet the specific needs of the residents and provide both necessities and amenities. Housing designed for elderly or handicapped people, for example, should include features like wide doorways, grab bars, and ramps.

Reducing negative effects on natural resources is a growing concern of local governments. Increasingly, regulations deal with stormwater runoff, flood management, wetland preservation, protection of endangered species, and preservation of open space, agricultural land, and forests. The requirements of these regulations must be incorporated into physical design. There is no consensus on housing goals, and they often conflict with one another. Social goals that promote housing for lower-income groups may conflict with fiscal goals by creating additional service problems for government. Protecting the environment may increase the costs of housing by requiring additional regulation of construction. Each local government must determine its own goals and priorities for housing.

Housing standards

In any housing analysis, it is necessary to distinguish between housing need and concepts such as demand and supply. Need is a social or evaluative concept, whereas supply and demand are economic terms. Housing need refers to the gap between what does exist and what should exist if adequate housing is to be provided for every household without regard to ability to pay.

Before need can be determined, housing standards must be established. Housing that does not meet the standards is inadequate. The following sections suggest eight standards of adequacy that can be used to evaluate housing in a community. Even when standards are established, however, it is difficult to evaluate housing objectively. First, the setting of standards in itself represents value judgments. Second, standards vary with time, place, and cultural values; our worst slums may be in better condition than average housing in developing countries, but they are still unacceptable to us. Third, the data to evaluate the standards may not be available.

Cost   The cost of housing is relative to income and is often calculated as a percentage of income. Although a ratio higher than 30 percent may indicate a housing problem, the real issue is how much money is left for other basic needs. Low-income or elderly households may have to restrict purchases for food, clothes, or health care because of high housing costs. Recently, affordability has become an issue for middle-income as well as low-income households because of inflation and high interest rates.

Condition   The physical condition of a unit is undesirable if it presents a threat to safety, health, or comfort. Units may be structurally unsound; contain hazards like faulty wiring, asbestos, or lead paint; be poorly weatherized; be rodent or insect infested; or lack certain facilities (like indoor plumbing) that are considered the norm in our society. Although the general condition of housing is good in the United States, the 1982 President's Commission on Housing found that certain groups suffered more housing inadequacies than the norm: low-income renters, rural households in the South, and black and Hispanic households.[34]

Crowding   Generally, any unit with more than one person per room is considered crowded. With declining household sizes and the reduction of urban population, crowding is not as severe a problem as it once was. Today the reverse is an increasing problem—oversized units. The growing number of elderly and single-person households is leading to the creation of more "accessory apartments"[35] and smaller additional units carved out of larger housing.

Design   Certain segments of the housing market, such as elderly or handicapped individuals, require specially designed units that provide amenities, services, and physical features adapted to their needs. The changing composition of the housing market may make specially designed units more important in the future.

Choice   A household should be able to select a housing unit suitable to its needs—one that is appropriate in size, cost, location, and form of tenure. Choice also includes the absence of discrimination. The vacancy rate is a useful indicator of the range of housing choice. Vacancy must be considered in relation to housing submarkets as well as in relation to the overall market. Types of vacancies should relate to types of demand. For example, a single-person household is not usually served by a three-bedroom unit.

Community facilities   The housing unit should be adequately provided for in the community at large; this extends the concept of condition from the unit to the man-made environment. Adequate community facilities and services include police and fire protection, mass transportation, water and sewerage, schools, and health, recreation, and social services.

Freedom from threats and access to opportunities are the more intangible features of a community. The amount of crime is a major characteristic of a neighborhood. Social and economic opportunities include access to friends, jobs, education, and entertainment or cultural activities.

Environmental factors   The condition of the air, water, and ground surrounding a home or a community must meet safety standards. Factors such as air pollution, hazardous dumps, polluted streams and groundwater, and even excessive noise (from airports or highways) should be incorporated into housing standards.

Control   Most people prefer to have control over their environment and to make choices about how they live within it. Good housing supports personal independence and dignity. As members of a free society, we expect a great deal

Figure 12–6   Lack of affordable housing is a problem that is no longer limited to lower-income groups. Small, well-designed houses respond to the continuing desire for a detached, single-family home, while keeping construction and maintenance costs down.

of personal freedom and may be dissatisfied with restrictions on how we can live—from landlords' regulations to covenants restricting innovations in physical design. Because they want to control their living situations, many people prefer to own their own homes and elderly householders often remain in their homes rather than move to congregate housing.

Determining housing need

There is no consensus today on the magnitude of housing need. The traditional approach to determining housing need has been to count up inadequate housing and the number of people paying too great a proportion of their incomes for housing, eliminate any overlaps, and call the resulting number *need*. Inadequate housing was defined as that which was dilapidated or in need of major repair, crowded, or lacking major plumbing facilities. The basic data was obtained from Census figures. (The Census no longer evaluates condition.)

The Kaiser Committee, using 1966 data and this approach, determined that there were 6.7 million occupied substandard housing units. Within ten years it would require 8.7 million units to eliminate them because 2 million more would become deficient. In addition, the committee estimated that 7.8 million poorer households would not be able to purchase housing without spending excessive proportions of their income.[36]

Defining housing need implies a responsibility to satisfy that need. At the federal level, in the 1980s, there has been no commitment to stimulate housing production, to provide significant subsidies, or to replace inadequate units. There has been no acknowledgment of housing as a priority or as a federal responsibility and thus no reason or incentive for quantifying a need. Need frequently is quantified to encourage or justify governmental programs. However, there has been no consensus on need because there has been no consensus on what governments should do in housing. Moreover, problems exist in many areas of housing, as has been discussed, and one group of advocates may focus on one kind of need, another on a different kind of need.

The 1982 President's Commission on Housing declined to project any specific housing need but did present data based on the 1977 *Annual Housing Survey*. From this data, 5.6 million households were identified as living in inadequate housing, representing 7.5 percent of all households. The commission also found that certain groups were disproportionately likely to occupy substandard housing. About 20 percent of low-income renters and 20 percent of black households occupied inadequate units. Other groups disproportionately affected included rural Southerners, urban Northerners in large metropolitan areas, female-headed households, and elderly persons.[37]

The major housing problem identified by the 1982 President's Commission was not the inadequacy of housing but the number of households paying a disproportionate amount of income to obtain housing. The commission found that this problem was particularly acute among very low-income renters (those having incomes below 50 percent of the area median). In 1977 there were 5.3 million very low-income renters paying more than 30 percent of their income for housing (of these, 1.2 million spent more than 50 percent of their income). An additional 1.4 million moderately low-income renters (80 percent of area median) paid more than 30 percent for housing. Together, 6.7 million lower-income renter households paid excessive proportions of income for housing.[38]

The *Annual Housing Survey*, produced by the Bureau of the Census and the Department of Housing and Urban Development (HUD) provides current information on rent ratios and condition of housing. In 1983, 8.1 million renter households were paying more than 35 percent of their income for housing that was not subsidized. (This data excluded those in public housing or receiving rent supplements).[39]

The *Annual Housing Survey* also provides information on the structural characteristics of housing supply, based on observation and on opinions of residents. According to this survey, the condition of housing is generally considered adequate. Structural characteristics include information about plumbing facilities, kitchen facilities, exposed wiring, water leakage, and rodent infestation. In evaluations based on structural characteristics, slightly more than 2 percent of households felt that their housing was poor. Evaluations based on neighborhood characteristics like condition of streets, crime, and trash yielded about the same percentage of households that felt their neighborhood was poor, although almost 10 percent expressed a desire to move, if possible. However, for black households, dissatisfaction was about three times as great; 6.2 percent of black households felt that the structural condition of their housing was poor.[40]

Overall need for new housing, without the replacement of inadequate units, has been projected to be about 24.5 million units in the 1980s. This number takes into account about 17 million new household formations, units that are demolished and additional vacancies. However, housing starts are projected to be considerably fewer than 24.5 million, at 19.3 million units. In fact, production has been considerably below the 2.4 million annually that might be required.[41]

It is worth noting, however, that the projected need for housing between 1980 and 1990 is about the same as that which was actually added to the supply between 1973 and 1983, estimated at 23 million units. Of these, 16 million were new construction and about 7 million were from other sources, such as mobile homes placed on a site for housing and conversions (including housing created from the rehabilitation of older industrial buildings and from the subdivision of larger units). During that decade also, about 5.5 million units were lost because of demolitions or disasters. Given the figures for 1973 through 1983, the projected number needed for 1990 may be achievable.

Starts have been projected to be 14.8 million single-family units and 4.5 million multifamily units.[42] In recent years, the great bulk of all new multifamily units have been either subsidized or condominiums, and in the future, it is not likely that enough rental units will be built. As rental units become an increasingly unattractive investment, the shortage of rental housing is expected to reach crisis proportions. Moreover, the rental market is being increasingly reserved for lower-income households, making the provision of new rental units even more unlikely without deep federal subsidies.[43]

There is general agreement that while the private market can be expected to accommodate most housing needs, the needs of some households will require government help. Of course, this includes very low-income households. Increasingly, however, it also includes elderly persons, handicapped individuals, and some nontraditional households, such as female-headed households with children. Minority households, mostly to the extent that they are also low income, also have special housing needs. Discrimination in housing today lies primarily in the failure to provide for low-income households.

Developing a housing plan

Once, housing planning for the suburbs consisted primarily of zoning land and reviewing subdivision plans. The central-city planner planned for public housing, urban renewal, and rehabilitation. Over the years, however, the scope of housing planning has increased considerably. The focus of housing planning has been altered and expanded by changing demography, rising housing costs, and fundamental changes in governmental responsibilities and programs for housing. Housing planners now must plan for group homes for the disabled, housing for the elderly, and emergency shelters and must develop ways to reduce housing costs for middle-income households. Even as federal funds decline, planners can be more creative and flexible in using existing federal subsidies. At the state and local levels, planners now have more opportunity to develop programs for housing.

This section provides direction for undertaking a comprehensive approach to housing planning. It includes an example of a simple housing market analysis, the elements of a comprehensive housing policy plan, and a discussion of housing costs and affordability.

Housing market analysis

A common element of many housing studies is a market analysis, which projects the number of housing units that will be required at some future time. The market analysis usually projects demand but can include need. A demand analysis is a reasonable projection of how the market is expected to perform. It includes a study of how many housing units currently exist and an estimate of how many of these are likely to be removed from supply and thereby will need replacement. The analysis also projects how many households will want housing. These factors together project probable supply and demand for the future.

Need components contribute additional policy considerations to the analysis. If it is assumed that 10 percent of existing units are physically inadequate and should be replaced, this number can be added to the supply requirement. However, it will mean that government programs must remove and replace these units. If it is determined that 20 percent of households will be paying too much rent, this can be identified as the number of housing subsidies required. Constraints on production such as building moratoriums or lack of sewer capacity may limit the projected supply and may become areas for government intervention. Any kind of need can be identified and added to the supply and demand analyses to help define housing concerns needing public attention.

The housing market area   Determining the boundaries of the market area is the first step in any housing market analysis. The area should be of reasonable size, should encompass social and economic linkages, and should be an area for which data are accessible. The market area is the base area for compiling all data. As defined earlier, the market area is an interdependent economic, geographic, and social entity within which all housing units are potentially competitive. It may be the area within which people commute to jobs, share local transportation facilities, or use the same communication networks. It is similar to a labor market area, a wholesale and retail trade area, or a newspaper circulation area. It is large enough to be a generally complete service area and small enough to encompass most daily travel.

For convenience of data collection, the area defined is usually coterminous with political jurisdictions or other established boundaries. It is useful to utilize Census geography and other defined regions for which information and statistics are available. It may be a Metropolitan Statistical Area (MSA), one or more counties, or several townships.

The components of change   Three factors determine future demand for housing: change in the number and composition of households; change in the number of vacant units, and change in the existing supply of housing. Projecting these three basic components for a given time period within a market area is the basis for any housing analysis. Each of these components can be altered by a community's decision to set social goals.

Change in households is derived in part from population change. Population change is a result of natural increase and migration. Migration is usually influenced by economic opportunity and jobs, but as the population ages, retirement is increasingly important.

For the purpose of planning housing, the Bureau of the Census and state and regional agencies can be called on to assist in area population projections. After population has been projected, it must be converted into households. First, group population is subtracted from total projected population. (Group population includes people housed in institutions, hospitals, military barracks, college dormitories, and prisons.) The resulting household population is divided by average household size to project the number of households at the future target date.

Declining household size has been a major factor in the housing market in recent years. The formation of households depends on both economic and social factors. The ability to pay for housing influences whether individuals establish separate households. When housing costs rise, people may more readily share housing, and children may remain with their parents longer. In recent years, the decline in birth rate and the increase in elderly, single, and divorced households has greatly reduced average household size; this, in turn, has generated much housing demand even in the absence of large population increases. The July 1985 provisional U.S. census information estimated that between 1980 and 1985, the U.S. population increased 5.4 percent, while the number of households increased 8.8 percent.

Change in the vacancy rate influences overall demand. A certain percentage of vacancies—usually 4 to 5 percent—is necessary to provide choice and mobility in any housing market. Too many vacancies will reduce demand for new units until the excess is absorbed. Too few will usually force prices up and generate demand for additional units. Rent control is sometimes viewed as a solution to the high housing costs that can result from too few vacancies. In practice, it can discourage the building of additional units—units that would increase the supply, provide more vacancies, and result in better housing prices.

Change in the number of existing housing units is the third factor that is considered in projecting housing demand. Housing units are continuously removed

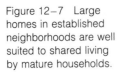

Figure 12–7 Large homes in established neighborhoods are well suited to shared living by mature households.

Step 1. Collect and analyze population data.

		1980 (census)	1985 (estimate)	1990 (projection)
a.	Population	250,000	285,000	325,000
b.	Group population	20,000	23,000	25,000
c.	Household population (a − b)	230,000	262,000	300,000
d.	Average household size	2.8	2.7	2.6
e.	Number of households (c/d)	82,100	97,000	115,400

Step 2. Collect and analyze housing data.

f.	Total housing units	85,000	101,000	121,500
g.	Occupied units	82,100	97,000	115,400
h.	Vacant units (f − g)	2,900	4,000	6,100
i.	Vacancy rate (h/f)	3.4%	4.0%	5.0%

Step 3. Determine average annual demand.

j.	Change in number of households (e for 1990 − e for 1980)	33,300
k.	Change in number of vacant units (h for 1990 − h for 1980)	3,200
l.	Units lost that must be replaced (m + n + o)	8,500
m.	Units lost to disaster	800
n.	Units lost to conversion	1,000
o.	Units lost to demolition	6,700
p.	Total number of units needed, 1980–1990 (j + k + l)	45,000
q.	Housing starts, 1980–1985	19,000
r.	Housing demand, 1986–1990 (p − q)	26,000
s.	Average annual demand, 1986–1990 (r/5)	5,200

Figure 12–8   Housing market analysis for hypothetical market area, 1980–1990.

from the existing supply because of natural disasters—such as fires, floods, or storms—conversions to other uses, and demolitions. Units are demolished because they have deteriorated beyond reasonable repair, to allow room for new development, or because they obstruct public projects such as highway construction or institutional expansion.

Conversions both add to and subtract from the housing supply. In some areas, housing is being converted to retail and office use; in others, old industrial buildings are being converted into housing. Other examples of conversion include vacation homes that become permanent residences and existing units that are subdivided to create new units. During and after World War II, subdivision of existing housing led to overcrowding, and public policy was designed to reduce density and limit the number of apartments in existing housing. Today, with the increasing numbers of elderly people and smaller households, public policy may begin to encourage the subdivision of existing housing.[44]

The replacement of units lost to supply is a significant portion of housing demand. The 1982 President's Commission on Housing reported that from 1960 through 1979, replacement of housing units lost constituted 31 percent of the demand for additional housing units.[45]

A sample housing market analysis   Figure 12–8 provides a simple illustration of a housing market analysis. First, a hypothetical housing market area is defined for which demand is to be projected to 1990. The beginning point is the most recent Census, which provides reliable data for starting the analysis.

For 1980 the information on population and housing units is available from the Census. Estimates for 1985 are derived from Census figures and from building permit information. The projections for 1990 are developed from trends, past information, and assumptions about the area.

The key projection is population for 1990. In the hypothetical housing market area shown in Figure 12–8 the population is expected to grow from 250,000 in 1980 to 325,000 by 1990. Household population for 1990 is projected population less group population. Dividing household population by 2.6, the average household size forecast for 1990, yields a figure for 1990 of 115,400 households, an increase of 33,300 over 1980.

In 1980 the vacancy rate reported by the Census was 3.4 percent, or 2,900 units. Since this is low, the increase in the vacancy rate to 5 percent by 1990 is desirable. A vacancy rate of 5 percent will equal 6,100 units by 1990, or an increase of 3,200 over the 2,900 vacant units reported in 1990.

After household population and vacancy, the third factor affecting housing demand is change in supply. In the example shown in Figure 12–8, disasters, conversions, and demolitions are expected to remove about 8,500 existing units from supply between 1980 and 1990. (Demolition permits and projected public works can be used to project data to 1990; public records can provide data from 1980 to 1985.)

Adding the three factors together—additional households, increased vacancies, and replacements—indicates that 45,000 additional housing units will probably be required between 1980 and 1990. A review of building permits and Census data on construction starts indicates that 19,000 have already been provided by 1985. This leaves a balance of 26,000 units between 1985 and 1990, or 5,200 per year.

This derived projection becomes the basis for developing public housing strategies. Government review or intervention may be necessary if an adequate amount of land is not zoned or serviced or if the housing industry is not providing enough units. Definitions of adequacy must then be added to the analysis, including standards for special needs. For example, a review of household incomes may indicate that many households cannot afford the costs of new housing and that therefore the housing may require some subsidy. Or the analysis may show that certain subgroups, such as elderly, homeless, or handicapped people, will be excluded from the market unless public action ensures that their housing needs are met at reasonable cost. If the availability of mortgage credit is a problem in the community, financing of housing may need to be examined. The performance of the housing industry must be reviewed to find out whether it can meet the projected demand.

Housing market analysis is a starting point for local governments in determining basic housing demands. Some housing needs may be identified and added to the market demand. The basic purpose of the market analysis is to establish a baseline demand and determine whether need remains, whether demand may be unmet, and what local government actions can have an impact on the situation.

Elements of a housing policy plan

The four elements of a housing policy plan are similar to those in any plan. First the planner must identify housing issues that need to be addressed in the community; he or she must then analyze the issues, establish goals and objectives, and prepare a course of action to implement the goals.

Identifying issues Although planning for housing began more than fifty years ago because of conditions in urban slums, the issues in housing today are broader. Here are some current issues affecting housing planning.

The physical condition of housing continues to be a primary concern for housing planners, but factors in addition to the general state of repair and the presence of adequate plumbing facilities must now be taken into account. Current standards of good physical condition include, for example, proper weatherization, which is a factor in energy costs, and the absence of asbestos and lead paint, both of which are safety hazards.

The cost of housing affects more than low-income people today; obtaining affordable housing is a problem for middle-income households as well.

Discrimination in the housing market against blacks and other minorities tends to take the form of exclusionary zoning policies, which are designed to discourage new low- and moderate-income housing.[46]

Regulating accessory housing

Accessory apartment regulations will vary according to the goals the community chooses to implement. If regulations are too restrictive, some homeowners may not be willing or able to convert legally. They must either convert illegally or not convert at all. Such regulations might include undue cost-generating requirements or a limit on the number of buildings that can be converted or on the ages of people that can live in the apartments.

When designing accessory apartment regulations, most communities try to maintain what they perceive to be the single-family residential character of their neighborhoods. The Cape Cod, split-level, and ranch styles of housing can be converted without significant exterior alterations. Many of the requirements for conversion concern the design characteristics of the portions of the building that are visible from the street. For instance, communities usually prohibit a house from having more than one entrance that faces the street or more than one exterior stairway that would be visible from the street. A performance standard requiring that the design of the new unit be in harmony with the surrounding residences gives the converter more latitude in designing a unit that is appropriate for its residents as well as for the community. This type of regulation presumably would result in more legal conversions than a less flexible requirement.

Communities usually limit the size of the accessory unit by specifying the maximum number of square feet that a new unit can have or the maximum percentage of the house that the converted unit can occupy. By doing this, they ensure that the accessory unit is, in fact, subordinate to the principal unit. These requirements distinguish a building converted into a principal unit and an accessory unit from the older two-family conversion. . . .

Regulations that define a family as having a maximum number of unrelated people, and that prohibit more than that number of unrelated people from residing in the principal and the accessory units combined, are unduly restrictive. . . . If the concern is with the number of people who reside in both units, it would be better to limit the number according to the amount of habitable floor space.

Accessory apartment regulations usually establish requirements for minimum lot size, parking, "infrastructure," owner occupancy of one of the units, and age of the building to be converted. A community has many opportunities to be creative so that regulations can achieve community goals without limiting the potential for conversion. . . .

Source: Adapted from Edith M. Netter, "Accommodating Accessory Apartments," *Urban Land* (April 1984), 34–35.

Regulation for environmental protection, added to existing development controls, is creating concern about the impact of excessive regulation on the cost of housing.[47]

Housing for elderly people is assuming increased importance because of the aging of the population. The concept of accessory housing has developed primarily in response to the needs of the elderly.

Providing for infrastructure is a broader concern today because of declining public investment in public works.

Problems and issues vary from community to community; they change as conditions and households change; and, in part, they are simply responses to popular causes, which change over time.

Gathering and analyzing data   After issues have been identified, the next step is to gather and analyze information that can reveal the causes and extent of the problems as well as their solutions. The analysis can be designed to follow trends and make projections regarding components of housing—supply, demand, and financial resources. The analysis may also reveal why the housing market is not meeting housing needs.

Information about the supply of housing must include the characteristics of existing stock, including tenure, availability, cost, and condition. Production trends and analyses of community facilities can also be included.

Demand is analyzed to determine the characteristics of the households that need housing. The changing characteristics of households forecast changes in housing needs. By 1983 the characteristics of U.S. households had already shifted in the direction of single and small households. More than 22 percent of all households were single persons, many of whom were elderly. And although 60.2 percent were married couples, only about one-fourth of all households were what was once considered the traditional household—a married couple with minor children.[48]

Comparing supply with demand will usually quantify the problem and identify the amount of new housing construction required. The private market will usually satisfy most housing demand in the United States. Government intervention is necessary when the private market fails, but such circumstances are seldom anticipated, in part because we are usually more responsive to current than to future need. Forecasts of supply and demand are important because they sketch out the dimensions of future problems.

An analysis of financial resources for housing would include the local availability of mortgages, interest rates, and any constraints on the operation of the market. Although local governments can do little to regulate financial institutions, they should make an effort to be aware of trends and policies.

Setting program objectives   The next step in establishing a policy plan is to set realistic and achievable objectives. These objectives are more likely to be acceptable and achievable if there is broad participation by those likely to be affected, whether they be providers, advocates, or consumers. Objectives can include targets for specific numbers of units or levels of service, dates for regulatory reforms, or funding guidelines for budgets. Including a time period for achievement is important. Long-range objectives are seldom achieved. Short-range objectives are most likely to receive attention and effort.

Implementing plans   Like all plans, a housing plan must identify the tools that can be used to address the issues and achieve the objectives. The tools in housing policy go well beyond physical design. They include

Identifying and using financial programs available at the federal and state

Figure 12–9   The origin, decline, and rehabilitation of a house.

1893–1930: Who built this house? The owner of the XYZ Hardware Company for himself, his wife, their four children, and two live-in servants.

1930–1979: Who lived in this house during its years of decline? Several large families usually simultaneously, on an income spiral from moderate to low to poverty level.

1979 on: Who lives there now? Young affluent professionals. No children. Two incomes to finance rehabilitation.

levels. The number of state programs is increasing, and federal programs are becoming more flexible. Federal and state resources include both capital programs, such as construction grants, and operating programs, such as grants for energy and rent supplements.

Proposing legislation at the state and local levels to correct a situation or create a new program. Changing legislation at the federal level is difficult for a local planner to achieve.

Reviewing and revising, where necessary, local land use, subdivision, building, and housing codes. This can also involve reviewing processing procedures and evaluating environmental regulations.

Developing capital and operating budgets that direct local funds to housing issues and problems.

Developing work programs for agencies to channel manpower to housing issues without requiring additional budgetary appropriations.

Housing cost

Since affordability of housing is a major concern, it is necessary to understand the real costs of housing. Misconceptions can lead to erroneous assumptions about how to reduce housing costs. Accurate housing costs are often difficult to obtain and vary appreciably according to location and the methods that are used to account for influences on costs.

Figures 12–10 and 12–11 present hypothetical housing development and occupancy costs. Development costs summarized in Figure 12–10 include land, construction, financing, and overhead costs (fees, profit, management, etc.). Land costs escalate with shortages of serviced land. Environmental restrictions or local land use regulations are often responsible for increasing improvement costs of land. The housing cost that has risen the most rapidly in recent years is the cost of land, particularly the improved cost. Construction costs include on-site labor as well as materials and equipment shipped to the site. Depending

Figure 12–10 Elements of housing development costs (figures are illustrative only).	

Cost component	Percentage of total cost
Land	
Typical range	15–25
Single-family example	
Acquisition	10
Development	10
Total	20
Construction	
Typical range	45–60
Single-family example	
Labor	18
Materials	37
Total	55
Financing (fees, profits, management, etc.)	
Typical range	5–10
Single-family example	5
Overhead	
Typical range	15–25
Single-family example	20

Figure 12–11
Elements of housing
occupancy costs
(figures are illustrative
only).

Cost component	Percentage of total cost	
	Renters	Owners
Mortgage payment (interest and principal)	55	65
Maintenance and repairs	5	5
Utilities	14	15
Taxes and insurance	12	15
Management	6	—
Vacancy, profit	8	—
	100	100

on local conditions, on-site labor may or may not be a major cost in housing. The industrialization of housing, therefore, will not always achieve significant reductions in the cost of housing. Building materials are often the largest single element in the cost of a house. This cost element is extremely difficult to control except through materials innovations, which require building code revisions, and through basic changes in housing design and characteristics, which require changes in attitude on the part of consumers. Financing costs are for construction loans. The final cost item, overhead, is necessary for any private-sector activity.

The occupancy costs of housing vary for owner- and renter-occupied units (Figure 12–11). Both require mortgage payments, which include principal and interest. The mortgage payment reflects the initial development cost of the unit, as well as interest, which has been a major factor in increased housing costs. A significant reduction in construction cost will have only a limited influence on occupancy cost, since all the other costs shown in the table affect occupancy cost. Maintenance and repairs, which usually consume 5 percent of occupancy costs, are most likely to be neglected when other housing costs rise beyond the consumer's capability to pay. Utilities are a major expense. As utility costs have risen rapidly, this item has assumed a larger share of housing outlays. Property taxes consume a large share of the housing dollar. Renters have the additional costs of management and owner profits.

When government tries to reduce the cost of housing, it usually reduces the costs of occupancy by providing rent subsidies, subsidizing interest, giving energy grants, or providing tax abatements. It is often harder to reduce development costs, but this is what regulatory reform is attempting. Development subsidies can also be provided.

The opportunities for local governments to affect housing are increasing, and the role of local government in housing is expanding. It is not clear at this time whether the federal government will ever again provide massive housing construction subsidies. It is more likely that housing advocates will increasingly try to influence local and state governments to intervene in housing. Along with increased government intervention, creativity and innovation in housing will be necessary.

1 U.S. Bureau of the Census, *Construction Reports,* Series C30.

2 U.S. Bureau of Economic Analysis, *Survey of Current Business,* July 1985.

3 The President's Commission on Housing, *The Report of the President's Commission on Housing* (Washington, DC: U.S. Government Printing Office, 1982), xviii.

4 Charles Abrams, *The Future of Housing* (New York: Harper & Brothers, 1946), 19–35.

5 Mel Scott, *American City Planning since 1890* (Berkeley: University of California Press, 1969), 6–10, 127–33, 255–60.

6 Nathaniel S. Keith, *Politics and the Housing Crisis since 1930* (New York: Universe Books, 1974), 12.

7 For more information about the history of the housing programs, see Keith, *Housing Crisis*; Mary K. Nenno, "Evolution of Local Housing Involvement," in Mary K. Nenno and Paul C. Brophy, *Housing and Local Government* (Washington, DC: International City Management Association, 1982), 1–46; J. Paul Mitchell, "The Historical Context for Housing Policy," in J. Paul Mitchell, ed., *Federal Housing Policy and Programs: Past and Present* (New Brunswick, NJ: Rutgers University, Center for Urban Policy Research, 1985), 3–17; and U.S.

Department of Housing and Urban Development, *Housing in the Seventies: A Report of the National Housing Policy Review* (Washington, DC: U.S. Government Printing Office, 1974), 5–30.

8   In the 1954 Housing Act, Section 220 extended and liberalized FHA insurance for housing in urban renewal areas. Section 221 was FHA insurance for displaced individuals. The 1954 act also redefined urban renewal to include rehabilitation as well as clearance. In the 1959 act, FHA insurance was extended to housing for the elderly (Section 231), and direct low-interest loans were made available to private, nonprofit developers of housing for the elderly (Section 202). In the 1961 act, direct-interest subsidies were extended to privately owned, moderate-income housing (Section 221[d][3]), and the first operating subsidies began for elderly public housing tenants. In the 1964 act, rent supplements were extended to all public housing families, and low-interest rehabilitation loans (Section 312) were created for owners. In the 1965 act, rent supplements were extended to very low-income households in private housing; some public housing began to be leased; and the Department of Housing and Urban Development was created, combining several existing housing finance and development administrations. The War on Poverty in the Johnson administration initiated a wave of new social programs. The Demonstration Cities and Model Cities Act of 1966 expanded the concept of redevelopment to many social and physical programs in a new approach to urban problems.

9   President's Committee on Urban Housing, *A Decent Home* (Washington, DC: U.S. Government Printing Office, 1969).

10 National Commission on Urban Problems, *Building the American City* (Washington, DC: U.S. Government Printing Office, 1968).

11 The major new federal housing programs were Section 235 and Section 236, providing subsidized debt service on owner- (235) and renter- (236) occupied housing for low- and moderate-income families. These provisions extended development opportunities to for-profit builders and owners.

12 President's Commission on Housing, *Report of the Commission*.

13 U.S. Bureau of the Census, *Annual Housing Survey*, Part A, 1983 (since 1983, replaced by the biennial *American Housing Survey*).

14 Keith, *Housing Crisis* 11.

15 For a full discussion of federal activities in financing housing, see President's Commission on Housing, *Report of the Commission*, 157–172.

16 See Henry J. Aaron, *Shelter and Subsidies: Who Benefits from Federal Housing Policies?* (Washington, DC: The Brookings Institution, 1972), 53–73. The President's Commission of 1982 estimated this deduction for homeowners at $28.7 billion in 1981 and projected a deduction of $57.4 billion by 1986. Steven F. Bloomfield, in "Shelter: A Neglected Agenda," *Urban Resources* 2 (Winter 1985), 47–49, computed the mortgage and property tax deduction for 1982 at $38 billion.

17 Civil Rights Act of 1964, Titles VI and VIII.

18 For reviews of state programs, see Marvin J. Tick and John Sidor, *State Actions to Promote Affordable Housing* (Washington, DC: Council of State Community Affairs Agencies, 1982); and Advisory Commission on Intergovernmental Relations and the Staff of the National Academy of Public Administration, *The States and Distressed Communities,* *The 1982 Report* (Washington, DC: Advisory Commission on Intergovernmental Relations 1982), a report funded by the U.S. Department of Housing and Urban Development.

19 ICF Incorporated, *State Housing Finance Agencies in the Seventies* (Washington, DC: Council of State Housing Agencies, 1981). This report provides a history of the development of these agencies.

20 President's Commission on Housing, *Report of the Commission,* 170.

21 John Sidor, *Affordable Housing and Infrastructure: The State Role* (Washington, DC: Council of State Community Affairs Agencies, 1984).

22 James C. Nicholas et al., *State Regulation: Housing Prices* (New Brunswick, NJ: Rutgers University, Center for Urban Policy Research, 1982).

23 In New Jersey, in response to the State Supreme Court *Mt. Laurel II* decision, the Council on Affordable Housing established goals for constructing low- and moderate-income housing in communities. On March 15, 1982, Governor King of Massachusetts signed Executive Order #215, withholding discretionary development funds from exclusionary communities.

24 William G. Grigsby, *Housing Markets and Public Policy* (Philadelphia: University of Pennsylvania Press, 1963), 47–76.

25 The U.S. Department of Housing and Urban Development reported in 1980 that only 1.3 percent of total existing rental stock had been converted. However, in certain major urban areas, as much as 8 to 10 percent of the stock was converted. U.S. Department of Housing and Urban Development, *The Conversion of Rental Housing to Condominiums and Cooperatives* (Washington, DC: U.S. Government Printing Office, June 1980).

26 Chester Rapkin, Louis Winnick, and David M. Blank, *Housing Market Analysis* (Washington, DC: U.S. Housing and Home Finance Agency, 1953), 9–10.

27 For detailed analyses of the relationship between financial institutions and housing, see President's Commission on Housing, *Report of the Commission,* 123–172; and an FNMA Symposium, *Housing Finance in the Eighties: Issues and Options* (Washington, DC: Federal National Mortgage Association, 1981).

28 The Depository Institutions Deregulation and Monetary Control Act of 1980 and Garn–St. Germain Act of 1982.

29 See Lawrence Litvak, *Pension Funds and Economic Renewal* (Washington, DC: Council of State Planning Agencies, 1981), 91–118.

30 President's Committee on Urban Housing, *A Decent Home,* 129.

31 Ibid., 46.

32 President's Commission on Housing, *Report of the Commission,* 4–9.

33 See Land Design/Research, Inc., *Planning for Housing: Development Alternatives for Better Environments* (Washington, DC: National Association of Home Builders, 1980).

34 President's Commission on Housing, *Report of the Commission,* 4–9.

35 "Accessory apartments" refers to housing units added to or converted from existing units. Accessory apartments include mother-in-law apartments, granny flats, echo housing and any secondary addition to a primary unit. See Patrick H. Hare with Susan Conner and Dwight Merriam, *Accessory Apartments: Using Surplus Space in Single-Family*

Houses Planning Advisory Service Report no. 365 (Chicago: American Planning Association, 1981).

36 President's Committee on Urban Housing, *A Decent Home*, 40–45.

37 President's Commission on Housing, *Report of the Commission*, 4–9.

38 Ibid.

39 U.S. Bureau of the Census, *Annual Housing Survey*. Part A: "General Housing Characteristics" (Washington, DC, 1983).

40 Ibid., Part B: "Indicators of Housing and Neighborhood Quality by Financial Characteristics."

41 ICF Incorporated, *Housing Needs in the Eighties* (Washington, DC: Council of State Housing Agencies, 1981).

42 Ibid.

43 See John C. Weicher, Kevin E. Villani, and Elizabeth A. Roistacher, eds., *Rental Housing: Is There a Crisis?* (Washington, DC: The Urban Institute, 1981); and George Sternlieb and James W. Hughes,

The Future of Rental Housing (New Brunswick, NJ: Rutgers University, Center for Urban Policy Research, 1981).

44 See Hare et al., *Accessory Apartments*.

45 President's Commission on Housing, *Report of the Commission*, 64.

46 Alan Mallach, *Inclusionary Housing Programs: Policies and Practices* (New Brunswick, NJ: Rutgers University, Center for Urban Policy Research, 1984), and Robert W. Burchell et al., *Mt. Laurel II: Challenge and Delivery of Low-Cost Housing* (New Brunswick, NJ: Rutgers University, Center for Urban Policy Research, 1983).

47 See President's Commission on Housing, *Report of the Commission*, 177, and Mary E. Brooks, *Housing Equity and Environmental Protection: The Needless Conflict* (Washington, DC: American Institute of Planners, 1976), 2.

48 HUD, *Annual Housing Survey*, Part A, 1983.

Part five: Management, finance, and information

13 Planning agency management

The purpose of this chapter is to provide an introduction to and overview of planning agency management. In general the emphasis will be on effectiveness rather than efficiency. This emphasis may seem paradoxical in an era (perhaps permanent?) of budgetary constraints. However, since every department of local government must now be efficient, the successful local agency is the agency that is effective—at solving problems, at helping the manager and elected officials to do a good job. Effectiveness is not based solely on doing good technical work, which should be the goal of any agency; being effective depends far more on a clear sense of mission, on leadership, on responsiveness to political leadership, and on implementing strategies to accomplish planning goals. "Accomplishing planning goals" is an operational definition of effectiveness. If government spends time and money developing plans, then those plans should guide day-to-day decision making. Plans should not gather dust on a shelf; they should be *used*. The agency that can help decisionmakers implement plans is an effective agency.

Planning agencies operate within a larger organization—local government—and local government in turn operates within yet a larger organization of governments at the metropolitan, state, and federal levels. The discussion will first consider the place of planning in the governmental structure. Then there will be an extensive exposition of strategic management planning. The remainder of the chapter will cover agency organization and functions, agency relations, work programming, staffing, the use of consultants, budgeting, office management, and administration of the planning commission and zoning board of appeals.

Planning commissions in the local government structure

Like any other local government function, such as police protection and fire protection, planning takes place within an overall governmental structure. The structure provides a framework for accomplishing governmental objectives by assigning authority, responsibility, power, and influence; by providing access to decisionmakers; and by assigning functions and procedures to a variety of units.

In addition to the traditional executive, legislative, and judicial branches of local government, a wide variety of boards, commissions, advisory groups, and councils handle particular local government functions. Twentieth-century local planning was first institutionalized in this sector of local government. (As chapter 2 notes, some of the earliest planning efforts were actually outside local government entirely, in cases where special committees or civic associations hired planning consultants to prepare plans for cities.) The first official permanent planning body was the Hartford Commission on a City Plan created by the state legislature in 1907. Since these early boards and commissions were outside the mainstream of local government, their influence varied considerably.

The early leaders of the planning movement were heavily influenced by the reform era in which they began their efforts. In the view of early twentieth-century reformers, local government was inefficient, ineffective, and corrupt. One way to protect the planning function was to place it outside the influence of public officials, many of whom had been accused of graft. Appointing a blue-ribbon group of business and civic leaders, which would then hire a planning consultant, would ensure that plan proposals would not be politically tainted.

As the city planning movement spread throughout the nation during the 1920s and 1930s, new conceptions about the appropriate function and placement of planning began to emerge. In *The Planning Function in Urban Government*, a 1941 book that was to become a planning classic, Robert Walker concluded that the scope and organization of planning had to change.[1] Walker saw that early planning had been limited to streets, parks, and zoning but that local government was expanding into new fields, such as health, welfare, and social services, with which planning agencies needed to be concerned. And, given the expanded role of government, the top officials of government needed to do their own top-level management planning in order to do their jobs well. In addition, Walker argued that city planning should become central planning and should be close to the chief executive—the office of the mayor or city manager—so that local government could do its own central planning and coordinate departmental planning. In Walker's view, an independent commission was too far removed from the chief executive to undertake such planning and coordination and should therefore be replaced entirely.

The planning commission as an institution did not, however, disappear. Instead, the planning function in most local governments underwent an evolution in which the municipality built up its in-house professional capacity by creating a planning department with a planning director appointed by the mayor or manager; and the planning commission remained as an advisory body to the chief executive and to the local legislative body. The department acted as a staff resource to the commission even though planning was an executive department. This is certainly an ambiguous structure but perhaps resulted from efforts to achieve both staff accountability and commission independence. The role of planning commissions include the following: holding public hearings on comprehensive plans or elements of comprehensive plans; holding public hearings on zoning amendments; reviewing new land subdivision plats to ensure conformance with subdivision regulations; and, in some cities, holding public hearings on and discussing the capital improvements program.

While planning departments were being integrated into the administrative structure of local government, many observers were concerned that planning commissions tended to be dominated by powerful economic and business interests, including the real estate industry, and were not representative of the public at large. Beginning in 1950 periodic national surveys of planning commissions showed that indeed they were not particularly representative.[2] By the mid-1960s, however, a widespread citizen association movement had begun. Almost every central-city neighborhood soon had a civic association to represent its interests with city hall, and during the 1970s suburban areas began to have their own associations, often concerned with growth and environmental issues. Although planning commissions may still be unrepresentative, citizen groups have become relatively sophisticated in getting their own ideas across. A number of cities, such as New York, Indianapolis, and Honolulu, have experimented with a variety of officially sanctioned neighborhood-level citizen planning boards.

Independent planning commissions have probably persisted because government officials find that they serve some useful purposes. A commission can act as a buffer between government officials and the general public; can relieve the local legislative body of time-consuming public hearings and details; can serve as a sounding board for new ideas; and can add a fresh perspective to competing viewpoints of staff, citizens, and developers.

Along with the planning commission, another common local government advisory body is the zoning board of appeals (sometimes called board of adjustment).

The board was created in very early zoning laws as a mechanism to hear appeals for variance from the strict interpretation of an ordinance. (See chapter 9 for additional discussion of the zoning board.) (It should be noted that Maryland, Washington, and Oregon have replaced the zoning board with a new administrative position, zoning hearing officers.)

Planning agencies in the local government structure

In the traditional and still widespread organizational arrangement, a planning department is a line agency (sometimes a mixed line-staff agency) within local government. The planning director reports to the mayor or manager, and the department prepares all general planning studies for the community. (The function and organization of this type of agency is discussed at length later in this chapter.) However, local governments organize and place planning, and especially planning implementation activities, in a number of agencies. In this section, a variety of alternative administrative arrangements will be discussed in the context of the historical development of planning within local government.

No sooner had planning begun to establish itself as a local government department (during the 1920s and 1930s), than it became useful, sometimes necessary, to divide the planning function. Beginning in the late 1930s, local governments began to deal with housing issues and frequently created housing authorities and agencies. Part of the reason for creating separate agencies was a legal mechanism that allowed separate authorities to have independent borrowing and financial powers; special agencies could therefore fund housing programs that state debt limitation statutes preventing local governments from funding. In addition, implementing, constructing, and managing a housing program required an entirely new set of government functions that were not really related to planning. For example, housing authorities dealt with architectural drawings, construction schedules, negotiation with landowners, condemnation proceedings, and the management of completed housing projects.

In the late 1940s and early 1950s, as federal aid for more comprehensive urban redevelopment was initiated, many local governments created redevelopment authorities—sometimes separate from housing authorities, sometimes combined—and often created separate urban renewal planning staffs that conducted detailed neighborhood-level surveys in potential renewal areas. Again, these agencies were organized partly for fiscal and legal reasons but also because the nature of the work was much more related to real estate development than to the activities typically associated with planning departments.

By the 1960s many observers, particularly federal officials responsible for renewal funding, began to feel that local government planning and implementation was becoming fragmented. In particular, it was felt that project planning did not relate sufficiently to overall development objectives of local government. That is, how did a project, or several projects, relate to an overall, communitywide renewal strategy? If a community was receiving federal money for land clearance, was it also taking steps to conserve areas by rehabilitation so that decline was arrested and future clearance was made unnecessary? During the 1960s federal funds were available for "community renewal programming," a planning program that attempted to pull together all the separate, often uncoordinated renewal projects of local government into a comprehensive program. In a number of communities the planning department was assigned this task and therefore reasserted a policy-oriented renewal program perspective. In some cities, however, this policy activity was considered so important that the community renewal program was placed in the mayor's office as a staff activity— above both planning and renewal agencies.

Although a number of cities, Boston being the most notable, combined the renewal, housing, and planning functions into a single superagency, this type of organization never became widespread.

In a number of metropolitan areas, the central city and the county have a joint city-county planning agency. (This hybrid plan seems to have been most popular in Kentucky, Tennessee, and Ohio.) Although the combined agencies have either a single city-county planning commission or separate planning commissions, they all have a single planning staff. Joint city-county agencies have generally been well accepted by local government officials at both the city and county levels, but conflicts do occasionally occur. For example, one governmental unit may feel that the planning staff is siding with the other governmental unit or doing more work for it.

During the 1970s a number of local governments experimented with creating a small planning staff in the mayor's, manager's, or executive budget office.

In the view of the chief executives of these communities, this arrangement had two advantages: First, it placed a portion of a planing staff under their direct control; and second, it meant that the central planning staff was in a position to implement the chief executive's policy preferences with all line departments—including planning. As a practical matter, a local government does not have to be very large or complex before the chief executive can see that there is a problem when planning or policy analysis skills are situated in a "distant" and large bureaucracy. Chief executives want these skills in their own offices because they realize that government departments frequently express their own policy preferences to the chief executive and that proximity facilitates this communication, However, in communities that placed planning staff in the mayor's or manager's office, the difference in perspective between the central planning office and line planning offices frequently created friction. In communities where the budget office was close to the chief executive, the central planning office was sometimes situated in the budget office during an era of experimentation with local government budgeting procedures and techniques.

Another development, particularly common in smaller communities or suburban jurisdictions, was the establishment of planning and development departments. These departments have all the traditional planning functions and also handle community renewal projects, which in smaller communities were never large enough to support a separate department.

During the 1980s older and larger cities began establishing new organizational forms for planning and the implementation of planning programs. For example, as local governments became increasingly concerned with economic development issues, many created economic development departments, which conduct programs to retain or attract industry and business. Working directly with local business groups and individual businesses, these agencies help local businesses expand, provide investment advice, plan incubator facilities, renew portions of downtowns, work on convention centers or sports stadiums, and assist local business (old or new) in dealing with local government bureaucracies.

A number of communities created economic development authorities with separate funding powers because of debt limitations on local government. Others, however, combined the planning and economic development functions into a single agency that does all long-range planning, land use control administration, capital investment planning, and economic development planning.

One organizational innovation (discussed at somewhat greater length in chapters 3 and 14) occurred in the mid-1970s in Atlanta, where a city charter combined the former planning and budgeting departments into a single department. However, this arrangement has not been emulated elsewhere.

What is interesting about the range of organizational adaptations over time is the recurrence of common themes and issues. For example, how many (and which) local government agencies are involved in planning, where is the planning function located, and who has the most direct access to planning expertise? Most local governments agree that it is necessary to plan for the future and that the planning department ought to be assigned this role. But a number of changes can occur that cause new agencies—or new versions of agencies—to be created. A new program emphasis may come along, and the governing board may feel that it deserves its own department. Established planning and implementation departments may be drifting in different directions and generating conflict; combining them into a single agency may be the solution. Where government debt limitations have come into play, one way to obtain outside funding is to create a new agency.

The location of the planning function in the departmental structure or in the mayor's or manager's office can influence planning processes and implementation in a number of ways. For the local governing board, neither of these alternatives may be acceptable. In a few communities, governing boards have created a staff position or a small office of planning—which is analogous to Congress creating its own advisory agency when the executive office already has a similar one. When different branches of local government want their own planners, perhaps planning has arrived.

Management planning: Strategic planning for planning

The 1980s have been a period of profound change in local government and in local government planning agencies. From a historical perspective, as discussed at greater length in chapter 2, the 1930s through the late 1970s was a period of expansion—in numbers of agencies, numbers of planners, expenditures, and most particularly, federal aid programs that supported local government planning. For most of the 1980s, however, local planning agencies have had to adjust to an entirely new environment: federal funds for local planning have disappeared, and state-mandated referenda have put caps on local government expenditures. These trends require that local planning agencies reassess their missions and programs to ensure that they are well managed—in other words, responsive, efficient, and effective.

At the simplest level, management can be defined as the planning, direction, and operation of an organization to achieve certain objectives. Rather than survey the vast literature on management in both the private and public sectors, this section will focus on planning, one of the most important management functions. Unfortunately, there is very little literature about management planning *for* planning agencies. A handful of references in the bibliography for this chapter deal with aspects of planning, but none offers a comprehensive model. In the literature that *is* available, one underlying theme is the need to develop strategies and implementation mechanisms to accomplish the purposes of planning. In other words, simply preparing and proposing a "rational" plan for a community will not ensure its implementation without thoughtful, specific, action-oriented strategies.

While the literature is sparse, its emphasis on strategy provides a good foundation for experimentation with the private-sector concept of strategic planning, which is coming into increasing use in the public sector. Before describing the use of strategic planning in planning agency management, however, it is essential to make a subtle, yet critical, distinction between early uses of strategic planning by local governments and the use of strategic planning by planning agencies that will be described in this section. Early local government efforts used strategic planning as an alternative to the traditional comprehensive plan. A comprehensive plan is a plan *for the community*. It is a plan for "out there" for the economy, urban development, transportation, and so on. Strategic planning, as it is used in the private sector and should be used in the public sector, is a plan *for the organization.* It is a plan for the organization to interact with and influence the environment. The discussion that follows covers strategic planning for planning agency management.

Basic steps in strategic planning

There are a number of different models of strategic planning in the private-sector literature. The discussion here is based on two primary sources: the author's experiences (with nonprofit strategic planning, management studies of planning agencies, and management training seminars) and the work of John

---

What is strategic planning?
Strategic planning is a systematic way to manage change and create the best possible future. It is a creative process for identifying and accomplishing the most important actions in view of strengths and weaknesses, threats and opportunities.

Implementation is the key to strategic planning, as opposed to long-range planning and goal setting. Strategic planning focuses on the allocation of scarce resources to critical issues. Development of the plan sets the stage for the crucial implementation phase.

Strategic planning is not always labeled "strategic," nor is it easily defined. It can be distinguished from other kinds of planning by its specific methodology, as well as by these key characteristics:

It is a focused process that concentrates on selected issues.

It explicitly considers resource availability.

It assesses strengths and weaknesses.

It considers major events and changes occurring outside the organization or jurisdiction.

It is action oriented, with a strong emphasis on practical results. . . .

Although variations are possible, the basic steps in strategic planning are as follows:

1. Scan the environment. Identify key factors and trends important for the future. Determine how external forces will influence events.
2. Select key issues. On the basis of the scan, choose a few issues whose successful resolution is critical.
3. Set mission statements or broad goals. Establish the direction for the strategy-development process by setting general goals.
4. Conduct external and internal analyses. Look in depth at outside forces affecting achievement of the goals. Identify strengths and weaknesses, along with availability of resources.
5. Develop goals, objectives, and strategies. Based on the external and internal analyses, decide what can be achieved with respect to each issue and how it will be achieved.
6. Develop an implementation plan. Be specific about timetables, resources, and responsibilities for carrying out strategic actions.
7. Monitor, update, and scan. Ensure that strategies are carried out. Adjust them as necessary in a changing environment. Be prepared to update the plan when major changes occur in the environment. . . .

Source: Donna Sorkin, Nancy B. Ferris, and James Hudak, *Strategies for Cities and Counties: A Strategic Planning Guide* (Washington, DC: Public Technology, Inc., September 1984, for the U.S. Department of Housing and Urban Development). Available from Public Technology, Inc., 1301 Pennsylvania Avenue, N.W., Washington, DC 20004.

M. Bryson.[3] Both sources rely heavily on the Harvard model of strategic planning.

Figure 13–1 shows one effort to distill Bryson's public-sector process; the steps shown in the figure are the basis for the discussion that follows.

Initial agreement The first step is essentially the decision to do strategic planning for a planning agency. This decision may derive from any of a number of factors: Recent funding cutbacks may require that the agency reassess its program. Perhaps the community has suddenly begun to grow very rapidly. Turnover of key staff, such as the planning director, might be another reason to initiate a plan. Changes at the political level—mayor or council—may require that the mission and direction of the planning department be reassessed.

It is important at this stage to obtain the commitment of key management personnel—this would include the planning director, assistant directors, and all division chiefs. Depending on the form of government, it might also require the involvement of key staff from the manager's office, the office of management and budget, and perhaps the chair of the planning commission. It is essential that all key players be committed to the process. It is not enough for the planning director to direct the involvement of subordinates; it is essential that subordinates understand why the process is being initiated.

At this point specific written products must be identified and deadlines established. If an agency is trying strategic planning for the first time—which is likely—the process should be kept informal. The object is to generate critical, strategic thinking about the agency. Because strategic planning already has a degree of artificiality built into it that may make some people uncomfortable, rigidity in format and products should be avoided. For most planning agencies, most of the products should be succinct memos containing both objective information and subjective opinions. Elaboration of points should be avoided.

Mandates The strategic planner must identify those things the agency *must* do. For planning agencies this would include state-legislated mandates. For example, Florida, California, and Oregon have state legislation that requires comprehensive plans and consistency between plans and zoning ordinances (and in Florida, between plans, zoning, and capital improvements programs). Some mandates

---

Management education Most planners come to planning with an undergraduate degree in a design, environmental, or social science discipline. The few that come from public administration have an understanding of basic management concepts. However, many planners learn management skills on the job, through the example and training of their superiors, or by reading. A planner who reads only technical planning literature is not likely to be prepared for the simplest of management tasks, such as managing his or her own time. Planners who are promoted to positions where they direct the work of others must turn to management literature if they are to be successful.

Fortunately, there is a vast literature on management. Most of it is written with the private sector in mind, but because much management is based on human relations, a good deal of the private-sector literature is applicable to public planning agencies as well. Planning students should be encouraged to take courses in the schools of business or public administration, and current staff members ought to be encouraged to take such courses part time. Because most planning agency work is intellectually oriented technical work, and the management of intellectual resources is the most difficult aspect of the management process, it is essential that good management skills be acquired.

are "softer" but nevertheless important. For example, the mayor may have been elected with a particular agenda, such as to improve the central business district, allocate more resources to neighborhoods, or push economic development. Individual local legislators may have strong views on planning issues in their own districts, which a planning agency can ignore only at its peril.

Mission and values   The third step in the strategic planning process to identify the organization's present mission, with particular emphasis on what "stakeholders" expect of the agency. Stakeholders include any group that may interact with or be vitally affected by the planning agency—citizens, the local building community, the governing body, neighborhood groups—and perhaps even a planner's peer group, insofar as the best of current practice sets standards for an agency's performance. Stakeholders' expectations must be identified because they form part of the environment in which the planning agency must operate and therefore will affect its work program, resources, and output.

An additional step suggested by some strategic planning literature is to have top managers ask themselves and the agency "how are we doing?" An unstructured opportunity for top managers to express their fundamental judgments and intuitive perceptions of the agency and its performance may in some cases be preferable to the more structured steps to be discussed.

Top management staff ought to have a good general sense of what the agency is doing well and what it is not doing well. Astute managers will sense the degree of respect accorded the agency, the quality of its work, the extent of its involvement in key decision making in the community, how well it fares at budget time in comparison to other agencies, and its standing in the governmental community.

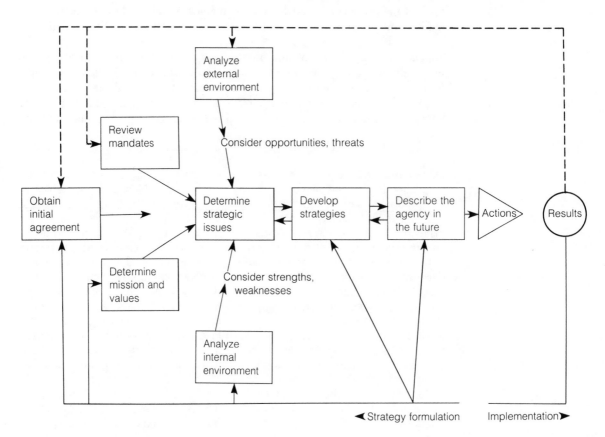

Figure 13–1   Strategic planning process.

Situation analysis The analysis of external and internal environments asks and answers four basic questions; some of the strategic planning literature refers to the four questions as constituting a "situation analysis."

1. What *external opportunities* can the agency take advantage of?
2. What *external threats* does the agency face?
3. What are the *internal strengths* of the agency?
4. What are the *internal weaknesses* of the agency?

In general, the agency can do little about external factors—trends in the national economy, how fast or slowly the metropolitan area is growing, the impact of the defense industry on the community, national population growth, and so on. Internal factors are those that the agency can control and can change with enough effort.

In business corporations, a situation analysis would be a highly complex undertaking including a great deal of quantitative analysis of the industry as a whole, sales and markets, return on equity, the relative competitive position of the company, state and federal regulatory climates, and even international political and economic trends.

A situation analysis for a planning agency, however, is more of an internal management audit, examining the agency's performance in relation to work products and management processes. The analysis is much more modest than the sort conducted in the private sector and much less quantitatively based. The output of such an analysis is likely to be a series of memorandums analyzing each department of the planning agency and an overall memorandum that emphasizes the results of critical thinking and evaluation. In some way a planning agency's first effort might best be described as a "think piece."

What would a situation analysis for a planning agency cover? Given the wide variety of agencies in the United States, such an analysis could cover almost anything that can affect an agency and its performance. The accompanying sidebar illustrates some, but certainly not all, of the kinds of judgments that might be contained in a planning agency situation analysis. Although a list of this length cannot cover the entire range of what might occur in a situation analysis, it can indicate the kinds of issues that ought to be addressed if a planning agency is to be well managed in the future. For example, the statements illustrate the importance of access to decision making. Because planning agencies are just one part of local government operations, departments can compete for attention. Elected officials may regard departments differently, depending on how useful their analytical work and advice is to those who must answer to their constituents. The statements also illustrate changes in the planning field or in the local urban environment that require the planning agency to shift its work program, its style of doing business, or its attitudes toward others. At times the statements that identify an issue suggest a new strategy: for example, if the private sector is somewhat suspicious of the planning agency, then the agency might consider finding a joint venture to prove the agency's worth.

Once the agency has completed a situation analysis, what is its next step?

First, the literature suggests that an organization must to some extent *adapt* to its environment. In other words, the agency must be realistic in assessing the implications of the situation analysis. What works in one community may not work in another, and there is no such thing as an ideal planning agency. A planning agency's style will have to fit in with the views of elected officials on a number of critical issues: for example, How much should government regulate the private building industry? If local government tries to balance the need to protect the environment with the desire to promote economic development, how can the planning agency adapt to this constant tension? How large a budget should the planning function have? In the last instance, planning agencies will

410 The Practice of Local Government Planning

have to cope with resource limitations by doing the best they can with the available staff and money; planning products and processes have to fit the available resources.

Second, the literature suggests that in general an organization must assess its opportunities and exploit them, deal with threats as best it can, build on strengths, and correct weaknesses.

Strategic issues and strategy development   An organization that has conducted a serious situation analysis has already begun identifying issues that are strategic to the organization's future. Although Figure 13–1 separates strategic issues and strategies, as a practical matter in a small planning agency these are likely to be discussed and studied together. What is essential in this part of the process is to carefully think through the *implications* of the external and internal factors that were identified in the situation analysis. Here are some examples of statements that examine the implications of the situation analysis:

New members (the majority) of the city council are action oriented, so a proposal to update the ten-year-old plan over three years won't fly. How can we build a staff and a program capable of responding to the council's agenda?

Financial questions will be among the most important issues to be debated and decided in the next three to five years. If our staff does not get a public finance analyst on board, we will be left out.

A recent landmark state court decision on development impact fees upheld

---

Sample statements from a planning agency situation analysis

External opportunities   The mayor is concerned about whether the city will be prepared if the new state infrastructure loan revolving fund legislation passes. The public works department is gearing up for the possibility by preparing to do maintenance inventories. Since there won't be enough money to do everything, the mayor needs help developing priorities and is considering using either the planning or the finance department to help establish them.

The Human Services Department doesn't do much planning and has put out tentative feelers about working more with the planning department in the future. We don't do social planning now, but should we take this opportunity to get involved with another department and expand our scope?

The Chamber of Commerce is interested in initiating a communitywide strategic planning and goals project, for which it would raise the funds. We have people with the technical and

participatory skills to work on such a project. Should we take this opportunity to develop a closer working relationship with the Chamber?

External threats   The local building industry is increasingly critical of local government regulation and especially of the amount of time required to get projects approved.

A number of staff people in the manager's office are working on various projects that are really "planning." Is a competing planning office being established?

In the past, our agency depended on state and federal grants to support the planning staff. This money is drying up fast and will be gone next year. The chance of getting an increased budget from city funds is nil.

While our staff gets support in its recommendations from the planning commission and the chief executive, the city council doesn't pay much attention to our work. Yet it is the council that establishes our budget.

the imposition of such fees only when the jurisdiction can measure the actual public service impact. We will have to mount a major study for our area in order to defend our own ordinance.

Our land use control administration system is slowing down while the volume of builder complaints goes up. We won't get more staff, so the process has to be streamlined. This may mean a drop in the quality of the reviews.

A critical step at this point is to review and refine the basic mission of the planning agency. In the private-sector strategic planning literature, the business planner asks, "What business are we in?" The response provides a foundation for objectives, strategies, and tactical plans. Although the top management of a planning agency must ask the same question, there will be practical constraints. For example, a public agency operating under state enabling legislation and created by a local ordinance may have many mandates and will not have complete freedom to "change the business."

Public planners need to think through the mission of the agency in operational terms: major functions, program content and emphasis, geographic focus, and the basic stance and style of the agency. For example, if an agency has very limited power, the mission may be to provide information to those who do have power. Or the mission may be to use the planning department's tools and techniques to achieve certain social or economic objectives. (Perhaps the most well-known example is the Cleveland Policy Planning Report, which in the 1970s took as its mission to focus on the needs of poor people—at the time an innovative mission statement.) A planning agency in a rapidly growing com-

---

At one time the planning department planned and the community development department implemented projects. Now so much gets decided through public-private negotiation that this divided responsibility doesn't work well anymore. Who should plan? Who should negotiate?

Internal strengths The mayor has from time to time asked us to do special projects; she seems to trust us, even with politically sensitive issues.

We are the best source of census and building statistics in the region.

We manage the planning commission agenda well; the business moves through much faster than it used to.

Our ability to analyze environmental issues is excellent.

Internal weaknesses When important decisions are made in this town, the planning department seems left out of the process. Maybe it is because on a couple of occasions we have been accused of being unrealistic and insensitive to political issues.

Our library doesn't seem to have up-to-date information, which means we sometimes lack confidence in our own studies and reports.

Our reports are long and filled with jargon. We suspect no one reads them.

Our planning commission seems honest and competent, but there is no one on it with sufficient political clout to go to bat for the department's recommendations.

Our agency has bright young people and politically astute top management, but middle management is filled with long-tenured, unimaginative people.

For the past two years or so we have spent an increasing amount of time doing "brushfire" special projects, yet we are still organized as though we do long-range planning (which we don't) and current land use administration.

munity, previously a boomtown with little planning, may choose a mission of "growth with quality." At first glance, this abstract statement may seem meaningless, but in application, it may mean that the agency accepts the fact of growth but will ensure, through plans, regulations, and impact fees, that new development pays for the effects of growth.

As another example, a planning staff may conclude that the key decisions in the community are capital investment decisions and choose to make the capital improvements programming process the critical operational mission of the agency. In the early 1980s, a number of cities shifted from being generalist planning organizations to being planning and implementation agencies for economic development.

In all of these cases, the planning staff perceived the planning environment as containing opportunities for adjusting the agency's mission with the objective of being a better planning agency, involved in the critical issues of the community.

Once the mission of the agency is clearly understood, it is possible to formulate objectives, subobjectives, and strategies. For example, assume that a planning agency's mission requires that one of its objectives is to be a primary source of information for decision making. The staff would ask a number of questions to analyze how to achieve this objective. What information and in what forms do decisionmakers need and want? What are the steps and costs associated with acquiring data? How do the agency's computer capacities have to be built up in order to store, retrieve, and manipulate the data? How much staff effort should be devoted to this objective? Do current staff members have the necessary technical skills, or will new staff have to be recruited? How will the agency market the information—through newsletters, data-retrieval services for a fee, periodic reports on particular topics? Finally, what type of evaluation method will be used to see whether the objective is being met? After considering such questions, the management staff would choose particular techniques and tasks to achieve the objective.

Here is another example: Assume that a suburban planning agency has determined that one of its basic missions is to help to obtain infrastructure financing by drafting an impact fee ordinance. For this basic mission to be achieved, a number of objectives or subobjectives must be established and achieved:

1. Using nationwide and locally generated data, develop benchmark data on the infrastructure costs of development.
2. On the basis of the assembled data, prepare a public relations program that includes a simple, nontechnical issues report and briefings for the planning commission and governing board; in addition, obtain the cosponsorship of the chamber of commerce for a one-day conference.
3. Assuming that consensus from the governmental and private sectors is obtained on the problem of infrastructure finance and on the appropriateness and necessity of shifting some costs to the private sector, and assuming a consensus that some system should be developed, develop a computer-based impact-measurement program.
4. Seek legal counsel to develop a legally defensible impact fee ordinance.
5. Seek the support of the local representatives to the state general assembly to amend the state subdivision act to allow communities to require off-site and oversized sewer and water improvements.
6. Develop a fast and efficient administrative system to conduct subdivision review and impose impact fees.
7. Create an advisory council from the metropolitan home builders association to advise staff on ordinance development and administration.

This list illustrates some key elements of the strategic approach to managing but one possible program. Note that in addition to developing a good factual base (where some planning agencies, unfortunately, stop), it is necessary to be sensitive to political and economic issues in the planning environment. Hence, the objectives include early consultation with the chamber of commerce, which is vitally interested in economic development, and efforts to obtain the early support of the governing board, without which additional work may be a waste of time. The list also illustrates the importance of reaching out to clients and users—to educate, consult, and probably negotiate matters that will vitally affect them. Public relations techniques are a valuable means of communicating an agency's objectives; long, dry reports are not enough. Efforts to obtain the support of the state's general assembly are a reminder that although state statutes are an external factor, it may be possible to take steps to change such constraints. The creation of a builder's association advisory committee is an example of an agency using client opinion to design a better—and more acceptable—system.

Implementation strategies As the top management staff of the planning agency has been going through the situation analysis, assessing the implications of the analysis, rethinking the agency's mission, and choosing strategic directions for various elements of the agency's program, a draft of the agency's strategic plan will begin to emerge. This document should be succinct, clearly state the mission, contain a small number of strategic objectives, and spell out strategies and tactics to achieve the objectives.

Some of the strategies will relate to agency stance and style, but some strategies must deal with the critical issue of implementing the community's plans and policies. It is at this juncture that the *strategic plan for the agency as an organization* relates to the *plans and policies for the community*. Top management should determine the extent to which the agency and its program are oriented to policy implementation. That is, are agency activities, especially technical work, clearly connected to the implementation of agency policies, proposals, and plans?

Unfortunately, the planning director and top management will have few models to which to turn for examples. Planning literature based on the traditional planning process has an enormous amount of information on research and analysis, goal formulation, plan making, and plan testing, but almost nothing on implementation. There is, of course, a large body of knowledge on the implementation of zoning, subdivision regulations, and capital improvements programming, but if a planning agency cannot implement its policies through one of these tools, it must develop other implementation methods. Just as a planning agency has a concept of a comprehensive plan, it should develop a concept of an implementation plan. The literature is so sparse that it is not possible to suggest a single, let alone a best, model,[4] but it is possible to summarize issues that need to be addressed.

First, an implementation plan may not be a formal "plan" at all. It may simply be a set of management policies, some of which are included in the agency's strategic plan and some of which are in a separate memorandum setting performance standards for the conduct of any study, plan, or program.

Next, planning agency management must inventory the policy and plan elements that have been adopted or are under preparation. It is axiomatic that an agency cannot implement a policy it does not have. Thus, is there an up-to-date comprehensive plan? Which specific policy areas (e.g., transportation, housing, infrastructure, and so on) have been completed, are under way, or are planned in a future work program? The management staff must ask whether the agency's strategic plan calls for new work elements and must determine the extent to which it has set priorities for future work.

Critical issues that need to be considered for each element of the agency's work program of plans and studies include the following:

1. *Involvement of client groups*. Has an effort been made to include elected officials at the earliest possible stage and throughout the process—not

merely at the end? Does the plan element involve the full range of client groups that may be interested in the substance of the plan? (Client groups can include other planning agencies, other government agencies and levels of government, the private sector, and quasi-public organizations.) Has the staff determined whether a particular client group might be considered a supporter or an opponent of potential public policy directions? What steps are planned to ensure continuing support or to gain new support?

2. *Emphasis on implementation.* Is the plan element specifically geared to implementation, and does it approach implementation constraints, opportunities, and resources as part of the work task? For example, does a study explicitly identify the officer, department, or agency responsible for carrying out a particular policy; does the document include rough financial estimates of implementation costs; and does the document specify how existing or proposed regulations need to be changed?

3. *Political astuteness and sensitivity.* Assuming elected officials have been involved in a project, what needs to be done to ensure official adoption (where necessary) of a policy or plan by the appropriate governing officer or body? Have the planners or analysts conducting a particular work task been thoroughly briefed about the political sensitivities that will be required? Does the agency understand or try to identify the priorities of

---

Putting a bias for action into planning agency management: A practitioner's perspective The popular book *In Search of Excellence* by Thomas Peters and Robert Waterman, Jr., reported that the first common characteristic of most successful businesses is a bias for action. Yet, unfortunately, some planners in local government agencies still appear to have a bias for inaction, since most of the critical problems they deal with are of such scale and complexity that they often require vague, impractical, or esoteric solutions.

Local governments are complex, and there is often a need for sophisticated planning and coordination mechanisms to facilitate order and understanding. But in many governmental planning departments, the process is greatly overdone. The resulting complexity leads to lethargy, inertia, and ineffectiveness.

Peters and Waterman observed that "chunking" is an underlying principle associated with a bias for action. Chunking "simply means breaking things up to facilitate organizational fluidity and to encourage action." Whether they are called teams, task

forces, project centers, or quality circles, these small groups have the same objective—to identify, attack, and manage problems on a priority basis. In essence, the right people are brought together on a problem and are expected to solve it.

Small groups, as noted by Peters and Waterman, "are, quite simply, the basic organizational building blocks of excellent companies." The best public planning agencies have for many years successfully applied the chunking principle. Arlington, Texas, has divided the city into three geographic areas, and it staffs each with a complete planning team that provides all platting, zoning, and planning services for the area. Baltimore, Maryland; Beaumont, Texas; Windsor, Connecticut; and San Jose, California, have project review committees or development teams that expedite the consideration of new development concepts and ordinances in addition to the review and evaluation of specific problem projects. Baltimore uses a permit expediter who troubleshoots for projects and has the authority to intervene directly in the permitting process. The City of Los Angeles uses a housing expediter to encourage development of housing for

key elected officials, who ultimately must choose policies? Does the agency seek ways to help those officials articulate policies? Does the agency seek out opportunities to provide information or advice quickly, thereby providing greater visibility for the agency? Are there mechanisms within the governmental unit (such as a mayor's or manager's cabinet) to coordinate policy among departments and provide an opportunity for planning department input?

4. *Interagency and intergovernmental relations.* Does the agency have a comprehensive grasp of the activities of all agencies and governmental units that affect development in the region? How does the agency monitor the policies of others? What are the channels of communication, and how are they used in the maze of interagency and intergovernmental relations? For example, do governing board or agency staff serve on advisory committees of other agencies? Does the planning agency use people from these agencies on its own advisory committees?

5. *Self-evaluation.* How does the agency monitor the implementation of its own policies? Are past policy successes and failures analyzed to determine guidelines for future action?

Local government planning is a far more complex and sophisticated undertaking than merely gathering good information, conducting technically competent

---

low- and moderate-income individuals or families. The common practice shared by all these cities is that the time associated with each problem project is kept relatively short. Each project is given priority attention by an appropriate individual or group until resolved.

A bias for action requires a commitment on the part of local government planners to the actual production or delivery of products and services. For years, some planners wasted time arguing whether planning is a process or a product. In addition, the planning profession's traditional emphasis and excessive concern with process has often resulted in creation of a general mindset that minimizes the role, value, and importance of planning results.

To build respect, support, and effectiveness, planners must concentrate on a limited and manageable number of definable, concrete, and solvable issues. Planners have to learn how to break down complicated issues and problems into a series of comprehensible and resolvable elements. Many decisionmakers in local government are not unlike the successful corporate president who disliked long memos

and told his staff to "boil it down to something I can grasp." Even the most complicated problems can be understood and resolved if presented as a series of simple problems that can be intelligently acted upon. An appropriate Chinese proverb is "settle one difficulty and you keep hundreds away." Successful planners have learned to place an emphasis on solving one difficulty at a time in order to increase their perceived and actual value and effectiveness.

Planning is a means to intelligent action and not an end in itself. It should be obvious that a bias for immediate action is a necessary characteristic for effectiveness and excellence in planning. Planners also need to cultivate political and administrative leaders and the good will, respect, and support of the private sector.

Source: Bruce W. McClendon, "Putting a Bias for Action into Planning Agency Management: A Practitioner's Perspective." Reprinted with permission from *Public Administration Review* (July/August 1986): 352–55. © 1986 by The American Society for Public Administration, 1120 G Street, N.W., Washington, DC. All rights reserved.

analyses, and proposing "good" plans. A planning agency that pays serious attention to implementation strategies is likely to be an action-oriented agency that is interested in results. Top agency management must strategically think through and manage the agency's work program. Moreover, careful staffing is necessary to ensure that the necessary skills are available. These skills include the ability to work comfortably with elected officials and interest groups; the ability to deal with people who hold conflicting views; the ability to negotiate and develop consensus; and the ability to accept the fact that not every good policy is implementable.

Description of the agency in the future   The final step indicated in Figure 13–1 requires the agency to try to create a vision of itself in the future. Where does the agency want to be? How will it develop the capacity to carry out its missions? What objectives will it reach? What new functions will the agency undertake, and which old functions will it discard or delegate to other agencies? In a sense this is a statement of where the agency will be if it achieves its strategic objectives and mission. There are planning organizations managed by leaders who can articulate the agency's mission to each and every staff member. There are planning directors who have created what the literature calls a "corporate culture" in which key people know what to do because they clearly understand the mission of the agency. Effective planning leaders create teams of staff members who work together in order to create a management environment that leads to effectiveness.

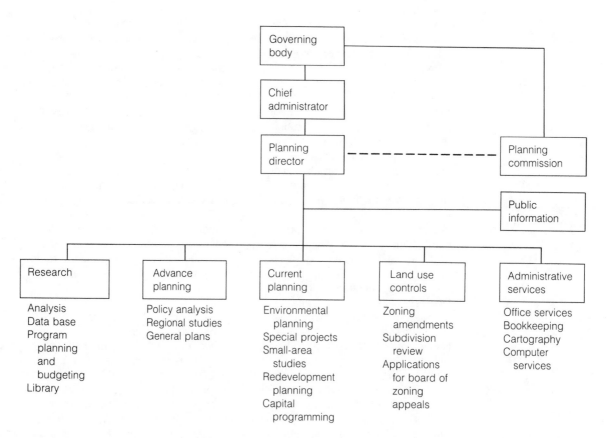

Figure 13–2   Typical organization of a local planning agency showing divisions that are common to many agencies.

After preparing a strategic plan for a planning agency, the manager must prepare detailed work programs and staffing and budgeting plans. These topics are covered elsewhere in this chapter.

Planning agency organization and functions[5]

The internal organization of planning agencies varies and is influenced by such factors as size, the position of the planning agency within the organizational framework of the local government, and the planning needs of the community. Figure 13–2 shows a typical organization of a planning agency with a traditional mandate.

In very small communities the staff may consist of a professional planner, an assistant planner, a draftsman, and a secretary. In such a small office the assignment of work is extremely flexible, and each staff member is involved in some way in almost all the activities of the office. As the number of staff members increases it becomes necessary to give various staff primary responsibility for certain kinds of work. The director, for example, is generally responsible for public functions, such as interaction with the mayor's office and the planning commission. One assistant planner may be responsible for collecting data for long-range plans, another for review of subdivision plats and zoning petitions. One secretary may serve as receptionist and typist, another will do all the filing and keep the financial records. As the office continues to grow, it will gradually become necessary to divide the agency into divisions, each with explicit responsibilities.

The division of an agency into departments has several advantages. First, it promotes efficiency by clarifying the responsibilities of each individual. Second, it promotes the development of skills through specialization. Personnel can be selected with training and experience suited to the needs of a particular unit: a landscape architect for the subdivision plat review division, an economist for the research division. Also, experience in a particular unit can allow persons with general skills to become specialists in specific aspects of agency work. The on-the-job training that is possible in a specialized unit also makes possible the effective use of nonprofessional personnel.

Another advantage of dividing an agency into specialized units is that it allows clients to more easily identify and contact key staff people. When an agency is loosely organized, all persons seeking information or a service tend to go to the director. If an agency has units with specific responsibilities, outsiders will go to the unit that relates to their needs. A builder goes to the subdivision plat review division. A school superintendent interested in population forecasts goes directly to the research division. Such direct contacts tend to foster more efficient communications between the agency and the various groups with which it needs to maintain contact, both in and out of government.

One of the most important advantages of dividing an agency is that it protects to some extent the continuity of long-range work assignments. Some agency work may take more than a year to complete; preparation of major reports and updating of comprehensive plan elements fall into this category. Every agency also has "brushfire" work—work that requires immediate attention. Brushfire work is usually no more important than other agency work, but its immediacy and public visibility often cause staff to be shifted from other tasks to work on the immediate problem. One consequence can be the virtual elimination of long-range planning, which is one of the most common complaints of agency directors. One solution is to designate certain units as responsible for long-range work and as not required to put out brushfires. In other words, agency organization can provide a mechanism that protects certain staff members from the disruption of day-to-day issues.

The division of an agency is not without hazard. It can reduce needed flexibility in the use of personnel if unit boundaries are observed too rigidly. When needs

Unofficial activities   Many . . . activities of the planning department are not recorded in any official list of duties. They include assuming the role of advocate for various groups and interests and geographic areas; generating new ideas about the physical environment and testing them before the public; and giving citizens a forum for voicing their complaints. Research into local physical, social, and economic conditions and the continuous provision of timely, easily understood information, regardless of whose cause it might help or hinder, can bring prestige and a measure of influence to those who provide it. It may be inherent in the nature of government that the more informal or voluntary activities serve the citizens as well as those that are required by law.

Source: Excerpted from Allan B. Jacobs, *Making City Planning Work* (Chicago: American Society of Planning Officials, 1978), 46.

arise that do not fit the responsibilities of one unit, it is often necessary to create task forces that cut across several units.

The division of an agency can also hamper personnel development. If division directors and their staffs concentrate exclusively on the work of their division, they may lose the comprehensive view of agency work that is necessary if each unit is to support the overall mission of the agency. Moreover, if a planner with a broad range of skills works for too long in a narrowly specialized unit, these general skills can become rusty and out-of-date; also, the ability to move upward or to another unit in the organization may be lost.

The most serious hazard in the division of an agency is that the arrangement will become so rigid that its organization predetermines the work program. The purpose of each division is to serve the overall mission of the agency—which is, ultimately, to respond to community needs. As these needs change, the agency's mission must change, and its internal organization may need to adjust. If staff within each subunit of the organization view their unit as an end in itself, the organization loses its ability to adapt to new situations.

There are several ways to divide an agency into divisions; these are as follows:

1. By function: the organization of the planning agency can be based on the major urban functions with which it is concerned. In an agency organized by function, land use, transportation, and recreation would be examples of internal units.
2. By process: agency organization can be based on the processes or skills necessary to carry out its work. In this case research and design would be examples of internal units.
3. By time: the agency can be organized according to the increments of time associated with its work. In this case, current planning, long-range planning, and continuing services would be examples of internal units.
4. By area: agency organization can be based on the major geographic units for which it has responsibility. In this case central business district planning, neighborhood area planning, and waterfront planning might be examples of internal units.

Few agencies are organized purely on one of these bases; in actual practice an agency blends several organizational arrangements to produce one that is most responsive to the needs of a particular community. Certain divisions are common to many agencies; these are public information, advance planning, current planning, land use control, research, and administrative services. These divisions are often subdivided into sections.

Public information

Although many plans get implemented through regulations and budgets, planning is an intrinsically *advisory* activity, which makes the function of public information extremely important. A planning agency of sufficient size and with adequate budgetary resources should have a professional public information officer; in large cities the mayor's office may have such a staff member to communicate with the media. In many planning departments, however, the planning director is responsible for this function.

Planning agencies must know how to deal with print and broadcast media, use community access cable television, prepare effective press releases, hold news conferences, give interviews, provide opportunities for field photos, publish agency newsletters, hold special conferences on critical planning issues, and effectively use public relations techniques.

Advance planning

The advance planning division is responsible for the development and maintenance of long-range plans. This may include the development of general plans or the updating of specific elements (for example, land use or transportation). The work of this division focuses largely on goal formulation and the definition of broad policies; it provides a framework or point of reference for other divisions in the agency. In crisis situations the advance planning staff may work on brushfire projects or may be loaned to other municipal departments to help them prepare plans.

Current planning

The current planning division is responsible for short-range developmental planning and brushfire situations. It may have sections responsible for small-area project plans, an urban design section, and a task force section specifically devoted to brushfire problems. Because the current planning division responds to the need for concrete advice on specific issues, its work tends to be narrowly focused and highly visible to decisionmakers. Sometimes this division is responsible for capital improvements programming.

Land use control

The land use control division administers the zoning and flood control ordinances, land subdivision regulations, and similar regulations; it also recommends periodic amendments to improve these mechanisms. Land use control personnel review all subdivision plats and zoning petitions and handle the agendas of the board of zoning appeals and the planning commission.

Research

The research (or "information") division supports the work of other divisions in a variety of ways. It often includes a section specifically responsible for maintaining a data base in such areas as population and housing. Microcomputers are used by the research division, and the division has staff to access the local government's computer system.

Research division data and forecasts are used by other planning divisions and by a variety of other agencies of government. The research division may be called on to support the decision-oriented work of the current planning division by conducting in-depth studies and policy analysis; or it may do general background studies in new technology, hillside development, housing abandonment, or other issues that are of interest to advance planning in the establishment of policy.

Administrative services

The administrative services division provides support to the other divisions of the agency. It includes such sections as drafting, library services, personnel, management, word processing, and desk-top publishing.

Other divisions

Given the wide variety in local government organization, planning departments may also have divisions dealing with economic development, urban design, capital improvements programming, annexation, housing, transportation, housing code enforcement, telecommunications, environmental impact assessment, community development (federal programs), technical assistance (consulting with cities by a county agency), one-stop permitting, and energy conservation. The list is potentially as long as the entire range of activities that local chief executives feel planning departments can handle.

In medium-sized communities the traditional divisions are often combined—

Figure 13–3   The formal and the informal organization. People will not stay put on the organization chart—the formal organization, that is. The real challenge is to bring the formal and informal organizations together.

for example, advance planning and current planning or current planning and land use control. In communities with serious fiscal problems, such consolidations may be essential.

Agency relationships: Operating in the planning network

There are very few communities in which all the planning is done by one agency acting alone. Rather, planning activities have expanded in a number of ways, both formally and informally. The result is a loose network of planning activities that permeates public institutions. The network includes the following components:

1. Planning within different units and levels of general government. This includes central cities, suburban municipalities, counties, townships, and state governments. This planning is usually general overall planning with a historical tendency to emphasize physical development.
2. Planning within the operating departments of general governments. This includes the planning that occurs within such departments as highways, health, recreation, and education at both the local and state levels. This planning is concerned primarily with the provision of a particular kind of service or facility.
3. Planning by regional agencies not responsible to a single general government. This includes such agencies as councils of governments, economic development districts, and other regional planning organizations. These agencies are primarily concerned with the coordination of plans and programs among various units of local government within a region.
4. Special-purpose planning agencies. These agencies, although they may vary widely in specific characteristics, have in common the fact that they deal with a particular service or program at a level that cuts across the boundaries of various units of government or the agencies within them. These special-purpose agencies include such organizations as areawide health planning councils and regional transportation study agencies.

Communication between a planning agency and other governmental units contributes to the agency's effectiveness. The day-to-day contact between a planning agency and other units is an important source of information for plan formulation and is also a means of gauging response to various plan proposals.

Agency relationships can be better understood if the organizational charts and other formal aspects of governmental structure are momentarily set aside. The official reports, news releases, laws, and other activities of a planning agency are only a part of its influence on public and private decisions in a community. The other part consists largely of informal contacts: the lunch meeting between a planner and an assistant director of the recreation department; a planner's sidewalk meeting with a developer; telephone calls between members of the planning staff and employees in local line departments and state agencies. This informal ebb and flow of information throughout the planning network and the local government is at the heart of an agency's vitality. This explains why planning based only on good analysis and information, as important as they are, can never be enough; "people skills" are extraordinarily important.

If informal contacts are the real substance of agency relationships, they are nevertheless conditioned by formal relationships. A planning agency that is a staff-level unit reporting to a city manager will tend to have a different relationship to line departments than would a planning agency organized as a line unit. The agency established as a staff-level unit would be perceived as more powerful than a line agency.

The sections that follow review the relationship of the planning agency to the individuals, agencies, and groups with which it has the most frequent and important contact.

The chief administrator

The relationship between the planning agency and the chief administrator is extremely important, especially in municipalities with the council-manager or strong mayor form of government. The influence of the chief administrator ranges from immediate operational issues to long-range policy questions. As the single person with the broadest influence on community decisions, the chief administrator can initiate new programs, lead publicly in the reconsideration of priorities, and throw the full weight of the local government administrative machinery behind a planning initiative.

The strong chief administrator is the chief planner for the community, in the sense that he or she oversees the development of strategies and action plans to respond to a broad range of community needs. Thus, the chief administrator who values planning will be especially interested in establishing the planning agency as a staff department. One authority has described this role for the planning agency as follows:

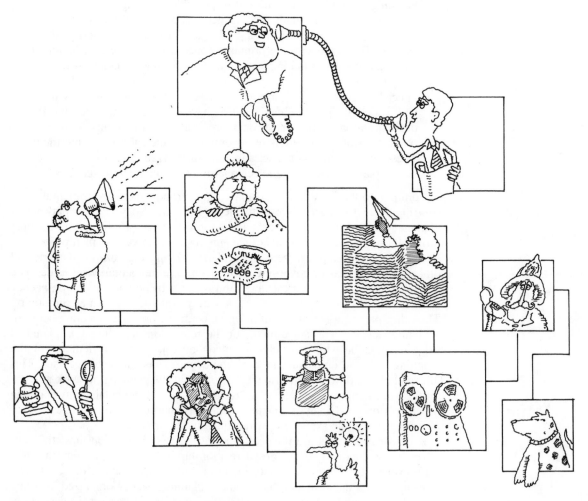

Figure 13–4   Position in the organizational structure does make a difference.

The notion of a staff role for planning is built on the assumption that the executive has central responsibility for developing policy, for coordination, and for directing and supervising the local government machinery through which development plans are carried into effect.[6]

When a planning department takes on an assignment from the chief executive, it must be aware that it will be working in a political environment characterized by ad hoc decision making, without enough consideration being given to overall and long-range policies. One planner who worked for a mayor on several policy studies makes the following observations about the principles that guide this kind of planning activity:

The first and overriding principle is that public persuasion follows only from a combination of strong policy and effective communication.

Second, the public impression of accomplishments by the chief executive will flow from one, two, or at most three projects or programs with which he has repeatedly been identified.

Third, it is essential that strategies of crisis management be devised so that crises can be defused.

Fourth, since crises and controversies are more noticeable to the public . . . it is important to try [to take] the initiative and . . . define the issues.

Fifth, . . . scenarios should be developed for the key programs and projects.

The key elements of policy are that it be consistent with the course of recent history, that the bureaucracy have the ability and the will to carry it out, that the decision be within the scope of what a chief executive can hope to affect, that it be within financial reach, that it be timely, and that the entire purpose and process of policy be explainable to the general public.[7]

The local legislative body

The local legislative body interacts with the planning agency in several ways. Because the council adopts the budget and passes local laws (including zoning ordinances), it is the final decision maker on the most fundamental policy issues in the community. Although the chief administrator develops and proposes the budget or makes recommendations on the programs that the budget supports, the council must give its approval. In effect, the council is the ultimate audience for the recommendations that emerge from planning activities.

Most of the interaction between the planning agency and the legislative body occurs in the context of zoning decisions. This is important for two reasons: First, the cumulative effect of zoning decisions has a profound impact on the physical development of the community. Second, the intensity and frequency of zoning activity make it the primary context for contact between the planning agency and the legislative body; it is here that the legislative body is most likely to observe the planning agency in action. Opinions that council members form about staff competence and integrity in the context of zoning actions may influence their willingness to accept planning agency advice in other contexts. Because zoning actions tend to be controversial and can be time-consuming and distasteful to the council, the conduct of the planning agency is particularly important.

Local boards and commissions

While the planning department has direct, formal relationships with the planning commission and the zoning board, it also has to interact with numerous boards and commissions in the governmental fabric of every urban community, many of which have responsibilities that relate to community growth and development. The list would typically include local school district boards, park and recreation commissions, and water or sewer utility district boards.

A major objective of planning agency contact with boards and commissions

Figure 13–5   The transportation department and the
planning department plan a subway.

is to influence them to pursue policies that support the overall plans for the
community. A new fringe area school, for example, needs to be located so that
it will serve a future—as well as the present—population distribution pattern.
The school should not be placed on a site that will be adversely affected by
planned changes in the street network. Moreover, the location of a new school,
the extension of public utilities, and the modification of bus services are all
examples of "priming actions," actions that influence many other developmental
decisions. Because their activities can affect overall community development, it
is important that the policies of independent boards and commissions support
comprehensive development policies adopted by general-purpose local governments.

Line departments

The line departments are the front lines of local government. They are the
departments that collect garbage, repair streets, and fight fires. Although the
planning agency has little or no contact with their day-to-day affairs, important
relationships do exist, primarily in several contexts: mandatory referral, a service
role, line department program planning, and capital budgeting.

   A mandatory referral state law or local ordinance requires that the planning
agency have the opportunity to review proposals of local government departments and comment on their appropriations to overall development plans. If a
good relationship exists between the planning agency and the line department,
the review may take the form of a continuing consultation that begins early in
the consideration of the project and continues through the selection of the site,
the design of the facility, and funding by the legislative body. If the relationship
is poor, the review may occur only after project plans have become so detailed
that the line department is reluctant to alter them.

   The planning agency can solicit the cooperation of line departments in at least
two ways. First, it can emphasize its service role, as a source of information and
skills that the line department can use to do a better job. The second way to
obtain cooperation from the line departments is to have the chief executive

require it. A chief executive who wants a strong, staff-level planning function will insist that department heads cooperate. This can be effective and it may be necessary, but coercion is a poor substitute for voluntary cooperation.

Program planning—planning for more effective delivery of services—often occurs in line departments. It may involve relatively simple tasks such as anticipating personnel and equipment needs for the summer recreation program; it may also involve developing entirely new programs such as establishing a paramedic squad. The initiation of new programs is likely to be conducted at the staff level in association with the chief administrator. The same would be true of program planning that considers the relative merit of alternative programs in order to better allocate resources; this type of program planning is a necessary prerequisite to budgeting. The annual budget (including both capital and operating budgets), is an important element in the administrative program-planning process for the achievement of community goals. Properly used, the operating and capital budgets authorize current action to meet community needs. They assign responsibility to various agencies and departments for accomplishing specific objectives and allocate the resources necessary for accomplishing those objectives.

The link between planning and budgeting has grown much stronger as planning has been accepted as an integral part of government operations. It is important to note that this new emphasis on budgeting differs from the traditional emphasis on capital budgeting. In the traditional view, the planning department's role in budgeting was to ensure that land acquisition and construction of major public facilities, such as schools, were scheduled so that they would be in place when needed. The larger view concerns itself, in addition, with the operational costs incurred year by year, as programs in education, garbage collection, police protection, and other areas are initiated or altered.

Development management

In numerous communities throughout the nation, in both suburban areas and mature cities, a more intimate relationship is emerging between the planning agency and other officials, administrators, and departments. Some planners refer to this relationship as *development management*. Development management is based on the realization that effective development (and redevelopment) requires a management team effort.

In the suburban context, for example, a growth management system may require that the planning agency conduct environmental assessments of new development; that the budget officer conduct cost-revenue studies measuring the fiscal impact of that development; that careful study and consultation with the municipal attorney be undertaken to determine the legal constraints on local action to control growth; and that the public works department be closely involved in programming and scheduling the construction of utility systems that will serve the development.

In the older city the goal is stabilization and renewal. Here the planning agency will be in close working relationships with a housing authority; the local economic development agency; social service agencies; numerous federal officials in regional offices who oversee federally funded local government programs; and quasi-public and private groups involved with commercial and industrial investments, job programs, or historic preservation.

In a certain sense every local agency is a planning agency, and all must work together if public policy objectives are to be achieved. Some cities with the council-manager plan have created cabinets of deputy managers to achieve this kind of top-level coordination.

Proposed Planning Work Program 1982/83

Project Title	Professional Staff Years 81/82	82/83	Project Title	Professional Staff Years 81/82	82/83
Regional Coordination and Continuing Activities			**General Plan**		
Board Referrals	2.1	2.1	Blue Ribbon Mobile Homes	.5	.2
Legislation	.9	.5	General Plan Information	1.0	1.0
Metropolitan Transit Development Board	.4	.0	General Plan Amendment 81-01 (GPA)	2.4	.0
Other Regional Coordination	.3	.3	General Plan Amendment 82-01 (Now GPA 82-04)	1.4	1.8
Advisory Board	.3	.0	General Plan Amendment 83-01	.0	1.2
Environmental Review Board Support	.2	.0	General Plan Amendment 83-02	.0	1.2
	4.2	2.9	General Plan Amendment 83-03	.0	1.0
			Housing	2.0	2.0
Government Structures			I-15 Corridor Plan	1.8	.0
Government Structures	2.3	1.0	Local Coastal Program	2.0	.0
			Specific Plan Review	.4	.2
Information Systems			Riding and Hiking	.5	.0
Demographic Estimates	1.0	.7	Bureau of Land Management Land Exchanges	.0	.2
Economic Analysis	1.0	.6	Otay Mesa GPA	.0	1.4
Land Use Information Systems	1.3	1.0	Bonsall Community Plan	.0	1.0
	3.3	2.3	Sycamore Canyon Off-Road Vehicle	.0	.4
				12.0	11.6
Transportation Projects					
Bike Lane Annual Program	.3	.3	**Facilities**		
East County Circulation Element	.7	.2	Capital Improvements Program Review (CIP)	.3	.1
Transportation Systems Element	1.5	1.5	Growth Information System/Facility Adequacy Policy	2.3	3.0
	2.5	2.0	Groundwater Policy/Implementation	1.0	1.0
			Water Resources Study	.9	.5
Environment			65402 Review	1.4	1.3
Energy Office	2.0	1.0	Facility Adequacy Policy	.5	.0
San Diego River	.3	.5		6.4	5.9
San Dieguito River study	.3	.0			
	2.6	1.5	**Zoning & Map Implementation**		
			Central Mountain	.5	.0
Ordinance			County Islands	.5	.5
County Code Amendments	.6	.6	Desert	.5	.3
Ordinance Subscriptions	.1	.0	GPA 81-01	1.0	.0
Process Simplification	1.3	1.6	GPA 82-01	.5	.0
Special Project	.7	.7	Mountain Empire	1.0	.5
Zoning Ordinance Amendments	1.7	1.7	North Mountain	.5	.5
	4.4	4.6	Pala Pauma	.5	.2
			Sand and Gravel Zoning	.6	.3
				5.6	2.3
			Total Professional Staff Years	43.3	34.1

"Below-the-Line" Projects

Project Title	Total Professional Staff Years	Project Title	Total Professional Staff Years
Billboard Regulations	0.5	Zoning Ordinance Revisions	2.0
Southbay Subregional Plan	1.1	General Plan Revisions	2.0
Southbay Circulation Element	1.2	Subdivision Ordinance Revisions	2.0
Fallbrook Plan Standardization	1.0	Series VI Population Forecast	0.4
Traffic Assignments	1.0	Commercial Industrial Standards	1.4
Circulation Element Mapping Coordination	0.5	Descanso Groundwater Study	0.5
Edgemoor Master Plan	0.2	Metropolitan Transit Development Board	0.4
Environmental Review Board (ERB)	0.4	Advisory Board	0.3
No Shooting Ordinance Revision County-wide	0.5	North County Metro Circulation Element	0.9
Community Planning Group Training	0.2	I-15 Corridor	1.5
San Luis Rey River	1.0	Local Coastal Plan Implementation	1.5
Sweetwater River	1.0	Riding and Hiking	0.5
		Valle de Oro Community Plan Update	1.0
		Poway Santee Boundary Adjustments	0.3
		Fallbrook Referrals	0.5
		Total	21.4

Figure 13–6 Sample work program showing allocation of staff resources for one year.

Intergovernmental relations

Today's planner works in a complex intergovernmental context in which decision-making authority is extremely fragmented, but where the actions of other governments at the local, metropolitan, state, and national levels can affect a particular community in profound ways. The following illustrations can only touch upon the complexity of intergovernmental relationships. Special districts may plan and operate sewerage and water systems, collect and dispose of refuse, operate port and toll roads, and operate hospitals and health facilities. Counties provide some police protection, build roads, operate social welfare services, run court systems, control land use in unincorporated areas, and manage open space and recreation facilities. Metropolitan councils of government and planning agencies plan and administer intergovernmental programs. State governments build highways, are responsible for higher-education facilities, manage state recreation systems, and administer a growing number of environmental regulations related to air, water, and land.

What are the practical implications for the local planning agency? It must spend a considerable amount of time monitoring the programs and actions of others, analyzing plans prepared by others, preparing position papers for local government, attending meetings, serving on advisory committees, and generally providing the technical background for the local manager and mayor who must take public positions on areawide and intergovernmental policies.

General administration

The daily management and administration of the planning agency requires establishing a work program, overseeing staff, devising and maintaining a budget, and following a variety of operating procedures. No matter how creative and professional a planning staff might be, it must attend to daily operations if it is to meet its work program objectives and stay within the budget. This section of the chapter will highlight some of the general administrative components of a smoothly run agency.

Work programming

If a planning agency is to plan for a community, it must first plan for itself by identifying its long-range strategic objectives (discussed earlier in this chapter) and by planning the tasks that need to be accomplished to meet those objectives. In addition to planning specific work elements for each project, it is necessary also to plan for continuing activities such as zoning administration and capital improvements programming, as well as for the inevitable special studies and requests. Work programming also enables the agency's director to allocate the financial resources and staff that will be needed to conduct the program.

A system of work measurement is a prerequisite to work programming. Although planners are professionals and unlikely to be required to punch a time clock, some type of record-keeping system is mandatory for all but the smallest agency. Tracking the use of staff resources helps the agency director manage current work and plan future work. A work measurement system classifies the agency's work into categories such as long-range planning, special studies, and zoning administration. Monthly time sheets for all staff members can be easily tabulated on most office microcomputers.

Unless an agency has been established only recently or significantly enlarged because of rapid growth in the community, it is unlikely to have enough resources at its disposal to conduct all the work that it deems necessary or desirable. The agency will therefore have to choose among competing projects—a task that will be easier if the director has a sense of the agency's strategic objectives.

However, most planners like to be comprehensive and will feel a certain degree of frustration in not being able to undertake certain projects because of budget limitations.

One useful way to divide an agency's work is to separate those things that it must do on a continuing basis (for example, zoning administration) from those that it may choose to do as opportunities arise. On the basis of past experience and data, staff and time estimates are then made for both continuing operations and particular projects for the coming year. Figure 13–6 summarizes one agency's activities for a year. Note that the current year is compared to a projected year; and that additional activities that may be desirable, but outside the expected budget, are also shown at the bottom of the chart. Analysis of Figure 13–6 shows that the agency was engaged in cutback management: its professional staff years show a decline by almost 10 persons, and the "below-the-line" projects add up to 21 staff years.

Although the work program will be prepared by the agency's director and top management staff, the planning commission, the chief executive officer, and the legislative body will all have a vote in determining which work is to be funded for the next fiscal year.

Staffing[8]

The pool of professional planners has grown substantially in recent years, and there is no reason why adequately funded agencies cannot be adequately staffed. What kind of staff do agencies employ, and how is that staff used?

The planning director   The position of the planning director is critical. Those who view the agency from the outside, whether citizens, political leaders, or other government employees, see the director as the person who speaks for the agency. The director's role is to influence those inside and outside the agency to cooperate to achieve common goals. Leadership within the agency includes at least the following four elements:

1. *Communication of goals to subordinates.* Communication from the planning director relies more on persuasion and explanation than on the exercise of authority. The director's aim is to ensure that staff members fully understand— and act on—agency objectives and that they develop personal objectives that support those of the planning department.
2. *Motivation of subordinates.* The director seeks to instill in staff a desire to get the job done. Motivation concerns both the quantity and quality of work. It can be promoted by such means as personal example, incentive, or clarity of direction. Motivation often depends on intangibles such as office atmosphere and rapport between management and other staff.
3. *Coordination of effort.* Few situations are more frustrating to staff members than to discover that they are working at cross-purposes. The director is responsible for allocating work so that sections function in mutually supportive ways. This involves, for example, timing of work assignments to ensure that the product of one task is ready when it is needed as input to another task. It also involves maintaining common goals to prevent work from overlapping or conflicting. In a poorly coordinated agency, for example, one might find the land use planning section and the zoning section both working on a study of how to accommodate a rapidly growing fringe area—with neither section being aware of the work of the other.
4. *Reporting on agency work and accomplishments.* To ensure that agency objectives continue to reflect community objectives, the director reports periodically to political leaders, the planning commission, and the public. The response to such reporting can be used to inform employees about acceptance of their work. If the work is well accepted, morale is strengthened and future work tends to be approached with greater dedication.[9]

The leadership function of the planning director also includes a political aspect. Public acceptance of the agency's work is influenced by the degree to which the community perception of the public interest is mirrored in the work of the agency. The director articulates the public interest in planning issues; if this is done well, it will tend to promote both public esteem for the agency and pride among agency employees.

The planning director plays a variety of roles, which vary with the community, agency priorities, and the composition of the staff. Ideally, a director's personal strong points should match the most critical needs of the agency. One author has summarized the roles of the planning director:

1. *Analyst.* Is an expert in the analysis of data and the application of the scientific method.
2. *Organizer.* Develops a constituency in support of the planning process. Assesses decision-making processes and determines how to participate in them to influence decisions.
3. *Broker.* Mediates issues and negotiates decisions.
4. *Advocate.* Assists client groups with information and advice.
5. *Enabler.* Provides indirect leadership, guiding others to achieve their objectives. Encourages and supports client groups to develop their own leadership skills.
6. *Educator.* Initiates outreach activities to educate the public on the purposes and functions of planning and to share training and experience with aspiring planners.
7. *Publicist.* Creates an awareness of planning. Publicizes information useful to the planning constituency.[10]

The typical planning director must give some attention to all these roles but usually finds that progress in some roles is achieved at the expense of progress in others. Typically, a person appointed as director has served previously in positions that emphasized the role of professional planner. Although the individual's rise through the ranks may reflect a history of achievement in largely technical roles, the director of a large agency can seldom become significantly involved in the technical details of programming a data-collection system, revising a complex site design proposal, or writing a technical report on the impact of freeway locations on air quality. Instead, the director is called upon to review the work of other staff members, to coordinate work within the agency, and to present agency activities to decision makers in a way that provides maximum impact. Ironically, successful directors often find that they must allow their own technical skills to wither to some degree in order to give appropriate attention to a wide variety of agency activities.

The director who is conscious of the various roles required by the position will be especially attentive to how the agency is perceived by key decisionmakers. The director can adopt a variety of strategies in establishing relationships with decisionmakers, including the following:

1. *The technical expert strategy.* Here the director emphasizes the use of planning techniques and skills to present objective advice to political decisionmakers. The strategy focuses on the nonpolitical or nonadvocacy role of the staff. It presumes both the presence of a high level of technical skill on the part of the staff and the willingness of decisionmakers to value technical information as a basis for decisions.
2. *The confidential-adviser strategy.* The director may be able to establish relationships with key decisionmakers that depend largely on personal trust. Strong faith in the director's personal judgment usually comes about only after some years of successful performance, during which the director comes to be viewed as trustworthy, discreet, and knowledgeable about community attitudes.
3. *The innovator strategy.* Some communities may benefit most from a director who is willing to suggest bold solutions to problems. The innovative planning director is highly visible to the public as an advocate of actions not previously considered. Community political leaders can observe the community's reaction to new ideas

and then adopt as their own those that gain broad acceptance. The risk of rejection is borne by the planner, who can be an asset to the politician who is willing to endure the initiation of controversy.[11]

These strategies do not exclude one another entirely, but most directors emphasize one at the expense of others. The choice reflects personal style, the needs of the community, the past history of the agency, and the preferences or styles of political leaders.

Staff composition   The composition of the agency staff should be tailored to the needs of the community and to the role of the agency in that community. A rapidly growing medium-sized city, for example, would probably want substantial skills related to land use control in both its legal and its design aspects. A rural multicounty planning agency might be especially interested in having some staff with skills in economic analysis. A central-city agency in an older city might want staff with special skills in housing, policy analysis, or planning for social services delivery.

Planning agency staff can usually be grouped into three broad classes: support, paraprofessional, and professional. The support staff category includes secretaries, bookkeepers, drafting room personnel, and similar positions. Support positions are usually filled under personnel guidelines or civil service procedures that are uniform for the community.

Paraprofessionals may be used to collect data, prepare rezoning application forms, conduct field surveys, and carry out other similar tasks. Such tasks do not require degrees in planning. Paraprofessional positions can be filled by persons who hold a college degree that is not related to planning; training occurs on the job.

At the entry level, professional personnel typically consist of two groups. The largest group consists of persons holding a master's degree in planning, which is widely accepted as a basis for entry at a professional level. Other persons who occupy professional positions have undergraduate degrees in engineering, architecture, or landscape architecture or graduate degrees in related fields such as economics, sociology, geography, or public administration. Above the entry level, full professional status is usually accorded those who meet the qualifications of certified planner, as set by the American Institute of Certified Planners, an institute of the American Planning Association.

Consultants   Most planning agencies, even large agencies with specialists on their staffs, occasionally find a need to seek outside professional help. A consultant is a way of dealing with such a situation.

Consultants are often specialists by both training and experience. Transportation planning, economic analysis, historic preservation, and health systems planning are just a few of the subject areas in which consultant specialists may be found. The agency using a specialist consultant not only gets the benefit of a product; it may also profit by having some staff members acquire informal training through contact with the consultant.

A traditional role for consultants is to provide planning services to those communities that do not have a resident professional staff. Consultants can, for example, prepare studies and long-range plans for such communities. They can also be put on retainer to attend regular meetings, conduct special studies, and give advice when needed.

How a city or agency seeks and hires a consultant is an important management issue. Some communities waste too much of their own and the consultant's time and money by trying to obtain detailed proposals from too many different companies. This practice drives up costs for the consulting firms, which eventually pass along the costs to the public.

A study of public and private needs in the consulting process recommends four ways to procure consultant services:

1. *Single-source.* The planning agency simply contacts a single firm with which it has had contracts in the past and proceeds with the project.
2. *List of prequalified candidates.* If an agency has long experience with several firms and knows the work of others very well, the selection can be made from among these two lists.
3. *Request for qualifications (RFQ).* The planning agency publicly announces an upcoming project and seeks information from firms about their qualifications and experience, list of projects, and references. Then the top three to five firms are interviewed and a final selection made.
4. *A two-step process.* In the two-step process, the agency develops a detailed work program—a request for proposal (RFP)—that it sends to a small number (3–5) of firms for a detailed response describing the methodology the company would use to approach the problem.[12]

Budgeting

A local planning agency's budget has to be prepared with several perspectives in mind. First, the proposed work program allocates staff time both to ongoing staff work and to special projects. Staff time on any given project translates into salaries, and the agency's director must plan the work program carefully to obtain the right combination of senior, middle-level, and junior-level staff members. Over several years of experience, an agency director will acquire a good sense of how the overall resources allocated to the agency are further suballocated throughout the staff.

Many local governments have position classification systems that specify the salary for a particular position at various levels of experience. In addition to professional salaries, budget allocations must be made for other personnel such as secretaries, draftsmen, and the wide variety of specialists a planning agency uses. Finally, funds must be allocated to nonpersonnel costs such as supplies, transportation, continuing education, and equipment purchase and rental. It is entirely likely that a first-draft work program and budget will exceed available money allocated to the department, and thus program cuts will have to be made. For the general result of this process, see Figure 13–6, which identifies "below-the-line" projects that cannot be funded.

The source of funds for local governmental planning has changed over the last several decades. At one time planning agencies were funded solely through the local government's general funds. A very small amount of money was generated through fees for processing permits, but generally this barely covered the cost of legal notices in newspapers. During the late 1960s and most of the 1970s there was an explosive growth in federal funds for planning. Federal programs in areas such as housing, renewal, community development, and coastal zone management not only funded the facility or program but also funded the planning that was required to receive the money. Between 1954 and 1980, as part of the HUD-administered "701" program, federal funds were available for general plans. Some agencies had between one-third and one-half of their budgets funded through federal programs.

During most of the 1980s, planning agencies have had to adjust to the almost entire withdrawal of federal funds for local government planning. The size of agency staffs has remained constant or decreased. A combination of factors, including high inflation rates, less federal funding for local government in general, and tax limitation referenda, resulted in cutback management. Currently, planning is supported almost entirely by local government funds, except for those agencies that use fees for processing permits to pay for land use control administration. Agencies are increasingly charging developers the actual costs of development review; for example, a fee of several thousand dollars might be imposed on a large planned unit development or shopping center. Of course, this method of raising planning funds has its perils when the general economy and development slow down.

Some planning agencies have tried to obtain funds through a variety of other techniques: providing technical assistance to lower levels of government, charging subscription fees for agency newsletters, and providing data services.

Another way to deal with budgeting constraints is to cut down the actual amount of work. If an agency has limited funds, it must spend less time on development processing—even if it charges higher fees. Many agencies have redesigned their zoning and land subdivision administration processes to cut the time and staff required for reviews. This change is welcome to the development industry, which advocates streamlining permitting.

Office management

This section highlights just a few of the numerous issues involved in agency office management.

Because planning agencies produce so much paper, modern office technology is virtually a necessity to keep the work flow going. In particular, microcomputers for data processing (tracking development fees and permits, keeping agency statistics, and so on) are coming into widespread use. Word-processing equipment allows planners and their secretarial support to be much more efficient in writing and editing agency reports, and microcomputer programs permit in-house desk-top publishing. Computers that have a computer-aided design (CAD) capability are also providing agencies with more flexibility. Ink-drawn maps are increasingly being replaced by computer-printed maps and graphics.

A planning agency's library also demands some management attention. The largest agencies need a full-time professional librarian to develop a classification system, keep up with acquisitions, and provide bibliographic services. Many medium- and small-sized agencies, however, have problems maintaining their libraries, which are not large enough to attract a professional librarian.

Many planning agencies have staff manuals that provide regulations on a host of personnel and office management topics, including work hours, annual and sick leave, lunch and other breaks, conflict of interest, telephone use, affirmative action, performance evaluation, use of government vehicles and equipment, and continuing education and conferences. A staff manual (sometimes called an office handbook) is particularly useful for orienting new employees. It is essential that these manuals be kept up to date.

Administration of planning commission and zoning board agendas

For local planning agencies that administer zoning and land subdivision regulations, one of the most time-consuming operational management functions is to keep the work flowing through the planning commission and zoning board of appeals. Because most state enabling laws relating to zoning and subdivision administration mandate publication of the time and topic of a meeting in a general circulation newspaper a specific amount of time before a meeting, and further mandate decisions within a certain period of time, it is important to adopt administrative procedures that help to maintain a steady work flow.

The first essential ingredient of a good administrative system for land use control is a series of forms for developers and applicants to complete as part of the initial application process. There are several advantages to having good forms. First, they shift some of the work to the developer's planner and architect and away from the planning agency. Second, asking a standard set of questions ensures that a lack of information does not become evident in the middle of a public hearing, thus causing delays. And a commissioner or board member will find a standard format easier to use, since the same information is always in the same place.

The staff should have its own internal set of forms for making recommendations to boards and commissions. Sometimes these forms can extract the most critical information from the developer's forms and then be used in their stead; again, the standardized format saves staff time and commission meeting time. The staff should also have a standard reporting format for each type of agenda item (rezoning, map amendment variances, planned unit development, and so on). These reports should be kept short, succinct, and free of jargon.

The staff should develop a system of obtaining, supplying, reproducing, and displaying graphic materials related to the board's agenda. The meeting room should contain a slide projector and overhead projector and screen, blackboards or flip charts, and other surfaces on which graphic materials can be mounted.

Finally, all commission and board members, particularly the chair, should receive and read manuals on the conduct of meetings. Where possible, new members should go through training exercises or should attend regional planning meetings, where effective meeting techniques are frequently presented.

Conclusion

This chapter has emphasized a set of interrelated principles about what managing a planning agency really means. There is a crucial difference between "administration" and "management." The first involves the day-to-day tasks that make an organization run smoothly. The second involves thinking about the most important issues that affect an organization's failure, success, or even survival. In the view of George A. Steiner:

There are two types of management. That which is done at the top of an organizational structure is strategic management. Everything else is operational management.

Strategic planning is a backbone support to strategic management.[13]

Peter Drucker has said that one of the tasks of top management is the formulation and implementation of strategy. He defined this activity as "the task of thinking through the mission of the business, that is, of asking the question 'What is our business and what should it be?'"[14] The planning manager must think through the mission of the agency and manage it in accordance with strategic objectives that help improve the agency's effectiveness.

1 Robert A. Walker, *The Planning Function in Urban Government* (Chicago: University of Chicago Press, 1941).

2 Surveys were conducted by the American Planning Association in 1950, 1965, 1979, and 1987, as part of its Planning Advisory Service Report series.

3 The author of this chapter provided staff resources for the American Planning Association in preparing its own strategic plans during the 1980s and tested some of these ideas in training seminars in 1983. A convenient place to begin with John M. Bryson's work is a special issue of *The Journal of the American Planning Association*: 53 (Winter 1987).

4 See, for example, Richard S. Bolan, "Emerging Views of Planning," *Journal of the American Institute of Planners* 33 (July 1967); Albert Z. Guttenberg, "The Tactical Plan," in Melvin M. Weber, ed., *Explorations into Urban Structure* (Philadelphia: University of Pennsylvania Press, 1964); Frank S. So, *Metropolitan Planning Policy Implementation*,

Planning Advisory Service Report no. 262 (Chicago: American Planning Association, 1970); and Jerome L. Kaufman, "Making Planners More Effective Strategists," in Barry Checkoway, ed., *Strategic Perspectives on Planning Practice* (Lexington, MA: Lexington Books, 1986).

5 This section of the chapter is adapted from James A. Spencer, "Planning Agency Management," in Frank S. So et al., eds., *The Practice of Local Government Planning* (Washington, DC: International City Management Association, 1979).

6 James H. Pickford, "The Local Planning Agency: Organization and Structure," in William T. Goodman and Eric C. Freund, eds., *Principles and Practice of Urban Planning* (Washington, DC: International City Management Association, 1968), 540.

7 This is an excerpt from a manuscript by William Lucy reproduced in David C. Slater, *Management of Local Planning* (Washington, DC: International City Management Association, 1984), 148.

8   The section on staffing is adapted from James A. Spencer, "Planning Agency Management," in So et al., *Practice of Local Government Planning*, 81–85.

9   Adapted from James M. Banovetz et al., "Leadership Styles and Strategies," in James M. Banovetz, ed., *Managing the Modern City* (Washington, DC: International City Management Association, 1971), 113.

10   Adapted from Edmund M. Burke, *A Participatory Approach to Urban Planning* (New York: Human Sciences Press, 1979), 269–74.

11   Adapted from Alan A. Altshuler, *The City Planning Process: A Political Analysis* (Ithaca, NY: Cornell University Press, 1969), 334–49.

12   Adapted from Efraim Gil et al., *Working with Consultants*, Planning Advisory Service Report no. 378 (Chicago: American Planning Association, 1983), 5–9.

13   George A. Steiner, *Strategic Planning: What Every Manager Must Know* (New York: Free Press, 1979), 4.

14   Ibid., 6.

Finance and budgeting

The purpose of this chapter is to provide a general introduction to the public finance aspects of urban planning.[1] Particular emphasis is placed on the role of the planning agency in local government finance management and decision making.

The first section of this chapter discusses sources of revenue with an emphasis on taxes and grants-in-aid.

The next section contains a discussion of the budgetary process in general, with emphasis on the operating budget. A step-by-step outline of the budgetary process is given, and various budget systems are described and evaluated.

Capital improvements programming is then discussed in detail, including the benefits of such programming, its financing, its fiscal policies, and the administrative process involved. Because the influence of intergovernmental relations and the political process on capital improvements programming is considerable, these topics are taken up in some detail. The section ends by relating capital improvements programming to a number of other planning tools.

The final section discusses the importance to planning of cost-revenue studies. The emphasis here is on the role of fiscal impact analyses. One method of this type of analysis is outlined, and policy issues involved in these analyses are discussed—particularly those equity issues that will continue to confront decision makers faced with increasing urban growth and dwindling resources.

Sources of revenue

Local public officials and experts in the public finance field spend vast amounts of time thinking and worrying about how government revenue will be found to pay for public services, including the programs and projects that planning agencies propose. However, the literature on taxes and revenue is so large that this overview can provide only an outline of the subject. Emphasis will be placed on basic principles and relevance to the urban planning function.

There is a legal foundation to the raising of revenue. Federal and state constitutions have provisions concerning governmental authority to raise revenue, as well as standards for equity and due process. Local governments derive power to tax from state constitutions and state statutes. Although some home-rule cities may have some flexibility in revenue policy, most municipalities may not impose a tax or fee without specific state authorization. State laws, statutes, and court decisions may govern the types of taxes that may be imposed, maximum rates, principles involved in uniform assessments, requirements for local ordinances or referenda, what a community may borrow in terms of both purpose and amount, and a large number of other requirements.

Revenue can be classified according to whether it is a tax, a user charge, an administrative fee, a license, a debt service, or a grant-in-aid. Some taxes go into a community's general fund and may be used for any lawful purpose. Other taxes or fees are earmarked—that is, may be spent only for a particular service.

The equity of a tax depends on the relationship between a *tax base* and a *tax rate*. Most taxes—such as property and income taxes—are stated in terms of a rate that is applied to a base. The base may be the value of a property, the amount of gross personal income, or an expenditure. Property taxes are usually stated as a percentage, as a mill (one-tenth of one cent), or sometimes as dollars per $100 or $1,000 of value. A tax rate on income may be either a flat rate or a progressive rate as income rises. The sales tax is an example of a percentage applied to a particular expenditure.

An important characteristic of any tax is the degree to which it is progressive, proportional, or regressive. If a tax rate increases as the tax base increases (for example, federal income taxes), the tax is considered to be progressive. If all persons pay the same rate of income tax for every dollar they earn, the tax is considered proportional. If persons with low incomes spend a larger proportion of their incomes on taxes than persons with higher incomes spend, the tax is considered regressive. For example, sales taxes are typically considered regressive, as is the United States social security tax.

Equity and distributional and economic effects create other tax-related issues. Some of these issues will be discussed in the section on the property tax; others are beyond the scope of this book. The issues raised in connection with equity and distributional and economic effects are illustrated by questions such as the following: What are the implications of the fact that owners of single-family houses must pay their own taxes, whereas those in rental units can shift their taxes to the owners of the units? What happens when business fees and taxes are simply passed on to the consumer in the form of higher prices? What are the effects of local and state tax rates on decisions regarding industrial and commercial location?

The property tax

The property tax historically has been one of the most important sources of local government revenue. State laws classify property as real property and personal property and further classify personal property as tangible and intangible. Generally speaking, real property is defined as land and all structural improvements. The real property tax is of greatest concern to urban planners because of potential impacts on urban development patterns.

The three essential steps in administering a property tax are assessing the value, setting the tax rate, and collecting the tax. The assessment function in local government involves locating, keeping track of, and recording all real property and improvements through maps, aerial photographs, and computer data banks. Although state laws normally prescribe how assessors conduct their work, assessment is partially an art. First it requires the determination of real, or market, value. Second, however, real property in the United States is seldom assessed at its full value for tax purposes. Thus, assessed value may be less than market value. In addition, state law may establish assessment ratios for various classes of property, for example, residential, business, and industry. The assessed-value figure may be further changed through the use of exemptions (for example, for veterans and elderly persons) and also may be altered by the equalization ratios designed to ensure that all properties in a given state are treated more or less equally, regardless of which governmental jurisdiction does the assessing. Finally, some state financial aid may be based on local assessments. For example, more state aid for education may go to local communities with poor tax base resources, but less aid may go to others that have a solid tax base but do not tax enough.

The tax rate is set by governments that have the power to tax real property. The rate is usually stated in mills or in dollars per $100 or $1,000 units. This rate is applied to the net value, following the application of all exemptions and equalization ratios.

Although the real property tax has been one of the most commonly used local taxes, it is also one of the most controversial. One issue is the degree to which property assessment is equitable. Local taxpayers are constantly comparing their assessed valuations with those of others in similar circumstances, and residents of rental properties may feel they are paying higher taxes than residents of owner-occupied properties, because assessment ratios in some states are higher on income-producing properties.

The interrelation between periodic reassessment of real property, the rampant inflation of the 1970's, and the decline in federal aid in the 1980s resulted in tax revolts in some parts of the country. Owners of single-family dwellings discovered that inflation had increased the value of their homes (doubling of value in less than a decade was common). As reassessments took into account the increased value of real estate, property taxes soared, and owners of what had once been modestly priced homes found themselves paying taxes on highly valuable property. This is a particular problem for elderly persons who have no intention of selling their homes for large profits but must nevertheless pay taxes far above originally anticipated levels.

Another problem is that real estate taxes tend to be regressive—to the disadvantage of low-income households. A family with a high income and a large, expensive house can presumably afford to pay taxes on it; moreover, housing costs do not make up a high proportion of the family's budget. Statistics show, however, that households with low and moderate incomes tend to pay a higher proportion of their incomes for housing costs; therefore, the proportion of their incomes paid for property taxes is also higher.

Local government's reliance on the property tax can cause serious problems in metropolitan areas when the wealth of communities (and therefore the tax base) varies considerably. Declining central cities and blue-collar suburbs find they cannot support essential public services, especially public schools, to the levels financed by high-income suburbs. Concern about potential educational inequalities has led civic and civil rights groups to institute legal action in numerous states. A number of state courts (for example, in *Serrano* v. *Priest*, 1971)[2] have held that relying on the property tax for school finance is discriminatory and therefore unconstitutional. Even in the U.S. Supreme Court, while not ruling in favor of such groups (*Rodriguez* v. *San Antonio School District*, 1973),[3] described reliance on the property tax as inequitable and chaotic. Efforts to solve these problems of school finance are still being made. One of the most popular solutions is to increase state aid to local schools on the assumption that the state has the widest possible tax base.

The fragmented governmental system and the property tax also cause a considerable amount of "fiscal zoning." On the one hand, communities compete for "high ratables"—that is, industrial and commercial properties that generate proportionately higher taxes than they do service costs. This competition generally does not lead to well-planned land use patterns in a metropolitan area as a whole. Moreover, the negotiating tactics used by some communities include "sweeteners" whereby the community as a whole installs expensive utilities to entice certain types of businesses or industries to locate there. On the other hand, communities are as vigorous in trying to keep out certain land uses (such as low- and moderate-income housing) that do not "pay their way." A variety of tactics are used, such as large-lot zoning, exclusion of apartments, unrealistically high building code standards, and the requirement of excessive public improvements. These practices have created a substantial amount of litigation that is beyond the scope of this discussion. The point here is that taxing and planning mechanisms need to be found that will lessen reliance on these inequitable and questionable practices.

Minnesota's fiscal disparities law is an interesting attempt to alleviate some of the problems created by tax competition and fiscal zoning.[4] The law provides that taxes obtained from industrial and commercial properties within a broad geographic area may still go to the governmental unit in which the facility is located. However, a portion of the tax revenues from new industrial and commercial properties is put into an areawide pool to be distributed among all

Guide to property assessment

Step 1   The assessor appraises and determines the market value of your property. The basis for all assessments in Cook County is *market value*. . . . This means the assessor determines what a willing buyer would pay you, as a willing seller, for your property. When this price is established, the *market value* of your property has been determined.

How is this done? Each year the assessor receives copies of all real estate transfer declarations, or sales, for all properties bought and sold in the county. These declarations indicate to the assessor what type of property was sold and the full sale price paid.

The assessor then matches these sales with their corresponding assessments through the use of sophisticated computers. He compares the assessments of similar homes in the same neighborhood where the sales took place. After analyzing this information, the assessor can predict what similar homes will sell for on the open market. This, then, determines the *market value* of those properties which have not recently been sold.

Step 2   The assessor employs a technique called *the classification system*. The system allows him to assess different types of properties at different percentages of full *market value*. This means that the assessor differentiates between properties, placing higher assessments on commercial/industrial properties and lower assessments on homes, in relation to the *market value* of those properties. In simpler terms, the assessor first determines the full *market value* of a property and then lowers that full value by a percentage determined by law.

Step 3   Your tax is computed. These definitions will assist you in better understanding the terminology used in computing taxes.

Assessed valuation   This is a percentage of the total value the assessor places on property. It includes land and building(s).

Equalization factor   The Illinois Department of Local Governmental Affairs requires that all assessed valuations in Cook County be multiplied by this factor in order to make assessments uniform throughout the state.

Equalized valuation   This is the result of the assessed valuation being multiplied by the *equalization factor*.

Tax rate   The rate is established as a result of levies by the local governmental bodies which have the authority to impose taxes on property located within the community.

Market value   Another term for market value is *fair cash value*—that is, what a willing buyer would pay a willing seller if a property were offered for sale on the open market.

Tax levy   This is the actual dollar amount that a local school district or local taxing agency requires to operate in any given year.

Example: single family residence

Market value...............................$40,000
Classification system ratio.............. 16%
Assessed valuation......................$6,400
Equalization factor 1.4153
Equalized value...........................$9,052
Tax rate 8.78%
Tax bill...$795

Source: Excerpted from Cook County Assessor, *Homeowner's Guide to Property Assessment* (Chicago: Cook County Assessor, 1985), 5–9.

governmental units. Over time, this should tend to equalize the tax benefits accruing to local communities, whether or not they have industrial or commercial land uses.

The property tax has been widely criticized also as having undesirable effects on urban land development patterns. For example, in suburban areas, urban sprawl and the pressures of the suburban land market may drive up the value of undeveloped land that is being used for agriculture or that contains environmentally sensitive systems such as stream valleys. When a tax assessor observes an overall pattern of conversion from rural to urban, the land may be assigned a higher value on the assumption that it is ripe for development. A farmer—whether interested in urban development or not—may then be faced with higher taxes. Many states are using a number of techniques to either halt or slow down this process of premature conversion. One technique is the use of open space or conservation easements whereby a community buys the development rights to a piece of property, thereby lowering its value. Another technique is a state law that allows preferential tax assessment for farmland. Under this system the assessor is required to assess farmland for its present use, not its potential use.

In the central city context, the problem with the property tax is that it creates strong disincentives for owners of deteriorating property to improve or rehabilitate the property. If the improvements increase the value of the property, property taxes increase as well. The idea of the site-value or land-value tax (which has been with us for three-quarters of a century) addresses this problem as well as the suburban one. The site-value or land-value tax is based on the idea that the value of land, not the value of buildings, ought to be taxed. It is argued that the land tax would control urban sprawl by increasing land value— and therefore taxes—at the urban fringe, thereby creating an incentive for a compact development pattern. In the central city, the land tax would not discourage rehabilitation by penalizing owners. However, the land tax has not caught on in the United States.

In summary, criticisms of the property tax are substantial, but the tax has persisted as a primary means through which local governments finance expenditures. However, public resentment against the tax has led a number of states (e.g., California and Massachusetts) to impose "caps" on rates.

The sales tax

The second largest locally generated source of revenue for cities is the local sales tax. It should be noted that state sales tax may be collected from a consumer at the same time. The latter rate can be, and usually is, substantially higher. A number of states also permit separate local taxes to be levied on cigarettes and gasoline.

Local governments turn to the sales tax as a form of revenue primarily because the property tax is reaching its practical and political limit as a revenue generator. The payment of a sales tax usually comes in small doses and therefore may be easier for local government to impose than the property tax.

An important planning issue is created by the fact that the sales tax can skew land use decisions. In states with local sales taxes, communities compete to obtain the land use "plums," such as major regional shopping centers, which, in addition to producing healthy real estate tax revenues, also contribute substantially to local sales tax revenues.

Income taxes

By the early 1980s four thousand local governments were collecting local income taxes. Like the sales tax, the income tax came about because of the limits of the revenue-producing potential of the property tax. Most such taxes have a flat rate, but a few have progressive rates.

As is the case with any tax, several issues need to be considered when local governments use income taxes. One issue is whether the tax base includes only personal income or also income from stocks, bonds, and a variety of nonlabor sources. Another issue relates to taxation of nonresidents. In fragmented metropolitan areas and in interstate metropolitan areas, many people question the equity of working in one community and living in another community when either one or both have income taxes. State laws on local income taxes handle these problems in a variety of ways, including using a different rate structure for nonresidents or having reciprocal tax credits between jurisdictions.

Miscellaneous local revenues

One major category of miscellaneous revenue is taxes and fees other than property, sales, or income taxes. There is a bewildering variety of such taxes; the purpose here is simply to identify a number of the more common ones. Localities can impose a variety of taxes on tobacco products, alcoholic beverages, utility services, and theater admissions. Fees for business licenses, which are a combination of regulatory and revenue-producing mechanisms, can be imposed also.

Another group of fees consists of largely administrative-regulatory fees such as building permit fees, fees for zoning and land subdivision changes, and plumbing and electrical fees. A few communities have tried to use these fees as impact taxes (that is, they have set fees well above regulatory costs to create a revenue source), but it is a relatively well-established point of law that such fees are intended to cover the costs of regulation and should not be used to raise revenue.

Cities and counties obtain revenues from a variety of user fees. For example, charges are usually made for water use and other services provided by the municipality, such as electric or gas supply, transit, bridges and tunnels, parking, airport facilities, and sewerage. Unless subsidized or defrayed by intergovernmental transfers, most user fees are used to pay operating expenses of a facility and to retire revenue bonds that financed construction.

Another category of tax revenues relates in part to the local level and in part to the county or metropolitan level. Local governments have created a host of special districts that carry out certain public functions. Sometimes these districts have been created to serve more than one governmental unit. Sometimes they have been created as a method of avoiding state-imposed tax limits on local governments. These special districts often have their own elected officials and separate taxing power. The services they provide include public schools, housing and urban redevelopment, flood control, sewer and water supply, parks and recreation, health facilities and hospitals, libraries, cemeteries, and airports, to name a few.

Two issues deserve mention here. First, creating a special district does not necessarily solve all financial problems. In both the short run and the long run, the public must pay the taxes. The overall tax load and accumulated debt are watched carefully by the financial community. A community's borrowing power may be limited if special districts have already imposed an excessive amount of overlapping taxes and debt on the same taxpayers. Second, although special districts have been created to carry out a public function and are presumably responsible to the public through either elected or publicly appointed governing boards, they have a tendency to be "out of control" in terms of urban development policy. For example, a community or metropolitan area can adopt a particular kind of growth plan, but this growth plan may or may not be supported by the special districts that build sewer and water lines—a key element in any growth control or planning strategy. One solution to this problem is for special districts to be legally affiliated with a metropolitan council of governments (COG).

(In addition, an officially adopted plan of a COG may require that special districts follow publicly adopted plans.)

Intergovernmental grants-in-aid

The dependence of local government on state and federal aid was considerable in the 1960s and 1970s. Almost every federal department that dealt with domestic issues made funds available to carry out local projects and services. In addition, the general revenue-sharing program funneled several billion dollars a year to local governments. In comparison with the traditional categorical programs related to a single function, revenue sharing gave local government a relatively free hand in spending funds.

By the mid-1970s there was some movement toward a type of special revenue sharing whereby numerous categorical grants within a single federal department were consolidated into a block grant program. One important program of this type was the Community Development Block Grant (CDBG) program administered by the U.S. Department of Housing and Urban Development (HUD). During the 1980s the federal government wound down many of its aid programs to local government. Currently, the major remaining programs for capital facilities relate to highway and transit projects. State and local government groups have lobbied hard for the continued deductibility of a variety of state and local taxes; deductibility is an indirect federal subsidy to state and local governments. The major tax reform that Congress passed in 1986 phased out the deductibility of sales taxes but retained the deductibility of state and local income taxes. However, the new law sharply curtailed tax-exempt status for a variety of state and local bond issues, which poses a problem for local governments: local officials see deductibility as a "help" in getting new local taxes passed in legislative bodies. With respect to bonds, tax-exempt status meant that local government paid lower interest rates to lenders. Many state governments are studying the feasibility of aiding local governments by building facilities to benefit local governments or establishing a variety of revolving loan programs.

The budgetary process

This section focuses on the budgetary process in general, with emphasis on the operating budget. The budgetary process for capital improvements will be discussed at greater length later in this chapter. Here the emphasis is on planning expenditures for current operating expenses for local programs and services, personnel costs, and other noncapital expenditures. It is during the budgetary process that *choices* are made among competing demands for resources.

The major purposes of a management-oriented budgetary process are financial control, management information, and planning policy implementation. Financial control relates to the traditional and legal requirements for ensuring that government funds are properly spent for public purposes. A good budgetary process requires the generation and manipulation of large quantities of data on staffing, activities, equipment, and similar subjects and is therefore a key management tool. In recent years planning policy implementation has been growing in importance as a purpose of the budgetary process. This represents an important shift from an "accountant mentality" to a policy orientation—that is, to the idea that government spending should be a key method of carrying out goals and objectives of the community.

Modern local government budgeting practice should be seen as part of an overall management system. One useful view of a management system defines it as having three levels of planning: strategic planning, management planning, and operational control.[5] Strategic planning deals with setting goals and objectives and the policies for reaching those objectives. Management planning is a level at which more detailed programs (such as budgets) are evaluated so as to make choices that are in line with adopted policies. Operational control involves carrying out tasks and programs.

This general scheme can apply to most kinds of planning activities within government. For example, the typical planning department would be involved in all three levels: at the strategic planning level in undertaking fundamental goals and objectives studies and helping to formulate proposed policies; at the management planning level through traditional comprehensive planning activities and capital improvements programming; and at the operational level through management of renewal or revitalization projects and the administration of land use controls.

What concerns us here is the interrelation of physical and fiscal planning in the management system. In local governments throughout the nation, the distribution of tasks varies considerably. The tasks can be distributed among the manager's office, the planning department, and the budget office. In a few communities there may be a combined planning and budget office; in other's there may be offices of management and budget. Whatever the organizational form, it is essential that two perspectives permeate the process. For the planning department involved in the budgetary process, it is essential that policies and plans be sensitive to financial considerations as early in the planning process as possible. For the budgetary office it is essential that financial management and planning be permeated with policy considerations.

Steps in the budgetary process

The actual steps a governmental unit follows in preparing its annual budget may vary considerably depending on its organizational structure, its size, and the availability of technical personnel. The following discussion focuses on the steps that normally take place in a budget cycle.

In general, a larger community takes a more sophisticated approach to each step and places more emphasis on the early steps, which emphasize policy analysis. The eight essential steps in the budgeting process are (1) fiscal analysis and policy choices; (2) expenditure estimates; (3) review of expenditure estimates; (4) revenue estimates; (5) budgetary forecasting; (6) preparation of the budget document; (7) budget review and adoption; and (8) budget execution.[6]

Fiscal analysis and policy choices If a budgetary process is to be sensitive to policy, local government cannot simply send out forms and ask what various departments want in the coming fiscal year. It is necessary to conduct an analysis of some essential factors before general policies can be set. Such an analysis has several components.

First, it is essential that the budgetary process be based on a sound understanding of local population and economic conditions. Whether a community is growing, stable, or declining will significantly affect the revenues available to that community as well as the service demands. Forecasting economic and population trends can point out a need to adopt particular fiscal policies. For example, a rapidly growing community may have to embark on a heavy capital investment program to provide the utilities and public facilities for an expanding population; however, its capacity to finance these facilities may be limited by the degree to which the local government has the power to borrow funds to serve a future population that may not yet be paying taxes. A mature or declining community may be faced with a declining population and economic base, which in turn leads to a declining local revenue; however, declining communities do not necessarily have declining service demands, particularly if the population contains a high proportion of low-income citizens.

Another step is to review current local government finances. This analysis investigates the revenues and expenditures generated by trends in tax assessments, sales or income taxes, grants-in-aid from other governmental levels, and potential changes in state laws concerning revenue sources. The key issue is whether the locality's financial structure can support the forecast service demands.

Another key element of the analysis is the review of major jurisdictional programs. For example, during the past several decades local governments, in addition to their physical housekeeping functions, have been increasingly involved in "people-oriented" programs in the fields of health, social welfare, and criminal justice. However, the resources available for such programs can vary from year to year depending on changes in federal or state programs, the degree to which local funds can be appropriated, and the launching of new programs or the winding down of others, such as Model Cities. If a local government has an effective management system, it is at this point that previously conducted program evaluations can help to determine the future of present programs.

Areas that are receiving increasing attention from local governments are labor relations and wage and price trends. As the union movement spreads throughout state and local government, labor relations plays an important part in budgetary policy. Even national and international problems, such as energy prices and policy, can significantly influence local expenditures.

Expenditure estimates   In the policy analysis of the first stage, some gross estimates are made concerning major trends in the local government's revenues and expenditures. At the expenditure stage, departments become much more involved in the detailed estimates. These estimates must, of course, be based on fundamental fiscal policies that have been set by the local government's administration and also must be based on work programs prepared by the departments. It is at this point that departments will need to make detailed analyses of programs and services, staffing and organization charts, salary costs, new equipment, level of effort for various programs, proposed new staff positions, and operating costs of recently completed capital facilities.

Review of expenditure estimates   It is during the review stage that budget making becomes a political and advocacy process on the part of department heads and others; these others sometimes include council members and others representing the local government. The task at this point is "to hammer out the allocation of resources among competing demands."[7] In other words, "rationality" is secondary to traditional bureaucratic infighting. In larger communities budget officers are assisted by budget analysts who go through these requests very carefully. In smaller communities the manager may rely far more on his or her own judgment about how much of what a department wants it actually gets.

Because the review of expenditure estimates provides an opportunity to test the relevance of specific expenditure proposals to policy objectives, it may be the most important step in the budgetary process. Recent experience suggests that a program budget approach may be the best way to ensure a policy-oriented budgetary process. (An example is discussed later in this chapter.) In a program budget approach, each department head is aware of basic policies and of specific program categories and subcategories that relate to carrying out the policies; expenditures are then allocated by program function.

Revenue estimates   Revenue estimates actually take place simultaneously with expenditure estimates. However, most of the responsibility for making revenue estimates rests not with the department heads but with the budget officer and the individual revenue-collecting departments. These revenue estimates go into the details of the means the municipality uses to raise revenue: building permits, administrative fees, income taxes, sales taxes, fines, water and utility fees, property taxes, business and license fees, regular state grants from such sources as motor vehicle taxes, and specific state and federal grant-in-aid programs that will be implemented during the coming budget year.

It is also essential that judgments and estimates be made concerning trends in revenue sources. Revenue sources of the municipality itself can be estimated and forecast by the use of municipal records. These are compared to population and economic forecasts, and further judgments are then made. In addition, it is necessary to carefully monitor program and regulatory trends in state and federal grant-in-aid programs. For example, judging from authorizations and appropriation history, how many years into the future is a particular federal program going to run? What are the purposes to which block grants may be put? Most important in this regard is that many federal and state grants require local matching funds. Can the local government raise the matching funds needed for the additional outside revenue?

Budgetary forecasting   Although most state laws merely require the adoption of the budget for one year, it is increasingly apparent to local government administrators that it is essential to forecast budget trends for a four- or five-year period into the future. This is particularly important in planning for capital facilities (discussed later in this chapter), and it is becoming increasingly important for operating budget purposes as well. The result of such a forecast in a growing community may be reassuring in that "all is well." However, for the more mature community, particularly in the East and Midwest, such an analysis may show that some hard budgetary choices need to be made. For example, some older cities are no longer committing themselves to new programs, and some cities are even funding capital improvements only on a pay-as-you-go basis.

The longer-range look at the operating budget also has the benefit of bringing long-term trends to the attention of the local legislative body. By generating discussion—if not debate—of potential new revenue sources and of how current capital investments could generate future operating costs, such forecasts may make it possible to avoid unpleasant surprises—such as budget deficits.

The budget document   The budget document represents the vast accumulation of estimates, projections, administrative decisions, and proposals presented by the local government administration to the legislative body. A good budget document ought to contain (in addition to the summaries of proposed expenditures by department, function, and program) the backup materials, policies, forecasts, and similar items that would enable the reader to reach an independent judgment concerning the soundness of the document. The budget document may contain supporting material such as a budget message, which emphasizes policy; a summary of the major fiscal analyses of revenue and expenditure estimates; forecasts of where the local government is headed financially; justifications for either expanding or contracting programs and services; and an accompanying narrative in text, tabular, and graphic form that helps explain the proposed policy choices.

Budget review and adoption   Budget review time is hectic for local legislative bodies. There are more work sessions, evening meetings, and public hearings than at any other time of the year. The mayor or the local government manager may make oral presentations, complemented by presentations by the budget officer and major department heads. Some councils have finance committees that do a great deal of this work.

It is at this point that formal public hearings are held. Since budgets must be adopted by specific legal dates, these hearings normally consist of relatively general presentations given under constraints of time. The participation of the public varies considerably from community to community. In larger jurisdictions public hearings are dominated by testimony and comments from chambers of commerce, labor unions, communitywide citizen and civic associations, and a sprinkling of neighborhood groups. Department heads, particularly the head of the planning department, have long since been meeting with neighborhood groups and discussing proposed plans and improvements. (Astute department heads in service agencies such as the park and recreation department and even police departments know that they must be out in the community at all times of the year listening for complaints, floating new program ideas, and engaging in partnership discussions in designing city programs at the earliest stages, not merely when the budget is published.) Participation by individual citizens is rare.

The final step in the process is a legal requirement: the council, by ordinance, adopts the annual budget. In some jurisdictions the capital budget may be adopted at the same time.

Budget execution This step takes place all year long and is the responsibility of the manager, the budget officer, and every department head. The technical functions of budget execution—such as accounting controls or audit systems—are beyond the scope of this chapter.

Evolving budget systems

The concept of a budget can be traced as far back as the medieval English parliament. The word *budget* comes from *bougette*, a leather bag carried by the monarch's treasurer that contained documents dealing with needs and resources of the nation.[8] Balancing needs and resources remains the modern purpose of budgeting.

In the United States the concept of municipal budgeting developed around the turn of the twentieth century in an age of urban reform. "Good government" groups realized that some method was needed to control rampant corruption in the handling of municipal revenues and expenditures. Early work, such as the model municipal charter and budget system proposed by the New York Bureau of Municipal Research, emphasized accountability and feasibility: where money was to come from, how much of it there was, and precisely how it would be spent. Detailed accounting procedures (for example, account numbers and categories) eventually developed. However, early municipal budgets followed a line item approach whereby categories of expenditure were divided into classes such as personnel, equipment, and insurance. This type of budget does not lend itself to use as a management tool.

In later years budgets and budgetary concepts evolved to emphasize the performance of particular services—thus the concept of the performance budget. In this type of budget, programs and services are divided into categories such as police protection, parks and recreation, traffic control, and other functions of government.

The planning-programming-budgetary system experience In the early 1960s the U.S. Department of Defense (DOD) began to evolve a system of analytical techniques based on systems analysis, operations research, and decision-making theory. The techniques developed by the DOD became the basis for the planning-programming-budgeting system (PPBS), which was expected to revolutionize municipal decision making. In fact, it did not.

The Pentagon "whiz kids" were less interested in how much a private is paid or how much a rifle costs than in the *mission* of a particular segment of the military. For example, if a particular mission of a branch of the Navy was "to protect vital sea lanes for commerce and military supply," how was that mission to be accomplished? What resources were required? What were the alternative ways in which the mission could be accomplished? Which alternative was most cost effective or cost efficient?

The PPBS approach has four distinctive characteristics: (1) it focuses on identifying the fundamental objectives of a program; (2) implications for future years are explicitly identified; (3) all costs are considered; and (4) systematic analysis of alternatives is performed.

In the mid-1960s an attempt was made to adapt the PPBS system to all departments of the federal government. (In subsequent years the effort faded away.) Proposals to have state and local governments adopt PPBS were made in the late 1960s. Any government that considered itself modern and well managed created PPBS systems. City staffs scurried about preparing "program memoranda" and spent sleepless nights inventing programs, activities, functions, and subcategories. Many technicians felt they were going through a meaningless ritual.

The experience with PPBS taught cities that highly structured, artificial systems cannot work if they undervalue the human element in government. Systems must be understandable to elected officials, must be accepted by the bureaucracy, and must contribute to a feeling among local government officials and technicians that they know what they are doing. Some good things came out of the PPBS experience, however. In particular, far more attention is being paid to basic goals and objectives; to identifying affordable approaches to programs that meet the objectives; to measuring what is being accomplished; and to understanding what is being achieved.

Zero-base budgeting   During the late 1970s another budget system that received attention was zero-base budgeting (ZBB). First developed by a private corporation (Texas Instruments), the concept was adopted by a number of state agencies and governments. Perhaps the most famous example of the adoption of zero-base budgeting was in Georgia during Jimmy Carter's governorship.

The essence of ZBB strikes at the heart of traditional "nonrational" budget making: the practice of taking last year's budget as a given and adding a little for inflation and expanding programs. Under ZBB, last year is a closed book; *everything* must be justified as though it were a new program.

The major steps of ZBB are as follows:

1.   The isolating of "decision units."
2.   The analysis of the decision units and the documentation of the analysis into "decision packages."
3.   The ranking of the decision packages in order of priority by management.
4.   The final compilation of the budget, based on the rankings.[9]

A decision unit is a cost center or activity that makes sense as an analytical unit. For each unit, goals and objectives must be specified, costs estimated, and performance criteria identified. Of critical importance is the definition of different levels of service so that decision makers can choose the level of service that the community wants to support. Under ZBB it thus becomes possible to choose levels of service that are *lower* than last year's, or at least to prevent automatic cost increases. In addition, it may be possible to perform the service in an alternative way.

One cannot predict the degree to which ZBB will be adopted by local governments, but it may be attractive to both mature communities with shrinking tax bases and rapidly growing localities whose service demands may grow at an exceedingly rapid rate if they are not well managed.

The Dayton system   A number of cities have developed budgeting systems that evolved out of the experiments with PPBS, zero-base budgeting, management by objectives, and other modern analytical techniques. One notable example is Dayton, Ohio, which has a long history of management experience. Dayton's budget method is called *Program Strategies*. The purpose of the system is to describe municipal services in a language that elected officials and the community can understand, while at the same time allocating resources (local, state, and federal) in such a way as to classify expenditures on the basis of policies and programs.

Dayton's *1986 Program Strategies* (its budget document), for example, identifies five broad policy categories: economic vitality, neighborhood vitality, community leadership, professional management, and urban conservation. In the budget narrative, each category includes a list of goals, objectives, and key issues; a report on progress toward achieving objectives; a community condition statement summarizing service and demographic indicators; departmental priorities for the current and next year; resource allocation and capital project tables; and a summary.

Figure 14–1, which shows a subcategory of the neighborhood vitality category dealing with neighborhood conservation, illustrates how the budget allocates resources according to policies. Ten major activities—from housing code enforcements to residential street lighting—are specified, along with which department is responsible for carrying out the work, an estimate of staff time, the budget allocation for the current and proposed year, and the percentage change. The figure shows how a city budget and management staff identifies all the municipal activities that can contribute to conserving residential neighborhoods.

Dayton combines its operating budget with the capital improvement's program to ensure that capital projects are in keeping with the policies of the program strategies. For example, Figure 14–2 shows the capital allocation plan for the neighborhood conservation elements just discussed.

Capital improvements programming

The 1909 Burnham plan of Chicago is the traditional benchmark for the beginning of modern city planning. The plan is usually mentioned together with the City Beautiful movement. What generally is not said is that the plan contained a discussion of how bond issues would be required to finance the plan's public works proposals. One urban historian has noted that Chicago built $300 million (about $3 billion in 1986 dollars) of public improvements to implement the plan in the first fifteen years.[10] In retrospect, it was an astonishing achievement.

Although the Chicago experience demonstrated that public expenditures are an important link in implementing comprehensive plans, it was not until the late 1920s that the concept of capital improvements programming began to emerge as a *continuing* element of municipal planning and fiscal management. A number of localities began to realize that planning capital improvements was a distinctly different process from annual budgeting. In essence, as capital improvements were increasingly financed by public borrowing, it was necessary to undertake financial analyses that projected the community's ability to pay in the future; that analyzed and projected ways to amortize debt; and that analyzed the options when the number of potential improvements exceeded the financial capacity of a community.

The Depression, when numerous jurisdictions became bankrupt, and World War II, when many communities postponed public improvements, gave impetus to the careful planning of public facilities. Basic concepts of capital improvements programming have come down to the present generally intact. The capital improvements program (CIP) has become a thoroughly tested, useful planning tool.

Neighborhood conservation: to preserve a high quality of housing choices, encourage investment in neighborhoods and eliminate unsightly and unsanitary conditions.

Operating allocation plan

Activity	Department	1985 staff	1986 staff	1985 budget	1986 budget	Budget % change
Housing and zoning code enforcement Reorganization to abolish two full-time positions. 1985 con-ained temporary positions not in 1986 authorized strength.	Urban development	58.5	55.5	$ 2,539,900	$ 2,570,650	1.2
Rehabilitation Loan Program CWDCª In 1985 $520,000 was received from state for home improve-ment loans, which helped reduce the amount required from CDBG.ª This source is not available in 1986.	City manager's office	0	0	400,000	500,000	25.0
Prosecution of housing viola-tions	Law	1	1	49,400	53,490	8.3
Solid waste collection and disposal Tipping fee increased by Montgomery County. Automated system purchase in 1986.	Public works	142.8	133.4	7,348,500	7,771,930	5.8
Street cleaning 1986 contains purchase of street sweepers.	Public works	25.6	25.6	1,295,700	1,488,000	14.8
Abandoned-vehicle removal	Police	3	3	82,800	84,280	1.8
Rodent control	Urban development	0	0	80,000	83,600	4.5
Weed control This program has grown in number of lots cut. While 1985 represents a level of official financing, the 1986 figure repre-sents actual time assigned. Department diverted staff from parks to vacant lot mowing.	Public works	3.6	11.9	110,700	226,810	104.9
Animal control	Public works	5	5	108,600	112,740	3.8
Residential street lighting	Urban development	0	0	735,000	735,000	0
Operating total		239.5	235.4	$12,750,600	$13,626,500	6.9

ªCity Wide Development Corporation.
ᵇCommunity Development Block Grant.

Figure 14–1   Portion of the Dayton, Ohio, budget dealing with neighborhood vitality.

Definitions

Capital improvements programming is the multiyear scheduling of public physical improvements. The scheduling is based on studies of fiscal resources available and the choice of specific improvements to be constructed for a period of five to six years into the future. The capital improvements *budget* refers to those facilities that are programmed for the next fiscal year. A capital improvements *program* refers to the improvements that are scheduled in the succeeding four- or five-year period. An important distinction between the capital budget and the capital improvements program is that the one-year budget may become a part of the legally adopted annual operating budget, whereas the longer-term program does not necessarily have legal significance, nor does it necessarily commit a government to a particular expenditure in a particular year.

The definition of a *capital improvement* may be different in different com-

Figure 14–2 Portion of Dayton, Ohio, budget: Capital allocation plan for conservation.

Activity	Department	1985 budget	1986 budget
Commercial nuisance abatement	Urban development	$ 0	$ 318,600
Funding source: $318,600 CDBG.[a] Inspectional Services has identified a number of commercial structures that are abandoned and in such poor condition that rehabilitation is no longer a viable option. These funds will provide for the demolition of a portion of these structures, removing these nuisance structures and clearing commercial parcels in neighborhood business districts for possible redevelopment.			
Sidewalk and curb repair	Urban development	1,000,000	1,000,000
Funding sources: $300,000 general fund/$700,000 special assessment. The City continues to support a citywide curb and sidewalk repair program. The City's portion of the funding pays for all overhead costs, intersection and alley mouth work. Individual property owners are assessed for repair of the walk and curb adjacent to their property. Emphasis will be placed on repairing curbs and sidewalks on streets that will be resurfaced in 1986 and 1987.			
FROC[b] alley resurfacing	Public works	50,000	75,000
Funding source: $75,000 CDBG. Many alleys in low- and moderate-income areas of the FROC Priority Board are deteriorated and in need of resurfacing. This project will address that need, resurfacing a portion of the alleys identified by the Priority Board. Only paved alleys will be resurfaced by this project.			
Wolf Creek—Junkyard removal	Urban development	0	75,000
Funding source: $75,000 CDBG. This allocation sets aside funds to implement a solution to the problems posed by the junkyard in the Progressive Wolf Creek neighborhood. The junkyard has been an eyesore and irritation to residents of the Wolf Creek Planning District for many years. Planning and Urban Development staff will evaluate the situation and make a recommendation as to what the City's options are to resolve this problem.			
Troy Street facade renovation	Planning	0	25,000
Funding source: $25,000 CDBG. These funds will be utilized to lower interest rates on loans from City Wide Development Corporation for facade improvements to businesses on Troy Street from Valley to Leo Street. Improvements will be required to meet guidelines to be established by the community and City staff.			
Prior year's projects	Various	50,000	0
1985 projects that received one-time funding: YWCA improvements.			
Capital total		$1,100,000	$1,493,600

[a]Community Development Action Grant.
[b]Fair River Oaks Council.

munities. The common definition of a capital improvement includes new or expanded physical facilities that are relatively large in size, expensive, and permanent. Some common examples include streets and expressways, public libraries, water and sewer lines, and park and recreation facilities. In smaller communities certain expenditures, such as the purchase of a fire engine, may also be considered a capital expenditure. There is an extremely important fiscal planning principle underlying this definition, which is that capital improvements should include *only* those expenditures for physical facilities with relatively long-term usefulness and permanence. Capital improvements *should not* include expenditures for equipment or services that prudent management defines as operating budget items and which ought to be financed out of current revenues. A number of large cities that invested financial "gimmicks" by placing noncapital expenditures into the capital budget during the late 1960s and early 1970s found themselves in serious financial difficulties by the late 1970s.

The benefits of a CIP

An effective capital improvements programming process can lead to many benefits to local government. Specifically, the CIP can ensure that plans for community facilities are carried out; can allow improvement proposals to be tested against a set of policies; can better schedule public improvements that require more than one year to construct; can provide an opportunity, assuming funds are available, to purchase land before costs go up; can provide an opportunity for long-range financial planning and management; can help stabilize tax rates through careful debt management; can avoid such mismanagement as paving a street one year and tearing it up the next to build a sewer; can offer an opportunity for citizens and public interest groups to participate in decision making; and can contribute to a better overall management of city affairs.

How capital improvements are financed

Because most capital investments involve the outlay of substantial funds, local government can seldom pay for these facilities through annual appropriations in the annual operating budget. Therefore, numerous techniques have evolved to enable local government to pay for capital improvements over a longer period of time than a single year. Most but not all of the techniques involve financial instruments, such as bonds, in which a government borrows money from investors (both institutional and individual) and pays the principal and interest over a number of years. Most of these techniques are carefully prescribed by state law. In addition, whether a governmental unit uses these techniques may depend on such financial factors as bond ratings given by bond rating services, current interest rates for municipal securities, and the current outstanding debt that the unit is already obligated to pay.

Public finance literature and state laws governing local government finance classify techniques that are used to finance capital improvements. These techniques are discussed below.

Current revenue (pay-as-you-go)   Pay-as-you-go is the financing of improvements from current revenues such as general taxation, fees, service charges, special funds, or special assessments.

Reserve funds   In reserve fund financing, funds are accumulated in advance for capital construction or purchase. The accumulation may result from surplus or earmarked operational revenues, funds in depreciation reserves, or the sale of capital assets.

General obligation bonds   Some projects may be financed by general obligation bonds. Through this method, the taxing power of the jurisdiction is pledged to pay interest and principal to retire the debt. General obligation bonds can be sold to finance permanent types of improvements such as schools, municipal buildings, parks, and recreation facilities. Voter approval may be required.

Revenue bonds   Revenue bonds frequently are sold for projects, such as water and sewer systems, that produce revenues. Such bonds usually are not included in state-imposed debt limits, as are general obligation bonds, because they are not backed by the full faith and credit of the local jurisdiction but are financed in the long run through service charges or fees. However, these bonds may have supplemental guarantees. The interest rates are almost always higher than those of general obligation bonds, and voter approval is seldom required.

Lease-purchase   Local governments using the lease-purchase method prepare specifications for a needed public works project that is constructed by a private company or authority. The facility is then leased to the jurisdiction. At the end of the lease period the title to the facility can be conveyed to the local government without any future payments. The rental over the years will have paid the total original cost plus interest.

Authorities and special districts   Special authorities or districts may be created, usually to provide a single service such as schools, water, sewage treatment, toll roads, or parks. Sometimes these authorities are formed to avoid restrictive local government debt limits and also to finance facilities serving more than one jurisdiction. They may be financed through revenue bonds retired by user charges, although some authorities have the power to tax.

Special assessments   Public works that benefit particular properties may be financed more equitably by special assessment: that is, by those who directly benefit. Local improvements often financed by this method include street paving, sanitary sewers, and water mains.

State and federal grants   During the 1960s and 1970s state and federal grants-in-aid were available to finance a large number of programs, including streets, water and sewer facilities, airports, and parks and playgrounds. During the early 1980s there was a significant change in federal policy, based on rising deficits and a political philosophy that encouraged states and local governments to raise their own revenues for capital programs. The result has been a growing interest in "creative financing." Some of the techniques are described in the following six sections.

Tax increment financing   Tax increment financing can be used to provide front-end funds in an area where large-scale redevelopment is feasible. First, a district that encompasses the proposed redevelopment area is designated and assigned a tax base equivalent to the value of all the property within the district. Computation of tax revenues is based on this initially assigned tax base, usually throughout the expected life of the project. In the meantime the area is redeveloped with the proceeds from the sale of tax increment bonds. These bonds are sold by the municipality or by a specially created tax district for acquisition, relocation, demolition, administration, and site improvements. Once the redevelopment is completed, the newly developed property has a higher assessed value and yields more tax revenue. The tax "increment" above the initially established level is used to retire the bonds. Once the bonds are retired, the tax revenues from the enhanced tax base are distributed normally.

User fees   Some types of user fees—such as tolls for bridges, tunnels, or roads—have been used by governments for many decades. More recently there has been an increasing interest in user fees to help pay for capital facilities and to possibly decrease demand. For example, fees are becoming more popular for park and recreation facilities such as tennis clubs, ice skating rinks, and exercise facilities. Sometimes communities use a sewer fee or tax, computed on the basis of water usage and paid as part of a water bill, on the theory that the more water used by a business or residence, the greater the demand for sewage treatment. A municipal water system may also have a schedule of water rates that sets a lower price for the basic amount of consumption and requires larger increments to be paid for at higher rates.

Impact fees and exactions   When reviewing new development, communities are increasingly using the land use control process to exact additional charges and fees to help pay for capital facilities. Traditional land subdivision regulations, for example, require a developer to install facilities within the development at the company's expense. These costs are, of course, passed along in the purchase prices of residences or in rents to business occupants. Recently, communities have begun to exact fees to pay for off-site or oversize improvements. Sometimes these fee systems generate money that goes into a common fund to pay for systemwide capital facilities.

Negotiated agreements   A local government operating under very tight fiscal constraints may not be able to construct capital facilities required by new urban development. An increasingly popular method of building such facilities is a negotiated agreement wherein the local government approves the development plan and the developer agrees to install major facilities so the development can go ahead. This is a "voluntary" approach, in contrast to a legislated approach. That is, the developer may feel that the local government does not have a clear legal right to demand such financing arrangements but that as a practical matter it may be the only way the project will be approved. For example, the local government may install water lines for a particular development at government expense, but the developer may have to pay for a sewer extension. Or the developer may agree not only to dedicate land for road widening (a traditional request) but also to pay for the construction costs. The general trend is for the developer to pay for facilities previously funded by local government.

Municipal finance   Experts have been developing new techniques related to municipal bonds—especially the marketing of the bonds. A variety of techniques such as zero-coupon bonds, put-option bonds, bonds with call provisions, and bond insurance may be attractive to either a municipality or the investment community. In general, these techniques aim to time interest payments according to market conditions. For example, put-option bonds and bonds with call provisions allow a municipality to redeem or call back bonds when interest rates are lower. The government then turns around and reissues new bonds at lower interest rates. The advantage of bond insurance is that it raises the bond rating, and the resulting interest costs are lower.

Privatization   As municipal governments rethink funding for public services and facilities, "privatization" has been receiving serious attention. In its most stark form, privatization means turning a public-sector service over to the private sector. At this extreme along a public-private continuum, a service would be provided by a private firm as an entrepreneurial, free-enterprise, risk venture. For example, some suburban communities have no public refuse collection system at all; refuse is collected and disposed of by private companies that charge fees to private customers. Further along the same continuum toward the public sector might be an arrangement whereby a local government would appropriate money for refuse collection, then contract with a private company actually to provide the service. This alternative is attractive to some communities that want to avoid higher union wage scales or public-sector strikes. Alternative delivery systems for public services will be the focus of a great deal of experimentation in the coming years.

Fiscal policies

Careful fiscal analysis and specific fiscal policies must be the foundation of a local CIP. Long-range financial studies and forecasts on which to base the analysis typically are conducted by the jurisdiction's finance officer or, in small communities, by the local government manager's office. At the minimum such analysis should include the preparation of tables showing the amortization of all outstanding debt. Since local government can issue bonds that mature over long periods of time, this analysis will have to look ahead for more than a decade. As a practical matter, more intensive forecasting and analysis are done for the next five-year period, focusing on the local general economic situation and the extent to which it may affect long-term local government revenues. For growing communities the analysis may show the degree to which various categories of revenue—property taxes, fees and licenses, state aid, income taxes, and other sources—will grow. For stable or declining communities, such as mature central cities, such an analysis may show that because the economic base of the community is declining (for example, manufacturing and retailing establishments are moving to the suburbs) the local tax base is also declining.

Anticipated revenues must then be compared with anticipated expenditures for capital improvements, personnel services, and pension plans, and other costs must be projected to determine whether projected revenues and expenditures are in balance or whether surpluses or deficits are forecast. Although the financial analysis provides useful information, what is essential is that it leads to the development of fiscal policies. These policies should address the major problems or implications identified in the financial analysis and should provide more specific guidance to the budget and planning departments as well as to the operating departments that propose capital improvements. Policies should address such issues as the maximum amount of debt the local government is willing to take on; the types of revenue devices that will or will not be used; the annual amount of debt service that the operating budget can absorb; the specific projects or facilities that must be made self-sufficient through user fees or other charges; and the degree to which the local government will seek state or federal grants-in-aid.

In recent years a number of communities have begun to adopt fiscal policies related to strategic community objectives. For example, mature central cities increasingly are adopting policies that relate expenditures to economic development objectives. These cities may adopt policies to finance improvements that are most likely to maintain or attract an industrial or commercial base, create new jobs for local residents, or generate private investments in neighborhood revitalization. Older cities that are in serious financial difficulty are even considering policies that target expenditures to certain areas and deliberately write off areas that may be beyond help.

In rapidly developing newer communities, fiscal policies are being adopted that will, for example, ensure that local governments achieve environmental objectives by purchasing critical environment areas, by acquiring parklands, or by creating greenbelts that will help shape urban growth. These communities are also paying more attention to the secondary impacts of capital investments: capital facilities, such as major sewer trunks and major expressways, may be located and planned in areas where the community wants growth to occur and be denied or delayed in areas the community does not want to see developed.

The CIP administrative process

Earlier in this chapter the annual budgeting process was described. The capital improvements portion of that process is often a distinct element that flows through local government in separate channels. In some communities the CIP process may actually occur earlier in the annual cycle than the annual budget. The separate channels for the CIP come about principally because the planning agency may be the key coordinator for capital expenditures, whereas a budget office or city manager's office may coordinate all operating expenditures. In addition, during the CIP process the planning commission may hold public hearings. Whatever procedure is used, the process normally takes several months to complete. Although the process varies from community to community, the description that follows can be considered relatively typical.

The first step in a CIP process is the analysis of the fiscal resources of the community—the revenue and expenditure projections discussed in the preceding paragraphs. This step typically is conducted by the finance office. After this analysis the local government manager or mayor meets with key aides and legislators to discuss the implications of the analysis for setting fiscal policies.

The next step is the directive issued by the chief executive officer to all department heads requiring that they submit proposed capital improvements projects to the agency administering the CIP—usually the planning agency or the finance office. The directive is accompanied by forms, deadline dates, and a list of key meeting dates. The directive also contains the fiscal policies discussed earlier.

The planning agency then usually provides the detailed project forms and instructions to departments for completing the project forms. If new procedures have been adopted, there may also be a CIP manual that describes the process and the products to be submitted. (See Figure 14–3.) The reason for this internal red tape is to ensure that essential information about each project is prepared and submitted in standard ways. Of particular importance, in addition to the obvious importance of cost estimates, is that statements of project justification be made. It is also essential that relationships between projects be cited—for example, that a particular new water main will be constructed in the right-of-way of a vacated street within a particular neighborhood conservation project. In addition, departments should be required to discuss how a particular project relates to previously adopted plans and policies.

Departments usually place priorities on proposals being submitted. Because a great many choices are made within functional areas, it is essential that the planning agency work particularly closely with departments.

Following the submission of all project proposals to the CIP agency, numerous meetings are held at which the planning director, finance officer, local government manager, mayor, and department heads discuss, critique, and hammer out project proposals. The objective at this juncture is to pull together a CIP that is sensitive to the policies that have been adopted; that contains projects related to community development objectives; and that results in a product that the manager or mayor can submit to the local legislative body. In some communities the administration's proposals are first presented to the planning commission, and public hearings are held. The general public seldom attends such hearings. The typical audience includes speakers and representatives from areawide citizen groups, neighborhood associations, chambers of commerce, downtown improvement interests, and similar organizations.

Communities that are trying to foster more effective citizen participation in the CIP process typically use a variety of techniques. Some communities, for

A. IDENTIFICATION AND CODING INFORMATION

1. Project Number	Agency No.	Update Code
687103		

3. Project Name: Damascus Library
4. Program: Culture and Recreation

2. RECOMMENDED: Dec. 15, 1986
REVISED:
ADOPTED:

5. Agency: Public Libraries
6. Planning Area: Damascus

7. PREV. PDF PG NO.: 1515
8. REQ. ADEQ. PUB. FAC. IDENT.

B.

Cost Elements	(8) Total	(9) Thru FY85	(10) Estimate FY86	(11) Total 6 Years	(12) Year 1 FY 87	(13) Year 2 FY 88	(14) Year 3 FY 89	(15) Year 4 FY 90	(16) Year 5 FY 91	(17) Year 6 FY 92	(18) Beyond 6 Years
1. Planning, Design and Suprv.	337	1	80	256	90	110	56				
2. Land	63			63	63						
3. Site Imprvmts. and Utilities	295			295		295					
4. Construction	1386			1386		703	683				
5. Furniture and Equipment	455	25		430	107	114	209				
6. Total	2536	26	80	2430	260	1222	948				

EXPENDITURE SCHEDULE (000's)

C. FUNDING SCHEDULE (000's)

	(8) Total	(9) Thru FY85	(10) Estimate FY86	(11) Total 6 Years	(12) Year 1 FY 87	(13) Year 2 FY 88	(14) Year 3 FY 89	(15)	(16)	(17)	(18)
CO BONDS	2011	26	80	1905	153	990	762				
CURRENT REV.	289			289	107	114	68				
STATE AID	236			236		118	118				

D. ANNUAL OPERATING BUDGET IMPACT $ (000's)

	(8) Total	(9) Thru FY85	(10) Estimate FY86	(11) Total 6 Years	(12) Year 1 FY 87	(13) Year 2 FY 88	(14) Year 3 FY 89	(15) Year 4 FY 90	(16) Year 5 FY 91	(17) Year 6 FY 92	(18) Beyond 6 Years
DEBT SVC	958	3	9	958	18	129	212	205	200	194	
MAINTENANCE	18			18				6	6	6	6
ENERGY	105			105				35	35	35	35
PRGM-STAFF	561			561				187	187	187	187
PRGM-OTHER											
COST SAVINGS	-180			-180				-60	-60	-60	-60
OFFSET REVS											
NET IMPACT	1462	3	9	1462	18	129	212	373	368	362	168
STAFF (WKYRS)	15			10				5	5	5	5

F. APPROPRIATION AND EXPENDITURE DATA (000's)

Date First Appropriation	71
Initial Cost Estimate	355
First Cost Est Current Scope (85)	2,274
Last FY's Cost Estimate	2,413
Present Cost Estimate (87)	2,536

Cumulative Appropriation	Expenditures/ Encumbrances	Unencumbered Balance
106	27	79

Appropriation Request, Budget Year FY 87: 686
Supplemental Appropriation Request Current Year FY 86: 0

G. RELOCATION IMPACT:

H. MAP Map Reference Code:

E. DESCRIPTION AND JUSTIFICATION   0016r   PROJECT NO. 687103   PROJECT NAME DAMASCUS LIBRARY

1. DESCRIPTION. The present project calls for the planning and construction of a library as part of a multi-use facility to include space for selected community service functions including a senior center and a day care facility. The project originally called for a library facility only. Because of the need for a larger building than originally planned, the facility will now be 20,000-25,000 square feet (including the 15,000 sq. ft. originally needed for the library). The Library Department, in cooperation with OMB and other County agencies, has made final site selection (on Route 108 across from the end of Route 124). This facility will serve a large geographic portion of the upper County.

2. JUSTIFICATION. Based on demographic projections, the Department's long-range Facilities Plan of January 1984 calls for the construction of a new community-sized library at the end of this decade. Although this area is now served by a storefront library, continued business and residential development will make this 7,000-square foot facility inadequate to meet the increasingly heavy demands being made by the citizens in this part of the County. Circulation increased by 12% and information questions increased by 4% in FY 86. The Library Board and the Damascus Library Advisory Committee both support the concept of a multi-use facility.

3. STATUS. Conceptual stage only. A potential 1.4 acre site had been acquired on the southeast corner of Maryland Routes 124 and 108 but was not adequate for the expanded facility. Acquisition of a new 9-acre site is underway. Temporary rental quarters opened in September 1973 and expanded to 7,400 square feet in FY 83. Costs at this point reflect only the library portion of this facility.

4. OTHER. Land costs of $56,000 for the original site were covered through the Advanced Land Acquisition Revolving Fund (ALARF) and will be repaid from this project in its design year along with the cost difference needed to purchase the newly selected site. Book acquisition schedule will be as follows: FY 88 - $107,000; FY 89 - $114,000; FY 90 - $68,000.

I. COORDINATION & OTHER INFORMATION (INCL SUBPROJS & WORK PRGM LISTS)

Because of potential service delivery and cost advantages, this facility will be co-located with the Damascus Day Care and Senior Centers (CIP # 885187). ***APPROPRIATION REQUEST IS FOR ARCHITECTURAL DESIGN AND ASSOCIATED COSTS FOR THIS PROJECT AND THE DAMASCUS DAY CARE AND SENIOR CENTERS.

Construction, site improvements, and utilities expenditures (cost elements #3 and #4) combined reflect an inflation adjusted expenditure estimate of $102 per sq. ft. per Council request.

* Operating Budget Impact in Section D reflects the ongoing costs of the current storefront library since the new building will replace and expand on that existing operation.

** Land costs reflect the cost of the original site and will be adjusted after the new site has been purchased.

Figure 14-3 Capital improvement project request, Montgomery County, Maryland.

example, may appoint ad hoc citizen committees to assist the planning commission or legislative body. To function adequately, these committees require extensive staff support and frequent meetings—during the entire CIP process and not just at the end. Some communities also hold public hearings at the neighborhood level to give an opportunity for more detailed small-area input. A fundamental problem in all these efforts is that schedules are, by necessity and by law, rigid and exact—and the citizen input cannot always be obtained quickly. Also, typical citizen groups are far more interested in their own neighborhoods than in broad policy or areawide decision-making processes. A number of communities use citizen polling and survey techniques to obtain opinions on local facilities and services.

The CIP is presented to the jurisdiction's legislative body by the chief executive officer, along with any special budget messages. Depending on local practice, the CIP and the operating budget may be discussed separately or together at this point. Normally, the legislative body holds numerous meetings and public hearings. For a legislative body the budget-making time of year is the busiest and most hectic time.

After the legislative body determines its own expenditure priorities and choices, the CIP is adopted. By "adopted" it should be understood that there is a significant difference between the first year of the program—the capital budget—and the remaining years. The choices for the first year are relatively firm. For subsequent years, an adopted CIP serves more as an expression of policy direction than as a firm choice about specific projects. It should also be understood that even though the CIP may be adopted with the annual operating budget, it will still be necessary for the legislative body to pass ordinances appropriating specific funds for specific projects during the budget year. Ordinances will also be required authorizing the issuance of bonds or other financial instruments.

The problem of choice: Priorities

Although the planning and management fields have had decades of experience with the CIP process, setting priorities continues to be a vexing problem. Choosing which projects will and will not be built is the most crucial step in the CIP process, yet it continues to be troublesome. For example, how does a local government decide which is more important—enlarging a water line, building a new library, purchasing more parkland, or repaving a street? In a more "quaint" era, planners simply evaluated each project in terms of the coverage of the comprehensive plan and the facility plans (that is, the park plan); the project was either in the plan or not. However, plans never specifically identified all the potential projects that could come up through the line departments of local government. Moreover, as comprehensive plans become more policy oriented they rarely identify specific projects. And some communities have plans that are completely out-of-date or are still under preparation. Communities have responded to this problem in a variety of ways, some of which will be discussed here.

One traditional and still widely used priority system divides proposed projects into four categories: essential, desirable, acceptable, and deferrable. These categories are usually further defined in terms of whether a project contributes to public safety, prevents hazards, satisfies a critical need, or would be of benefit but is not essential. Another type of priority system labels projects according to criteria such as protection of life, public health maintenance, conservation of natural resources, and replacement of obsolete facilities.

A moment's reflection shows that these systems cannot be particularly helpful, because the real criteria remain unarticulated. What is the dividing line between essential and desirable? Is it more important to reduce operating costs or to replace obsolete facilities?

One response to the priority problem that has been tried by some communities is the construction of scoring or point systems (one example from New Orleans is shown in Figure 14–4) whereby a project is evaluated in terms of a particular criterion (for example, contributing to public safety) and a score, for example, between 1 and 10. Using the internal logic of such systems, it is to be assumed that projects that get a high score are more desirable. It cannot be overemphasized that such numerical systems should be cautiously used. They cannot substitute for judgment, and, if not carefully constructed and applied, they can do more harm than good.

Minneapolis has a priority evaluation rating system that its planning office believes is invaluable in achieving a balanced program. The Capital Long-Range Improvements Committee (CLIC) uses citizen task forces to evaluate capital improvements proposals. The CLIC considers the city's financial capability and annually makes project recommendations, including bond expenditure limits. Proposals are rated on a scale of 0 to 50 points according to fourteen factors. Among the community objectives are economic development, further defined as the extent to which the proposed capital improvements "will encourage capital investment, improve the City's tax base, improve job opportunities, attract consumers to the City, or produce public or private revenues," and public benefit, defined as the extent to which the proposed capital improvement "is justified in terms of number of people to be benefited."[11] The CLIC also receives advice and recommendations on capital improvements from the city planning commission. The planning commission prepares a checklist that contains many policy-related items for departments to follow in making referrals to the commission. Significantly, if a project proposed for a particular year was in the five-year program, it gets additional points—thus a project that is just suggested "at the last minute" is penalized.

Priority setting is a particular problem for the small community that has few professional staff members and must rely more on lay persons for decision making. An example (Figure 14–5) prepared by a consultant for Franklin, Massachusetts, shows a simple easy-to-use checklist for priority setting.

Priority-setting systems in older communities are likely to undergo changes in the coming years. Older communities have street, bridge, water, and sewer systems that are decades old and, depending on the condition, require extensive maintenance, rehabilitation or replacement—circumstances that came to be known in the mid-1980s as the "infrastructure" problem. Media interest was so strong that network news shows and popular news magazines ran stories on "America in Ruins." The media and some planning literature concentrated on comprehensive needs assessments with mega-billion-dollar price tags.

On a more mundane but far more practical level, public works officials and specialists are studying and experimenting with realistic needs assessments and discovering better means for communities to maintain their capital plant in an era of fiscal restraint. In many localities, priority systems will depend on facility-maintenance strategies and options, which can range from replacing a facility to doing nothing about it. (A range of such options and strategies are presented in the accompanying sidebar.) Thus, for many communities that adopt facility-maintenance strategies, priorities for capital facilities will be closely related to the condition of the capital plant, the fiscal resources available to the community, the options that it chooses, and the ultimate capital policy decisions.

This discussion emphasizes priority-setting systems because public officials, budget officials, and planners in many communities are struggling with the challenge of choosing a small, limited number of projects from a long list of needs or demands. Although choices in many communities will be made on purely political grounds, an increasing number of local governments want a more systematic assessment of the benefits of public capital expenditures. If a community cannot build everything, it must build what is most important and what will most contribute to its physical, social, and economic development objectives. Developing priority systems is an extremely difficult task, and such systems may always have a degree of artificiality. However, it is possible to develop realistic priority systems; some of the considerations are listed in the accompanying sidebar.

The CIP process and intergovernmental relations

The pattern of intergovernmental relations in metropolitan areas has profound effects on urban planning. The vast literature on metropolitan area problems and intergovernmental relations cannot even be reviewed here. What is relevant for purposes of this chapter are two basic factors and the implications that flow from them. First is the fact that the vast majority of metropolitan areas contain small, fragmented municipal governments and a number of separate special districts; second is the recent dependence of metropolitan areas on state and federal grant-in-aid programs. As these programs decline, serious local revenue problems must be faced.

Criterion	3	2	1	0	P	S	W	T
Public health and safety	Project is needed to alleviate existing health or safety hazard.	Project is needed to alleviate potential health or safety hazard.	Project would promote or maintain health or safety.	No health or safety impact is associated with project.	A		3	
External requirements	Project is required by law, regulations, or court mandate.	Project is required by agreement with other jurisdiction.	Product will be conducted in conjunction with another jurisdiction.	Project is City only and not externally required.	A		3	
Protection of capital stock	Project is critical to save structural integrity of existing City facility or repair significant structural deterioration.	Project will repair systems important to facility operation.	Project will improve facility appearance or deter future expenditure.	No existing facility is involved.	A		3	
Economic development	Project will encourage capital investment, improve the City's tax base, improve job opportunities, attract consumers to the City, or produce public or private revenues.			Project will have no significant economic development impact.	A		3	
Operating budget impact	Project will result in decreased costs in the operating budget.	Project will have minimal or no operating and maintenance costs.	Project will have some additional operating costs, and/or personnel additions will be necessary.	Project will require significant additions in personnel or other operating costs.	A		3	
Life expectancy of project	Meets needs of community for next 20 years or more.	Meets needs of community for next 15 to 19 years.	Meets needs of community for next 10 to 14 years.	Meets needs of community for less than 10 years.	A		3	
Percentage of population served by project	50% or more	25% to 49%	10% to 24%	Less than 10%	B		2	
Relation to adopted plans	Project is included in formal plan that has major/council approval.	Project is included in written plan adopted by City board/commission.	Project is included in written plans of City staff.	Project is not included in any written plans.	B		2	
Intensity of use	Project will be used year-round.	Project will receive seasonal and as-needed use.	Project will receive only seasonal use.		B		2	

Figure 14–4　System for establishing priorities among proposed capital projects, city of New Orleans. Codes: P = priority; S = score; W = weight; T = total.

Governmental fragmentation and the CIP process are related because certain important facilities, especially sewage treatment plants and their related major sewer trunk lines and major expressways and highways are built by either state or special-district governments and not by local governments. These key facilities can trigger, accelerate, or retard the speed and pattern of urban growth—in other words, they are the growth shapers. Other governmental bodies plan and construct these facilities, but it is the local government that must then provide the local capital facilities and public services to serve the growth generated. Thus, local government may not always have complete control over its destiny.

A number of steps have been taken to coordinate planning and development at the metropolitan level. Many planning agencies are adopting metropolitan development policies and trying (often struggling) to influence key investment decisions. However, even though many metropolitan agencies are governed by locally elected officials, the primary focus of the metropolitan agency is on areawide problems and not necessarily on local impacts of capital investment decisions. A handful of metropolitan agencies have begun areawide capital

Criterion	3	2	1	0	P	S	W	T
Scheduling	Project to be started within next year.	Project to be started within 2 to 3 years.	Project to be started within 4 to 5 years.	Project is uncertain.	B		2	
Benefit/cost	Return on investment for the project can be computed and is positive.		Return on investment cannot be readily computed.	Return on investment can be computed and is negative.	B		2	
Potential for duplication		No similar projects are provided by public or private agencies outside of City government.		Project may duplicate other available public or private facilities.	B		2	
Availability of financing	Project revenues will be sufficient to support project expense.	Non-city revenues have been identified and applied for.	Potential for non-city revenues exists.	No financing arrangements currently exist.	C		1	
Special need		Project meets a community obligation to serve a special need of a segment of the City's population, such as low/moderate-income, aged, minority, or handicapped persons.		Project does not meet particular needs of a special population.	C		1	
Energy consumption	Project will reduce amount of energy consumed.	Project will require no increase in energy consumption.	Project will require minimum increase in energy consumption.	Project will require large increases in energy consumption.	C		1	
Timeliness/external	Undertaking the project will allow the City to take advantage of a favorable current situation, such as the purchase of land or materials at favorable prices.			External influences do not affect the timeliness of the project.	C		1	
Public support	Public has demonstrated a significant desire for the City to undertake the project, through neighborhood surveys, petitions, or other clear indicators.		City staff reports that the project is desired by the community to be served.	Public has not expressed a specific preference for this project.	C		1	

Figure 14–4 *continued.*

improvements assessments that attempt at least to identify capital investments being made by various governmental levels and point out needed improvements.

At the local government level a number of steps can be taken to exchange information. A local governmental unit can survey capital investment plans of overlapping governments and special districts regarding capital improvements that will be built within the jurisdiction. This activity can inform local officials, who then may want to take political action; it also provides an opportunity to coordinate projects that will be built by different units in the same part of the community. Some communities have organized intergovernmental bonding committees that attempt to keep each other informed as to bonds that will be issued by the governments involved. This is a particularly important step, because when a community's bonds are rated by investment services, the amount of overlapping debt on taxpayers is a relevant factor in the safety of the security.

State and federal grants-in-aid present another set of problems for local government. Although local governments react favorably to state and federal programs

Figure 14–5   Priority-setting checklist proposed for the town of Franklin, Massachusetts.

The following checklist should help in considering the secondary consequences of building capital facilities or making other capital outlays. All questions are structured so that yes answers indicate an impact consistent with town policy as expressed in "Planning for Franklin," the Residents' Master Plan Studies, 1974–76.

		Yes	No	Not applicable
1.	Will this project either leave unchanged or slow the rate of population growth in Franklin?	——	——	——
2.	Is the amount of growth that this project is designed to serve consistent with the most recent projections of the planning board?	——	——	——
3.	Will this project either leave unchanged or increase the ratio of jobs in Franklin to residents of Franklin?	——	——	——
4.	If the project is likely to stimulate residential development in an area, as opposed to townwide,			
	a. Will that development be totally in the center or suburban district?	——	——	——
	b. Will that development be partially in the center or suburban district?	——	——	——
	c. Can the stimulated growth in that area be serviced with roads, schools, utilities, etc., without further town investments?	——	——	——
	d. Are existing development controls adequate to relieve all other concerns about the stimulated growth in that area?	——	——	——
5.	If the project is likely to slow residential development in an area, as opposed to townwide,			
	a. Is that area in the rural district?	——	——	——
	b. Are one or more public service systems in the area being used at or near capacity?	——	——	——
6.	If the project is likely to stimulate commercial or industrial development in an area, as opposed to townwide			
	a. Is that area now zoned for commerce or industry?	——	——	——
	b. Can the stimulated development be adequately serviced with roads, utilities, etc., without further town investments?	——	——	——
	c. Are existing development controls adequate to relieve all other concerns about the stimulated growth?	——	——	——
7.	If located in a rural district, will this project itself be free of characteristics leading to an urbanized "character"?	——	——	——

that can help them undertake capital improvements projects, there are some problems that require careful attention from local officials and planners dealing with capital investments.

One such problem is that grant progams can distort economic choices and skew local decision making. Since money may be available for certain capital improvements but not for others, local governments tend to choose projects that can be funded in part through grant programs. Capital facilities that do not have a grant program to support them may go begging. Grant formulas for the balance between federal or state and local cost can also skew decision making. For example, for more than a decade the federal urban mass transportation system program provided that the federal government would pay up to 80 percent of the cost of a transit capital program. On the other hand, an interstate highway going through a locality would be funded by a federal formula that provided for the federal government to pay 90 percent of a highway project. Clearly, it cost local government more to build transit than highways.

The U.S. Congress's cycle of providing authorizations and appropriations or grant-in-aid programs can also be troublesome to local government. For example, Congress may pass a new grant program with a span of five years and with a total authorization of a lump sum or up to certain amounts for each year of the

---

Options for facility maintenance

Options for specific facility segments
1. Do nothing, except emergency repairs when, and if, a need for them arises.
2. Apply preventive maintenance effort.
3. Rehabilitate the item.
4. Replace it.
5. Abandon/sell/lease it.

Basic maintenance strategies
1. Do nothing/crisis maintenance. Do only that maintenance that has to be done. This is a purely reactive approach.
2. Worst first. Repair (or replace) those infrastructure components that are in the worst condition, thus basing choices primarily on information on the condition and problem level of capital facilities.
3. Opportunistic scheduling. Repair or replace those components when other related work is scheduled.
4. Prespecified maintenance cycle "standards." Select and follow a repair cycle, such as resurfacing particular types of roads every so many years.
5. Repair components "at risk." Identify and repair those infrastructure segments most likely to have near-future major problems, even though the current condition of the segment

is not known to be a significant problem.
6. Preventive maintenance. Install a systematic maintenance program to reduce the need for later and presumably more costly and more disruptive repairs. Such a program typically involves a scheduled program, including regular inspections, and relatively light maintenance.
7. Reduce the demand and wear and tear on the facility. Reduce the need for maintenance activity by reducing the demand for the activity and thus the wear and tear (e.g., on the roads, bridges, water, or sewer system). A variation is to alter the original construction or rehabilitation design so as to make the item easier and less costly to repair.
8. Economic comparison of alternatives. Undertake some form of systematic economic analysis to decide which segments to repair and in what way. The analysis is intended to help the agency select which of the previous maintenance strategies, and what specific maintenance treatment, is appropriate.

Source: Harry P. Hatry, Annie P. Millar, and James H. Evans, *Guide to Setting Priorities for Capital Investment* (Washington, DC: The Urban Institute, 1984), 27.

program. However, until Congress appropriates the money for a particular program in a particular year, that money is not available. Moreover, appropriations may be below annual authorization levels. To add to the misery of local government financial planners, Congress also has the habit of appropriating money several months into a fiscal year, which forces local governments to try to carry out programs and spend money designed for a twelve-month period in, for example, seven or eight months. In the mid-1980s, the federal deficit and a desire to return certain functions to local government led to congressional proposals to cut or eliminate federal grant programs. The uncertain fiscal environment created by such proposals made long-range financial planning difficult, if not impossible, for local governments.

The local CIP process is also heavily influenced by other types of federal programs. For example, as both major metropolitan areas and small communities have discovered, environmental standards for water quality management require local governments to spend enormous amounts of money to maintain and improve water quality. New and major improvements in sewage treatment plants and the construction of major trunk sewer lines may require local communities to postpone other capital investments. In addition, the secondary impacts of federal, capital-related programs are not yet well understood, let alone controlled. For example, a federal or state environmental requirement forces a local government unit to build a trunk sewer line in a particular location. Although this capital investment achieves certain environmental objectives, it can also open up vast areas of land for urban development. Local land use plans may not have proposed or anticipated such development.

As can be seen even from this short discussion, local government capital investments can be greatly influenced by other levels of government. The degree to which local government units can use capital investments to shape urban

---

Desirable "technical" characteristics for a priority-setting process

1. Be understandable. The information provided should be clear both to participants and to users of the process. For example, unclear evaluation criteria or esoteric scoring procedures are less likely to be helpful.

2. Be comprehensive; that is, consider all major consequences of a project.

3. Minimize double-counting of evaluative criteria. (If two criteria are highly interrelated and the selection process does not take this fact into consideration, double-counting can result.)

4. Provide valid, accurate information. When numerical information is provided, it should be accurate and meaningful. When qualitative information is used, it should be clearly presented and accompanied by an appropriate rationale so that users will know what has been evaluated.

5. Articulate clearly the key value judgments in the procedures made by nonelected officials (e.g., if weights are developed by persons other than the elected officials).

6. Provide information not only on the relative ranking of projects but also on the individual merits or value of the projects. Without the latter information, project selectors will not know which projects are worth funding. (If a set of projects is not worthwhile, the fact that one is top ranked does not make the projects worthy of funding. Similarly, even low-ranked projects may be worth funding if they have a high payoff.)

7. Be insensitive to minor differences in ratings. Procedures, for example, that automatically reject a proposal because of small differ-

growth will determine the extent to which the CIP serves as an effective management tool.

The CIP process and the political process

The procedures discussed in this chapter for the CIP and the local budget emphasize concepts, techniques, and bureaucratic routines that are essential to a well-managed local government. The neat, rational process described does not really explain completely the complex political process that is taking place simultaneously, often outside the bureaucratic technical process. A favorite pastime of some academics (albeit unsophisticated ones) is to take planning and management literature describing such routines and then compare real-world case studies to the routines. These analyses always come to the conclusion that "things don't always work that way." However, this does not mean budgetary processes are obsolete, unrealistic, or naive—it simply means that the process is more complicated.

The purpose of this section is to make some generalizations from the literature (see the bibliography to this chapter) that describe the complexity of local government budgetary decision making.

One set of observations relates to common patterns within a government's technical bureaucracy. For example, heads of operating departments are far more interested in their own departmental priorities than in citywide policy issues. Thus, the public works director is more interested in sewer construction than in park acquisition. Also, given the fact that most department heads are running ongoing programs and services, they are more interested in solving current problems than in building an infrastructure for an urban land use program. Generally, but not always, the department administrator's time horizon

---

ences in ratings among raters would be a problem.

8. Accept proposals that meet a critical need while rejecting proposals that fail to satisfy any critical requirement. Ratings should be designed to spotlight projects that are urgent or critical. Norfolk, Virginia, for example, includes as a criterion an "overriding consideration factor" to cover any major and far-reaching consideration not otherwise covered adequately. Either positive or negative points of up to 20 may be assigned; this factor must be documented.

9. Consider possible interdependencies among projects. Some projects may benefit each other, thus increasing their joint value or reducing their total cost; examples are street and water projects that could save money if done jointly. In other cases, some projects together may add problems; an example is scheduling a bridge for major rehabilitation at the same time a major sewer project is planned under the street that is the major alternative route to the bridge.

10. Be practical in terms of cost, time, and personnel available. Late or overly expensive information would, of course, be a major problem for any priority-setting system.

Note: In developing this list, the study team found quite useful Theodore Wang and William Beine's Project Report to the National Bureau of Standards, "The Development of Criteria for Project Prioritization," Washington, DC, 8 February 1978.

Source: Harry P. Hatry, Annie P. Millar, and James H. Evans, *Guide to Setting Priorities for Capital Investment*. (Washington, DC: The Urban Institute, 1984) 30.

is shorter than the planner's. Naturally, all department heads ask for more than they expect to get; projects listed near the bottom of a priority list may be of next to no importance. Moreover, politically astute department heads frequently establish informal relationships with elected officials, especially council committees related to their own areas of interest; therefore, they have built a consensus on certain projects.

Another general observation is that not all decision making is postponed until the time of year when the CIP is being prepared. Many investment decisions are made outside the annual CIP process. For example, emergencies may occur in the middle of the budget year and require expenditures to be made. New programs and projects may become possible because of a new state law or federal program. Decisions on capital investments may be made as political promises during campaigns and then implemented after new officials take office. A few major capital investment decisions may be made when a comprehensive plan is adopted. More commonly, however, key investment decisions are made when neighborhood or district plans are prepared.

Some of the literature deals with the role of elected officials in the budgetary process. In general, elected officials are engaged in constant negotiations with public and private interests that want or oppose certain improvements. The continuing bargaining process makes the elected official reluctant to make commitments too many years in advance. Therefore, programs for future years are not as firm as they appear. One of the bargaining devices that is frequently resorted to is to program an improvement for a particular future year. As the next budget cycle comes around, the project may move up a year and sometimes can be moved back a year. Many projects bounce from year to year in the capital program but never arrive in the capital budget. Because elected officials are involved in this negotiating process, they also have some reluctance to explicitly identify and publicly announce all capital investment policies and priorities. They want to maintain flexibility and the opportunity to change their minds.

Certain investment decisions and styles of decision making are irresistible to elected officials and therefore are inevitable. These are a desire to keep tax rates down; a desire to spread capital improvements throughout the community so that each neighborhood "gets something"; a tendency to give in to vocal community and neighborhood groups—sometimes ignore such opinion; a tendency to balance expenditures and allocate cuts and additions across the board among all local government departments; a tendency at times to avoid seeking certain federal or state grants if there are too many strings attached; and a strong tendency to guard the capital investment decision-making process so jealously that technicians do not really participate and often do not know why certain decisions are made.

The relationship of the CIP to other planning tools

Comprehensive planning   "Master" plans were once so specific that they identified particular facilities. Now, plans are more policy oriented and may provide only a general guide to investment decisions. Nevertheless, community or neighborhood level plans and plans for small communities may still contain a degree of specificity that makes it easy to know whether a particular improvement does or does not conform to policy.

Plans prepared for particular functional elements—the park plan and the public library plan, for example—can also be quite specific with respect to improvements. In fact, some plans go so far as to make broad cost estimates regarding implementation of proposals. This practice is to be recommended because it gives elected officials a far better idea of what it might cost to follow a planner's recommendations.

At the suburban fringe a growing number of communities are constructing so-called growth management systems in which the CIP is an important component. Such communities carefully try to relate the comprehensive plan to the CIP and to zoning and subdivision regulation. Permits for development are based on whether or not certain community facilities are either in place or programmed in the CIP.

It is interesting to note that in several older central cities (e.g., Philadelphia, Baltimore, and Pittsburgh), the CIP is the centerpiece of the planning program. In these cities the CIP is a very important activity, and annual and multiyear development programs and policies are designed to be interrelated with annual capital budget decisions.

The relationship between the planning function and the budgeting function is taken a step further in Atlanta, where a department of planning and budget is responsible for both urban and financial planning. Local law specifically requires the preparation of development programs relating to capital investments for one-, five-, and ten-year horizons.

In 1985 the Florida state legislature mandated that all local governments prepare a capital improvements element for their comprehensive plans (previous legislation mandated a comprehensive plan). This CIP must contain policies for the construction, extension, or increase in capacity of public facilities as well as identify how existing facility deficiencies can be corrected. Estimates of costs must be made, timetables set, and revenue sources identified. The act also requires that local governments develop standards to ensure the availability and adequacy of facilities for new development.

Zoning and subdivision regulation In many communities, the CIP is also becoming more closely related to traditional zoning and subdivision regulation. A number of communities are adopting policies that permit or deny zoning and subdivision permits on the basis of whether there are adequate public facilities. These policies are based on the desire to extend utilities in the most efficient way and to prevent urban sprawl. Some growth management systems permit private developers to install public facilities at their own expense if these facilities are not scheduled until later years.

Subdivision regulation administration (see chapter 8) also relates to the CIP in that there has been a historical trend to require developers to install utilities and other public facilities at their own expense. This policy in effect shifts some of the costs for capital facilities out of the public budget and into the budget of the private developer and therefore to the eventual home buyer. In addition, although state laws are relatively silent on the point, it is widely known that extensive negotiations go on between private developers and public bodies regarding who pays for major public facilities required by new urban development. This is particularly true with respect to planned unit developments and other large-scale developments such as shopping centers and industrial parks. When local government perceives that there are economic development or tax advantages to encouraging industrial and commercial development, local government will frequently pay the cost of utility extensions in order to promote private investment.

Special assessments In more mature communities special assessments are the principal way of financing purely local street and utility improvements. Special assessment districts are set up whereby properties that benefit from a particular improvement (for example, a new street) actually share the costs of providing it. This is another technique that shifts capital facility costs away from public budgets. In some cases, the technique is used to finance downtown improvements, such as parking or pedestrian facilities.

Economic development and renewal   Economic development and renewal projects often require large capital investments, such as new streets, utilities, and parks. Chapter 10 covers many of the substantive issues that economic development raises. The point here is that extensive coordination is required between the CIP and federal, state, and private funds to be expended in a particular area. As noted earlier, extensive negotiations may go on between public bodies and private developers in joint developments. Public bodies may be willing to pay for certain improvements in order to make private investment possible.

Mandatory referral   A number of state enabling acts and local charters include provisions stating that when capital facilities are built by either the government unit or independent special districts, the plans for such capital facilities must be referred to the local planning commission or planning department for comment. When the capital facility is being built by the governmental unit itself, the planning agency comments may have some force. However, when independent governmental units are constructing facilities, recommendations are usually only advisory.

Annexation   At the urban fringe, land development companies that own and want to develop land seek to have the land annexed to a municipality to save on certain urban services, such as police protection, fire protection, and public utilities. A few states, such as Illinois, allow annexation agreements that permit local governments and private developers to negotiate public facility improvement costs. Even in states without such enabling laws, governments frequently exercise such negotiating powers because they have a strong bargaining position, in that they provide public services that developers need. Again, the issue here is the shifts and balances between private and public expenditures for capital facilities. In Texas, if communities refuse to annex, private developers are permitted to form municipal utility districts to provide services.

Official maps   Several states permit local governments to adopt official map ordinances, which specify the location of particular improvements such as a park site or the right-of-way for a future street. The designation of such sites on an official map puts private property owners on notice of the government's intention to construct a public facility. Within the designated areas, the local government may deny zoning and building permits in order to prevent the eventual cost of acquisition from becoming prohibitive. However, there is usually a strict time limit (between one and three years), by the end of which a public body must purchase or condemn the land.

Cost-revenue studies as a management tool[12]

The topics covered so far in this chapter—revenue sources, intergovernmental aid, the budgeting function, and capital improvements programming—relate to fundamental communitywide policy issues. This section deals with the public revenues and costs from a somewhat narrower perspective, showing how they are related to the regulation of new development or redevelopment.

A number of techniques are used to analyze a particular development at a specific time and place. Because of the changing fiscal condition of local governments, such techniques will continue to be critical to planning. Communities are increasingly shifting to developers the cost of improvements through development exactions and inpact fees. The economic interests of developers and the legal tests courts may apply to test the reasonableness of such demands make the accurate measurement of impacts extremely important.

The concept of comparing public costs and revenues for a particular development proposal had its roots in the planning field in the 1930s. During the

1920s many properties had been "prematurely" subdivided into residential neighborhoods—meaning that they remained forever vacant. A number of communities tried to renew these "dead" subdivisions by preparing simple analyses showing how much more money would flow into the local government treasury if the land were developed with improvements instead of remaining tax delinquent.

Beginning in the 1950s, cost-revenue concepts were used in both central city and suburban planning situations. In the central city context, urban renewal project reports would frequently contain estimates showing how little tax revenue was being generated by a deteriorated neighborhood and how much it cost to service the neighborhood; these reports would then compare revenues and expenditures of the area after the proposed renewal.

The 1950s was a time of aggressive annexation in many suburban communities. Because planning agencies did not control the precise location of development, they had to take annexation requests from wherever they came and in whatever location. The cost of extending major sewer and water lines and serving new populations encouraged planners and public administrators to study the costs and revenues of annexing a particular area.

In the late 1960s and early 1970s the focus of cost-revenue studies shifted to the problem of growth management. This came about through a combination of factors: inflation and the resulting increasing public costs for all services; a greater desire to manage growth; shifts in the housing market from single-family dwellings to multifamily dwelling units; and the increasing popularity of planned unit developments with combinations of uses. These changes all contributed to a growing awareness on the part of planners and urban administrators that it was necessary to measure more carefully potential tax revenues and potential public costs at the time new development was being approved.

Growing interest in the fiscal impact of development has developed concurrently with similar emphases in the field of environmental planning, where development proposals are evaluated to determine their impact on a variety of natural, economic, and social systems. Thus, studies of the cost-revenue aspects of development are increasingly referred to as examples of *fiscal impact analysis*.

Basic concepts

A widely used comprehensive methodology of impact analysis developed at Rutgers University defines the fiscal impact study as "a projection of the direct, current public costs and revenues resulting from population or employment change to the local jurisdiction(s) in which this change is taking place."[13] Researchers familiar with the techniques emphasize the conceptual limits and boundaries of such studies. For example, fiscal impact analyses usually consider only *direct* impact and not secondary impacts that may take place as money flows through the local economy. In any event, no one knows how to predict secondary impacts. Moreover, the analyses emphasize *current* dollar costs, and this emphasis is limited, to *public*, not necessarily private costs of public actions. In essence, fiscal impact analysis is the estimation, tallying, and comparison of costs and revenues. Most fiscal impact studies limit themselves to costs and revenues related to the local jurisdiction and do not necessarily include other or higher levels of government. The bottom line on any analysis is either positive or negative. It is positive if the revenues that a particular development will generate are larger than the public service costs. It is negative if the public service costs are larger than the anticipated revenues. Thus, obviously, local governments are reluctant to approve developments unless there is a positive fiscal impact on the community.

Cost-revenue analysis, which focuses on municipal revenues and services, should not be confused with cost-benefit analysis, which assesses nonmonetary issues as well, or with cost-effectiveness analysis, which assesses the most economical way of carrying out a particular public service. The distinction between average and marginal costs is another technical factor that deserves mention. Average-cost analysis estimates the cost of providing a public service to *all* present and future residents. Marginal-cost analysis determines how much *more* it will cost to serve the next *increment* of population growth. Over the long term, the average cost is more important; over the short term, marginal cost may be more important to a governmental unit.

The Rutgers methodology identifies six basic types of fiscal impact analyses: per capita multiplier, case study, service standard, comparable city, proportional valuation (these represent average costing approaches), and employment anticipation (representing marginal costing methods).

The per capita multiplier method of analysis is the most common (over 70 percent of the studies in the original Rutgers project used this method). Forecasting of future costs and revenues is based on average cost per person and average school cost per pupil, which in turn is based on population of pupils residing in particular housing types. Highly reliable population and school data are needed to support this method.

In the case study method, a particular development—the case at hand—is analyzed through an examination of the characteristics of the development. Then various department heads are interviewed to determine the range of possible future local costs to serve that development.

The service standard method is a more detailed approach, similar to the per capita multiplier method. The service standard method goes into the details of personnel requirements within the specific service categories. Data are derived from the U.S. census of governments.

The comparable city method is rarely used, but it may be used more frequently in the future if data about particular communities increase. Basically, the method emphasizes changes in population size or growth rate by comparing the community at hand with other communities of similar size, growth patterns, and so on.

The proportional valuation method, used for nonresidential studies, assigns a proportion of municipal costs to a new nonresidential facility on the basis of its real property valuation in comparison with that of the community as a whole.

The employment anticipation method, another technique for nonresidential developments, is based on the assumption that municipal costs are related to the number of employees of an establishment and that this relationship is the best measure for determining public costs.

The six categories just described are classified according to the varying ways in which *cost* is calculated. *Revenues* are calculated similarly for all types of studies.

The per capita multiplier method

A comprehensive manual that would explain the technical detail of fiscal impact studies would be as long as this entire book. This chapter can only highlight some of the general procedural and data requirements for but a single method—the per capita multiplier method. The steps outlined in this section are used to calculate the costs that a particular development might generate.

The first step in calculating costs is to determine what locally generated data are available. Both municipal and school district budgets should be obtained and analyzed. In particular, it is useful to know school district populations, which are frequently divided into elementary and high school populations and can also be divided by grade. Local government expenditures should be divided into service categories—for example, general government, public safety, public works, health and welfare, and recreation and culture—and should be separated into operating expenses and debt service expenses.

The next series of steps relates to analyzing the characteristics of the development. For example, what is the total area, and what portion is residential and what portion nonresidential? Within the residential portion, the dwelling units need to be classified by type (single-family, town house, apartment) and, further, by number of bedrooms. It is also essential to classify the dwelling units according to cost and rental per dwelling unit. Once these data have been combined with previously generated data from the school district, basic multipliers can be used for each housing type. For example, data collected at the local (and sometimes state) level will show the mean number of children that can be expected to reside in various types of dwelling units. These multipliers can be applied to the development to determine the number of school-children that will be generated. Then, using average per pupil expenditures from the local school district, it is possible to calculate the total costs for public schools that the development will generate.

Whereas school costs are typically calculated on a per pupil basis, a different base is used to calculate nonschool municipal costs. Municipal costs are analyzed according to the proportion of service cost that can be assigned to existing residential and nonresidential land uses. Those costs that can be assigned to residential areas, on the basis of the ratio of their property value to total local real property value, are divided by the current local population to determine a per capita cost multiplier. The cost multipliers for various municipal functions are then applied to the development. Next, data from the U.S. census that show multipliers for various housing types can be used to determine the total population of the development. The total population times the per capita cost is then calculated for each public service category.

If the development contains nonresidential uses, such as a shopping center, costs must be assigned to that portion. Earlier in the process, when total municipal cost data were analyzed, costs were allocated to residential and nonresidential uses on the basis of real property value. To assign costs for nonresidential uses, the real property value of the use at hand is compared with the total nonresidential value in the community. For example, if the value is 1 percent of the total value of nonresidential uses in a community, then 1 percent of the costs of municipal services can be allocated to that use.

Finally, all estimated and projected costs that can be assigned to the development are computed. The analyst's attention then turns to estimating revenues that the development will produce. When revenues are calculated, major emphasis is placed on general revenue categories such as the property tax. Revenues for utility services typically are not considered, since they are user chargers and almost by definition cover the cost of operating services.

The property tax, the most important source of revenue to be calculated, needs to be allocated to the school district and to the municipality. In addition, a variety of miscellaneous revenues, such as building and zoning permits, come from the development. Estimation of real property income is accomplished by calculating the costs of the dwelling units and applying the various ratios and multipliers that were discussed in the revenue section of this chapter. Thus far the analyst is dealing with sources of revenue that go directly from the resident to the governmental unit or to the school district.

A second, more complex, set of calculations must be made concerning intergovernmental transfers. Many grant-in-aid programs on both the federal and state levels are based on population. If the development increases the population of a community, the community will receive more aid, such as the state motor fuel tax funds. Similarly, the amount of state aid to a school district depends on enrollment or attendance. If enrollment increases, state aid will also increase.

All revenues are tabulated; these revenues include those going directly to the municipality and to the school district and the governmental transfers to both units. At this point, total revenues can be compared to total costs.

How are the results of such a study used? If the study result is positive, presumably both the developer and the community are happy. If the result is negative, however, some steps can still be taken. For example, a number of models of impact analyses have been developed that make it possible to change the outcome by adjusting some of the inputs. For example, since it is generally acknowledged that multifamily dwelling units have fewer school-age children than do single-family dwelling units, a developer might decrease the number of single-family units and increase the number of apartment units. This alone might change the balance. Or, if the development is largely multifamily, it is possible to change the mixture of dwelling unit sizes so as to have fewer large apartments with children.

Some policy issues

The sketchy description presented in the preceding section cannot do justice to the complex technical and analytical steps involved in fiscal impact analysis. But it can provide a basis for consideration of policy issues that arise when these techniques are used.

One issue relates to the technical validity of such studies. Typically, the studies are carried out by municipal personnel who are not necessarily familiar with the intricacies of analysis, methodological pitfalls, and data limitations. The probability of making errors is high enough to require that the analyst be very careful. All assumptions must be stated; all data sources must be identified; and data sources, particularly local ones, should be described so that it is clear whether data are based on a long history of data collection and analysis or on a one-shot look at a current fiscal year.

Another issue relates to how a particular development might fare in various communities. For example, a moderate-income development planned for a high-income community might generate a negative result in an impact analysis, but that same development in a moderate-income community might generate a small surplus.

Fiscal impact analysis raises profound questions of equity. The effective municipal planner and urban administrator must manage the community's resources efficiently, but can they do so at the cost of individual constitutional rights? Fiscal impact analysis can provide information for more rational decisions, but local planners and administrators cannot blindly ignore social implications. One authority has observed that users of fiscal impact analysis must realize that not every land use can be a municipal benefit; although local governments can assess relative fiscal merit, they cannot always exclude land uses that impose a liability. Moreover, "courts have recognized that municipalities also have to provide housing for those who work nearby, answer regional as well as local needs, and provide residential opportunities for those who are economically disadvantaged."[14]

In short, we do not need an analytical tool that will discriminate against people. Yet the tool will be used more in the future if, as it now appears, the public is less willing to make transfer payments or invest in public goods.

Conclusion

Detailed understanding of public finance and public facility maintenance and construction will be essential for the local government planner in the foreseeable future. Although professional specialization and practice within the planning field will continue to be common, both generalists and specialists will need this knowledge if they are to contribute to the technical and policy discussions in local government planning. Neither a planner's most creative proposals for community facilities nor the most professionally proficient citizen effort to identify public needs will be sufficient: The planner will need to know how much something costs, where the money is coming from, and who will pay.

A number of converging factors have created a need for creative thinking in public finance: changing conceptions of the roles of the federal, state, and local government; devolution of responsibility from the federal to the local level; tax reform; federal deficits; and the particular problems faced by communities that are either old and declining in resources or new and rapidly growing. Fortunately, many local governments have the services of dedicated professionals in planning, management, public finance, and public works, all of whom will contribute to innovative ways of planning—and paying for—public services and facilities. Many local governments will reconsider the level of services that they will, or can, provide. New methods of public-private cooperation will be arranged. New ways of monitoring and maintaining facilities using new technology and materials will be developed. State and local governments will experiment with a variety of revenue-raising mechanisms beyond traditional property and sales taxes. Interlocal governmental agreements within metropolitan areas will create new ways of providing public services at lower costs.

Increasingly, planners will participate in local government management teams representing planning, public works, management, and public finance, to develop new ways of helping communities grow, work, and renew.

1 For detailed coverage of local government finance, see the following book in the Municipal Management Series: J. Richard Aronson and Eli Schwartz, eds., *Management Policies in Local Government Finance* (Washington, DC: International City Management Association, 1987).

2 *Serrano* v. *Priest*, 487 P.2d 1241 (1971), 96 Cal. Rptr. 601.

3 *Rodriguez* v. *San Antonio School District*, 411 U.S. 1, 93 S.Ct. 1278 (1973).

4 Minn. Ex. Sess. Laws 1971 Ch. 24. Codified at Minn. Stat. Ch. 483F (1974).

5 James C. Snyder, *Fiscal Planning and Management in Local Government* (Lexington, MA: Lexington Books, 1977), 78 ff.

6 The organization of this discussion is based on Richard W. Lindholm, David S. Arnold, and Richard R. Herbert, "The Budgetary Process," in Aronson and Schwartz, *Management Policies in Local Government Finance* (1975 edition), 68–87.

7 Ibid., 72.

8 Lennox L. Moak and Kathryn W. Killian, *A Manual of Techniques for the Preparation, Consideration,* *Adoption, and Administration of Operating Budgets* (Chicago: Municipal Finance Officers Association, 1973) 5.

9 David L. Leininger and Ronald C. Wong, *Zero-Base Budgeting in Garland, Texas.* Management Information Service Report vol. 8, no. 4A (Washington, DC: International City Management Association, April 1976), 2.

10 Mel Scott, *American City Planning since 1890* (Berkeley: University of California Press, 1969), 102.

11 City of Minneapolis, Capital Long-Range Improvements Committee, *CLIC* (Minneapolis: City of Minneapolis, 1971).

12 This section draws on the following work: Robert W. Burchell and David Listokin, *The Fiscal Impact Handbook: Estimating Local Costs and Revenues of Land Development* (New Brunswick, NJ: Rutgers University, Center for Urban Policy Research, 1978).

13 Ibid, 1.

14 Ibid., 8.

15 Information for planning

Data versus information

If data alone could be used to solve planning problems, there would be little reason to include a chapter on information in this book.[1] However, for many planning problems, more data may be available than can be assimilated, especially for day-to-day analysis and decision making. The phrase "data rich and information poor" accurately describes many organizations.[2]

Developing information for planning involves not only locating data, but also evaluating its relevance and analyzing and communicating its importance. Only when the meaning in a set of data has been discovered and translated into useful concepts does data yield information.

The purpose of this chapter is to discuss the process of identifying, collecting, evaluating, analyzing, and communicating data for planning decisions.

It is important to note from the outset that this is not a chapter about computer-based planning and information systems, automated data retrieval systems, or geographic-based data systems. Nor is it about organizing a research unit, for which the reader is referred to chapter 11, "Basic Studies for State and Regional Planning," in *The Practice of State and Regional Planning*.[3] Although these are important concepts and systems, this chapter focuses on a broader range of information-development issues and sources.

Problem definition

Developing information for planning begins with a definition of the problem. Data that are not based on a careful definition of the problem and evaluated for veracity will provide little basis for accurate planning decisions. Simply put, if you don't know what a problem is, you can't collect the data to solve it. However, once the problem is identified, there is no guarantee that it will remain the same during the planning process. Experience teaches planners to be skeptical about definite answers and easy solutions. The problem may change or take on additional dimensions while data are being collected and analyzed. Thus, it is important to reconsider the problem definition while assembling the data to ensure that the proper facts are being collected.

Problem definition is difficult because objectives may be unclear or in conflict, and agencies often have to respond to shifting public opinion. To undertake a profitable data search, it is necessary to define the problem in tangible terms, specify its technical and political dimensions, and identify the involved or potentially affected groups and individuals.

In many cases the problem is assigned, and the planner's job is simply to collect relevant data. But assuming that the planner is involved in the early stages of a planning issue or that the problem has not been clearly specified, what should be done to define it?

Analysts and writers have presented numerous ways to develop a problem definition, but most processes involve the following seven steps:[4]

1. *Develop a preliminary definition of the problem.* Problem definition

begins with verifying the existence—and importance—of a problem. The goal is to specify the precise nature of the problem and to identify interested groups and individuals. What is the core of the problem? How important is the problem? Who is interested in having it solved, and how much are they willing to invest in its resolution? The basic problem statement developed in this first step can be further refined as new issues and data are uncovered.

2. *Specify the boundaries of the problem.* How wide ranging is the problem? Is it local or regionwide? How long has it existed? Is it part of a larger problem? Who else might be involved in the issue? Answering these questions can provide clues about possible sources of data, including groups and individuals who may already have collected relevant data.

3. *Develop a fact base.* Developing planning information is usually an incremental process. The planner collects some initial data, and, if it looks promising, collects more. It is of little use to collect a large data set if it does not address the problem squarely. It is useful, then, to assemble a fact base as a way to reveal the dimensions of the problem, including facts about the problem itself as well as data on related variables such as demographic, economic, and political trends.

4. *List goals and objectives.* Problems seldom develop in isolation, and their solutions relate to the general goals and objectives of the local government and the community. The goals and objectives of decision makers can guide planners in identifying the types of data likely to be of use in solving the problem.

5. *Identify the range of solutions.* The nature and extent of alternative solutions considered will affect the type of data collected, assuming the data are to be used not only to identify the problem but to devise and assess potential solutions. The potential scope of solutions needs to be made clear early in the planning process to ensure that appropriate data are collected from the outset.

6. *Define potential costs and benefits.* Which individuals or groups are likely to gain or lose if the problem is resolved in various ways? What do those affected by the problem see as potentially good or bad solutions? The answers can be used to identify additional quantitative data that should be collected; just as important, they can identify data needed about the political aspects of the problem.

7. *Review the problem statement.* Does the problem statement suggest potential alternatives and thus the range of topics on which data need to be collected? The results of steps 1 through 6 may indicate that the problem statement needs to be revised—and consequently that the list of data to be collected needs to be reconsidered.

The seven steps of problem definition require some assembling of data, but this is not to suggest that a large-scale data-collection effort occur at this stage. The early work should be limited to collecting secondary data, making back-of-the envelope calculations, estimating magnitudes and relationships, and identifying additional data needs. Practical approaches to data collection at this stage include locating facts in reference sources, gathering data through a quick phone survey of other planners, using known values to estimate unknowns, and obtaining estimates from experts.

Sources of planning data

Listing all the sources of planning data is impossible because of the varied and changing nature of problems encountered in planning practice. Main sources include the U.S. census, federal and state agency reports, local agency files, and the work of other planners. Locating the data that fit the particular problem and then putting the pieces together is the primary activity at the outset of most analyses, especially when time is short.

Rather than begin with a list of data sources that will be out-of-date as soon as it is published, this section offers ways to think systematically about sources of planning data.

The accompanying sidebar is a data source checklist that gives an overview of the range of sources of planning data. The major headings suggest the broad categories of data sources outside of a planner's own agency. Although some large planning agencies have data collection divisions, many agencies can maintain only basic data on continuing problems and issues. When new or larger problems arise, these agencies undertake searches for specific facts needed to

---

Data source checklist

Libraries
Local libraries
University libraries
State libraries
Federal depository libraries
Agency libraries
Interlibrary loans

Federal agencies
Census Bureau and State Data User
  Centers
Department of Agriculture
Department of Commerce
Department of Health and Human
  Services
Department of Housing and Urban
  Development
Bureau of Labor Statistics
Internal Revenue Service
National Center for Health Statistics
Social Security Administration

State agencies
State planning agency
State departments of transportation,
  health, education, etc.
State budget bureau
State archive
State reference library
State license bureau (automobile and
  other)

Local agencies
Local and regional planning agencies
Departments of public works, building
  inspection, zoning, etc.
Community development departments
City and county assessors' offices

County extension agencies
Law enforcement agencies
Public health offices
Social service agencies
School districts
Housing authorities

Other public and quasi-public bodies
Water and sanitary districts
Gas and electric companies
Telephone companies
Transit districts
Park and recreation districts
Public health districts
Economic development districts

Survey research organizations
University-affiliated organizations
Private firms
Radio and television stations
Newspapers

Private organizations
Chamber of commerce
Boards of realtors
Voters' leagues
News media organizations
F. W. Dodge Division of McGraw-Hill
  Information Systems Company
Rand McNally
Sanborn Map Company
R. L. Polk Company
Donnelly Marketing Information
  Services
Conference board
Consulting firms

address those problems. Success depends on creativity in thinking about a problem and ferreting out the most appropriate and reliable data.

Evaluating information quality

Since at least some of the data used for any planning decision will be obtained from secondary sources, careful evaluation of data quality is essential. As the checklist in the accompanying sidebar indicates, *how*, *why*, and *by whom* the data were collected are useful clues to its veracity. As a general rule, data that were systematically collected through a random sample as part of an ongoing process by trained, experienced staff under a skilled administrator are more likely to be valuable. As would be expected, however, planners must sometimes compromise because of constraints on time and resources.

Libraries

The primary source of one-stop shopping for data is the municipal, county, or university library. Libraries are also maintained by most states and major agencies. Federal reports and statistics can be examined at federal depository libraries located in major cities. Local, university, and state libraries are sources for U.S. census data; indexes, abstracts, and guides; government publications; and laws and statutes. Agency libraries are sources for internal reports and often maintain general libraries on the agency's primary area of concern. For example, the state department of education may have a library of education statistics, and the state department of health may have a library of vital statistics. If the most accessible library does not have a certain report or data set, the item can often be obtained through an interlibrary loan.

Federal agencies

Although reports and statistics from federal agencies can often be obtained from a library, if time is available the federal agency should be consulted directly, because most libraries hold only a fraction of what a federal agency produces. Most planners are already familiar with data from federal agencies such as the U.S. Census Bureau, the Department of Housing and Urban Development, the Department of Commerce and its Bureau of Economic Analysis, the Department of Health and Human Services, the Department of Agriculture, and the Department of Labor and its Bureau of Labor Statistics, but numerous other agencies can provide planning data, including the Statistics of Income Division of the Internal Revenue Service, the National Center for Health Statistics, and the

---

Data quality checklist

How were the data collected?
Systematically/Haphazardly
Random sample/Nonrandom sample
Impartial third party/Program personnel

Why were the data collected?
Ongoing monitoring/Response to a
  crisis
To respond to an internal need/To fulfill
  an external requirement

When were the data collected?
After planning/During a crisis
Recently/In the past

Who collected the data?
Trained/Untrained personnel
Experienced/Inexperienced
  personnel
High-level/Low-level staff
Highly/Not highly regarded staff
Organized/Unorganized director
Skilled/Unskilled communicator

Social Security Administration. The *Federal Statistical Directory* is a telephone directory listing federal agencies that provide statistical data, and a detailed list of sources and agencies can be found in an appendix of the *Statistical Abstract of the United States.*

State and local agencies

It would be fruitless to attempt to list all state and local agencies that collect and provide planning data. Most states provide a directory of agencies, but even then planners learn only through experience who has which data and how to get it. Agencies of potential help to local planners include the state planning agency, the bureau of the budget or its equivalent, the state archives, the state reference library, and the state departments of transportation, health, and education. Analysts in these agencies can often provide reports on similar problems elsewhere in the state and in other states as well. The key is to develop contacts with the right individuals before the data are required.

Local agencies are also sources of planning data. Beyond planning-related units such as zoning and code enforcement departments, organizations such as school districts, housing authorities, assessors' offices, and similar groups collect data that planners need.

Other public and quasi-public bodies

Most agencies, public and private, regularly collect data on their own activities. For example, the transit agency can provide data on traffic conditions; the park district often can provide data on park use and sometimes even on user attitudes and characteristics; and water, sanitary, and other utilities can provide data on population characteristics. Before initiating a data collection effort, think carefully about specific organizations that may already have what you seek. Even if they do not have precisely what you want, they can often indicate other sources that do.

Survey research organizations

Many research organizations collect data continuously on particular topics. Universities often have survey research centers, either as independent units or affiliated with departments of urban affairs or political science. In addition to surveys undertaken for specific clients that may be released for public use, these units sometimes conduct annual or biennial omnibus surveys that provide a wealth of planning-related data. These data may be available on disk or tape as well as in printed form. The survey research unit is often able to reformat the data or produce custom reports from the data on file at reasonable rates.

Similar data and services are also available from private firms, with the difference that the data more often are proprietary. Nonetheless, private survey research firms should be contacted, for they often have high-quality data sets on a variety of planning topics.

Radio and television stations and newspapers and magazines often conduct their own surveys. Although these surveys tend to cover popular topics, they do include planning data such as citizen opinions on development issues, housing and office vacancy rates, and average rental rates.

Private organizations

A sage once said that if you find three people with the same interest, an organization certainly exists to further that interest. A number of such special interest organizations regularly collect and make available planning-relevant data. Local and state chambers of commerce assemble data on business activities and trends; boards of realtors collect housing data; voters' leagues produce community guides; the F. W. Dodge Division of McGraw-Hill collects data on the construction industry; Rand McNally produces city maps and population data; the Sanborn Map Company provides detailed city block maps for insurance and other purposes; the R. L. Polk Company and the Donnelly Company produce a variety of city directories; the Conference Board collects data on emerging business trends and issues; and numerous consulting firms regularly provide information on population and economic trends, parking and transportation issues, retail sales volume, office and hotel occupancy rates, and similar topics. A list of private companies that have repackaged census data to meet special user needs is available from the Census Bureau's National Clearinghouse for Census Data Services.

Identifying and gathering data

Since most planners have received some training in identifying and collecting data, this section of the chapter will review that process and offer guidelines for locating data through library searches and in government publications.

Library searches

Although computer-based library retrieval systems are becoming more widely available, for some time to come most planners will have to rely on the traditional library search to locate data. This process can yield great amounts of valuable data in a day or two if a systematic search process is followed. For most topics, planners will be familiar with the basic concepts; if not, specialized dictionaries or encyclopedias are available on planning, urban development, community development and environmental management, and many other topics. A list of these resources can be found in the American Library Association's *Guide to Reference Books*. These specialized dictionaries and encyclopedias can lead to other sources, both books and individuals, and can provide the key words and subject names to facilitate a search for related information.

Understanding how others have dealt with similar problems is important. Skimming the contents of key journals for the past year or two can reveal both experts and data sources, but skimming more than several journals is not practical. Instead, consult indexes, abstracts, and guides to planning and related fields: Indexes list the contents of journals and newspapers; abstracts contain summaries of articles; guides are annotated bibliographies that often contain an introduction to the topic and instructions about locating information sources. A number of indexes, abstracts, and guides are published on planning and related areas, and even more specialized indexes are available for education, law and transportation. Consult the following as a beginning step: *Public Affairs Information Service (PAIS) Bulletin* and *Index*, *Index to Current Urban Documents*, *ABC Political Science and Government Index*, *Social Sciences Citation Index*, and the *New York Times Index*.

Abstracts go beyond indexes in that they contain summaries of journal articles. Depending upon the size of the library, it may have abstracts for urban affairs, economics, sociology, and management, to name a few areas. Dissertations and masters theses are also summarized in abstracts and can provide information about research that has not yet been reported in journals or books. However, dissertations located through the *Comprehensive Dissertation Index* usually have to be ordered from University Microfilms at the University of Michigan, so they take a while to obtain.

Guides to the literature are published in numerous fields of interest to planners. Scanning the shelves in a library reference room might reveal guides to energy, housing, urban development, and the like. *Recent Publications on Government Problems* by the Merriam Center Library in Chicago is a guide to publications on more than a dozen planning topics.

Government publications

U.S. government publications can provide a great amount of planning data if you have access to the right documents. A documents librarian can help locate relevant publications. To conduct the search yourself, begin with the *Monthly Catalogue of United States Publications,* which lists publications by author, agency, subject, and title. If your library does not hold the necessary documents, they can be ordered from the Superintendent of Documents (the *Monthly Catalogue* provides an order number). Other major resources for locating government documents include *Government Reports Announcements and Index,* published by the National Technical Information Service, and the *Congressional Information Service Index* and *Abstracts.*

U.S. Bureau of Census reports are especially valuable to planners. Although most planners have used the reports from the Census of Population and the Census of Housing, the Census Bureau's annual *Census Catalogue and Guide* can be used to locate other data. It lists and describes all products issued since 1980, lists the State Data Center organizations, and provides other pertinent information. The types of data found in the decennial censuses of population and housing—too numerous to list here—cover population and housing characteristics for cities and larger areas.

Planners who have not yet used the Census Bureau as a resource should begin by calling one of its dozen regional offices or its public information office or Data Users Services Division in Washington, D.C., to request an information packet. Obtain its brochure *The Census Bureau: America's Fact Finder,* a copy of *Data User News,* and a *Monthly Product Announcement.* Ask to be included in the Census Bureau mailing list for *Data Users News* and the *Monthly Product Announcement. Data Users News* has up-to-date information on Census products and services, plans for future services, how to order data, and important phone numbers. The *Monthly Product Announcement* includes new publications, news about workshops on Census topics, and advice on how to order. Census data are available as printed reports, maps, microfiche, computer tape, floppy disks, and online. Note that data collection, reporting, and publication formats are being changed for some Census data in anticipation of the 1990 census.

A Census Bureau State Data Center (SDC) has been established in all fifty states, the District of Columbia, Puerto Rico, and the Virgin Islands. These centers make Census Bureau data available for public use. Many centers provide customized data services and detailed statistics not readily available from other sources. Contact the Census Bureau for the SDC lead agency in your state.

In addition to the decennial census, the U.S. Bureau of the Census collects data on selected topics every five years, biennially, annually, and monthly. Every five years, censuses are conducted and published on the following activities: agriculture, construction, foreign trade, governments, manufacturing, mineral industries, retail trade, service industries, transportation, and wholesale trade. These data are updated through monthly, quarterly, annual, or biennial surveys and are reported in publications such as the following: *American Housing Survey* (*Annual Housing Survey* before 1984), *Annual Retail Trade Report, Annual Survey of Manufacturers, Current Population Reports, Current Housing Reports, Current Industrial Reports, County Business Patterns, Quarterly Summary of State and Local Tax Revenue,* and *Current Construction Reports.*

If an issue is currently under debate in Congress, a House or Senate committee might be assigned to the topic as well as a government agency or commission. Agencies and their missions can be located in the *United States Government*

Manual; names, addresses, and telephone numbers of government personnel can be found in the *Congressional Directory* and the *Congressional Staff Directory*.

Among the guides to official statistics are the *Guide to Federal Statistics: A Selected List*, the *American Statistics Index*, the *Guide to U.S. Government Statistics*, and the *Statistical Reference Index: A Selective Guide to American Statistical Publications from Sources Other than the U.S. Government*. Also useful are the *Statistical Abstract of the United States*, which contains general statistics and a list of other sources of data, and the *Census of Governments*, which contains summary statistics on a wide range of planning topics.

State and local data are available in sources such as *PAIS*, *Government Reports Announcements*, *The Index to Current Urban Documents*, *The Municipal Year Book*, *The County Year Book*, *Book of the States*, *National Civic Review*, and the *Monthly Checklist of State Publications*. Also consult the U.S. Census Bureau reports on city and state government, including the *State and Metropolitan Area Data Book*, the *County and City Data Book*, *City Government Finances*, and *State Government Finances*. Consult also the *Directory of Federal Statistics for Local Areas*, which has an *Urban Update*. The *National Directory of State Agencies* and *State Administrative Officials Classified by Function* provide names, addresses, and telephone numbers of state agencies and officials.

Basic data sources

Any planning unit, no matter how large or small, needs a shelf of basic data sources. The breadth and depth of that shelf will vary, depending on the agency's mission and whether it has a library or reference center. Candidates for that shelf would include basic census documents on population, the economy, and housing, as well as material on the specific subject areas in which the agency works. Although it would be impossible to produce a comprehensive, up-to-date list of data sources for specific planning topics, this section includes prototype lists for several areas of planning—population and the economy, urban development, housing, and the environment.

Population and the economy

The *U.S. Census of Population* and the *U.S. Census of Housing* are basic data sources that should be on the shelves of every local planning agency. Census of Population reports for the municipality, region, and state contain data on numbers of inhabitants by jurisdiction, population characteristics, and social and economic characteristics. Current population estimates and projections are available in the Census Bureau's *Current Population Reports* series.

In addition to the general economic and social data contained in these reports, more detailed and current wage and salary data for the nation, states, counties, metropolitan areas, and larger cities can be obtained in the annual *County Business Patterns* report by the Bureau of the Census. Similar nonfarm civilian wage and salary data are available from the U.S. Department of Labor in its publications *Employment and Earnings* (monthly) and *Employment and Wages* (quarterly).

Since basic analyses include both tallies (which the documents just mentioned can provide) and comparisons and projections, local planning agencies should also obtain the *County and City Data Book* and the *OBERS BEA Regional Projections for States* and *for Metropolitan Areas*.[5] The *County and City Data Book* is just that—a compilation of basic population and economic data for counties and cities. The two BEA reports contain projections, Volume 1 for the nation and states and Volume 2 for 330 U.S. metropolitan areas: (243 MSAs, 15 NECMAs, and 17 CMSAs comprising 55 PMSAs).[6] These reports include historical data from 1969 and projections to the year 2035 for population, personal income, earnings, and employment by place of work and by industry.

These data should be supplemented by detailed labor force and labor market statistics, usually available from a state agency such as a bureau of employment services, and metropolitan area population projections made by a state department of development or data users center.

The *Statistical Abstract of the United States* is a good reference, because it contains general social and economic data on more than 30 topics and a list of more than 1,000 other statistical publications. Each local planning agency should also have the *Municipal Year Book* and the *Census of Governments* (if they are not already available in a nearby office). The *Year Book* provides comparative data on municipal services and levels of expenditure: and the *Census of Governments* also provides comparative data on local government activities. *American Demographics* contains articles on current issues and publishes an annual guide to demographic data sources.

Urban development [7]

Many of the issues planners face relate directly or indirectly to development proposals, feasibility studies, and impact assessment. These areas provide an example of the wide range of data sources to which planners need access.

At the federal level, the Office of Policy Development and Research of the Department of Housing and Urban Development (HUD) publishes many useful studies on a wide range of topics. *Recent Research Results,* HUD's newsletter, describes its current projects and publications as well as other selected publications in the housing area.

A number of major organizations produce books and reports for developers that are also valuable for planners. The Urban Land Institute (ULI), one such organization, has a publication list of approximately 80 titles covering a variety of topics, and selected volumes are updated regularly. Key ULI publications

---

Key information sources for a planner's reference shelf

U.S. Census of Population. Reports by state, region, and locale. Data on numbers of inhabitants, population characteristics, social and economic characters.

U.S. Census of Housing. Reports by state, region, and locale. Data on housing characteristics by census tract and city blocks.

Current Population Reports. Selected reports on topics of local relevance.

County and City Data Book. General comparative data on population and economic conditions of counties and cities.

U.S. Department of Commerce, Bureau of Economic Analysis. *1985 OBERS*

BEA Regional Projections. Vol. 1: State Projections to 2035. Washington, DC, 1985.

————. *Vol. 2: Metropolitan Statistical Area Projections to 2035.* Washington, DC, 1985.

Statistical Abstract of the United States. General social and economic statistics for the United States and a list of other data sources.

Municipal Year Book. Comparison data on municipal services and expenditures and local persons to contact.

Census of Governments. Comparison data on local government organization, structure, and finance.

include *Development Handbooks* for office buildings, shopping centers, down-towns, residential areas, industrial areas, and recreation. The ULI annual *Development Review and Outlook* covers important issues and building types for major metropolitan areas. Other organizations that regularly publish on development issues include the Center for Urban Policy Research at Rutgers University and the Brookings Institution in Washington, D.C.

In addition, a number of organizations have developed online population and housing census data and provide related analytic services. These data can be obtained for almost any place in the United States, by census tract, concentric circle, zip code, and so on. Printouts and graphic services are also available. Fees are charged for these services, but when time is short the service may be well worth the cost. Organizations providing these services advertise widely in planning and related journals.

If specific cost, income, and expense data are required, sources such as R. S. Means and F. W. Dodge publish construction cost data and estimating manuals and provide related services. The Institute of Real Estate Management publishes income and expense books for office buildings, apartments and other types of housing, as well as books on managing office buildings and shopping centers.

Housing[8]

Planners' involvement in housing ranges from planning to finance, from sub-division design to rehabilitation, and from needs analysis to the economics of the construction industry. Dozens of sources of information could be generated for each of several housing and user group subareas: for example, housing for elderly persons, housing and minority needs, or sex discrimination in housing.

The first source to consult would be at the federal level: the U.S. Department of Housing and Urban Development publishes handbooks and reference material as well as information on housing programs and experimental program research. The Bureau of the Census publishes data and specific analyses on housing conditions, trends, and needs. The key publications are the *Census of Housing* and the biennial *American Housing Survey*. The *Census of Housing* is a survey of all households; it reports the number of dwelling units, number of rooms, and condition of plumbing, as well as ownership and rental data by census tract and city block. A sample of households is asked for more detailed data about living conditions and building characteristics. The *American Housing Survey* contains data from sample surveys of counties and metropolitan areas. It provides data on general housing characteristics, housing and neighborhood quality, financial characteristics, households that have moved, urban and rural housing units, and energy characteristics.

Even more detailed data can be found in the Census Bureau's *Current Housing Reports,* which cover such topics as housing vacancies and housing characteristics. *Quarterly Housing Reports* are also available from the Census Bureau on a variety of topics such as the market absorption of apartments and the charac-teristics of apartments completed. These publications typically are based on sample data for regions and metropolitan areas. Also at the federal level, the Department of Housing and Urban Development publishes an *Annual Report* and monthly *Housing Statistics,* which provide national data and data for selected locales.

Federal legislative committee hearings and reports are continuing sources of information on legislative needs and reviews as well as on housing conditions. Key committees from which to seek information include the House Committee on Banking, Finance, and Urban Affairs; the House Subcommittee on Housing and Community Development; and the Senate Committee on Banking, Housing, and Urban Affairs.

Because of the federal movement away from direct investment in housing, many state housing, planning, and finance agencies have begun to build and subsidize housing, to conduct housing research, and to publish their findings. Increasingly, these agencies are additional sources of housing information.

The Journal of Housing, published by the National Association of Housing and Redevelopment Officials, is a source for current information on federal, state, and local housing activities and emerging trends. Construction data are available in *Dodge Construction Contract Statistics* and *Engineering News-Record.*

Environmental issues[9]

The federal government provides substantial data on environmental issues. The Center for Environmental Research Information in Cincinnati, Ohio, is an office of the U.S. Environmental Protection Agency (EPA) that disseminates research results of the Office of Research and Development (ORD). The National Technical Information Service (NTIS) of the U.S. Department of Commerce is the central source for sale of U.S. government-sponsored research, development, and engineering reports. Its catalogue of more than one million titles contains many reports on environmental topics and can be obtained from NTIS in Springfield, Virginia.

A number of key reports are also available, including *Environment Reporter,* published by the Bureau of National Affairs, Washington, D.C., which contains "Current Developments," a weekly review of pollution control and related environmental management problems. *Environmental Quality,* the annual report of the Council on Environmental Quality, and *Environmental Planning Quarterly,* a publication of the Environmental Division of the American Planning Association, are sources of information on current environmental issues, legislation, and related publications. *State of the Environment Report 1985* by the Organization for Economic Cooperation and Development (OECD) focuses on air, water, and land quality; the condition of wildlife, forests, and the marine environment; and hazardous wastes. It is intended to encourage public and private efforts to ensure that economic growth does not occur at the expense of the environment.

Data on other topics and practices are available from various federal agencies too numerous to name here. As an example of the extent of information available in one area, the U.S. Energy Information Administration publishes monthly, quarterly, and annual reports on coal, petroleum, natural gas, nuclear fuels, electric power, and mineral production. Similar data are published by some state departments of natural resources and are also available from trade associations such as the American Petroleum Institute, the American Gas Association, and the National Coal Association. Utility organizations such as the American Public Gas Association and the American Public Power Association might also be consulted. For facts on specific topics, the planner must be able to conduct a good library search as well as use survey research, interviewing, and other data collection methods.

Data collection

Data that does not already exist in reports or in the files of an agency can be collected through a number of methods, primarily survey research techniques, interviewing, and observation. A number of good texts describe how to conduct formal surveys, carry out systematic interviews of individuals involved in planning issues, or collect information by observation.[10] The three sections that follow present the basic principles, purposes, and advantages and disadvantages of these methods.

Survey research

When planners and analysts speak of survey research, they usually mean a systematic survey of a local population to collect policy-relevant data not available elsewhere. Usually these data are collected from a sample of a target population rather than from the entire target population. Unfortunately, over the years, a lot of nonscientific data collection has been called survey research. Survey data collected from a skewed or limited sample will not yield information that can be generalized to the whole population. It will yield data only about the group that has been sampled—people walking past the corner of Fifth and Vine, members of the local athletic club, or subscribers to *Planner's Weekly*.

Why not collect data on everybody? Won't that ensure that the data are correct? Although saving money is one reason for sampling, there are other reasons, including timeliness and accuracy, for using this approach. A sample survey permits data to be collected more quickly. Given limited resources and a data-collection team of fixed size, a survey of 10 percent of the target population can be conducted much more quickly than a census of the entire target population. Sample surveys can also yield data that are more accurate than a complete census. Because a sample survey is conducted in a shorter time, the data are more likely to be available when needed, and intervening factors will not create differences between responses received at the beginning and at the end of the survey period. In addition, when the survey method calls for interviewers or other staff, better results are obtained by training fewer, more highly qualified personnel than by training a large team, and the smaller team requires less supervision.

To provide useful information, a survey must be designed to collect data from a *representative* sample of the population. That is, all the individuals in the relevant population must have a known probability of being selected. If the sample is a random one drawn from a complete list of names for the full target population, the results are reasonably reliable and can be used to draw conclusions about the entire target population. Some compromise inevitably occurs; the list may not be complete, or the sample may not be entirely random. However, good survey research practices ensure that the results are approximately correct and allow the degree of error to be estimated.

If survey data are required, for example, to obtain citizen opinions on a planning decision or update population and household data for a rapidly changing neighborhood, the planning agency can contract for survey research services or undertake its own research. Private companies and university research units provide commercial survey research services in most communities. Deciding whether to conduct outside or inside survey research depends on funds and skills available and often on timing. There is no fixed rule. Sometimes a commercial unit can conduct a survey more quickly, less expensively, and more accurately than a planning agency, especially if the agency does not regularly conduct surveys. Although some planning agencies do normally conduct their own surveys, an in-house survey is not necessarily the least expensive route. For example, even if several summer interns are available, training and supervisory costs, as well as start-up costs for what may prove to be a one-time event, must be taken into account. On the other hand, an agency that plans to conduct regular surveys may want to establish an in-house mechanism for doing so. For a first survey, it might be wise to hire a consultant to help design both the survey approach and the analysis of the results.

Types of surveys   Before conducting a survey it is necessary to decide how the results will be used. Will they be used to describe a single point in time or a situation over a period of time? The first type of survey is cross-sectional; the second is longitudinal. A cross-sectional survey collects data on a single population or on several target populations. The characteristics of these populations can then be examined on a number of variables—for example, income, education, homeownership, or age—and comparisons can be made among the populations and their subgroups. When data are being collected to compare subgroups, it is a good idea to take a larger sample from those subgroups that may make up only a small fraction of the population, such as certain minority groups or elderly citizens. This can help ensure enough responses to permit statistically meaningful analysis. These "oversampled" groups must then be adjusted mathematically back to their proper proportion of the population when the results are reported as comparisons among subgroups.[11]

Longitudinal surveys collect data on one or several subgroups over time, to permit comparison, for example, between responses before and after the introduction of a policy. Trend analyses can be made using data for several time periods. Planners are often asked to produce such analyses only after a policy has been initiated; it is then necessary to construct "before" data from existing records.

After the type of survey is chosen, the next step is to determine the survey method.

Survey methods   Each of the three basic survey methods—mail, telephone, and in-person—has advantages and disadvantages. Mail surveys are the most common of all approaches, and their familiarity is also their drawback. Recipients tend to ignore them, and without a great deal of follow-up effort, a 15-percent response rate is average. However, for a hotly debated local issue, the response rate may be higher. A variety of techniques can be used to encourage recipients to respond. First, mail surveys that are brief are more likely to be completed. Second, methods can be used to attract—and retain—the attention of recipients. For example, the survey might have a cover letter from a prominent person; respondents might be given token gifts (such as a magazine subscription or theater tickets); or those who do not respond might be called on the telephone and encouraged to participate. An advantage of mail surveys is that they require less staff time to administer than do other data-collecting techniques.

Telephone surveys are becoming more popular as the costs of other survey approaches increase. Respondents to this approach are obviously limited to persons with telephones. If the telephone book is used as the source of names, individuals with unlisted numbers will not be surveyed. A technique called random-digit dialing permits calls to be made within specific geographic areas without the need for a list of telephone numbers. Although telephone surveys require a staff of several persons if the calls are to be completed within a reasonable period of time, new computer systems allow interviewers to code respondents' answers as they are given, thus reducing staff time for data entry and coding. Much survey research by commercial firms is now conducted by telephone. Properly conducted telephone surveys can yield relatively high response rates, but the list of questions must be kept reasonably short and uncomplicated.

In-person interviews are a third method of obtaining data for planning. Interviews are preferable when data are being collected about complicated issues or issues with a visual component. Interviews need to be used in situations in which respondents tend not to have telephones, are not well educated, or do not usually answer mail surveys. They are also used when the survey data are to be related to physical data about the housing unit of the respondent (e.g., the condition of the structure).

As would be expected, in-person interviews are the most expensive form of survey research. Higher response rates and more detailed data have their costs. Nonetheless, there are times when this is the most reasonable approach. Interviews do, however, require larger and more highly trained field and supervisory staffs than other methods, if the data are to be collected quickly enough for timely decisions.

Questionnaire construction A planning agency that wishes to conduct its own survey may want to obtain help with questionnaire design and construction. A number of texts are available on the topic, but a consultant might also be considered. The survey should be pilot tested before being used in the full study. Be sure that respondents can understand and answer the questions and also that the data can be analyzed.

Sample selection How large a sample to take is the question most often asked by beginning analysts. The principle is to take a sample only large enough to yield data at the level of accuracy needed. That is, if an agency wants to know the median income in an area plus or minus $500 and is willing to risk being wrong in 5 out of 100 samples, it will need a smaller sample than an agency that wants to know the median income plus or minus $100. Technically, sample size is related to the confidence interval (plus or minus $500) and the confidence level (5 out of 100) that are acceptable to those undertaking the survey. These concepts are discussed in most basic planning methods textbooks. For most local planning studies, a sample that results in 400 usable returned questionnaires yields data that give a good approximation of the value for the full population. Of course, the sample has to be unbiased and random. Simple random sampling uses a random number table or takes every *nth* element from a list. Several other sampling methods are available also: Stratified sampling can be used to select random samples from subpopulations of the target population. In large areas, cluster sampling is used to reduce expenses, by, for example, first sampling census blocks and then sampling households from those blocks. *Survey Research Methods* by Earl Babbie remains one of the best basic references on this topic.

Interviewing[12]

Interviewing selected, key individuals is an important way to identify and collect data. In contrast to mass-interviewing survey research, "elite" or "specialized" interviewing is used to obtain nonstandardized information from individuals who have specialized knowledge of an event or process. Elite or intensive interviewing would be inappropriate for collecting a sample of citizen opinion, gathering data for statistical analysis, or obtaining other types of sample data.

Planners use personal interviews to collect data under a variety of circumstances—for short-term projects; for new topics; when there is little or no literature; when respondents would be reluctant to put certain answers in writing; when quantitative data are difficult to obtain; and when hired interviewers might be insensitive to the complexities of an emerging problem. Interviewees may include agency personnel, experts, program participants, and persons who have access to unpublished materials. Some interviewees may have facts; others may have experience. Interviewees may be chosen for *whom* they know as well as for *what* they know. Even if they do not have the sought-after facts, they may be able to identify someone who does.

In most cases it is more efficient to seek basic data from staff persons who are not too highly placed. Executives and higher-level managers are less likely to have time to obtain basic data for the interviewer. On the other hand, these individuals may need to give their approval before the required data can be released. The more senior members of an organization may have a more sophisticated understanding of the political arena, but they may also be more reluctant to speak openly. Individuals at or near the operational level of a bureaucracy usually speak more freely and may be more interested in the interview than their superiors would be.

Remember that an interview provides one person's view of a situation. Although you may in fact be seeking the interviewee's interpretation of a rule or regulation, there may be no absolute truth. The elite or intensive interview should not be the only source of data, and it is wise to check the findings from the interview against other facts. The credibility and reliability of the source must be judged. The following questions can help in evaluating interview data.[13]

1. Is the account plausible, reasonable, and coherent?
2. Is the story consistent, or does it contain contradictions?
3. Is the account specific, precise, and detailed?
4. Does the story fit together? Does it correspond to known facts?
5. Is the account based primarily on direct experience or is it a second- or third-hand account?
6. Does the expert have any ulterior reason to present a particular view of the situation?
7. Did the interviewee have reason to give an account that would please you?

Interviewing   There are few hard and fast rules for arranging and conducting a successful interview. The tips that follow provide some general guidelines.

It is sometimes possible to obtain an interview without an appointment. In other cases a phone call may be necessary, in still others a formal request on letterhead. So that the expert recognizes your name when you request an interview, first send a letter that briefly introduces you, spells out the reason for the interview, and indicates that a phone call will follow. It helps if you have been referred by someone, so that you can say, "I'm calling at the suggestion of Senator Getzels."

If you happen to reach the expert by telephone when arranging an interview, use this as an opportunity to open the conversation. The more you learn before the face-to-face interview, the more penetrating your questions will be. Be prepared for the individual who prefers to talk by telephone. In some cases, you can engage the expert's interest in your topic to such a degree that you will be invited in for a personal visit.

When conducting the actual interview, it is probably best to begin with simple, factual questions and move toward more complex ones. Save more difficult or controversial matters for near the end of the interview, but try to end on a pleasant note by returning to more neutral issues or by summarizing some of the positive aspects of the interview.

The questions themselves should be devised in advance. Keep the questions simple, short, and clear. You may want to use an interview guide to jog your memory, but the value of elite interviewing is the opportunity to follow up on new issues as they are raised and probe for additional information.

You can encourage the expert to continue, to explain, or to go into detail by attentively taking notes, nodding your head, paraphrasing responses, and using other similar cues. It is important, however, to maintain control of the interview. If the expert gets sidetracked, do not hesitate to say that time constraints require you to get back to the main topic. However, before doing this, make certain that the expert is really off the track and not merely shifting to an important, related issue.

A friendly, knowledgeable, attentive, and perhaps skeptical interviewer is generally most effective. Skepticism should be expressed by probing and asking for more details rather than by adopting an adversarial role. However, do not allow inadequate answers to stand. Ask for evidence and examples.

8. Would any current budgetary or political issues have prevented the expert from responding candidly?
9. Is the expert knowledgeable, informed, and clear-headed?
10. Is the interviewee self-critical?

Observation

Observation is another important source of planning data. Observation means monitoring behavior rather than asking direct questions about attitudes. Do usage patterns indicate a preference for particular types of recreation facilities? Are teenagers observing the curfew? Data collected by observation include those obtained through windshield or sidewalk surveys, mechanical counts (e.g., of traffic volume), recording user preferences, and viewing photographic records and satellite images.

Observational studies are more often used to monitor policies than to collect basic data. Although observation can provide quick insights into the operation of a program or into problems experienced by a group or organization, you

---

An appropriate ending to an interview can assure continued contact with the expert and can direct you to sources of additional information. As you conclude the interview, summarize the main points, ask the expert to agree or disagree, repeat what the expert has promised to forward to you, and ask for the names of other people and documents that may be helpful.

Send a thank-you letter that can be used to ask for additional information, to remind the interviewee about promised materials, and to keep the lines of communication open and your name in mind.

Interviewees are usually busy and will try to keep the interview as short as possible. If time is particularly short, a tape recorder will save the time otherwise spent taking notes. The more complex the issue, and the greater the quantity of data provided, the more useful a recording is to ensure accuracy. Knowing that the interview is being recorded also permits you to listen carefully and to follow up any unexpected comments or inconsistencies. On the other hand, transcribing tapes is time-consuming and costly, and information is sometimes lost as a result of malfunctions. In addition, a tape recorder may inhibit frankness, especially when the interview concerns sensitive issues. Instead of recording

on the spot, it may be preferable to take brief notes and use them immediately after the interview to reconstruct the conversation on tape or paper.

It is best to rely on written notes, even if a tape is made. Listening to the tape takes as much time as the interview, although it can be used to check quotations, facts, and figures. Because notes cannot be taken verbatim, concentrate on impressions and major points. While reviewing the notes immediately after the interview, record additional ideas or questions generated by the interview, summarize the main points covered by the expert, analyze the relationship of this new information to previously collected data, and list unresolved points to be checked through a follow-up phone call.

The interview can also be used as an opportunity to collect other data— annual reports, rules, regulations, and other such documents; if you find out about these documents before the interview, you can request them by name. During the interview you may learn about additional data sources such as internal reports, memos, or agency files, or about relevant documents from other agencies.

should be aware that it can also cause those being observed to change their behavior. Observation can be time-consuming and difficult to quantify, and it is usually based on small samples. Its accuracy depends on the consistency of the observer. Although the data collected may be anecdotal, they can provide insights into problems and illuminate data obtained from other sources.

Basic data analysis[14]

As noted earlier, *data* collected about a planning issue must be converted to *information* before it can be used. Even after a planner has analyzed the data, interpreted the facts, and developed conclusions and recommendations, these products must be communicated effectively to decision makers and clients. Statistical analysis is one way to communicate planning information, but when the goal is to communicate with lay audiences or public officials, statistics need to be supplemented with other methods. Descriptive data analysis, is one possibility; it is a process used to examine patterns and relationships in a set of data to determine what the data describe.

Graphic techniques

Simple graphic techniques are a basic part of the analysis and communication of data; visual displays are often clearer and more accessible than tabular summaries of numerical data. Figure 15–1 summarizes one typology of common comparisons and their associated graphic displays.[15] Figures 15–2 through 15–7 illustrate the six types of graphic presentations.

In addition to graphs, organization and flow charts can be helpful in communicating information. An organization chart shows formal and informal relationships at a given time. A flow chart portrays an entire process, or alternative processes, and identifies important steps in those processes.

All graphics should be properly documented, self-contained, and self-explanatory. The title should provide a clear and complete explanation of what the graphic shows. The title might be kept short to catch attention, with a subtitle to complete the thought. Labels, sources and explanatory notes, keys, and the date of preparation should make it possible for users to answer many questions for themselves.

Use graphics as one of several aids to understanding. Once the data have been plotted, don't look only for confirmation of your hypothesis; be alert to other interpretations. Observe trends, patterns, and cycles. Note historical events that may explain apparent aberrations. Look for the highest and lowest points and ensure that they can be plausibly explained and that they are not exaggerated by the measurement scale.

Maps are an excellent means of communicating information that has spatial dimensions. Figure 15–8 shows the location of chain food stores in Atlanta in 1960 and 1980. The geographic dispersion of stores over the twenty-year period is clearly communicated.

Geographic units shown on maps represent data groupings in the same way that income or age groupings summarize tabular data. Note that important information can be concealed by inappropriate groupings—for example, presenting data by municipality rather than by census tract. Transparent overlays showing conditions or impact by area can be used with a base map depicting basic features. This technique is especially helpful in communicating information about physical changes over time. For example, the location of chain food stores in Atlanta in 1980 could have been displayed on an overlay to the 1960 map.

Preparing any graphic is an iterative process that typically involves trial and

Continued on page 493

Figure 15–1 Common statistical comparisons and corresponding forms of graphic presentation.

Type of comparison	Corresponding graphic form
Components or proportions of the topic being examined	Pie chart
Number of items or differences	Bar chart
Frequency distributions of characteristics	Histograms and dot diagrams
Co-relationships between variables	Scatter diagrams
Time-series or trend data	Time-series curves

Figure 15–2 Sun City neighborhood populations, 1980. A pie chart like the one shown in this figure illustrates percentages of the whole. Pie charts are a valuable graphic technique because they are familiar to most people and present differences dramatically.

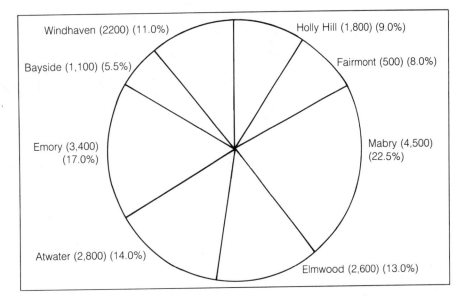

Figure 15–3 Number of households by race and ethnic group, Holly Hill, 1980. A bar chart such as this one can be used to show the magnitude of and to compare mutually exclusive categories. Bar charts provide information about quantities as well as about relative proportions.

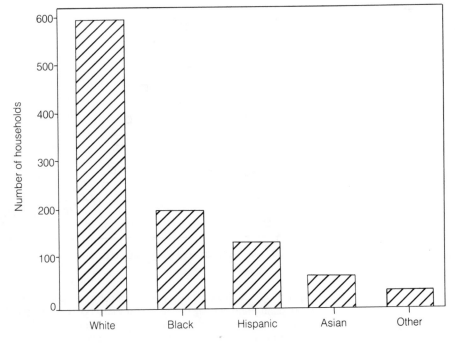

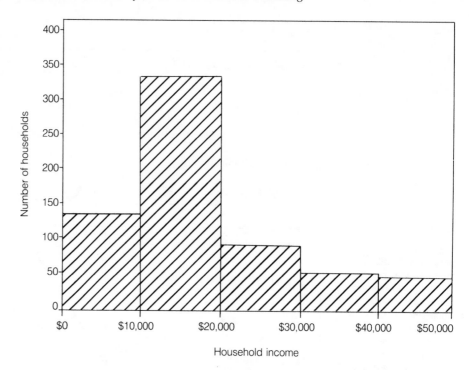

Figure 15–4   Number of households by income, Bayside, 1980. Like a bar chart, a histogram shows both magnitudes and differences among categories. Bar charts are drawn with spaces between the bars, because the categories are not continuous (e.g., race or religion), whereas histograms are drawn with the bars touching, because they represent continuous categories (e.g., income). The histogram shown in this figure illustrates the number of households in each of five income categories for a given neighborhood.

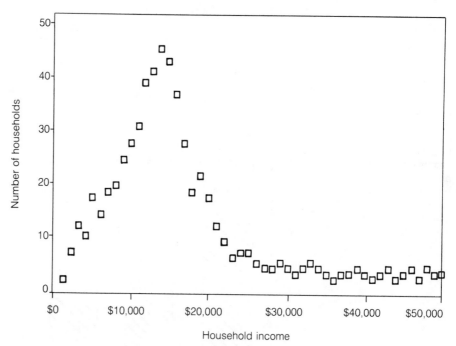

Figure 15–5   Number of households by income, Bayside, 1980. The dot diagram in this figure portrays graphically the number of households in a neighborhood by thousand-dollar income categories. Dot diagrams are used in much the same way as histograms, but they are used when the variables have many categories—for example, when income data are plotted by thousand-dollar rather than by ten-thousand dollar increments. The points in dot diagrams are sometimes connected to produce a line graph.

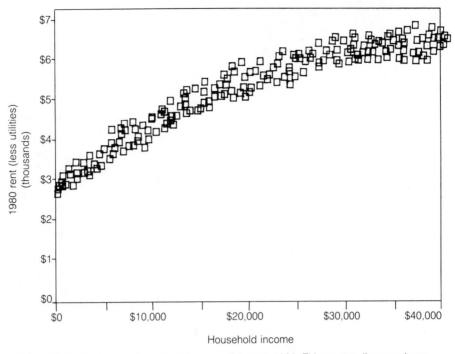

Figure 15–6   Rent versus household income, Fairmont, 1980. This scatter diagram shows the relationship between annual household income and annual rent payments. Unlike a dot diagram, a scatter diagram plots ungrouped data—which could be grouped to produce a dot diagram. Although this diagram might be the most useful in an investigation of the affordability of housing in a particular locale, additional graphics would be necessary to interpret the patterns revealed in the diagram. For example, the relationships shown in the scatter diagram might be investigated separately for each race or compared with similar data for other neighborhoods.

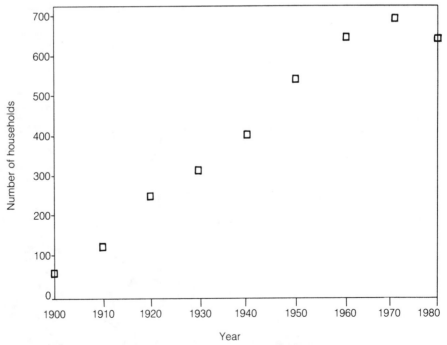

Figure 15–7   Number of households residing in Bayside, 1900–1980. Time-series diagrams such as the one in this figure show change over time in the quantity of a variable—for example, size of population, unemployment levels, or tax rates. Data may be plotted for each year or for selected years, and more than one time series can be shown on an individual diagram—for example, the number of households in each neighborhood in a municipality for the past nine decades.

Figure 15–8 Location
of chain food stores in
Atlanta, Georgia, 1960
and 1980: Ownership
change and location
dispersion.

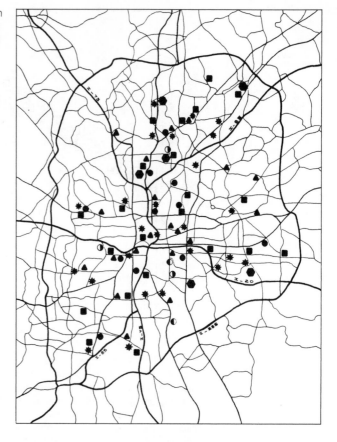

Legend
Kroger ●
Colonial Stores ★
A & P ▲
Big Apple ■
Winn Dixie ⬢
Food Town Stores ◗

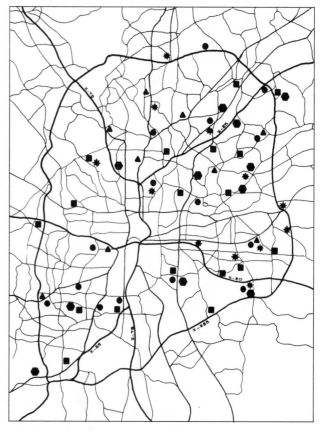

Legend
Kroger ●
Big Star ★
A & P ▲
Food Giant ■
Winn Dixie ⬢

error, but graphic techniques can be extremely valuable in capturing the attention of an audience and communicating key information.

Tables

Tables are another important means of communicating information, but it takes practice to develop tables that convey the meaning of data precisely, concisely, and consistently.

Since planners often work with ordinal or interval data, which are generally positive in sign, it helps to visualize a table as the upper right quadrant (x positive, y positive) of the coordinate system. Data should be ordered from low to high values along the x axis beginning at the zero point (intersection) and similarly from low to high along the y axis. With this layout, a positive correlation will yield data that tend to fall on the diagonal from lower left to upper right, and a negative correlation will run from the upper left to the lower right, a widely used convention.

Complex tables are more easily interpreted and compared if percentages are computed for all cells but the number of cases is given only for column or row totals. As in Figure 15–9, row totals permit individual cell values to be recomputed if necessary. It is also important to indicate the missing observations (MO) or data that could not be collected, as well as the data that are not applicable (NA)—for example, questions about automobile ownership that are skipped by persons who do not own a vehicle.

To make visual sense, most data need to be collapsed into categories such as five-year age groupings or five-thousand-dollar income categories. The percentage of cases falling into each category should be reported, with the percentages based on the number of respondents rather than on the total number of questionnaires sent out.

Data categories must be mutually exclusive (not overlapping) and exhaustive (include all possible values). For example, income categories should be given as $0 to $9,999 and $10,000 to $19,999 to avoid the problem of deciding where to place a person who earns $10,000 per year. To include all possible values, the upper category might be $90,000 and above.

The following guidelines are useful for preparing tables:

1. Give all tables a title and a subtitle if necessary.
2. Divide the data into mutually exclusive and exhaustive categories.

Figure 15–9 Sample table showing influence of proximity to Champaign–Urbana. This typical table layout presents data from an investigation of the influence on newcomers of the convenience of a nearby city.

Town and period moved	None (%)	Some (%)	Strong (%)	Total (%)
Mahomet				
1970–1976	8	50	42	100 (361)
Pre–1970	38	42	21	101 (272)
Total	21	47	33	101 (633)
St. Joseph				
1970–1976	13	41	47	101 (215)
Pre–1970	24	38	38	100 (178)
Total	18	40	42	100 (393)
Tolono				
1970–1976	38	36	26	100 (202)
Pre–1970	49	29	22	100 (250)
Total	44	32	24	100 (452)

Mahomet:	St. Joseph:	Tolono:
MO[a] = 54	MO = 103	MO = 11
NA[b] = 172	NA = 105	NA = 194
Gamma = 0.54	Gamma = 0.21	Gamma = 0.16

[a]MO = Missing observations
[b]NA = Not applicable (have always lived in town).

3. Use categories of similar width whenever possible.
4. Order variable values from low to high, from left to right, and from bottom to top.
5. Round off the cell data to whole percentages (that is, report 67% rather than 66.8%). Report the total of the rounded cell percentages as the column or row percentages. Rows or columns will not always sum to 100%, but that is acceptable.
6. Report the number of "missing observation" responses.
7. Cite sources.

Basic statistics

Along with graphic techniques and tables, statistics are a valuable means of communicating planning information to clients and decision makers. The three sections that follow cover several important aspects of statistical analysis: descriptive statistics, association or correlation, and measures of significance.

Descriptive statistics

Descriptive statistics are measures that summarize attributes of a data set. The most common descriptive statistics are the mean, median, and mode as indicators of central tendency; and the range, variance, and standard deviation as measures of variation. Standard statistics texts cover descriptive statistics in detail.

In the production of planning information, the mechanics of calculating statistics are less important than identifying key variables and the measures of the variables that will yield insights. Figure 15–10 shows a table of grouped data exploring possible instances of redlining—systematic discrimination through the denial of loans or insurance coverage to properties in specific geographic areas. The table appears to show that when households are grouped by neighborhood of applicant, neighborhoods with lower average household incomes show lower approval rates. However, when statistics for individual applicants are computed, the average income of approved borrowers is shown to be only slightly higher than that of those not approved (Figure 15–11). This finding should raise questions about whether the location of properties is a factor in loan approval or denial. To explore this issue further, the planner should probably obtain additional data on approval rates by location and income of applicant for several time periods.

Association or correlation

It is often helpful to know the relationship between two variables or among three or more. To detect association or correlation, you might begin by examining

Figure 15–10 Sample table showing average housing income, loan applications, and approval rates for neighborhoods in Sun City in 1980.

Neighborhood of applicant	Mean 1980 neighborhood household income ($)	Number of loan applications	Approval rate (%)
Windhaven	9,500	40	35
Bayside	17,800	40	80
Emory	6,400	30	10
Atwater	23,200	80	75
Elmwood	25,800	90	85
Mabry	15,800	60	75
Fairmont	16,200	50	70
Holly Hill	17,500	60	80

frequencies, which would reveal how often particular values occur in the set of data. For example, which variables have values that vary sufficiently to suggest that they should be examined further? Is frequency of accidents or license suspensions a meaningful variable? Next, you might cross-tabulate two variables (one independent and one dependent) to detect patterns in the data. Do persons who have had a driver education course within the past five years have different frequency-of-accident records from those who did not take a course? Do the values of the variables change in a consistent manner? As the value of one variable increases, does the value of another increase or decrease? For example, do persons with higher education levels have higher or lower accident rates?

Once you understand basic relationships, you can examine the effect of other (control or test) variables. Such variables might alter the apparent relationship between two variables. For example, an initial comparison of data might show a relationship between race and quality of housing—that black households occupy lower-quality housing. However, when the data are controlled for a third variable such as income, the relationship between race and housing quality may no longer hold. Households with similar incomes may occupy similar housing, no matter what their race.

Putting the data in tabular form reveals associations, and basic statistics can be used to summarize the data in the contingency tables. For example, Figure 15–12, which shows the final exam results for male and female students in a planning information class, suggests that females were more likely to pass the final exam than males. A correlation coefficient can be computed to measure the strength of this association or correlation. Gamma (also called Yule's Q) is a handy measure for this purpose when ordinal data are being used. The computation of gamma is too complex to be included here; for the final-exam example, it equals .39.[16]

A gamma of .39 indicates a moderate positive association between sex of the test taker and passing the final exam; that is, females are more likely than males to have passed the final exam. The value of gamma can range from −1.0 to +1.0 with 0 indicating no relationship, +1.0 indicating a perfect positive relationship (all persons with high scores on one variable have high scores on the other variable, and all persons with low scores on one variable have low scores on the other), and −1.0 indicating a perfect negative relationship (all persons high on one variable are low on the other, and vice versa). (In this instance, the two-category nominal variable "sex" can be considered an ordinal variable, with males arbitrarily classified as "low" and females as "high.")

A finding that females are more likely to pass the final exam would probably

Figure 15–11 Sample table showing average household income of applicant, location of property, and approval rates for neighborhoods in Sun City in 1980.

Neighborhood of property	Mean 1980 household income of applicant ($)	Approval rate (%)
Windhaven	16,500	25
Bayside	18,400	79
Emory	16,300	5
Atwater	19,500	90
Elmwood	20,600	92
Mabry	17,900	74
Fairmont	17,500	75
Holly Hill	18,200	81
Mean income of loan applicant		$16,500 per year
Mean income of approved loan applicant		17,400 per year
Range of income of approved loan applicants		14,800 to 62,300 per year

merit further investigation. One explanation for the different pass rates might be attendance at a review session. Controlling the data for review session attendance is one way to investigate this hunch. Controlling the data means dividing them into two groups: students who attended the review session and students who did not. Figure 15–13 gives the statistics that result when the data are regrouped in this way.

This step in the analysis indicates that the same percentage of males and females passed the exam within the group of persons attending the review session (75% passed) and within the group that did not (33% passed). The results of controlling or testing for a third variable are not always this clear, so the partial correlation coefficient, which explains mathematically the statistical impact of the test variable, should be computed to determine whether and how the test variable had an effect. (Readers who have not had a statistics course should consult a statistics text to learn how to compute a partial correlation coefficient.) After the results of controlling the data for a test variable have been obtained, the data would be recast to show the importance of attending a review session rather than the apparent importance of the sex of the test taker. The new figures are shown in Figure 15–14. Displaying the data in this way demonstrates that there was a much higher proportion of successful exam takers among those who attended the review session than among those who did not. This appears to be a clear and important finding.

The discussion so far has assumed that 335 persons took the exam. But suppose these persons were a 10-percent random sample of 3,350 persons who took the exam. Another question then arises: Was the sample representative, or was it for some reason an odd sample? Do the sample results validly represent the larger population?

Measures of significance

Inductive or inferential statistics are used to indicate, among other things, how confident we can be that the results obtained from a sample resemble those that

Figure 15–12   Sample table showing student test performance in a planning information class.

Sex of student	Final exam performance		
	Fail (%)	Pass (%)	Total (%)
Female	34	66	100 (205)
Male	54	46	100 (130)

Gamma = 0.39

Figure 15–13   Sample table controlling for whether the test taker attended the review session.

Did attend review session	Exam performance	
	Fail	Pass
Female	40	120
Male	10	30

Gamma = 0.0

Did not attend review session	Exam performance	
	Fail	Pass
Female	30	15
Male	60	30

Gamma = 0.0

Figure 15–14 Sample table showing final exam performance and review session attendance.

Attendance at review session	Final exam performance		
	Fail (%)	Pass (%)	Total (%)
Yes	25	75	100 (200)
No	67	33	100 (135)

Gamma = 0.72

would be obtained from a survey of the entire population. Although we can never be absolutely certain that any given sample accurately describes the population, we can estimate the number of samples out of 100 (the confidence level) that will yield results that fall within a certain range of the actual value (the confidence interval).

Returning to the previous example, inferential statistics would allow us to determine how likely it is that the findings were not the result of a nonrepresentative sample but reflected test score differences in the population of 3,350 test takers. If the inferential statistics indicated that 95 out of 100 times the difference was not due to chance, the finding would be called statistically significant at the .05 level, or in lay terms, we would say that there was a 5 percent chance of being wrong ($1.00 - 95/100 = .05$). That a difference is "statistically significant" (i.e., probably did not occur by chance) does not necessarily mean that it is "intellectually significant" or important. Here the planner must make

---

Communicating information Most planners communicate with their clients in writing. What makes a good report? The information must be clear, concise, and free of jargon; it must also be accurate, fair, and well documented.

Clarity and simplicity Give information to your client in clear sentences, using no more words than necessary. Unless it is forbidden, write in the active voice, using "I" and "you." The active voice ("The mayor rejected our proposal") is almost always better than the passive ("Our proposal was not approved"). Active constructions are usually simpler, and they also avoid ambiguity. Avoid jargon and language that might confuse listeners or insult those holding views other than your own. Use graphics to enliven your presentation. Large-scale graphics are necessary to address a group; for a presentation to one person or a small, informal group, copies of a handout are sufficient.

Accuracy Verify the facts. Check your calculations. Use several sources of data. Reconcile inconsistencies. Don't go beyond the data. Separate fact from opinion. Accuracy also means com-

pleteness. You can't include every detail, but in selecting those to report, do not ignore facts that conflict with your personal position.

Fairness and documentation Present facts that support alternative viewpoints. Provide enough documentation to allow your facts to be checked. Be critical of your work's shortcomings but not apologetic. Report the assumptions you made and the shortcuts you took.

Personal communication Don't miss an opportunity to present information in person, with the written report as backup. Anticipate questions, comments, and criticisms. Make a strong effort to be receptive to these and respond tolerantly and openly. Make your presentation interesting. Address your listeners' concerns early; present a summary rather than a full written report; try to defuse controversy by preparing listeners in advance for your ideas. If you don't know the answers to a question, make a commitment about when you will provide it. Finally, leave behind copies of your written analysis, or, if the group is large, a written or visual summary of the major findings.

a judgment. Was the difference of 42 percentage points (75 percent of reviewers passed, versus 33 percent of nonreviewers) a statistically *and* intellectually significant finding?

One last question remains. Did attending the review session cause the students to do better on the exam? In this case the answer appears to be "Yes." However, determining significance does not determine cause. On the one hand, attending the review may have given students either answers or a better understanding of the material. On the other hand, those who attended may have been a self-selected group of superior students; if so, what actually went on at the review may not have caused the better test results. To develop causal explanations requires a solid data base, a strong theory supported by statistical association, and successful attempts to rule out rival hypotheses. There are, then, four separate aspects of statistical analysis that must be understood: strength of relationship, statistical significance, research importance or intellectual significance, and causality.

Conclusion

This chapter addressed the problem of converting data into planning information. The chapter began by noting that a clear problem definition is essential to specify the types of data needed to produce usable *information*. Although sources of basic planning data were identified, the primary focus was on the process of finding and collecting relevant data.

The chapter then shifted from secondary data sources to the collection of original data. The basics of survey research, interviewing, and observation were described. The chapter then discussed basic data analysis methods, including graphic display techniques and maps. An overview of several statistical concepts was provided to alert the reader to basic methods, problems, and pitfalls.

If a single message underlies this chapter, it is that data does not speak for itself. Planning information is produced through a process that includes a clear statement of the problem, careful efforts to uncover existing data from a variety of sources, systematic collection of original data when necessary, and careful translation of data into easily understood written and graphic displays. Not only must planners understand the information they produce from various data sources, they must also be able to communicate the information precisely and concisely to clients, decision makers, and the public.

1　A number of the concepts discussed in this chapter have appeared in earlier work by the author, in particular in Carl V. Patton and David S. Sawicki, *Basic Methods of Policy Analysis and Planning* (Englewood Cliffs, NJ: Prentice-Hall, 1986). Jane Patton provided valuable assistance in verifying and updating sources and references for this chapter.

2　Stanley M. Altman, "The Dilemma of Data Rich, Information Poor Service Organizations: Analyzing Operational Data," *Journal of Urban Analysis* 3 (April 1976): 61–75.

3　Connie O. Hughes and Donald A. Krueckeberg, "Basic Studies for State and Regional Planning," in Frank S. So, Irving Hand, and Bruce D. McDowell, eds., *The Practice of State and Regional Planning* (Chicago: American Planning Association, 1986).

4　This section is based on Chapter 4, "Verifying, Defining, and Detailing the Problem" in Patton and Sawicki, *Basic Methods of Policy Analysis and Planning*, 103–38.

5　The projections program acquired the acronym "OBERS" when it began as a cooperative effort between the Office of Business Economics (now BEA) and the Economic Research Service in the Department of Agriculture. Now the projections are prepared solely by BEA, but the OBERS name is retained for continuity.

6　MSAs = Metropolitan Statistical Areas; NECMAs = New England County Metropolitan Areas; CMSAs = Consolidated Metropolitan Statistical Areas; PMSAs = Primary Metropolitan Statistical Areas.

7　Harvey Rabinowitz, Associate Professor of Architecture at the University of Wisconsin–Milwaukee, suggested many of the most important data sources in this section.

8　Leonard Heumann, Professor of Urban and Regional Planning at the University of Illinois at Urbana, provided many of the primary data sources in this section.

9　G. William Page, Associate Professor of Urban Planning and Associate Scientist at the Center for Great Lakes Studies, at the University of Wisconsin–Milwaukee, identified the key information sources for this section.

10 A basic source is Earl R. Babbie, *Survey Research Methods: A Cookbook and Other Fables* (Belmont, CA: Wadsworth Publishing Co., 1973); but see also Herbert Hyman, *Interviewing in Social Research* (Chicago: University of Chicago Press, 1975) and Eugene J. Webb et al., *Unobtrusive Measures: Non-reactive Research in the Social Sciences* (Chicago: Rand McNally, 1966).

11 The mathematics of this process are too involved to present here. Readers who would like additional information should consult a survey research text.

12 This section is based on Patton and Sawicki, *Basic Methods of Policy Analysis and Planning,* 62–71.

13 See Lewis Anthony Dexter, *Elite and Specialized Interviewing: Handbooks for Research in Political Behavior* (Evanston, IL: Northwestern University Press, 1970), and Jerome T. Murphy, *Getting The Facts: A Fieldwork Guide for Evaluators and Policy Analysts* (Santa Monica, CA: Goodyear Publishing Co., 1980).

14 This section is drawn from Patton and Sawicki, *Basic Methods of Policy Analysis and Planning,* 71–91.

15 Stanley M. Altman, "Teaching Data Analysis to Individuals Entering the Public Service," *Journal of Urban Analysis* 3 (October 1976): 211–37.

16 For a discussion of the use of gamma, see James A. Davis, *Elementary Survey Analysis* (Englewood Cliffs, NJ: Prentice-Hall, 1971).

Part six:
Plans and
planners

16 The values of the planner

Are the professions accomplishing the opposite of their central goals? Contemporary criticism often says yes. In the view of some people, doctors cause illness; teachers keep children from learning; lawyers break laws; ministers lead people to Hell; and planners produce unexpected disasters.

Professional people often fuel criticism by conferring a remote and elevated status on the professions. The aura of knowingness, the command of mysterious forces, the privilege of the expert, the hard and narrow path of access to professional standing—these have built illusions of professional infallibility, of problems invariably solved if professional advice is sought and followed.

Once the consumers of professional advice discover its limitations, they discover also the need to be active participants in how the advice is developed and used. The aloof professional is replaced by the accountable professional. The passive consumer is replaced by the consumer who affects professional decisions. The professional gives less case-by-case advice and more instruction on how to be your own professional.

As a new profession, not quite a hundred years old in its modern American form, planning scarcely had time to build the walls of illusion around its exclusive professional competence before the siege came. Now the beleaguerment of the professions is leveling those walls. The expansion of malpractice responsibility, commercial advertising of professional services, pressure toward competitive bidding for services, and citizen review of professional standards are leading us to the unwalled profession.

As long as the professions stick to their central aim, society will continue to want and need them. That central aim is to muster the best knowledge, skill, and imagination in solving complex problems and in making the solutions work. The active client sets the priorities among problems, judges whether the best method has been used, and in addition judges whether the solution is effective, whether its cost is too high, and whether the solution gets in the way of other good things.

Clemenceau's saying that war is too important to be entrusted to generals was revised by Charles de Gaulle when he said that politics is too serious a matter to be left to the politicians. The saying can be applied to any profession. To get effective results, however, it is important not to leave the professionals out. The aim of planners is like the aim of other professionals: to translate our experience into ideas and to test our ideas in experience, solving problems as we go.

This chapter examines the values of a planning profession that some say does not exist. Samuel Johnson once replied to an elaborate argument that proved that matter did not exist. He kicked a large stone with great might and said, "I refute it thus." The planning profession is often kicked with great might.

Planning values

Many debates in planning, as in other fields, pose choices as either–or. Is planning scientific or is it not scientific? Can we forecast the future or is it unknowable?

The place of values in the work of planners is itself debated in these terms. On the one hand, do, or should, planners work objectively, keeping their own preferences out of their advice, serving their employers as neutral technicians? Yes, of course. Who selected them to work for their own program? On the other hand, do, or should, planners express their own vision in their work? Give priority to matters that they think are important? Fight for whatever they think best? Yes, of course. Why hire an independent-minded professional if what you want is someone to take orders?

Planners in practice strike a balance between these conflicting views, a balance that differs with the personality, temperament, and convictions of the planner. Although the balance will vary with the client's or community's rapport with the planner, it is hazardous to let the balance tip to one extreme or the other.

If the balance tips toward neutrality, it is deceptive. As a whole person, the technician cannot be empty of views, values, and biases. Even the collection of facts requires choosing questions to ask, choosing methods of getting answers, and making judgments about their validity. Different values will yield different choices. The technician's biases may be subtle, quiet, and hidden, but they are there. An attempt to be neutral merely produces passivity.

Tipping the balance toward active promotion of the planner's values risks creating an idiosyncratic program that is not responsive to the community. That responsiveness, coupled with an explicit acknowledgment of the planner's values, leadership, and fairness in presenting contrary evidence, contributes to making opposing tendencies complementary rather than conflicting.

How do the values of planners sort out? Which are deemed by planners to be more important than others? The following discussion shows that many planning values are in competition with each other and with values of the broader community as well. This is not a report of a consensus among planners. It expresses views based not on a scientific poll but on years of knowing many planners and many plans and listening to many planning debates.

The techniques planners use to balance competing values are not special to the planner, be they old-fashioned horse-trading or new fashioned cost-benefit analysis. Planning brings to these techniques a concern for long-term consequences and an interest in devising solutions that consider the costs and benefits to people outside the immediate circle of decision making.

The planner's values are not specific to the planner. They are widely held and generally shared. Everyone favors health, happiness, prosperity, and justice. Planners used to advertise the objective of a city plan as that of making the

The politics of city planning

Certainly I was involved in the politics of city planning. Every city planner is. Overall, however, the best "politics" is top professional work, forcefully presented and defended.

City planners should not be neutral, and I do not believe their clients, at the level of local government, expect them to be without values or opinions. After they have arrived at some position, some point of view, some desired direction, one would hope to see it reflected in both public plans and day-to-day recommendations. Why hide it?

Further, city planners should be willing to stand up for their points of view if they want to be effective. They should be prepared to "mix it up." They must do more than recommend. Within a democratic process they should advocate and search for ways to carry out their plans. I believe, too, that they should value and nurture their utopian predilections. They are nothing to be ashamed of.

Source: Excerpted from Allan B. Jacobs, *Making City Planning Work* (Chicago: American Society of Planning Officials, 1978), 313.

Figure 16–1

community a better place to work, live, and play. What is now specific to the planner is an inclination to stand up for those public values that are fragile and hard to maintain in competition with values that more predictably command acceptance.

Health

Health, strongly and universally valued, is a composite of subsidiary values. Planners worry about the more fragile of these values. Although planners do not lack interest in the needs of people who are physically ill, they are more likely to emphasize environmental health, preventive programs, clean air and clean water, surroundings and services that nurture self-development, and the integration of handicapped people into the larger society. Even with respect to individual physical illness, planners turn to the more fragile values: ensuring that poor people have access to services and controlling priorities and costs.

Conservation of resources

The numbers and influence of people who support the conservation of resources have markedly increased. Understanding of the problems is widespread. But the understanding and commitment that are required to produce policies for sustainable development[1] have still reached only a small segment of society. Conservation remains a fragile value.

Norbert Weiner, the mathematician who introduced cybernetics, told a planning conference some years ago that "no firm can underwrite the growth of a redwood forest. [If it is] to be grown by anybody, it can scarcely be by an organization of less respected prominence than the State or perhaps the Church." Planners must have that concern for the more remote future that leads them to address issues such as soil erosion, deforestation, energy use, materials recycling, water allocation, and the rural-urban balance. It is hard to save a swamp from development, but planners try.

Efficiency

Efficiency is a popular value. All of us want to see it, especially in those who serve us. Although the work of planners probably is done as efficiently as the work of other professionals, the special significance of efficiency for planners is not in the efficiency with which plans *are produced* but in the efficiencies that plans *can produce*. The solutions that appeal to planners, for example, are those that produce multiple services from one investment: using school facilities after hours for recreational and community activities, or buying more land than is needed for a highway right-of-way to use for other public purposes. Such solutions are often resisted by administrators of specific functions, who may value the competing efficiency of concentrating every resource on one function.

Efficiency leads planners to oppose urban sprawl, which results in overbuilt sewer, water, and transportation facilities that provide too much, too soon to patchy development. Efficiency is the value that evokes an intelligent stinginess in capital improvements programming.

Beauty

Beauty is a value that shares eternal life with its companion, truth. The life they share, however, is often poverty-stricken. Planners, who deal with public expressions of beauty, cope with two responsibilities in trying to alleviate that poverty.

One is that public beauty must satisfy public taste. Common denominators need not be low, and a high common denominator is a reasonable aspiration. However, some lasting delights in our environment require hospitality toward, or at least tolerance of, heretical and prickly designs that have only a small audience at first but earn more general appreciation in time. We can choose individual delights in music or poetry, but the environment is shared. The wide diversity among high cultures and pop cultures and their basis in emotional rather than physical needs make it difficult to strike this communal balance.

The second responsibility is using the power of urban design to affect our lives. Urban design is long lasting, highly visible, and capable of causing psychological uplift or oppression. Although a community obviously can put up with sterile and ugly environments, it will cherish developments, large and small, that fulfill with zest and delight the complex demands of our public living space.

Equity

Social equity is profoundly influenced by public plans and the way they are carried out. Can people who earn low wages live near where they work? Are

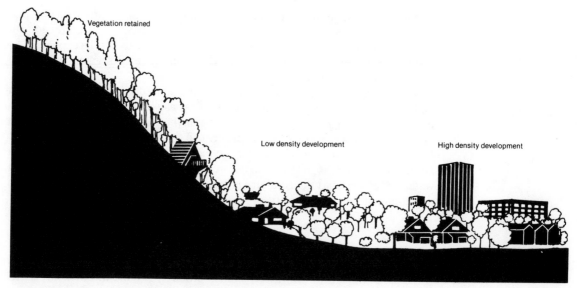

Figure 16–2   The conservation of resources is a value
. . . that remains fragile.

they cut out of jobs by business location decisions? Is police protection as good in a poor neighborhood as in a better-off one? Do schools give poor children enough chance to become not-so-poor adults? Are homes available on a fair basis?

Recent progress toward greater equity has been particularly remarkable in the realm of principle. Legislation, judicial findings, and public attitudes now buttress the general value of equity. Many policy questions involving equity concern the implementation of principles: How can resources be allocated to obtain more equitable results? Although such allocations are political decisions made case by case, they are strongly influenced by planning analysis and recommendations.

A neutral planning stance on equity issues ignores the windfall and wipeout effects not only of land use decisions but also of capital expenditures and service programs. It is a paradox that those who hold most strongly to the value of individualism are often the most skilled in exploiting the organized structure and resources of government, law, and finance. Those who must make it on their own—owing to poverty, physical handicap, geographic location, lack of education, lack of employment opportunities, or discrimination—often are the least skilled in exploiting government, law, and finance. Fairness in the planning process requires that steps be built in to redress the imbalance.

Pluralism and individuality

To assert that planners value pluralism and individuality seems to run counter to much evidence. Haven't planners produced the American suburb of dreary sameness? The urban renewal project that replaces small-scale diversity with super-block rigidity? The expressway that slices up an old neighborhood? The zoning ordinance that isolates every land use in its own unmixed district?

Planners have indeed contributed to each of these visions of what development should be like. To a large extent they have done so in response to the values and dictates of the majority. And to some extent they have done so because, as citizens, many planners share these values. For example, majority views of the need to protect and separate residential areas from business and industry were the foundation of zoning regulations. The design of subdivisions was based on a widely held view that an urban neighborhood should almost be self-contained—like a village transplanted into the city.

Yet planners have also concerned themselves with satisfying a plurality of tastes and with meeting minority needs. Planners worked to get public support for mass transit during its long decline; adopted the planned unit development to counteract the imposed uniformities of a zoning ordinance; promoted rehabilitation and conservation instead of wholesale clearance; favored scattering public housing in existing neighborhoods; and did much to give environmental concerns the status of a majority value.

Like other values, individuality cannot be asserted absolutely. Its importance—as well as the need to balance pluralistic values against values held in common—is expressed in a comment by Jean Renoir, the film director: "You see, in this world there is one awful thing, and that is that everyone has his reasons." Our plans should accommodate more of those reasons. But if we cannot arrange for the city of all virtues, we can arrange for each city to be true to its own individuality: "It's the best place in the world to live in if that's the kind of place you like."

Democratic participation and democratic responsibility

Democratic participation means not only electing officials but also participating in public decisions. No other local government activity generates more citizen participation than does planning. The planning agency holds public hearings, conducts attitude and opinion surveys, arranges neighborhood meetings, and appoints citizen advisory committees. Unpaid citizens serve on planning commissions and publicize alternative decisions to test public reaction. Planners are concerned with the quality of participation and the substantive understanding on which it is based. Genuine participation has to begin before ideas are crystalized—long before a hearing is held on unchangeable proposals with contracts about to be let. It must proceed without the condescension of technician-knows-best, the selective packaging of facts that will sell best, or glib replies to questions that may trip up the project.

The most effective participation will not produce automatic decisions. Elected officials have the democratic responsibility of resolving the tough situations in which some participants gain and some lose, of balancing a neighborhood interest against a communitywide interest or a communitywide interest against a regional interest. Public-policy disputes often reveal heavier support for a facility in someone else's backyard: a nuclear plant but not in my town, an expressway but not in my neighborhood, a halfway house but not on my street. Resolving these conflicts is a political responsibility. Genuine and widespread participation should yield better decisions—although they may not please all participants.

Rational management

Planning is integral to good management. Management needs to anticipate events; it is weak if it merely responds to them. The tempo and complexity of change have rapidly established administrative and management planning as distinct executive responsibilities. A central goal of both the administrative planner and the public planner is the gradual replacement of seat-of-the pants judgments with reasoned judgments. The evolution of planning method has stressed the validity and pertinence of information, the logic of analysis, the worth of evaluating the consequences of alternative decisions, and the effectiveness of standards and policies in achieving goals.

Figure 16–3 "The planner is a leader . . urging progress with quiet but unrelenting persistence."

This evolution has been greatly assisted by computer technology—a situation that gives the impression at times that decisionmakers also will be replaced by machines. Although the models and the computer games should help us understand what happens and why, should help us deal with complex relationships, and should improve our guesses about the limits of action and the opportunities for solution, it is not rational for us to hope for or to fear a conspiracy that will completely replace wisdom with knowledge. Planning solutions, like scientific hypotheses, can be methodically tested, but it takes a certain amount of inspiration—not just a formula—to come up with either one.

A rational balance does not require a choice between inordinate faith in computer products and strictly intuitive decision making. An appreciation of the limitations of computers and mathematical models can make these models more, rather than less, helpful. If we know the assumptions and guesses and "fudge factors" that helped put the model together, we also know the points at which professional and political judgments must enter if we are to make use of what the model tells us. A brief story may illustrate this point. President Franklin D. Roosevelt is said to have mixed his martinis by pouring gin into a graduated beaker and holding the beaker up to eye level to see that the prescribed amount came exactly to the line. Then he would pour the right proportion of vermouth into the beaker and hold it up again to see that it came exactly to the line. He would then stir. But before serving he upended the gin bottle over the beaker and vigorously sloshed in a lot more. The most rational rationality is leavened with emotion.

Planning issues

A few general planning issues that are discussed perennially are reviewed here. The intent is not to settle them once and for all but to illustrate how opposing tendencies can be balanced so that a conclusion can be reached.

The far-off goal and the immediate decision

Plans are made to reach a goal that is generally years away. The usefulness of a plan, however, is in helping to make decisions today. The burden of problems that need answers now will not be lightened by the posting of a sign that says "Plans being prepared." Neither will our decisions improve much if the emphasis is reversed: "We don't know where we're going, but we've got to move fast."

Two steps that are important in themselves will also reduce the conflict between making plans and making decisions. One is to ensure against stop-and-go planning. When an intensive general planning effort is funded, reports are produced, and some recommendations are carried out. Then the job is considered done, the planning budget is cut, and the staff assigned to general planning is reduced. However, as the general plan that the staff must consult becomes obsolete, day-to-day decisions require more and more of the staff's time, and the quality of staff advice on day-to-day issues declines. When the advice becomes poor enough, there may be a decision to fund another general planning effort. How much more effective it would be to strive for a successful balance between long-range planning and daily decision making—to eliminate the peaks and valleys in favor of ongoing, serious general planning.

The second step is to develop all the connections that Martin Meyerson referred to as *the middle-range bridge:*[2] the activities that connect long-range plans with short-range implementation. Planning is part of management, and management is part of planning. Plans must be translated into programs and budgets, and the effects of carrying out plans must be checked to measure success and find the surprises.

If such measures succeed, there will still be a balancing problem: keeping the planners from skimping on help with immediate decisions and keeping the decisionmakers from skimping on support for long-range planning.

Incrementalism, ad hocism, and comprehensive planning

Incrementalism has been proposed as one solution to the difficulties of comprehensive planning. Incrementalism is based on the following ideas: Long-range, comprehensive planning is not only too difficult but is also inherently bad; problems are harder to solve when you group them together and are easier to solve when you take them one at a time; solutions are best negotiated with the few people who have a direct interest, not with the many whose interests have a remote connection to the problem at hand; genuine reform is accomplished in small bites, not in whole swallows; and small increments of change can be better fitted to people's needs than can the tyranny of a grand design.

Some of the weaknesses documented in examples of comprehensive planning seem to bear out the promises of incrementalism. Many long-range proposals have been put forward in the form of an "end state," a condition to be reached in, perhaps, thirty years, in which all the problems are solved, all the resources are allocated, and all the books are balanced. Cheerful people will encounter no lot that is vacant, no building that is crumbling, no stream that is dirty. No doubt the planners responsible for these misleading visions did not intend to mislead; they understood the projected plans as generalized forecasts of the consequences of alternative policies. But because forecasts oversimplify the future, as myth oversimplifies the past, forecasts can mislead. Planners can mislead somewhat more intentionally by fearing to forecast the persistence of problems; promises are easy when the delivery date is so far off.

Long-range plans also tend to design solutions that are too uniform for the diversity of cases that will come up. The attraction of ad hoc solutions is in tailoring each one to fit the problem, in making each solution a spontaneous invention that is uninhibited in its improvised answers. Unlike long-range plan-

---

Alternative futures for decision making   We are not going to find technological fixes to any of the problems in our culture that matter. . . . These are social problems, but we keep on looking for technological fixes. . . .

If you look at the evidence from the last ten years there has not been a significant increase in standards of living in the United States. What has been happening . . . is a transfer towards those families that now have two wage earners instead of one.

We are not going to get a major rise again in the standard of living. We are going to have to learn to manage stability, not growth. . . .

Rapid growth [is] no longer necessarily in the interest of those who are getting it any more than decline was in the

interest of those experiencing that. With rapid increases in marginal costs, rapid growth may be the best way to wreck your city. . . .

Management means the dealing with incomplete, uncertain information and making the best decision that one can. It means that one of the key priorities is preserving enough social cohesion that people will go along with decisions that are not ideal, but merely optimal. It means that one works with imperfect people. And one recognizes that decision making is not a tidy, decent, cleancut process, but a messy, untidy, unsatisfactory, and gutsy process.

Source: Excerpted from Robert Theobald, "Strategies for the Future," speech reprinted in *Public Management,* January 1979, 15, 16.

ning, ad hocism gets rid of the burden of worrying about tomorrow. The difficulty is that today's solutions can become tomorrow's problems; another layer of ad hoc solutions can multiply the problems further for the day after.

Incrementalism embodies a truth about how things get done but not necessarily a truth about how the right things get done. When we deal with complex events, the "right things" will always be elusive, but they are more approachable comprehensively. The environmental-impact approach to evaluating proposals took hold because incremental solutions satisfied a narrow interest in the short run but not the broader environmental interests in the long run. The extension of impact analysis to social and economic issues returns us to one of the original, central concepts of comprehensive planning: the plan was intended as the basic reference in evaluating all of the impacts of a particular proposal. In the 1920s this sort of impact analysis was called *mandatory referral*. Although that phrase is now little used, it conveys the relationship between a specific incremental step and the general comprehensive plan. Don't be put off by the word *comprehensive*. It doesn't mean implementing all proposals at once. It doesn't mean being paralyzed by John Muir's realization that "when we try to pick out anything by itself, we find it hitched to everything else in the universe." Refer to the plan to see how the specific step fits related objectives. Refer to it to see how it fits the objectives of the entire community and the wider region. To be a good incrementalist, you should know what, in the long run, is to be accomplished bit by bit.

Public decisions and private decisions

Our communities operate in a mixed political economy. Public dollars and private dollars mix in the development of a project. Public policies and private policies mix in determining that project's design and operation. Public policies help determine private profits. Private policies help determine the success of public programs.

The mix of dollars and policies is often settled by negotiation. A suburb and a developer will hammer out agreement on the size of a development; its density, housing types, and kind of shopping area; funding for the sewer; dedication of land for a school; and length of time for the completion of the development. An older community wants to create jobs and will offer incentives for business development such as special zoning permissions, tax allowances, new services at city expense, or public acquisition of land with a writedown of costs.

Benefits do flow both ways—to the public and to the developer; but with so much money at stake, clear precautions must be established to lessen the opportunities for corruption and to keep public and private interests from blurring to the public detriment.

Precautions include the adoption of guidelines to limit the negotiator's discretion and to set standards for acceptable development agreements. Approvals should not be recorded as bare conclusions but should be accompanied in the public record by statements of the findings that justify the approvals. The proceedings and record of negotiations should be public, although the early and tentative stages may involve business confidences that must be protected. Development opportunities that are created by public action should be open to competitive offers, including competition based on design quality or on meeting special housing needs.

At times, extravagant gifts of publicly created value have been granted private entrepreneurs in the name of entrepreneurial rights. But a heavy burden of requirements, imposed on the developer in the name of public-interest regulation, has also accumulated. Developers add up the demands for installed utilities, land for schools and recreation, fair housing, low-income housing, design standards, art, performance bonds, and assurances of holding to a fixed schedule, and then protest that, translated into costs, the requirements will stop the development.

These debates are not effectively resolved by an exchange of slogans between free enterprise on the one hand and the public interest on the other. Active community development does need the partnership of both public and private sectors; some public investments and incentives to private development are justified, and a public concern for the marketability of that development is needed. The balance between public and private rights and responsibilities will be better struck if all the costs and benefits and markets are explicitly and publicly examined, case by case.

Who is the client?

The quick answer to the question of who is the client is that the planner's client is whoever pays the planner's salary. The professional does owe diligent service to the client-employer. Ethical performance requires that a planner not serve at the same time two employers who may have conflicting interests.

One difficulty in identifying the planner's client is that the planner may often have *one* employer with conflicting interests. For example, in one community a planner may be recruited, interviewed, and recommended for appointment by a committee of a planning commission. The planner is appointed by the mayor or city manager and then confirmed by the council. Once on the job, this planner reports, let us say, to the city manager, providing studies and advice on many aspects of the manager's business. The planner also advises the planning commission on its decisions and the council on its legislation.

Where interests or views differ, whom does the planner serve? One refuge is in the standards of the profession. The same thorough and dispassionate analysis will be presented to all participants; the same careful analysis of alternative decisions will be made for all. Hazards, opportunities, and possible compromises in resolving issues are conscientiously disclosed.

This model of the conscientious professional answers the problem only partially. The decisionmakers want more than the facts and analysis: they want a recommendation. Given that it is impossible for a planner to be completely neutral, even the analysis steers gently toward a particular recommendation. Make it explicit, the decisionmaker asks, and give your justifications.

Ethical codes say that planners serve the public interest primarily and must fit the client-employer's interest to the public interest or else not serve that client. This guideline is needed most when the public interest is hardest to identify. It is needed most, then, when the guidance it offers is least clear.

The public interest is an amalgam of many interests. These include the interests of democratic majorities; improving the conditions of poor or handicapped people; protecting resources; economizing in the use of public funds; living up to our laws; protecting health and safety; preserving human rights—in short, doing all the things that affirm our abiding values. Even the ability to pursue private interests is part of the public interest, given our view of government as the servant of the individual.

We cannot codify a consensus on a permanent balance among these competing elements of the public interest nor a permanent balance between the public interest and the right to pursue private interests. It is a planner's professional responsibility to achieve such a balance and use it as a personal guide.

Some planners have found a persistent imbalance in the so-called public interest, especially as public decisions affect poor and minority groups. Some have become advocate planners, supporting the interests of those groups that do not normally command articulate, knowledgeable, skillful, and aggressive representation. Advocate planners have cited precedents for such advocacy by pointing to planners who have "advocated" for builders and developers, for example, or for transportation interests.

Localism and interdependence

The problems of metropolitan areas are not fragmented, but the governments are. The neatness of creating a metropolitan government was once looked to as a solution and has been adopted in a few places, but most people are looking to solutions that leave local government a little more complex. Metropolitan councils of governments (COGs) have been set up as a modest layer to work for the coordination of plans and programs. States have been setting up regions within the state and taking a more active role in some local decisions that have effects beyond local boundaries. Highly urbanized counties have sought a new identity as local urban governments.

Councils of governments have tried to achieve coordination primarily through elected officials representing autonomous units. The states have acted, especially on environmental issues, when state governments have found that localities have not acted to set environmental goals or work toward them. Counties have acted to serve the clusters of cities within their boundaries by initiating or stepping up urban services.

These efforts all seek more centralization or coordination on a metropolitan basis. At the same time, there has been greater interest in decentralizing some of the decisions within large central cities—giving neighborhood councils at least the power to review and advise.

This interplay of governments often illustrates the point that administrators wish to coordinate all of the units that are below theirs in size or authority but do not wish to be coordinated by units that are above theirs.

Ethical Principles for Planning, adopted by the Board of the American Planning Association, 26 April 1987 This Statement of Ethical Principles for Planning was prepared by the American Planning Association (APA), whose purpose is to advance the art and science of planning—physical, economic, and social—at the local, regional, state, and national levels. By distributing this Statement, APA seeks to promote ethical principles in planning and public discussion of ethical practice. APA members who are also members of its professional affiliate, the American Institute of Certified Planners (AICP), are subject to a separate AICP Code of Ethics and Professional Conduct, which provides for an enforcement procedure. This Statement is intended to complement the AICP Code.

APA encourages the adoption of the principles in this Statement by legislatures through ordinances or statutes, by public planning bodies through incorporation into bylaws, and by employers of planners, who may include them in personnel manuals and other employment policy documents.

1. Serve the public interest.
2. Support citizen participation in planning.
3. Recognize the comprehensive and long-range nature of planning decisions.
4. Expand choice and opportunity for all persons.
5. Facilitate coordination through the planning process.
6. Avoid conflict of interest.
7. Render thorough and diligent planning service.
8. Do not seek or offer favors.
9. Do not disclose or improperly use confidential information for financial gain.
10. Ensure access on an equal basis to public planning reports and studies.
11. Ensure full disclosure at public hearings.
12. Maintain public confidence.
13. Respect professional codes of ethics and conduct.

Note: The full text explains each principle in detail.

Figure 16–4 "The planner is dedicated. . . . He has seen the light."

Planners work at each of these levels, balancing a loyalty to localism and to decisions that originate among those who are closest to the problem with a loyalty to coordination and to decisions that span all parts of the problem. The advocate planner is redefined for this purpose as the advocate for a particular level of governmental decision.

Coordinative and functional planning

Comprehensive planning does not comprehend all the planning that must be done. Each function of government carries out its own specialized and detailed planning: health planning, transportation planning, school planning. These types of planning will be studied by the general planning agency in their interrelationships, for their secondary effects, and for their relative priorities. The specialized departments study and plan for their functions—as they should—as though nothing else mattered.

Better planning is done when there is sound, mutual respect between the people responsible for these two kinds of planning. The general planner, as the one working with all the departments, has the burden of making the relationships go well by seeking to understand the needs and reasoning of the various departments and by providing useful services to them.

Planning objectives and constitutional ends

Planners are often painted in the colors of frustration—as having marvelous plans but facing insuperable obstacles. The search for more effective tools to implement the plans, therefore, continues.

Implementation, however, must fit the framework of values that is embedded in the Constitution. Justice William Brennan said that if a "policeman must know the Constitution, then why not a planner?"[3] Chief Justice Rehnquist added, in a 1987 case, that some lessening of "the freedom and flexibility of land-use planners" is a necessary consequence of a decision that upholds a constitutional right.[4]

The recent Supreme Court decisions in takings cases show, however, that knowing the Constitution is an intricate and continuing study. Due process, removal of discrimination, freedom of belief and expression, and individual privacy are constitutional values to be observed in the preparation of plans. A large part of the planner's obligation lies in documenting the legitimacy of the public interest to be served. Another large part lies in designing regulatory means to advance that public interest substantially without triggering a constitutional challenge. Constitutional rights are well worth some frustration.

Who owns the city?

Planners' values are tested regularly as they are confronted with the daily question "Who owns the city?" Is it the old settled families who would like to profit from growth and development, or the recent arrivals who want to cultivate an oasis of quiet enjoyment? Is it the entrenched establishment that prescribes Spanish-tiled roofs, or newcomers with divergent tastes? Is it the low-income families finding enjoyment in an older neighborhood with family-owned stores, or the gentrifiers with skylights and boutiques? The drivers on expressways or the riders on buses? The parishioners who want to cash in and replace their old church, or the historic preservationists who want to protect it? The hospital that wants to expand, or its neighbors who want more homes and less traffic? The developers of beachfront lots or the fishermen or the bathers? The local homeowners or the day-trippers? The landlords or the tenants? The shoppers or the shopkeepers? The sculptor or the people who live with the sculpture?

And who is to pay for building the city and running it? Today's taxpayers, with property taxes, income taxes, sales taxes, or user fees? Developers and their customers, with regulations, impact fees, assessments, and linkages? Tomorrow's taxpayers, with indebtedness, deferred maintenance, exhaustion of resources, or decrease in services?

Politicians are responsible for evaluating and resolving conflicting claims. Planners sometimes seem intent on cornering the politicians and trapping them into making the correct decisions through the power of rational analysis. But rational analysis is infused with values that need to be displayed as clearly as other facts. Planning, like other professions, presumes to bring some order to a sector of human experience. Planners bring some order to community change, satisfying a sense of progress. The valued ends of progress are community goals that emerge from debate around the political table. Planners share community goals, but their concerns emphasize longer-run consequences and the coordination of independent decisions. As a result, planners often represent minority values and find themselves speaking for the voiceless majority that will people the future.

1   Lester R. Brown et al., *State of the World: A Worldwatch Institute Report on Progress toward a Sustainable Society* (New York: Norton, annual).

2   Martin Meyerson, "Building the Middle-Range Bridge for Comprehensive Planning," *Journal of the American Institute of Planners* 22 (Spring 1956): 58–64.

3   *San Diego Gas & Electric Co.* v. *City of San Diego,* 450 U.S. at 661 (1981). Brennan, J., dissenting.

4   *First English Evangelical Lutheran Church of Glendale* v. *County of Los Angeles, California,* U.S. No. 85-1199, decided June 9, 1987.

Bibliography and resource guide

This bibliography and resource guide is highly selective and represents informed judgments about basic and introductory references. Many additional books, periodical articles, and other references are cited in the endnotes to the individual chapters. Immediately below are listed eight professional associations and resource agencies that are of particular interest to planners and managers. Shown for each organization are name, address, and a condensed listing of services that bear on planning. Next is a listing of periodicals and other publications that are of value as continuing reference and information sources. Shown for each publication are name, frequency of issue, publisher, and annotation. The balance of this bibliography consists of additional references listed by chapters; this listing— mostly books—emphasizes general works that are deemed helpful for students and practitioners.

Associations and agencies

American Institute of Architects (AIA), 1735 New York Avenue, N.W., Washington, DC 20006. Urban design, environmental planning, professional policies and standards.

American Planning Association (APA), 1313 East 60th Street, Chicago, IL 60637. Organization for professional planners and appointed and elected officials in local government. Activities include research, professional standards and development, and a wide variety of planning publications.

Council of Planning Librarians, 1313 East 60th Street, Chicago, IL 60637. Issues bibliographies on a wide variety of local and regional planning subjects. More than 600 bibliographies available; complete list on request.

International City Management Association (ICMA), 1120 G Street, N.W., Washington, DC 20005. General management, planning and programming services, relationships of planning and budgeting, occasional reports on planning topics.

National Technical Information Service (NTIS), 425 13th Street, N.W., Washington, DC 20004. Clearinghouse for public sale of U.S. government publications, including those of the U.S. Department of Housing and Urban Development, the U.S. Department of Transportation, and the U.S. Department of Energy. Publishes weekly newsletter listing its acquisitions.

The Urban Institute, 2100 M Street, N.W., Washington, DC 20037. Research, analysis, and publications on a wide range of topics in urban affairs, many directly related to planning.

Urban Land Institute, 1319 18th Street, N.W., Washington, DC 20036-1810. Research activities and publications on a range of topics in public policy, residential development, and land development.

Urban and Regional Information Systems Association (URISA), 319 C Street, S.E., Washington, DC 20003. Major interests are data sources, data usage, data management and reporting, and information systems; publishes a bimonthly newsletter with developments in government information systems.

Periodicals

AIA Journal. Monthly. American Institute of Architects. Occasional articles deal with planning topics, especially urban design.

Architectural Record. Monthly. McGraw-Hill. Articles on building design; of particular interest are articles on large industrial structures.

Environmental Comment. Monthly. Urban Land Institute. Environmental law, land use regulation, and growth control.

Housing. Monthly. McGraw-Hill. Edited primarily for the private sector; topics include residential development, small commercial development, and economics of the housing industry.

Journal of the American Planning Association. Quarterly. American Planning Association. Professional and scholarly coverage of planning and urban affairs through articles, commentary, and extensive book reviews.

Journal of Housing. Monthly. National Association of Housing and Redevelopment Officials. Articles, reports, and news stories on community development, housing, federal legislation, and related areas.

Land Economics. Quarterly. University of Wisconsin at Madison. Covers land economics, land and buildings as commodities, and assessment, taxation, and regulation on the value of land.

Land Use Law & Zoning Digest. Monthly. American Planning Association. Covers public regulation of zoning, subdivision regulation, and other aspects of land use, with abstracts of state and federal court cases, coverage of proposed and adopted legislation, brief articles on legal developments, and thorough documentation and indexing.

Landscape Architecture. Quarterly. American Society of Landscape Architects. Coverage includes open space and recreational development, urban parks, and water-related development.

Law reviews. These periodicals issued primarily by law schools, include occasional articles on zoning, housing, real property taxation, and related planning topics.

The Municipal Year Book. Annual. International City Management Association. Occasional surveys and analyses of planning subjects as well as regular coverage of local government finance and other subjects of direct interest to planners.

Planning. Monthly. American Planning Association. Wide coverage of city and regional planning with articles, listing of job openings in planning, news reports and analyses, question-and-answer section, and book reviews and book notes.

Planning Advisory Service. Monthly. American Planning Association. Reports based on extensive research and analysis cover almost every conceivable subject in city and regional planning.

Urban Land. Monthly. Urban Land Institute. News and trends in land use and land development, particularly central business districts.

2 Historical development of American city planning

Arnold, Joseph L. *The New Deal in the Suburbs: A History of the Greenbelt Town Program, 1935–1954*. Columbus, OH: Ohio State University Press, 1971.

Black, Russell VanNest. *Planning and the Planning Profession: The Past Fifty Years, 1917–1967*. Washington, DC: American Institute of Planners, 1967.

Cherry, Gordon E., ed. *Shaping an Urban World: Planning in the Twentieth Century*. New York: St. Martin's Press, 1980.

Chudacoff, Howard P. *The Evolution of American Urban Society*. Englewood Cliffs, NJ: Prentice-Hall, 1981.

Ciucci, Giorgio, et al. *The American City: From the Civil War to the New Deal*. Cambridge: MIT Press, 1979.

Clawson, Marion. *New Deal Planning: The National Resources Planning Board*. Baltimore: Johns Hopkins University Press, 1981.

Conkin, Paul K. *Tomorrow a New World: The New Deal Community Program*. Ithaca, NY: Cornell University Press, 1959. Published for the American Historical Association.

Frieden, Bernard J., and Marshall Kaplan. *The Politics of Neglect: Urban Aid from Model Cities to Revenue Sharing*. Cambridge: MIT Press, 1975.

Gelfand, Mark I. *A Nation of Cities: The Federal Government and Urban America 1933–1965*. New York: Oxford University Press, 1975.

Gerckens, Laurence C. *Shaping the American City*. Columbus, OH: The On-Call Faculty Program, Inc., 1985.

Glaab, Charles N., and A. Theodore Brown. *A History of Urban America*. 3d ed. New York: Macmillan, 1983.

Goldfield, David R., and Blaine A. Brownell. *Urban America: From Downtown to No Town*. Boston: Houghton Mifflin, 1979.

Graham, Otis L., Jr. *Toward a Planned Society: From Roosevelt to Nixon*. New York: Oxford University Press, 1977.

Gutheim, Frederick. *Worthy of the Nation: The Planning and Development of the National Capital City*. Washington, DC: Smithsonian Institution Press, 1977.

Haar, Charles M. *Between the Idea and the Reality: A Study in the Origin, Fate, and*

Legacy of the Model Cities Program. Boston: Little, Brown & Co., 1975.

Hargrove, Erwin C., and Paul K. Conkin, eds. *TVA: Fifty Years of Grass-Roots Bureaucracy*. Champaign: University of Illinois Press, 1984.

Hines, Thomas S. *Burnham of Chicago: Architect and Planner*. New York: Oxford University Press, 1974.

Housing and Home Finance Agency. *Chronology of Major Federal Actions Affecting Housing and Community Development, July 1892 through 1963*. Washington, DC: U.S. Government Printing Office, 1964.

Krueckeberg, Donald A., ed. *The American Planner: Biographies and Recollections*. New York: Methuen, 1983.

_____. *Introduction to Planning History in the United States*. New Brunswick, NJ: Rutgers University, Center for Urban Policy Research, 1983.

Lubove, Roy. *Community Planning in the 1920s: The Contribution of the Regional Planning Association of America*. Pittsburgh: University of Pittsburgh Press, 1963.

_____. *The Progressives and the Slums*. Pittsburgh: University of Pittsburgh Press, 1962. Westport, CT: Greenwood, 1974.

Martin, Roscoe C., ed. *TVA: The First Twenty Years*. University: University of Alabama Press, 1956.

McKelvey, Blake. *The Emergence of Metropolitan America, 1915–1966*. New Brunswick, NJ: Rutgers University Press, 1968.

_____. *The Urbanization of America, 1860–1915*. New Brunswick, NJ: Rutgers University Press, 1963.

Miller, Zane L. *The Urbanization of Modern America: A Brief History*. New York: Harcourt Brace Jovanovich, 1973.

Mohl, Raymond A., and James F. Richardson, eds. *The Urban Experience: Themes in American History*. Belmont, CA: Wadsworth Publishing Co., 1973.

Muller, Peter O. *Contemporary Suburban America*. Englewood Cliffs, NJ: Prentice-Hall, 1981.

Newton, Norman T. *Design on the Land: The Development of Landscape Architecture*. Cambridge: Harvard University Press, 1971.

Reps, John W. *The Making of Urban America: A History of City Planning in the United States*. Princeton, NJ: Princeton University Press, 1965.

Schaffer, Daniel. *Garden Cities for America: The Radburn Experience*. Philadelphia: Temple University Press, 1982.

Scott, Mel. *American City Planning since 1890*. Berkeley: University of California Press, 1969.

Stein, Clarence S. *Toward New Towns for America*. Cambridge: MIT Press, 1966.

Sutcliffe, Anthony, ed. *The Rise of Modern Urban Planning: 1800–1914*. New York: St. Martin's Press, 1980.

Teaford, Jon C. *City and Suburb: The Political Fragmentation of Metropolitan Areas, 1850–1970*. Baltimore: Johns Hopkins University Press, 1979.

_____. *The Twentieth-Century American City: Problem, Promise, and Reality*. Baltimore: Johns Hopkins University Press, 1986.

Toll, Seymour I. *Zoned American*. New York: Grossman, 1969.

Tunnard, Christopher. *The Modern American City*. Princeton, NJ: Van Nostrand, 1968.

Tunnard, Christopher, and Henry Hope Reed. *American Skyline: The Growth and Form of Our Cities and Towns*. New York: Houghton, 1955.

Wilson, James Q., ed. *Urban Renewal: The Record and the Controversy*. Cambridge: MIT Press, 1966.

Wilson, William H. *Coming of Age: Urban America, 1915–1945*. New York: John Wiley & Sons, 1974.

3 General development plans

Altshuler, Alan. "The Goals of Comprehensive Planning." *Journal of the American Institute of Planners* 21 (August 1965): 186–95.

American Law Institute. *A Model Land Development Code*. Complete text, adopted by the American Law Institute 21 May 1975, with Reporter's Commentary. Philadelphia, 1976.

Branch, Melville C. *Comprehensive Planning: General Theory and Principles*. Pacific Palisades, CA: Palisades Publishers, 1983.

Bryson, John M., and Robert C. Einsweiler, eds. "Symposium: Strategic Planning." *Journal of the American Planning Association* 53 (Winter 1987): 6–97.

Chapin, F. Stuart, Jr., and Edward J. Kaiser. *Urban Land Use Planning*. 3d ed. Champaign: University of Illinois Press, 1979.

Godschalk, David R., David J. Brower, Larry D. McBennett, and Barbara A. Vestal. *Constitutional Issues of Growth Management*. Chicago: American Planning Association, 1979.

Jacobs, Allan B. *Making City Planning Work*. Chicago: American Planning Association, 1980.

Kent, T. J., Jr. *The Urban General Plan*. San Francisco: Chandler Publishing Co., 1964.

Livingston, Lawrence, Jr. "California General Plan Requirements: A New Weapon for Challenging Local Government Land Use and Development Decisions." *Urban Lawyer* 16 (Winter 1984): 1–15).

Perloff, Harvey S. *Planning for the Post-Industrial City*. Chicago: American Planning Association, 1980.

Richard L. Ragatz Associates. *Comprehensive Plan Monitoring: Guidelines and Resources for Oregon Communities*. Salem, OR: Department of Conservation and Development, 1983.

Roeseler, W. G. *Successful American Urban Plans*. Lexington, MA: Lexington Books, 1982.

4   District planning

California Office of Planning and Research. *Economic Practices Manual*. Sacramento, CA, 1978.

_____. *General Plan Guidelines*. Sacramento, CA, 1982.

_____. *Specific Plans: How Some California Communities Use Them*. Sacramento, CA, April 1981.

Hagman, Donald. *Urban Planning and Land Development Control Laws*. St. Paul, MN: West Publishing Co., 1971.

Sedway/Cooke. *Downtown San Francisco Planning Program: Phase I*. San Francisco: San Francisco City Planning Department, 1979.

Sedway/Cooke. *Land and the Environment: Planning in California Today*. William Kaufmann, Publishers, 1975.

Slater, David C. *Management of Local Planning*. Washington, DC: International City Management Association, 1984.

Smith, Herbert. *The Citizen's Guide to Planning*. Chicago: American Planning Association, 1974.

ULI–the Urban Land Institute. *Downtown Development*. Washington, DC, 1980.

5   Environmental land use planning

Adams, Thomas. *Rural Planning and Development: A Study of Rural Conditions and Problems in Canada*. Ottawa: Commission of Conservation, 1917.

Bailey, L. H. *The Country Life Movement in the United States*. New York: Macmillan, 1915.

DiNovo, Frank, and Martin Jaffe. *Local Groundwater Protection: Midwest Region*. Chicago: American Planning Association, 1984.

Graham, Edward H., Jr. *Natural Principles of Land Use*. New York: Greenwood Press, 1944.

Hopkins, Lewis D. "Methods of Generating Land Suitability Maps: A Comparative Evaluation." *Journal of the American Institute of Planners* 43, no. 4 (1977): 386–400.

Hopkins, Lewis D., et al. *Environmental Impact Statements: A Handbook for Writers and Reviewers*. IIEQ no. 73-8. Illinois Institute for Environmental Quality, report no. PB 226 276/AS. Springfield, VA: National Technical Information Service, 1973.

Howard, Ebenezer. *Garden Cities of To-Morrow*. Reprint. F. J. Osborn, ed. Cambridge: MIT Press, 1965. (Original published 1898.)

Juneja, Narendra. *Medford: Performance Requirements for the Maintenance of Social Values Represented by the Natural Environment of Medford Township, New Jersey*. Philadelphia: University of Pennsylvania, Department of Landscape Architecture and Regional Planning, Center for Ecological Research in Planning and Design, 1974.

Kockelman, William J. "Some Techniques for Reducing Landslide Hazards." *Bulletin of the Association of Engineering Geologists* 23, no. 1 (1986): 29–52.

Leopold, L. B., et al. *A Procedure for Evaluating Environmental Impact*. Geological Survey Circular no. 645. Washington, DC: U.S. Geological Survey, 1971.

Marsh, George Perkins. *The Earth as Modified by Human Action*. New York: Arno

Press, 1970. (Original published in 1874 as *Man and Nature*.)

Marsh, William M. *Landscape Planning: Environmental Applications*. Menlo Park, CA: Addison-Wesley Publishing Co., 1983.

McHarg, Ian L. *Design with Nature*. Garden City, NY: Doubleday, 1971.

Powell, John Wesley. *Report on the Lands of the Arid Region of the United States*. Reprint. Wallace Stegner, ed. Cambridge, MA: Belknap Press, 1962.

Robinson, G. D., and Andrew M. Spieker, eds. *"Nature To Be Commanded. . . ."* Earth-Science Maps Applied to Land and Water Management. Geological Survey Professional Paper 950. Washington, DC: U.S. Government Printing Office, 1978.

Shopley, J. B., and R. F. Fuggle. "A Comprehensive Review of Current Environmental Impact Assessment Methods and Techniques." *Journal of Environmental Management* 18 (1984): 25–47.

Spirn, Ann Whiston. *Granite Gardens: Urban Nature and Human Design*. New York: Basic Books, Harper Colophon Books, 1984.

Steiner, Frederick. "Resource Suitability: Methods of Analysis." *Environmental Management* 7, no. 5 (1983): 401–420.

Steiner, Frederick, and Kenneth Brooks. "Ecological Planning: A Review." *Environmental Management* 5, no. 6 (1981): 495–505.

Thurow, Charles, William Toner, and Duncan Erley. *Performance Controls for Sensitive Lands: A Practical Guide for Local Administrators*. Planning Advisory Service Report no. 307/308. Chicago: American Planning Association, 1975.

Toner, William. "Ag Zoning Gets Serious." *Planning* 50, no. 12 (1984): 19–24.

_____. "Land Use Controls: Agricultural Zoning." In Robert E. Coughlin et al., eds. *National Agricultural Lands Study. The Protection of Farmland: A Reference Guidebook for State and Local Governments*. Washington, DC: U.S. Government Printing Office, 1981.

U.S. Environmental Protection Agency. *Chemical Emergency Preparedness Program: Interim Guidance*. Draft. Washington, DC, 1985.

Waugh, Frank A. *Rural Improvement*. New York: Orange Judd Co., 1914.

_____. *Country Planning: An Outline of Principles and Methods*. New York: Harcourt, Brace & Co., 1924.

6 Transportation planning

Aldridge, Meryl. *The British New Towns. A Programme without a Policy*. London: Routledge & Kegan Paul, 1979.

Altshuler, Alan, with James P. Womack and John R. Pucher. *The Urban Transportation System: Politics and Policy Innovation*. Cambridge: MIT Press, 1979.

Black, John. *Urban Transport Planning: Theory and Practice*. Baltimore: Johns Hopkins University Press, 1981.

Bly, P. H. "Effects of the Recession on Travel Expenditure and Travel Patterns." In G. R. M. Jansen et al., *Transportation and Mobility in an Era of Transition*. New York: Elsevier North-Holland Publishing Co., 1985, 15–36.

Institute of Transportation Engineers. *Trip Generation*. An ITE Information Report. Arlington, VA, 1983.

Jones, David. *Urban Transit Policy: An Economic and Political History*. Englewood Cliffs, NJ: Prentice-Hall, 1985.

Kirby, Ronald F., et al. *Paratransit: Neglected Options for Urban Mobility*. Washington, DC: The Urban Institute, 1975.

Lave, Charles A., ed. *Urban Transit: The Private Challenge to Public Transportation*. Cambridge, MA: Ballinger Publishing Co., 1985.

Manheim, Marvin. *Fundamentals of Transportation Systems Analysis*, Cambridge: MIT Press, 1979.

McDowell, Bruce D. "Role of Metropolitan Planning Organizations in the 1980s." *Transportation Research Record* 1045 (1985): 41–44.

Meyer, John, and Jose Gomez-Ibanez. *Autos, Transit, and Cities*. Cambridge: Harvard University Press, 1981.

Meyer, John, John Kain, and Martin Wohl. *The Urban Transportation Problem*. Cambridge: Harvard University Press, 1965.

Meyer, Michael D., and Eric J. Miller. *Urban Transportation Planning: A Decision-Oriented Approach*. New York: McGraw-Hill, 1984.

Morlok, Edward. *Introduction to Transportation Engineering and Planning*. New York: McGraw-Hill, 1978.

National Cooperative Highway Research Program. *Quick-Response Urban Travel Estimation Techniques and Transferable Parameters: A User's Guide*. NCHRP Report no. 187. Washington, DC: Transportation Research Board, 1978.

Pushkarev, Boris S., and Jeffrey M. Zupan. *Public Transportation and Land Use*. New York: A Regional Plan Association Book, 1977.

Teal, Roger. "Transit Contracting—The State of the Industry." *PTI Journal* 1 (May/June 1987): 6–9, 18.

Transportation Research Board. *Highway Capacity Manual*. Special Report no. 209. Washington, DC: National Research Council, 1985.

U.S. Department of Housing and Urban Development. Office of International Affairs. *French National Urban Policy and the Paris Region New Towns: The Search for Community*. Washington, DC, April 1980.

Warner, Sam Bass. *Streetcar Suburbs: The Process of Growth in Boston 1870–1900*. Cambridge: Harvard University Press and MIT Press, 1962.

Krier, Rob. *Urban Space*. New York: Rizzoli, 1979.

Lynch, Kevin. *A Theory of Good City Form*. Cambridge: MIT Press, 1981.

Lynch, Kevin, and Gary Hack. *Site Planning*. 3d ed. Cambridge: MIT Press, 1984.

McHarg, Ian. *Design with Nature*. Garden City, NY: Doubleday, 1971.

Rowe, Colin, and Fred Koetter. *Collage City*. Cambridge: MIT Press, 1978.

Shirvani, Hamid. *Urban Design Review: A Guide for Planners*. Chicago: American Planning Association, 1981.

Spirn, Anne Whiston. *Granite Gardens: Urban Nature and Human Design*. New York: Basic Books, Harper Colophon Books, 1984.

Tunnard, Christopher, and Boris Pushkarev. *Man-Made America: Chaos or Control?* New Haven: Yale University Press, 1963; New York: Harmony Books, 1981.

Watkin, David. *A History of Western Architecture*. New York: Thames Hudson, 1986.

Whyte, William H. *The Social Life of Small Urban Spaces*. Washington, DC: The Conservation Foundation, 1980.

7 Urban design

Alexander, Christopher. *The Timeless Way of Building*. New York: Oxford University Press, 1979.

Alexander, Christopher, Sara Ishikawa, and Murray Silverstein. *A Pattern Language: Towns, Buildings, Construction*. New York: Oxford University Press, 1977.

Barnett, Jonathan. *The Elusive City: Five Centuries of Design, Ambition, and Miscalculation*. New York: Harper & Row, 1986.

———. *Introduction to Urban Design*. New York: Harper & Row, 1982.

Clay, Grady. *Close-Up: How to Read the American City*. New York: Praeger, 1973; Chicago: University of Chicago Press, 1980.

Girouard, Mark. *Cities and People: A Social and Architectural History*. New Haven: Yale University Press, 1985.

Hedman, Richard, with Andrew Jaszewski. *Fundamentals of Urban Design*. Chicago: American Planning Association, 1984.

Kostof, Spiro. *A History of Architecture: Settings and Rituals*. New York, Oxford University Press, 1985.

8 Land subdivision regulation

Bucks County Planning Commission. *Performance Streets: A Concept and Model Standards for Residential Streets*. Doylestown, PA, 1980.

De Chiara, Joseph, and Lee E. Koppelman. *Time-Saver Standards for Residential Development*. New York: McGraw-Hill, 1984.

———. *Time-Saver Standards for Site Planning*. New York: McGraw-Hill, 1984.

Freilich, Robert H., and Peter S. Levi. *Model Subdivision Regulations*. Chicago: American Society of Planning Officials, 1975.

Friedman, Stephen B. "Rural and Small Town Subdivision Regulations." In Judith Getzels and Charles Thurow, eds. *Rural and Small Town Planning*. Chicago: American Planning Association, 1979.

Green, Philip P., Jr. "Land Subdivision." In William I. Goodman and Eric C. Freund, eds. *Principles and Practice of Urban Planning*. Washington, DC: International City Management Association, 1968.

Hagman, Donald G., and Julian Conrad Juergensmeyer. *Urban Planning and Land Development Control Law*. 2d ed. St. Paul, MN: West Publishing Co., 1986.

Hershey, Stuart, and Carolyn Garmise. *Streamlining Local Regulations: A Handbook for Reducing Housing and Development Costs*. Management Information Service Special Report no. 11. Washington, DC: International City Management Association, 1983.

Institute of Transportation Engineers. *Recommended Guidelines for Subdivision Streets*. Washington, DC, 1984.

Kendig, Lane, with Susan Connor, Cranston Byrd, and Judy Heyman. *Performance Zoning*. Chicago: American Planning Association, 1980.

Lamont, William, Jr. "Subdivision Regulation and Land Conversion." In Frank S. So, Israel Stollman, Frank Beal, and David S. Arnold, eds. *The Practice of Local Government Planning*. Washington, DC: International City Management Association, 1979.

Mandelker, Daniel. *Land Use Law*. Charlottesville, VA: The Michie Co., 1982.

National Association of Home Builders. *Cost Effective Site Planning*. Rev. ed. Washington, DC, 1982.

————. *Land Development 2*. Washington, DC, 1981.

————. *Subdivision Regulation Handbook*. Washington, DC, 1978.

Porter, Douglas R., ed. *Growth Management: Keeping on Target?* Washington, DC: ULI–the Urban Land Institute, with the Lincoln Institute of Land Policy, 1986.

Sanders, Welford. *The Cluster Subdivision: A Cost-Effective Approach*. Planning Advisory Service Report no. 356. Chicago: American Planning Association, 1980.

Sanders, Welford, Judith Getzels, David Mosena, and JoAnn Butler. *Affordable Single-Family Housing: A Review of Development Standards*. Planning Advisory Service Report no. 385. Chicago: American Planning Association, 1984.

Sanders, Welford, and David Mosena. *Changing Development Standards for Affordable Housing*. Planning Advisory Service Report no. 371. Chicago: American Planning Association, 1982.

Seidel, Stephen R. *Housing Costs and Governmental Regulations: Confronting the Regulatory Maze*. New Brunswick, NJ: Rutgers University, Center for Urban Policy Research, 1978.

Snyder, Thomas P., and Michael A. Stegman. *Paying for Growth: Using Development Fees to Finance Infrastructure*. Washington, DC: ULI–the Urban Land Institute, 1986.

So, Frank S. "Public Works Planning." In Sam M. Cristofano and William S. Foster, eds., *Management of Local Public Works*. Washington, DC: International City Management Association, 1986.

So, Frank S., David Mosena, and Frank S. Bangs, Jr. *Planned Unit Development Ordinances*. Planning Advisory Service Report no. 291. Chicago: American Society of Planning Officials, 1973.

Soil Erosion and Sedimentation Control. Prepared by Beckett, Jackson, Raeder, Inc., Ann Arbor, for the Michigan Departments of Natural Resources, Agriculture, and State Highways and Transportation and the U.S. Soil Conservation Service. Reston, VA: Environmental Design Press, 1981. (Out of Print. Contact Beckett & Raeder, Inc., Ann Arbor, MI.)

Tourbier, Joachim, and Richard Westmacott. *Water Resource Protection Measures in Land Development, A Handbook*. Newark, DE: University of Delaware Water Resources Center, April 1974.

ULI–the Urban Land Institute. *Residential Development Handbook*. Washington, DC, 1978.

————. *Residential Erosion and Sediment Control: Objectives, Principles, and Design Considerations*. Washington, DC: Urban Land Institute, American Society of Civil Engineers, and National Association of Home Builders, 1978.

————. *Residential Storm Water Management: Objectives, Principles, and Design Considerations*. Washington, DC: Urban Land Institute, American Society of Civil Engineers, and National Association of Home Builders, 1975.

————. *Residential Streets: Objectives, Principles, and Design Considerations*. Washington, DC: Urban Land Institute, American Society of Civil Engineers, and National Association of Home Builders, 1974.

Vranicar, John, Welford Sanders, and David Mosena. *Streamlining Land Use Regulation: A Guidebook for Local Governments*. Prepared by the American Planning Association with the assistance of the Urban Land Institute for the U.S. Department of Housing and Urban Development. Washington, DC: U.S. Government Printing Office, 1980.

Weitz, Stevenson. *Affordable Housing: How Local Regulatory Improvements Can Help*. Prepared for the U.S. Department of Housing and Urban Development. Washington, DC: U.S. Government Printing Office, 1982.

Yearwood, Richard M. *Land Subdivision Regulation.* New York: Praeger, 1971.

9 Zoning

Anderson, Robert M. *American Law of Zoning.* 3d ed. Vol. 1. Rochester, NY: Lawyers Co-Operative Publishing Co., 1986.

Babcock, Richard F. *The Zoning Game: Municipal Practices and Policies.* Madison: University of Wisconsin Press, 1966.

Bassett, Edward M. *Zoning: The Laws, Administration, and Court Decisions During the First Twenty-Five Years.* New York: Russell Sage Foundation, 1936. Salem, NH: Ayer Co. Publishers, 1974.

Brower, David J., Candace Carraway, Thomas Pollard, and C. Luther Propst. *Managing Development in Small Towns.* Chicago: American Planning Association, 1984.

Burchell, Robert W., and James W. Hughes. *Planned Unit Development: New Communities American Style.* New Brunswick, NJ: Rutgers University, Center for Urban Policy Research, 1972.

Burrows, Lawrence B. *Growth Management: Issues, Techniques and Policy Implications.* New Brunswick, NJ: Rutgers University, Center for Urban Policy Research, 1978.

De Chiara, Joseph, and Lee E. Koppelman. *Site Planning Standards.* New York: McGraw-Hill, 1978.

Department of Transportation and Federal Aviation Administration. *Airport—Land Use Compatibility Planning.* Washington, DC: U.S. Government Printing Office, 1977.

Godschalk, David R., David J. Brower, Larry D. McBennett, and Barbara A. Vestal. *Constitutional Issues of Growth Management.* Chicago: American Society of Planning Officials, 1979.

Gruen, Victor. *The Heart of Our Cities: The Urban Crisis: Diagnosis and Cure.* New York: Simon & Schuster, 1964.

Hendler, Bruce. *Caring for the Land: Environmental Principles for Site Design and Review.* Chicago: American Society of Planning Officials, 1977.

Howard, Ebenezer. *Garden Cities of To-Morrow.* Reprint. F. J. Osborn, ed. Cambridge: MIT Press. (Original published 1898.)

Jacobs, Jane. *The Death and Life of Great American Cities.* New York: Random House, 1961.

Mandelker, Daniel R. *The Zoning Dilemma.* Indianapolis, IN: Bobbs-Merrill Co., 1971.

McHarg, Ian L. *Design with Nature.* Garden City, NY: Doubleday, 1969.

Nelson, Robert H. *Zoning and Property Rights: An Analysis of the American System of Land-Use Regulation.* Cambridge: MIT Press, 1977.

Schaenman, Philip S., and Thomas Muller. *Measuring Impacts of Land Develoment: An Initial Approach.* Washington, DC: The Urban Institute, 1974.

Shelton, David C., and Dick Prouty. *Nature's Building Codes: Geology and Construction in Colorado.* Special Publication for the Colorado Department of Natural Resources, 1979.

Thurow, Charles, William Toner, and Duncan Erley. *Performance Controls for Sensitive Lands: A Practical Guide for Local Administrators.* Planning Advisory Service Report no. 307/308. Chicago: American Society of Planning Officials, 1975.

Venturi, Robert, Denise Scott Brown, and Steven Izenour. *Learning from Las Vegas.* Rev. ed. Cambridge: MIT Press, 1977.

Williams, Norman, Jr. *American Land Planning Law: Land Use and the Police Power.* Vol. 1. Wilmette, IL: Callaghan & Co., 1974.

10 Economic development

Ady, Robert M. "Shifting Factors in Plant Location." *Industrial Development* (November/December 1981): 13–17.

The AmeriTrust/SRI. *Choosing a Future.* Cleveland: The AmeriTrust Co., 1984.

An Assessment of U.S. Competitiveness in High Technology Industries. Washington, DC: U.S. Department of Commerce, International Trade Commission, February 1983.

Beynon, Roger. "The High Tech Race: Not to the Penny Pincher." *Texas Business* (June 1985): 14.

Biermann, Wallace W. "The Validity of Business Climate Rankings: A Test." *Industrial Development* (March/April 1984): 17, 23–25.

Birch, D. L. *The Job Generation Process.* Cambridge: Massachusetts Institute of Technology, MIT Program on Neighborhood and Regional Change, 1979.

Bluestone, Barry, and Bennet Harrison. *The Deindustrialization of America: Plant Closings, Community Abandonment, and the*

Dismantling of Basic Industry. New York: Basic Books, 1982.

Boyer, Richard, and David Savageau. *Places Rated Almanac: Your Guide to Finding the Best Places to Live in America*. Chicago: Rand McNally, 1985.

Boyle, Ross M. "New Directions for Economic Development in an Information Based Economy," *Economic Development Review* (Winter 1984): 57–64.

Burns, James J. "International Siting Priorities for a High Technology Firm." *Industrial Development* (May/June 1984): 10–12.

Directory of Incentives for Business Investment and Development in the United States: A State-by-State Guide. 2d ed. Washington, DC: The Urban Institute, 1986.

Friedman, Stephen B. *Assessing Public Incentives for Private Development*. Management Information Service Report, vol. 13, no. 12. Washington, DC: International City Management Association, December 1981. (Available in the city manager's office of many communities.)

Grant, Alexander, & Co. *General Manufacturing Business Climates of the Forty-Eight Contiguous States of America*. Chicago: Alexander Grant & Co., Annual.

A Guide to Industrial Site Selection. Washington, DC: Society of Industrial Realtors and The National Association of Industrial and Office Parks, 1979.

Hack, George D. "The Plant Location Decision-Making Process." *Industrial Development* (September/October 1984): 31–33.

Harding, Charles F. "Business Climate Studies: How Useful Are They?" *Industrial Development* (January/February 1983): 22–23.

Industrial Real Estate. 4th ed. Washington, DC: Society of Industrial Realtors Educational Fund, 1984.

Joint Economic Committee 1982. *Location of High Technology Firms and Regional Economic Development*. Washington, DC: U.S. Government Printing Office, 1982.

Latham, William R., III, and Paul J. Hockersmith. "Investor-Owned Electric Utilities as Information Sources." *Industrial Development* (March/April 1984): 30–36.

Leonhardt, Derr. "Environmental Aspects of the Site Location Decision." *Industrial Development* (July/August 1984), 23–27.

Leontief, Wassily, and Faye Duchin. *The Impacts of Automation on Employment: 1963–2000*. New York: New York University, Institute for Economic Analysis, 1984.

MacDonald, Douglas. "Incubator Fever." *New England Business* (September 2, 1985): 62–70.

MacDonnell, Arthur. "How Silicon Valley Lures 128 Engineers with Sports, Arts." *New England Business* (May 21, 1984): 45.

Markensen, Ann, et al. *High Tech America*. Boston: Allen & Unwin, 1986.

Real Estate Research Corporation. *Emerging Trends in Real Estate*. Chicago, Annual.

Reich, Robert. *The Next American Frontier*. New York: Times Books, 1983.

Ryans, John K., Jr., and William L. Shanklin. *Guide to Marketing for Economic Development: Competing in America's Second Civil War*. Columbus, OH: Publishing Horizons, 1986.

Snyder, David Pearce, and Gregg Edwards. *Future Forces*. Washington, DC: Foundation of the American Society of Association Executives, 1984.

Sternlieb, George, and James W. Hughes. *Shopping Centers: USA*. New Brunswick, NJ: Rutgers University, Center for Urban Policy Research, 1981.

ULI–the Urban Land Institute. Community Builders Handbook Series: *Downtown Development*, 1980; *Industrial Development*, 1978; *Office Development*, 1982; *Recreational Development*, 1981; *Residential Development*, 1980; *Shopping Center Development*, 2d ed., 1985. Washington, DC.

———. *Development Review and Outlook*. Washington, DC, Annual.

———. *Downtown Retail Development*. Washington, DC, 1983.

U.S. Department of Commerce. *U.S. Industrial Outlook*. Washington, DC: U.S. Government Printing Office, Annual.

---

11 Social aspects of physical planning

American Institute of Planners. *The Social Responsibility of the Planner*. Washington, DC, 1973.

Bachrach, Leona L., ed. *New Directions in Mental Health Services. Vol. 17: Deinstitutionalization*. San Francisco: Jossey-Bass, March 1983.

Birch, Eugenie Ladner, ed. *The Unsheltered Woman: Women and Housing in the 80's*. New Brunswick, NJ: Rutgers University Center for Urban Policy Research, 1985.

Burdge, Rabel, and Sue Johnson. "Socio-cultural Aspects of the Effects of Resource Development." In James McEvoy III and Thomas Dietz, eds. *Handbook for Environmental Planning: The Social Consequences of Environmental Change*. New York: John Wiley & Sons, 1977, 241–278.

Christensen, Kathleen. *Social Impacts of Land Development*. Washington, DC: The Urban Institute, 1976.

Davidoff, Paul. "Advocacy and Pluralism in Planning." *Journal of the American Institute of Planners* 31 (September 1965): 311–328.

Dear, Michael J., and S. Martin Taylor. *Not on Our Street: Community Attitudes to Mental Health Care*. London: Pion Ltd., 1982.

Finsterbusch, Kurt. *Understanding Social Impacts: Assessing the Effects of Public Projects*. Monograph no. 110. Beverly Hills, CA: Sage Library of Social Research, 1980.

Finsterbusch, Kurt, and Charles P. Wolf. *Methodology of Social Impact Assessment*. 2d ed. New York: Van Nostrand Reinhold, 1981.

Forester, John. "Critical Theory and Planning Practice." *Journal of the American Planning Association* 46 (July 1980): 275–286.

Fried, Marc. "Grieving for a Lost Home: Psychological Costs of Relocation." In Leonard J. Duhl, ed. *The Urban Condition*. New York: Basic Books, 1963.

Gilmore, John. "Boomtowns May Hinder Energy Resource Development." *Science* 191 (February 13, 1976): 535–540.

Kaufman, Jerome. "An Approach to Planning for Women." In Karen Hapgood and Judith Getzels, eds. *Planning, Women, and Change*. Planning Advisory Report no. 301. Chicago: American Society of Planning Officials, 1974.

Krumholz, Norman, Janice Cogger, and John Linner. "The Cleveland Policy Planning Report." *Journal of the American Institute of Planners* 41 (September 1975): 298–304.

League of California Cities. *Social Element Planning in California*. Sacramento, CA, January 1977.

Murdock, Steve H., and F. Larry Leistritz. *Energy Development in the Western United States: Impact on Rural Areas*. New York: Praeger, 1979.

Peters, James. "Job Targeting: What Planners Can Do." *Planning* 49 (October 1983): 26–30.

Schill, Michael H., and Richard P. Nathan. *Revitalizing America's Cities: Neighborhood Reinvestment and Displacement*. Albany: State University of New York Press, 1983.

Shifman, Carole. *Increasing Housing Opportunities for the Elderly*. Planning Advisory Service Report no. 381. Chicago: American Planning Association, 1983.

Wolch, Jennifer R., and Stuart A. Gabriel. "Dismantling the Community-Based Human Service System." *Journal of the American Planning Association* 51 (Winter 1985): 53–62.

Wolpert, Julian. "Social Planning and the Mentally and Physically Handicapped: The Growing 'Special Service' Populations." In Robert W. Burchell and George Sternlieb, eds. *Planning Theory in the Nineteen Eighties: A Search for Future Directions*. New Brunswick, NJ: Rutgers University, Center for Urban Policy Research, 1978, 95–111.

12   Planning for housing

American Institute of Planners. *Housing Planning*. Washington, DC, 1971.

Florida, Richard, ed. *Housing and the New Financial Markets*. New Brunswick, NJ: Rutgers University, Center for Urban Policy Research, 1986.

Hammer, Greene, Siler, Associates. *Regional Housing Planning: A Technical Guide*. Washington, DC: American Institute of Planners, 1972.

Hare, Patrick, with Susan Conner and Dwight Merriam. *Accessory Apartments: Using Surplus Space in Single-Family Houses*. Planning Advisory Service Report no. 365. Chicago: American Planning Association, 1981.

ICF Incorporated. *Housing Needs in the Eighties*. Washington, DC: Council of State Housing Agencies, 1981.

———. *State Housing Finance Agencies in the Seventies*. Washington, DC: Council of State Housing Agencies, 1981.

Johnson, M. Bruce, ed. *Resolving the Housing Crisis: Government Policy, Decontrol and the Public Interest*. Cambridge, MA: Ballinger Publishing Co. for the Pacific Institute for Public Policy Research, 1982.

Land Design/Research, Inc. *Planning for Housing Development: Alternatives for Better Environments*. Washington, DC: National Association of Home Builders, 1980.

Mitchell, J. Paul, ed. *Federal Housing Policy and Programs*. New Brunswick, NJ: Rutgers

University, Center for Urban Policy Research, 1985.

National Commission on Urban Problems. *Building the American City*. Washington, DC: U.S. Government Printing Office, 1968.

Nenno, Mary K., and Paul C. Brophy, eds. *Housing and Local Government*. Washington, DC: International City Management Association, 1982.

Nicholas, James C., et al. *State Regulation: Housing Prices*. New Brunswick, NJ: Rutgers University, Center for Urban Policy Research, 1982.

The President's Commission on Housing. *The Report of the President's Commission on Housing*. Washington, DC: U.S. Government Printing Office, 1982.

President's Committee on Urban Housing. *A Decent Home*. Washington, DC: U.S. Government Printing Office, 1969.

Roudebush, Janice, and Leslie J. Wells. *Low and Moderate-Income Housing. Part I: Increasing the Supply and Accessibility*. Planning Advisory Service Report no. 350. Chicago: American Planning Association, 1980.

_____. *Low and Moderate-Income Housing. Part II: Conserving What We Have*. Planning Advisory Service Report no. 351. Chicago: American Planning Association, 1980.

Sanders, Welford, Judith Getzels, David Mosena, and JoAnn Butler. *Affordable Single-Family Housing: A Review of Development Standards*. Planning Advisory Report no. 385. Chicago: American Planning Association, 1984.

Shifman, Carole. *Increasing Housing Opportunities for the Elderly*. Planning Advisory Service Report no. 381. Chicago: American Planning Association, 1983.

Sidor, John. *Affordable Housing and Infrastructure: The State Role*. Washington, DC: Council of State Community Affairs Agencies, 1984.

_____. *Affordable Housing, Land Supply and Land Development*. Washington, DC: Council of State Community Affairs Agencies, 1983.

Sternlieb, George, and James W. Hughes, eds. *America's Housing: Prospects and Problems*. New Brunswick, NJ: Rutgers University, Center for Urban Policy Research, 1980.

Tick, Marvin J., and John Sidor. *State Actions to Promote Affordable Housing*. Washington, DC: Council of State Community Affairs Agencies, 1982.

U.S. Bureau of the Census, *U.S. Census of Housing*.

_____. *Annual Housing Survey* (since 1983, *American Housing Survey*).

_____. *Construction Reports*, C-20 Series.

U.S. Department of Housing and Urban Development. *Developing a Local Housing Strategy: A Guidebook for Local Government*. Washington, DC: U.S. Government Printing Office, 1978.

_____. *FHA Techniques of Housing Market Analysis*. Washington, DC: U.S. Government Printing Office, 1970.

_____. *Housing in the Seventies*. Washington, DC: U.S. Government Printing Office, 1974.

Weicher, John C., Kevin E. Villani, and Elizabeth A. Roistacher, eds. *Rental Housing: Is There a Crisis?* Washington, DC: The Urban Institute, 1981.

13 Planning agency management

Bair, Frederick H. *The Zoning Board Manual*. Chicago: American Planning Association, 1984.

Branch, Melville C. *Continuous City Planning: Integrating Municipal Management and City Planning*. New York: John Wiley & Sons, 1981.

Catanese, Anthony James. *Planners and Local Politics: Impossible Dreams*. Beverly Hills, CA: Sage Publications, 1974.

Jacobs, Allan B. *Making City Planning Work*. Chicago: American Planning Association, 1978.

Jones, Warren W., and Albert Solnit. *What Do I Do Next? A Manual for People Just Entering Government Service*. Chicago: American Planning Association, 1980.

Lucy, William. *Close to Power: Setting Priorities with Elected Officials*. Chicago: American Planning Association, 1988.

McClendon, Bruce, and Ray Quay. *Mastering Change: Winning Strategies for Effective City Planning*. Chicago: American Planning Association, 1988.

Slater, David C. *Management of Local Planning*. Washington, DC: International City Management Association, 1984.

Solnit, Albert. *The Job of the Planning Commissioner*. Chicago: American Planning Association, 1987.

Steiner, George A. *Strategic Planning: What Every Manager Must Know*. New York: Free Press, 1979.

Vranicar, John, Welford Sanders, and David Mosena. *Streamlining Land Use Regulation: A Guidebook for Local Governments*. Chicago: American Planning Association, 1980.

Walker, Robert A. *The Planning Function in Local Government*. 2d ed. Chicago: University of Chicago Press, 1950.

Whetten, David A., and Kim S. Cameron. *Developing Management Skills*. Glenview, IL: Scott, Foresman & Co., 1984.

Zucker, Paul C. *The Management Idea Book*. San Diego: West Coast Publishers, 1983.

14   Finance and budgeting

American Society of Planning Officials. *Local Capital Improvements and Development Management: Literature Synthesis*. Washington, DC: U.S. Department of Housing and Urban Development, 1977.

Aronson, J. Richard, and Eli Schwartz, eds. *Management Policies in Local Government Finance*. 3d ed. Washington, DC: International City Management Association, 1987.

Bamberger, Rita J., William A. Blazar, and George E. Peterson. *Infrastructure Support for Economic Development*. Planning Advisory Service Report no. 390. Chicago: American Planning Association, 1985.

Burchell, Robert W., and David Listokin. *The Fiscal Impact Handbook: Estimating Local Costs and Revenues of Land Development*. New Brunswick, NJ: Rutgers University, Center for Urban Policy Research, 1978.

Golembiewski, Robert T., ed. *Public Budgeting and Finance: Behavioral, Theoretical and Technical Aspects*. 3d ed. New York: Marcel Dekker, 1983.

Hatry, Harry P., Annie P. Millar, and James H. Evans. *Guide to Setting Priorities for Capital Investment*. Washington, DC: The Urban Institute, 1984.

Moak, Lennox L., and Albert M. Hillhouse. *Concepts and Practices in Local Government Finance*. Chicago: Municipal Finance Officers Association, 1975.

Petersen, John E., and Ronald Forbes. *Innovative Capital Financing*. Planning Advisory Service Report no. 392. Chicago: American Planning Association, 1985.

Peterson, George E., Rita Bamberger, Nancy Humphrey, and Kenneth M. Steil. *Guide to Financing the Capital Budget and Maintenance Plan. Vol. 6*. Washington, DC: The Urban Institute, 1984.

Snyder, James C. *Fiscal Management and Planning in Local Government*. Lexington, MA: Lexington Books, 1977.

Steiss, Alan Walter. *Local Government Finance: Capital Facilities Planning and Debt Administration in Local Government*. Lexington, MA: Lexington Books, 1975.

Wildavsky, Aaron. *Budgeting: A Comparative Theory of Budgetary Processes*. Boston: Little, Brown & Co., 1975.

_____. *The Politics of the Budgetary Process*. 4th ed. Boston: Little, Brown & Co., 1984.

15   Information for planning

Babbie, Earl R. *Survey Research Methods: A Cookbook and Other Fables*. Belmont, CA: Wadsworth Publishing Co., 1973.

Blalock, Hubert M., Jr. *Social Statistics*. Revised 2d ed. New York: McGraw-Hill, 1979.

Dandekar, Hemalata C. *The Planner's Use of Information: Techniques for Collection, Organization, and Communication*. Stroudsburg, PA: Hutchinson Ross, 1982.

Davis, James A. *Elementary Survey Analysis*. Englewood Cliffs, NJ: Prentice-Hall, 1971.

Dexter, Lewis Anthony. *Elite and Specialized Interviewing: Handbooks for Research in Political Behavior*. Evanston, IL: Northwestern University Press, 1970.

Dillman, Don A. *Mail and Telephone Surveys: The Total Design Method*. New York: John Wiley & Sons, 1978.

Dixon, Wilfred J., and Frank J. Massey, Jr. *Introduction to Statistical Analysis*. 4th ed. New York: McGraw-Hill, 1983.

Farley, William B., and Frederick Mosteller, eds. *Statistics and Public Policy*. Reading, MA: Addison-Wesley, 1977.

Hoaglin, David C., Richard J. Light, Bucknam McPeek, Frederick Mosteller, and Michael A. Stoto. *Data for Decisions: Information Strategies for Policymakers*. Cambridge, MA: Abt Associates, 1982.

Hughes, Connie O., and Donald A. Krueckeberg. "Basic Studies for State and Regional Planning." In Frank S. So, Irving Hand, and Bruce D. McDowell, eds. *The Practice of State and Regional Planning*. Chicago: American Planning Association, 1986.

Hyman, Herbert. *Interviewing in Social Research*. Chicago: University of Chicago Press, 1975.

Kish, Leslie. *Survey Sampling*. New York: John Wiley & Sons, 1965.

Krueckeberg, Donald A., and Arthur L. Silvers. *Urban Planning Analysis: Methods and Models.* New York: John Wiley & Sons, 1974.

Murphy, Jerome T. *Getting the Facts: A Fieldwork Guide for Evaluators and Policy Analysts.* Santa Monica, CA: Goodyear Publishing Co., 1980.

Patton, Carl V., and David S. Sawicki. *Basic Methods of Policy Analysis and Planning.* Englewood Cliffs, NJ: Prentice-Hall, 1986.

Spear, Mary Eleanor. *Charting Statistics.* New York: McGraw-Hill, 1952.

Tanur, Judith M., ed. *Statistics: A Guide to the Unknown.* 2d ed. San Francisco: Holden-Day, 1978.

Tufte, Edward R. *The Visual Display of Quantitative Information.* Chesire, CT: Graphics Press, 1983.

Webb, Eugene J., Donald F. Campbell, Richard D. Schwartz, and Lee Sechrest. *Unobtrusive Measures: Nonreactive Research in the Social Sciences.* Chicago: Rand McNally, 1966.

16   The values of the planner

Bair, Frederick H., Jr., and Richard Hedman. *And on the Eighth Day.* Chicago: American Society of Planning Officials, 1967.

Bolan, Richard S., and Ronald Nuttall. *Urban Planning and Politics.* Lexington, MA: Lexington Books, 1974.

Braybrooke, David, and Charles E. Lindblom. *A Strategy of Decision: Policy Evaluation as a Social Process.* New York: The Free Press of Glencoe, 1963.

Davidoff, Paul, and Thomas A. Reiner. "A Choice Theory of Planning." *Journal of the American Institute of Planners* 28 (May 1962): 103–15.

Harris, Britton. "The Limits of Science and Humanism in Planning." *Journal of the American Institute of Planners* 33 (September 1967): 324–35.

Hiltner, Seward. "Planning as a Profession." *Journal of the American Institute of Planners* 23 (Fall 1957): 162–67.

Marcuse, Peter. "Professional Ethics and Beyond: Values in Planning." *Journal of the American Institute of Planners* 42 (July 1976): 264–74.

Meyerson, Martin. "Building the Middle-Range Bridge for Comprehensive Planning." *Journal of the American Institute of Planners* 22 (Spring 1956): 58–64.

Rondinelli, Dennis. *Urban and Regional Development Planning.* Ithaca, NY: Cornell University Press, 1975.

List of contributors

Persons who have contributed to this book are listed below with the editors first and the authors following in alphabetical order. A brief review of experience and training is presented for each author. Because many of the contributors have published extensively, books, monographs, articles, and other publications are omitted.

Frank S. So (Editor, and Chapters 1, 13, and 14) is deputy executive director of the American Planning Association. He has worked previously in local and areawide planning agencies. He is senior editor of the companion volume to this book, *The Practice of State and Regional Planning*, and of the 1979 edition of this book. He holds a bachelor's degree in sociology from Youngstown State University and a master's degree in city planning from Ohio State University.

Judith Getzels (Editor, and Chapter 1) is director of research at the American Planning Association (APA). She has designed and reported on APA research projects, including studies of capital improvements planning, public-private partnerships, and planning for the changing needs of women. She holds a bachelor's degree from Radcliffe College and master's degrees from the University of Chicago and the Illinois Institute of Technology.

Jonathan Barnett (Chapter 7) is director of the graduate program in urban design at the City College of New York and is a partner in the firm of Jonathan Barnett, Steven Kent Peterson & Associates. A graduate of Yale, the University of Cambridge, and the Yale School of Architecture, he was formerly director of urban design for New York City and has been a consultant to cities including Pittsburgh; Cleveland; Kansas City, Missouri; and Charleston, South Carolina. He has authored many books and articles about urban design. Dr. Barnett is a Fellow of the American Institute of Architects and a member of the American Institute of Certified Planners.

Frank Beal (Chapter 3) is general manager of corporate planning for Inland Steel Industries. He is responsible for long-range planning for the corporation. He was formerly director of the Illinois Institute of Natural Resources, a state agency responsible for conducting research and providing information on the energy resources and environmental and natural resources of the state. He has served as special assistant on energy and environmental affairs to the governor of Illinois, and he previously worked as deputy director of research for the American Society of Planning Officials. Mr. Beal holds a bachelor's degree from Antioch College and a master's degree in urban planning from the University of Illinois.

Alexander J. Darragh (Chapter 10) is manager of Economic Development Advisory Services in Laventhol & Horwath's Chicago office. He is currently serving as project director on a variety of economic development projects for utilities, chambers of commerce, city and county governments, private developers, and corporations. His areas of expertise include strategic planning, target industry analysis, and organizational development. Mr. Darragh is a member of the board of directors of the American Economic Development Council and speaks frequently at national and regional conferences on emerging trends in economic development. He holds bachelor's and master's degrees in urban economic geography from Queen's University in Kingston, Canada, and a master's degree in urban planning from Northwestern University in Evanston, Illinois. Prior to joining Laventhol & Horwath, Mr. Darragh was an assistant vice president at The Fantus Company.

Richard Ducker (Chapter 8) is an associate professor of public law and government at the Institute of Government at the University of North Carolina at Chapel Hill. He is also assistant director of the institute. Since coming to the institute in 1977, he has presented numerous workshops and programs for planners and board members and has consulted with state agencies and local governments in planning and land use matters. Dr. Ducker has a master's degree in urban planning from the University of Wisconsin and a law degree from the University of California at Los Angeles.

Stephen Belais Friedman (Chapter 10) is manager of Real Estate Advisory Services in Laventhol & Horwath's Chicago office. He is responsible for project conceptualization, market and financial feasibility analysis, and financing and implementation strategies for numerous development projects. He has worked extensively with cities and not-for-profit institutions on redevelopment strategies. He also has worked for numerous private developers in the economic planning of multiuse developments for downtowns and waterfronts. Mr. Friedman is vice chairman of the Chicago Metropolitan Section of the American Planning Association and is an officer of the Ely Chapter of Lambda Alpha International, the Honorary Land Economics Society. Mr. Friedman holds a bachelor's degree from Goddard College in Plainfield, Vermont, and a master's degree in urban and regional planning from the University of Wisconsin at Madison.

Laurence Conway Gerckens (Chapter 2) is emeritus professor of city and regional planning at Ohio State University, national historian for the American Institute of Certified Planners, and executive secretary and founder of the Society for American City and Regional Planning History. He holds certificates and degrees from the Cooper Union Art School, the University of Cincinnati, and Cornell University. Currently a freelance professor of American planning history, Mr. Gerckens recently taught full courses in planning history at Georgia Tech, the University of Toledo, the University of Michigan, and the University of Hawaii, and he has guest lectured at more than sixty universities in the United States and abroad. Mr. Gerckens is a member of the American Institute of Certified Planners.

Elizabeth L. Hollander (Chapter 3) is commissioner of planning for Chicago. Prior to her appointment as commissioner in 1983, she served as executive director of the Metropolitan Housing and Planning Council and as associate director of the Task Force on the Future of Illinois. She holds a bachelor's degree from Bryn Mawr College and has done graduate work at the Kennedy School of Government, Harvard University. She has also chaired several special committees concerned with housing and planning issues. She is a board member of the

Northeast/Midwest Institute and vice-president of Lambda Alpha International, the Honorary Land Economics Society.

Elizabeth Howe (Chapter 11) is associate professor of urban and regional planning at the University of Wisconsin at Madison, where she teaches social planning. She has been an active member of the Faye McBeath Institute on Aging and has done extensive research on the ethics and roles of urban planners. Her recent research has focused on homesharing by elderly people and on social development planning in Third World countries. Ms. Howe currently serves on the Madison Plan Commission.

Eric Damian Kelly (Chapter 9) is a lawyer and city planner with the firm of Kelly & Potter, P.C., which has offices in Pueblo, Colorado, and Santa Fe and Albuquerque, New Mexico. He holds a bachelor's degree with honors in political economy from Williams College and Juris Doctor and master of city planning degrees from the University of Pennsylvania. Since 1975 he has been a member of the adjunct faculty of the graduate planning program in the College of Architecture and Planning at the University of Colorado. Mr. Kelly has worked with local governments and private interests on zoning and land use issues in ten states, primarily in the Sun Belt.

Constance Lieder (Chapter 12) has been secretary of state planning in Maryland since 1979. She heads the cabinet department for comprehensive physical planning, capital budgeting, intergovernmental coordination, and socioeconomic data. She has been a university professor, has consulted nationally on housing and development, was president of the American Institute of Planners, and was a founding board member of Women Executives in State Government. Ms. Lieder holds a bachelor's degree from Wellesley College and graduate degrees from the University of Michigan, the Harvard Graduate School of Design, and Princeton University.

Carl V. Patton (Chapter 15) is professor of urban planning and dean of the School of Architecture and Urban Planning at the University of Wisconsin at Milwaukee. Previously he was head of the Department of Urban and Regional Planning at the University of Illinois at Urbana–Champaign, director of the department's Bureau of Urban and Regional Planning Research, an associate in the architecture and planning firm of Richardson, Severns, Scheeler, & Green, and a planner with Ladislas Segoe and Associates. He holds a bachelor of science degree in community planning from the University of Cincinnati, a master's degree in urban planning from the University of Illinois at Urbana–Champaign, and a Ph.D. in public policy from the University of California at Berkeley. Dr. Patton is a member of the American Institute of Certified Planners.

Leslie S. Pollock (Chapter 3) is a co-founder and principal consultant of Camiros, Ltd., a city planning consulting firm in Chicago. He has authored or contributed to the development of over two dozen comprehensive plans for communities of various sizes across the country. He has served as chair of the Wilmette, Illinois, plan commission and is currently a member of that community's village board of trustees. He holds bachelor of architecture and master of urban planning degrees from the University of Illinois at Urbana–Champaign, and he has taught planning at the University of Illinois and Loyola University of Chicago.

Jeffry D. Reckinger (Chapter 3) is a policy planner in the Department of Planning, Chicago. Previously he worked for the University of Illinois Center for Urban Economic Development and for federal and local governmental agencies. He holds a bachelor's degree from Harvard University and a master's degree from the University of Illinois at Chicago.

Sandra Rosenbloom (Chapter 6) is professor of planning and David Bruton Centennial Professor of Urban Design in the graduate program in community and regional planning at the University of Texas at Austin. She has worked extensively on the role of the private sector in financing and delivering transportation services and on the transportation problems of elderly and handicapped people. She holds a doctorate in political science from the University of California at Los Angeles.

Paul H. Sedway (Chapter 4) is a principal in Sedway Cooke Associates. His firm, founded in 1963, has offices in California, Texas, and Florida. Mr. Sedway holds bachelor's and law degrees from Harvard University and a master's degree in city planning from the University of California at Berkeley. He has taught planning at Berkeley for eighteen years and has served as vice-president of the American Institute of Planners and as a member of the board of the American Planning Association.

Israel Stollman (Chapter 16) is executive director of the American Planning Association and of the American Institute of Certified Planners. He was executive director of the American Society of Planning Officials prior to its consolidation with the American Institute of Planners, chairman of the Department of City and Regional Planning at the Ohio State University, and planning director in Youngstown, Ohio. He holds a bachelor's degree from the City College of New York and a master's degree in city planning from the Massachusetts Institute of Technology.

William Toner (Chapter 5) is University Professor of Public Administration at Governors State University in University Park, Illinois. He holds bachelor's and master's degrees from California State University at Fullerton and is currently pursuing his doctorate in geography at the University of Chicago. He has written extensively on rural planning, environmental planning, agricultural protection, and a host of other planning issues. He also has served as consultant to local, regional, and state governments as well as to the federal government. He was formerly on the board of directors of the American Planning Association.

Illustration and table credits

Chapter 1 Figure 1–1: Sam M. Cristofano and William S. Foster, eds. *Management of Local Public Works* (Washington, DC: International City Management Association, 1986), 72.

Chapter 2 Figure 2–1: Historic Urban Plans, Ithaca, NY; Figures 2–2 through 2–6: Courtesy of the Library of Congress; Figure 2–7: Courtesy of the J. C. Nichols Company, Kansas City, MO; Figures 2–8 through 2–10: Courtesy of the Library of Congress; Figure 2–11: Courtesy of the American Planning Association; Figure 2–12: Courtesy of Paul Farmer/Department of City Planning, City of Pittsburgh; Figure 2–13: Courtesy of the Greater Boston Convention & Visitors Bureau; Figure 2–14: Pier 17, photo by Joel Greenberg for South Street Seaport; Schermerhorn Row, courtesy of South Street Seaport, New York, NY.

Chapter 3 Figure 3–1: Left, David Macaulay, *City* (New York: Houghton Mifflin, 1974, 12, and London: William Collins, Ltd.); right, courtesy of Camiros, Ltd., Chicago; Figure 3–2: Top, Harold M. Mayer and Richard C. Wade, *Chicago: Growth of a Metropolis* (Chicago: University of Chicago Press, 1969), 276–277; bottom, photo by Kee Chang, Chicago Association of Commerce and Industry. Figure 3–3: Courtesy of Alameda City, CA; Figure 3–4: Courtesy of Camiros, Ltd., Chicago; Figure 3–5: Courtesy of Thomas & Means Associates, Alexandria, VA; Figure 3–6: International City Management Association, *Effective Supervisory Practices* (Washington, DC, 1978), 64; Figure 3–7: Courtesy of Thomas & Means Associates, Alexandria, VA.

Chapter 4 Figure 4–1: Adapted from Sedway Cooke Associates, *San Francisco Downtown Conservation Plan and Program, Phase 1 Summary* (San Francisco: Department of City Planning, November 1979); Figure 4–2: Sedway Cooke Associates, *Novato Downtown Plan and Program* (City of Novato, CA, 1970); Figure 4–3: Sedway Cooke Associates, *San Francisco Downtown Conservation Plan and Program,*

Phase 1 Summary (San Francisco: Department of City Planning, November 1979); Figure 4–4: Sedway Cooke Associates, *University of California at Berkeley Westside Study* (Berkeley: University of California, 1982); Figure 4–6: Sedway/Cooke, *The New Capital City for Alaska: General and Specific Plans* (San Francisco, 1982; prepared for the New Capital Site Planning Commission, Anchorage, AK); Figure 4–7: Sedway Cooke Associates, *Chula Vista Bayfront Plan and Program* (City of Chula Vista, CA, 1983).

Chapter 5 Figure 5–1: Courtesy of the U.S. Environmental Protection Agency; Figure 5–2: Courtesy of the U.S. Department of Agriculture; Figures 5–3, 5–4: Courtesy of Camiros, Ltd., Chicago; Figure 5–5: Adapted from Michigan Department of Natural Resources, *Assessment of Groundwater Contamination: Inventory of Sites* (Lansing, MI, July 1982); Figure 5–6: Courtesy of the U.S. Environmental Protection Agency.

Chapter 6 Figure 6–1: Courtesy of the Washington Metropolitan Area Transit Authority; Figures 6–2, 6–3: Adapted from John Black, *Urban Transport Planning: Theory and Practice* (Baltimore: Johns Hopkins University Press, 1981; Kent, England: Croom Helm Ltd., 1981), 119, 85. Figures 6–4, 6–5: Transportation Research Board, *Highway Capacity Manual*, Special Report no. 209 (Washington, DC: National Research Council, 1985), 3-9, 12-6; Figure 6–6: Courtesy of the Washington Metropolitan Area Transit Authority; Figure 6–7: Niagara Frontier Transportation Authority photo by Joe Ciffa; Figure 6–8: Courtesy of the Washington Metropolitan Area Transit Authority; Figure 6–9: Courtesy of the Northern Virginia Transportation Commission; Figure 6–10: Frank S. So et al., eds. *The Practice of Local Government Planning* (Washington, DC: International City Management Association, 1979), 224; Figure 6–11: Louis J. Pignataro, *Traffic Engineering: Theory and Practice* (Englewood Cliffs, NJ: Prentice-Hall, 1973), 452.

Table 6–1: Transportation Research Board, *Highway Capacity Manual*, Special Report no. 209 (Washington, DC: National Research Council, 1985), 12-9.

Chapter 7 Figure 7–1: Werner Hegemann and Elbert Peets, *The American Vitruvius: An Architect's Handbook of Civic Art* (New York: Arno Press, 1968; reprint of 1922 edition); Figure 7–2: C. B. Purdom, *The Building of Satellite Towns* (London: J. M. Dent & Sons, 1925); Figure 7–3: Regional Plan Association, *Regional Survey of New York and Its Environs. Vol 7: Neighborhood and Community Planning* (New York: Arno Press, 1974; reprint of 1929 edition); Figure 7–4: Courtesy of the London County Council; Figure 7–5: *Archigram 4*, Spring–Summer 1964; Figure 7–6: Plan of Tannin, ©Copyright 1985 by Andres Duany and Elizabeth Plater-Zyberk, architects.

Figure 7–7: Courtesy of the Borough of Brooklyn, NY; Figure 7–8: Courtesy of the San Antonio Convention & Tourist Bureau; Figure 7–9: Courtesy of the Greater Boston Convention & Visitors Bureau; Figure 7–10: Courtesy of the Denver Metro Convention & Visitors Center; Figures 7–11, 7–12: Courtesy of The Rouse Company, Columbia, MD; Figure 7–13: Photo by David Danelski.

Chapter 8 Figure 8–1: Drawn by David Povilaitis; Figure 8–2: Courtesy of the Watershed Management Committee, Guilford County, NC; Figure 8–3: Reprinted with permission from *Subdivision Regulation Handbook* (Land Development Series), Copyright 1978, National Association of Home Builders, 15th and M Streets, N.W., Washington, DC 20005; Figure 8–4: Adapted from Buck's County Planning Commission, *Performance Streets: A Concept and Model Standards for Residential Streets* (Doylestown, PA, 1980), 26; Figure 8–5: Drawn by Randy Barnett for the newsletter of the North Carolina chapter of the American Planning Association; Figure 8–6: Reprinted with permission from "Layout and Design, Cluster Housing," from *Project Development Update*, National Association of Home Builders, 15th and M Streets, N.W., Washington, DC 20005; Figure 8–8: Reprinted with permission from "Lotting Option," from *Project Development Update*, National Association of Home Builders, 15th and M Streets, N.W., Washington, DC 20005; Figure 8–9: Courtesy of Triangle Engineering, Raleigh, NC; Figures 8–10, 8–11: Prepared by Robert M. Leary and Associates for Charleston County, SC, 1975; Figures 8–12, 8–14: Mack Little and Frank Rupp, *Residential Stormwater Management* (City of Raleigh, NC, Conservation Division,

1976), 11, 26; Figure 8–15: Courtesy of Beckett and Raeder Inc., Land Planning, Landscape Architecture; Figure 8–16: Adapted from "Why Does Cluster Work?" *Builder* 1 (August 1978): 26–27; Figure 8–17: Reprinted with permission from "Zero Lot Line Atrium Houses," from *Project Development Update*, National Association of Home Builders, 15th and M Streets, N.W., Washington, DC 20005.

Chapter 9 Figure 9–2: Courtesy of the Town of Palmer Lake, CO; Figures 9–3, 9–4: Photos by Eric Damian Kelly; Figure 9–6: Courtesy of Hart-Freeland-Roberts, Inc., Nashville, TN.

Chapter 10 Figure 10–1: Courtesy of the Fairfax County Development Authority; Figure 10–3: The AmeriTrust/SRI, *Indicators of Economic Capacity* (Cleveland: The AmeriTrust Company, December 1986), 12; Figures 10–10, 10–11: Courtesy of ULI–the Urban Land Institute.

Table 10–1: U.S. Department of Commerce, Bureau of the Census, *Statistical Abstract of the United States: 1962, 1977, 1984, 1986* (Washington, DC: U.S. Government Printing Office); Table 10–2: Grant Thornton, *The Seventh Annual Study of General Manufacturing Climates* (Chicago, 1986). Reprinted by permission of Grant Thornton, Copyright 1986.

Chapter 11 Figure 11–1: Left, photo by Jon Crispin; right, courtesy of Thomas & Means Associates, Alexandria, VA; Figure 11–2: Courtesy of The Bettmann Archive, Inc.; Figure 11–3: Photos by Jessie Ewing; Figure 11–4: Left, photo by Richard Reinhold; right, courtesy of the Coastal Colony Corporation, Manheim, PA; Figure 11–5: Photo by Mike Portney; Figure 11–6: Courtesy of the Portland Development Commission.

Table 11–1: Judith G. Rabkin, Gregory Muhlin, and Patricia W. Cohen, "What the Neighbors Think: Community Attitudes Toward Local Psychiatric Facilities," *Community Mental Health Journal* 20 (Winter 1984): 309.

Chapter 12 Figure 12–1: Photo by Dan Ransohoff, reprinted by permission of The Cincinnati Historical Society; Figure 12–2: page 372, top and middle, courtesy of Thomas & Means Associates, Alexandria, VA; bottom, courtesy of ULI–the Urban Land Institute; page 373, top left, courtesy of the *Journal Of Housing*; top right and bottom left, courtesy of the National Association of Housing and Redevelopment

Officials; bottom right photo by Louis B. Schlivek; Figure 12–3: International City Management Association photo files; Figure 12–4: Drawing by David Povilaitis; Figure 12–5: Courtesy of Thomas & Means Associates, Alexandria, VA; Figures 12–6, 12–7: Courtesy of ULI–the Urban Land Institute; Figure 12–9: Drawing by David Povilaitis; Figure 12–11: Courtesy of ULI–the Urban Land Institute.

Table 12–1: U.S. Department of Commerce, *Construction Reports*, Series C20.

Chapter 13   Figure 13–1: Adapted from J. M. Bryson, R. E. Freeman, and W. D. Roering, "Strategic Planning in the Public Sector," in B. Checkoway, ed., *Strategic Perspectives on Planning Practice* (Lexington, MA: Lexington Books, 1986); Figures 13–3, 13–4, 13–5: Drawings by David Povilaitis; Figure 13–6: Paul C. Zucker, *The Management Idea Book* (San Diego: West Coast Publishers, 1983), 63.

Chapter 14   Figures 14–1, 14–2: *1986 Program Strategies* (Dayton, OH: City of Dayton, 1986), 69, 70; Figure 14–3: Adapted from *Adopted Capital Improvements Program, Montgomery County Government, Fiscal Year 1986*, vol. 1 (Rockville, MD: Montgomery County Government, 1987), 1516; Figure 14–5: Peat Marwick Main & Co., *Rebuilding New Orleans:*

Financing Public Facilities (New York: May 1982), 8.

Chapter 15   Figure 15–1: Abridged from Stanley M. Altman, "Teaching Data Analysis to Individuals Entering the Public Service," *Journal of Urban Analysis* 3 (October 1976): 217; Figures 15–2 through 15–8 and Figures 15–10 through 15–14: Carl V. Patton and David S. Sawicki, *Basic Methods of Policy Analysis and Planning* (Englewood Cliffs, NJ: Prentice-Hall, 1986); Figure 15–9: Carl V. Patton and Kenneth E. Stabler, "The Small Town on the Urban Fringe: Conflicts in Attitudes and Values," *Journal of the Community Development Society* 10 (Spring 1979): 87.

Chapter 16   Figure 16–1: Richard Hedman, *Stop Me before I Plan Again* (Chicago: American Society of Planning Officials, 1977); Figure 16–2: Charles Thurow, William Toner, and Duncan Erley, *Performance Controls for Sensitive Lands: A Practical Guide for Local Administrators,* Planning Advisory Service Reports no. 307/308 (Chicago: American Society of Planning Officials, July 1975), 73; Figure 16–3; Richard Hedman and Fred Bair, Jr., *And on the Eighth Day. . . .*, 2d ed. (Chicago: American Society of Planning Officials, 1967); Figure 16–4: Hedman and Bair, *And on the Eighth Day. . . .*

Index

Data collection, processing, and analysis. *See* Information use
Day care facilities, 358
Dayton, Ohio
  budgeting system, 446–47, 448, 449
  Dayton Plan, 51
Deed restrictions. *See* Covenants
Deinstitutionalization of mentally handicapped, social planning for, 342–47
Delano, Frederic Adrian, as chairman of National Planning Board, 38
Democratic process, relationship to values of planner, 504–05
Demographics
  relationship to social planning, 332–38
  see also Central cities, immigration and demographics
Demonstration Cities and Metropolitan Development Act of 1966, 47
Denver, Colorado, Civic Center, 195
Development bonds, 315–16
Development management
  guidelines for large-scale suburban development, 188–89
  land development definitions, 206–07
  land use analysis, 100–01
  minimum lot area requirements, 45
  model code for, 70
  phased development controls, 278–79
  public investment in, 192–97
  relationship to planning, 425
  relationship to regional design, 194–97
  residential suburbs, 7
  Sun Belt cities, 6
  and urban designers, 176
Discrimination in housing, 45, 48, 51, 52–53, 368, 370, 379, 383
District planning, 95–115
  Anchorage, Alaska, 113
  assessment of options, 107–112
  and capital improvements program, 114–15
  citizen participation in, 98
  design studies, 102–03
  development start-up, 99
  economic and market analysis, 103–04
  financial resources survey, 105–06
  housing and residential analysis, 104–05
  implementation program, 114–16
  land use analysis, 100–01
  overview, 95–96
  plan presentation, 116
  planning document, 112–16
  problems in, 96–97
  program prerequisites, 98
  public facilities and services analysis, 105
  regulation analysis, 105
  relationship to comprehensive plan, 97
  scope and content, 106–07
  traffic and circulation studies, 101–02
  types and elements, 97–98
  use of information in, 99–106
Douglas Commission. *See* National Commission on Urban Problems

Downtown areas. *See* Central business districts; Urban redevelopment; Urban renewal
Drucker, Peter, and strategic planning, 433

Earth Day, 1970, 119
Eastlake, Ohio, zoning referendum, 52
Economic base studies, 303–06
Economic development, 50, 287–329
  analysis for land use requirements, 103–04
  boomtowns, 350–52
  business climate, 294–96
  business location profile, 306–07
  business retention and expansion, 317–18
  and capital improvements program, 466
  central cities, 4–5, 324–26
  commercial districts, 321–22
  downtown development plan, 300
  economic capacity indicators, 296
  and economic restructuring, 289–90
  and employment trends, 290–93
  factors in investment decisions, 307
  financing, 297–99, 314–16
  foreign competition, 288, 296
  and foreign reverse investment in the U.S., 288–89
  functions distribution, 302
  and gentrification, 352–56
  geographic shifts in economic activity, 290–93
  and globalization of the U.S. economy, 288–90
  growth analysis, 302–14
  high-growth suburban centers, 8
  incubator facilities, 320–21
  industrial parks, 321
  information sources, 304–05
  marketing, 297, 301, 323–34
  office parks, 321, 323
  overview, 287
  planning process for, 299–302
  relationship to real estate development, 305, 308–14
  relationship to services and infrastructure, 296–97
  relationship with developers, 326–28
  research parks, 321, 322–23
  rural areas, 9
  small business assistance, 318–20
  social impacts of, 247–56
  state assistance programs, 293
  strategy for, 299–314
  target industry identification, 308–08
Economic Development Administration, 293
Economic forecasting, 305–06
Education issues
  baby boom generation, 332
  school costs, 469
  school-centered city plan, 38
  suburbs, 6, 7
EIA. *See* Environmental impact assessment (EIA)

Municipal Management Series

**The Practice of
Local Government
Planning
Second Edition**

Text type
Times Roman, Helvetica

Composition
EPS Group Inc.
Baltimore, Maryland

Printing and binding
Arcata Graphics Book Group,
  Kingsport Press
Kingsport, Tennessee

Design
Herbert Slobin